Insecure Prosperity

Insecure Prosperity

SMALL-TOWN JEWS IN

INDUSTRIAL AMERICA, 1890–1940

EWA MORAWSKA

PRINCETON UNIVERSITY PRESS

PRINCETON, NEW JERSEY

Library of Congress Cataloging-in-Publication Data

Morawska, Ewa T.
Insecure prosperity : small-town Jews in
industrial America, 1890–1940 / Ewa Morawska.
p.   cm.
Includes bibliographical references and index.
ISBN 0-691-03735-3 (cl. : alk. paper)
1. Jews—Pennsylvania—Johnstown—History.
2. Johnstown (Pa.)—Ethnic relations.
I. Title.
F159.J7M835   1995
974.8'77—dc20   95-30471   CIP

This book has been composed in Galliard

Princeton University Press books are printed on acid-free paper, and meet the guidelines for
permanence and durability of the Committee on Production Guidelines for Book
Longevity of the Council on Library Resources

Printed in the United States of America by Princeton Academic Press

1 2 3 4 5 6 7 8 9 10

TO THE MEMBERS OF JOHNSTOWN'S
JEWISH COMMUNITY, MY PARTNERS AND
SUBJECTS IN THIS PROJECT, AND,
WITH A SPECIAL GRATITUDE, TO DR. ELMER
AND BETTY MATCH, ISADORE AND RUTH GLOSSER,
AND THE LATE BEN ISAACSON

CONTENTS

ILLUSTRATIONS

MAPS

PHOTOGRAPHS

TABLES

WHAT THIS BOOK IS ABOUT, WHAT IS DIFFERENT ABOUT IT,

AND WHO HELPED IN ITS MAKING

> You should understand that in a town like this, most [Jewish] people were
> not so conscious then of cultural opportunities, careers for themselves
> and that sort of thing. They didn't think they were denied here,
> provided they made a living, and were living decently.
> Other things were much less important.
>
> —*Isadore S., native-born Johnstowner*

> Jews here? They were quiet people. . . kept a low profile.
>
> —*Louis M., Anglo-Protestant, retired superintendent*
> *at the local steel mill*

> You're asking how it felt that we were "multiple outsiders" in Johnstown?
> Did we feel insecure? I tell you. . . [compared to Eastern Europe]
> it was a much much more secure insecurity.
>
> —*Louis G., immigrant from Ukraine*

THIS BOOK is about the ways Jewish—predominantly East European—
immigrants and their children made their lives in a small steel town in the
coal-mining region of western Pennsylvania during the half-century between the 1890s and the outbreak of World War II. We will see how they
incorporated themselves into the economy by building an ethnic entrepreneurial niche within it, and how they pursued within this niche their main
life goals—the achievement and maintenance of what they viewed as a satisfactory standard of living, and the enjoyment of the company of their fellow ethnics; how they built and slowly transformed their inclusive, multi-
purpose congregational community; and how they negotiated the local
political system from a position of economic and sociocultural marginality.
While this is primarily a single case study, it is also intentionally comparative: the Johnstown case is compared with itself over time, and also with
pertinent findings for the same era reported by the existing studies of
American Jews in big urban centers with large Jewish populations.

Most sociohistorical studies of East European Jews in the United States have been conducted in rapidly growing metropolises like New York, Boston, Philadelphia, and Chicago. And with good historical reason: indeed, a solid majority of Jewish immigrants who arrived in America at the turn of the century settled in big cities. Still, no less than 20–25 percent made their homes in smaller towns (with less than 100,000 residents), and many others resided in such places for a number of years before moving on to bigger cities. So far, there have been very few studies of the adaptation of Jews outside the metropolitan centers.

This gap in the research alone tempted me to undertake a historical investigation of Jewish experience in a small town. But I had an additional incentive of a more general sociological nature. Studies of East European Jews who settled in large numbers in big, economically expanding, and culturally vibrant cities depict four interrelated developments that began early in this century and intensified during the interwar period, transforming Jewish-American communities in the process. The first development was the rapid collective climb by metropolitan Jews up the mainstream educational and occupational ladder during the first decades of this century. This spectacular collective ascent, accomplished in two generations, from the ranks of the industrial proletariat (a position already occupied by many Jewish immigrants before their emigration) to the white-collar strata has been explained as a happy convergence of the demands of the American urban economy and the supply, on the part of the Jews, of particular skills and cultural predispositions like educational zeal and a strong drive toward personal achievement. These images are also firmly embedded in popular ethnic stereotypes.

The second development pointed out by these studies has been the significant increase of Jewish participation in various forms of mainstream American public life, civic-political and associational. The third transformation—already incipient in the urban-industrial centers of turn-of-the-century Eastern Europe, where many immigrant settlers in American metropolises originated—has reportedly been the quickening pace of "the secularization of Jewishness," that is, the progressive disjoining of its once inseparable ethnic and religious dimensions. Fourth and closely related has been a rapid diversification and increased complexity of social relations. These combined processes, which qualitatively transformed Jewish-American communities by making their outward sociocultural forms resemble American middle-class patterns, made up what has been called in American Jewish historiography "the master pattern" of Jewish-American life during the four decades preceding World War II.

I was interested in testing this master pattern in a different configuration of circumstances, preferably in a situation that constrained rather than induced change in the group and individual lives of American Jews: in a small town relatively remote from metropolitan centers, with an undifferentiated economic base and a small number of Jewish residents. In particular, I wanted to find out how—that is, by what concrete ways and means, at what pace, and in which specific configurations—Jewish immigrants and their American-born children, men and women, members of different local synagogues, who had lived in such an environment went about fusing the old-country approaches, customs, and lifestyles with those of their new, American surroundings.

My original intention was to combine, in one comparative project, a study of the adaptation patterns in such a constraining social environment of Jews, Slavs, and Hungarians—former neighbors in Eastern Europe. (Most historical studies of the latter peoples in America, by the way, far less numerous than those of American Jews, are also concentrated in the large cities.) John Bodnar recommended a location: Johnstown, a steel-producing town surrounded by a ring of coal-mining townlets in the hills of western Pennsylvania, approximately seventy miles southeast of Pittsburgh, with a stable population of about 50,000 between the turn of the century and the 1930s. Initial on-site research after I arrived in this country in late 1979 indicated that the town was indeed suitable for my purposes. Because of its geographic location it had remained relatively isolated from the outside world throughout the time period I was interested in. Johnstown's economy was heavily dependent on the steel and coal industries that employed the great majority of the adult male population; these industries grew rapidly until World War I but subsequently began to decline. Until the Second World War the town had remained nonunion under the enforced patronage of the Bethlehem Steel Company. Finally, it had an autocratic political order and a rigid social stratification system with sharp ethnic cleavages between the established Anglo-Protestant elite and West European groups on the one hand, and, on the other, new ethnic groups, mostly of East European backgrounds—Slavs and Hungarians (the great majority), and Jews (between 1,000 and 1,300 in total number after mass migration ceased in 1914 until the outbreak of the Second World War).

I began research on all these East European groups at once, but the enormous amounts of local material I was collecting soon persuaded me that a joint East European study was not feasible. In addition, my initial information showed the enduring concentration of Johnstown's Jews in small business; the limited schooling of the American-born generation; the virtual absence of Jews in local public life; and the persistence of the traditional congregational character of their ethnic community, all of which indicated that the pattern of their adaptation differed considerably from that reported in the big cities. As a result, my investigation of this group's experience increasingly turned toward comparisons with its big-city Jewish-American counterparts.

I decided, therefore, to research separately, and complete first, the "peasant-immigrant" project; it was published in 1985 under the title *For Bread with Butter: Lifeworlds of the East Central Europeans in Johnstown, Pennsylvania, 1890–1940.* I simultaneously continued the "Jewish" one.

(Since these two East European groups transplanted to Johnstown from the old country, and maintained throughout the interwar period, their traditional relationship of economic exchange—Slavic and Hungarian working-class families were the bulk of the clientele of Jewish stores in town—different aspects of their mutual relations are discussed in the present study.)

I think that this separation was a wise decision, and that a long maturation made the Jewish study a better or fuller product. In any case it turned out to be a much more time-consuming (twelve years) and more complicated venture than the earlier undertaking, for both professional and personal reasons. The last decade has been for me a time of intense professional "Americanization," or, more accurately perhaps, Westernization, as I absorbed, through extensive reading and thinking, theoretical and research agendas in several disciplines at once, with each field itself in motion: sociology, American social history, especially immigration and ethnic studies, and American Jewish history.

Personally, these last ten years have been equally, or even more, intense. I am the offspring of a mixed marriage, my mother an ecumenically minded Catholic publicist and writer, rather estranged intellectually from the nationalistic orientation common among Polish Roman Catholics; and my father a Jew, a Holocaust survivor who after the war became a marxist philosopher and joined the Communist party, from which he was subsequently expelled as a "Zionist-revisionist." I came to this country as a "Pole of Jewish background," religiously indifferent and basically ignorant about lived Jewish culture, but acutely conscious of this "Jewish background" in a classical, pathetic East European blend of defensiveness, fear, and pride; "political" is perhaps the best description of this difficult identity, void of cultural content, but nevertheless deeply felt. During the last decade I first became intellectually fascinated by Judaism, then formally converted and became involved in modern (read: liberal Conservative) Jewish life. In no small measure, this personal transformation has occurred as an effect of, or, better, concomitantly with, my Johnstown Jewish research.

This book is intended for two different (though partially overlapping) audiences: for the scholarly one, composed primarily of sociologists and historians, and perhaps historical anthropologists; and for a larger reading public interested in Jewish, and, more generally, immigrant/ethnic history, mainly in America, but also in Europe and Israel. For scholarly readers to locate this book in the intellectual landscape of the academic disciplines mentioned above, I briefly introduce here the general approaches, along with the major theoretical concepts and methodological assumptions, informing this study. The still more basic philosophical premises underlying my conception of the nature and knowability of human society are spelled out—forced out, actually, by the profound postmodernist doubt penetrating into all branches of the social sciences—in appendix I, entitled "(Self-)Reflections of a Fieldworker." Having declared myself a neo*modernist,* the prefix due to my recently raised epistemological self-consciousness, I also try to account in that essay for the intertwining of my fieldwork and personal involvement, and for its possible consequences for my presentation of the Johnstown story. Readers who see no reward in the kind of exercise that follows, especially when encoded in a hard-to-digest sociologese, should proceed to the closing section of this preface, or directly to chapter 1.

This study, then, belongs to the genre of historical sociology that conceives of society and culture not as separate structures, but as reciprocal constructions, each constituted by and constituting the other; and views purposive and responsive actors, concretely located in time and space, as central in this ongoing reciprocity, or structuration, in maintaining sociocultural forms as well as transforming them. Long-term and immediate sociocultural configurations shape the material and nonmaterial resources (such as skills and knowledge, social networks, mental schemas) used by social actors in pursuit of their purposes; the familiarity with and practical use of these resources by the actors enables them, in turn, to shape the world in which they live: directly, its micro-structures, and, through the mediation of the latter, also at the macro-level.[1]

The capacity of actors to access, and deploy toward their purposes, material, social, and symbolic resources empowers them in their interactions with the social world. This understanding of "power" as the generic capacity of human agency to appreciate the world and act upon it—the *power to*—informs the structuration analyses throughout this study. The capacity to produce the effects on the sociocultural environment, however, is usually unequally distributed among different collective and individual members of society, and these power disequilibria among social actors affect the processes and outcomes of structuration. The notion of power as the capacity of groups or individuals to appropriate a larger share of valued resources, and to define the socioeconomic and cultural space within which others can move—the *power over*—finds expression in this study regarding Jews' position in, and relations with, the larger Johnstown (American) society. Although the analysis does not center explicitly on power relations in the sense above, they are present throughout this book as the boundaries delineating the field of maneuver for Jewish residents within the existing economic and sociopolitical order controlled by Bethlehem Steel Company's managers and the established Anglo-Protestant elite. Also and more explicitly, the notion of *power over,* interpreted primarily in terms of "authority" understood conventionally as power viewed as legitimate or "natural" by those subject to it, has been applied to the analysis of social relations—particularly gender and intergenerational—within the Jewish community (see the methodological appendix at the end of this book for the discussion of reasons, evidential and personal, for my preference for this interpretive framework). Whereas the idea of "the double structure" informing this study posits human action and its social environment as (in Giddensian) substantively and causally equivalent,[2] each the condition-and-consequence of the other, in a practical application of this approach in research, and in particular regarding differentially powered relations of Jews with the outside society and within the Jewish community itself, I found a greater epistemic gain in starting by identifying what Fernand Braudel called "the limits of the possible" for human action circumscribed by time- and place-specific opportunities and constraints of the social environment in which this action takes place, then reversing the direction of impact by looking at social actors' purposes and pursuits in this context, and then repeating this reciprocal movement again and again as my investigation continued. Throughout the book, however, historical analysis remains focused on the ways and means (or hidden and open "transcripts" in the language of *power over* theory) used by the powered-over—ethnic (Jewish) actors in their relations with the dominant society, and Jewish women and children inside their ethnic community—to maneuver in their situation in the pursuit of the desired goals, rather than on the relations between the "dominating" and the "dominated."

Turning to the particular subject matter of this study: studies on American immigration and ethnicity (a specialized subfield of research in both sociology and history) offer different theoretical models of the adaptation to the dominant society of immigrants and subsequent generations, or, translated into the terms of structuration approach, of ways and effects of the interaction between opportunities and constraints on the part of the host environment, and the material, social, and symbolic resources available to the actors—ethnic Americans. Their range, to continue the translation, embraces the following approaches, in chronological order of appearance: the least agentic representation, assuming the (host) society to be the main player-shaper in the process of adaptation (the classical assimilation model, positing the dislodgement of ethnic bonds, customs, and identities by the higher-level—ethnic-neutral or all-American—ones of the dominant society); the "double structure" model wherein ethnic lifestyles and sociocultural patterns emerge in the interplay between newcomer-actors and the host environment (the ethnicization approach); and the most recent interpretation, centering on ethnic actors who "construct" their ethnic group identity and institutions (the "invented ethnicity" model).[3]

The approach used in this study is the middle one, that of *ethnicization* understood as the process of blending from inside the ethnic group of the old (country of origin) sociocultural patterns with the new—traditions and lifestyles of the dominant (host) society.[4] In yet another respect the ethnicization approach corresponds well with the overarching theoretical orientation informing this study: the double contingency of this process on the social actors and their environment allows for flexibility and variety in the blends of ethnicization. As a general interpretive framework for the analysis of processes of adaptation to the host society, the ethnicization qua

structuration approach also reaches downward, so to speak, extending um-
brella-like over the lower-level concepts informing the discussion of particular aspects of the experience of Johnstown's Jews: their economic pursuits, life-orientations, family and communal life, relations with the larger
society. They will be introduced in the pertinent chapters; a couple of
them, however, require some advance clarification, because they have been
used in quite different ways in the sociological literature.

Thus, in the analysis of ethnicization that occurred in the area of Jewish
Johnstowners' public, or communal, life, I have used concepts of social
differentiation and secularization, and of the *Gemeinschaft/Gesellschaft*-
types of social relations (the former denoting inclusive and wholistic forms
of social participation, involving the entire person and all/several realms of
life, and the latter fragmented and task-specific interactions), but emphatically *not* in the dichotomizing and teleological sense in which they are
used in conventional modernization theory.[5] Rather, subordinate to the
notions of ethnicization and, more generally, structuration informing this
study, these concepts have been used to denote open-ended, uneven developments, whose time- and place-specific "faces" are products of the
interaction of people with their surroundings.

Regarding the concept of schemas as practice-organizing symbolic resources of Johnstown's Jews, following William Sewell's recent elaboration,[6] I take them to consist of a variety of representations and prescrip-
tions shaped by group past history (the lived one, and that encoded in
collective memory, both in the Great and Little Traditions), and current
experience. Taken together, these various schemas make up what Ann
Swidler calls a "cultural tool kit," or a group repertoire—likewise open-
ended and pliable—of guideposts for social practice.[7] I assume these
schemas to exist at various levels of consciousness: some of them are cognitively known to their actor-carriers, who can explain them relatively easily;
others are so deeply sunk in everyday life that conceptualizing and verbaliz-
ing them requires a considerable effort—Bourdieu's *habitus* belongs to this
category (I use it in this study interchangeably with Hans Kohut's notion
of *experience-near* thoughts and feelings; in historical-sociological studies
the use of Wittgenstein's *unarticulated understanding* has been more
common); and others yet are of a mixed nature—partly near the surface,
partly submerged. Finally, I consider these schemas to be generalizable as
well as transposable or flexible—that is, transportable and adjustable to
new situations by reconfiguring, absorbing new elements, and forming different patterns.

Whereas the ethnicization-as-structuration interpretive framework acknowledges the macroscopic, long-term social environment (including
economic and social relations, political organization, and material and
symbolic culture) as an element of the context of origin, or background, of
smaller-scale, shorter-term social life, it is the latter that is conceptualized
in terms of structuration or mutual reconstitution, and investigated

through close-to-the-ground, thick analysis. Since it conceptualizes social life as a ceaseless activity of shaping-and-reshaping through everyday social practice, this approach does not, and cannot, constitute a conventional theory with tightly knit causal statements linking particular levels or aspects of social life, but, rather, to use E. P. Thompson's phrase, exemplifies "an empirical idiom of discourse."[8] Put differently, it represents what Theda Skocpol has called a *problem-oriented* sociohistorical analysis, seeking not to rework an existing theoretical paradigm or to generate an alternative one, but, rather, to make sense of people's concrete experience and clarify its peculiarities through comparisons with contrasting settings, relying in this undertaking on whatever conceptual tools seem effective and pertinent.[9]

The sources and research methods of this study, as well as the representativity of the Johnstown case, are discussed in detail in appendix I. Here, I will just say the following. As I look back at the twelve years of labor it took me to complete this study of a small group of people in a small town, I feel overwhelmed by the enormous scope of the local (ethnographic and archival) and comparative (largely secondary) sources I worked with, and I find it hard to believe I had the *Sitzfleisch*, not to mention the determination, to carry on with, or, more precisely, sit through this undertaking. Sources pertaining to the lives of Johnstown's Jews were, of course, of primary importance and the most plentiful, and I located and squirreled away each and every piece of information that seemed of potential use. I ended up with a basement full of files, of which no more than 25–30 percent, I believe, has been actually used for this book.

During the first two and a half years of my research I practically lived in Johnstown, talking to members of the local Jewish community individually, in thematic groups (we had meetings on business life, Jewish life in a small town, and on the situation of women), and at congregational meetings (at which I reported on the progress of the project, and answered and asked questions), while at the same time carrying on research on the local sources, and reading on different aspects of American immigrant/ethnic and, specifically, Jewish history, general and in particular localities. After a one-year break during which I was completing the "Slavic" study, for the next four years I visited Johnstown regularly for extensive periods to continue research. I worked on historical records, talked to my informants, and traveled to various cities to look at specific archives; moving among the sources, I checked and linked data on particular aspects of the lives of Johnstown's Jews. After that, and throughout the writing phase of this study, I visited the town occasionally, continuing to use the shuttle routine, that is, checking the information from one source against that from the other, and often repeating the round. While in Philadelphia, I also often used the telephone, asking my informants, by then also good friends, to check a detail in the congregational records or in the local newspaper, or else to clarify a specific issue. I called, too, a number of ad hoc informants—old-time Jewish residents of the localities I used as comparative references for the Johnstown story or authors of historical studies of these places—asking for additional information or a bibliographic reference. When the manuscript was finally completed, I took it, as I had promised I would, for inspection to the old-timer board members of the Beth Sholom Congregation. I waited, I must admit, with a certain anxiety, for their opinion—not about the particulars, but whether the story by and large "sounded true" to them. It did, by and large, and it felt good.

This book is composed of six chapters and the epilogue (the methodological appendix has already been mentioned). Chapter 1 deals with the economic and sociocultural backgrounds of the Johnstown immigrants. It presents a composite picture of life in the rural shtetls in turn-of-the-century Eastern Europe, and it has been constructed backward, as it were, from the issues and themes that emerged in the course of my research in Johnstown. (In this chapter and throughout the book, the spelling of Yiddish words has been conformed to the YIVO Institute standards.) Chapters 2 and 3 are devoted primarily to Johnstown's Jews' economic existence, at work and in their homes, in the initial period of their settlement in the city, and during the interwar decades, respectively. Chapter 4, the bulkiest of all, discusses Jewish communal life, focusing, in particular, on the continuity and change in the functioning of group institutions, public and private religious observance, and patterns of intragroup social life. Chapter 5 deals with Johnstown's Jews' participation in the organized and informal activities of the local society. Chapter 6 is about schemas that, as recollected by the Johnstowners, gave meaning to and guided their actions in the shared condition of their lives, namely, insecurity of their economic fortunes and civic station. In the epilogue, I outline the major changes in the surrounding circumstances and inside the Jewish group in Johnstown in the postwar era, and the present-day situation of the Jewish community. When the Princeton University Press requested that the submitted book manuscript's length be reduced, the bibliography (65 pp.) became the first victim of this operation. It is available upon request from the author.

My historical-sociological consciousness still deplores, and I wish to put it on record, the necessity of cutting into pieces or chapters what for the actors of the Johnstown story has been one continuous experience. Given this continuity in the lived experience of the people about and with whom these chapters talk, as well as my theoretical and methodological positions regarding the study of social life, the separation of discussions of the actions and schemas has been particularly absurd, but it was necessitated by the unusual density of material. The placement of the schemas at the end of the book by no means suggests that I consider them derivative or of secondary importance: rather, since I intended to discuss these schemas in one encompassing frame that required back-and-forth references to issues dealt with in different chapters, it made sense to locate it at the point in the study where readers would have already become familiar with its entire content.

This study has been a collaborative endeavor, and I should like to acknowledge and heartily thank those to whom this book is dedicated, the members of the Johnstown Jewish community who were at once my partners and subjects in this project. There are too many of them to be enumerated here (nearly 160 persons either were interviewed or in some other way contributed to this study); they are listed, as requested by Beth Sholom board members who collaborated in this study, in appendix II at the end of the book. This seems the appropriate place to explain that in the text my informants appear under their first names and surname initials. Having presented, as was agreed at the beginning of the project, the completed book manuscript to two old-time Johnstowners—members of the board of directors of the congregation—I suggested changing these identifiers. They did not think it was necessary; in fact, as one of them put it, "[local] people will have fun guessing who said what." I nevertheless changed both first and last names in two instances: when the details of bankruptcy records and the lowest-income budgets are quoted.

My very special thanks go to specific people mentioned in the dedication: Dr. Elmer Match and the late Ben Isaacson, my priceless first guides into the Johnstown Jewish community who made it possible for this project to take off and keep moving, and my "fellow travelers" to other small-town Jewish communities in western Pennsylvania with a presentation of our project; and Isadore and Ruth Glosser, without whose sustained interest and faith in my endless undertaking, and generous assistance in its subsequent phases, my fieldwork would not have been carried to its conclusion.

I wish to express thankful appreciation to my Johnstown friends who helped to start this project by recording life stories of the local Jewish community's members, and with whom we later worked extracting from these narratives their major themes: Nathan Edelstein,* Phillip Eisenberg, Mildred Ginsburg, Harriet Katz,* Betty Silverstein,* and also Rabbi Rav Soloff, Harriet Soloff, and David Rosen. To several people I returned, and returned again, as I moved along with my project, asking more questions and repeating old ones; I learned a great deal from them, and some of our conversations still ring in my "inner ears": Blanche and Abe Beerman, Dr. Meyer Bloom,* Bella Coppersmith,* Millard Cummins, Isadore and Jen Greenberg, Arthur Hagadus,* Esther Jacovitz, Henry Kaplan,* Abe Kleinstub,* Bob Kranzler, Rose Leshner and Lillian Leuin, Irving London,*

* An asterisk following the name indicates the person was deceased by the time of this writing (September 1994).

Golda Morrow and her children, Helene, Ben, and Harry, Helen Paul, Harry Rabinowitz,* Seymour Silverstone,* Naomi Sky-Holtzman, Isadore Suchman, Dr. Israel and Rita Teitelbaum, and Betty Weissberg. My sincere thanks go to the former rabbis of Johnstown's congregations who graciously shared with me their time and memories: Rabbis Ralph Simon, Hayim Perelmuter, Nathan Kollin, Mordecai Brill, Morris Landes, and Leonard Winograd in whose history of Johnstown's Jews, *"The Horse Died at Windber": A History of Johnstown's Jews of Pennsylvania* (1988), I found many valuable details I would not have discovered by myself. Most helpful too, especially at the beginning of my project, was the dedication book *Jewish Center of Johnstown Rodef Sholom Synagogue* (1954) prepared for the fiftieth anniversary of this congregation by four of its members, Saul Spiegel, Betty Rabinowitz, Meyer Levin, and Morton Glosser. And I could not have written the epilogue to this book without the information about the present-day situation of Johnstown's Jews provided by Dr. Jon Darling.

I also gratefully acknowledge kind assistance in different parts of this project of non-Jewish Johnstowners, especially Atty. Samuel DiFrancesco Sr.,* Atty. Andrew Gleason, Jack Penrod, Robert Franke, Walter Suppes, Alberta Long, Marian Varner, Sandy Stevens, Edward Howells, Ethel Jane Naylor, Bruce Williams, Patricia Raines, and Ruth Whitehead. I am especially indebted to the staffs of the *Johnstown Tribune*, Cambria County Courthouse in Ebensburg, and Meadowvale Media Center and public schools in Johnstown, where I spent long months gathering information about various aspects of the history of Johnstown's Jews. Jeff Shiley from the Geography Department at the University of Pittsburgh in Johnstown prepared expert maps of residential and business premises of local Jews over the half-century before World War II, and Deanna Knickerbocker computer-mastered drawings of maps of Eastern Europe and western Pennsylvania.

Similar thanks are due as well to all those who helped me with the archival and other work related to this study, especially at the National Archives in Washington, Federal Archives and Records Center in Philadelphia, Dun and Bradstreet Company's library in New York, Jewish Historical Society archives in Waltham, Massachusetts, The Central Zionist Archives in Jerusalem, and YIVO Institute for Jewish Research in New York (at this last, I thank especially Dina Abramowicz, Marek Web, Chana Mlotek, and Eve Sicular). I am also greatly indebted to Professors Victor Karady, Szabtai Unger, Israel Bartal, and to Rachel Rubinstein and David Broun, for their kind assistance in particular matters concerning turn-of-the-century East European Jewish history. My heartfelt thanks go as well to Dr. William Glickmann, without whose patient help, broad historical knowledge, and excellent memory I would never have been able to recover the meaning of the invaluable source in my study, the five-hundred-page-long handwritten Yiddish-language minutes of the board meetings of the Rodef Sholom Orthodox Synagogue in Johnstown during the first quarter of this century.

Of the many other contributors to this project, I should like to acknowledge with great appreciation my academic colleagues, and others whom I had not met, who most kindly responded to my phone calls and provided the information I needed about other American cities and their Jewish communities for comparisons with particular aspects of the Johnstown case: Moses Rischin, Deborah Dash Moore, and Ron Bayor (about New York); Edward Miggins, Thomas Campbell, John Grabowski, and Judah Rubenstein (about Cleveland); Amy McCandless and Solomon Breibart (about Charleston, South Carolina); and Max Einstandig and Martin Schwartz (about Terre Haute, Indiana).

Three more sine qua non kinds of assistance in the making of this book must be noted here with profound gratitude. My friend and mentor in American Jewish history, Jonathan Sarna, spent hours, hundreds of them it seems, on the phone thoughtfully answering my questions and raising his own, and miraculously producing obscure bibliographic references I had unsuccessfully chased for weeks. He also read, and reread, chapter after chapter of my evolving book manuscript, invariably offering insightful comments and useful criticism. So did Charles Tilly, my second intellectual patron—in this case, in historical sociology as practiced in this country. His critical comments were usually aimed at the foundations of the products submitted for his evaluation, but since more often than not these criticisms were well taken, big chunks of what I thought was sound and solid enough resoundingly collapsed in front of my nose, forcing me to begin building da capo. I also wish to express here my admiration and thanks for the wisdom shared with me by Dr. Samuel Lachs and Michael Walzer, with whom I have been privileged to study the Talmud; this experience, I believe, enhanced my understanding of the lifeworlds of Johnstown's Jews. Warm thanks go also to my colleagues, historians and sociologists, who read and commented on one or more chapters of this book-in-the-making: Moses Rischin, Deborah Dash Moore, Barbara Laslett, Ivan Light, Samuel Klausner, Renee Fox, Charles Bosk, Alice Goldstein, Michael Katz, Eviatar Zerubavel, and Leonard Dinnerstein.

Michael Joyce and Kathleen Much patiently struggled with the linguistic infelicities of my non-native English writing through the earlier drafts of the chapters, and Virginia MacDonald formatted, aligned, and brought to user-friendly shape the WordPerfect version of the book manuscript. I thank them very much as well as the expert editorial team at Princeton University Press, and especially Lauren Lepow whose talented gentle-touch copyediting made my intricate narrative style more palatable to the English-language reader.

Finally, I cannot thank enough all those who provided me with assistance, in space and money, through the many years that were needed to complete my Johnstown project: the John Simon Guggenheim Foundation, the Institute for Advanced Study in Princeton, the Memorial Foundation for Jewish Culture, the University of Pennsylvania Research Foundation, and the Center for Advanced Study in the Behavioral Sciences in Stanford, California. In this company, with heartfelt gratitude, I wish to acknowledge as well the financial support in this project of two Johnstown Jewish families: the Abe and Janet Beerman Foundation and the David M. Glosser Foundation.

Insecure Prosperity

In the Shtetls and Out

THIS PRESENTATION of old-country backgrounds of the immigrant settlers in Johnstown, Pennsylvania—let me reiterate what has been noted in the preface—is a composite portrait, based on various sources, that has been assembled "backward," from the issues and themes that emerged during my research on the history of this town's Jewish community.[1] It centers on Eastern Europe, home of the great majority of the Johnstowners: by 1914, over 90 percent of the Jewish population in the town and vicinity was of East European origin; the remainder were German Jews, the earlier settlers. This reconstruction focuses on the economic and sociocultural resources and interpretative cultural schemas organizing Jews' everyday lives in turn-of-the-century Eastern Europe that, in a more or less modified form, the immigrants reapplied in their adaptation to the local American environment, and passed on to their children.

WAYS OF LIFE

It was only in the five decades preceding World War I that Eastern Europe entered the process of accelerated urban-industrial transformation. This was a protracted, uneven, and incomplete transformation, fraught with contradictions. It was initiated and executed from above by the old feudal classes; constrained by the dependent character of the region's economic advance, which lacked internal impetus and was significantly influenced by and subordinated to the far more developed core countries of Western Europe;[2] and encumbered by the ubiquitous remnants of a feudal past in social forms and political institutions. The abolition of serfdom and alienation of noble estates (1848 in Austro-Hungary and 1861/63 in Russia), executed without rearrangement of the socioeconomic order, combined with a demographic explosion, impoverished and dislocated large segments of the population previously occupied in the countryside: landless peasants, lesser gentry and tenants of their properties, rural petty traders and craftsmen. East European historians estimate that the combined permanent and seasonal migrations, in large part directed toward nearby and distant urban-industrial centers, affected no less than 25–30 percent of the total region's population between 1870 and 1914. This mass movement notwithstanding, by 1910 the majority of East Europe's population—over 70 percent in Russia (including Congress Poland), 81 percent in the Galician

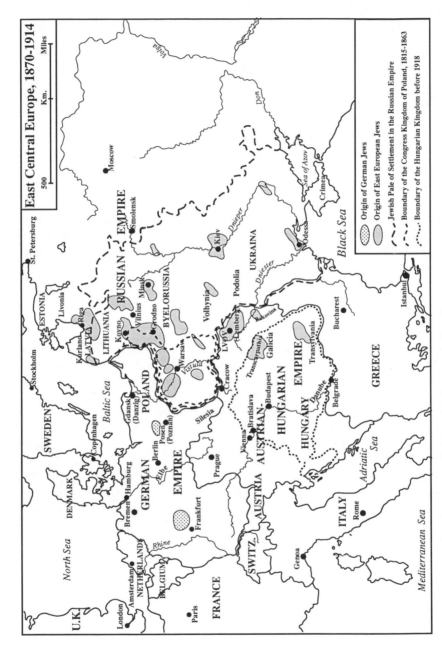

Map 1.1. Areas of Old-Country Origin of Johnstown's Immigrants

East Central Europe, 1870-1914

Legend:
- Origin of German Jews
- Origin of East European Jews
- Jewish Pale of Settlement in the Russian Empire
- Boundary of the Congress Kingdom of Poland, 1815-1863
- Boundary of the Hungarian Kingdom before 1918

and 66 percent in the Hungarian parts of the Austrian Monarchy—was still employed in agriculture.[3]

Constrained as they were from within and without, the urbanization-industrialization processes transforming the region as a whole also caused major relocations, restructuring, and consequent pauperization of significant segments of Jewish society. These experiences were particularly harsh for the inhabitants of the so-called Pale of Jewish Settlement in the Russian Empire, though more so in the more easterly parts of this territory than in semiautonomous Congress Poland in the west. The Jews of the Pale, home to nearly three-quarters of the approximately seven million Jews in Eastern Europe, were victims of a series of expulsionary decrees and restrictive legal statutes issued during the thirty-five-year period following the assassination of Tsar Alexander II in 1881. The hostile policies of the tsarist regime fomented popular violence against Jewish persons and property. The first large-scale pogrom in Odessa in 1871 was succeeded over the following decades by hundreds of others—particularly in 1881–1884 and 1903–1906—most of them in southern and western Ukraine, but some in Lithuania, Byelorussia, and sporadically in Congress Poland. In the Galician and the Hungarian parts of the Austrian Monarchy, however, the Jews, while subject to generally similar structural dislocations as their coreligionists in the rest of the region, enjoyed legal protection granted by the Emancipation Act of 1867, which had removed the disabilities that had persisted since Joseph II's *Toleranzpatent* of 1782. In Galicia, however, the Polish ruling class, supported from below by fellow nationals, obstructed rather than facilitated the implementation of the constitutional laws by tolerating, if not actually encouraging, the practice of residential and occupational exclusion and harassment of Jewish citizens. The political and civic constraints accompanying East European economic transformations were felt least by the Jews of semiautonomous Hungary, where the official attitude was not to exclude but, in fact, to encourage Jewish citizens to become part of the Magyar nation, and where occasional anti-Semitic excesses in the provinces were publicly deplored by the government.[4]

The residential provenance, preemigration occupational pursuits, and sociocultural milieus of the immigrants who were to establish the Jewish community in Johnstown indicate that in the unevenly changing landscapes of Eastern Europe and Jewish society, most came from vestigial environments that were less—or, rather, less directly—affected by these transformations. Some of these characteristics are presented in table 1.1. The majority, 80 percent, of the future Johnstowners had lived in the Russian Pale: over one-half in Lithuania-Byelorussia, and the rest split between the Ukraine and Congress Poland; the remainder were about equally divided between Galicia and the northeastern part of Hungary. By 1910, more than 50 percent of all Jews in the Russian Pale of Settlement were already concentrated in cities with populations over 50,000—large by contemporary East European standards. The largest cities (Odessa, Kiev, Vilno,

TABLE 1.1

Regional Origin, Population Size and Ethnic Composition of Place of Residence, and Occupations of Future Johnstowners (Men)[a] in Turn-of-the-Century Eastern Europe

Regional Origin[b]	(%)	Town's Population	(%)	Ethnic Composition (% of population Jewish)	Occupation	(%)
Russian Pale	80	Cities over 100,000	7	29	Traders	36
Lithuania-Byelo-		Cities 45,000/50,000–			Artisans	43
russia	(53)	100,000	8	56	Factory	
Congress Poland	(15)	Towns 10,000–25,000	15	50	laborers	15
Ukraine	(12)	Towns less than 10,000	64	61	Furriers	5
Galicia	11	Villages	6	—	Other	1
Hungary	9					
N = 120		N = 107			N = 87	

Sources: Naturalization dockets, Cambria Country Courthouse, Ebensburg, Pennsylvania; lists of arriving passengers, 1880s–1914, National Archives, Washington, DC; local interviews.

[a] In this and all other tables percentages are in rounded figures.

[b] A few emigrants from the areas north of Lithuania (outside of the Russian Pale) are included in "Lithuania-Byelorussia," and a few from Romania in "Hungary."

Ekaterinoslav, and Minsk in Russia; Warsaw and Lodz in Congress Poland; Lvov in Galicia; Budapest and Szeged in Hungary) witnessed six- to sevenfold growth of the Jewish population during the last four and a half decades preceding World War I.[5] But among the future Johnstowners whose old country residence I was able to identify, this proportion was only 15 percent. The solid majority, 70 percent, either had lived in small towns of less than 10,000 inhabitants or had been *yeshuvnikes*, countryside Jews residing in the *derfer*, villages and hamlets. Although the majority of bigger-city dwellers had lived in Lithuania-Byelorussia, where Jews were more urbanized-industrialized than in other parts of the Pale, most of the residents of this region in my sample resided in small towns.

The shtetls then—little, predominantly Jewish towns dispersed throughout the countryside—were home to most of those who eventually came to the Johnstown area before World War I. Influenced in part by popular representations,[6] post–World War II American-Jewish historical and sociological literature has treated the shtetl as the symbolic manifestation of East European "Jewishness" and as a yardstick by which to measure the subsequent transformation of the immigrants and their descendants. As such, the shtetl has been subject to opposite interpretations: depicted as a stronghold of stability and vital tradition in the early postwar decades, it later was portrayed as a decaying social world crumbling under the impact of destructive external forces.[7]

As often happens in the social sciences after a paradigmatic representation has fully swung from one extreme to the other, more recent studies have moved toward more differentiating and equivocal representations of the shtetl. One such refining point is particularly relevant for this discussion. Although the way of life and attitudes of turn-of-the-century small-town Jewry were in general more traditional than those in larger urban centers, the shtetls were not as uniform as stereotypes made them. Depending on the province, particular location, and economic function, more or less industrial shtetls whose occupational composition and patterns of social life more closely resembled those of the bigger cities coexisted with agricultural ones more deeply rooted in the countryside economy and premodern social relations.[8]

Following this distinction, I evaluated the character of the shtetls in which the prospective Johnstown immigrants had resided by inspecting the available historical encyclopedias, "shtetl finders," and *yizker-bikher*, the Jewish memorial books,[9] as well as a collection of taped life histories of my Johnstown informants. I decided to treat as "industrial" 15–20 percent of the identified towns with populations up to 20,000 ($N = 76$) in which pre–World War I settlers in Johnstown originated. The criterion for inclusion in this category was mention of at least one manufacturing establishment typical of the "Jewish" industries of Eastern Europe: production of textiles of all varieties; glove, brush, bristle, soap, candle, and match making; tanning, and so forth. This is, of course, a rather dubious measure of industrialization, considering that such enterprises often employed no more than twenty to fifty workers in toto, but it is the only one available.

Accordingly, the great majority of shtetls in which most of the prospective emigrants lived were of the rural type. Inspection of the lists of passengers arriving at U.S. ports, which usually (but alas, not systematically) noted both the place of birth and the last residence of the immigrants and their children, suggests another aspect of the traditionalism of lifestyles of the future Johnstowners. Namely, among those for whom this information was provided ($N = 53$), over 70 percent appear to have been rather stationary: their birthplaces were also their places of last residence before they left for America. This does not mean, however, although most of my immigrant informants did not recollect specifically, that they did not move around in between, whether in search of a livelihood, forced by expulsions, or for personal reasons.

Like urbanization, industrialization of the region also affected the Jewish minority. By the beginning of this century, the proportion of Jews occupied in manufacturing as factory and workshop employees was estimated at a considerable 35–40 percent in Russia (with the largest concentration in northwestern Lithuania and Byelorussia), in Congress Poland, and in central Hungary, and about 25 percent in much less industrialized Galicia.[10] In rural shtetls, however, Jews were chiefly occupied in small shopkeeping, artisanry, or peddling, gaining their livelihood from trade with residents of the surrounding countryside. Such was also the employment of the great majority, 80 percent, of the men (passenger lists and naturalization records did not record information about women's occupations) who eventually settled in the Johnstown area before World War I and who were old enough to pursue a gainful occupation; the proportion of industrial laborers was only 15 percent (see table 1.1 for a more detailed distribution).

The economic pursuits of the shtetl Jews—the recollections of my informants did not differ in this regard from the accounts published in immigrant memoirs and recorded oral histories—were usually a family enterprise, commonly involving not only men and women, but also children, as soon as they were able. (The 1897 Russian census reported 21 percent of the total population of adult Jewish women as employed, but this estimate did not include wives and daughters occupied in small family businesses.)[11] In many of these families, too, work had not yet, or not completely, been separated from home. In the shtetl Antopolie in Byelorussia, the family of Bella C., who came to Johnstown in 1907 as a ten-year-old, "had a little bit of a store in a square [where we lived], and both parents worked there." As a little kid Bella used to "sell kerosene from the pantry of the house, made cigarettes by hand, and sold syrup, and rice, and also potato peels for the cows." Elsewhere in Russia, David R. worked as a tinner, while his wife Hanna had a stall in the market where she repaired rubber boots and raincoats, and, if necessary, took her repairs home to finish. Renee G.'s mother in Deva, a little town in Hungary, raised geese, selling them and their feathers in the local market. Lejbe M., a *milkhiker*, milkman, in the shtetl Radzvilitz in Lithuania, took his teenage son, Samuel, with him on his daily rounds in the area. Adolf and Sarah K., *yeshuvnikes* in a village near Munkač in northeastern Hungary, owned a piece of land and a tavern combined with a little store where the entire family worked. And, just as typically, members of Max W.'s family in the shtetl Zaritovo near Minsk were *dorfgeyer*, countryside peddlers; his mother "would go to the peasants to buy eggs and sometimes would carry a bag of grain she would buy from some peasants. . . . Besides buying things from the peasants [she] also sold them kerosene and salt and in the course of time the girls [his sisters] started to sell fancy prints by the yard to women in the villages."[12]

The economic activities undertaken on behalf of the family by Jewish women, wives specifically—especially when independently conducted— gave them a considerable measure of authority within the household. In a minority of cases, this authority involved major initiatives and decisions concerning economic matters, as in the home of Renee G. in Deva, Hungary, who, rather than her husband Moshe, was acknowledged as the business head of the family and was accorded supervisory power beyond her own realm of selling geese and feathers. In most households, however, women's authority in economic matters, even when considerable, was ultimately subordinate to that of the men, not least because there were among the latter practically no people of the Book or Talmudic scholars withdrawn from daily activities in pursuit of a livelihood; I will return to this point below.[13]

1.1. Shtetl Zablodow, south of Bialystok, Grodno Province. Collection of the YIVO Institute for Jewish Research.

1.2. Zager, north of Kovno, Kovno Province. Collection of the YIVO Institute for Jewish Research.

1.3. Market day, Krasnobrod, southeast of Lublin, Lublin Province. Reprinted from Bernard Newman, *The Story of Poland* (London: Hutchinson, 1940).

1.4. Jewish-owned grain store, Yeziori, east of Grodno, Grodno Province. Collection of the YIVO Institute for Jewish Research.

A recurrent theme in the recollections of my immigrant informants was the pervasive poverty and never-ending struggle to make ends meet—the most direct and most vexing effect of the region's economic restructuring on them and their families. The families of the prospective Johnstowners included a few that were better off, such as Martin S.'s in Vorono near Zempleň in Slovakia, who were "well-off . . . owned a well-prospering store and had servants in the house"; or the above-mentioned *yeshuvnikes* near Munkač who owned land and ran a tavern in the village. Early-twentieth-century ethnographic studies, such as those of Limanowa in western Galicia and Sniatyń in Bukovina in the Carpathian Mountains, provide estimates suggesting that the size of the well-off group in local Jewish societies was between 15 and 20 percent of the total population. In my sample, this proportion was no more than a third of this—not surprising, considering that it consisted of immigrants looking for better fortunes far away from their homes.

According to my informants, their families, while often struggling at the subsistence level, were not, however, such desperate paupers as to be forced to ask their local Jewish community for Passover charity to help them celebrate the holiday in the proper way. An 1898 survey of Jewish communities in the Russian Pale of Settlement indicated that an average of about 15 to 20 percent of shetls' residents fell into this category.[14] My informants' families apparently occupied a somewhat higher position, in a large category that in the language of American social stratification studies could be called a middle-to-upper lower class. It was the ever-precarious position of "chasing after *parnose* (livelihood)" on a day-to-day basis, money sometimes accruing in a series of more fortunate business operations, but more often suddenly disappearing when little or nothing materialized. In this or another form, most immigrant reminiscences of their situation in the old country contained this message. Harry R.'s father, for example, in the shtetl Vilkomir in Lithuania, rarely knew whether he would earn enough for the family's current needs, and if he accumulated some capital, "it was usually by luck." Similar experiences echoed in the recollection of Bella C. from Antopolie in Byelorussia: "With everybody working [in the store] we still could hardly make the ends meet, because even if it [business] did better, you were sure it was not going to last long."[15]

In such a situation, efforts to make ends meet required a perpetual bricolage, a snatching at occasions as they presented themselves. Much as one tried, however, the ceiling of the possible was very low, given the even worse poverty of the surrounding countryside. At the end of the last century in Galicia, a region generally poorer than other provinces of Eastern Europe, about 50,000 peasants annually died of starvation; such catastrophes did not occur in Jewish society, even among the most deprived, partly because of well-organized intragroup assistance, but also because of a somewhat higher general standard of living.[16]

In that segment of East European societies within which the future Johnstowners originated, Jews up until World War I continued to perform their traditional role as economic middlemen, positioned in the "status gap" separating two major classes: the peasantry and the gentry.[17] The demise of noble estates worked by serfs eroded this function of the Jewish minority vis-à-vis the gentry, although the latter still used Jewish services in marketing their produce and, in those parts of Eastern Europe where Jews were not forbidden countryside residence, quite commonly leased them their lands as business enterprises. With the exception of a couple of immigrants whose families leased land from the gentry and who recollected them in the role of landowners, my informants recalled the ruling class in a generalized image as part of the dominant order. That order combined several elements. First, the political system: as we have seen earlier, in most of Eastern Europe, it was, if not openly hostile, then potentially threatening to the Jews. Second, the predominantly agricultural socioeconomic structure wherein trade- and money-related occupations, particularly when performed by an ethnoreligiously different group, had been held in contempt—by 1900, Jews constituted 75 percent of the entire commercial class in Russia and Congress Poland, 80 percent in Galicia, and 65 percent in Hungary.[18] Third, toward the end of the nineteenth century there was an intensifying nationalism of the primordial and exclusionary type manifested by the middle and upper classes. And, last but not least, the dominant order was informed by the institutions and hegemonic ideology of the Christian religion. Strong ethnic communal bonds and the sh...ed Great

Tradition of God's Chosen People shielded Jews on the inside, as it were, from social and emotional effects of their multiple estrangement from the larger East European societies. Despite these internal protections, most of my immigrant informants, and, for that matter, also their American-born children who learned from their parents, represented the position of the Jewish group vis-à-vis the dominant system in Eastern Europe as one of powerlessness, and the accompanying feelings as profound collective insecurity.

While in the relationship with the gentry the middleman role of the Jews—former arendators administering the villages on noble estates—had weakened, in that with peasants it actually was strengthened. Jews bought peasant produce to be distributed across the region and exported outside, and they sold to the rural households both services and manufactured goods prepared by local artisans or brought from city factories; the shtetls thus served as centers of this two-way market exchange, tying the country-side to the larger network of production and distribution.[19] Propinquity and familiarity with peasants, and knowledge of the local languages learned through contact with the non-Jewish residents of the countryside—these were recurrent themes in the recollections of the immigrants themselves and of their American-born offspring reporting on their parents' memories. We will somewhat more closely examine this relationship between Jews and Slavic and Hungarian peasants, because it was transplanted with the emigrants to Johnstown and, modified in some respects and reversed in others, persisted there through the 1930s.

Economic exchange was the main sphere and focus of everyday interactions between the two groups. It was conducted chiefly on market days. So routine was this tradition-sanctioned occasion that if it fell on a Jewish holiday, the village priest would announce from the pulpit that "no trading would take place this week."[20] Trading continued through the rest of the week as peasant customers came to stores in the shtetls to purchase or order items they needed, while Jews traveled through the countryside buying agricultural produce and selling their wares. Other forms of contact between the two groups had developed around economic exchange: peasants visited local Jewish store owners or innkeepers to get news and ask for advice (even in matchmaking), *klezmorim* (folk musicians) were hired to play at peasant weddings, Jewish midwives attended peasant women at childbirth and distributed remedies to the villagers in sickness, peasant servant girls worked in better-off Jewish homes in the shtetls, and *Shabes goyim* (Gentile men) took care of the household tasks forbidden Jews on the Sabbath and holidays.[21] Set in close proximity and a long historical tradition, this economic symbiosis bound the two groups in daily interactions and made for considerable familiarity in their relationship. It was, however, familiarity with built-in distance, characteristic of the relations of groups in societies segmented by the ascriptive statuses and social roles that clearly and differently defined particular collectives, and by profound cultural divergence between them. This simultaneous propinquity and distance in the relationship of *shtetldike* Jews with their non-Jewish neighbors has been captured in the almost identical titles and leitmotivs of two recent socio-historical studies of Jewish inhabitants of two regions in Eastern Europe: the "native aliens" Jack Kugelmass describes in turn-of-the-century rural Poland, and Livia Rothkirchen's "deep-rooted aliens" in the Subcarpathian Rus.[22]

Peasants were basically disdainful and mistrustful of their Jewish economic partners, although this attitude was not wholly unequivocal. As already mentioned, commercial functions performed by a group ethnically and/or religiously distinct from the majority of the population were seen in agricultural societies as treacherous and exploitative in nature, and the two major classes, the gentry and the peasantry, shared this perception. Since business and commerce were viewed as the Jewish domain, by extension Jews themselves were considered deceitful and cunning. At the same time, however, peasant perceptions of Jews also contained a detectable element of ambivalent admiration for such qualities as the resourcefulness, intellectual cleverness, and solidarity of the Jewish traders. This recognition was expressed in such standard references in the East European peasant parlance as "Jewish smarts," "wise as a Jew," and "to stand for each other like one Jew for another." It was commonly observed in all parts of Eastern Europe and readily acknowledged by the peasants themselves that, even when they had the option of dealing with a Christian merchant, they usually preferred to conduct their economic affairs with the Jews.[23] This preference was a reflection of the region's tradition-sanctioned sociocultural division of labor as well as of popular appreciation of Jewish mercantile talents and efficiency. A strong reinforcement of disdain and mistrust felt by the peasants toward their Jewish neighbors came from the realm of religious images and beliefs. The "sins" of theological Jews against the Christian God were collectively transferred onto their contemporaries. As repeatedly witnessed in Jewish immigrant memoirs and recollections, the slur "God killers" was commonly used against them when peasants were drunk, angry with them for some reason, or religiously aroused, particularly during the Easter season, by hearing an especially moving sermon about Christ's martyrdom and crucifixion. By implication, the sinners are equated with evil, and this, in Christian imagery, has had a ready symbol in the figure of the devil. And in fact, the Jews' likeness to and collusive connections with the devil and the "spirits" were common themes in turn-of-the-century East European peasant tales, sayings, proverbs, and pictorial representations.

Again, however, these perceptions of Jews, while basically deprecatory, were not unambivalent, and in the area where theological religion interfused with folk magic, they even contained certain positive elements. Inasmuch as they believed in the Jews' supernatural connections, peasants, according to contemporary ethnographers, ascribed to the Jews certain magical powers, evil, but also beneficent influences, such as good luck or health.[24]

Because of this intermingled cognitive and emotional content of peasants' attitudes toward their Jewish neighbors—in both aspects of which predominated elements of disdain and resentment with an admixture of wondrous awe—their routine daily relations based on the established patterns of service exchange easily broke down into acts of verbal abuse and behavioral aggression. Low as their position was, at the bottom of the social structure in East European societies, peasants, as one of the two major classes, felt secure in relation to Jews, who were a minority in the status gap, and superior, as part of the dominant body cultural-religious: the agricultural, Christian Eastern European countryside was their territory, in which the Jews were a rooted but nevertheless alien insertion. This component of security/domination in the peasants' relation to the Jews found expression in disparaging labels used commonly throughout Eastern Europe by the Gentile rural and urban classes alike: *Zhidek* (Slavic) and *Biboldo* (Hungarian), with the belittling meaning perhaps closest, although not quite equivalent, to the English "Jewboy." This perceived vulnerability of Jews vis-à-vis the generally unfriendly surrounding population made them all the more suitable social objects for peasants from which to generate a sense of self-importance and power in their otherwise subordinate position in East European society. The customary means for doing so were the "jokes" played on Jews, a common diversion of peasant children and youth: pulling at Jewish boys' earlocks and siccing dogs after them, mimicking Jewish speech and prayers, breaking windows and extinguishing candles in the synagogue on the Sabbath, throwing stones and dead birds into *Sukkoth* booths, and the like.[25] Under the instigation of nationalist agitators or zealous local clergy, such confrontations would occasionally turn into public "blood" accusations, collective attacks on Jewish shops, and, ultimately, full-fledged pogroms.

Now for the counterpart of this relation—the Jewish perceptions of the surrounding peasantry. Here, too, the recollections of my Johnstown informants generally coincided with those recorded in the immigrant memoirs and other sociohistorical studies using oral history interviews. In the realm of mundane things and relations, the Gentile environment in general, and the inhabitants of villages surrounding the shtetl in particular, were seen by the Jews primarily in instrumental terms as suppliers of *parnose*—material livelihood, through the means of everyday economic exchange. Just as for peasants, however, the two groups' mutual familiarity—resulting from such accustomed repetitive interactions derived from ascription-based group functions, and reinforced by differences in appearance, language, and customs—maintained rather than diminished the distance and sense of otherness felt by Jews toward their economic partners. This otherness of the peasants in Jewish eyes was a negative one, underlaid by disdain, uneasiness, and suspicion. But if similar feelings in peasant

attitudes toward Jews were evoked by their perception of the latter as endowed with some supernatural characteristics and beyond their grasp, the
Jewish perceptions of peasants were the reverse: peasants represented the
base-natural, uncivilized and uncultured. The term *goy*, referring generally
to Gentiles (non-Jews), was actually used to denote "peasant" in the everyday idiom of the shtetls all across Eastern Europe. And that meant people
and things (*goyish*) that were backward, ignorant, driven by corporeal, un-
restrained instincts and physical aggression.[26]

In part, despite Jews' marginality and acute collective insecurity vis-à-vis
the dominant class system, their perceptions of peasants reproduced those
held as self-evident by members of the upper echelons of East European
social structure.[27] More directly, however, in the eyes of the shtetl, the
goyim-peasants represented everything a Jew, including members of the
proste or uneducated strata of Jewish society, did not want to and should
not be, and this value-laden distinction was inculcated in children from
infancy.[28] Yet more forcefully perhaps, a sense of superiority Jews felt toward peasants emerged from the former's religious convictions. They held
Christianity to be idolatrous, and especially so the rituals observed by the
peasantry, their cult of icons, statues, devotionalia, and other "graven
images" representing the Christian deity.

Contrasting Jewish and *goyish*, and the disdain for the latter notwithstanding, the Jews' negative attitude toward peasants generally lacked intensity and passion. Rather, it was accompanied by a feeling of pity, resulting from their observation of the wretched conditions of the latter's
existence; in immigrant recollections, shtetl Jews, however poor themselves, by and large saw their own standard of living as higher than that of
the villagers. And, perhaps even more important, pity arose from a sense of
the superiority of their own values and their whole way of life. "It never
occurred to us," recollected an immigrant who grew up in the town of
Neustadt in northern Lithuania, "that the Gentile world [around] was happier . . . on the contrary, we considered our world happier and finer." And
Joseph K. from northeastern Hungary who as a thirteen-year-old came
with his parents to western Pennsylvania: "We thought they were unfortu-
nate . . . we [were poor but] were above them, this was the feeling [toward
peasants]."[29]

Side by side with disdain built upon a sense of material and cultural superiority (yet softened by the feeling of pity), the second component in the
attitude of the shtetl Jews toward *goyim*-peasants was fear and mistrust.
Underlying it was that generalized sense of insecurity they felt as a minority
group occupying the actual position of inferiority and powerlessness in
East European societies. Specifically in their relation to peasants, this dread
among inhabitants of the shtetls was fortified by their perception of the
threatening, uncontrollable physicality of their Gentile neighbors, who
were easily aroused to aggressive acts by momentary upset or inebriation,
or by religious or other incitement. This brewing tension beneath accus-

tomed everyday peasant-Jewish contacts was played out in Gentile children's hurtful "jokes," in individual acts of adult verbal or physical violence, and finally in pogroms, and kept the Jews in a state of ever-present
anxiety. From their parents and the shtetl community children learned
early this sense of unceasing apprehension in relation to the Gentile environment. As a result of all these experiences, there developed in the common Jewish attitude toward peasants a sort of compartmentalization: one
element of it, accommodating demeanor, was directed outward and displayed in their relations with the countryside population; the other element, a sense of disdain for and superiority over the peasants, was turned
inward, expressed and reasserted among one's own within the shtetl community. (As my interviews indicate, however, Hungarian Jewish rural residents, supported by official Budapest policy, apparently did not experience
this unabated anxiety in their local environment.)[30]

The restructuring of Eastern Europe in the process of urbanization-
industrialization was accompanied across the region by social and cultural
ferment. This was expressed in a variety of political and ideological forms,
from nationalism to populism and socialism, each offering a different vision
of building modern society to replace the descending old order. Ferment
also spread among Jews, who were affected by similar general dislocations
and subject to additional problems because of their special-minority status.
The *Haskalah* (Jewish Enlightenment, or modernism, whose followers
were called the *maskilim*), Zionism, socialism—each in its way was opening
traditional Jewish life. These innovative ideas and organizations, however,
were most influential in larger, socially heterogeneous urban centers.[31]

In no more than 15 percent of the small towns in all regions of Eastern
Europe combined, and in about 28 percent of those in more "mobilized"
areas of Lithuania-Byelorussia, and the Ukraine, from which the immigrants came to the Johnstown area, did I find recognized *Haskalah* ideo-
logues, or established Zionist organizations, or a Bundist (i.e., Jewish-
socialist) cell. (For each identified locality I checked the period *until* the
departure of its resident[s]; about two-thirds of the future Johnstowners
who came to Johnstown before World War I left Eastern Europe before
1905.) The recollections of my immigrant informants indicated that they
were aware of these movements; visiting speakers held meetings and propagated their ideas, and local people gathered to discuss the new concepts;
some young men, often *yeshive* students, surreptitiously read secular literature. But in only half a dozen immigrant families in Johnstown was there
apparently someone personally involved in these activities.[32] Asked about
their own or their parents' religious orientation and political sympathies in
Eastern Europe, the Johnstowners usually described themselves as "just ordinary Orthodox Jews."

Indeed, by any measurement, the families of the future immigrants were
overwhelmingly *proste yidn*, commoners from the lower socioeconomic
strata of Jewish societies, without much learning, whether traditional (reli-

gious) or secular. Respectful of scholarship, they did not pursue it themselves. In the opinion of one typical immigrant, apprenticed in artisanship at the age of thirteen because of his family's economic needs, this avenue of achievement was *far di andere*, for the others, those of greater means and higher ambitions. Most of them never received education beyond traditional *kheyder* instruction in the essentials of reading the Hebrew Bible and prayerbook, and reciting blessings—the mandatory program for boys. The girls, exempt as females from most public religious practices and participation, memorized a few Hebrew prayers required of women at home, and learned some reading and writing in Yiddish. No more than 10 percent of the pre–World War I adult settlers in Johnstown attended public schools in East Europe, specifically in the regions under Austro-Hungarian rule; only a couple of young men and one woman attended a gymnasium.[33] Apart from three or four self-taught Talmudic scholars, a still smaller proportion could name among their family members men with higher Jewish learning traditionally rewarded with *yikhes*, respect and prestige—a rabbi, a *khazn* or cantor, or a *yeshive-bokher*, a student in a Talmudic academy—and none of these completed their studies.

Although religiously unlearned by the standards of Judaic scholarship, the "ordinary Orthodox Jews" in turn-of-the-century rural shtetls still lived lives more, or more exclusively, bound by tradition than those of their contemporary fellow ethnics who relocated to larger cities, undertook industrial employment, and more readily came under the influence of growing secular movements.[34] Among the characteristics of this traditionalism were virtually complete nonvoluntarism of group membership; undifferentiation of folk (ethnic) and religious identity and practices; a high degree of influence on social and cultural life exerted by group religious symbols and institutions, or, in Peter Berger's language, a wide scope of coverage of the "sacred canopy";[35] and inclusive communalism. Nonvoluntary membership and the interpenetration of Judaism (religion) and Jewishness (peoplehood) were sustained by the external situation, namely, the organization of the larger society based on ethnoreligious ascription, and this was even more pronounced in the countryside than in the modernizing cities: for example, to contemporary ethnographers' inquiries about their collective identity, turn-of-the-century Polish (Catholic) peasants commonly answered, "I am of Polish religion." On the inside, this traditionalism was upheld by the Judaic Great Tradition, binding God and His people Israel, and by the actual functioning of local Jewish communities.[36] In the small shtetls dotting a countryside populated by Russian (Polish, Ukrainian, Slovak, etc.) Christians, it was practically impossible to be a Jew other than among, with, and like other Jewish people; conversely, Jewishness was naturally expressed or realized through the religion-related cultural symbols and social institutions. "In our town . . . religion was the framework of everyday life . . . even some young people who went astray [i.e., involved themselves in secular studies or social movements] did so within the religious sphere"—this representation from the memorial book of the shtetl

1.5. *Groyse shul*, Antopolie, east of Brest Litovsk, Grodno Province. Collection of the YIVO Institute for Jewish Research.

Antopolie in Byelorussia, from which a chain of families came to settle in Johnstown, was typical.[37]

Organization of public life in the shtetls was communal and synagogue-centered—a pattern mirrored in the surrounding society, where the church was the focus of public village life. If a minimum of 2,000 to 2,500 Jews lived in a shtetl, one would most likely find there, as in Antopolie, one *groyse shul*, a big synagogue used on the Sabbath and holidays. There were also two or three *boti medroshim*, smaller buildings or often just large rooms for the men's daily prayers and religious study, each with its customary patrons; a ritual slaughterhouse; a *mikve*, ritual bath; and a few *khedorim*, religious schools for children. As women had no place in the public sphere of Orthodox Jewish religion, they were relegated to a remote place in the synagogue (usually the balcony), separated by the *mekhitse*, curtain, from the main floor, which was reserved for the men. At best, the women could participate in the religious functions as participant observers; in Derazhnya in the Ukraine, for example, when the boys were trained by the cantor for Kol Nidre chant (public declaration, chanted at the beginning of Yom Kippur services, canceling all forced and harmful personal vows) in one of the smaller prayer houses, the girls "would get in on these rehearsals, standing on the sidelines," and in this way learned "every voice in the chant."[38]

In addition to their religious functions, the prayer houses served as centers of social and cultural activities. In Zhitkovitch in Byelorussia, "Men [eagerly] went to shul. . . . This fulfilled an obligation as well as being a way of social contact." And so they commonly gathered there *tsvishn minkhe un mayriv*, between the late afternoon and early evening prayers, for storytelling, and, after the market day, to discuss business over a glass of apple brandy. The women, many of them likewise involved in market trading, were excluded from these gatherings of their husbands and sons; they talked about the same subjects as men, as well as family matters, seated on the doorsteps of their houses, or inside over a cup of tea. The prayer houses were used for communal assemblies to listen to *magidim*, visiting preachers, for celebrations occasioned by religious holidays and involving dancing (*simkhas-toyre*) and plays (*purim-shpiln*), as well as for performances staged by traveling theatrical troupes, usually based on biblical stories. In these cultural-social events women participated, too, as observers, seated in a separate section of the *shul*, or looking on through the windows.[39]

The shtetl synagogue served also as a meeting place for the *khevres*, charitable societies providing various kinds of assistance: in sickness and death, to the poor, the orphaned and the widowed, the old, the transient, and to *yeshive* students. Such *khevres* were virtually universal in Jewish communities across the region; the Jewish Colonization Association's 1898 survey found nearly 2,500 charitable organizations in the Pale of Settlement. Membership in the *khevres* was restricted to men; the women engaged in charitable activities individually or in informal cooperation with others: visiting new mothers, making and distributing clothing and food to the needy before the Sabbath and holidays, passing out coins the family members put into the *pushkes*, charitable boxes at home, to traveling collectors for Jewish causes.[40]

The *khevres* were not truly or wholly voluntary associations: giving to or assisting others in need is perhaps the root religious precept of Judaism inculcated into children, boys and girls equally, from the earliest age by word and practical demonstration. The Jewish term for charity, *tsdoke*, implies a social obligation intrinsic to membership in the group, rather than, as in Christian *caritas*, a voluntary act of benevolence. Moreover, Jews believe that charitable deeds are the best means of accumulating "credits" toward the afterlife: "*Tzedokah* delivers from death" (Prov. 10:12), that is, gains one a place in *oylem*, the world to come.

The acts of *tsdoke* have eight degrees or rungs, teaches Maimonides; the most meritorious acts of charity are ones that "help men to help themselves," that is, anticipate and prevent need by making people self-sufficient. In practical matters such as gaining a livelihood, the righteous deed would be, means permitting, apprenticing the needy person at a trade, or providing employment or a loan to establish an independent business. *Tz'enah Ur'enah* (the popular Yiddish version of the Torah with paraphrased Talmudic commentaries for the instruction of the unlearned, especially women) commented on Lev. 26:37, "A man shall fall on his brother," thus: "Our sages say that every person of Israel is a guarantor for the others. . . . For this reason, the people of Israel are likened to nuts: when one nut is taken out of the box, all of them move about."[41] Sustained from without by the insecurity of their minority position and from within by religious sanction, a socially embedded network of interfused institutional and personal assistance created, as Arcadius Kahan called it, a "mini-welfare system" inside the shtetl communities.[42]

The practice of *tsdoke* can be considered as a link between the public (institutional) and private (family) spheres of the religious lives of East European Jews, and it had been the women, or women's charitable works, precisely, that made this connection. Practically excluded from the formal-religious public life of the shtetl, by exercising the acts of *tsdoke*, even in an informal way, on behalf of the community, women gained a certain presence and authority in communal affairs. The locus of their intrinsic authority, however, was the home.

At home, women were responsible for the family's proper nutrition, a matter of as much existential as religious importance among Orthodox Jews. This involved, first and foremost, daily maintenance—and instruction therein of the daughters—of the rules of *kashrut* (Jewish dietary laws), one of the prime precepts of traditional Judaism. In my informants' recollections observance was strict in the shtetls; here, also, remembrances coincided with those recorded in immigrant memoirs describing similar environments—in content, that is, because in form the latter have been more elaborate and stylized. The woman's responsibility in the home also included weekly preparation for the Sabbath: cleaning the house, usually with the help of the girls, and preparing the customary meal, as well as lighting the candles at the onset of the holy day. And, of course, they cooked and baked for all other holidays in the Jewish religious calendar, which were observed scrupulously in the shtetls. Reminiscing about women's role in religious observance in the home, my informants' most common images were of mothers (or grandmothers) lighting the Sabbath candles and reciting the customary blessing; on the preceding day, collecting coins from everyone able to contribute to the charity *pushkes*; and busying themselves in the kitchen preparing food for seasonal holidays. These holidays provided occasions for socializing, open-house style, managed again by the women as food distributors. Not as universal finally, but not uncommon, was a custom among shtetl women such as Leah P., a "very *frum*, pious or observant, person," the mother of Sarah F. On Sabbath afternoons Leah spent time reading a Yiddish book of legends adapted from parts of the Bible, or from *Tz'enah Ur'enah* the explicated fragments from that day's Torah reading.[43]

Asked about the religious observance of their fathers, or other adult males, at home, my informants most commonly recalled *davenen* (praying) at the beginning and the end of the day, *kidesh*, a blessing over wine recited at the opening of the Sabbath, and the ritual of *havdole* at its closing. Besides the scrupulous practice of *kashrut* in the homes, Sabbath memories appear to have been most deeply engraved in the minds of my immigrant informants, perhaps because it was this fundamental observance that, as we will see later in this study, they had abandoned, or radically truncated, shortly after coming to America, and so the contrast was particularly stark.

How secularized Jews had become in some large urban centers of Eastern Europe at the turn of the century is evidenced by contemporary observations of most stores remaining open on the Sabbath—in Lemberg, for example, and even more so in rapidly expanding Odessa, where an estimate put store openings at 90 percent. Reportedly, many an Odessan Jew also carried money and chatted in cafés smoking cigarettes; the first and third activities are explicitly forbidden on the Sabbath, while visiting cafés was a violation because nonkosher food was served.[44] No such things apparently occurred in the shtetls in which the prospective Johnstowners originated (nor, for that matter, have I heard anything of the kind from those few who lived in the bigger cities). According to my informants' recollections, on Sabbath all weekly activities ceased in the shtetls, and this cessation was observed by all residents: "Nothing [forbidden] was done, nothing"; "Shabes was strictly Shabes."

A very significant factor upholding this widespread observance of the traditional Sabbath ritual (as well as other religious practices) was the effective social control within the local Jewish communities. "In Zager they [the shtetl people] would kill you for violating Shabes": thus Hyman M. sharply contrasted the way of the Sabbath observance in his hometown with the situation in Portage, Pennsylvania, where he had settled.[45] Similar references to the consensual shtetl opinion were recurrent in my informants' remembrances of religious conduct, particularly on the Sabbath. This public opinion not only pronounced judgment on actions (or nonactions) that had already taken place, but it was also quite effective in preventing nonconformist behavior. Leo Baeck called this type of religiosity *Milieufrömmigkeit*—the devoutness of the environment, in conformity with the prevalent mores. And indeed it was in great measure because of traditional Judaism's wide scope of "social coverage" and of the interfusion between the religious and folk (ethnic) membership, combined with effective intragroup controls, that the strong grip of religious observance seems to have persisted in the lives of Jews in those shtetls.[46] In no small measure, if somewhat paradoxically, it was also upheld from the outside, by the cooperation of Gentile economic partners who, their animosity notwithstanding, adjusted to the rhythm of the Jewish liturgical cycle and religious practices—a situation that did not continue in America.

POPULAR WORLDVIEWS

Know-how in countryside trading and familiarity with the peasant-economic partners of the rural shtetls, along with a strong sense and practice of communal bonds and collective responsibility upheld by religious precepts and effective social control, can be seen as resources used by Jews to pursue family livelihoods and guarantee the persistence of the group. We now consider the counterpart of these resources, namely, more or less un-reflexive popular mental schemas that, shaped by past experience of the Jewish people encoded in their collective memory, and by shared life situations in turn-of-the-century Eastern Europe, imbued with meanings the social world of shtetl residents and guided their everyday practice.

These schemas consisted of folk wisdom, expressed in customs, sayings, proverbs, and the like, deeply penetrated by religious symbols and references. As in the lower, uneducated segments of societies in general, symbolic religion in the Orthodox rural shtetls was of a popular nature. (The conventional term "folk religion" does not seem appropriate in this context, because of the constitutive role of the concept of folk-as-peoplehood in the understanding of Judaism, whether scholarly or not.) Still, because of Judaism's special emphasis on continuous religious learning, which was required even of the most ordinary members of Jewish society, an unusually large portion of the Great Tradition was absorbed into the popular religion in the shtetls, although most residents would not have been able to articulate it in a coherent way.

The basic and most embracing component in these schemas of shtetl Jews was the taken-for-granted assumption of God's creative presence in the universe, and the elemental "yes of the heart" to life grounded in *bitokhn*—confidence in God's beneficence and the fundamental goodness of His works, expressed in the Yiddish version of the well-known Talmudic dictum *Gam zu letoyve*, "This, too, is for the good" (B.Talmud: *Taanit*, 21b). This fundamental trust, however, did not necessarily imply a belief in God's involvement in people's everyday affairs. In this matter, and specifically regarding pursuit of a livelihood, the schema contained a range of options. At one end was the hopefully dependent "God will provide" (Gen. 22:8), joined with admonitions to uphold pious trust in the Almighty; this stance was also jokingly travestied in a popular Yiddish saying: all right, God will help, but *vi helft nor Got biz Got vet helfn*—if only God would provide until He provides. At the other was the more collaborative "God [may] grant one a successful life, but one has to work hard," derived from the well-known verse of *Pirke Avot* (The Ethics of the Fathers, 1:14), "If I am not for myself, who is for me. . . ?" Although the former idea recurred most often in the religious literature designed for women, such as the pedagogical reader *Tz'enah Ur'enah* or traditional *tkhines*—prayers for particular occasions—by the end of the nineteenth century more collaborative interpretations also appeared, for instance, that informing a new *tkhine* (of maskilic origin), expressing at once the reliance on God and a call to action: "Although you, Lord of the Universe, are our protector, yet you have written in the Holy Torah that human beings should not depend on miracles."[47]

Contained within this base frame of fundamental confidence in God's beneficent presence in the universe were the directives—more conscious and elaborated in the minds of their carriers—for human, and specifically Jewish, conduct in life. The major one has been the call to sustained and purposeful action, as implied in the above-quoted precept from *Ethics of the Fathers.* The *magidim* preaching in the shtetls taught that "God's influence is manifested in granting to men the primitive clay of life [to] work it into manifold forms," each person to make the best use of it according to his circumstances, "for [they] will be held accountable regarding it"; and *Tz'enah Ur'enah* echoed: "Man resembles God in this, for just as God chooses His own path, His own desires, so man, too, can choose which way to go, what sort of life to lead." Since the time humans spend in this world is short, and the work is great, their lives should have *takhlis*—concrete purpose(s) or projected goal(s) within the range of socially accepted, and gender-specific, pursuits in the Jewish community, toward which they should strive as much as they can in their life situations. (It should be noted in this context that Judaism considers Torah study as a distinctly active pre-occupation and meritorious *takhlis*, and therefore, particularly in a traditional community, a reflective, studious lifestyle would perfectly meet the normatively prescribed conduct.)[48]

The human world was represented as a field of inherently contradictory forces carrying multiple potentialities and significations, and therefore always relative and underdetermined. All cultures acknowledge the conflicts and ambiguities of life. Jewish culture, however, seems to have been predicated on this recognition, inviting and thriving on it; it informs the midrashic part of Talmudic scholarship as well as the folk-religious worldview of the shtetl, conditioned by the centuries-long ever-precarious experience of a minority in diaspora.[49]

The Torah has "forty-nine faces," taught the rabbis, each verse saying "Interpret me!" and generations of scholars did just that, uncovering compound layers and variants of meanings to be elucidated in the never-ending process of interpretation, each answer subject to further checking and revision.[50] Reading the explications of particular Torah portions from their *Tz'enah Ur'enah*, the shtetl women commonly found them concluded with such statements as ". . . but others [rabbis] say that the opposite is true" or "a different explanation of the same is. . . ."

This acknowledgment that things have many, oftentimes contradictory meanings, that one and the same event contains plural, frequently opposite possibilities, was also expressed in Yiddish folk wisdom. Countless maxims delighted in this antithetical quality of life and the intrinsic ambiguities of human experience: "Every part has its counterpart"; "No choice is a choice." The same wisdom was brought to the fore in the teachings of the local sages, like that of the Ladier Rabbi, repeated throughout the shtetls: "A man should so master his nature that he can habituate himself to both the positive and negative aspects of every character trait. For example, he should be both conservative and progressive, a man without fear and yet a man of peace, a man of strong personality and yet a meek one."[51]

Related to the representation of human life as a field of crisscrossing paths and multiple potentialities was a deeply embedded belief that the world, in a phrase of Rabbi Ishmael ben Elisha (second century C.E.), "re-volved in a wheel of fortune" (B.Talmud; *Shabbat*, 151b). In *Tz'enah Ur'enah*, women read on that theme: "A person should not rejoice [too much] over the fact that he has amassed money, for a time will come when it will be gone, [for] everything has an appointed season."[52] To-gether with the base frame of the universe as an ongoing (re-)creation by God, whose "ways are mysterious and man cannot understand them,"[53] the revolving-wheel model of the world posited the impossibility of full rational mastery of life and of systematic means-to-ends manipulation of events toward desired purposes. At best, such self-determination was con-sidered only partially feasible, with ready acknowledgment of the incom-prehensible and with a place always left for unpredictable, adverse, or pro-pitious developments.

The Jews' precarious situation in turn-of-the-century Eastern Europe furnished experiential credence to the recognition of limits to rational mas-tery of life and the vicissitudes of fortune encoded in the Great Tradition,[54] and generated similar acknowledgments in Yiddish popular culture. There were sayings familiar in all shtetls, such as *Yidishe ashires iz vi shney in merts* (Jewish wealth is like snow in March, here today, gone tomorrow), or *Dem yidns simkhe is mit a bisl shrek* (A Jew's joy is not without fright). They expressed a sense of chronic uncertainty and limited control over the course of their lives as middlemen in a sluggishly changing and impover-ished economy, and as a politically dependent, and usually unwelcome, ethnoreligious minority. In everyday speech, whenever things were going well, people interjected disclaimers acknowledging the limitations on one's mastery of life events: *keyn ayn-hore* (no evil-eye), intended to exorcise bad luck in reports on a task successfully accomplished; *borekh HaShem* (Bless God) or *Got tsu danken* (thanks to God); statements concerning plans to be undertaken were punctuated with *as Got volt helfn* (God willing; with God's help).[55]

The combined "practical logic" of these world-schemas, validated by ex-perience of life in the shtetl, directed human pursuits not into fixed routes with precalculated means and firm-set goals, but, rather, onto twisting paths, (re)adjusted through intelligent evaluation of changing situations. *Got heyst oykh keyn nar nit zayn*, God never told anyone to be stupid—this Yiddish saying implied a similar directive: within the limits of human power, one should use reason by scrutinizing circumstances in order to understand their meaning and possible options. Then, appropriate action could be undertaken, and what was a limitation might become an opportu-nity. It was through this continuous, searching attention to the possibilities of purposeful action contained in concrete situations that *takhlis* was to be sought after.

In the world that revolved in a wheel of fortune where humans could never fully master the course of their lives, religious prescription of collec-tive responsibility and mutual assistance assumed an additional meaning as a safety regulation. On a verse in Deuteronomy (15:10), "You shall surely give him, and thy heart shall not be grieved when you givest unto him," *Tz'enah Ur'enah* expounded: "This means that the world goes in a circle; today this one is rich, tomorrow the other is rich. . . . The rich man should therefore be sure that he is generous to the poor man, lest God turn over the circle and the rich man become the pauper, while the poor one turns wealthy."[56] Embedded in such a worldview, the most meritorious of the acts of *tsdoke* as specified by Maimonides, those that "help men to help themselves," also had an obvious pragmatic rationale besides fulfilling the principal religious obligation.

GET THEE OUT!

American Jewish historians have recognized that of all the new social movements that emerged in Eastern European Jewish society toward the end of the previous century—*Haskalah*, Zionism, socialism—mass emigration to America definitely had the greatest, and broadest, impact.[57] The "American fever" of 1880–1914 did not affect Jewish communities alone but swept across the whole of Eastern Europe, mobilizing millions of people from virtually every ethnic group. During these three and a half decades almost seven million immigrants arrived in the United States from Russia and Austro-Hungary, of whom two million were Jewish, and the rest mainly Slavs and Hungarians, most of them peasants.[58] Structural dislocations and increasing poverty, the "demonstration effect" facilitated by chain-migration assisted by local networks on both sides of the ocean, and the myth of America as the Golden Land—all these were common forces setting in motion Jewish and non-Jewish peoples in the region. But there were also significant differences between these two emigrations.

While they constituted less than one-tenth of the total population of the Russian Pale, Galicia, and Hungary combined, Jews proportionally furnished three times as many American emigrants from all these territories, nearly 30 percent. Between the 1880s and World War I about 27 percent of all East European Jewry left for America, as compared with less than 10 percent of non-Jewish East Europeans. (It should be noted, however, that non-Jews, and peasants in particular, moved in continuous seasonal labor migrations within and around the region, mostly into the agricultural parts of Lower Austria and eastern Germany.)[59]

Why did such a great proportion of the Jews go to faraway America so much more? The greater availability in Central Europe of seasonal employment in agriculture for peasants was very likely a contributing factor, as well as the fact that poverty among the peasants was reportedly more acute and more widespread than among Jews. In the overwhelming majority of peasant families, funds were simply unavailable for a transatlantic voyage. Another, probably more decisive factor was the vexing civic-political condition of the Jewish minority in those parts of the region where it was most heavily concentrated. The intensity of Jewish emigration to America indeed varied considerably, its general pattern reflecting the legal-political treatment of Jewish minorities in particular countries: worst in Russia, better in Galicia, and relatively good in Hungary. Thus, in the Russian Pale, the Jews (11 percent of the population) made up over one-half of the total number of emigrants to America in the years 1880–1914. Each new wave of pogroms sent off ever greater number of Jews; after running at about 50,000 annually at the turn of the century, Jewish emigration from Russia increased to double that figure in 1905, and by 1907 it had trebled. In Galicia, the Jews (12 percent of the population) made up nearly one-fourth of all American emigrants; but in Hungary, the overall share of Jewish emigration in all departures to America equaled the proportion of Jews (4 percent) in the population of the country. There are, however, no data for the northeastern and southernmost provinces, where the prevailing civil-political climate was less hospitable to the Jews and in which the majority of Jewish emigrants originated; their rate of emigration from these territories could have been higher.[60]

Adding to economic distress, political discrimination and open anti-Semitism made thousands of Jews willing to make a radical break and get out far and for good. Strikingly different demographic profiles of Jewish and non-Jewish East Europeans arriving at U.S. ports suggest that the intention of the majority of the Jews was permanent resettlement. Of the non-Jews, nearly 80 percent were young and single men, and only 10 percent were children under fourteen. By contrast, Jewish emigration was a family venture—the sexes were about equally represented, the proportion of married men and women was roughly the same, and the percentage of children under fourteen was two and a half times larger (25 percent). The contents of immigrant letters sent to relatives and friends in Eastern Europe shortly after arrival in America—I inspected a sample of Polish and Yiddish correspondence from the years 1890–1891—seem to confirm the conclusion above: whereas letters by Poles contained frequent references to their intended return, although the exact time was most often unspecified, the Jews essentially did not mention this possibility, focusing, rather, on planning the transatlantic voyage of those who remained behind.[61]

Some interpretations of turn-of-the-century mass emigration of Jews from Eastern Europe point out its "ideological" dimension—this term is used to create an analogy with other contemporary movements, such as Zionism, socialism, and the like. This extra dimension, absent among the non-Jewish migrants, was the symbolic joining of the collective movement to America with one of the most powerful images in the Jewish Great Tradition, that of the Exodus of the Jewish people from Egyptian slavery, and their march toward the Promised Land. Through such linkage, a mass emigration of Jews from Russia to America acquired, according to this interpretation, a transhistorical dimension: not only the relocation of the physical persons across horizontal space, it became also, as Irving Howe called it, a "vertical liberation" (from bondage) of the Jewish people. Although this was no doubt a blasphemous transference from the viewpoint of Judaic lore, the immigrant memoirs and autobiographies indicate that such connections had indeed been made in several East European Jewish communities. For example, in Mary Antin's city of Plotsk in Congress Poland, those who decided to leave for America "to begin life all over again" would conclude their Passover *Haggadah* with "Next Year in America!" "our promised land," in place of the customary "Next Year in Jerusalem!"[62]

Spreading across Jewish society, the American fever also mobilized inhabitants of the rural shtetls, although likely with lesser intensity than residents of the more urbanized-industrialized areas. No comparative data exist, but this conclusion is suggested by the provenance in the Pale's northwestern provinces of the majority of immigrants, as well as by the occupations they declared at the ports of entry in the United States. It has also been argued that the emigration from the commercial-agricultural sector of the "Jewish" economy was less because of its disproportionate concentration in the grain and cattle trade, which had little transferable value in America.[63]

The future Johnstowners were, then, it appears, part of a smaller group among emigrants leaving for America. In several characteristics, they resembled the general emigrant population as presented above, but they also had distinct features. Like the latter, they mostly came from the Russian Pale, and, within it, the majority had lived in the northwestern provinces; most of them, too, were leaving their homes for basically economic reasons, and with no intentions of returning. A somewhat greater proportion of the prospective male Johnstowners than of the general population of emigrants, however, departed as married men with wives, 52 percent and 45 percent, respectively.

Like Jewish emigrants in general, the majority of whom had had their passage paid by (62 percent) and were going to join (74 percent) relatives,[64] those who settled in Johnstown relied very heavily on kin connections in organizing travel across the Atlantic and the initial stay in America. For example, Miriam Goldberg wrote in 1891 from New York to her sister's niece in Lipno in Congress Poland, the area from which a group of emigrants had settled in and around Johnstown: "About Bella [a cousin], let her just come to America and let her not delay the trip. Please give her my address. I shall meet her in Castle Garden and take her home with us until her husband will be able to make a living for the two of them." And Isaac Hartboit to his wife in the same area, announcing that he would send tickets to his family as soon as possible: "Dear wife, please get some bedding ready. You should make 2 quilts, 3½ yards long and 3 yards wide. The rest of the bedding may be the same as it is at home. The more of it you have, the better." Or Edith and Sara Pilap to their parents in Rypin, in the same year of 1891: "Dear Mother, do not think that the country here [New York] is like a village at home. Many people from Rypin live here and that is why Sarah [sister] wants to be here. . . . With God's help, we shall send a steamship ticket for father even before Passover. And I hope that after our dear father will arrive here, we shall be able to send for our dear mother and our little brother, even before the summer."[65] Social networks within and between towns in the surrounding area supplemented family aid in assisting the emigration; thus most Johnstown immigrants originated in distinct territorial patches in each province of the region (see map 1.1). Take, for example, the shtetl of Antopolie in Byelorussia, from which, as mentioned earlier, a chain of *landslayt* came to settle in Johnstown. Between the turn of the century and 1914 nearly one-third of the town's Jewish inhabitants emigrated, the majority to America.[66]

As already noted, while telling their life stories, most Johnstowners mentioned the economic hardship suffered by their families in Eastern Europe and the hope of making a better life in America as the main cause of their decision. In the follow-up interviews I tried, as gently as possible, and only with the immigrants who seemed to have particularly lucid memories of their old-country lives, to find out whether that mobilization to leave for the better world had perhaps any deeper symbolic framework of the kind suggested earlier, the "Exodus Connection." Basically, however, excepting some references to the millennial tradition of Jewish people's moving from place to place fleeing oppression, my informants did not describe a sense of "vertical liberation," although they may have had such a feeling at the time of emigration. Rather, their recollections, focused on a desire to escape poverty and make a better life, expressed the attitude of get-up-and-do when an opportunity arises. "Who changes his place changes his luck," they averred, a folk rendition of the Talmudic maxim to the effect that a wisely selected change of environment may change a person's life (B.Talmud; *Shabbat*, 6.9); an immigrant from Galicia was actually given this very advice when he approached a local *tsadik* for an opinion regarding emigration. The Antopolie rabbi urged people "[with the help of God] to take things in their own hands" in matters where good reason dictated action, and advised those who asked him about emigrating to America, "Go . . . you will make a living there," adding, "Observe the Sabbath" (an unusual approach, since the Orthodox leaders tended, rather, to discourage Jews from going to this "unkosher land").[67] Wolf G., who came to America from Congress Poland at the age of twenty-one, had left with his wife thinking, "No one knew how it was going to turn out, but we saw others [who had gone earlier] were doing well, so, God willing, we should try do the same, to make our lives better. . . . There was a Hasid rabbi in Europe, he said when he dies he won't be asked, 'Why were you not Moses, but why were you not Susya,' this was his name [Meshullam Zusya, a famous

Hasidic preacher from Hanipol in the Ukraine], meaning what did you make of your own life. . . . Well, there was not much to do at home, and [so] we went."[68]

As we have seen, those leaving the rural shtetls shared several character-istics with the general population of Jewish emigrants heading for America; but they were also taking along some distinct resources. Their backgrounds were in very small towns amid the countryside rather than, as seems to have been the case with a majority of their emigrant fellow ethnics, in more ur-banized centers. Correspondingly, the great majority of the future Johns-towners, 80 percent, were occupied in petty trade and rural artisanry, while nearly two-thirds, 64 percent, of the total number of East European Jews who had arrived in America between 1880 and 1914 had been employed as skilled workers prior to emigration (most of them had been employed in small shops, but they were protoindustrial wage workers nevertheless).[69]

As rural traders and artisans, the prospective Johnstowners, unlike Jew-ish residents of larger urban-industrial centers, had everyday dealings and familiarity with peasants who were simultaneously migrating to America in great numbers. As a matter of fact, as peasant-emigrants' letters and memoirs attest, not infrequently Jews extended their role of middlemen for peasants' affairs by arranging for passage across the border and getting tickets to the port of departure, and for the ship to America.

Last but not least, the social life and, presumably, mentalities of the resi-dents of these rural shtetls were still largely traditionalist, that is, character-ized by a low level of social institutional differentiation or communalism and involuntarism of membership; and by the fused folk and religious iden-tities, and a wide scope of "sacred canopy" in the symbolic-cultural sphere. The difference in this regard from the general population of Jewish emi-grants was not that the latter did not contain quite large numbers and groupings of traditionalists, but that there were practically no "moderns" or secularists among the immigrants who were to establish the Jewish com-munity in Johnstown.

These, then, were the economic and sociocultural resources with which the immigrants confronted and adapted to their new American environ-ment. We now look at these people's routes to Johnstown, Pennsylvania, and ways in which they organized their lives in that town and vicinity dur-ing the early phase of their settlement.

CHAPTER 2

Fitting Old-Country Resources into a New Place: The Formation of a (Multi-)Ethnic Economic Niche

THIS CHAPTER discusses the ways in which Jewish immigrants settled, and incorporated themselves into the local economy in Johnstown and vicinity by purposely using specific sociocultural resources familiar to them from the rural shtetls in Eastern Europe. Recent studies of immigration and ethnicity have distinguished two modes by which immigrants and their offspring adapt to the American economy. One is incorporation directly into the mainstream primary or secondary economic sectors; the other—an indirect or, as some students of contemporary immigrants' adaptation call it, "adhesive" way—occurs through participation in ethnic economic enclaves defined as the realms of production and/or distribution in which immigrants are largely employed by and work with members of their own ethnic group. These studies have also demonstrated the socially embedded nature of these incorporation processes. That is, immigrants rely extensively on kin and ethnic networks in entering employment and in initial occupational mobility, especially in the secondary sector of the mainstream economy, and in ethnic economic enclaves.[1]

The Johnstowners entered the local economy in their new environment in the second, indirect manner, by forming, through mutual assistance, a close-knit ethnic economic niche. The arrangement differed, however, from the ethnic subeconomies established in big urban centers, and especially in New York—then home to nearly two-thirds of the entire East European Jewish population in America. In New York, conventionally considered representative in American Jewish studies, the majority of gainfully occupied Jews at the beginning of this century were industrial wage workers, most of them in the largely (German) Jewish-owned and rapidly expanding garment manufacturing industry.[2] In the quite different economic and social environment of Johnstown, a small town in western Pennsylvania, Jewish settlers reconstructed a facsimile of the old-country petty-entrepreneurial niche, linked within by family and social bonds among local Jewish retailers, and to the outside by connections with fellow ethnic wholesalers in the larger area.

This concentration in entrepreneurial employment sustained through the internal networks of mutual assistance was a configuration that Johnstown's Jews shared with their fellow ethnics in other smaller American cities. At the beginning of this century, in urban centers with populations of over 250,000 and with large concentrations of Jewish immigrants, an average of 60 percent of gainfully employed Jews worked in manufacturing industries (in New York this proportion was highest); by contrast, in places with fewer than 100,000 inhabitants an even greater number, about 70 percent, were employed in trade and service occupations. But while ethnic entrepreneurial niches in these towns primarily served external, local mainstream markets, in Johnstown Jews had reestablished economic exchange with their former customers, East European peasants-become-industrial laborers in the local mills and coal mines, forming a multiethnic trading enclave within the local economy.[3]

The vast literature on the sources and sustaining factors of ethnic entrepreneurship that has accumulated in recent decades concurs in its emphasis on the interplay between conditions originating in the host environment and sociocultural resources internal to a group in question. The former include economic opportunities, and sociopolitical or religious disadvantage/discrimination; the latter, the experience, skills, and predispositions of the individual members, informal and institutional support networks, and socially sanctioned life-goals and role models encoded in a group cultural system and transmitted through the socialization process.[4] For analysis of the contributing components in ethnic entrepreneurship, a distinction between ethnic and class resources has also been useful. The former denote "the social features of a group, which coethnic business owners utilize in business, or from which their business benefits [as well as] values, knowledge, skills, information, money and work attitudes [and] solidarity." Class resources of entrepreneurship can be material and cultural: the former are private property of the means of production and distribution, wealth, and investments in human capital; the latter are "bourgeois values, attitudes, knowledge, and skills transmitted intergenerationally in the course of primary socialization to a class culture." The two kinds of resources may be simultaneously present, overlap, or even fuse in the same ethnic group, but the distinction is useful in comparisons of ethnic and nonethnic business and entrepreneurial niches.[5]

For a great number of Jewish immigrants from Eastern Europe external opportunities in the economic structure of American cities where most Jews settled combined with group experience of urban living and industrial employment in the country of origin. This concurrence enhanced class-ethnic resources and facilitated the emergence of a large industrial ethnic enclave in New York, and also in big urban centers such as Philadelphia, Boston, and Chicago. In Johnstown and vicinity, too, the external economic and sociopolitical conditions interacted with specific class-ethnic resources, including in this case entrepreneurial know-how, predispositions, and group solidarity—transplanted from rural shtetls. This particular combination had led to the reestablishment of a (multi)ethnic economic niche. In what follows I have tried to capture the important elements of this process, starting with an outline of Johnstown's environment, and then following the pursuits within this framework of pre–World War I Jewish settlers: how they first procured and then sustained entrepreneurial employment, how they conducted their businesses, and how they maneuvered within their niche in order to achieve their purposes.

"A GOOD PLACE FOR BUSINESS": BUILDING OF THE ETHNIC ENTREPRENEURIAL NICHE

Located in Cambria County in western Pennsylvania, situated along the Conemaugh River and surrounded by the Allegheny-Kiski mountain chain, Johnstown—a smoky city of molders and miners—was by 1910 counted among the nation's top six steel-producing centers. The major impetus for its industrial expansion was Cambria Iron Works (later Bethlehem Steel), founded in Johnstown in 1852. Its mammoth mills turned out 125,000 tons of steel rails and over 300,000 steel ingots annually by the end of the century, and almost four times that amount by the outbreak of World War I. This pivotal industry was supported by the smaller Johnstown Steel Rail Company, the National Radiator Company, brick-, clay- and machinery-manufacturing enterprises, and by nearly fifty coal mines in nearby boroughs and townships. An additional one hundred coal mines operated nearby in adjacent Indiana, Somerset, and Westmoreland Counties. All of them served primarily the needs of Cambria/Bethlehem plants.[6]

Map 2.1. Location of Johnstown in Western Pennsylvania

The demographic growth of the Johnstown area progressed concurrently with its industrial expansion. During the thirty years from 1880 to 1910, Johnstown grew from a borough of barely 8,000 inhabitants to a town of over 50,000; between the turn of the century and World War I, the population of Cambria and the three adjacent counties more than doubled. The population of the fifteen largest towns within a fifteen-to-twenty-mile radius of Johnstown grew more than fourfold in the same period (the number of inhabitants ranged from 1,500 to 8,000). As elsewhere in the country where expanding industries attracted large numbers of immigrants, southern and eastern Europeans significantly contributed to the demographic growth of the Johnstown area. Between 1890 and 1910 the number of foreign-stock persons from Russia and Austria-Hungary increased from about 2,000 to nearly 12,000, or 22 percent of Johnstown's population. In the rest of Cambria County and in the three adjacent ones, it grew approximately tenfold, constituting, by the outbreak of World War I, about one-fifth of their total population. Of these numbers, the overwhelming majority—about 95 percent in the city of Johnstown and 99 percent in the surrounding counties—were Slavs and Hungarians.[7]

With rapidly expanding operations, the steel and coal industry in Johnstown and vicinity directly or indirectly provided a livelihood for most of the area's growing population. About three-quarters of the town's male labor force were manual workers, and of this number no fewer than two-thirds worked at Cambria/Bethlehem mills and coal mines, and 30 to 40 percent of the rest were employed in establishments servicing them. Not surprisingly, given this economic profile, Johnstown entered this century with a lesser share of its population employed in white-collar jobs than was the case in the big cities. Expectedly, too, the area's economy held few employment opportunities for women; in 1900, only about 11 percent of Johnstown's females over fifteen years of age were gainfully occupied, as compared with 27 percent in New York, 28 percent in Philadelphia, and 22 percent in Pittsburgh. The rest of Cambria and surrounding Indiana, Somerset, and Westmoreland Counties were even more occupationally homogeneous: not counting farmers, close to 80 percent of the employed male population were manual workers, the majority of them miners.[8]

With the greater part of the male blue-collar workforce in Johnstown employed at Cambria/Bethlehem plants, and most of the workers in the surrounding area in the mines providing coal for their needs, the company held an unrivaled power. After crushing independent labor organizations in its mills and coal mines in the 1870s, Cambria/Bethlehem Steel Company managed to keep the workforce captive for nearly seventy years, until 1941. Although some of the smaller independent coal mines in the surrounding counties unionized at the beginning of the century, they remained under the tight control of their owners, with law and order maintained by the ubiquitous Coal and Iron Police.[9] The influence of the local potentate, the Cambria/Bethlehem company, penetrated far beyond the economic sphere into the social, political, and cultural realms. Its managers, all members of the established, mostly Anglo-Protestant elite, routinely held public office in Johnstown and took a leading part in the region's political life. The city's major newspaper, the *Johnstown Tribune*, served as a loyal publicity agent for the company and traditionally supported its policies.

Another characteristic of the Johnstown area, closely related to the nature of its industrial base, was a large and stable percentage of native-born; despite the influx of new immigrants during the three decades preceding World War I, this group made up over three-quarters of the local population. Of these, one-half were native-born Americans of native parentage, and one-fourth were persons of West European origin. Both groups were openly nativist and strongly conscious of their separateness and superiority. The social organization of turn-of-the-century Johnstown reflected pronounced ascriptive divisions between the "old" and the "new" ethnic groups, and was replicated in all important spheres of life. Southern and eastern European laborers, constituting from 50 to 60 percent of the local miners and 30 to 40 percent of the steel workers by the outbreak of World War I, were concentrated in nationality gangs employed in the plants, or in departments reserved for foreigners. Most new immigrants lived in a few sections of town, the so-called foreign colonies. Social interaction and cultural participation were similarly compartmentalized. Without unions, and with unconcealed nativism among the longer-established population, Johnstown and the surrounding area had practically no institutional channels to provide for regular social and cultural interaction between the old and the new ethnic groups. Even if they shared the same class position, new immigrants from southern and eastern Europe remained quite separate from Americans and West Europeans, routinely frequenting different houses of prayer, social halls, and picnic grounds.

Finally, the exclusionary ethnic-ascriptive bases of local social organization, informed by strong nativist sentiments on the part of the dominant groups, were also reflected in political life. With the exception of a handful of persons who held low-level offices in the immigrant sections of Johnstown and the surrounding boroughs and townships, new immigrants were conspicuously absent from local politics, which was dominated by the established Anglo-Protestant elite and residents of West European ethnic stock. In sum, fragmented, ethnic-based ties and identities prevailed in the social and cultural organization of Johnstown and vicinity. The American and new immigrant worlds largely functioned as separate, hierarchically ordered social entities.

Like the majority of East European Jewish immigrants arriving in the United States between the 1880s and 1914, those who eventually settled in the Johnstown area headed for New York or other large cities in the eastern part of the country. Local interviews and the passenger lists of ships coming to U.S. ports indicate that slightly over 20 percent of the eighty-six

turn-of-the-century immigrants for whom I was able to gather this information went directly to Johnstown or surrounding towns. Nearly half
stopped in New York, about 15 percent headed for cities in Pennsylvania—
mainly Philadelphia or Pittsburgh—and a similar proportion for big cities
in Massachusetts, New Jersey, and Maryland. Excepting those who joined
their relatives immediately upon arrival, the immigrants spent an average of
five to six years elsewhere before settling in Johnstown. There was no common pattern apparent in the whereabouts of these people before their arrival in Johnstown: approximately half had come after a sojourn in large eastern cities, and the other half had stopped in various small towns, mostly in
the eastern and western parts of Pennsylvania.[10] Most of them followed
their kin and friendship contacts, their routes indicating the extent of the
social networks they built over the years.

It is unlikely that the prospective Johnstowners knew in advance the details of Johnstown's economic and sociopolitical characteristics. But some
of its features, as described by the pioneer settlers, appeared to them similar
enough to their old-country experience, and suitable to their current purposes and preferences, to warrant their making a home there. There were
of course a few classic cases of mistakes and accidents that brought people
to Johnstown. Jacob G., en route by train from Philadelphia to Youngs-
town, Ohio, misheard the conductor, got off in Johnstown, and stayed.
Israel N. met the son of Johnstown's rabbi at the Pittsburgh railroad station and was "talked into" going to that town. Moshe Yitzhak G., a peddler based in York in eastern Pennsylvania, periodically made long-distance
trips to collect scrap metal in the coal-mining towns in western parts of the
state. When his horse died in Windber, a few miles from Johnstown, he
decided to stay. A few people, no more than four or five altogether, were
sent to Johnstown by the Industrial Removal Office (I.R.O.)—a branch of
the Baron de Hirsch Fund organized in 1891 to decongest New York by
helping employable Jewish immigrants move to other localities.[11]

More typically, however, three motives surfaced repeatedly in the recollections of my informants as they reconstructed their own or their parents'
route to this area. One—for those who had lived in New York—was a dislike of the Lower East Side, where the majority of East European Jewish
immigrants resided at the beginning of the century. Its vibrant social and
cultural life notwithstanding, everyday existence there was dreary, housing
conditions were appalling, and all the hustle and bustle of the big city was
tiresome and annoying to people from the shtetls—townlets or small towns
with immediate rural surroundings. For the parents of Louis F. from
northeastern Hungary, Moses S. from Buczacz in Galicia, and Robert K.
from Czerków in that same province, of Sarah H. from near Bialystok in
Congress Poland, or for Harry M. from Zager in Lithuania, and for Samuel T. from Złatopolie in the Ukraine, "New York was too big," "a bad
place to raise children"; "It was in those days a real rat race, very difficult
[to live] in these tenements that were so crowded, ten people to one room

. . . "; "With rural background, they were attracted to a more rural area [and New York was all grey and stone]"; "[In New York people were] always in a hurry, rush, rush, and so preoccupied with their business that they did not care to ask about your health, your life . . ."; "they were happy to leave."[12]

A second common motive was the desire for self-employment in some kind of business—a "natural" inclination, as my informants put it, in people who themselves, or whose families, had been occupied in small trade and artisanry in Europe. In New York the majority of East European Jews were manual workers employed in the huge garment manufacturing enclave, and the chances of establishing oneself successfully in an independent enterprise were slim. These odds were somewhat better in two other large cities within the immigrants' social net—Philadelphia and Pittsburgh, where the ethnic industrial enclaves were smaller and less embracing; there too, however, the proportions of Jewish workers employed in manufacturing industries were a high 60 percent and 40 percent, respectively (see table 2.2). But the steel and coal towns in Cambria and the surrounding counties in western Pennsylvania, as the immigrants were advised by relatives and *landslayt*, were "a good place for business."

And so, having worked for a few years in Baltimore, then in Philadelphia's clothing factories, Isaac C. came to Johnstown when his cousin, a store owner in Atlantic City, told him about that town as "a very good location to go on one's own." Similarly, Philip E.'s father, who was just married and had been occupied at odd jobs between New York and Newark, heard from his new brother-in-law that "Johnstown was a good town to make an independent living," and decided to move there. After their window-cleaning business failed in New York, Moses S.'s partner left that city in search of a better place and, shortly after arriving in Johnstown, wrote to him "what a great place it was." And since, after four years of residence in New York, Moses' wife "was only too glad to get out of there," he joined his partner in 1910. Robert K.'s father, a waiter in a New York kosher restaurant, heard from relatives peddling in Altoona in western Pennsylvania that the nearby coal-mining town of Beaverdale had "good opportunities for clothing business." And Harry M., employed as a watchmaker in a Philadelphia factory, moved with his family to Portage in Cambria County, a few miles from Johnstown, after his uncle, who had a couple of small stores in the area, wrote to him, "Come over here and you will make a fortune . . . [the town] has good location for business and there is no jeweler."[13]

A third and related motive for moving to the Johnstown area was the large and growing population of East European peasant-immigrants, now industrial laborers in local mills and coal mines, who had to be clothed and fed, and whose languages, habits, and needs were known to the Jews from the old-country shtetls. And so Louis I. came in 1903 to Boswell because, according to his relatives, it was "a prosperous town with many Gentile

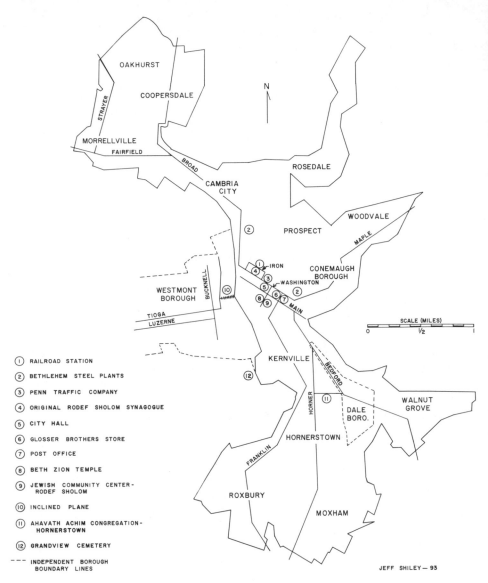

Map 2.2. Overview of Johnstown with Locations of Major Public and Jewish Buildings

miners from [Eastern] Europe," and "[since] he spoke their languages, it looked like the best thing to do." Similar reasoning—good prospects for self-employment and familiarity with prospective customers—led Abraham K. to nearby Beaverdale, and Harry M. to Dunlo near Johnstown, because both men "knew how to communicate with these people." As did Jack S.'s father, who "had an ambition to be in business for himself" and, while working as a salesman in a Jewish store in Richmond, Virginia, kept saving money "with a lookout for a prosperous area." When "Mr. Epstein, a wholesaler from Baltimore, advised [him] to check Johnstown," he went there in 1910, and seeing "how many people [there were] on the streets, immigrant workers coming and going with their lunch buckets, going to the mills, to the coal mines . . . I made up my mind to stay."[14]

By 1910, approximately 700–750 Jews, including immigrants and their children, resided in Johnstown, and about 100 more Jewish families lived in the towns and boroughs in the rest of Cambria and adjacent parts of the three surrounding counties.[15] A small group among the residents of Johnstown—about 10 percent of the entire Jewish population in that city—were German Jews who had arrived earlier, mostly from the Hesse-Darmstadt province in Westphalia and from Poznania in the German-ruled section of partitioned Poland. At the beginning of this century this German group, now well established in the city, numbered about thirty families closely connected by marriage and business relationships. By the outbreak of World War I, the overwhelming majority, 90 percent, of Jewish residents of Johnstown (and practically all in the surrounding area) were East Europeans.

Table 2.1 presents the family and household characteristics of the East European and German Jewish households, gathered from the manuscript schedules of the 1910 census. Table 2.2 shows the occupational distribution of the East European immigrants and second generation in Johnstown at the beginning of the century. The sources used recorded only a small fraction of the married or widowed females who were actually working; the participation of immigrant women in the household economy will be discussed later in this chapter. For comparison, data on the employment of local German Jews, and Jewish occupations in the same period in selected big cities, are also included.

An average East European immigrant household in Johnstown at the beginning of the century comprised a nuclear family, with parents in their early thirties and four children;[16] in comparison, German Jews were older and their families considerably smaller. Slightly over one-fifth of East European households kept boarders: they were most often *landslayt*, usually adolescent or young men recently arrived from Europe.

Jewish immigrants' position in the Johnstown economy was from the beginning strikingly different from the occupational distribution of the general population. While in the latter the proportion of people occupied in the commercial and service sector in 1910 was 18 percent, and of the self-employed in these occupations 11 percent, the respective shares among East European Jews were a very high 95 percent and 84 percent (including proprietors, independent artisans, and peddlers working on account).[17] Among the earlier German settlers, all of the gainfully employed in the city at the beginning of the century were also occupied in trade; about 40 percent were independent merchants, and the rest of the German Jewish adult men worked in their stores as managers, buyers, and salesmen.

TABLE 2.1
Family and Household Characteristics of Johnstown's Jews, 1910

	East Europeans	Germans
Median Age		
M	32.8 (130)	50 (31)
F	30.5 (98)	40.2 (27)
% Married[a]		
M	72 (94)	83 (26)
F	91 (89)	91 (27)
N (living) children per family[b]	4.1	2.7
% Nuclear families	64 (72)	78 (25)
% Extended family households	15 (17)	4 (1)
% Households with boarders	21 (24)	18 (6)

Sources: Manuscript schedules of the 1910 census; local interviews.

[a] Median age at marriage for East European Jewish immigrants was 23.7 for men, and 21.5 for women; for German Jews, 35 and 24, respectively (and for over half of the men the marriage recorded in 1910 was their second marriage).

[b] Number of (living) children born to East European immigrant women in particular age categories was as follows: 1.6 (under 25); 3.0 (25–29); 4.7 (30–34); 5.7 (35–39); 5.3 (40+). Lestschinsky gives the average number of children in the Jewish immigrant families from Russia at the beginning of this century as 5.6 (Jacob Lestschinsky, "Economic and Social Development of American Jewry," in *The Jewish People: Past and Present* [New York: Jewish Encyclopedic Handbook, 1955], 4:64).

In towns and boroughs in the surrounding counties, this occupational concentration of Jewish immigrants was greater yet: all the gainfully employed for whom I was able to gather this information were either store owners or peddlers, most often a combination of the two (in over 80 percent of the cases, the census recorded possession of a horse).[18] Contrastingly, at this time only 16 percent of East European Jews in New York, 18 percent in Philadelphia, and 34 percent in Pittsburgh were self-employed in trade.

Indeed, most East European Jews who had come independently to the Johnstown area, or had been brought there by their kin and acquaintances, so that they could "go on their own" did exactly that. This was possible in part because another expectation they brought with them was also fulfilled: they did find a large population of Slavs and Hungarians, their former neighbors and trading partners in Eastern Europe, whose languages, habits, and needs they knew, and who could again become their customers. The families of East European peasant-immigrants become industrial laborers—95 percent of Slavic and Hungarian adult males entered the local labor market as manual workers—constituted the bulk of the clientele of Jewish enterprises.

Founded on mutual familiarity from the old country, and sustained by the economic and sociopolitical conditions prevailing in the area, the pri-

TABLE 2.2
Occupational Distribution of Johnstown's Jews, 1910
(with Comparative Data for Large Cities)

	Johnstown			New York	Phila-delphia	Pitts-burgh
	% East Europeans (Men and Women Combined)		% German Men[a]			
	Immigrants (N = 137)	Second Generation (N = 68)[b]	N = 28			
				% Russian Jewish Men		
Self-employed in trade[c]	83	4	42	16	18	34
Storeowners	(33)	(4)	(42)			
Independent artisans	(23)					
Peddlers	(27)					
Commercial employees	12	93	58	9	10	15
Professionals	1	—		2	1	1
Occupied in manufacturing industries	4	3		73	71	55
Managers	(1)			(9)	(10)	(8)
Employees	(3)	(3)		(64)	(61)	(42)

Sources: The data for Johnstown from 1900 and 1910 manuscript schedules of the U.S. Census; 1910 and 1915 Johnstown business and city directories; tax assessments of Jewish persons and properties, 1910 and 1915 (located at Cambria County Courthouse in Ebensburg, Pennsylvania; local interviews. Information about (Russian) Jewish occupations in New York, Philadelphia, and Pittsburgh has been compiled from Jacob Lestschinsky, "Economic and Social Development of American Jewry," in *The Jewish People, Past and Present* (New York: Jewish Encyclopedic Handbook, 1955), 4:78–83; Joel Perlmann, "Beyond New York: The Occupations of Russian Jewish Immigrants in Providence, R.I., and Other Small Jewish Communities, 1900–1915," *American Jewish History* 72 (March 1983): 388–89. See also n. 2 in this chapter.

[a] No German Jewish women were recorded as gainfully employed; a discussion of East European women's involvement in business can be found below in this chapter.

[b] Children of immigrants over 15 years old.

[c] See also n. 17 in this chapter.

mary form of interdependence was between East European Jews as commercial dealers, and Slavs and Hungarians as their customers. This was supplemented by another, secondary type of relationship between the former
as employers and the latter as their employees. Together, these relations
made up a specific (multi)ethnic economic enclave wherein the two groups
established a pattern of "distant proximity" based on economic exchange
and corresponding social roles—a pattern similar, though not identical, to
that which informed their contacts in Eastern Europe.[19]

As it had been in the shtetls, economic exchange was the primary sphere
and focus of the relations between Jewish and Gentile immigrant groups.
It was facilitated by their continued residential proximity in the new settlements in Johnstown, and by the location of Jewish businesses: several were
found within a few blocks of the downtown section near the railroad sta-

tion through which every week hundreds of immigrant families came from nearby coal-mining colonies to do their shopping. In small surrounding towns their shops were equally accessible. The type of business carried on by Jewish entrepreneurs in Johnstown's foreign sections and the adjacent coal towns, and by those peddling their wares around the area, was well-tailored to the needs of working-class immigrant families: wares included work clothes for men, fabric and notions for women who sewed at home for themselves and their children, secondhand furniture, and jewelry items—"shiny, like those [sold] at the *odpust* [church patron's festival] in Europe"—pleasing to peasant tastes; foreign money was exchanged and steamship tickets sold from the counters of general stores. The establishment of Helma W.'s parents in Cambria City, one of the immigrant sections of Johnstown, was typical: "We had a large stock of clothing . . . and shoes for all the family and they [Slavic and Hungarian people] would come in with seven or eight kids and string them out on the benches and all [the] family would buy [whatever they needed]." Isaac R. peddled with a horse and buggy "among foreign [Slavic] people [in coal towns] around Johnstown," selling them "everything, jewelry, holy pictures, draperies, sheets."[20]

The manner of trading was also familiar. Like many Jewish immigrants, Olga S.'s father, first a peddler, then owner of a clothing store in one of the small towns in Somerset County, had a working knowledge of "several Slavish languages [which] came [in] very useful." And when miners were short of money, the transactions were frequently conducted in kind, old-country style, like those of Hyman K. from Creekside in Indiana County: "They gave me chicken and I gave them shirts." More commonly, the merchandise was sold on credit, with installments paid every two weeks, when the workers received their paychecks from the mills and coal mines. Seymour R.'s father, owner of a secondhand furniture store, whose customers were "mostly Polish, Slavish, Hungarian . . . sold [them] on credit . . . and went around collecting debts, fifty cents here, a dollar there." Zeinwel S., a storekeeper in one of Johnstown's foreign colonies, kept a "little book in Yiddish, with customers, what they owed [him] . . . not by their names, but by the description of the persons." He did know the names of his regular customers, but there were simply "too many Peter Hudaks and Mary Yarcheks" to distinguish them in this way in the book, hence such descriptions as "'a tall man with a beard who lives down the alley,' 'a little woman with a crippled foot,' 'big, fat woman with six kids.'"[21]

Most of the enterprises owned by East European Jewish immigrants in Johnstown at the beginning of the century were small family establishments; those that were somewhat bigger employed fellow Jews. Before World War I, there was only one Jewish-owned manufacture in the city, a small cigar factory in Cambria City, the neighborhood most densely populated by Slavs and Hungarians. This establishment was owned by Harry L., an immigrant from the Ukraine who could communicate in several East

2.1. Main Street in Johnstown, beginning of the century. Johnstown Area Heritage Museum.

2.2. Mr. William Teitelbaum in front of his clothing store in Cambria City, ca. 1912. Collection of the Teitelbaum family. Note signs in Slovak and Hungarian.

44

2.3. Mr. Oscar Suchman in front of his men's furnishings business on Washington Street, downtown, ca. 1915. Collection of the Suchman family.

European languages. From its foundation in 1900, it was operated by a Slavic and Hungarian workforce—young female employees recruited from Cambria City and adjacent areas.[22] Much more typical, however, of the employer-employee relationship between the two groups was the frequent use in Jewish homes of East European Gentile maids—another transplant from the old-country tradition, facilitated by their residential proximity in the new settlements and everyday business contacts. When Jews did employ servants—at the beginning of the century the wage for such help in Johnstown was $1.50–$2.00 per week with board—they were Slavs and Hungarians. The enumeration of members of East European Jewish immigrant households in the manuscript schedules of the 1910 census showed the presence of these domestics in nearly one-fourth of homes, and more were hired part-time on an hourly basis.[23]

In sum, the local situation, particularly the predominance of expanding heavy industry employing thousands of Slavic and Hungarian laborers who had to be fed and clothed, offered the Jewish immigrants an excellent opportunity to utilize their old-country sociocultural resources to undertake small trading—the occupation they had known best from individual and collective experience ascribed to the ethnic qua class position of Jews in the East European countryside. (Neither the city's major employer, Cambria/Bethlehem Steel, nor the smaller coal-mining companies in the surrounding counties were eager to hire Jewish workers, who were considered unfit for arduous manual labor; but this discriminatory attitude was not of great significance, since Jews themselves did not seek this kind of employment.) These resources' effectiveness in enabling the immigrants to pursue their preemigration occupations was indicated by a high rate of matched jobs: among men who had been old enough to work before they left Eastern Europe, almost half had reportedly continued the same type of employment in Johnstown: storekeeping, peddling, and artisanry, mostly in items of everyday wear. Another fifth undertook a similar pursuit; say, storekeeping instead of peddling, or peddling in place of artisanry.[24]

Benjamin I. described his father's approach after he had settled in the Johnstown area at the beginning of the century. It was one of individual initiative—that is, appreciating the situation in terms of practical possibilities it contained, and then "making a wise choice and acting intelligently." Such initiative served many immigrants well as a schema-resource in finding opportunities suitable to their skills and current circumstances. Thus Abe K., from a shopkeeping family in a Galician shtetl, did not give up when he was prevented from opening a general store in a town near Johnstown where the local coal company held the monopoly on selling to its workers. Instead, he looked around and soon "set up a place half a mile away, and the miners [previously exploited by the company store] came in right away and bought food and clothing." Samuel I., immediately after his arrival in western Pennsylvania, "looked around for the places that were similar to [his native] Lithuania, found a small niche [in a coal-mining town], bought a little store and the right merchandise [i.e., wares suitable for the needs of his prospective customers as he knew them], and started to do business. From that, he ventured out, went into hides and sheepskins [his occupation in the old country]. . . . This was intelligent: look around and find an opportunity." As turn-of-the-century Jewish settlers perceived it, the situation in America, and in the Johnstown area specifically, was much more amenable to purposeful action than had been circumstances they knew in Eastern Europe, and this felt comparative advantage invigorated immigrants' efforts to find and pursue promising avenues of economic endeavor. Isadore S.'s immigrant relatives from Galicia appreciated their new situation as compared with what they had left behind: "Whatever options they had here, they went after them [. . .] the circumstances [in America] permitted them to do it, because the marketplace was so structured that it did not deny them this opportunity."[25]

Old-country class-ethnic know-how in small entrepreneurship and trading with the peasantry, and individual "intelligent" initiative in search of the most suitable employment opportunities—these resources were certainly useful. However, as indicated by various sources about local Jewish business before World War I, and as confirmed by my informants, they were not sufficient to launch and maintain the immigrants in business. Another, equally significant or perhaps even weightier factor abetting the concentration of immigrants in small entrepreneurship was what Mark Granovetter has called the social embeddedness of the economic action,[26] namely, a social network of intragroup mutual assistance sustained by prag-matic considerations, and by the normative code that was part of their cultural heritage. Expanding and solidifying as the number of participants grew, this network facilitated the entry of new members into the ethnic entrepreneurial niche and supported those already in it.

In the process of establishing an economic support network and forming an entrepreneurial niche, men, and specifically male heads of households, were the main actors at all stages and levels of this development: they searched out business opportunities in the new place, exchanged advice, and arranged for the money necessary to start and continue an enterprise, through both personal and local institutional channels. I noted a few cases of women extending a loan from their personal funds to their (male) rela-tive to help him in business, but more commonly such operations, even when money belonged to a woman, were conducted between men. It also sometimes happened that a new (male) arrival in Johnstown asked a resi-dent female relative to connect him with an appropriate (male) person who could assist him in entering the Jewish entrepreneurial network; or the owner of an already-functioning business who needed a loan to keep it afloat asked a female relative to put in a good word with a potential (male) lender. On such occasions, women served as mediators—sometimes more than one mediator was involved—but the ultimate gatekeepers were men.

Although close physical proximity does not appear to be a necessary con-dition for constructing and maintaining personal and institutional net-works supportive of an ethnic economic niche, it certainly fosters this pro-cess. The residential arrangement in Johnstown, as in most other American cities where immigrants from Europe had settled since the 1880s, provided for, and in fact enforced, such closeness. Jews could not afford to live in sectors inhabited by Anglo-Americans and members of longer-established West European groups, nor were they welcome there. Instead, like other new arrivals at the turn of the century, they settled in the immigrant sec-tions of town. These neighborhoods, located near the mills and in the downtown area close to the railroad station, thickened every year as more newcomers joined their kin and acquaintances. Maps 2.3, 2.4, and 2.5 show where the homes and businesses of East European Jews at the begin-ning of the century were located; the Germans all lived and worked in the center-city business district.

As indicated by the 1910 manuscript schedules of the census, the largest proportion, nearly 40 percent, of new Jewish immigrants were concen-trated in the neighborhood between River Avenue and Iron Street next to the railroad station, north of Washington Street, and, close by on its south side, in similar tight residential clusters, within a few blocks between Johns, Union, and Lincoln Streets. Almost one-fourth lived in the two largest Slavic and Hungarian neighborhoods: Cambria City and Woodvale. Alto-gether, over 60 percent of them resided in Johnstown's "foreign colonies"

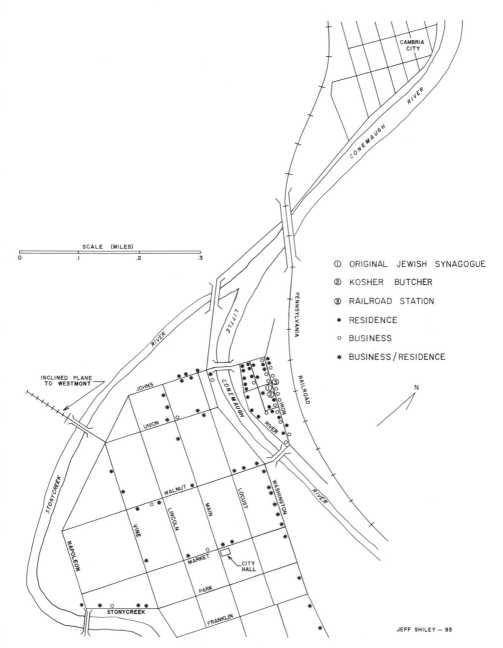

SCALE (MILES)

① ORIGINAL JEWISH SYNAGOGUE
② KOSHER BUTCHER
③ RAILROAD STATION
• RESIDENCE
○ BUSINESS
＊ BUSINESS/RESIDENCE

CAMBRIA CITY

CONEMAUGH RIVER

LITTLE

PENNSYLVANIA

RIVER

INCLINED PLANE
TO WESTMONT

JOHNS

UNION

CONEMAUGH

RIVER

RAILROAD

IRON

N

WALNUT

LINCOLN

MAIN

LOCUST

WASHINGTON

RIVER

VINE

STONYCREEK

NAPOLEON

MARKET

CITY
HALL

PARK

STONYCREEK

FRANKLIN

JEFF SHILEY — 93

Map 2.3. Residential and Business Locations of Johnstown's Jews, 1910s
(Downtown Area)

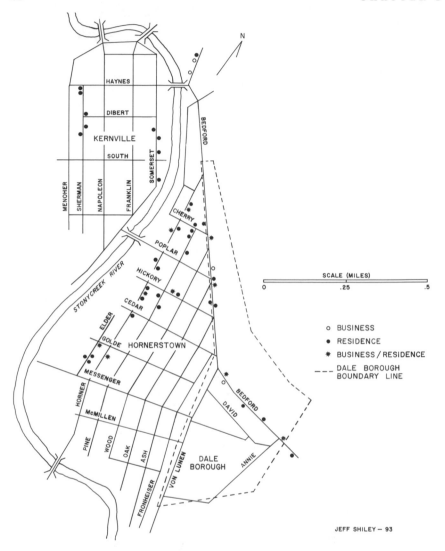

Map 2.4. Residential and Business Locations of Johnstown's Jews, 1910s (Kernville, Hornerstown, Dale Borough)

(in comparison, more than 80 percent of the Slavs and Hungarians were thus concentrated). The remaining Jewish domiciles were about equally divided between the area not far from the railroad station on the edges of the downtown business district along Washington, Clinton, and Franklin Streets, and further south in Hornerstown, house-to-house near the intersection of Bedford and Poplar Streets, and along Horner down to Cedar Street.

As listed in Johnstown's business guide of 1910, nearly two-thirds of the

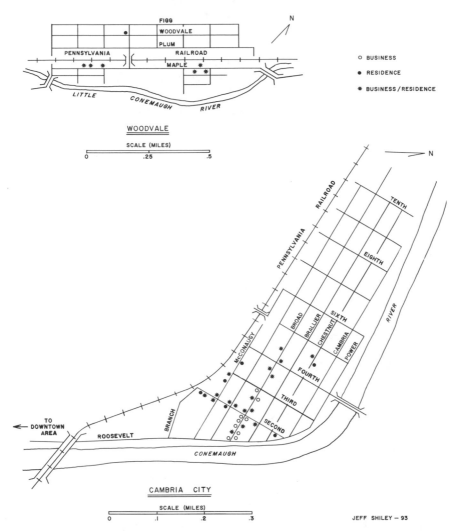

Map 2.5. Residential and Business Locations of Johnstown's Jews, 1910s (Cambria City, Woodvale)

Jewish shops had the same address as the domiciles of their owners; the rest were located in the downtown area within a few blocks south and east of the railroad station. About half of the immigrant peddlers lived in the Iron Street/River Avenue area, and the other half resided in Hornerstown, which for the next couple of decades was referred to by the local Jewish community as "the peddlers' place." In the surrounding towns and boroughs where Jewish immigrants settled at the turn of the century this residential closeness was even more pronounced, with their homes and stores

located on or near the main shopping street. A half dozen Jewish families
within a few blocks was enough for the local population to name the area
"Jew-town," "Jew-hill," or the like.

Just as they came to the Johnstown area relying on family and informal
social contacts and advice, once they had arrived there and found lodging
in close proximity to their fellow ethnics, practically all immigrants used
intragroup means of assistance in procuring initial employment. Kin and
landslayt—acquaintances from the same shtetl—were the two main providers. This informal assistance was supported by, and in part channeled
through, the communal institutions the immigrants created to serve their
religious and social needs. In this initial assistance in starting up business,
as well as in the later support to stay on in this occupation, the helping
resources were also, like entrepreneurial know-how, of a mixed ethnic-class
character, but with a different meaning. The ethnic contribution derived
from a group-specific sociocultural heritage, institutional and normative,
while the class element was expanded, as it were, by the entrepreneurial
experience and economic means gained in the United States by immigrant
businessmen that added to their original old-country skills.

The small and tightly knit group of German Jews in Johnstown did not
have a temple and met for services in the private quarters of one of its members; the congregation, under the name of Beth Zion, was institutionally
organized, and a permanent rabbi installed, only in the 1920s. Their only
(semi)formal association before World War I, the Progress Club (founded
in 1885), administered the burial ground in the municipal cemetery and,
until they purchased their own at the beginning of the century, East Europeans were also interred there. But apart from this service, a one-time financial donation to the Orthodox *Khevre Kadisha* (burial society), and a
contribution to the local B'nai B'rith's relief collection for the victims of
Russian pogroms in 1905, the German Jewish community was not a significant personal or institutional ethnic support resource for the new immigrants. A couple of German merchants maintained some informal contacts
with one or two of their longest-established East European counterparts,
such as attending *bar mitzvah* celebrations of each other's sons, and half a
dozen or so American-born children of immigrants found employment in
larger German Jewish owned stores in the city.[27]

But the East Europeans primarily relied on assistance from within their
own group. Large numbers and the social heterogeneity of their fellow ethnics in the big urban centers, especially in New York, from the early years
of immigrants' settlement fostered proliferation of various institutions that
provided assistance to immigrants in need: different kinds of traditional
mutual help societies linked to the synagogue; *landsmanshaftn* or secular
philanthropic and loan associations; workmen's organizations, and the
like.[28] In Johnstown, the small number of Jews and their sociocultural homogeneity instead fostered continuation of the old-country tradition of the

inclusive *khevre*, the religious congregation, as the main institutional center of communal activities.

Such was actually the character of the Rodef Sholom Orthodox Synagogue, located in the town's most Jewish neighborhood in the Iron Street/River Avenue area. The first rabbi, who was also a *shoykhet* (ritual slaughterer) and *moyel* (performer of circumcision), arrived in the city from Russia in the early 1890s and settled in the Jewish immigrant colony on River Avenue; at first the religious services and other group meetings were conducted in his home. The synagogue was constructed in 1904–1906 in the same neighborhood on Iron Street. Nominally independent, but closely affiliated with the *shul*, were three other organizations actually functioning in an informal manner. One was the *Tikvah Zion* society (perhaps—I was unable to ascertain—affiliated with the Mizrachi or religious Zionists), which took care of the religious education of children. The second was the local Israel Isaiah lodge of the B'rith Abraham fraternal organization, which provided insurance to its (male) members, as well as ad hoc business assistance, mostly through the exchange of information. The third one, somewhat of a novelty in comparison with the shtetl tradition of excluding women from even the most loosely organized activities, was the *Hakhnoses Orkhim* society for assistance of transients, staffed and managed by women of the *khevre* Rodef Sholom (women's participation in the public life of the local Jewish community, with comparisons with the situation in the big cities, will be discussed in chapter 4).[29]

Conveniently situated next to the railroad station, the synagogue served as an information center for immigrants getting off the train who "naturally went right in there." "The *shames* [sexton], always around the *shul*, would tell them where to go next, for a meal or some money to go on traveling, or what else they might want." David F.'s kosher butcher shop, established in 1903 on Iron Street, next to the station, also served as a referral service for passengers just off the train. If they were transient, travel assistance was provided by women of the *Hakhnoses Orkhim*. Among those who wished to stay, many became dues-paying members of Rodef Sholom—by 1910, it already had about a hundred such affiliates from Johnstown and the surrounding towns. Others elected merely to attend services and send their children for religious instruction. In the decade preceding World War I, nearly fifty additional names appeared in the congregational records as contributors of *nedorim*—donations pledged for *aliyes*, the honor of being called for public reading of the Torah. The newcomers were checked by a special committee composed of established members, who investigated the newcomers' provenance, family status and reputation, and economic standing, and filed a report to the congregation.[30] This practice of institutional clearance simultaneously served to integrate the new arrivals into the social web of the community, and, by recognizing their life situations, needs, and intentions, to bring them into its economic network.

2.4. Rev. Hyman Kaminsky, the first religious leader of the Rodef Sholom Congregation, and his home at River Avenue in which services and *kheyder* classes originally took place. Reprinted from the *Jewish Center of Johnstown Rodef Sholom Synagogue*, Anniversary Book, 1954.

2.5. Rodef Sholom Orthodox Synagogue on Iron Street, dedicated in 1906. Reprinted from the *Jewish Center of Johnstown Rodef Sholom Synagogue*, Anniversary Book, 1954.

2.6. One of the earliest weddings in the Rodef Sholom Congregation: Mr. and Mrs. Israel and Rachel Beerman, April 1, 1900. Reprinted from the *Jewish Center of Johnstown Rodef Sholom Synagogue*, Anniversary Book, 1954.

THE ETHNIC ECONOMIC NICHE AT WORK

Most new arrivals first started as peddlers.[31] Typically, after they settled either with relatives or on their own nearby, newcomers were directed to one of the Jewish wholesalers (East Europeans)—first in Altoona, some thirty miles from Johnstown, which had an older Jewish community with two established jobbers in dry goods and clothing, and then in the city itself. There between 1910 and 1915 three Jewish wholesale establishments—in dry goods, produce, and scrap metal and junk—had also appeared, which had been opened by earlier arrivals after some years of peddling and a few more in retailing. These same men, like other economically established merchants, usually occupied leadership positions in the local synagogue, and, if they were not themselves members of the committee "clearing" the newcomers, they knew about them from this or another source; in this way, informal assistance was linked to the main institution in the emerging community.

If he collected junk—rags, rubber, or scrap metal—all a peddler needed was a backpack, or, preferably, a horse and a buggy. If he sold merchandise—"socks, shoes, buttons, *shpilkes* [pins], kerchiefs, pots, pants, what have you . . ."—all he needed was some advance capital or credit to buy the first load. This he might procure with his own savings, as did Morris S., who brought with him two hundred dollars saved from earlier work in Baltimore. Alternatively, he might enlist the aid of the relatives who arranged for his coming—like Samuel M., who got a similar amount of start-up money from his uncle, a jeweler in Johnstown. Others got a boost from the wholesalers themselves, in the form of a "grub stake"—one to two hundred dollars' worth of merchandise advanced to a vendor, secured by the signature of a relative or a friend. Hyman K., for instance, who came to the town of Creekside in Indiana County in 1900, "had association with *landslayt* in Altoona who put him in contact with [a man in] junk business. . . . [With his own savings] he bought a horse and a wagon, and Mr. Harry S., a wholesaler who took care of all the peddlers around, trusted him with two hundred dollars [in merchandise]. With this he went on the road, to the coal towns."[32]

From peddling—which, as the interviews indicate, usually lasted two to five years—most immigrants moved to a stationary business and opened small stores or artisan shops. This course of action, too, was assisted by an intragroup network of information, reference, and financial help that plugged the immigrants into the emerging ethnic grid of trading in the specialties of the local wholesalers. At the beginning of the century, the start-up capital needed to open a small business establishment in Johnstown or one of the surrounding towns ranged from $500 to $700 for a storeroom to about $1,000–$1,500 if one was to start on a "bigger scale."

Most commonly, assistance was provided by relatives. Elliot L.'s uncle, the family pioneer in the area, first employed his nephew in his clothing business in Altoona, offering room and board in exchange for the young man's services. Then, after a few years, he "set him up in 1909 on his own in Dunlo [near Johnstown] with $500 which he had saved for him from his [unpaid] earnings." Sarah H.'s father came with his brother in 1911, bringing about $1,000 saved from their work in a New York garment factory; with this money, they bought a small general store from their cousin who had just opened another one. The father of Joseph P. came to join his wife's family who advanced him money to open a similar store in Colver—which "was found [for him] by a brother-in-law . . . who had talent for finding out places as a likely spot to make a living." Similarly, David K., who first peddled in Indiana County and then opened a business in the coal town of Bolivar, subsequently brought over his three younger brothers and set each of them up in little stores around the area. Julius and David K. were likewise placed in business in the towns around Johnstown by their uncle, who "picked [the locations] where he knew they could make a living . . . and furnished the merchandise [to get them started]." And

Samuel B. opened a store in Cresson in 1913 with a loan of a few hundred dollars obtained from his wife Sarah's brother, a storekeeper in nearby Portage.[33]

Another common pattern was to combine kin and ethnic resources. Abe F. opened a shoe store in Johnstown in 1908 with his own savings of $340 and an additional $1,000 borrowed from his brother and from two local Jewish friends already established as merchants, both active leaders of the Rodef Sholom Congregation. Jacob C. first worked for his cousin as a salesman, part-time in his store and part-time on the road as a peddler, and then, having saved some money, "let a *landsman* [of his] from a nearby town persuade him to open a men's clothing store in Ebensburg . . . since there was no [such establishment] there." The same wholesalers who "took care of the peddlers" later helped them to start their own businesses by giving advice on location and advancing the first merchandise. Abraham K., for example, was told "to go here rather than there [as he originally intended]" because—in the opinion of a jobber who had befriended him and who was also a leader in the local synagogue—"it was a better place." Commonly, "[a peddler] worked his territory for some time and then would go to a jobber and say: 'I've been working there for a while and I know the area . . . I now want to open a store. There is a storeroom in Nanty-Glo, it is a good town. . . .' [The jobber] knows him [has references], so he supplies him with merchandise for a start."[34]

First used for entry into the employment network, intragroup resources of an ethnic-class nature also served as the primary means of assistance for immigrant entrepreneurs to remain in business, or, if it failed, to restart it or find work with a fellow ethnic merchant. A secondary support resource employed toward the first two of these purposes was, so to speak, purely class in character, i.e., financial assistance obtained from mainstream local banks and commercial credit. At the beginning of the century it was used, however, only by a few longer-time residents and better-established merchants.

Most of the East European businesses operated as family-run enterprises whose pecuniary strength (net worth), as assessed by the Dun and Bradstreet Company, fell into the lowest brackets on the $-worth scale used in its ratings. In fact, compared with the enumeration provided in the 1910 Johnstown manuscript census, the D & B listing for that year covered no more than 54 percent of the total number of Jewish entrepreneurs identified by the census. Merchant-peddlers and most owners of artisan shops were omitted, most likely because they were too small and unstable even to be considered as businesses. Table 2.3 shows an assessment conducted five years later: over one-third of the appraised East European Jewish businesses received no rating, and a similar proportion was valued at less than $1,000. For comparison, the table also shows D & B evaluations of German Jewish enterprises in the city, evidently better-off economically than those of the recently arrived immigrants.

TABLE 2.3
Jewish Enterprises in Johnstown, 1915:
Assessments by Dun and Bradstreet Credit Company

Estimated Pecuniary Strength, 1915							
East European Businesses N = 75					German Businesses N = 12		
No Rating (%)	Less Than $1,000 (%)	$1,000– $3,000 (%)	$3,000– $10,000 (%)	Over $10,000 (%)	$10,000– $20,000 (%)	$35,000– $75,000 (%)	$75,000– $125,000 (%)
36	35	12	9	8	20	50	30

Suggested Credit, 1915							
East European Businesses				German Businesses			
High	Good	Fair	Low	High	Good	Fair	Low
—	10	24	66	40	50	10	—

Sources: Manuscript schedules of the 1910 Census, Johnstown; Johnstown city directory, 1910; Dun and Bradstreet Company's business credit-rating reports from Johnstown, Pennsylvania, 1915 (D & B Company archives, New York).

Not surprisingly, then, the company's appraisers advised prudence in extending credit to East European Jewish business owners. The majority, two-thirds, were considered worth only "limited credit." Without doubt, the small size and newness of these businesses were reason enough, but the fact that they were owned by Jews—"Hebrews" or "Israelites" in the D & B evaluations—suggested, in the opinion of the company, additional caution, because of the implied deviousness inherent to that race's marketplace conduct. Thus, recommendations describing the financial standing, local reputation, and business practices of the assessed Jewish entrepreneurs in Johnstown and vicinity contained remarks such as the following (very similar, incidentally, to those made by the company raters about German Jews a few decades earlier): ". . . a Hebrew, industrious, seems energetic [. . .] how much capital he has being Jew [we] cannot always tell"; ". . . a reliable man but is an Israelite and sharp and shrewd"; ". . . are Hebrews, shrewd and pushing, doing a pretty fair business so far as we can learn and pay their bills [but] we are unable to place an estimate"; ". . . doing fair business and making some money [but] cannot estimate worth . . . as they are Israelites, the real facts are hard to get."[35]

Because most of the immigrant businesses were opened and run on limited capital, keeping them afloat involved a good deal of financial maneuvering to meet coming payments and renew inventory. For these purposes, the immigrants needed credit, occasional loans, and other kinds of mercantile assistance, and they turned for it primarily to members of their own group. Johnstown had no Jewish free loan society to help immigrant entrepreneurs, and no formal *landsmanshaftn* associations extending economic assistance such as those that flourished in large American cities. When they needed some ready cash to keep their businesses going, the immigrants borrowed it informally within the local Jewish community.

Relatives, again, were the first resource approached. My estimation, based on the listings of names of Jewish residents in city directories and business guides for Johnstown and vicinity, and checked in interviews to establish their family connections, indicates that by World War I more than 40 percent of East European immigrant families in the area were related to each other either by blood or by marriage, and so the pool of potential assistance was quite large. Unless they got along very badly, which did occasionally happen, the relatives usually "maintained close contact, and helped each other," "as they were set up in similar business[es], and at homes [whenever they gathered] discussed what their needs were." Because it involved money, this kind of "kinwork" was not the domain of women, although, if they had the means and opportunity, they also participated in this assistance, primarily as go-betweens.[36] Fellow merchants among the immigrants' closer acquaintances were another support resource, often combined with family assistance.

The sums lent, as shown on the promissory notes registered with the prothonotary's office at the county courthouse, usually did not exceed a few hundred dollars. Morris L., owner of a general store in the coal-mining town of Nanty-Glo, in 1911 borrowed $302 and $385 from his two brothers—storekeepers in two nearby towns—and $99 from a Jewish merchant in Johnstown, and paid them back in the same year. Between 1903 and 1907 the peddler Julius K. obtained three such loans from three Jewish storekeepers in Johnstown—for $500, $315, and $575, all of which he repaid by 1909. Sam M., a grocer in one of the city's foreign colonies, borrowed $300 from a fellow storekeeper in his neighborhood and repaid it within two years.[37] Registering these transactions in court was, however, a rather unusual practice in immigrant business circles. Most often, they were conducted informally "on a handshake," based on personal knowledge of the borrowers, their circumstances, and their reputation—an internal credit system similar to those reported among German Jews in Cincinnati, San Francisco, and small Louisiana towns in the mid-nineteenth century.[38]

If not from their own relatives or closer acquaintances, immigrant businessmen sought economic assistance from the better-off merchant–synagogue officers and community leaders; by 1915 there were about five or six such persons, who also assisted their fellow ethnics in arranging for citizenship papers, collateral to purchase a house, and the like.[39] "When you needed a loan, to buy the inventory or because payments were slow [from customers; many Jewish stores sold on credit], they [merchant–synagogue officers] helped out, with a few hundred dollars or so [loaned on a personal note], to be repaid in three or four months. It was based on trust from knowing the person." "My father [Moses B., dry goods wholesaler in Johnstown, who supplied local merchants, and member of the officer board of Rodef Sholom] knew practically all [Jewish] retailers in town as they bought from him, and knew what they could pay, so when someone had a little problem with his business, he would advance them [so much] money, or sign for them to get a loan from the [local] bank where he had some connections. . . . When they [retailers] missed a few payments, we didn't stop trading with them, didn't lose contact . . . we didn't turn them down by refusing credit [. . .] we'd say, 'we'll carry you, we'll give you more merchandise . . . ,' they will be slow [in paying] but they'll pay, we knew them, so we cooperated, this was the principle." "Moses G. [owner of a wholesale scrap metal and junk business to whom most of Jewish peddlers in the area sold their collections, also an officer of the synagogue] would tell them [peddlers] when the prices went up, like for copper or brass or pewter, these were the best, and glass, too, so that by looking for these, they could put away some more money."[40]

It was also predominantly within the Jewish business network, by means of ethnic-class resources, that merchandise for immigrant stores was purchased and credit obtained. Of the seven supplier-creditors of Morris R.'s general store in Boswell before World War I, six were Jewish—half of them from the local area, and the rest from Pittsburgh and Philadelphia. A bigger establishment of the brothers R. in Johnstown, Great Eastern Clothing Company, had over thirty suppliers. Of these, three-quarters were certainly Jewish (the rest were listed under ethnic-neutral company names, and I did not classify them)—about one-half from New York, one-third from Philadelphia and Pittsburgh, and the rest from the local area.[41]

If despite the advances of merchandise and extensions of credit, a business failed and the enterprise had to be refinanced or sold out, in most cases it was done within the group. For instance, Max S.'s unprofitable enterprise in Gallitzin was sold in 1911 to three local Jewish merchants: the horse and wagon to David R., a peddler from the area; the (clothing) stock and store fixtures to David K. from Johnstown; and the storeroom to his brother-in-law, Isadore F., owner of a general store in a neighboring town. In 1912, Harry S., a wholesaler from Altoona, bought out at a public sale the entire stock of the bankrupt clothing establishment of Zeinwel S. in one of Johnstown's foreign colonies; in another one the contents of Samuel M.'s defaulted general store were purchased by Jacob H. from Pittsburgh. In nearby Windber at the same time, two partners, Samuel B. and David A., sold their entire enterprise: store, stock, and fixtures, to Henry S., a Jewish fellow merchant from the same town.[42]

When one business did not work out, most immigrants tried another, again seeking loans from different members of their family clans in the area, or, as often, by using the assistance of their (Jewish) creditors and merchandise suppliers. "Ups and downs [in business] were ordinary, it was expected, not only among retailers, but also among their suppliers, they knew it was a way of life." Oscar S. restarted his business several times when it failed or was not bringing sufficient returns: "in such circumstances, they usually settled the situation, they got them back into business to allow them to survive [. . .] 'So you failed today, you owe me $3,000 or whatever. You were doing all right before, well, so look, give me so much now [a negotiated percentage of debts owed], and we will wipe it clean. I'll give you [some new] credit, and we'll start all over again.' " And a similar recollection from another Johnstowner, Isadore G.: "When a merchant didn't make out . . . he'd go to a wholesaler and say: 'You know I've been in business here for a while . . . I'll straighten it out with you and my other creditors, but [now] give me some merchandise and I will start up again.' . . . And, unless he was no good at all [that is, had repeatedly proven himself to be incompetent or unreliable], the jobbers did it."[43]

I have noted earlier that this wide-scope mutual assistance-as-resource was generated and upheld by pragmatic considerations on the one hand, and, on the other hand, group institutional and normative tradition. In practice, these two motives of the support extended to fellow-ethnic entrepreneurs were of course intermingled, but they may be analytically distinguished. The former could be seen as a class motive of group business assistance, not unlike the pragmatic reasons the informal support networks reported as well among nonethnic small entrepreneurs operating on limited financial capital and subject to sharp market fluctuations in the urban economies of nineteenth- and early-twentieth-century North American cities.[44]

In the recollections of my Johnstown informants, pragmatism was surely an important reason for reliance on assistance from fellow entrepreneurs, who facilitated entry into the intragroup business network and thus realization of the purpose that had brought the immigrants to the Johnstown area. Reflecting national trends, fluctuations in local steel and coal industries caused massive layoffs alternating with rapid expansion of the labor force; these fluctuations also affected Jewish businesses, which were directly dependent on a working-class clientele. The social support network enabled small business establishments subject to chronic economic cycles in the dominant industry to stay afloat, or at least remain within the entrepreneurial niche. From the perspective of the suppliers, this assistance, too, had a pragmatic meaning. As Isadore S. explained, "[It] was not only a matter of personal knowledge and trust, it was also in the interest of the suppliers . . . because, if you had fifty merchants as clients in Johnstown and ten of them failed, now you could only sell to forty, but you help them back into business, and you could still sell to fifty. . . . So it was also an economic calculation, to keep them alive and well." "Had we stopped giving credit"—Moses B.'s wholesale dry goods establishment customarily "carried" delinquent retailers and helped out those who had failed—"we'd lose a lot of customers, and we would not have been successful ourselves."[45]

But this pragmatic orientation of Johnstown's Jewish entrepreneurs derived from their generally insecure class position (even the local economic tycoons were big fish in a small pond, really), blended with a group-specific or ethnic component, a multilayered one. One such specific grounding of class pragmatism was that the precariousness of fortune, characteristic of petty entrepreneurship in general, was reflected in the Jewish case at the symbolic level in the traditional representation-schema of the world "revolving in the wheel of fortune." This strongly felt popular belief, so poignantly realistic in the rural shtetls, was transplanted to the Johnstown environment and basically retained its validity, despite a new sense that authentic opportunities for gradual improvement were available. Indeed, the sense of opportunity further strengthened the reliance on in-group mutual help. Perhaps at a deeper level yet lay the minority group pragmatism of a people whose chronically precarious position in the past—encoded in collective memory—fostered reliance on each other. Blended into the *habitus* through frequent invocation and longitudinal use—an "automatic reflex" and a "natural impulse" as my informants called it—group normative prescription to turn to each other "just in case" was not eradicated in an American environment like early-twentieth-century Johnstown's—an environment that was at best indifferent, if not hostile, to "Israelite" newcomers. This aspect of the ethnic component of pragmatic mutual assistance also had a more positive, or less defensive, expression. People with whom I talked about their recollections of those beginning years repeatedly mentioned a desire to establish, as one person put it, "the Jewish environment to live in and make friends, and [for] the Jewish community here to grow, and so the more people [were] helped in starting and staying in business, the better [for these purposes]."[46]

Minority group pragmatism that sustained mutual assistance in business (and in other matters) was upheld as well by the situation of recent immigrants who had settled in a place where economic and sociocultural life was patterned by ascriptive divisions. "If not to the family, which was natural, or to other Jews, where else would you go here?"; "It was more comfortable [to deal with members of Jewish group], there was a common language, not just Yiddish, but also in trade, the way it was done"; "[Jewish] jobbers, they put [small merchants] in business, they were lenient with credit. . . . They conversed with them and they knew how each of them was doing [financially and otherwise]. . . . They knew each other, so it was practical."[47]

But the most explicitly "ethnic"—in terms of the distinction being used here—reinforcement of internal mutual assistance derived from the religiously grounded normative schemas-prescriptions regarding social conduct within the Jewish community. As noted in chapter 1, basic to this behavioral code was the injunction to act on the principle rendered by *Tz'enah Ur'enah* as "All Israel are sureties for one another." Of all acts of *tsdoke*, assisting a fellow Jew "to help himself" to become and stay economically self-sufficient was considered the most meritorious *mitsve*. "Our home [like many others] was always open, people were coming to discuss all kinds of matters what[ever] came up"—Abe B.'s father, although not among the wealthiest merchants in Johnstown, ran an established grocery store in one of the town's "foreign colonies" and was an active and recognized leader of the *shul*. "He gave advice, told people where to seek help when needed, or, means permitting, provided himself." In response to my question about his father's motives, he replied, "It was a mixture: a *mitsve*, a natural thing to do, and also, the situation they had [there], it was [mutual assistance within the group], the best way [to act]"; "It [mutual help] was so ingrained in the Jewish people, from early childhood: 'give something,' 'help out, it's a *mitsve*,' [so] they naturally expected that information, and help, would be provided."[48]

As more immigrants settled in the area and joined the group's business support network, it expanded and solidified into an ethnic entrepreneurial niche wherein small stationary merchants and owners of artisan shops, employees of these enterprises, and traveling vendors were tied to each other horizontally by kin-*cum*-business connections and vertically to the suppliers of credit and merchandise. These bonds were reinforced by shared participation in the religious and social life of the community. This combination of horizontal and vertical interconnections channeled most Jewish entrepreneurs into a few lines of trade and services, in which they came to occupy a share much greater than their proportion among the local workforce employed in this sector. Table 2.4 shows the concentration in particular lines of commerce of East European Jewish entrepreneurs (excluding peddlers, but including self-employed artisans) in Johnstown in 1915, and the proportion of Jews in the selected occupations (including professions) in that city from 1915 until 1940.

By the outbreak of World War I, Jews, constituting about 1.5 percent of the local population, made up somewhat less than one-tenth of the total number of self-employed in the trade and service sector in Johnstown. The overwhelming majority—close to nine-tenths of East European small entrepreneurs—were concentrated in five lines of business. Most of them were in apparel and shoes (including ready- and custom-made garments and furnishings, and general stores carrying work clothing, shoe dealers, and shoemakers), and the remaining were in notions, jewelry, furniture, and foodstuffs—the merchandise in which local Jewish jobbers also specialized. The same items—clothing, hats, gloves, fabric and millinery pieces, notions and jewelry—were also carried by the peddlers. In 1915 there were about three dozen Jewish-owned apparel and shoe stores, two dozen groceries and notions, and over a dozen each of tailor, furrier and millinery, and jewelry shops in Johnstown. Although few in number, these enter-

TABLE 2.4

Concentration of Jewish Entrepreneurs in Particular Lines of Trade and Services,
and the Proportion of Jews in Selected Occupations in Johnstown, 1915

| | Concentration of Jewish Businesses in Selected Lines of Trade | | Jewish-owned Businesses as Percent of City Total |
	East Europeans (%)	Germans (%)	(%)
Apparel and shoes			
(ready- and custom-made)	47	70	51[a]
General merchandise	7	20	26
Dry goods and notions	14	⎫	35
Jewelry	10	⎬ 10	41
Furniture	3	⎭	13
Foodstuffs	13		6
Other	6		
	N = 106	N = 13	

Sources: Johnstown's city directories and business guides, 1915; local interviews.

[a] In ready-made apparel business this proportion was 65%; among tailors and furriers, 29%, in shoe business, 15%.

prises constituted between one-fourth and one-half of all establishments in the city involved in these lines of commerce. About a dozen German Jewish businesses were even more selective, concentrated in three lines of trade.

THE FAMILY ECONOMY

As noted earlier, in all stages of the development of Johnstown's Jewish entrepreneurial niche at the beginning of this century, men were the main actors, even though women occasionally served as the mediators between a (male) relative in need of some kind of business assistance and a potential (male) provider thereof. Once established by the male head of the household, however, the actual functioning of the business usually involved the entire nuclear family as the collective work and accumulating unit: husband, wife, and all capable children.

The cooperative family economy has been a common strategy in virtually all groups in the nineteenth and early twentieth centuries, and, for that matter, among present-day immigrants as well. In interpreting its purposes, some social historians have emphasized most of all the necessity to offset the externally imposed economic uncertainty, while others pointed to the immigrants' desire to improve as much as possible their family's material standing.[49] Recollections of my Johnstown informants about what moved them to act in the way they did during those initial years can be interpreted in terms of Alfred Schutz's distinction between two types of motive. They tended to mention the former element as the "because" motive, referring to the surrounding conditions that influenced people's actions, and the latter as the "in-order-to" motive, denoting the wished-for future state of affairs or the goal to be brought about by the actions undertaken.[50]

Earlier in this chapter I have discussed the surrounding conditions, and specifically the fluctuations in local industries that affected Jewish businesses—the "because" motive of economic cooperation within Johnstown Jewish families (and beyond them within the larger immigrant community) that guaranteed a safety net against the ups and downs of economic cycles. The practical goal or *takhlis* that motivated them to such collective efforts consisted, first and foremost, in establishing an economic independence that would provide for everyday family welfare. In this early period, it meant a level of material sufficiency above the bare survival well remembered from the shtetls, a level that in the longer-term future could serve as a base on which to build. Build what exactly the immigrants did not know at that time, or did not remember when asked to recollect it several decades later; ". . . just wanted to get established so as to go on [from that point]" was a typical recollection.

Cooperative family economies were enacted by Jewish immigrants in small towns like Johnstown as well as in large urban centers like New York, Philadelphia, or Chicago. But in these different environments the family economies were differently organized. In the big cities, where Jews were massively employed in manufacturing—New York, of course, was the prime case—the way the cooperative family economy functioned derived basically from the separation of home and (industrial) work. Although at the turn of the century it was not uncommon for immigrants employed in the "Jewish" garment industry enclave, particularly married women and their teenage children, to do finishing homework in their tenement apartments, by 1915 this practice had greatly diminished, and, in any case, the majority of Jewish wage earners worked outside the home in factories and shops. This separation, and the strong social disapproval of married women's industrial employment that prevailed in New York's Jewish community (and, for that matter, in Eastern Europe as well), effectively eliminated most of the latter from the labor market in the ethnic economic enclave. According to contemporary reports (1907–1910), less than 10 percent of married Jewish women had worked for wages. Instead, the majority, 58 percent, of Jewish housewives were found to have kept board-paying lodgers, thus contributing from within the home to the family budget.[51]

In the Jewish entrepreneurial niche in the Johnstown area, the cooperative economies of the majority of immigrant families were based, as in the rural shtetls they came from, on a shared home-and-work territory: as noted earlier (and illustrated in maps 2.3–2.5), two-thirds of stationary businesses in 1910—1915 operated from their owners' homes. While immigrant public opinion, in large urban and small-town Jewish communities alike, decidedly frowned on married women's working for wages in industry, their involvement in business, and particularly family-run enterprise—a continuation of East European tradition—was considered appropriate.[52]

Such was in fact the prevailing pattern among Johnstown Jewish families of East European backgrounds; in the small number of enterprises owned by German Jews whose lifestyles by that time more closely resembled the middle-class American pattern, the participation of wives was more limited. The proportion of lodger-keeping homes—the housewives' way of contributing to the family budget—was less than half that of the New York figure; of course, in accounting for this large difference, we must bear in mind the incomparably larger population of new immigrant arrivals— potential lodgers—in the Jewish communities in major eastern cities. Boarder keeping was most frequent in the families of peddlers, who were usually relatively more recent arrivals in the area and not yet well established, suggesting that this mode of augmenting immigrant family incomes was temporary.

One-tenth of married or widowed Johnstown women were recorded in 1910–1915 local sources as storekeepers, constituting slightly over one-tenth of the total number of East European Jewish immigrant storekeepers in the city. Over half of this number were widowed heads of households, and the rest were running either a second store owned by the family, or an adjunct business (usually dressmaking or millinery) allied with the family's main firm listed under the husband's name. Actually, however, a much greater proportion of immigrant women, unrecorded in standard sources used by historians to gather information about their subjects' occupations, actively participated in the family economy by working full- or part-time in family stores side by side with their husbands. My conservative estimate of the proportion of such East European female coworkers, based solely on interviews, is about 65 percent (see table 2.5 for quantifiable information on the involvement of wives in household economies).

Most Jewish shops were open from early morning till late evening, thirteen to fifteen hours a day, to accommodate customers who worked shifts in the mills and coal mines. Since the majority of them were attached to the domiciles of their owners, immigrant wives divided their time between household chores (if there was no live-in help) and tending the store. Like their husbands, these women had a working knowledge of the languages spoken by their Gentile East European customers, and familiarity with their needs and preferences. Selling merchandise was the most common activity of women working in the store, but if they had other marketable skills, these were also put to use. Jennie G., for example, expert at sewing, "[made] for the store aprons and [items] for children," and also took fan-

TABLE 2.5
Participation of East European Immigrant Wives and
Widows in Household Economies, 1910/15

N = 91	%
Contributing as:	
Shopkeepers	11
Commercial employees (sales, clerical)	1
Keepers of boarders	21
Wives "helping" in family stores (estimate)	65

Sources: Manuscript schedules of the 1910 census, Johnstown;
Johnstown business guides and city directories, 1910, 1915; local
interviews.
    Note: A historical study of Jews in Providence, Rhode Island, in
1915 found 11% women to have been shopkeepers, and 17% keep-
ing boarders; the total proportion of "working wives" was 31%
(Alice Goldstein, "Mobility of Natives and Jews in Providence,
Rhode Island, 1900–1920," *Rhode Island Jewish Historical Notes*
8 [November 1979]: 79; Judith Smith, *Family Connections: A
History of Italian and Jewish Immigrant Lives in Providence,
Rhode Island, 1900–1940* [Albany: SUNY Press, 1985], 48).

cier custom orders from clients: "Hungarian stuff, wedding dresses, lawn
dresses with embroidery."[53]

    The scope and areas of married women's authority in matters of family
economy, considering their active participation therein, and in the social
and cultural activities in the homes and in the community, will be discussed in greater detail in the following two chapters dealing with the
interwar decades. Here, I would like merely to point out the complexity—
contradictoriness, really—of immigrant women's position in the family
economy, already in the formative period of Johnstown's Jewish commu-
nity/entrepreneurial niche.

    In comparison with the situation in the rural shtetls, where (lower-class)
married women's independent entrepreneurial activities were common, the
economic autonomy of the immigrant wives had evidently diminished. The
majority of them were in prime childbearing age, so in most homes there
were babies and little children, which made it difficult for young mothers
to pursue "separate careers." Then, too, the environment was new, and the
role of striking out into new terrain was in the Jewish tradition reserved for
men; the area, dominated by heavy industry, was known as a "men's
place," uncongenial to women's public—that is, out-of-home—activities,
whatever they might be. For all these reasons, the Jewish entrepreneurial
network in Johnstown was, from the beginning, a male-dominated one.
Therefore, while the majority of Johnstown immigrant wives were economically active, for most of them those activities were pursued together
with their husbands.

At the same time, however, because of the entrepreneurial nature of immigrant family economy, Johnstown wives continued to share with their
husbands/coworkers the common territory of home/business. Their experience contrasts with that of their counterparts in New York and other big
cities with a high rate of Jewish industrial employment; there, as has been
discussed, home and work were separated, and, as soon as financial conditions permitted, married women were relegated to the home, to what had
become a gendered "domestic sphere." Even though most of the Johnstown women performed the roles of assistants rather than partners, their
position as coworkers and the physical commonality of the home/work
ground gave them a direct insight and a say in business matters. On occasion, the wife's participant-advisory authority in family business was further enhanced by particular circumstances, for example, if one or more
of her own male relatives occupied high status positions in the Jewish
community.

Besides women, children also joined in the cooperative family economy
at a young age, first starting as helpers in the parental store under the supervision of the adults. Compared with the offspring of Gentile East Europeans, only 20 percent of whom continued education beyond the sixth
grade before World War I, sons and daughters of Jewish immigrants remained in school longer, most commonly until the completion of elementary education—about 75 percent of those traced in Johnstown school
records between 1900 and 1915—while working part-time.[54] Table 2.6
shows the percentages of Jewish boys and girls fifteen years old and older
who in 1915 were reported by the local sources as continuing their education, staying at home with parents, and employed. Considering that many
girls recorded as "at home with parents" were most likely helping in the
stores of their parental or more distant family, the proportions of boys and
girls employed in some fashion in the ethnic entrepreneurial niche were
probably not much different. More boys than girls, however, stayed in
school beyond the age of fifteen. During the first one and a half decades of
this century, slightly over one-fifth of East European Jewish families sent
their children to high school. Of those who entered, about half discontinued secondary education and half graduated; about 6 percent of the
family households sent their children to college. Unfortunately, comparisons with educational data reported from big cities are often more confusing than enlightening because different investigators have used different
age categories, or presented their findings in terms of school grades completed. The latter did not match at that time the age of the students, especially in the immigrant groups, including Russian Jews, whose elementary-
school children the 1909 Immigration Commission Report classified as
retarded in about 42 percent of cases. The only comparable data I was able
to find—for Russian Jewish children fifteen and older in Providence,
Rhode Island, in 1915—indicate proportions recorded as working, for

TABLE 2.6

Participation of Immigrants' Children (Age 15+)
in Household Economies

N = 149	Sons (%)	Daughters (%)
Recorded as:		
at school	17	10
at home	12	38
working	71	52
	Sons and Daughters (%)	
in parental business	42	
in other Jewish-owned stores	39	
in mainstream jobs	9	
unknown	10	

Sources: Manuscript schedules of the 1910 Johnstown census;
Johnstown business guides and city directories, 1910, 1915;
Johnstown public school records, 1890–1915; Johnstown High
School records, 1900–1915.

both gender groups, as having been basically similar to those in Johnstown, 67 percent and 58 percent, respectively.[55]

Table 2.6 also shows a very high, nearly exclusive, concentration of immigrants' children recorded as working within the Jewish entrepreneurial niche. Only a small minority, 9 percent each of the employed young men and women, all German, held mainstream jobs as clerks or salespeople, while about 80 percent were occupied in the parental business, worked in other Jewish-owned firms, or were self-employed in trade (for the remainder, the place of employment could not be identified). If they worked in the parental business, young people usually did not receive regular pay, except for a weekly allowance and, if the situation permitted, occasional extras on special request; those employed elsewhere as a rule turned in most of their earnings to their parents.[56]

The range and concrete applications of autonomy and decision-making authority of immigrants' sons and daughters in matters related to the collective family economy, and in sociocultural activities in the homes, informal social circles, and in Jewish communal institutions—like the position in this regard of immigrant wives—will be discussed at greater length in the two following chapters. One observation should be made at this point, and a comparison of the Johnstown group with their big-city fellow ethnics employed in the ethnic industrial enclaves is again illuminating. In New York, the separation of home and work in the majority of Jewish families required that young people participating in the cooperative household economy go out to work, thereby escaping the reach of parental control for most of the day on weekdays. As reported in memoirs and life histories of American-born New York Jews growing up at the beginning of this century, this experience was usually felt as liberating and assertiveness-building, particularly for young women brought up in the restrictive tradition of their parental homes.[57] In this context, the second generation's wages or salaries, even when they were largely contributed to the family budgets, at the same time symbolized and reasserted their earners' newly gained independence. In Johnstown, on the contrary, the second generation's immersion in their (nuclear or extended) families' businesses, more often than not conducted on the home territory, subjected them to a parental authority doubly enforced in work and home life, without leaving much space for personal independence.

JOHNSTOWN'S JEWS BY THE OUTBREAK OF WORLD WAR I: ACCOMPLISHMENTS

During the initial phase of their "adhesive" incorporation into Johnstown's society and economic structure, the immigrants utilized effectively—"intelligently," in the group's own language—their personal experience and preferences, as well as collective sociocultural resources of a combined class-and-ethnic character, which they in part transplanted from the old country and in part created in the new American environment. The most important of these group resources were know-how in business dealings with their former peasant neighbors, the East European industrial laborers; the strong intragroup support networks sustained by pragmatic considerations as well as by the religiously grounded code of social conduct toward fellow Jews; the cooperative family economy largely based on the commonality of home and work; shared cognitive schemas for the interpretation of and practical guidance in life situations encoded in the group's cultural meaning-system.

A few indicators may be interpreted as evidence of the effectiveness of these combined resources: residential persistence, continuance in business, material well-being of the family, and establishment of a permanent group institutional framework. Thus, during the first decade of this century, Jewish immigrants persisted in Johnstown at a rate of 67 percent, and in the following five years at 72 percent—considerably higher proportions than the 39 percent rate among local Slavs and Hungarians in the period 1900–1910, and 33 percent and 44 percent among Jews in Boston and New York, respectively.[58] Expectedly, immigrants less established in town, peddlers and store employees, were more inclined to leave: they constituted two-thirds of the departing group. A good number of the peddlers, however, I found in the adjacent towns, while among those who persisted in Johnstown over 40 percent had moved into stationary businesses during these years.

Given the limited financial capital Jewish enterprises were run on, and the instability of the local market dependent on the fluctuations in steel and coal industries, their owners' high rates of persistence in business also attest to the effectiveness of the combined resources commanded by members of the Jewish economic niche. From among East European Jewish entrepreneurs (including peddlers) who had persisted in Johnstown between the beginning of the century and the conclusion of World War I, about 40 percent had remained in the same line of business, while nearly 30 percent had switched at least once (and often more frequently) to other kinds of enterprises. Those whose businesses failed had either left town or gone to work for local Jewish merchants, but the majority—nearly two-thirds—stayed on in the area and maintained their entrepreneurial status, restarting same line of business, or, more commonly, trying a somewhat different one. Compared with business turnover among Gentile merchants in Johnstown, the persistence of Jewish ones was indeed impressive: within the decade between 1900 and 1910, about 70 percent of non-Jewish store-owners disappeared from business guide listings. Among East European Gentile immigrant merchants, business turnover was even higher: withdrawals were close to 60 percent every three to four years during the period from the turn of the century through World War I. Their old-country experience did not equip them with the know-how and group tradition of trading, and, partially in consequence, the employment support networks of Slavic and Hungarian immigrants were in the mills and coal mines, where most of them worked; having failed in business, they could easily get (re)plugged in to a group of laborers of the same nationality.[59]

Finally, the accomplishments of those who stayed on in the area also evidenced how effectively the East European Jewish entrepreneurs applied personal and group resources in pursuing their desired goals. As my informants conceived of these accomplishments, they were realized within two spheres: that of familial material well-being and that of group institutional life.

Regardless of whether they were still peddlers or had already established stationary businesses, people coming from impoverished shtetls saw their living conditions in the foreign quarters of Johnstown, drab as they were by middle-class American standards, as a considerable improvement, and this alone was felt as an achievement. Having joined her father, a storekeeper, in 1909 in his rented apartment in a Jewish neighborhood on River Avenue, Bella C. wrote to her sisters in Antopolie in Byelorussia describing their home: "It had two bedrooms upstairs, and a bathroom . . . all our furniture was secondhand, [but] to me it looked as though we moved into a palace—there was a rocking chair, and I never saw a rocker before, and a little rug on the floor, and when I saw that I thought by mistake they threw it on the ground so I picked it up and put it on the table . . . and when I walked into the kitchen I saw a [coal] stove but to me it looked like a machine, I never saw that, because it was all built-in in Europe . . . and I wrote home and they thought we lived on an estate." And Meyer B., who came as a young boy in 1912 from a small town in Lithuania: "[Father was peddling and] we rented a house and didn't live lavishly, but we ate well . . . in Europe, I remember, eating chicken indicated a holiday, we ate chicken on a Shabes and a holiday, and now in America we could have afforded it every day. This is why I loved eating chicken."[60] Indeed, in 1912 a live chicken cost eighteen cents; a local peddler made approximately fourteen dollars a week.

Within such a frame of reference, immigrants were satisfied with the achievements they accomplished by means of combined personal, family, and group resources. As one of my informants recollected the common way of life, and perceptions, at that time among Johnstown Jews, "Because of [old-country] ways and ingrained habits of frugality . . . we didn't lack for what we felt we needed or could [then] recognize as a need."[61]

By the outbreak of World War I, their possessions and occupational standing located the majority of the East European Jewish families in the lower middle class or petty bourgeoisie. Thus, only slightly over one-tenth of them could be classified as "major proprietors"—those whose real property was assessed for tax purposes at at least $5,000, and whose personal property at at least $1,000. And about the same proportion could be classified as "major merchants"—those whose assessed occupational valuation, based on incomes from performed professions, exceeded $750. In comparison, more than half of the German Jews were in the "major" proprietary-entrepreneurial category. Since the beginning of the century, the proportion of real estate owners among East European Jewish families had increased fivefold, to 28 percent, but it still lagged behind the city average of 34 percent; among Slavs, however, the figure was considerably lower still, 19 percent. The average valuation of East European Jewish homes in 1915 was $2,630, more than 50 percent lower than that of German Jews in town but almost double that of the Slavs and Hungarians.[62]

Along with family well-being, the institutional establishment of the Jewish community was deemed an accomplishment, the source-and-effect of the group's sociocultural resources. Particularly significant was the construction and maintenance of the synagogue, Rodef Sholom, and the upkeep of affiliated services, financed by the contributions of individual households. The capital involved was modest, and the realization of projects required, as the congregational records indicate, continuous renegotiations, nudging, reminders of dues, even (usually effective) threats of suspension from membership leveled against particularly persistent slackers. Yet while the much more affluent German Jewish community in Johnstown had neither a congregational building nor permanent rabbinical leadership, with the help of their monthly dues of $1.50 and extra donations, East European immigrants did build early on a large *shul* with a *kheyder* and an adjacent *mikve* for $10,000 in construction costs, plus $2,450 for the lot. They also supported a permanent rabbi-*shoykhet* for $30 a month and a *shames* for $10, a congregational secretary and *Talmud Torah* teacher (of 250 children in 1916) for $100 a year each; and they purchased—as custom required—tickets for seats in the synagogue for the *Yomim Neroim* (High Holidays) ranging in cost from $50 to $200. Guest *khazonim* (cantors) were regularly invited to lead prayers on those and other holidays of importance for $200–300. Families routinely contributed little monies to the *Hakhnoses Orkhim* society, which was always busy with transients, and to the local needy on Purim and Passover.[63] Compared with the communal investments of Jews in large American cities, those made by Johnstown's immigrants were unspectacular, small-scale like the town itself and its Jewish community. But its members looked upon them with a sense of achievement and pride.

Insecure Prosperity

THE INTERWAR PERIOD witnessed rapid expansion of the white-collar sector in the American economy: the number of office and professional jobs that required training beyond mandatory schooling more than doubled between 1910 and 1930. This development was accompanied by a proliferation of specialized educational institutions, and by the spread of a new "secular religion," as one commentator called the American urban middleclass's "unprecedented interest" in extended schooling, particularly college education, as "the safest and most promising route to occupational training and social status in a changing world."[1]

Parallel trends were observed among American Jews in the large cities. The interwar period has often been called in American Jewish historiography a "watershed era" to emphasize the profound structural transformation of U.S. Jewry of East European origin. These years saw the emergence and growth of a modern middle class of clerical and professional workers employed in the mainstream American economy. Data from the large urban centers document this transformation: a survey of Jewish occupational distributions in New York, Chicago, and Philadelphia (combined) in the first and third decades of the twentieth century shows the proportion of industrial workers decreasing by almost half (from 61 to 34 percent), and that of clerical and professional occupations nearly tripling (from 11 to 29 percent). For the most part, it has been argued in Jewish social-historical studies, this professionalization occurred as a result of "the 'invasion' of higher learning institutions of all kinds by Jewish students," who used advanced education "to climb from the proletarianization of the immigrant generation to a modern educated urban middle class." This passion for learning among upwardly mobile Jews was particularly notable in New York, where the opportunities for upward social mobility through extended schooling were multiple: the dynamic growth of white-collar employment, particularly in public education, communications, and sales and marketing; the existence of free city colleges (CCNY, Hunter, Brooklyn) that made it possible for large numbers of even economically insecure but aspiring families to provide their children with a college education; and, last but not least, the presence within the Jewish community of a vast ethnic market for, and employer of, various professional services. In the mid-1930s, over 30 percent of college-age Jewish youth in New York were enrolled in institutions of higher learning (as compared with the national average of 15 percent), and, among the employed aged sixteen–twenty-four, 66 percent were found in clerical/professional occupations.[2]

Conditions conducive to a similar transformation of Johnstown Jews during the interwar period were lacking both in the surrounding environment and within the Jewish group itself. Several factors served to uphold rather than weaken the occupational patterns established during the previous decades. In the surrounding environment, such preservative effects were due primarily to the continued predominance of heavy industry and stagnant occupational structure in the region, and to the proximity of Slavic working-class families as established customers of Jewish businesses. As a corollary of these outside circumstances, intraethnic business networks and cooperative family economies solidified inside the local Jewish community, encompassing the immigrants and their American-born offspring, and contributing to their residential stability and social inwardness. In the experience of Johnstown's Jews, unlike their big-city fellow ethnics, the achievement of middle-class status was not a matter of upward mobility on the occupational ladder attained by, as one historian put it, "investing in themselves" through advanced education;[3] the percentage of college-goers among the second generation in the 1930s was about half the figure reported in New York. Rather, Johnstown's Jews' route toward middle-classdom led through material accumulation and improved lifestyles realized by collective family efforts within the ethnic entrepreneurial niche.

Participation in this niche, and collective family economy, allowed for the majority of Jewish households to afford lifestyles within the range considered "the American middle-class standard" by contemporary economists, and it is in this area—the operation of family businesses and the material comforts it permitted—that we shall primarily look for signs of ethnicization. This middle-class standard of living allowed by ethnic entrepreneurship, however, was an unstable achievement, an insecure prosperity—now present, then threatened, then returning again. This instability was a chronic condition resulting in part from local Jews' class position as small traders, and in part from the peculiarities of Johnstown and the situation of its Jewish residents.

The specifics of the economic operation and insecure prosperity of Jewish households—sales, loans, property tax assessments, incomes, family budgets, and the like—are very dense. For this reason, I refer here to the sociocultural forms and meanings in which these economic activities were embedded, as in the presentation of the emergence of the ethnic entrepreneurial niche, only briefly as *resources* for these undertakings and for the realization by its members of their desired life-goals. Necessarily, I have relegated to the subsequent chapters a discussion of the functioning of social institutions in the Jewish community, and of the shared cultural practices and symbolic schemas its members used to interpret the world

and act upon it, as well as of the transformation over time of group sociocultural life.

JOHNSTOWN'S LIMITED OPPORTUNITIES AND THE PERSISTENCE OF
THE JEWISH ENTREPRENEURIAL NICHE

The spectacular expansion of the Cambria Steel mills and of the adjacent
coal mines, together with a rapid increase in the population of Johnstown
and its surrounding towns, constituted two major factors in the area's development from the late nineteenth century through World War I. But
with the end of war in Europe, accelerated growth in the American steel
and coal industries exhausted itself. Although growth in the automobile
and aviation industries in the following decades furnished the steel industry
with increasing orders, it never again achieved the same rate of expansion.
As it became easier and cheaper to use the rich ores of the Great Lakes
region, Johnstown's industrial advantage was reduced. Furthermore, increasing competition in transportation, the area's rough and difficult terrain, and isolation from the main routes connecting the East Coast with the
interior parts of the country diminished the region's role as a supplier to
remote markets. As shifting markets gradually tipped the scales in favor of
other regions, the Johnstown area began to decline in importance as a
major industrial center.

   This process was accompanied by a slowdown in demographic growth:
whereas between 1890 and 1910 the population of Johnstown increased
by over 150 percent and that of the fifteen largest coal towns in Cambria
and the closer parts of Indiana, Somerset, and Westmoreland Counties by
more than 300 percent, between 1910 and 1920 the rates were 22 percent
and 44 percent, respectively. Between 1920 and 1940 the population of
the city of Johnstown actually decreased by 1 percent, although it grew in
the immediately adjacent boroughs. In the same period, the population of
the fifteen largest surrounding towns decreased by 4 percent.[4]

   The Johnstown area's continuing dependence on steel and coal, along
with slackened industrial growth after World War I, did little to diversify
the occupational structure. To be sure, mechanization in the mills and
mines increased the number of higher-skilled jobs. But in general character, Johnstown and the surrounding counties remained distinctly blue-
collar during the interwar decades. Seventy percent of Johnstown's employed population in 1920 were wage workers, and even by the outbreak
of World War II this figure remained a high 63 percent; the percentage was
even higher—about 75 percent in 1940—in the rest of Cambria County
and in Indiana, Somerset, and Westmoreland Counties. Among the city's
male labor force, no less than three-fourths continued to be employed in
manual occupations throughout the interwar period, and about two-thirds

of all gainfully employed men in Johnstown worked in steel manufacturing and mining. Of these, the Cambria Steel Company—superseded in 1923 by the Bethlehem Steel Company, which purchased Cambria's properties in the area—employed approximately 70 to 75 percent, while an additional 10 percent worked in the mills of the smaller local U.S. Steel plant.[5]

As in the rest of the country, languid growth in the steel and coal industries was accompanied by rapid fluctuations of demand and consequent unsteadiness in production levels. Because of frequent shifts in the volume of industrial production, the size of the workforce employed in local manufacturing and mining expanded and contracted by as much as 15–20 percent between good and bad seasons. The Depression of the 1930s further destabilized the demand for labor. In the second half of 1931, for instance, unemployment among workers in Johnstown and vicinity was nearly 25 percent; it subsequently decreased somewhat, only to reach an all-time high of 34 percent by the beginning of 1934.[6]

The size and growth of the white-collar strata depended directly on the uneven prosperity of the local mills and coal mines. Not surprisingly, the Johnstown area failed to witness the surge in white-collar jobs seen in large American cities during the same period. Between 1920 and 1940 the total number of professionals and self-employed persons in trade and services in Johnstown grew by 11 percent, while those employed in sales, clerical, and kindred occupations increased by only 17 percent. In actual numbers— even more telling of the area's constrained development and skewed occupational profile—between 1920 and 1940 the ranks of professionals and self-employed in trade and services expanded by no more than a few hundred people (from 3,084 to 3,414), while those of the salaried employees in commercial and service establishments increased by less than a thousand (from 3,702 to 4,505).

Dependent on the same heavy industry, Johnstown remained also a "man's place": between the beginning of the century and World War II, the proportion of women in the workforce grew from 11 percent to only 19 percent, over two-thirds of them employed in clerical and sales occupations. In all, by the outbreak of World War II, persons employed in white-collar occupations constituted slightly over 35 percent of all males and females gainfully employed in the city of Johnstown, and about 25 percent in the rest of Cambria and the three surrounding counties. For comparison, in 1940 the share of the white-collar sector was 47 percent in New York, 41 percent in Philadelphia, and 42 percent in nearby Pittsburgh, also a steel city but much larger and more occupationally diversified. The proportions of women in gainful employment in these three cities were 37, 31, and 28 percent, respectively.[7]

As the region's largest producer and employer, Cambria/Bethlehem Steel Company retained its leading role in the region's public life, as well as firm control over the labor force. The two major strikes for recognition of independent unions, in 1919 and 1937, ended in failure. In both cases, the company's efforts at suppressing the labor unrest were loyally assisted by joint campaigns undertaken by the *Johnstown Tribune* and the Citizens' Committee, the latter made up of city officials and business and community leaders.[8]

Even though they were by now firmly settled in and around Johnstown, and their communities formed a permanent component of local society, East and South Europeans by and large remained separate from the dominant groups of "old" Americans and people of West European origin; as before, the latter constituted the solid majority: about three-quarters of the area's residents.[9] The ongoing "cultural division of labor" in the mills and mines, persistent residential segregation, the lack of class and supraethnic institutional networks to serve as bases for social integration, and unconcealed nativism—all these forces continued to divide the area into separate sociocultural worlds. Throughout the interwar period, the rate of intermarriage uniting residents of East European stock (Christian and Jewish combined) with native-born Americans of native parentage or persons of West European origin was less than 5 percent.[10]

Finally, in its cultural outlook, interwar Johnstown exhibited characteristics typical of self-contained, relatively isolated small towns. It offered, to be sure, popular entertainment such as sports, cinema, vaudeville theater, and dance halls. In 1927 the city acquired its own (junior) branch of the University of Pittsburgh where 600–800 students were enrolled, the majority of them in summer and evening courses. Yet, tucked away in the hills and valleys of western Pennsylvania, with its 50,000-odd inhabitants, most of whom were old-time, well-settled residents, Johnstown was not New York, with its exciting cultural life, rapidly expanding educational institutions, new people and ideas, and all the accompanying intellectual stimulation. Nor was it Philadelphia or even Pittsburgh, which offered similar stimuli on a smaller scale. It was, on the whole, insular and parochial, largely absorbed in its own day-to-day life and preoccupations, and its predominantly blue-collar character gave it a distinctly pragmatic, down-to-earth cultural ambience.

Like the town's general population, the size of the Jewish community remained roughly constant during the interwar period, numbering between 1,200 and 1,300 people (less than 2 percent of the city's population), or about 300 (in 1925) to 340 (in 1940) households. As before, East Europeans constituted the overwhelming majority, over nine-tenths of the entire group. The surrounding towns of Cambria County, and the closer parts of Indiana, Somerset, and Westmoreland Counties, contained an additional 700–800 Jews in toto, including immigrants and their American-born children, practically all of them of East European origin. The Johnstown Jewish community was also residentially stable. Nearly two-thirds of the households present in town in the 1920s were the families of settlers from the beginning of the century. A similar proportion, 60 percent, of the families residing in Johnstown in 1925 also lived there in 1940; the roughly one-fifth who left Johnstown were replaced by a similar number of newcomers. (Interestingly, as my informants remembered, among those who left, only a handful moved to large urban centers in search of careers on a bigger scale; the majority apparently resettled in small cities in Pennsylvania or surrounding states.) A significant proportion of Jewish households in the city continued to be related through blood or marriage; about 40 percent shared the same name with at least one other family, and over one-third of the East European and more than two-thirds of the German Jews were related to each other by marriage, either in the parental (immigrant) or the American-born generation.[11]

As in the earlier period, too, Jews remained residentially concentrated, though now in more prestigious parts of the city to which they were gradually relocating during the interwar decades—in part because of the prevailing divisive sociocultural climate of Johnstown, and in part because they themselves wanted to live next to each other.[12] The areas of Jewish settlement are shown in maps 3.1, 3.2, and 3.3.

By the outbreak of World War II, about one-fifth of the East European Jewish families still resided in the original foreign colonies, either in the Iron Street–River Avenue area, where the Orthodox synagogue was located, or in the Slavic sections; one-tenth lived on the edges of the downtown commercial district; and 15 percent were in Hornerstown—the old "peddlers' place." The majority, or nearly 60 percent, had moved to better neighborhoods, over one-half of this number to the most affluent, genteel Westmont section of town, up on the hills.[13] As the maps show, they clustered side by side within particular blocks in the new neighborhoods. In Kernville, for instance, a pleasant residential neighborhood not far from downtown—an in-between location on the upward-prestige route to Westmont—practically all Jewish families in the late 1930s resided on one or two blocks of four streets: Somerset, Dibert, Napoleon, and Sherman. In uphill Westmont, the residence of the "truly arrived," most Jews lived in a small area along Luzerne and Tioga Streets, and Second and Third Avenues, and the rest farther up between Clarion and Wyoming Streets; once again, they were concentrated within one or two blocks on each street.

The American-born generation, when they set up their own households (and this, as we shall see, they did rather late), resided in a close proximity to their parents: in 1925, nearly two-thirds, 63 percent, of such households were on the same street or within a few blocks of the parental residence, and another 15 percent were in the adjacent neighborhoods (ten–twelve blocks away); in 1940, this combined proportion was still a high 60-odd percent (see table 3.5).

The sluggish growth of the Johnstown economy was reflected in the Jewish group's characteristics. Its basic occupational profile as formed at

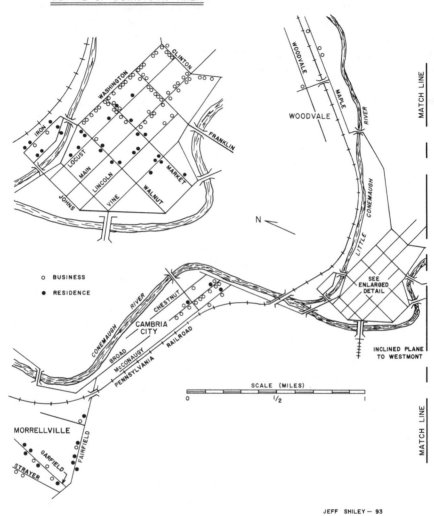

DETAIL OF DOWNTOWN AREA

○ BUSINESS

● RESIDENCE

N

SCALE (MILES)

0   1/2   1

JEFF SHILEY — 93

Map 3.1. Residential and Business Locations of Johnstown's Jews, 1930s
(Downtown Area, Woodvale, Cambria City, Morellville)

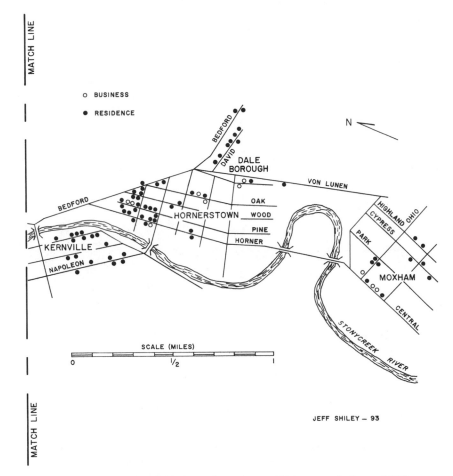

JEFF SHILEY — 93

Map 3.2. Residential and Business Locations of Johnstown's Jews, 1930s (Kernville, Hornerstown, Dale, Moxham)

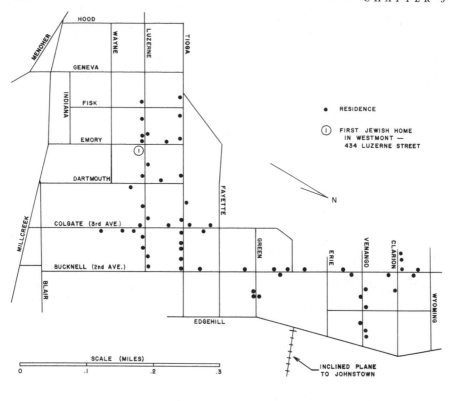

Map 3.3. Jewish Residences in Westmont Borough, 1930s

the beginning of the century, namely, its pronounced concentration in an entrepreneurial niche, persisted throughout the interwar period. Table 3.1 shows the occupational distribution of foreign- and American-born Jews in Johnstown (East European and German origin combined) in 1925 and 1940, with comparative data for New York, Pittsburgh, and Detroit, and for selected small and middle-size cities whose Jewish communities' demographic profile was surveyed in the 1930s.

As the table shows, from the 1920s until the outbreak of World War II, no less than nine-tenths of Johnstown's Jews, both generations, and men and women combined, pursued commercial occupations—about 40 percent as self-employed and 50 percent as employees, with no difference between East Europeans and Germans—a proportion much larger than that reported not only in the large cities, but also in small towns for which the data are available. Persons self-employed in professions made up, by the outbreak of World War II, a total of about 8 percent, less than the respective proportions in both large cities and small towns surveyed in the 1930s; most of them were American-born, and the majority of East European

3.1. Mr. and Mrs. Tobias and Fanny Callets' home on Luzerne Street (the first Jewish residence in this neighborhood, 1918). Collection of Mrs. Rose Leshner.

3.2. The Jewish Community Center Rodef Sholom's interim location on Tioga Street, 1947–1951. Reprinted from the *Jewish Center of Johnstown Rodef Sholom Synagogue*, Anniversary Book, 1954.

TABLE 3.1

Occupations of Jews in Johnstown and in Selected Cities and Towns, Interwar Period

	Self-employed in Trade and Services (%)	Sales/ Clerical (%)	Professional (%)	Manufacturing (%)	Other (%)
Johnstown 1925					
Immigrants (N = 184)	74	19	2	5	—
storeowners	(49)				
indep. craft.	(15)				
peddlers	(10)				
American-born (N = 230)	13	76	7	4	—
Total (N = 414)	40	51	5	4	—
1940					
Immigrants (N = 102)	84	11	3	2	—
storeowners	(63)				
indep. craft.	(11)				
peddlers	(10)				
American-born[a] (N = 326)	21	68	9	2	—
Total (N = 444)	38	52	8	2	—
New York (1937)[b]		49[c]	11	35	5
Pittsburgh (1938)		60	12	25	3
Detroit (1935)		60	10	27	3
Surveys of middle-size and smaller cities (average) (1934/5–1937/8)		69	12[d]	17	2

Sources: Johnstown city directories and business guides, local interviews. Data for other cities calculated from Nathan Goldberg, "Occupational Patterns of American Jews," *Jewish Review* 3 (January 1946): 274–75, 280–83, and idem, "Economic Trends among American Jews," *Jewish Affairs*, October 1, 1946, 12–16; Henry Meyer, "The Economic Structure of the Jewish Community in Detroit," *Jewish Social Studies* 2 (April 1940): 130; Maurice Taylor, *The Jewish Community of Pittsburgh: 1938* (Pittsburgh: Federation of Jewish Philanthropies, 1941), 98, 103–5; Jacob Lestschinsky, "Economic and Social Development of American Jews," in *The Jewish People. Past and Present* (New York: Jewish Encyclopedic Handbook, 1955), 4:87, 91–93; *American Jewish Year Book* 39 (1937/38): 55; Sophia Robison, ed., *Jewish Population Studies* (New York: Conference on Jewish Relations, 1943), 13–16, 31–33, 65–66, 77–78, 85–86, 98, 102–6; Samuel Koenig, "The Socioeconomic Structure of an American Jewish Community," in *Jews in a Gentile World*, ed. Isacque Graeber (New York: Macmillan, 1942), 208–11.

[a] American-born men and women have been combined, because their occupational distributions were similar in their most outstanding feature, i.e., the predominance of commercial employment in sales and clerical occupations. Young men were, however, over three times more likely than women to hold professional jobs.

[b] In all comparative data immigrants and American-born, men and women are combined.

[c] In all comparative data trade and services self-employed, clerical and sales are combined.

[d] A higher proportion of professionals in other smaller-city Jewish communities in comparison with Johnstown's Jews could have been the result of several factors, e.g., a more open social and political climate in these places in comparison with Johnstown (see chapter 5 on this issue), the absence of the ethnic economic niche, or nearby metropolitan centers, facilitating movement of people and ideas.

origin. Only a negligible minority, 2 percent, worked in manufacturing (including two partner-manufacturers of ladies' garments, and no more than five laborers). This proportion was considerably smaller than the figures reported in either larger or smaller cities where light industries employed Jewish wage earners.

Upward occupational mobility—as noted earlier, one of the main themes in the collective experience of big-city second-generation American Jews during the interwar period—occurred among Johnstown Jews on a very limited scale. Table 3.1 shows occupational distributions of immigrants' children recorded as employed in the 1925 and 1940 city directories, the majority of whom held sales and clerical jobs. Although between 1915 and 1940 the proportion of clerical workers and salespeople employed in the mainstream white-collar sector nearly doubled, from 9 percent to 17 percent, the decided majority of American-born Jews of East European and German origin alike worked with the parental generation in the ethnic entrepreneurial niche. Tracing the occupational careers of the offspring of Jewish merchants who had persisted in Johnstown between 1910/15 and 1935 revealed a basically similar pattern: the majority, over 70 percent, of American-born men and women found themselves in sales and trade-related clerical occupations, and nearly nine-tenths of this number worked in the ethnic entrepreneurial niche.[14]

Tables 3.2 through 3.4 illustrate the absence of occupational mobility among American-born Jewish Johnstowners during the interwar period from a different angle—that is, educational achievement, and specifically the effects, or lack thereof, rather, of advanced schooling on their occupational careers. (The micro-social context and attitudes toward education prevailing in the local Jewish community will be discussed in the next chapter).

As already mentioned, between the two world wars there was among young Johnstown Jews, regardless of ethnic origin, no rush to college similar to that observed in the large cities, especially New York. I used two different measures to estimate college attendance in the prewar Jewish community: the proportion of families sending their children to college during the 1920s and the 1930s, and a more conventional measure comparable with data from national and other ethnic studies and from the local censuses, the percentage of persons eighteen to twenty years old still in school in 1925 and in 1935. The two calculations turned out similar figures. As table 3.3 shows, by the early to mid-twenties the proportion, 11–12 percent (double that of the earlier period), was higher than both the share of Johnstown's youth in this age category attending college and the respective national figure as reported by the 1920 census, and much higher yet than the proportion in the same year in Cambria City, one of Johnstown's foreign colonies most densely populated by Slavs and Hungarians. It was lower, however, than in two downtown wards densely inhabited by middle-class Anglo-Protestant households. By the mid- to late thirties, my

TABLE 3.2

High School Attendance of American-Born Jews in Johnstown, 1920s–1930s

	1920s (%)	1930s (%)
% of general city population 16–17 years old continuing education	33[a]	80
Jews (estimate)	61[b]	89
2 Anglo-Protestant, white-collar wards	60	n.d.
4 Slavic, working-class wards	23	n.d.
Johnstown senior high school quits[c] (estimates for 1935–1937)		
non-Jews (average of all class and ethnic groups)		42
Jews		26
N Jews traced through Johnstown High School records 1920–1930: 146; 1931–1940: 187		

Sources: Johnstown High School, Westmont High School, and Dale High School—permanent student records, 1920–1940; The Spectator and The Phoenician—high school yearbooks, 1920–1940; U.S. Department of Commerce, School Attendance: 1920, Census Monograph 5 (1924): 247, 264–65; Fourteenth Census of the United States: 1920, Population, 2:866; ibid., State Compendium: Pennsylvania, 83; Sixteenth Census of the United States: 1940, Characteristics of the Population (Pennsylvania–Texas), 254–55; Sixteenth Census of the United States: 1940, Population, vol. 2, pt. 6, 159; Martin Trow, "The Second Transformation of American Secondary Education," International Journal of Comparative Sociology 2 (1961): 152–53; Biennial Survey of Education in the United States, 1936–1938, U.S. Office of Education (Washington, DC: Government Printing Office, 1942), 138–39; Historical Statistics of the United States, Colonial Times to 1957 (Washington, DC: Government Printing Office, 1960), 207, 214. Over-age rates in John Folger and Charles Nam, Education of the American Population, 1960 Census Monograph, U.S. Department of Commerce (Washington, DC: Government Printing Office, 1967), 6, 77–78. On problems of incompleteness and reliability of census and school records, see Joel Perlmann, "The Use of Student Records for the Study of American Educational History," Historical Methods Newsletter 12 (Spring 1979): 66–74.

[a] Data for general city populations, and for Anglo-Protestant and Slavic wards, come from the 1920 and 1940 census data on school attendance of 16–17-year-olds; other data in this table represent averages for the decades of the 1920s and the 1930s.

[b] [1]A slightly higher proportion (70%) was reported in that period (1925) for Russian Jews in Providence, Rhode Island—the city 5 times larger than Johnstown, and the Jewish group about 20 times larger (general enrollment in high school of those aged 16–17 was likewise higher, 50%). As in Providence, however, the proportion of girls and boys attending high school was not very different, with the former slightly more likely to attend (Joel Perlmann, Ethnic Differences, Schooling, and Social Structure among the Irish, Italians, Jews, and Blacks in an American City, 1915–1935 [New York: Cambridge University Press, 1989], 26, 29, 142–48).

[c] These figures include also those who left town without follow-up record.

TABLE 3.3
College Attendance of American-Born Jews in Johnstown, 1920s–1930s

	1920s (%)	1930s (%)
% of general city population 18–20 years old attending college[a]	7–8	12–13
Jews (estimate)	11–12	16–17
2 Anglo-Protestant, white-collar wards	16–17	n.d.
4 Slavic, working-class wards	2–3	n.d.
% of U.S. population 18–20 years old attending college	8	15

Sources: U.S. Department of Commerce, School Attendance: 1920, *Census Monograph* 5 (1924): 247, 264–65; *Fourteenth Census of the United States: 1920*, Population, 2:866; ibid., *State Compendium: Pennsylvania*, 83; *Sixteenth Census of the United States: 1940*, Characteristics of the Population (Pennsylvania–Texas), 254–55; *Sixteenth Census of the United States: 1940*, Population, vol. 2, pt. 6, 159; *Biennial Survey of Education in the United States, 1936–1938*, U.S. Office of Education (Washington, DC: Government Printing Office, 1942), 138–39; *Historical Statistics of the United States, Colonial Times to 1957* (Washington, DC: Government Printing Office, 1960), 207, 214; University of Pittsburgh, Office of the Registrar; enrollment statistics, Hillman Library, Archives of the Industrial Society, 1920–1940.

[a] The figure for Johnstown, and for Anglo-American and Slavic-American wards, are estimates, based on the 1920 and 1940 census data on school attendance of 18–20-year-olds, adjusted for the national over-age rates in senior high schools, and checked against the available relevant information in Johnstown's high school records.

TABLE 3.4
Impact of Schooling on Occupational Careers of American-Born Jews in Johnstown, 1920–1936

	Total %	Men %	Women %
Ever enrolled in college and employed in:			
professions and semiprofessions	36	34	30
(ethnic) business	64	66	70

	Men and Women (%)
High school graduates and employed in:	
ethnic economic niche	75
mainsream clerical/sales	13
professions and semiprofessions	12[a]

N = 146 traced through Johnstown business guides and city directories

Sources: University of Pittsburgh (main and Johnstown capuses), Carnegie Institute—Office of the Registrar, 1920–1936; Johnstown High School, Westmont High School, Dale High School—permanent student records and high school yearbooks, 1920–1940; Johnstown city directories, 1920, 1925, 1929, 1937, 1940—occupations of Jewish high school graduates; local interviews.

[a] Of this number about one-third were women, almost exclusively teachers.

estimates showed the proportion to be about 16–17 percent, about one-third higher than the percentage of Johnstown's 18–20-year-olds reported by the 1940 census to be pursuing college education, but only slightly higher than the national figure in that year (the 1940 census did not provide educational information for particular neighborhoods in Johnstown).

While most young Jews in Johnstown did not go to college, an increasing majority during the interwar period obtained secondary education (see table 3.2). As I estimated from the available, although unfortunately incomplete, local high school records (for day students), by 1925 the majority of sixteen- to seventeen-year-olds pursued secondary schooling—almost double the proportion for the town's general population in that age group, and about equal to that reported in the 1920 census for the two downtown wards with a heavy concentration of middle-class Anglo-Protestant households. By 1940, nine-tenths of sixteen- to seventeen-year-old Jews attended high school. I calculated the proportion of senior high school dropouts for 1935–1937, bad Depression years, but with more reliable records, for some reason, than the rest of the decade. It turned out to be somewhat over one-quarter, or about 60 percent less than in a sample of a general (all occupational and ethnic groups) senior student population in those years.

Most striking, however, is evidence, shown in table 3.4, of the absorbing force of the ethnic entrepreneurial niche almost regardless of educational attainment. Among a small minority of American-born Jews who attended college between 1920/21 and 1935/36, only slightly over one-third, without significant gender difference, subsequently pursued professional occupations, while the rest for the most part found business-related employment in the Jewish economic enclave. The occupational careers of high school graduates followed a similar pattern: three-quarters of them, men and women alike, found themselves employed within the entrepreneurial niche created by their parents.

Now, a closer look at the operation of this absorbing ethnic economic niche. It was sustained by the prevailing socioeconomic conditions in the Johnstown area, and, inside the Jewish group, by combined resources such as residential stability and proximity of its members, social support networks established in the earlier period and enforced by pragmatic as well as by group normative considerations, and professional know-how. These intragroup resources remained, as before, of a mixed class and ethnic character, or, more accurately, they were of the class-built-into-ethnic type, with the emphasis still on the latter. The know-how or class skills of Jewish entrepreneurs in dealing with American market conditions expanded over time, and this development—their learning of modern capitalist resources—can be viewed as ethnicization. This learning process occurred when immigrants applied shared mental schemas or symbolic "coping tools" transplanted from the old country and modified (or ethnicized) in the American environment, but it occurred primarily within, and in reliance on, a group of fellow ethnics. In the case of the East Europeans, it also occurred in the context of their dealings with customers familiar from the old country—a familiarity that greatly facilitated a good product-consumer relationship, as economists call one of the important aspects of occupational expertise in commercial pursuits.[15] Nevertheless, as we shall see, a distinguishable class-based resource, although for a considerable proportion of the local Jewish business community still mediated by ethnic representatives, evidently increased in importance. Three tables in this section, 3.5, 3.6, and 3.7, show some of these sustaining internal factors that are calculable in statistical figures.

Little more than one-tenth of Jewish businesses during the interwar period were wholesale establishments and larger department stores. Most of the Jewish-owned enterprises in Johnstown were small-scale undertakings: small stores, artisan shops, and peddling enterprises; peddlers, by then called traveling vendors, still made up one-tenth of the self-employed group. The majority of businesses run by Jewish entrepreneurs were individually owned. In this case, records show a considerable difference between those owned by East Europeans and those owned by Germans, with a significantly larger proportion of the latter conducted as partnerships. We could reduce this difference by including a number of East European enterprises that were run as informal (unrecorded) partnerships; but the small German group also had two characteristics, noted earlier, that facilitated joint business ventures: in comparison with East Europeans, establishments of German Jews were generally larger, and there was a much higher rate of family ties in their ownership.

Established in the earlier period, the concentration of Jewish businesses, both German and East European, in a few lines of trade continued through the interwar period. Table 3.6 shows the clustering of Jewish merchants (retailers, including self-employed owners of artisan shops such as tailors, milliners, and furriers) in the selected lines of trade, calculated from city directories' and business guides' listings in the late 1920s and the late 1930s; these data are compared with the distribution of Gentile merchants in the city, as well as the proportions of Jews in these lines and in professions. Jewish and Gentile merchants were, so to speak, reversely concentrated, specializing in different areas of business. While most of the Gentile merchants operated food and automotive businesses, the majority of Jews worked in four lines: apparel/shoes, dry goods, jewelry, and furniture. Foodstuffs, a common trade line among East European Jewish immigrants in the early phase of their settlement in Johnstown, attracted fewer retail merchants during the interwar period, although a few well-established stores remained, and "traveling vendors" in this specialty continued to move around the area, somewhat like shtetl Jews in the old country. In recollecting reasons for diminished interest in the foodstuffs trade, my

TABLE 3.5

Family and Household Characteristics That Sustained Jewish Entrepreneurial Niche, 1920–1940[a]

Social Characteristics	1900/10–1920/25	1925–1940
% of families persisting in Johnstown:	62	60
% of households related by blood or marriage	1920–1940	
sharing family name with at least one other	41	
with different family names related through marriage		
East Europeans	34	
Germans	68	
	1925	**1940**
% of working children 16+ years old living with parents	73	52
residential proximity to parents of independently living working children 16+ years old[b]		
same street or within a few blocks	63	51
adjacent neighborhood (within 10–12 blocks)	15	11
Economic Characteristics		
% of intragroup business partnerships (registered)	**1920s**	**1930s**
East Europeans	16	9
Germans	35	38
% of East European wives involved in family business (estimate)[c]	60–65	
% of adult children in sales/clerical occupations employed in:	**1925**	**1940**
parental business	30	20
other Jewish-owned stores	57	63
total within the ethnic niche	87	83
mainstream jobs	13	17
% of immigrant employees occupied in the ethnic niche	87	90

Sources: Johnstown city directories, 1920–1940; manuscript schedules of the 1929 business census, Cambria County, Pennsylvania, National Archives, Washington, DC, Suitland Branch, Rg. 29, Entry 317, Box 1381, files 2312, 2371–72, 2374; Box 661, files 6 and 17; local interviews.

[a] Unless otherwise indicated, the figures comprise both East European and German Jews.

[b] A study in Providence, Rhode Island, found a lesser, but still considerable proportion (46%) of adult independent children residing in the same neighborhood as their parents, in 1940 (Judith Smith, *Family Connections: A History of Italian and Jewish Immigrant Lives in Providence, Rhode Island* [Albany: SUNY Press, 1985], 112–13, tables 3-6, 3-7, 3-8).

[c] In a 1935 study of the Jewish community in Detroit, over 50% of wives of the entrepreneurs were reported as actively participating in family business. See Henry Meyer, "The Structure of the Jewish Community in Detroit" (Ph.D. diss., University of Michigan, 1939), 72–73.

TABLE 3.6

Concentration of Jewish and Gentile Merchant Populations in Selected Lines of Business, and the Proportion of Jews in the Total Number of Johnstown's Merchants and Professionals, 1920s–1930s

Lines of Business	Jewish (%)		Gentile (%)		Jews as % of Total	
	1920s	1930s	1920s	1930s	1920s	1930s
Apparel/shoes[a] Jewelry Furniture Dry goods/general stores	73	67	11	15[b]	43	44[c]
Food Automotive	19	19	74	70	3	4
Other	8	14	15	15		
Professions doctors dentists lawyers					8	9

Sources: Johnstown business guides and city directories, 1925, 1929, 1933, 1937; U.S. Bureau of the Census, *Census of American Business: 1933*, Retail Distribution, vol. 2 (Washington, DC: Government Printing Office, 1935), 146–47; idem., Wholesale Distribution, 3:136; U.S. Bureau of the Census, *Census of American Business: 1935*, Retail Distribution, vol. 2 (Washington, DC: Government Printing Office; 1937), 140; idem., Retail Distribution, 3:224–26, 229–30; idem., Wholesale Distribution, 3:xix; U.S. Bureau of the Census, *Sixteenth Census of the United States: 1940*, Retail Distribution: 1939, vol. 1, pt. 3 (Washington, DC: Government Printing Office; 1943), 424–25, 775, 823; idem., Wholesale Trade: 1940, 2:94.

[a] Included in this category are self-employed owners of artisan shops (furriers, milliners, shoemakers, etc.).

[b] I checked for comparison the distributions of total merchant populations in particular lines of trade in the two closest large cities: Pittsburgh and Philadelphia in 1939. In both places, these distributions were similar to that in Johnstown: 69% and 61%, respectively, of all merchants concentrated in food and automotive trade, while those in the "Jewish" lines made up 13% and 17% of the total (U.S. Bureau of the Census, *Sixteenth Census of the United States: 1940*, Census of Business, vol. 1, Retail Trade: 1939 [Washington, DC: Government Printing Office, 1943], 779–81). In Pittsburgh, however, and also in Detroit (another large city for which comparable data are available), a considerably larger proportion of Jewish merchants traded in foodstuffs: nearly one-third. See Maurice Taylor, *The Jewish Community of Pittsburgh: 1938* (Pittsburgh: Federation of Jewish Philanthropies, 1941), 117; Henry Meyer, "The Structure of the Jewish Community in Detroit" (Ph.D. diss., University of Michigan, 1939), 194–95, 313.

[c] In other, large and small American cities during the 1930s, Jews were similarly, or even more highly, concentrated in these lines of business, ranging from 50% to 75% (see, e.g., Jacob Lestschinsky, "Economic and Social Development of American Jewry," in *The Jewish People, Past and Present* (New York: Jewish Encyclopedic Handbook, 1955), 86–87, 90–93; Taylor, *The Jewish Community of Pittsburgh*, 117, 122, 194–95, 313; Marshall Sklare, *The Jews: Social Patterns of an American Ethnic Group* (New York: Free Press, 1958), 75, 78–79; Robert Shosteck, *Small-Town Jewry Tell Their Story* (New York: B'nai B'rith Vocational Service: 1953), 14.

informants mentioned first and foremost this specialty's comparatively low profitability ("quick turnover, little money"); the appearance by the 1920s of a number of food stores owned by Slavs and Hungarians, traditional trade partners of Jewish merchants, did not seem to be of much concern. A small group (six–seven) of established Jewish wholesalers in town also clustered in a few lines of trade: dry goods, shoes, metal junk, and produce—especially fresh fruit and vegetables, sold later by individual peddlers.[16]

In all of their trade specialties, the proportion of Jews exceeded their share of the general merchant population by several times. In comparison, Johnstown's Jewish professionals, like businessmen concentrated in a few specialties, had a much lesser, if any, ethnic weight. Even though, as elsewhere, their proportion in particular professions considerably exceeded Jews' share in the town's general population (about 8 and 2 percent, respectively), the share of Jewish doctors, dentists, and lawyers (combined) in the entire population of similarly occupied professionals did not compare with the figure of 60 percent in New York, or even 22 percent in Cleveland (where Jews constituted in 1938 about 8 percent of the general population).[17]

As already noted, the economic and sociocultural conditions prevailing in the Johnstown area during the interwar period also made for the persistence of a multiethnic enclave that had formed at the beginning of the century, involving East European Jewish and Gentile families. As before, the primary relationship was between the providers of services (Jews) and their customers (Slavs and Hungarians); the second, supplementary relation was between the former as employers and the latter as employees.

By the late 1930s, as we have seen, a majority of Jewish residents of Johnstown had moved their homes to better parts of the city. But 70 percent of the East European Jewish stores remained either in the old foreign sections of town and in the area close to the railroad station—which continued to serve as a shopping center for customers from nearby coal towns—or had moved to parts of the city where the Slavs and Hungarians had formed secondary ethnic communities (see map 3.1).[18] And so through the interwar period, Slavic and Hungarian families constituted the bulk of the clientele patronizing Jewish businesses: David S.'s, Israel B.'s, and William R.'s clothing and furniture stores, and Jacob G.'s soft drinks bottling business in Johnstown; Barry H.'s steamship agency in Cassandra; Barney S.'s, Aaron E.'s. Samuel I.'s, Julius K.'s, Morris L.'s clothing stores in Twin Rocks, Nanty-Glo, Boswell, St. Michael, and Beaverdale; and the life insurance company managed by Julius F., a resident of Johnstown, who "spoke eight [East European] languages" and traveled around the area "among coal-mining towns selling policies to the foreigners." Working for their parents or in other Jewish-owned stores, the native-born children of the immigrants regularly waited on their customers, and often "learned enough Slavish [just what was needed] to sell." The department store of the five Glosser brothers, conveniently located not far from the railroad station and carrying low-priced merchandise for working people, catered to "Slavish, Polish, Russian, Hungarian . . . groups [who] felt at home in the store." Born after World War I to one of the founders of this establishment, Isadore G. worked part-time in the store in the 1930s and can still remember "the many, many foreign-born mothers who would come in with their *babushkas* and the long dresses on, while the children waited outside . . . and they would bargain over prices [like in the old country]. . . . They [Slavic people] would rather shop in our store than in [American ones] because in the latter they were not well accepted."[19]

In fact, a great many East European peasant-immigrants did prefer the familiar Jewish business, not only over the American ones where the language and the manner of dealing were alien and where they felt uncomfortable, but also, as in the old country, over the stores of their own Christian countrymen. This habitual inclination was noted (and lamented) by Johnstown's Rusyn-language newspaper *Chranitel*, which in 1920 devoted a lengthy article to this issue, "Svoj ko Svojemu"(Support your own). It repeatedly appealed—clearly to no avail, or the reiteration would not have been necessary—to the local Rusyn community: "Cas uze in johnstownskim Rusinam spojenymi silami napomahatim . . . narodny ruski stor" (It is time for the Johnstown Rusyns [to start] with united strength to support their own Rusyn stores). It is interesting to note, however, that the same paper also carried regular advertisements—in Rusyn and Slovak—of local Jewish businessmen.[20]

As table 3.7 shows, money loans from Jewish merchants to Slavic and Hungarian borrowers, so common in the East European countryside, ceased to play a significant role in the economic exchange between the two groups. What persisted was the debtor-creditor relationship. According to the manuscript schedules of the 1929 business census, about one-half of Jewish retail stores in the area sold their merchandise on credit, the proportion varying from 30 percent for clothing and shoe shops to nearly 80 percent for those carrying furniture and household items.[21] As in the earlier period, the working-class customers of Jewish stores usually tried to repay these debts in full on a biweekly basis, when the steel workers and coal miners received their paychecks, or else—for more substantial purchases—in installments over a long period of time.

The basic form of East European Jewish-Gentile relations, that of economic exchange between commercial dealers and their customers, expanded during the interwar period to encompass professional services provided by American-born Jewish doctors, dentists, and lawyers. Interviews with these professionals indicate that East European Jews and Gentiles formed the bulk of their clientele in the 1930s. Peasant-immigrants and their American-born children sought out Jewish medical and legal services for the same reasons they patronized Jewish stores and because—"they would say, 'I want a Jew-doctor or a Jew-attorney'"—they considered

3.3. Mrs. Miriam
Weisberg, wife of Max,
in front of their family
store in Cambria City,
early 1920s. Collection
of Mrs. Ruth Glosser.

them "to be endowed with some special powers." This perception might
be seen as a (more or less) secularized version of old-country peasant beliefs in Jews' supernatural connections.[22]

The secondary type of economic relationship linking East European
Jews and Gentiles in regular contacts was that of employers and employees.
Also a transplant from the old country, as noted in the previous chapter it
reemerged in Johnstown soon after the immigrants settled there at the turn
of the century, and continued through the interwar period. On the part of
Slavs and Hungarians, it involved mostly women—unmarried girls of the
foreign- or American-born generation. As in the earlier period, more affluent Jewish homes employed Slavic and Hungarian maids, and young
women of this extraction were also hired as employees in larger Jewish-
owned establishments in town; at Glosser Bros.' department store, Slavic
and Hungarian clerks and salesgirls made up in the 1930s one-third of the
payroll. In the cigar factory, which operated in one of the town's foreign
colonies from the beginning of the century until the 1930s, East European

3.4. Advertisement of Berman's store "Clothing on Credit," corner of Franklin and Main Streets, downtown, 1930s. Collection of the Berman family.

Gentile workers constituted most of the labor force; and in the ladies' garments factory, established in Johnstown in the late 1930s by two Jewish manufacturers from Philadelphia, the majority of the four hundred workers were second-generation women of Slavic and Hungarian backgrounds.[23]

The evidence presented so far of the continued heavy concentration of Johnstown Jews in trade and related occupations within the ethnic entrepreneurial niche indicates the effectiveness of intragroup social networks as an employment resource. Besides securing employment, the same networks served also as sources of apprenticeships for the young and the newcomers, and of business information and assistance. As noted earlier in this chapter, these were mixed, ethnic-class (with the accent on the first term) resources, in that factors such as the supply of jobs, trade credit, financial loans, and business information derived from the suppliers' class position as entrepreneurs, solidly established after twenty to thirty years of practice in the area; yet at the same time these very supplies were accrued and distributed through participation in the ethnic economic niche. Similarly, the motives of the assistance-providers had retained their mixed, class-ethnic character. On the one hand, there was the pragmatism of entrepreneurs who needed the support of the lesser members of their class, especially in the face of chronic business fluctuations. On the other hand, there had persisted certain traditional group ethnoreligious schemas or perceptions, in particular a representation of the world as moving in a "wheel of fortune"

in which human fortunes rose and fell in alteration (see chapter 6), a strong
normative precept obliging them to charitable deeds and intragroup mutual assistance, and, as my informants referred to it, a deep-rooted impulse
to "close ranks" based on a shared sense of group civic insecurity (see chapter 5). All these factors of group-specific cultural derivation combined to
call for sustained support of their fellow ethnics in need.

The institutional growth of the community during the interwar decades
expanded and further solidified the organized base of this internal support.
The synagogue remained the center of organized Jewish life in Johnstown
and vicinity (its social functioning will be discussed in greater detail in
chapter 4). As before, the Orthodox Rodef Sholom, founded by East Europeans at the beginning of the century, had the largest membership. In
1922, a splinter group of Hornerstown residents founded their own small
Orthodox *shul*, Ahavath Achim, in the same neighborhood; and in 1924,
the German Jews, who until then had met privately for religious services,
purchased a building on Vine Street downtown for their Reform Beth Zion
Temple. An array of other organizations appeared, such as Y.M.H.A.,
Pirche Zion Society (later Masada), additional lodges of the fraternal B'nai
B'rith Society, local branches of the Hadassah and the Council of Jewish
Women (with junior groups), as well as the Jewish War Veterans, the Jew-
ish Social Center, and, by the outbreak of World War II, the Johnstown
Jewish Community Council, which also took on activities of the United
Jewish Appeal.[24]

Another factor enhancing the intragroup resource pool for work-related
assistance-seekers was the slowly increasing number of more affluent mer-
chant-owners of bigger enterprises. They were not numerous, a dozen or
so altogether, but they were reliable; as in the earlier period, most were
actively engaged in the organized life of the community, and were therefore also accessible through communal channels. By the 1920s, the two
ethnic parts of the Jewish community, Germans and East Europeans, while
still socially separate, had by and large come to share business support networks.

Reliance on fellow ethnics in seeking employment was considered a matter of course in the Jewish community. Having calculated that a striking
80-odd percent of the young men and women during the 1920s and 1930s
worked in the Jewish entrepreneurial niche, I asked my American-born informants whether they had ever tried to obtain outside employment. They
commonly answered in the negative, pointing out characteristics of the situation in prewar Johnstown that they apparently perceived at that time as
natural, namely, the marginal position in the dominant local society of the
Jews on the one hand, and, on the other, the latter's encapsulation in their
ethnic community. As Betty and Helen N. explained it, for example, the
reasons for this proactive withdrawal were twofold: "We didn't want to test
anti-Semitism, although perhaps there was a little less of this than we

thought, and besides, it was natural, Jews were in business, and there were also the Glossers."[25]

As table 3.5 showed, among American-born young men and women who worked in the Jewish economic niche during the interwar decades, about 60 percent were employed in establishments (other than parental businesses) owned by their fellow ethnics. Of this number, a large proportion worked at the Glosser Bros.' department store; started at the beginning of the century as a small clothing shop by the five Glossers, immigrants from Antopolie in Byelorussia, it had by the early 1930s grown to be the second-largest department store in the city, after the one owned by Bethlehem Steel Company, the local "Saks Fifth Avenue." Not counting part-time and seasonal help, it employed about five hundred workers, of whom nearly one-third were Jewish. In fact, it apprenticed to business the majority of American-born Jewish young men and women in town. "Almost every Jewish person [in Johnstown before World War II] got their basic training at the store. We called it 'Gee Bee Tech.'" Young people usually started working part-time at Gee Bee when still in high school, during summer vacations and the busy holiday seasons, at two dollars per day, and after they finished their education, many continued as regular employees for a few years; the store's payroll records from the 1930s showed the average length of employment of clerks and salespeople to have been 3.5 years. While it provided assured employment and practical business training for local Jewish youth, the impact of the Gee Bee department store was not unambiguous; as my informants admitted, half resentful and half admiring of the Glosser family's business acumen, the store's rapid expansion and competitive advantage in the assortment and pricing of merchandise hurt smaller merchants who catered to the same clientele.[26]

Two other large Jewish-owned department stores, Nathan's and Schwartz Brothers, served predominantly an affluent, native-born American clientele, and while the majority of the workforce in these stores, each employing 300–350 people, was also native-born American (mainly women of Welsh, Scotch, German, and Irish backgrounds), between 30 and 40 percent of the department heads and managers were Jewish. Both these department stores went out of business during the Depression. Smaller-size establishments in a "larger business" category had on their payrolls from one to two dozen people, depending on current economic conditions in the local area. And still smaller establishments also hired help from outside of the owners' households, with staffs between five and ten.[27]

Financial assistance in conducting business was another area in which intragroup social networks continued to serve as an important resource. Closer and more remote relatives, in terms of both degree of kinship and geographic proximity, remained the primary recourse when merchants needed help to strengthen their troubled enterprises. As indicated by the dispositions in a sample of last wills filed at the Cambria County Court-

3.5 and 3.6. Glosser Brothers' department store, and a page from its payroll book, 1930s. Collection of the Glosser family.

3.7. Schwartz Brothers'
department store, 1930.
Collection of
Mr. Martin Schwartz.

house, such loans, ranging from a few hundred to several thousand dollars,
often remained outstanding for a number of years. Max W., for example,
deceased in 1943, acknowledged in his testament debts to his two sons-in-
law, residing out of town, and to his daughter, a Johnstown teacher, in the
total amount of $5,300, which he had received from them after the flood
in March of 1936—another of the recurrent Johnstown floods that badly
damaged the downtown section, including Jewish businesses.[28]

Besides kin, the larger group also served as an assistance resource for
hard-pressed merchants. Interest-free small loans were provided by the
B'nai B'rith Beneficial Society lodges, and by the Free Loan Society estab-

TABLE 3.7
Claimed Personal Loans and Liabilities of Jewish Merchants,[a] 1920–1940

Promissory Notes on Personal Loans Obtained from and Issued to Individuals		Debts Owed to Business Creditors, Banks, and Individuals	
Involving	(%)		(%)
Jews	66	to business creditors (whole-salers, jobbers, manufacturers)	46
Americans	26	to banks and commercial estab-lishments	29
Slavs or Hungarians	8	to individuals	25
		Total to fellow ethnics (estimate)	65–70

Sources: Judgment notes (secured claims) recorded at the Cambria County Courthouse, Ebensburg, Pennsylvania, Judgment dockets, 1920–1940; bankruptcy records, 1920–1940 (debts exclusive of unpaid taxes, rent, and wages to employees), U.S. Bankruptcy Court, Western District of Pennsylvania, Pittsburgh; and Federal Archives and Records Center, Philadelphia.

[a] East European and German merchants combined.

lished after the 1936 flood. They usually ranged from $100 to $300 (as the next chapter will show, Jewish organizations suffered chronic financial insufficiency, so the aid was correspondingly limited), to be repaid in weekly installments of a few dollars a week. Applicants for such loans were required to obtain two endorsements from community members.[29] Much more commonly, the needed assistance in loans and mercantile credit was provided by friends and acquaintances from the local Jewish entrepreneurial niche as well as from broader-scope ethnic business networks, extending to nearby Greensburg and Altoona, and further to Pittsburgh, Philadelphia, and New York. Table 3.7 shows the ethnic composition of the providers and receivers of personal loans on promissory notes issued to and by Jewish merchants in town during the interwar period, and the composition of liabilities claimed in the bankruptcy records of Jewish entrepreneurs in the vicinity in the same period, with the proportion of Jews among creditors and individuals claiming unpaid debts.

Personal loans—the table shows only those secured by promissory notes registered in the courthouse—ranged from $500 to $6,000 and usually involved local people, the majority of them Jewish. As in the earlier period, more common yet was financial assistance provided "over the table" to Jewish merchants by the more affluent members of their group, who were usually also community leaders, and secured "by a handshake" or "private note." When his Great Eastern Clothing Company store in Johnstown found itself in trouble in 1923/24, Isaac R. borrowed money from a fellow merchant, Isadore M.: "I loaned him [almost $2,000 in small sums], sometimes $100, sometimes $200 in cash, on and off, to help him out." "Jewish merchants in town, when they might use some help, would come to the store"—Isadore G.'s family owned a large department store in Johnstown, and was also actively involved in the *shul* and other Jewish organizations. "[They came] when they needed some money to see them through a tough time or whatever, and borrowed money, leaving a note that they would pay it back." Similar emergency assistance to fellow merchants was extended by Morris B., owner of a dry goods wholesale enterprise and a board member of Rodef Sholom; Moses G., owner of a metal junk wholesale business and patron of the Ahavath Achim *shul* in Hornerstown; and Max W., an old-time established storekeeper in town and one of the founders of the Iron Street synagogue—the same Max W. who borrowed money from his relatives when his own business was in trouble.[30]

The data on the liabilities of Jewish merchants were gathered from the bankruptcy records. As we shall see later in this chapter, filing for bankruptcy (not necessarily carried through) remained a common occurrence among local Jewish business owners, so that this evidence, supported by the information gathered in the interviews, can serve to represent the whole group.

As compared with the earlier period, a considerably greater proportion of debt was owed to local banks: 29 percent versus 12 percent. This ethnicization, an expansion of class resources used in conducting business, indicated that Jewish entrepreneurs—especially those of East European origin, since their German counterparts had already relied on this kind of resource in the earlier period—were being increasingly incorporated into the mainstream financial system. Still, as my interviews indicate, a considerable number of Jewish store owners, while seeking a bank loan, used a fellow ethnic intermediary—most often one of the well-established merchants with "some personal connection" in the local (mainstream) financial establishment. Bill B., son of the owner of a prospering wholesale establishment, put it this way: "In this town, you needed connections [apparently also outside one's own ethnic group], the banks at that time were quite liberal with [business] credits, but they wanted to know you." Indeed, as Abe B. recalled, Bill's father did arrange for a bank loan for his father when the latter had "some business troubles."[31]

But despite the increased frequency of reliance on business loans provided by mainstream financial institutions, the majority of business operations of Johnstown Jews were financed within the group, by fellow ethnics—a situation that reflected, again, the enduring marginality of the Jewish group in the larger society, and the reliability of intragroup resources. As bankruptcy records indicate, the creditors of Jewish stores in Johnstown and vicinity were either local wholesalers or fellow Jews from nearby Altoona, and from Pittsburgh, Philadelphia, and New York.

In Bill B.'s words, "The informal network was of crucial importance in business." This opinion reappeared regularly in my informants' discussions of their pre–World War II entrepreneurial experience. The setting in which contacts between jobbers and retailers took place fostered the intermingling of business and social relations, entangling persons in a web of reciprocal obligations. Retailers' visits at local wholesale establishments were customarily accompanied by an exchange of news about current events in the Jewish community and of inquiries about the well-being of the family and business. Encounters with out-of-town jobbers and their representatives were similarly personalized. When Samuel and Morris T., Johnstown furriers, traveled to New York on their seasonal buying trips, they were usually treated to tea and conversation about "Jewish matters," and information about people and trade was exchanged. Similarly, when Julius K., a clothing merchant in the coal-mining town of St. Michael, and Aaron E., a general store owner in Nanty-Glo, were visited by Jewish salesmen from Pittsburgh and Philadelphia, they "invited them home, sat down together, and talked about different things," and "they oftentimes stayed overnight." In such situations, credit leniency and wholesalers' assistance over difficult times were expected as a matter of course.[32]

When, despite private loans and credit extensions, the enterprise failed, the bankrupts, like David B. and Samuel E., owners of two small clothing stores in Johnstown, were often "put back in business with the encouragement of the creditors" (usually at 20–25 percent settlement of the claims, and not uncommonly by so-called friendly adjustment, that is, without court supervision), and with money borrowed from relatives and Jewish fellow merchants; if legal advice was needed at any point in these proceedings it was usually provided by local Jewish lawyers. And when, despite efforts to revive it, the business was sold, as bankruptcy records indicate, it was most often purchased by Jewish merchants from the area. So, for instance, the stock and fixtures of Morris R.'s failed clothing store in Boswell were bought out in 1920 by Tobias C., owner of the Empire Clothing Company in Johnstown; and in 1929 the bankrupt scrap metal and junk establishment of Israel L. and Sons was split between the brothers G., Harry D., and Hyman B. This last purchaser was a former shoe-store owner in Johnstown, who subsequently, according to his testimony in the bankruptcy hearing, went on to make a living from "buying bankrupt stocks and selling them."[33]

"A GOOD LIFE FOR THE FAMILY":
ECONOMIC STRATEGIES AND HOUSEHOLD MANAGEMENT

The business world of Johnstown's Jewish community can be depicted as a matrix: local opportunity structure and the dominant social order on the outer sides, and the situation in the ethnic entrepreneurial niche as a dense inner network, within which operated Jewish family households, the basic work and accumulating units. We now look more closely at how they functioned economically.

While most—nine-tenths—of the Jewish businesses in Johnstown were headed by men, their operation by and large remained a collective family effort, involving wives and all able children. In comparison with the earlier period, however, the *takhlis*—or, to reapply Alfred Schutz's useful concept, the in-order-to purpose of this shared effort—was not, as in the earlier period, primarily the establishment of a permanent economic foothold in the area, sufficient to feed and house the family, but, building upon this base, the attainment of a materially comfortable existence, or what in the local Jewish community came to be perceived as a "decent" standard of living.

In the big cities, as East European Jews moved up from the laboring into the white-collar strata, married women withdrew from economic activities; as one New Yorker recalled a common status concern among upwardly mobile Jews during the interwar period, "the man was ashamed [if his wife worked]."[34] In Johnstown in the 1930s, the proportion of merchants' wives actively engaged in some way in conducting family business remained, as I estimated, about 65 percent, similar to the percentage in the earlier period. As before, these women were for the most part of East European origin, including second-generation married immigrants' daughters who either were still childless or had children old enough to be at school for a few hours a day; to this number a minority of female-headed enterprises, mostly run by widows, should be added.

The concentration of Jews in small business and the existence of an ethnic entrepreneurial niche facilitated continued economic involvement on the part of married women. Unlike working for others in the outside world (what the New Yorker quoted above presumably had in mind), business activity, either independent, or better yet, with one's husband, had not ceased to be considered by Jewish public opinion as a respectable pursuit for a wife. Married women's economic participation in the Johnstown Jewish entrepreneurial niche was, therefore, both a socially approved and an expected contribution to the realization of long-term family goals aimed at a decent middle-class standard of living. As my interviews indicate, most of these women, also American-born, genuinely enjoyed their participation in family business matters. Ida B., for instance, "always liked business and was good at it"; when the children were very small, she stayed at home, but soon she "got help for the children and went back to business"; the mother of Frieda C. "worked in the [family] store, and she greatly enjoyed it."[35] Let us take a closer look at the authority the participant-wives had in carrying on family businesses.

As married women of the nouveau-riche Jewish middle-class in the big cities increasingly withdrew into the home, they lost whatever measure of authority they might have had in family economic affairs that derived from participation in earning a livelihood. The majority of Johnstown wives continued to be actively involved in family enterprises, and this in a double sense, in that they both contributed to household income and shared with their husbands the social space of work—or, differently stated, family inter-

actions were extrapolated into the business place. This involvement provided Johnstown wives some measure of influence in matters economic.
Inasmuch as business and household economies could be separated, however (we will see that they were to a considerable extent conflated), regardless of women's involvement in the store, in the domain of business
men remained the bosses in most cases, in immigrant as well as second-
generation families: "It was not a partnership, really," "we worked for
them rather than with them" as my informants put it, matter-of-factly acknowledging the situation. I have encountered only one rebel—one vocal
rebel, that is—but even this woman evidently repressed her resentment
over the imposed authority hierarchy in family business matters: "I started
teaching him [her husband, after they married] business [. . .] I loved
working in the store [. . .] but he got ahead of me [even though they had
help for the children]."[36]

There were a few silently recognized female bosses in family businesses;
interestingly, immigrant women decidedly prevailed in this small group
(the one rebel, for that matter, was also Russian-born), as if—but this is
merely a conjecture—they still carried in them the image of the role models
of their own or other independent merchant-mothers in the Eastern European shtetls. Renee G., for example, as everyone in her family acknowledged, was "the brains of the business," an originally small soft drinks
bottling firm in one of Johnstown's Slavic colonies that was subsequently
transformed into a large and prosperous Pepsi-Cola franchise. Her mild-
mannered, self-effacing husband was involved primarily in preparing and
selling the merchandise. Similarly, in the families of Israel T., Elmer M.,
and Raphael R., "mother(s) really ran the store [and father(s) 'listened']."
In a few other cases, wives were genuine partners of their husbands, like
Chaia Tzippa G., a "smart, shrewd businesswoman," who entirely ran her
family's grocery store and, in addition, "bartered [there] food for scrap"
for a junk metal enterprise managed by her husband Moshe Yitzhak; Ida
T., who "shared in all decisions" in running the family furrier shop; or
Gitel H., likewise a full-and-equal partner in the family's general store in
Cambria City. But even in those few instances where women either ran the
business entirely—that is, made all important decisions—or were equal
partners in it, the public image of subordination, of merely "helping," was
carefully maintained. As Martin G. succinctly put it, "The men knew how
important women were [in business], but in those days you did not come
out and say it."[37]

"Helping" was also the term used, regardless of generation, by most of
my female informants with whom I talked about the extent, and areas, of
their decision-making authority in running family businesses, as they enumerated various storekeeping activities, usually (although not exclusively)
left in their purview: selling and, generally, dealing with customers, that is,
talking with them and advising on purchases, and bookkeeping (if there
was any). In addition, depending on the line of trade, wives assisted their

husbands in buying merchandise: they offered opinions that the latter usually listened to and often considered in the final decision; but these final
decisions were men's, even when they reflected their wives' recommendations.[38] The women themselves, even the most active in business, complied
with this subordination, as they themselves admitted in their recollections:
"This was how things were at that time."

The intragroup credit network, discussed earlier, was virtually an all-
male affair, with no input by women, whether immigrant or American-
born. But regardless of whether they did or did not work in family stores,
women participated in the exchange of personal loans. A few, possessing
some personal funds, served as providers—like the mother of Fanny K., for
example, who with five hundred dollars she saved from household expenditures set her husband up in a peddling business after his store went
bankrupt during the Depression. More commonly, women functioned as
go-betweens if money was borrowed from their own relatives. Such finan-
cial-mediation kinwork by wives could have momentarily enhanced their
influence in matters of family business but did not alter the pattern of decision making described above; as in the earlier period, however, if the wife's
relatives were affluent and influential in the community, their position, as
my informants believed, would have more permanently reflected on that
woman's impact on business decisions in her own family, unless, of course,
she was timid or self-effacing.[39]

As in the earlier period, immigrants' offspring living in parental homes
continued to participate in family businesses. As children, they had already
became familiarized with their parents' store and often ran little business
errands; upon reaching adolescence, they regularly worked part-time—
after school hours and during busy holiday seasons—at the counters or
cash registers, without or with minimal pay. Of the adult (over sixteen years
of age) young men and women listed as clerks and salespeople, 30 percent
were employed in parental businesses in 1925, and 20 percent in 1940 (see
table 3.5). Most of the remaining, as already noted, worked for other Jews,
often relatives, in the ethnic entrepreneurial niche, but helped in parents'
stores on busy days or when needed for some other reason. As long as the
young people stayed in their parents' home, they continued to contribute
a substantial portion of their earnings to the family budgets. And, as can
be seen in the same table, they stayed there for an extended period of time
(I combined East Europeans and Germans because there was not much
difference between them): about 70 and 50 percent, respectively, of the
sixteen-year-old and older members of the American-born generation recorded as working in the 1925 and 1940 Johnstown city directories resided with their parents.[40]

Young people residing with their parents, even more than their mothers,
remained subordinate to the male head of the household in family business
matters. It seems that, in comparison with the earlier period, whatever little
voice immigrants' children had in conducting business affairs diminished

to the extent that their parents, formerly dependent on their offspring for communicating, particularly in writing, with the English-speaking environment, had mastered the new language. This diminution of young people's influence in family business matters generally affected—such was my impression from the interviews—daughters considerably more than their brothers, and that because young men apparently acquired a new voice, soft though it might have been, from their advisory initiatives concerning new or ethnicized ways of conducting business; young women, trained in clerical skills in high school, were commissioned with "helping" tasks, like their mothers.

These new—my informants used the terms "modern" and "American"—entrepreneurial ideas that American-born young men often desired to implement in the family business were not easily accepted, however, by the immigrant generation. In any case, a recurrent theme in the interviews suggested some subdued but persistent disagreements between sons and fathers in these matters. These disputes usually occurred in small businesses; by contrast, Gee Bee department store adopted modern business methods quickly and effectively. Henry K., for example, working in his family's general store, would have preferred that his father abandon once and for all the "old-fashioned" way of buying large quantities of the same merchandise and holding on to it even when it sold poorly. In Israel E.'s business, as his sons Nathan and Lester complained, there was a chronic "lack of credit supervision" that caused problems with cash flow; while Isadore S., in the opinion of his son, should have made more systematic use of "modern bookkeeping." While young men's persuasions did have some effect, they did not, in my informants' recollections, radically alter their fathers' ways of conducting business.[41]

In the previous chapter, while comparing the organization of cooperative family economy at the beginning of the century in Johnstown's immigrant households and the large cities such as New York, I noted the impact of outside employment of immigrants' sons and daughters in strengthening the children's autonomy and influence in parental homes. During the interwar period, when big-city, better-educated American-born Jews entered mainstream white-collar occupations en masse as they continued to contribute to family incomes, their independence and authority vis-à-vis their parents increased further. In Johnstown, a similar development was prevented by the continued absorption of the second generation into the ethnic entrepreneurial niche, either in family businesses in which fathers played the dominant role, or, if they worked for other Jews, in close-knit networks of a still largely *Gemeinschaft*-like community with extensive social control.

In good or even average times in the local mills and coal mines, the cooperative family economy conducted within the specialized ethnic entrepreneurial niche permitted, as we shall see shortly, the majority of Jewish households in Johnstown to realize their primary goal of a comfortable standard of living. However, the material consumption that constituted this standard was generally considerably more modest in scale and variety than that reported among more demanding upwardly mobile Jews in the big cities.[42] In the latter, consumer appetites in Jewish communities noticeably increased in the 1920s, paralleling the new nationwide trend among middle-class urban Americans toward "conspicuous preoccupation with leisure and the enjoyment of consumption" that was fueled by the expansion of both the psychology and the industry of consumer advertising.[43] And so a contemporary observer noted about New York Jews that "it is generally admitted by department store heads, theatrical producers, and restaurant men, that Jews are among the most lavish spenders [in the city]," while a present-day historian has pointed to a common "pretense of not having to count each penny," and called the representatives of this new consumer orientation—*pleasurniks.*[44]

While hardly all New York Jews were *pleasurniks*, the point was that there existed a large, and growing, group of such ostentatious, avid consumers. In Johnstown, there were, really, no *pleasurniks*, even among the most affluent by local standards. First, the average annual family income in the Johnstown Jewish community (1929 estimate, primary and secondary areas of settlement combined) was about one-third lower, and after adjustment for the lower cost of living, about one-fifth lower than the respective figure for New York Jews (1930 average estimate, for six neighborhoods differing in status combined, ranging from the Lower East Side to the Upper West Sides). More significantly, however, the ceiling of the possible at that time in a place like Johnstown—that is, the average income of Jewish families residing in the best neighborhood in town—was about two and a half times lower than in its New York counterpart.[45] Second, the town's consumption and leisure opportunities were much more limited than those in big urban centers, and in New York especially, and so there were far fewer potential objects of lavish spending. In seeking a comfortable standard of living, Johnstowners were decidedly not lavish but thrifty spenders. "The goal was not business expansion, but a comfortable life for the family"; "the main thing was earning a living, and living decently, which meant a decent home, [good] food on the table, nice clothes, and a few little luxuries"—these recollections of American-born Arthur T. and Isadore S. were fairly typical of my informants.[46]

The social-cultural sources of inspiration, so to speak, for Johnstowners in defining and updating this "decent" lifestyle will be discussed in the following chapter; here, we look at family budgets and the distribution of spendable incomes among particular categories of expenditures making up this desired standard. The statistical data presented below (tables 3.8 and 3.9) on the amounts of sales and income drawn from family businesses combine enterprises owned by the immigrants and by those of their offspring who were married and living independently, because, as my calculations of these figures indicate, there was not much difference between the

TABLE 3.8
Pecuniary Strength[a] of Jewish Businesses
(Average for 1920, 1925, and 1929)

	East European (%)	German (%)
Over $75,000	8 ⎫	
$35,000–$75,000	12 ⎬ 28	51
$20,000–$35,000	8 ⎭	
$10,000–$20,000	13	
$3,000–$10,000	18	
Less than $3,000	41	
	(N = 136)	(N = 13)

Source: Dun and Bradstreet credit ratings, Johnstown's merchants, 1920, 1925, 1929—D & B library, New York.

[a] "Pecuniary strength," as defined by Dun and Bradstreet Credit Company, expressed merchants' net $-worth, i.e., total assets minus total liabilities as reported biannually to the local D & B branch. The category "Less than $3,000," includes merchants listed in a report but without the assignment of a $-value to their businesses.

TABLE 3.9
Net Sales of Business[a] and Estimated Spendable Annual Income from Store Operation, Johnstown, 1929

	Net Sales		Annual Spendable Income[b]
	East European (%)	German (%)	
Over $100,000	10 ⎫		⎫ Over $3,000
$50,000–$100,000	8 ⎬ 36	66	⎭
$30,000–$50,000	18 ⎭		$2,500–$3,000
$20,000–$30,000	28		$2,000–$2,500
$10,000–$20,000	17		$1,500–$2,000
Less than $10,000	18		Less than $2,000
	(N = 143)	(N = 12)	

Sources: Manuscript schedules of the 1929 business census, Cambria County, National Archives, Washington, DC, Suitland Branch, Box 1381, files 23/12, 23/71–74; Box 6617, files 16–17. Estimates of annual spendable incomes have been based on sources—too many to enumerate here—listed in nn. 47, 48, 53, and 54 in this chapter.

[a] Estimations include retail and wholesale establishments in Johnstown and vicinity. Among the wholesalers (N = 15) seven reported net annual sales over $50,000, while the remaining—mostly peddlers—produce vendors had annual net sales between $10,000 and $20,000. Families owning more than one store are counted once, and their net sales are combined. New stores (opened in 1929) are excluded.

[b] Includes salaries of part-time employees and remuneration of family members working in the store.

two; but I noted dissimilarities when I found any, and I have also commented on family budgets of those second-generation independent households that made their livelihood from salaried employment in the ethnic entrepreneurial niche. The main focus of the following presentation is, as before in this study, businesses and households of East European Jews (hereafter generally referred to simply as "Jews"), although I have also included some comparative data for German Jewish ones.

According to the Dun and Bradstreet Company's credit reports, during the 1920s an average of 28 percent of East European Jewish merchants reported the net worth of their businesses as greater than $20,000. As before, establishments owned by German Jews had on the whole a greater dollar value, with the respective proportion nearly twice as large; generally, the German business group was stronger in the upper-middle categories within the scheme used by the D & B assessors, but East Europeans—the very few that there were in this category—dominated in the uppermost stratum.

As indicated by the information in the business census conducted nationwide in 1929 by the U.S. Department of Commerce, almost two-thirds of Jewish merchants in Johnstown and vicinity made less than $30,000 in sales that year; a difference between the establishments of foreign- and American-born businessmen was that sales in the stores managed by the latter concentrated more in the upper range of this category. Excluding large department stores, the average dollar value of net sales of the wholesale and retail businesses combined was $47,096, and of the retail (the majority) establishments alone, $31,337. For German Jewish stores—all retail—this figure was $79,405. Jewish entrepreneurs, at least those in the Johnstown area, were more successful than Gentile ones. Data for the general business population from the same census showed one-half of all retail stores in the country as having handled a business of less than $12,000, with average net sales below $5,500. In Johnstown and vicinity, Jewish businessmen (including wagon vendors) reporting revenues of less than $10,000 constituted about one-fifth of the total number of Jewish merchants surveyed, mostly foreign-born, with average net sales of $6,200.[47]

Net sales below $30,000, the revenue of the largest proportion of Jewish enterprises reported for 1929, provided, when combined with various strategies of cost cutting and/or supplementary earnings, the majority of small business owners with a materially sufficient livelihood. Excluding department stores and larger wholesale establishments, the estimated average spending income of Jewish stores in 1929, after subtraction of actual business expenses and the money needed to restock—assuming the same amount of sales for the following year—was, as I calculated from the reports filed by the merchants themselves, $2,200–$2,300. In comparison, the national figure in that year for small retail businesses was $1,600.[48] For enterprises in the two lowest categories, reporting net annual sales below

$10,000 in the bottom one, and $10,000–$19,000 in the one above, income was between $1,000 and $2,000, depending on overhead and turn of stock during the year; for the next category up, with net sales of $20,000–$29,000, it was between $2,000 and $2,500; for the brackets just above this, $30,000–$49,000, the amount of spendable income ranged from $2,500 and $3,000; and in the top two categories, it was over $3,000. Since, as I calculated from the 1929 business census, about two-thirds of the enterprises in the next-to-lowest category reported sales close to its upper bracket, they can be included in the class of $2,000 in spendable income (i.e., the lower range of the next higher group). All in all, then, somewhat over one-fourth of the total number of East European Jewish households reporting to the 1929 business census had spendable income below that figure. In comparison, about three-quarters of East European Gentile families in Johnstown in the mid-twenties existed on such earnings.[49]

As already noted, the financial situation—the volume of sales and spendable income derived from it—of enterprises owned by American-born married heads of separate households was generally similar to that of the immigrant generation. A greater proportion of such second-generation independent households (over 60 percent) relied for their livelihood on husbands' salaried employment; of this number, about two-thirds held higher-level positions, mostly in the Jewish entrepreneurial niche, such as buyers and senior salesmen, section managers in department stores, or supervisors in two local Jewish factories. As I estimated from the 1929 census and interview information, there were in the ethnic niche by the end of the decade about fifty such positions, some in larger retail businesses, and more in wholesale establishments and department stores; Glossers', the largest employer, had twenty to twenty-five such senior-level jobs. These positions were customarily filled by married men, and since the majority of immigrants were self-employed in business, these jobs went largely to the American-born, usually close or more distant relatives of the owner(s), so that the top ranks of the larger establishments were for the most part occupied by members of the *mishpokhe* or extended family. Such higher-level jobs usually paid between $40 and $45 a week, or $2,080–$2,340 annually. In a few cases salaries were even higher, $50 a week or $2,600 per annum, depending on the size and prosperity of a business, and on the personal generosity of fathers, uncles, brothers-in-law, and the like.[50]

In 1920, an annual income of $2,000 was set by private and government-sponsored studies as a "fair American standard of living" necessary for a minimum level of comfort for an urban middle-class family. A similar investigation, conducted in 1926 in New York among families of office workers, set this minimum budget at $2,400 for a five-member household, while a study of family expenditures for professional workers and government employees in Washington, D.C., set it higher, at $2,700.[51] These minimum budgets considered necessary for maintaining a "fair American standard of living"—standards, more accurately—by different middle-class strata, covered expenses for food, clothing, housing and home furnishings, household operation, health care, life insurance, religious and organizational membership, and recreation. Outlays for home furnishings and household operation contained in these American-standard budgets also included such widely available new consumer amenities as electric lighting and other household equipment, including radios, refrigerators, and electric washing machines. Considering that, despite all these changes, the overall cost of living in the United States actually decreased by nearly one-fifth between 1920 and 1929, and that it was generally lower in small towns than in large cities—in western Pennsylvania, lower by over 20 percent, owing to less expensive food and housing as well as the lower cost of light and fuel—an income of $2,000 can be taken as the minimum-level budget for a middle-class standard of living in the Johnstown area at the end of the decade.[52]

Such estimates were reaffirmed by my informants from a then broad middle-income category. A major difference between immigrant and (married, living separately) American-born generations in interwar Johnstown was, it appears, not so much in the amount of spendable money each group believed to be necessary for "decent" living, but in the ways it was spent—an issue I will return to below. And so an annual income of $1,700 "sufficed" for second-generation Nathan E. and his wife, but they "had to live very close"; similarly, about $1,600 in yearly revenues from Isadore G.'s father's small kosher butcher store in Hornerstown "made for a living," but it was a frugal existence. On the other hand, when Russian-born Joseph E., a truck vendor of fruit and produce in the same neighborhood, had about $2,500 in disposable income, the family "lived nicely and did not lack anything"; and young, recently married Sidney and Molly O., the former employed at Glossers' as a buyer at $40 a week, considered, as they recollected, his annual income somewhat over $2,000 to have been "all right," but "tight." Expectedly, a larger budget, above $3,000 and usually around $4,000, appeared necessary for a comfortable life for major merchants and professionals.[53]

With annual sales below $30,000—the business revenues of the majority of East European Jewish enterprises in Johnstown and vicinity in 1929—achieving a spendable income of over $2,000 required quite a bit of maneuvering from the owners' family households, even in the upper third of this category. One commonly practiced strategy was the reduction of expenses involved in running the store. Studies on the operation of retail businesses conducted in the 1920s on a large, national sample of establishments by the Harvard Bureau of Business Research showed the average total overhead costs (rent, fuel and light, interest, employees' salaries, and all other expenses) for solvent stores in the lines of trade in which Jews concentrated to have been 27 percent of net sales.[54] In Johnstown and vicinity, according to the manuscript schedules of the 1929 census, average overall business expenses in Jewish enterprises were 17 percent of sales, and even less for those with annual revenues below $20,000: 11 percent in the > $10,000 group, and 14 percent in the $10,000–$19,000 one. Not uncommonly, particularly in the smallest immigrant-owned establishments run in old-country shtctl style, overhead expenses were almost eliminated: Harry P., for instance, ran his general store in Johnstown, which had net sales of $7,000, with business expenses of less than 2 percent; Ephraim M. in Crescent operated his shoe store on 3 percent of $13,400 annual sales. Even in the higher sales categories, business expenses were often radically reduced: Joseph C., an American-born owner of a grocery store in Morellville, the secondary Slavic settlement in Johnstown, reported overhead of 8 percent of his yearly sales of $29,225; Isadore K., a store owner in the downtown section of the city, incurred business expenses of 11 percent of his annual net sales of $35,085.[55]

Conducting business from the house, with the front room turned into the store and the kitchen in the back, was an effective way to eliminate extra rent. It was practiced widely in Jewish *gesheftn*—small businesses—in Eastern Europe, and replicated in the foreign colonies in Johnstown and in the surrounding towns. Over one-third of all Jewish merchants, practically all of them immigrants, reporting to the 1929 census combined the store with the domicile (see also maps 3.1 and 3.2). In the two lowest sales groups, the proportion of those who paid no store rent, or a minimum amount ($300–$400, the usual annual charge for the ground floor in a rented house in the immigrant sections of town), was 60 percent. Ben Z., for instance, owner of a general store in Woodvale, operated it, with annual sales of $10,000, from his own house purchased in 1915; Morris B., a resident of Cambria City, a Slavic neighborhood in Johnstown, reporting sales of $8,200, rented a room for his clothing store on the main street there for $400 a year; and Nathan L., making $7,000 in annual sales, paid rent of only $200 for his ladies' and gents' furnishings store in nearby Nanty-Glo.[56]

Another way to reduce business expenses in small enterprises was to do away with regular salaries for store employees. Twenty-eight percent of all East European Jewish businesses (excluding department stores) reported no workers receiving regular salary. In the two lowest sales groups, this proportion was nearly one-half. Commonly, however, these stores employed family members, either unpaid or remunerated irregularly, depending on current business (this way of reducing expense-augmenting income could not, of course, be practiced by young American-born merchant families who were still childless or had one or two small children). Thus, Solomon T., a Johnstown furrier, had his wife, Ida, and son Morris work regularly without remuneration, as did Hyman R., owner of a clothing store in town, who employed part-time but without regular pay his three sons, Sam, Harry, and Abe, all of them living in their parents' home. In his bankruptcy hearing in 1928, Moses L. in Portage said that his clothing store was run by the family trio: himself; his wife, Etta, who waited on the customers; and "[his sixteen-year-old] girl, Frieda, [who] did cashier's work after school." Neither of the women received any payment. In the 1922 bankruptcy hearing of Max S., a grocer in one of Johnstown's foreign colonies, the owner, accounting for his expenses, explained that all "clerk work" was done by "[his] girl . . . paid $15 a week when business was good, [and] nothing when it went badly."[57]

In stores with regularly paid workers, the mean salaries were lower by more than one-third than the 1929 national average for regular clerical and sales employees, males and females combined.[58] Average annual salaries of paid Jewish employees (including part-time workers and family members) in the Johnstown area were $865 (for men), $557 (for women), and $711 (for men and women combined). American-born young men and women who worked for pay in their parents' stores received on the average 20 percent less than those employed in other establishments ($622 versus $778 annually).[59] Salaries of immigrants' children working in parental stores, reported to the census as part of business expenses, were, however, largely returned to the family budget.

Contributions of young adults who lived in their parents' homes but were employed elsewhere—the majority of the second generation in the interwar period—were used as another means of stretching family budgets. The amount usually ranged between 50 and 65 percent of weekly earnings received by young people, and, as my informants' matter-of-fact tone suggested, this practice did not evoke any particular resentment; at any rate, I did not detect any in their recollections. The household of Abe M., a merchant with net sales of $22,942 in 1929, represented a common case: the younger children, still in high school, worked part-time in the store, for which they received a 25-cent weekly allowance, while two adult ones, brother and sister, employed at the Glosser Bros' department store, paid their mother $10 and $7 from their respective $17 and $13 weekly paychecks—an amount that increased the family budget by about $800 annually.[60] After young people had married, they often rented a part, or, if it was a duplex, one side of a parental house while saving for their own and in this way temporarily continued their long-standing contributions, although on a diminished scale.

Peddling on the side—not an infrequent practice in the interwar period among owners of the smallest shops—was another way of augmenting income. It was usually conducted on weekends, with the adult or teenage sons often accompanying the merchant while his wife tended the store; in good industrial times and with luck, such persistent part-time traveling vendors could make up to $1,000 annually. Some merchants among owners of stores with bigger business revenues used extra money to purchase inexpensive real estate in working-class neighborhoods and rented it out, although only a small proportion invested in this commodity on a bigger scale.[61]

Yet another way to elevate spendable income was to adjust the amount of merchandise purchased and of debts paid to current business. As my informants recollected, purchases in most small Jewish stores owned by the immigrants before World War II were not planned in advance but made "on the needs [of the store]." "[The shopkeeper] looked around and saw what he had; when he ran out of pants, he bought them, or when salesmen came from New York [with the merchandise], he looked at the shelves [in the store] and took [from the seller] some of this, and some of that." As the bankruptcy hearings suggest and the interviews confirm, systematic book-keeping was seldom practiced among small immigrant storekeepers: most of them drew from the cash registers for current household needs as they arose. And when it happened that they found themselves without ready cash, they delayed payments to the creditors, "maybe $500 or $600 of debts outstanding," relying on the latter's leniency based on their private contacts and in-group support.[62]

Like other decisions involved in running a commercial enterprise, strategies of cutting business costs in order to stretch family income up to the level of a "fair American standard"—or, as the Johnstowners called it, a "decent living"—remained in most cases regardless of generation the purview of the men, although their wives usually participated in the decision-making process; and, of course, by working in the store without remuneration, wives "decided" on this particular method of reducing costs by enacting it. In comparison with business financial management, the executive power of wives in managing household expenditures was greater and more, though by no means completely, autonomous. We now look at what the Johnstowners described as the common pattern of gender authority in Jewish households in terms of money disbursements of the average family income at the end of the 1920s.[63]

Interviews and the interwar bankruptcy records indicate that in good times—that is, relatively steady economic conditions in the area—the annual family expenditures in the immigrant and independent second-generation households whose businesses brought between $20,000 and $50,000 in net sales (about one-half of the entire number of enterprises) ranged between $2,000 and $2,600; the majority of the salaried husbands in American-born families living separately drew, as noted earlier, incomes in a similar range, $2,080–$2,340. Let us, then, look at the disposition and control of the annual budget of $2,200–$2,300, the average spending income accrued from store sales in the middle-range category as specified above, and of the higher-level employees at the end of the twenties.

If the family rented a house in one of the "better" neighborhoods in Johnstown like Kernville or Dale, the rent was about $400–$450 a year. Second-generation couples, who by the late 1930s were still predominantly renters of apartments rather than houses, preferred to live in Westmont—in terms of location the ultimate realization of a "decent" life—although rent there was higher, $500–$600; by 1940, 30 percent of the immigrant, but over 40 percent of independent American-born, households resided in this section. Expenses on light and fuel were approximately $70 in immigrant budgets, and about 35–40 percent less in second-generation ones because of the smaller size of their homes. If there was a car, about $50 was needed for car payments; according to my informants, "maybe 25 percent, maybe 30 percent" (they were not sure, and I could not locate independent sources) of Jewish families in the 1930s, and about equal proportions in each generational group, owned an automobile other than a peddlers' truck. Life insurance policies—one for each family member—usually cost $200–$250 in annual premiums in immigrant homes, and about half as much in American-born households; the majority of second-generation families were either still childless or had one small child. In immigrant households, while husband and wife usually talked these matters over, decisions about expenditures and responsibility for them in most cases belonged to the husbands. In the next generation this authority, while still hierarchical, pluralized to a certain degree, in that women acquired some service-type responsibilities. Namely, as I was told, it was not uncommon for American-born wives to "take care of the household bills," meaning that they kept track of, calculated, and actually paid them, but the funds, of course, had to be obtained from their husbands.

Without much generational change, however, male heads of households continued to allocate and pay synagogue dues, pledges, and charitable donations; combined, these cost about $150–$200 annually and included annual membership, moderately priced seats for High Holidays services, and Hebrew school for any children of the appropriate ages. Extreme savings measures, such as reducing rent payments by moving to a cheaper place or giving up all life insurance policies, were practiced only when all other means were exhausted—for instance, during the particularly bad years of the Depression. However, postponing, fractioning, and rescheduling synagogue and other related remittances were common ad hoc means of enhancing household budgets; on the other hand, extra expenses in this category accrued when the first/next child started Hebrew school or there was fund-raising for a concrete cause. Expenditures on food and household operation in Jewish families remained in daily practice within the planning and executive authority of wives, but in an ultimately subordinate way, like the American-born married women's "secondhand" control of household bill payments. In immigrant and second-generation households alike, and regardless of wives' engagement in the family business, husbands, as the ultimate directors of family finances, commonly "gave" their wives an agreed sum of money "for the household." In the period discussed here it was in immigrant homes[64] usually between about $15 and $20 a week, or around $800 and $1,050 annually; in smaller-size homes of American-born couples annual expenses in this category were around $800. From this amount, $12–$18 a week was usually spent on food, and the rest, $150–$200 over the year, on cleaning products, toiletries, and non-prescription medications. When at particular occasions some additional money was needed, wives took it themselves directly from the cash register in the store; for instance, small sums requested by schoolchildren, or minor donations for current activities of the congregational Sisterhood, were usually drawn in this way.

Most of the time, however, women's task, and not a small challenge, was to plan and calculate these routine expenditures so as to keep costs as low as possible without reducing substance, and at the same time "update," as my informants put it—or ethnicize—family lifestyles by changing diet, making food more aesthetically appealing, and setting a more ornate table, which in turn called for greater expense. It appears that the main factor affecting the scope of the increased spending involved in updating one's home style, assuming such growth was financially possible, was not the generational position of the families but, rather, their place of residence in town, and specifically relocation to Westmont.[65] The funds used by wives for expenditures on food and household operation, or savings, were also the source of pennies dropped regularly into charitable *pushkes*. This old-country custom, practiced in the majority of East European Jewish homes throughout the interwar period, remained completely under women's control; the annual sums collected in this way ranged usually, as I estimated, from $5 to $15. (In the next chapter we shall discuss the concrete forms and "contents" of ethnicizing of home life as well as the tensions between the updating and saving efforts in women's house management.)

Similar financial maneuvers and inherent conflicts as in the case of managing costs of food and household operation, and a similar subordination of wives' executive control to their husbands' ultimate authority, had been involved in dealing with expenditures on attire and home furnishings—two other areas of women's initiative and acknowledged influence in immigrant as well as second-generation households. The average immigrant family spent $150–$200 annually on clothing; adult gainfully employed children generally paid for their own from the part of their earnings they retained. Clothing costs were even less if the wife and mother, or one of the grown daughters, was an expert and willing seamstress, or if the family business specialized in shoes or clothing and some items could be acquired from the store. In second-generation households, the top of the range was elevated to $250, and that because although these families were smaller, garments, or some of them at least, were purchased in one of the better and more expensive local department stores such as Penn Traffic, rather than more thriftily at Glossers', for instance, where prices were less by 50 percent or more. In expenditures on shoes and clothing, generational position seemed to have had a greater impact overall than residential location in that a tendency toward reducing costs was more pronounced in immigrant households than in American-born families. Typically $150–$200 was spent on home furnishings, larger and costlier items paid on installment plans, such as a new living room set or a piano—a status symbol for socially aspiring members of the Jewish community. Here again, second-generation families generally purchased less in volume than immigrant ones (because of the smaller space to be furnished), but they tended to prefer "more American goods," those reflecting local mainstream middle-class fashion, which were therefore more expensive.

Occasional purchases of more expensive items of clothing, such as a winter coat or a suit, or costlier home furnishings, brought into sharper relief the ambiguities inherent in Jewish wives' authority in the financial management of their households. As noted earlier, married women's continued involvement in running the stores, and the shared social space of family and work relations, to some extent strengthened their voice in business matters. At the same time, however, this close overlap of family and work roles and interactions enhanced husbands' authority in matters of household management carried on by the women, or, more accurately, reasserted this authority as ultimate. And so, for instance, in the home of Joseph and Hannah S., an immigrant household quite typical in terms of gendered patterns of decision making during the interwar period, the wife decided, that is, picked out what she thought was nice and financially feasible: furniture, window curtains, tableware. Then her husband checked the price; in this particular family, Joseph "agreed most of the time" to what Hannah selected, but should he have said "no," unless she persuaded him to change his mind, a "no" it would have been. Customary practice in this regard in the home of Johnstown-born Abe B. and his wife Janet was similar: she calculated and chose, and he gave his approval before the purchase was made.[66]

Concerning second-generation women's authority in managing expenditures on the house and the table, two observations are worth noting at this point. One concerns young unmarried daughters residing in parental homes. In contrast to the disputes between American-born sons and their fathers about modern ways of conducting business, there seems to have been no particular disagreement between daughters and their immigrant mothers regarding ideas for "updating" home life, probably because the latter were themselves interested in such alterations when they moved to better neighborhoods.[67]

The other observation concerns immigrants' daughters after they married—specifically, to men occupied as salaried employees—and established their own households. I pointed out the reciprocal, enhancing effects of the shared social space of home and work on the executive authority of husbands and wives managing the household finances and family business; this situation did not obtain in those second-generation households, the majority, where the husband did not run his own enterprise but worked in someone else's establishment. In such households, if the situation in Johnstown resembled developments reported in New York middle-class homes in the 1920s–1930s, the separation of home and work spheres and a corresponding division of gender responsibilities would have contributed to considerably increased autonomy of wives' authority in the home, in no small measure because of the withdrawal, or substantial weakening, of their husbands' voice. Nothing of the kind seems to have happened in Johnstown (or I failed to record it), most probably because employee households remained immersed in the ethnic entrepreneurial niche and its dense social networks, in which the shared (home/work) social space with its implications for authority patterns prevailed.[68] In big cities like New York, young women's premarital employment in mainstream institutions outside the ethnic milieu—an experience unknown to most of their Johnstown counterparts—was probably also a factor. The strengthened independence in decision making they gained through such employment became transferred, after they married and withdrew into the home, to more assertive ways of managing the household.

The last item in the average household budget was recreation. In this area of shared decision making, immigrant wives had a more nearly equal voice than in matters of consumer purchases, and their married daughters had even more influence. The annual expenditure for this purpose in immigrant homes ranged from $50 to $75 and included small weekly allowances paid to the younger children helping in the store; the older, gainfully employed ones used their own monies for entertainments that were not collective family activities. How to use the little free time left over from work was planned and discussed, as my informants recollected, between husband and wife, and decisions were made together (unless I missed something again, there was apparently very little marital disagreement in this regard). Decisions about another, more ambitious form of recreation—piano lessons for a son or a daughter—were made in a similar fashion. In the middle-budget group, a private music teacher was generally hired, if at all, for only one child, at about $50 a year for weekly lessons. In this case, however, disagreements about the worthiness of the expenditure seem to have been more frequent, with the wife usually in favor of the lessons and the husband reluctant; it was often (not always) her "yes" that won over his "no," even if she had to procure monies on her own. In second-generation homes, recreational expenses absorbed $50–$100; in the majority of families, there were not yet any children old enough to receive little allowances as in immigrant homes, but the couple did go out more: to dances, the cinema, or local vaudeville theater, occasionally to a restaurant, and on longer-distance trips.[69]

All these expenditures—allowing for a comfortable lifestyle and an acceptable level of participation in communal activities—added up to just about $2,300, leaving nothing for savings, a down payment on a house, or (in the case of immigrant parents) for college for the children. (In the 1920s and 1930s, the annual cost of maintaining one child at the University of Pittsburgh was $400–$500, including tuition, room, and board.)[70] If some money was to be put aside, cuts had to be made in the above expenditures. The most flexible were those managed by women, that is, those made flexible by women's skillful management: spending on food, household operation, clothing, and home furnishings. While husbands' final approval was needed for major purchases in these areas, cutting costs for these items was the wives' autonomous prerogative. In the husbands' executive domain in household finances, as noted earlier, the remittance of synagogue dues and various fund-raising pledges were easily postponed, or, in business, payments of debts for store merchandise had to be partially delayed or rescheduled. Another common source, unavailable for young second-generation households, was the additional income accrued from gainfully employed children or other household members.

Similar budget-expanding maneuvers were needed if a family purchased a house. The decision-making process was in this case also two-layered, as it were, in that the husband and wife usually discussed a range of money assigned for this undertaking, approximate mortgage payments, and the location of the house, but the final decision almost invariably belonged to the man. Given a fifteen-year mortgage, annual payments for a medium-priced ($4,000) house bought during the 1920s in Kernville or Dale would have been $850.[71] After we deduct the $400 formerly spent on rent, mortgage payments would have added about $500 to the $2,300 basic budget. Savings and/or college for a child would have required even more financial maneuvering from the homeowners in this budget group, a combination of some cuts in expenses with other income besides that from store sales. Budget increments above what came from the latter were also needed if a family chose to purchase a house in the prestigious Westmont section of Johnstown, where real estate prices ranged from $5,000 to $12,000.

Benjamin N., for instance, a merchant with annual sales of about $23,000, drew from his store about $2,200 a year for living expenses and other payments, including slightly over $1,000 for a house in Westmont, and $150 for a new Buick purchased on a six-year installment plan. With all other expenses in amounts closer to the higher cost brackets for particular items in the average budget, the N. family's annual expenditures added up to about $3,000—that is, $800 more than the drawings from the store's cash register. Contributions from the salaries of two adult children employed in a Jewish-owned department store in the city made up this sum.[72]

In the two lowest sales categories (less than $20,000 annually), which made up 35 percent of the East European Jewish firms reporting to the 1929 business census, nearly two-thirds had a spendable store income below the minimum budget for a comfortable existence by "a fair American standard" for a middle-class family; the average for this group was $1,475. Among second-generation families living separately whose heads were employed in salaried occupations, the proportion with incomes below $2,000 was around 40 percent. For such immigrant households to be able to spend $2,300 in the way illustrated earlier, not only would they have to cut costs in household expenditures, but at least two of the adult male or three of the female children residing at home would have to have regularly paid work from which they contributed a customary one-half to the family budget. And in fact, almost one-half of the family households in this category had young people at home gainfully employed either in parental stores or on the outside.[73] In second-generation households where a young husband earned less than $2,000, family budgets could not be augmented to reach, let alone exceed, the minimum level of a "fair middle-class standard" through the employment of children. The only available option was for the wife, if she did not yet have a baby, to take up sales or clerical employment, often part-time, in one of the larger Jewish-owned firms in the city—for example, with a relative. My estimate from the interviews suggests that among childless American-born couples in independent households supported by salaries of husbands employed at lower-level jobs in the niche, about 30 percent of the wives had indeed worked at some point after marriage.

Households whose family businesses reported net annual sales of over $50,000 and accrued spendable income of more than $3,000, along with professional households (mostly second-generation), had, naturally, much more comfortable budgets. But even the top group in this category did not approach the luxurious lifestyles of arrivistes among New York East European Jews—and, for that matter, neither did the small German group in Johnstown, who were generally more affluent than the East Europeans. Along with the interviews, old photographs kept by my informants, last wills, and bankruptcy records (a couple of leading merchants did file for bankruptcy during the Depression) all indicate that financial expenditures in these households grew, first of all, on housing and home furnishings; then on a car, clothing (in that it was regularly bought at the better local stores), life insurance (multiple policies for each family member and at higher values than in the average budget), and recreation (more travel, a summer cottage on nearby hills).

Instructive as it would be as an insight into the actual lifestyles of the immigrant families, it was unfortunately impossible to collect quantified data on material acquisitions by Jewish households during the period of rising standards of living between the First and Second World Wars. The interviews could not be used for this purpose because too many of my informants did not accurately remember what was obtained when, and I could not help their memory by showing contemporary written records; the bankruptcy records, while they do occasionally contain listings of possessions in homes of particular cases, are also much too incomplete. Instead, then, we shall look more closely only at the acquisition and value of homes purchased by local Jews during the interwar period, and at the net values of estates left during the interwar period by deceased members of the Jewish community as recorded in their wills—two indicators of Jewish households' economic standing for which information has been more systematically available (see table 3.10).

TABLE 3.10
Selective Indicators of Material Accumulation by Jewish Households, 1920–1940

	1925 (%)	1940 (%)
Proportion of Homeowners[a]		
Entire group	34	40
East Europeans	33	39
Germans	41	50
Proportion of Major Proprietors (Real Property)		
Entire group	22	14
East Europeans	21	15
Germans	55	42
	1922–1926	*1938–1941*
Average Prices of (Residential) Real Property Purchases by Jewish Families[b]		
All homes	$7,300	$8,800
in Westmont		$10,300
in Kernville-Dale		$5,600
East Europeans	$5,900	$8,400
Germans	$8,700	$9,300
Clear $-value of estates left by immigrants (East Europeans)[c]		
average	$10,000–$12,000	
range	$2,500–$28,000	

Sources: Johnstown city directories, 1925, 1940; Johnstown street guide, 1940; Cambria County Courthouse, Ebensburg, Pennsylvania: real estate transactions recorded in deed books 1922/1926; 1938/1941; last wills records 1920s–1940s. U.S. Bureau of the Census, *Census of the United States: 1940*, Housing (Pennsylvania), vol. 4 (Washington, DC: Government Printing Office, 1943), 44, 89.

[a] In comparison, the proportion of homeowners among the Detroit Jews—the only data for the interwar period I located—increased between 1920 and 1935 from 26% to 31%. See Oliver Zunz, *The Changing Face of Inequality: Urbanization, Industrial Development, and Immigrants in Detroit, 1880–1920* (Chicago: University of Chicago Press, 1982), 116; Henry Meyer, "The Structure of the Jewish Community in Detroit" (Ph.D. diss., University of Michigan, 1939), 116.

[b] Tax valuations of real property, often used in this context, are not presented here, because as a result of the 1936 flood in Johnstown that affected large parts of the downtown business district, taxes levied on buildings there had been significantly decreased (interview with Mr. Michael Jerome, Cambria County Courthouse, Ebensburg, Pennsylvania, Real Estate Department, 6/28/1987).

[c] I checked wills from the 1920s through the 1940s so as to increase their number ($N = 66$).

Compared with that for the pre–World War I period (28 percent), the proportion of homeowners among Jewish families increased, reaching one-third, similar to that for the general population of Johnstown in 1925; by the outbreak of the Second World War it was 40 percent, above the average for the city. The share of homeowners in 1940 was, expectedly, higher among the immigrants than among second-generation families living independently: 55 and 29 percent, respectively. As before, the figures for German Jews were higher than those for the East Europeans. Not surprisingly, there were also differences between particular locations in town: in the old foreign colonies, for instance, the proportion of homeowners among Jewish residents was 36 and 28 percent in 1925 and 1940, respectively, while in prestigious Westmont, 52 and 38 percent; the decline was due to the presence there on the eve of World War II of a considerable number of young second-generation renter-households. Perhaps more interesting, though, the share of homeowners among merchant families in the two lowest sales groups as reported in the 1929 business census (35 percent) did not differ from the proportion for the whole Jewish group in the city. Nearly half of them, however, were old-time residents of Johnstown who had purchased their homes before the First World War; in comparison, in the local Slavic and Hungarian communities, only 28 percent of the total number of resident households were homeowners in the 1930s.[74]

Major proprietors—those whose real property was valued for tax purposes at over $7,500 and/or who declared "money at interest" in the amount of $2,500+—constituted, like the major merchants, a minority among Johnstown's Jews during the interwar period. The proportion of such individuals or family households was again considerably larger among Germans than among East Europeans; in the latter group, nearly all were of the immigrant generation (the Depression depleted their number in both groups, but note should be taken of a significant decrease in taxes levied on real property in Johnstown following the 1936 flood).

The average value of homes purchased by Jewish families between the mid-twenties and the end of the following decade increased by about 20 percent, from $7,300 to $8,800; the average cost of houses bought by East European and German Jews, which in the earlier period had differed by more than one-third, reached near-parity by 1940. The reasons for this equalization were a relocation of the former into better sections of town, and especially to Westmont where house prices were the highest, and also the presence among East European Westmont residents of the most affluent merchants, who invested in high-value property. The cost of homes purchased by young second-generation families was on the average about 20–25 percent lower than that of those owned by immigrants, mainly because of a larger number of more affluent merchants among the latter.

The prices paid by Jewish home buyers as recorded in the deed books in 1938–1941 ranged quite widely, from about $4,000 to $14,000, depending on the neighborhood: in Westmont, for instance, the average was

$10,300, while in the second-best Kernville and Dale neighborhoods the average was $5,600. At the same time (1940), the average value of houses owned by Johnstown's homeowners in general was $4,000, or more than 50 percent lower than the figure for Jews, with that in Westmont $8,900 or 2 percent lower, and in the Kernville-Dale sections $4,800 or 17 percent lower. But compared with the cost of houses purchased by Jews in the big cities in the same period—I sample-checked the announcements placed in the local Yiddish newspapers of real estate bought and sold in Chicago in the 1920s—the highest prices paid by Jewish homeowners in Johnstown were no more than a third of the big-city prices.[75]

During the interwar period, Johnstown's Jews conducted over 1,000 real estate transactions recorded in the deed books in the county courthouse. Two-thirds of them, however, were performed by only about 30 families, with the average number of transactions per family 28 (and 10 families having conducted over 50 real property transactions each). As noted earlier, the purpose of real estate buyers in this group was to use property as a means of obtaining additional income; of course, the scale of investment did not even compare with huge operations conducted by New York Jewish builders, who by the 1930s constituted as much as 40 percent of all real estate constructors in the city. The remaining one-third of the Johnstown purchases were usually for the buyers' private use. Excluding those of the families owning multiple properties, the mean mortgage loan taken out between 1920 and 1940 was $5,000, and it took the borrower on average 17 years to pay it off, the time ranging from 3 to 30 years—expectedly, the Depression greatly contributed to delays in payoff.[76]

Inspection of immigrants' wills indicate that, excluding the most affluent merchants, the values of estates left by East European immigrants to their relatives ranged between $2,500 and $28,000. The average amount was about $10,000–$12,000 of clear value—that is, clear of unpaid debts left by the deceased and claimed against the estate. It should be noted, however, that these figures exclude families in the lowest income bracket, in which the deceased, usually the husband/father, did not have much to leave—a few hundred dollars, perhaps, after all debts were subtracted—and therefore dispositions concerning his estate were never recorded in the courthouse. The figures do enable us to form some sense of the scale of material accumulation achievable in interwar Johnstown by a large middle economic stratum within the Jewish entrepreneurial niche; translated into the average annual income ($2,300) of a family household in this group, the (clear) values of estates represented from one to about twelve times this sum, or, on the average, between four and five times the average annual income. It must be added, however, that the average number of beneficiaries was seven to eight; thus, if the figures $10,000–$12,000 are taken as a base, each of them was heir to a much more modest $1,300–$1,600. In the top bracket of $28,000, per capita value would have been more substantial, $3,500–$4,000, the worth of a nice house in a good neighborhood. Expectedly, estate values were much higher for the three German Jews among the deceased: the owner of a high-price department store whose estate was worth several hundred thousand dollars; the owner of a prosperous enterprise started in the 1880s that traded in leather products and served the entire region, who left about $250,000; and the owner of a well-established clothing store who left around $80,000.

As shown above, the annual budget above $2,000, with income of the majority of Jewish households accrued through combined strategies of family cooperatives, permitted their members a materially comfortable existence at a "fair American standard" for the middle class. It was, however, comfort without slack, dependent on steady business in little stores. And this steadiness could not be relied on. A deeper slump in local industrial production causing larger than usual layoffs in the mills, or a more prolonged strike in the coal mines—recurrent events in the Johnstown area, particularly during the Depression of the 1930s—repeatedly forced Jewish households to shift from business to business, to retrench by giving up some comforts, or to go more deeply into debt.

"SOMETIMES RICH AND SOMETIMES POOR": THE INSTABILITY OF HOUSEHOLD ECONOMIES

The rest of this chapter illustrates the insecurity of the "little luxuries," as my interviewees called them, that the Jewish entrepreneurial niche afforded its household-members and points out the sociocultural resources they used for coping with this situation.

As in small businesses in general, financial instability was a routine experience for most Jewish enterprises in the Johnstown area, making everprecarious their more affluent lifestyles.[77] Table 3.11 presents the available data that illustrate considerable capital fluctuations of Jewish-owned enterprises during the interwar period: Dun and Bradstreet Company's credit ratings, and petitions of bankruptcy filed at the Cambria County Courthouse.

The table shows shifts in the net financial worth of Jewish stores reporting to D & B Company, calculated as the proportion of establishments that received a different credit classification at least once during the interwar period. I checked only at five intervals (1920, 1925, 1929, 1935, and 1940), and D & B ratings classified the stores surveyed not by the exact amount of declared net capital, but by ranges such as $3,000–$5,000 or $5,000–$10,000. Therefore, the figures presented here most likely underestimate the actual amount of financial fluctuation. Of the total number of stores traced, about one-fourth maintained the same net financial worth classification, while nearly three-quarters shifted (including the "no rating" category), most of them back and forth between the categories; enterprises of immigrant and second-generation families have been treated jointly,

TABLE 3.11
Fluctuations of Businesses Owned by Jewish Merchants, 1920–1940[a]

	(%)	*N*
Pecuniary strength classification:		115[b]
maintained the same	27	
changed	73	
to higher	(17)	
to lower	(13)	
back-and-forth	(43)	
Filed for bankruptcy	32	248
and: left town	23	
moved to employee status	17	
shifted to different line of business	37	
continued in the same line of business	23	
Persisting in the same line of business:		
1920–1929	49	124
1929–1937/39	52	122
Employment shifts of storekeepers discontinuing business:		185
left town	31	
moved to employee status	19	
shifted to different line of business	44	
unknown[c]	6	
Homes sold by sheriff and regained:		130
homes lost	24	
homes regained	49	

Sources: Johnstown business guides and city directories, 1920, 1925, 1929, 1933, 1937, 1939; Dun and Bradstreet Company's credit ratings, 1920, 1925, 1929, 1935, 1940 (D&B Business Library, New York); U.S. Bankruptcy Court, Western District of Pennsylvania, Pittsburgh, and Federal Archives and Records Center, Philadelphia; judgment dockets, 1930–1940; deed and mortgage books, 1930–1940; real property tax assessments, 1925, 1940—Cambria County Courthouse, Ebensburg, Pennsylvania; local interviews.

[a] East European and German, and immigrant and American-born merchants combined.

[b] Figures in this column indicate numbers of names/merchants traced for particular calculations.

[c] The information was contradictory about eleven merchants and they were left out.

since differences between them did not exceed a few percentage points in each category. A comparison of German- and East European–owned establishments indicates that while the former also shifted between categories, especially—downward—during the Great Depression, this movement occurred at a higher dollar-value level.

These financial fluctuations of Jewish businesses, which tended to reflect the ups and downs in local industrial production and employment, are evidenced in the merchants' own accounts of their situation. "In business, so much is a gamble"—this perception of Johnstown-born Henry K., who worked with his father in a small shop catering to a working-class population, was repeated by others, and these recollected perceptions are confirmed by sales figures I gathered from independent contemporary sources. And so, for example, Samuel I.'s clothing and dry goods store in Boswell did very well, with annual sales of $40,000–$45,000, until 1922, when a prolonged coal strike started in the area; then it "fell into trouble." Samuel Z., a jeweler in Johnstown, had a similar experience: in 1922, his annual sales were $35,000, or about $700 a week, but then they fell by nearly one-half, so that during 1923 he "had to drive one sale after another," averaging returns of no more than $1,200 for six to seven weeks or $200 a week. Abraham S., owner of a general store in the city, was likewise affected by "bad times" in the mills during 1923, when within half a year he lost about $10,000 in sales. The following year was better, but still "some months were good, and some were bad," with weekly sales "sometimes $600–$700, sometimes $1,300 or $900." Asked whether Moses L., manager of a junk metal shop in Hornerstown, was a wealthy man, his son, who had worked with him, replied: "Sometimes he was, and sometimes he was very poor." A very Jewish answer, that, applying to the concrete life experience a traditional group symbolic scheme of *galgal hozer b'olam*, the revolving wheel of the world; but I checked Moses L.'s business records and, indeed, between 1927 and 1928, when the volume of steel production decreased by 10 percent, his weekly receipts ranged widely from a low of $300 to about $900.[78]

The Depression, of course, destabilized enterprises even further. In 1935, the proportion of major merchants—those whose businesses were rated by Dun and Bradstreet Credit Company as having a net worth of over $20,000—dropped to 10 percent among East Europeans, an almost triple decrease since 1925 (among German Jews, it decreased by one-third, to 57 percent). By 1940, it expanded again to 17 percent (for German merchants, it remained about the same). And at the other end of the spectrum, the proportion of merchants receiving "no rating"—their businesses apparently too much in flux—increased between 1925 and 1935 from 19 to nearly 40 percent, and then went down again to 21 percent in 1940 among storekeepers of East European origin (and from none to 29 percent, and to 31 percent among German Jews).[79]

The major reason for such deep plunges in the pecuniary strength of businesses was, naturally, sharp fluctuations in the volume of trade. The average annual sales in "Jewish" lines of trade in Johnstown and fifteen surrounding towns decreased by nearly 45 percent between 1929 and 1933, and then increased by 29 percent by 1935. In the following year, a disastrous flood caused over $28 million worth of damage to business and residential buildings in the central section of town where many Jewish stores were located. By 1939, sales grew again by almost 30 percent. It should be noted, however, that in comparison with "Gentile" trade lines reported in local business censuses conducted in 1933, 1935, and 1939,

"Jewish" ones remained on the average 17–18 percent higher through the entire period.[80]

Business fluctuations that repeatedly undercut limited financial capital on which small businesses operated made bankruptcies a frequent occurrence among petty entrepreneurs; as mentioned earlier, such failures were also common among prewar Jewish storekeepers in Johnstown. Table 3.11 shows the proportion of merchants, among a total of 248 Jewish shop owners listed in business guides between 1920 and 1940, who during that period filed for voluntary or involuntary bankruptcy (not necessarily carried out). It was a significant 30-odd percent, of whom nearly one-fifth initiated this procedure more than once; and this figure does not include common out-of-court settlements. Not surprisingly, a majority—nearly 60 percent—of bankruptcy filings took place during the Depression. Immigrant and American-born shopkeepers have been treated jointly in this calculation, but the former filed for bankruptcy somewhat more often, by about 15 percent; this difference might have been even greater if it were not for the equalizing effects of the Depression. Among German Jewish merchants the proportion of potential—that is, formally registered—bankrupts was similar, about 30 percent of the small total.

A recurrent theme in the bankruptcy court's hearings of Jewish petitioners throughout the interwar period was inactive or deteriorating business with unpaid customers' bills and overdue credit, the result of irregular work in the mills and coal mines, seasonal layoffs, or prolonged strikes. Hyman B.'s shoe shop in Johnstown failed in 1924, because, as he explained, "since last winter . . . people wasn't working and I wasn't doing any business." Filing for voluntary bankruptcy in 1928, Hyman G., owner of a dry goods store in Portage, called himself "a victim of circumstances," the "bad years" following the 1922 coal strike. Uncollectible credit from "the working class [presently] under poor circumstances"—customers of Joseph R.'s secondhand furniture store in Johnstown—was, according to his testimony in 1926, the major cause of his failure. As the bankruptcy records indicate, the current liabilities of East European Jewish stores in the area usually did not exceed $10,000–$15,000, and many were less.[81] But often a hundred-odd nonpaying debtors owing a small merchant a total of a few thousand dollars were enough to undermine a business, like that of David G., owner of a clothing store in one of the foreign colonies in Johnstown during the 1920s (see the partial list, quite typical, of debtors, 80 percent of them with Slavic and Hungarian names, and the small amounts owed).

Despite unstable capital and common financial difficulties of the Johnstown Jews' small businesses, their enterprises were not only more prosperous but also more persistent through the interwar period—including the Depression years—than were non-Jewish stores. Thus, about half the Jewish merchants, without a significant generational difference, had stayed in the same line of business (see table 3.11). Among Gentile storekeepers—I

PERSONAL PROPERTY.

	Dollars	Cents
Jack Steeme		
Borobohaok	8	95
Shvazerko		60
Mrs. Patula	27	51
Xerbia	46	50
Piluary	26	23
Tutosh Co.,	26	14
Vanbush Co.,	16	25
Gregorovich	11	2.
Ragaria	3	52
Pirko	121	50
Uhen	35	40
Kulbask	1	87
John Vargo	30	23
Macho	65	10
Martin Kinet	18	19
Ignots Kinet	23	28
Krankot	8	86
Smondrai	6	35
Lehvar	7	96
Frank Neudze		55
Seeley	15	95
Milo Tomanhek	32	83
Carl Kane	46	83
Andy Sarech	10	55
Karick Wjerva	21	53
Sam Lucatchick	21	80
Lichick	43	75
Elenitr	13	89
Waltor	5	98
Mihal Olota	29	03
Mike Banje	12	55
Jucob Pishter	27	63
Mackara	14	90
Mrs. Votaler		80
Mihelovitch	2	41
Martinovich	7	48
Frank Lubich	6	20
Steve Broxa	3	30
Ivan Budelich	2	06
John Stelvick	3	05
Ruehnitoa		43
M. Anjusky	9	75
Pere Zallik	4	86
Andy Bendick	1	05
Andy Reno	8	83
Paul Pishter	2	15
Mrs. Hall	8	93
Mr. Vonaef	3	29
Pete Uran	13	42
M. Ovas	9	25
Mrs. Uhrin		75
Frank Herbo	6	88
Vortek Valya	1	25
Toma Valurnek		60
Mike Komadizk	1	00
Lovra Gerdovich	2	70
	1	20
kloliko	4	75
Total	888	65

Petitioner.

3.8. List of Slavic and Hungarian credit recipients in David G.'s store, 1920s. Federal Archives and Records Center, Philadelphia.

traced persons with English-sounding names in the business guides for the two lines of trade in which non-Jews predominated, food and automotive—this proportion was considerably lower, about one-third, and lower still, about one-fourth, among entrepreneurs of Slavic and Hungarian backgrounds occupied in the same specialties.

Among Jewish entrepreneurs who did not (for reasons unspecified) remain in the same line of trade between 1920 and the end of the 1930s, the largest proportion had retained self-employed status by trying other kinds of business(es); about one-fifth took up salaried employment, and approximately one-third left town—all in all, no fewer than three-quarters remained within the ethnic economic niche (see table 3.11). Those whose businesses were officially pronounced bankrupt apparently followed a similar path: nearly two-thirds of them either resumed the same kind of business or took up a different one in Johnstown or the vicinity, and about one-fifth went to work for other Jews in the area. In comparison, studies of the general population of small retail bankrupts in Chicago and Poughkeepsie, New York, during the interwar years, showed fewer than 30 percent of such post-bankruptcy persisters.[82]

A combination of factors made this occupational perseverance so much greater than among non-Jewish merchants. Studies of American small businessmen in the prewar era consistently show a high proportion of them (50–66 percent) entering this occupation as a temporary retreat from other kinds of wage or salaried employment to which they subsequently returned. In addition, a similarly high percentage (50 percent and above) of the general population of new storekeepers did not have any previous commercial experience. Coming from other class and ethnic backgrounds, they had no resources facilitating entrepreneurial pursuits, such as social capital—namely, access to personal business networks—and cultural capital in the form of socialized values and predispositions.[83] In comparison, Jewish businessmen in the Johnstown area had a multiple advantage. First, on the outside, the continuing predominance of heavy industry based on manual labor, and the limited supply of white-collar jobs in the region, offered Jews few alternative—or desired—opportunities for work. Second, inside the by now well-established occupational niche within the trade sector of the local economy, they could readily rely on class-ethnic individual and collective resources. And third, consumer habits and preferences of their clientele, working-class families of Slavs and Hungarians, were usually traditional and less volatile than those of higher-status customers. In this regard, Johnstown storekeepers also differed from their big-city fellow ethnics—merchants and manufacturers alike—in that the latter often entered those areas of light industry/trade most susceptible to the mercurial whims of fashion and style. Rapid proliferation after World War I of chain stores in the large cities further increased turnover rates of small businesses, especially those trading in foodstuffs—one of the specialties of big-city Jewish storekeepers (see note b in table 3.6).

Some illustrations from the Depression years—a particularly insecure time in the national and local economies can be used to bring out the practical advantage members of the Jewish entrepreneurial niche had in coping with the instability of their small businesses.

"Everybody owed everybody," I repeatedly heard from my informants as they talked about keeping their businesses afloat during the Depression. The intragroup loan network, useful, and used, ever since it had been established at the beginning of the century when someone's enterprise needed propping up, now involved most merchants in the niche in a back-and-forth exchange whose flow depended on the current conditions of particular businesses.[84] If a business failed, or went formally bankrupt—as already noted, such occurrences, while not uncommon previously, increased in frequency in the 1930s—the owners effectively used individual resourcefulness, cooperative family economy, and some forms of assistance from fellow ethnics to reemploy themselves in the entrepreneurial niche.

As my respondents recollected the twists and turns of their family fortunes, Jewish entrepreneurs did not lose spirit when they lost their business. Rather, they remained hopeful that, if they "kept at it," they would stand back on their feet—*im yirtse HaShem*, God willing, as those from more traditional homes customarily qualified their plans even when relating events from years long past. As Isadore S. recalled, the attitude toward such downturns was "go back and try again, keep trying." And, as city and business directory records show, try they did. A stint as a peddler was one solution. Julius K., Sam M., and Morris R., for instance, after their stationary enterprises failed in particularly bad Depression years in the local economy, temporarily returned to peddling, which they had done in their first years in Johnstown at the beginning of the century. And so did American-born Louis M., who, although reluctantly, took up a *greeners'* (recent arrivals') job: "*Az me ken nit vi me vil, tut men vi me ken*" (if you can't do what you want, do what you can)—he used a Yiddish saying while reminiscing about that interim occupation but mentioned also that he "looked for something better." David B., whose ladies' and children's apparel store in Johnstown failed shortly after the onset of Depression, peddled for a couple of years, and in 1933 he started a ladies' furnishings shop that he kept until 1940. Some others opened makeshift small shops selling secondhand furniture and household utilities that became very much in demand after the 1936 flood. And Seymour R. thus recollected his father's entrepreneurial initiatives in that same period: "[From one business], when it didn't work out, he thought he might go into fabrics, it looked like a reasonable thing to do then, workers were laid off, so the women sew clothes at home, and also there was a Jewish [dry goods] wholesaler in town . . . [so] it made sense."[85]

Jews whose livelihoods were jeopardized by an economic downturn and who were not trying to open or restart their own business, or did not have such determination—a more frequent case in the American-born than in the immigrant generation—went to work for their fellow ethnics. We have seen that employment resources within the ethnic occupational niche effectively secured employment for young members of the local Jewish community entering the labor market, or newcomers who did not establish independent enterprises. These resources practically eliminated unemployment among Jews in the Johnstown area, even during the Depression. Thus Samuel G. and Harry C., after the bankruptcies of their clothing stores in Berlin, Somerset County, and in South Fork, Cambria County, in 1930 and 1931, both moved to Johnstown, where until 1940 they worked as salesmen in Jewish-owned stores. Brothers Isadore and Joseph O. in 1931 lost their men's furnishings store near the railroad station in Johnstown, but they stayed on in town and became salesmen at Gee Bee; in 1940, Isadore went back into the clothing business for himself, and Joseph came to work for him. Nathan B. worked in the early 1930s as a department manager at Gee Bee, then opened his own clothing and furnishings store; it failed in 1938, after which he returned to work at Glossers'. "Gee Bee Tech" was particularly useful during the Depression for the occupational training and the reliable source of employment it provided to young members of the Jewish community, and to job-seekers from the larger local society as well. While many small retail stores struggled hard to keep afloat, and two other Jewish-owned department stores catering to a more affluent, native-born clientele lost business, Gee Bee's trade in low-priced merchandise considerably expanded, and its payroll, including part-time workers, increased by over 40 percent. The availability, and flexibility, of part-time work at the expanding Gee Bee department store was very helpful to families whose high school–age children could, after school and during vacations, contribute to household incomes thinned by recurrent waves of economic depression.[86]

Interestingly, contemporary studies of unemployment in New York, Pittsburgh, and Detroit conducted in the 1930s reported the unemployment rate among Jews as oscillating around 15 percent—a substantial proportion in comparison to almost zero in Johnstown, but still less than half the 30–35 percent national average for major industrial centers. This difference was ascribed to a higher concentration of Jews in trade in comparison with the general population, and, implicitly, to Jewish businesses' serving as an employment resource for fellow ethnics in need of jobs in bad times.[87] Looking for data to compare with my Johnstown findings, I stumbled upon evidence that seems to confirm both this supposition and a more general thesis about Jewish self-help repeatedly noted in studies of this ethnic group. Business census data for 1929, 1933, 1935, and 1939 indicate that in the Bronx and in Brooklyn, the two boroughs in which about two-thirds of New York City Jews were then concentrated, the number of employees in retail stores in "Jewish" lines of trade actually increased during the

Depression, while in Manhattan, for instance, it diminished. It may well have been that a number of laid-off Jewish industrial workers and former employees of mainstream offices and department stores in Manhattan found temporary employment in businesses owned by fellow ethnics.[88]

The solid intragroup support network combined with the *takhlis*-oriented resourcefulness of individual entrepreneurs and entire family collectives reliant on this assistance to create an efficient safety net against unemployment in the Jewish entrepreneurial niche. Nonetheless, the profound economic crisis of the 1930s affected the incomes of most member-households, including those of the more affluent families. In their reminiscences of the Depression years my informants distinctly remembered them as "difficult," and "worse than before and after," but, in striking contrast to Johnstown's Slavic and Hungarian working-class families whose recollections I listened to in an earlier study, most of them did not recall this period as a struggle at the survival level to obtain basic food, clothing, and shelter. There were a few family households who on an on-and-off basis, depending on how bad a given year was, received traditional communal support for Passover supplies; but, also in accord with tradition, to the present day the names of the recipients have been kept confidential.

Regrettably, there are for the Depression period no systematic data on spendable incomes accrued from businesses like those for 1929, but an indirect estimate can perhaps be made. In Detroit in 1934, the average income of Jewish small proprietors was reported as $1,600, and, as I estimated, in Johnstown it oscillated about the same figure.[89] In households with the lowest incomes, the situation was very difficult indeed. For instance, Abraham M.'s little secondhand furniture store in Johnstown took in only $7,000 in 1931, or about 40 percent less in sales than in 1929. To keep their business going and feed the family, Abraham and his wife engaged in barter trade with working-class customers who cultivated little agricultural plots at the outskirts of Johnstown using old-country skills; after the flood in 1936 the M.'s secondhand furniture business, dealing in sought-after items, revived, and its sales more than doubled. Ephraim B.'s father's income from peddling had been "sufficient" for family needs in better times but dwindled dramatically during the worst years of the Depression. His mother "made do" by mending clothes previously purchased and dressing the children in hand-me-downs, and although nobody went hungry, neither was there an abundance of food on the table (it should be considered that keeping a kosher kitchen, as was done in most Jewish homes in interwar Johnstown, added expense).[90]

Families in lower-middle and middle income categories—presumably about the average of $1,600 quoted above, whether derived from independent business or salaried employment—were also forced to tighten their household budgets, by cutting down, or even eliminating in very bad years, some expenses that had become part of their "decent" lifestyles. Moses S. recalled the frequent appearance of "old-country dishes, made of flour, potatoes, and kasha" on the table, but since mother was an excellent cook and they were tasty, the children didn't really mind. Lena S., too, was "canning and baking at home, to save money, and even grew tomatoes and beans in a little garden in the back of the house"; the siblings Martin G. and Esther J. "were still dressed all right" but did not get their customary new clothes for Rosh Hashanah, the new year, until their father's business improved after 1936. And although Israel and Helma N. did not discuss business problems with their children, and home life "went on more or less as usual," Betty, Helen, and Harold remembered their parents worried, father pacing the room at nights, and mother waiting for sales on Saturday evenings at Gee Bee to buy food; the oldest daughter, who thought she would like to go on to college, was told to take a commercial course at the high school and forget her unfeasible ideas. Except for Lena S.'s, the remaining three families, we may add, owned their homes: the first in Kernville, the second in Hornerstown, and the third in Westmont.[91]

Adjusting to circumstances when there was not much they could do to change them, as soon as things picked up, member families of the Jewish entrepreneurial niche moved to regain lost ground and keep up socially recognized standards of a "decent" lifestyle. To reformulate somewhat the deprivation thesis,[92] it appears as if it was, precisely, the shared insecurity of Jewish households' prosperity—embedded in the uncertainty inherent in the petty-entrepreneurial nature of the ethnic economic niche—that fixated the model of accomplishment placing the main emphasis on the goal of a materially comfortable existence. Relocation to better neighborhoods and holding on to home ownership amid sharp turns of the economy are good illustrations of the determination with which this was pursued. Thus, among storekeepers whose pecuniary strength in D & B Company's credit ratings shifted back and forth several times during the 1920s and 1930s, the proportion of homeowners was the same as among Johnstown's general Jewish population, and 24 percent of this group had in those years moved to Westmont, the most prestigious section of town, half as renters, and half as owners. As we have seen earlier, it look the home buyers several years to pay off their houses, and no less than 60 percent of all Jewish homeowners in Johnstown during this period took out second and additional mortgages; Westmont in particular was called "the mortgage manor." Expectedly, sharp economic downturns during the Depression hurt them considerably: as shown in table 3.11, 24 percent of the home-owning families lost their houses during the 1930s. By 1940, however, as soon as industrial and business conditions improved in the local area, half those families were again owners of real property.[93]

This chapter has shown how specific local conditions, especially the stagnant economy and undifferentiated occupational structure, made for the persistence and solidification of the inclusive Jewish entrepreneurial niche established at the beginning of the century. It has demonstrated, further, how their external and intragroup circumstances shaped what the local

Jewish community perceived as the most valuable life accomplishments, and how they were to be achieved—accomplishments that differed from the pattern of success rapidly becoming dominant during the interwar period among American Jews in large and expanding cities, particularly New York. The following chapter looks at the patterns and contents of social-cultural life inside the Jewish community in interwar Johnstown, which were also, as I try to show, quite different from big-city ways.

CHAPTER 4

Small Town, Slow Pace:
Transformations in Jewish Sociocultural Life

STUDIES OF interwar American Jewish history have linked the collective ascent of East European big-city dwellers, by means of advanced formal education, into the mainstream white-collar service and professional strata with the accelerated transformation (led by the second generation) of sociocultural patterns brought from the old country. The processes traced in these studies involve rapid diversification and secularization of institutions, lifestyles, and worldviews within the Jewish group, and, more specifically, the acculturation of these to lifestyles of the American urban middle class—"modernization" and "Americanization," as these developments have often been called. These transformations began in the first decade of the twentieth century as the traditional ways were breaking down, or—from a different point of view—catching up with the practices and institutions of the middle strata in the host society. They spread and intensified in the following decades, setting "the master pattern" whereby—in the words of commentators—"a new [American] Jewish community came into being in the period between the great wars."[1] In terms of the interpretative model used in this study, sociocultural transformations reported in big-city studies represented the type of a relatively quick-pace ethnicization absorbing in its makeup a large dose of host, middle-class American influences that, blending with immigrants' old-country social patterns and cultural/religious customs, produced qualitatively different, "new [American] Jewish communities." The ethnicization model, it should be recalled, does not assume across-the-board dislodgement of the old patterns: even when the transformations in question became the dominant trend among, say, New York Jews during the interwar period, there remained differently situated subgroups wherein the ethnicization processes occurred at a different pace and with a different proportioning of old and new sociocultural elements.

The circumstances prevailing in Johnstown slowed down the pace and scope of change and sustained traditional elements in the sociocultural life of the local Jewish community. Referring to this community as "new" in spirit and practice would not have occurred to those who moved to Johnstown from large cities during the 1920s and 1930s; in reconstructing their life histories, they recalled, rather, how they initially found the town "kind of tranquil," and Jewish sociocultural life "less varied," "constrained," "more traditional," not very "*veltlekh*"—worldly or secular. It certainly contained more—and more diversified—lifestyles and outlooks than those found in the shtetls the immigrants had left at the turn of the century, but these innovations were limited. First, compared with the big urban centers, especially New York, Johnstown's spectrum of practices and orientations in Jewish society was much narrower; some forms were simply absent or marginal. Religious practice—as we shall see momentarily—remained more or less traditional. There were no true secularists and practically no associations that were not related, somehow, to the synagogue. There were no Jewish socialists, labor activists, or politicians; intellectuals were but a few old men self-taught in traditional Jewish learning; and college-goers were drawn from a few small clusters of families who set no trend for others. Second, what had been common practices among Johnstown's Jews—religious life in the synagogues and at home, and the social and cultural activities revolving around them—were changing more slowly and haltingly than in the larger, more cosmopolitan cities with more heterogeneous Jewish populations. With its constrained economic dynamics, relatively undifferentiated social structure, settled, small-town cultural aura, conservative social habits, and persistent near-ascriptive ethnoreligious divisions, Johnstown did not provide much in the way of external stimuli for bolder innovations.

Nor did the situation within the Jewish group. The small size of the group, and its enduring occupational homogeneity and encapsulation in the entrepreneurial niche sustained largely *gemeinschaftliche* relations in most shared activities, as well as efficient social control. The integration of immigrants and their American-born children at work, in residence, and in the group's social life was not conducive to the formation of sharply delineated "generation units," as Karl Mannheim called the different age cohorts whose distinct experience provided bases for shared outlooks and behavior.[2] Johnstown Jews' participation in the civic-political affairs of the dominant local society and in closer personal relationships with its members was, as we shall see in the next chapter, very limited. Last but not least, the economic volatility of small and even larger businesses placed a low ceiling on new undertakings.

What follows is a reconstruction, within these external and intragroup contexts, of what I believe were characteristic features of Jewish sociocultural life in prewar Johnstown. "Sociocultural life" is one of those loose concepts that cover virtually all human activity. In selecting the areas for investigation, I focused first and foremost on those that appeared to have been major components of a larger "meaningful entity" of Jews' existence in Johnstown. Second, I looked at those for which comparative information exists to permit an evaluation of continuity and change in local Jewish institutions and lifestyles from the two ends of the old/new spectrum, preemigration and contemporary, as reported for American Jews in big urban centers.

In order to structure this dense, close-to-the-ground presentation, I have fragmented into three parts what, in the Johnstowners' experience, formed one integrated piece. The first deals with public, or organized, religious and social life; the second with private, home-based religious practices, and social activities in primary group circles. The last part brings out the micro-social contexts—family, and local Jewish and general communities—responsible for the absence among Johnstown Jews of a "passion for [advanced] learning"—such passion as had become an increasingly pervasive schema-motive in the achievement drive and a major resource for socioeconomic upward mobility among their big-city fellow ethnics during the interwar period.

Religious and Social Life (Public)

Two related developments in Jewish-American life have been emphasized and documented in studies conducted in New York, of course, and in such cities as Philadelphia, Cleveland, Milwaukee, Los Angeles, Baltimore, Rochester (N.Y.), and Buffalo, all with general populations over 300,000 and more than 20,000 Jews. One was the decoupling of previously interfused ethnic and religious components in Jewish group life and self-identification. *Yidishkeyt*—as a folk or a people with common history—became separable from Judaism, and this "secularization of Jewishness" was reflected in the de-synagogization of American Jews and a rapid proliferation of religion-unrelated social and cultural institutions. The other development, the Conservative movement in Jewish religion, fused into the Orthodox synagogue's structure and public worship some contemporary American/Protestant patterns of church organization and forms of communal prayer.[3] Each of these developments involved a considerable role expansion for women in group public life, spurred also by macrosocietal changes; in turn, women's institutionalized entry and delimited empowerment in the public sphere fostered the above transformations.[4]

In Johnstown, the external and intragroup situations outlined above did not make for an environment conducive to quick advancement of these two transformative processes before World War II. After providing well for the family, the next major concern named by my informants when they recollected the shared orientations of local fellow Jews was to "keep a good Jewish environment to live in and raise children." Asked what they thought were the ways of doing this in prewar Johnstown, practically all my respondents, men and women, immigrants and the American-born generation alike, and regardless of residence in primary or secondary settlements, pointed to participation in the synagogue, indicating as motives four elements they could not really disentangle: the personal need to uphold Jewish traditions; socially sanctioned expectations; the expressive functions of membership, in other words, the enjoyment of social contacts and self-identity maintained through this association; and the instrumental purposes, that is, practical assistance, business and otherwise, provided by the

4.1. Beth Zion Reform
Temple on Vine Street.
Collection of Dr. Meyer
and Sally Bloom
Archives at Beth Sholom
Temple.

interfused economic/congregational networks developed since the beginning of the century.

This affiliative orientation coincided with the "churchliness" of the
larger local society, which was pronounced in public life. A bird's-eye view
of interwar Johnstown would show the imposing structures of the mills in
the center, and a dense net—over a hundred—of parishes around them and
further away at the city's edges. Indeed, according to the 1926 and 1936
U.S. religious censuses, average church membership among all Christian
denominations, as reported by the town's ecclesiastical authorities, was
over 80 percent, as compared, for example, with less than 60 percent in
Pittsburgh, 55 percent in Philadelphia, and 45 percent in New York. In
Johnstown, church membership was taken for granted by the town's public
opinion, and when the ethnic groups appeared in the local paper, it was
most frequently in connection with their holidays and parochial festivities.[5]

Among New York Jews, according to estimates from the early 1920s,
formal synagogue affiliation varied, depending on the neighborhood, from
a minuscule 2 percent to 44 percent, or 23 percent on the average. In
nearby Pittsburgh, with a Jewish population fifty times the size of Johnstown's, formal synagogue affiliation in the mid-1930s was only about 25 to
30 percent. In both cities, scores of independent, secular organizations

4.2. Ahavath Achim Orthodox Synagogue at the corner of Cedar and Oak Streets in Hornerstown, interwar period. Collection of Dr. Meyer and Sally Bloom Archives at Beth Sholom Temple.

with cultural-educational or social-recreational purposes permitted Jews to stay institutionally attached to the group, and to express and sustain their Jewish identity. In Johnstown, even during the Depression when paying dues was particularly problematic, 75 to 80 percent of all Jewish families in the city, with no significant generational difference, were retained by one or another of the three local synagogues; these institutions' upkeep was bolstered by emergency contributions from the personal funds of the most affluent merchant–community leaders. About four-fifths of the affiliated belonged to Rodef Sholom, founded as an Orthodox *khevre* at the beginning of the century by East European immigrants. The remaining synagogue members were divided between its offshoot, the Orthodox Ahavath Achim (founded, as previously noted, in 1922 by a small group of immigrants from one neighborhood who found the Sabbath walk across town to the old shul too tiresome), and the Reform Beth Zion Temple (formally instituted in 1924), which was predominantly German, but which some East European families joined in the interwar period.[6]

The not-quite-voluntary nature of membership is suggested by an observation from the rabbi who led Rodef Sholom in the 1930s. Those who were not formally affiliated tended to "remain at the fringes, as it was difficult in a small group like this to stay out, you'd make yourself conspicuous . . . and also it wasn't practical." The nonaffiliated appeared a few times a year on the *yortsaytn* (death anniversaries) of their closest relatives to recite *kadish* (the memorial prayer); on High Holidays; for a special religious service such as a *bris* or a burial; or in some kind of practical difficulty.[7]

With such an encompassing membership, both formal and fringe, the three synagogues functioned as the foci of the group's communal life. In the big, economically expanding cities with large, socially differentiated Jewish populations, the rapidly growing number of secular Jewish organizations in the 1920s–1930s made the synagogue an increasingly "subsidiary part in the totality of Jewish life."[8] In Johnstown, secular Jewish organizations—their number increased in the interwar period—while nominally separate, "stemmed from the synagogue," "connected around," as my informants interpreted the significant overlap between their leadership, members, and social activities. Although frequented by others, the Jewish Social Center, for example, founded and managed by Rodef Sholom's leaders of both the immigrant and American-born generations, was "practically totally the Iron Street [Rodef Sholom] shul's affair." Similarly, the Jewish War Veterans group drew its members and activists mostly from the Rodef Sholom pool, and so did the popular Hadassah, an association of Zionist women, and a couple of Zionist youth groups, which frequently used the synagogue's space for their meetings. The Johnstown lodge of the Workmen's Circle—an organization known in the large cities for its staunch secularism and socialist leanings—had a membership (half a dozen) composed of self-employed small traders and artisans most of whom were affiliated with the Ahavath Achim Orthodox Synagogue and made occasional contributions toward its communal purposes. The local branch of the Council of Jewish Women, on the other hand, though open to the whole group, "rather belonged to the Temple": the majority of its officers were activists of the Beth Zion Sisterhood, and the association held its meetings, as well as social events "for Beth Zion's benefit," in the Temple's building. In community relations, that is, in dealings with non-Jewish local society, the group was represented by leaders affiliated with the synagogue—the rabbis and the officer boards—until the Jewish Community Council, organized at the outbreak of World War II, took over this function. And virtually the only Jewish undertaking in the interwar period that attracted a larger outside audience, a lecture series held in the Johnstown High School building, carried a name identifying its sponsors' religious affiliation: the Beth Zion Forum.[9] The traditionally broad-scope, congregational character of Johnstown's Jewish community was reflected in its members' collective identities. The synagogues' names were used as inclusive adjectives: my question, for example, about a list of names I had compiled from some source, or a particular public event, was usually answered with "This was Rodef Sholom [or Temple, or little shul—Ahavath Achim]," denoting the whole (sub)group as well as the organizations and activities within that synagogue's orbit.

In large, metropolitan Jewish settlements during the interwar years, specialized Jewish welfare and social service agencies professionally staffed by men and women of the American-born generation increasingly assumed the traditional functions of synagogues in looking after the needs of local residents. In Johnstown, these needs primarily involved business and employment assistance to members of the entrepreneurial niche, and, in case of illness or other incapacitation, a good word and a helpful hand. In addition, while big-city Jews' increasing involvement in mainstream American institutions dealing with social welfare enabled them to acquire firsthand knowledge about the workings of modern organizations, most of Johnstown's Jews, minimally involved outside their ethnic group as they were, did not directly experience even a small-town version of modern organizational life. As a result of these combined circumstances, ethnicization qua differentiation of social institutional life in the local Jewish community proceeded far more slowly than in the big and expanding cities with large and heterogeneous Jewish populations whose American-born, middle-class representatives participated in growing numbers in public affairs of the dominant society.

In the big cities, the Anglo-Protestant style philanthropic institutions had by the 1930s largely replaced the old-country type charitable societies. But in Johnstown, after the 1936 flood severely damaged the downtown business district, the traditional *Gemilut Hasadim* (free loan society) was organized at Rodef Sholom by a group of the shul's (male) leaders to help affected storekeepers back on their feet. Besides that, however, as we have seen in the previous chapter, economic assistance was for the most part delivered informally: if not by kin, it was provided within the congregations by the leader-owners of larger establishments (although the "big shots" served the group at large). During the Depression the "Temple's" Council of Jewish Women established a committee on social service, with one professional caseworker paid by the outside Family Welfare Association, but only a few needy cases were reported. They were "not really 'cases,'" I heard in this connection—in a comment that illuminated the traditional character of even this "modernized" mutual assistance institution—"we just looked after these needy families." Side by side with this new agency, the traditional, synagogue-linked *Moes Chitim* committee distributed Passover funds, mostly to area peddlers.[10]

The *Kranken* committee, for the visitation of the sick, an old-country tradition reestablished at Rodef Sholom at the beginning of the century, also continued through the interwar period. Its activities were recorded (in Yiddish) at the synagogue's monthly meetings: for example, in February 1924, "In the name of the *khevre* [congregation—the traditional East European name was still used] M. Glaser Slutzker and Meir Fishin visited

Moshe Beterman when he did not feel good." The small *khevre* to assist transients, *Hakhnoses Orkhim*, had also endured, but its operation was "updated," as my women-informants described it, that is, made more efficient: once a month, the collected donations were deposited in bulk at the kosher butcher shop near the railroad station, and the owner used the money to feed the passersby, or buy them a train ticket for their continuing journey.[11]

There were not enough Jews in the area, nor was there enough steady money, to create another institutional innovation established in large Jewish settlements—the organization at an even higher level of complexity than the specialized agencies that replaced traditional *khevres*: an overarching Jewish Federation, to plan and supervise fund-raising and distribution for national and world Jewish causes.[12] Through the interwar period, most actions for such purposes were conducted by synagogues and their satellite associations, whose volunteer representatives, organized in two- or three-member ad hoc committees, canvassed house to house, collecting modest contributions and asking for pledges. In the early 1930s, a joint Rodef Sholom and Beth Zion committee launched a mini-analogue of the United Philanthropies as the German Relief Fund Campaign to help victims of Nazi persecution; this initiative was subsequently (1938) transformed into the United Jewish Appeal. It was only at the outbreak of World War II that the federated Jewish Community Council was organized to take over these fund-raising functions.[13]

The transformation of the East European Orthodox *khevres* into the Conservative synagogue-centers that began to sweep through larger Jewish settlements in the decade 1910–1920 has been considered in American-Jewish historiography as the major, and perhaps most tellingly symbolic, expression of "modernization"—that is, acculturation to American socioreligious patterns of religious institutions and worship as known to the immigrants in the old country. Interpreted in the ethnicization framework, the emergence of the synagogue-centers was an outcome of a transformative absorption of a large dose of the host society's elements into the traditional old-country ways of worship and socializing. These new institutions, seen as "the hallmarks of second generation Jews' social and economic arrival" adopted programs shaped by "American middle-class norms. . . . As each synagogue center grew, the primacy of its religious origins receded." This observation of progressive internal secularization drawn from the secondary Jewish settlements in New York City also applied to other large cities in that period, so that among Jews themselves it earned "the humorous epithet of 'a pool with a school and a shul.'"[14]

These innovations arrived in Johnstown late, and when finally instituted at Rodef Sholom (Ahavath Achim did not follow), it was a halfway, or even quarter-way reform—"Consorthodox," retaining a good deal of the distinctly old-country flavor of public worship.[15] The Center also turned out to be a mini-substitute for the real thing: a *synagogue*-center raµer than a synagogue-*center*, again with the traditional emphasis on the first part of the combination.

The idea of building a new, "American" synagogue appeared for the first time in 1920 in the minutes of Rodef Sholom's board meetings. The all-male board of officers was still entirely of immigrant stock (the second-generation men joined in the second half of the decade), and the minutes were recorded in Yiddish—with a characteristic admixture of English terms written in Hebrew characters: The "*khevre* is to rise new *geld* for a *naye*, up to day *shul*." The matter was taken up again at several meetings during 1921 and 1922, but no action was taken. In 1924, it reappeared under the name Jewish Community Center, this time recorded in a mixture of Yiddish, English (in Hebrew characters), and Hebrew: the Center, "to house the shul, Talmud Torah [religious school], and meeting rooms," was to be "modern and *kedat Moshe ve Yisroel*" (the formula used in the traditional wedding ceremony, meaning: according to *halakhah* or the Talmudic law).[16] "Modern" referred to the building's new, more prestigious location and decorous exterior, and, on the inside, to the old-new institution's specialized functions, each assigned separate space; this modernity apparently was meant to symbolize both to the congregation's members themselves and to outsiders the group's entry into middle-class American society (the term my informants sometimes used in this context was "advancement"). The invocation of *halakhah*, and the use of the traditional terms *khevre* and *shul* reflected the simultaneous desire to preserve Orthodox traditions in the form and content of worship as practiced by the congregants.

A down payment was in fact made that year on a $15,000 lot in a respectable downtown section of Johnstown, but six years later the property was sold, as it was clear the project exceeded the financial resources of the congregation. Annual expenditures for the Rodef Sholom Synagogue, including upkeep of the building along with the *shakhthoyz* and *mikve*, and salaries for the rabbi, cantor (who also performed the function of ritual slaughterer), recording secretary, *shames* (sexton), and teacher of the Hebrew school, amounted to $10,000 to $12,000. In comparison, the national average for urban Jewish congregations in 1926 was over $16,000; in New York City in the late 1920s, the average figure for East European synagogue centers was $30,000, but many had budgets of over $50,000. At Rodef Sholom, membership dues, religious school tuition, and income from the purchase of synagogue seats on the High Holidays were not sufficient to cover costs, and not stable enough either; actually, the amounts available for synagogue expenses varied from month to month, as member families adjusted and rescheduled payments according to their current economic situations.[17] The congregational budget was therefore regularly supplemented by special donations, subscriptions, and pledges, including the major, traditional collection on Yom Kippur and fund-raising campaigns run several times a year at social occasions or by volunteers who visited people at home.

Women participated in these congregational and related social activities. About the same time that the issue of the "*naye*, up to day *shul*" appeared at the congregational meetings, the exclusively male officer board of the synagogue decided "to give women and daughters of the khevra Rodef Sholom [. . .] the full right to hold entertainments and socials in the building for the benefit of the shul." Whether the decision was propelled by the women themselves my informants could not clearly recollect: "Not necessarily; money was needed for the shul, so it was a way to get it" was the most specific I heard. This was an innovation for Rodef Sholom, but in comparison with the better organized, more autonomous and expansive appropriation of social space by women in the large urban centers, it did not appear impressive.

In the big cities, growing educational and occupational opportunities provided Jewish (and other) women with skills useful outside of the home in the public arena. In upwardly mobile Jewish households, once the man's income sufficed for a middle-class lifestyle, the married woman withdrew from regular employment, thus gaining a degree of free time that could be invested in other activities. Spurred by the twin developments of intragroup institutional differentiation and "secularization of Jewishness" in large Jewish settlements in big urban centers, religion-neutral ethnic organizations with various purposes proliferated, and social space was created wherein middle-class women could, and did, invest their time and energy, especially in the areas of social work and education-related activities. This autonomous female public presence and activity in large urban Jewish settlements remained circumscribed within delineated fields such as philanthropy and social work, and education-related pursuits. Yet so spectacular did it become in the interwar period that some commentators on the Conservative movement at that time called it a "quiet revolution."[18]

In Johnstown, there was a similar general trend toward an increased involvement of women in congregational life, but like all other transformations of social and cultural (religious) life of the local Jewish community, this (sub)process of ethnicization was throughout the interwar period weighted considerably more toward tradition. In this case, the traditional emphasis meant a smaller public space designated for women, and a lesser degree of autonomy for their activities therein. For the great majority of Johnstown's Jewish women, white-collar occupations meant, as we have seen, "helping out" in family or other Jewish businesses in the ethnic entrepreneurial niche, so that the available free time was limited. A handful of young women professionals, mostly public school teachers and a few nurses, had insufficient authority as a group—and no apparent desire, either—to take over the leadership of women's organizations and promote a more substantial appropriation of public space; in addition, several of them were also occupied after work in family businesses. The small Jewish group's institutional structure was much less differentiated, with predominantly *Gemeinschaft*-type internal relations and traditional authority. By consensus, the group remained synagogue-centered, so that both old and new associations, including women's, had more nominal than actual autonomy; in practice, they were influenced by the congregational leadership, which was all male in the town's major congregation. Finally, while the previously closed public space opened for women's participation, the practice of religious "Consorthodoxy" (see below) set narrow limits to this territory.

But even if initiated and overseen by men, and more limited in scope than in the big cities, the entry of Johnstown's women into group public-religious space was an innovation unheard of in the shtetls, where women were merely observers. As it transformed the old-country organization of communal life through the admixture of middle-class American patterns, women's involvement in congregational life became part of its ethnicization. It was, actually, a double transformation: the very appearance of women in an area previously reserved entirely for men, as well as the role of innovation managers (see below) the former played in this newly gained territory, ethnicized—that is, in that historical context, secularized—congregational activities.

Thus, in addition to running the traditional *Hakhnoses Orkhim* society to assist itinerants, women of both generations, organized in the Hebrew Ladies Aid Society, began in the 1920s regularly to sponsor social events. The smaller and more routine events were usually planned and managed by the women alone. In the preparation and execution of big programs, particularly those important for fund-raising purposes, men and women collaborated in special joint committees. These committees were constituted at synagogue meetings at which the "ladies" were not present, and they operated according to the conventional modern middle-class division of roles in such instances—the men supervised and handled the finances and "the press" (the local paper), while the women attended to the event's aesthetics and catering.[19]

Besides card games on Sundays, and the traditional schnapps-and-herring receptions for bar mitzvah and *bris* celebrations, as the decade progressed the synagogue building housed a variety of new secular and secularized religious functions with mixed Jewish and American elements, organized by the women: kosher bake and rummage sales, plays by the children on biblical and Jewish-American folk themes, traditional religious and secular Yiddish musical performances, Columbus Day programs, Thanksgiving gatherings, Hanukkah dances, and Purim celebrations. The Hebrew Ladies Aid Society appeared also in the 1930s in the "little shul," old-fashioned Ahavath Achim, but there its role was limited to preparing and serving traditional food at religious celebrations—the main congregational socials—or at special occasions, when a small group of synagogue children was "showing a *yidishe* play" (in English).[20]

I asked my oldest informants, the women-organizers of activities, if they could perhaps remember where all these new ideas and practices originally came from and how they spread. As they recalled, it was mostly by imitation, secondhand—"adjusted to the means, as we were small"—of things done in the larger Jewish settlements, observed through personal and organizational contacts and visits. Johnstown's innovations were largely based on those of Pittsburgh and Philadelphia, where Jewish community centers were already well established; and those of nearby Altoona, where the Johnstowners had many relatives and business connections, and where the synagogue-center project was already well under way. They were also stimulated by the Jewish press. About 20–25 percent of households received *Forverts* and *Tageblat*, later *Morgen Zhurnal*, from New York, and the English-language *Jewish Criterion* and *American Jewish Outlook* from Pittsburgh, and subscribers circulated the papers to others. The two Yiddish papers were quite different ideologically: the former was socialist-secular, the latter "a little more modern liberal" Orthodox-religious. Each in its way propagated the "Americanization of Jewish life." *Forverts*'s socialist leanings did not concern Johnstown readers; in fact, they explicitly denied that their reading it "had anything to do with socialism. . . . There were no socialists here. It was a Yiddish paper, and had good stories and Jewish news, [also commercial advertisements] that's why." The local American environment—that is, the *Johnstown Tribune*'s genteel "Town's Social Chronicle" and reports (with photographs) of festivities in the prestigious Protestant churches, as well as radio programs—must also have provided models for imitation. As for the little shul's timid innovation of Ladies Aid, the original inspiration seems to have come from the big shul-mother, but the inspired individuals were apparently the men: the project was proposed and approved at the all-male synagogue meeting.[21]

As the Depression set in, congregational finances became even more precarious—in February 1934, for example, the Rodef Sholom bulletin reported only 25 percent of member families as having "paid their dues and pledges on time." The project of a new synagogue center was abandoned, to be revived a full fifteen years later and finally realized in 1951/52. Instead, a mini-substitute was organized in 1931 as the "Jewish Community Center–Rodef Sholom": one large room with a mezzanine rented in a downtown building, with a bar, card tables, and a space for social events. The president of the Center was an American-born man, from one of the earliest and more affluent member families of Rodef Sholom; board officers, drawn from both the immigrant and second generations, included two native-born women, also from among the most influential families in the congregation.

The Community Center Rodef Sholom continued to mix the religious with the secular, including a few more innovations such as community Passover seders, confirmation performances by Sunday school students, and New Year's Eve dance parties. There were also locally produced Broadway-style mini-musicals. These were adapted, it seems, from similar productions at theaters in bigger cities, and the biggest hit was apparently a program titled "Gay Nineties and Gayer Thirties," presented in 1933 in the midst of the Depression. The Center Rodef Sholom served also for meetings and social functions of the local Zionist organizations, men's, women's, and youth's.

These ethnicized events reflected the gendered power structure in the local Jewish community. Thus, for example, the UJA dinners organized by men in which women participated but did not bid took place in Fort Stanwix, the best hotel in town, to emphasize the event's importance. But similar fund-raising occasions organized by the women's Hadassah or the Ladies Auxiliary were more modestly located in the Jewish Center (women catered, and men pledged their donations), or, for special occasions, in the Capitol Hotel, less prestigious than Fort Stanwix (where, again, men did the bidding).[22]

Not far away, the old synagogue was by then managed by men from both generations. It was only in 1952, when the new synagogue-center was opened in Westmont, that the Rodef Sholom Ladies Auxiliary could appoint its five representatives to the board of directors; they participated there not, like men, as individuals, but as a collective body. In comparison, in the big cities individual women began to join the boards of directors of Conservative synagogues by the early 1940s. The old shul housed the religious services, Hebrew and Sunday school, congregational meetings, and *bris* and bar mitzvah receptions—as time went on, more "*balebatishe* [my informant used the old Yiddish expression for the new middle-class respectability of the celebrants], usually a sweet table [. . .] prepared at home." These celebrations, however, as my informants emphasized, were nothing in comparison with the upwardly mobile New Yorkers' *narish-keyt*—foolishness, that is—lavish spending on "exhibitions of vanity and frivolity . . . devoid of the least spirituality," accompanying such and similar occasions. These events were interspersed with such ethnicized American middle-class novelties as "Jewish Home Beautiful," a secular-religious program organized by the synagogue women and depicting various holiday tables, or regular "businessmen's luncheons" prepared and served—to the very husbands and fathers with whom they often worked in the stores—by the Ladies Auxiliary. The revenues from the latter went for "the needs of the shul [. . .] it was like fund-raising, and also practical: why pay elsewhere?" This arrangement itself, and the women's management of it in the synagogue's space, undoubtedly already represented the organization of social life quite different from the gatherings of the shtetl traders before the evening prayers in the *boti medroshim* after the market day over a piece of dark bread with a herring, washed down with a little schnaps. These Rodef Sholom luncheons, however, were certainly still a long way from the "modern" American dining clubs frequented by successful Jewish businessmen in the metropolitan cities.[23]

Like Rodef Sholom, during the 1920s the Beth Zion Reform Congregation, too, contemplated the project of relocating to a more prestigious area, and transforming the Temple into a "Social Center" with meeting rooms and schoolrooms, an auditorium, and a social hall. For similar, financial reasons, the plan had to be abandoned (it was realized in 1951), and the Temple remained housed in an adapted residential building downtown, purchased from a member, the widow of the owner of a chic Johnstown department store. Small membership and an even smaller number of children, no pressing social welfare needs in the area, and ultimately the lack of space limited the usual social activities at the Temple mostly to card games, tea parties, and community dinners. For special occasions, such as the Valentine Cabaret Party or the New Year's Eve dance, outside facilities were rented at the Jewish-owned Hendler Hotel or, better yet, at the Fort Stanwix Hotel.[24]

Much more than at Rodef Sholom, the "German" Beth Zion's inner life was in the hands of its female members, the Sisterhood and the Council of Jewish Women (both organizations enrolled practically every one of them). This greater women's visibility in the Temple resulted in part from what Beth Zion shared with other U.S. Reform congregations—although, as we shall soon see, Johnstown's Reform, like all other reforms in this town, was from the start a muffled undertaking. On the one hand, a relative gender equality in institutional functioning, patterned after the Anglo-Protestant model, mobilized women for action, while, on the other, the low intensity of public religious practices, likewise modeled on the culturally dominant denomination, removed the men—traditionally central in Jewish worship—from the scene.[25]

But another factor in the situation within the small Beth Zion Temple seems to have had a greater immediate effect on gender roles and relations in this congregation: namely, the powerful economic position and equally strong personality of the widow-benefactor of the Temple, and, for similar reasons, of her only daughter. Throughout the interwar period, the Nathan widow, Maggie, as she was known—I also heard people refer to her as the "Mother to the Temple"—not only was a member of but pretty much directed Beth Zion's board of trustees. The rich heiress, her daughter Hulda, was married to the chief manager of the Nathans' department store. Active, like her mother, in both the Jewish Women's Council and the Temple Sisterhood, she personally arranged in the early 1920s for the hire of a permanent Hebrew teacher at Beth Zion when her two boys reached the age for religious instruction. Beth Zion was not unique in this regard: for similar reasons inherent in the largely informal functioning of the socioreligious institutional network, in Rodef Sholom, too, the high economic status of women's families—their own or that of relatives—enabled them to exert a backstage but not necessarily whispered influence on public socioreligious matters, and this influence was more powerful than what the Sisterhood could manage through solely institutional channels. But Rodef Sholem women pulled strings less spectacularly than did Maggie and Hulda. In the 1930s Hulda indeed served for a few years as the Temple's president. Still, as one peruses Beth Zion's news bulletin, *Temple Tidings*, the women activists, with the exception of Maggie, appear under their husband's first names; Hulda, even as president, appears as as Mrs. Nelson Elsasser. The distribution of the Sisterhood's and Brotherhood's responsibilities shows the former in charge of internal affairs, the latter of outer-directed activities. The director of the Beth Zion Forum, a lecture program directed at the outside society and attended by Beth Zion women, was Mr.—not Mrs.—Nelson Elsasser; as my interviews suggest, the women did not aspire to such outside representation, and it was understood and accepted that in a town such as Johnstown, with a male-centered economy, company-controlled conservative politics, and traditional social life, men were more effective in such roles.[26]

Intertwined with the transformation of the traditional East European *shul* into an increasingly secularized synagogue-center was the ethnicization ("modernization" and "Americanization" have been, again, the terms commonly used in the literature) of the organization and style of Orthodox religious education and public worship. The idea was to make these practices "celebrate God in an American accent," as one poetically minded student of this transformation put it—that is, to make them resemble native (middle-class Protestant) forms of religious behavior: improved, professionalized, and properly housed religious instruction that included secular Jewish history and culture and educational recreation; orderly and decorous weekly religious services with English-language sermons, organ playing, and congregational singing; and gender-mixed family seating in the synagogue. The groundwork for the main product of this reconstruction, the Conservative synagogue, was laid during the decades of mass immigration by leaders of East European birth but trained in West European (mostly German) rabbinical schools and public universities, with the assistance of American-born, moderate-Reform Jews. The project, as its promoters saw it, had as its goal "civilizing" the East Europeans and their religious Orthodoxy in such a way as to make both of them "thoroughly American" while simultaneously maintaining the Jewish tradition. Initiated "from the top," the Conservative reform—which broke its original ties with Reform Judaism as the latter moved toward what traditionalists saw as much too "Christian"(Protestant) forms of worship—soon became a grassroots movement within the East European congregations. The end of World War I, in American Jewish historiography's conventional wisdom, marked a watershed in making the Conservative synagogue the leading religious-institutional form among East European Jews.[27]

In Johnstown, in the late 1920s Rodef Sholom continued to be an old-style East European *shul*, with long services in Hebrew and a cantor singing the life out of himself. Women sat separately in the balcony, while men "noisily *davened* (prayed), each at his own pace, wrapped in traditional *taleses* (prayer shawls), and *shnuddered* (bid money) for the *aliyot* (honors of being called up to the Torah)." "A lot of conversation [went on] during services, and a crowd of children raising Cain in the sanctuary, the cantor or rabbi pounding on the bima, *Shah!* (silence!), trying to keep order. . . ." (In his recollection of these scenes, an American-born Johnstowner used a mixture of Yiddish, Anglicized Yiddish, and Hebrew terms.)[28] Next to the synagogue there was a *shakhthoyz,* a place for ritual slaughter, where every week children from Johnstown and the surrounding towns brought chickens to be killed for the Sabbath meal; and a *mikve,* the traditional ritual bath, used by a group of older immigrants mostly from the neighborhood (it closed down after the 1936 flood).

In the early 1920s it was decided, "for the needs of the young generation," that the Rosh Hashanah sermon was to be delivered in English. Less than a decade earlier, a guest preacher who addressed the children in English was interrupted and publicly insulted; the event, and the issue itself, caused a great commotion in the congregation and reverberated at the *khevre*'s meetings for a long time afterward. So changes were under way, but the traditional religious practices still held strong, even among the socially arrived residents of prestigious, Anglo-Protestant Westmont: about the same time that English began to creep into the shul, a group of well-respected immigrant men from that neighborhood high on the hill above the center city sent a *shaylah* (ritual question) to the *beth din* (rabbinic court) in Pittsburgh about the permissibility of using the inclined plane (rail-trolley moved by cable winch) on the Sabbath to get to and from the synagogue. The court pronounced it lawful, provided a Gentile was riding at the same time who could push the up and down buttons, and the Westmonters followed the ruling.[29]

The majority, about 80 percent, of the six- to thirteen-year-old children of Rodef Sholom members attended religious classes: the weekly afternoon Hebrew and/or Sunday school. The former, with few exceptions, was attended by boys only, the latter by boys and girls—a major innovation compared with the practically total exclusion of girls from religious instruction outside the home that had obtained in the shtetl. The proportion of religious school enrollment in Johnstown was similar to that in Jewish agricultural colonies (New Jersey). It was higher than the average (65 percent) for urban places with a similar number of Jews, less than 2,000, and much higher yet than the average in cities with over 50,000 Jewish residents (37 percent).[30]

Like public worship, the manner of religious instruction during the 1920s at Rodef Sholom had become "updated" while retaining a good measure of old-country flavor. In 1924—about the time that the issue of a "modern American *shul* according to *halakhah*" was on the synagogue's public agenda—a permanent task force to improve and supervise the *kheyder* or Hebrew school, as it was now to be called, was formed. Although formally independent, the school was for all practical purposes part of the *khevre* Rodef Sholom. The board of directors, all-male and volunteer (the leaders of the congregation), expected suitable male applicants to respond to Rodef Sholom's ad for a "teacher [with] a command of the English language as well as being a good Hebrew scholar," placed in New York's *Yidishes Tageblat*. Meanwhile, however, a local young woman was employed for a small remuneration as a "temporary assistant teacher." Even if temporary, the appointment of a female teacher to the Hebrew school was certainly a departure from traditional Orthodox custom—made easier, it seems, by the established presence in the same synagogue building of the Sunday school managed by the *Tikvah Zion* society and, from its inception in 1911, staffed by women instructors. The position was soon given to an appropriately traditional person: a Russian-born *talmid khokhem* (Talmud scholar), a relative of one of the most affluent and influential families, recently arrived from Eastern Europe. It was apparently agreed—I was not able to ascertain whether his rich-and-mighty relations influenced the decision—that so learned a person should not be employed in a shop. In fact, he was a better Hebrew scholar than an English-speaker, and there formed around him a small group of men inclined to religious study when they were free from work.

The Talmud Torah instructors spoke to the children in English, but the school scene, with all pupils together in one room in the basement of the old synagogue—"rowdy, lots of monkeyshine going on" and the teacher distributing smacks with a ruler—was not unlike one in Eastern Europe; in fact, despite the official renaming, it was still commonly referred to as *kheyder*. Sunday school was taught by young, predominantly female, volunteers (the school's own alumni), each in charge of a group of children sitting together in the main sanctuary, with some sections in the women's balcony because of a lack of space; they were just as rowdy, but no rulers were used.[31]

As the 1930s started, there was already, as my informants recollected, "a mood among many at the Rodef Sholom shul to become Conservative, in an unspecified way . . ."—a sense rather than a program—"just readiness to modernize the old ways." It was felt particularly among the American-born men and women active in the congregation and among some male and female members of the immigrant generation who viewed themselves as more "progressive" or "American." In the big cities, it was usually a newly formed group of professionals who were leaders of the Conservative movement among East European Jews. In Johnstown, however, occupational status was not the common denominator; advocates of change included both professionals and merchants. More important was place of residence, and especially uphill Westmont, the location of the truly arrived in the eyes of local Jewish opinion. In 1931, the first American-born and Conservative rabbi was invited to the pulpit of Rodef Sholom—as one commentator put it, men "led" the initiative and women "assisted"—and under his leadership the congregation became "officially Conservative." As Rabbi Ralph Simon himself recalls, the seven years he spent at a New York Orthodox yeshiva before receiving training at the (Conservative) Jewish

Theological Seminary helped him to "navigate"—and ethnicize—Johnstown's congregation.

The changes he introduced included "prayerbooks with texts both in Hebrew and English, weekly sermons in English and on various topics such as contemporary Jewish life in America and in Palestine, the elimination of the auctioneering of the *alyiot*, the choral society, mixed (family) seating in Friday evening late services, shortening somewhat of the Sabbath morning and High Holiday services." But, as before, the prayers were conducted predominantly in Hebrew; "those who chose to use the Orthodox prayerbooks did so, and they *davened* at their own pace as it suited them, sat or stood when their prayerbooks so indicated, oblivious to any other [English] prayer activity going on." On Saturdays and High Holidays women sat separately upstairs, and although uncommon, it was not a surprise when a boy delivered his traditional bar mitzvah speech in Yiddish rather than English.

The major area of change, as Rabbi Simon remembered, "was not in liturgy and religious rituals, which remained Orthodox, but in religious instruction, and in cultural and social programs," including adult education, with special classes for women in elementary Hebrew and Jewish (public) worship, updated curricula for the religious school adding interpretation to the traditional Hebrew readings, Passover community seders at the Social Center. In addition, he organized a regular lecture series on religious and other Jewish topics by out-of-town speakers, most often rabbis—an ethnicized analogue of sorts of the *droshes*, sermons by *magidim*, visiting preachers in the shtetls, but in-group directed and more traditional in subject matter than the Reform Beth Zion Forum.

The innovations in seating arrangements and the adult classes for women in the Hebrew language and synagogue rituals, introduced at Rodef Sholom by the Conservative rabbi, created more public space for women in the religious life of the synagogue, and they stepped into it. But their increased participation in public religious life could by no means be considered a "feminization of the synagogue," a development reported in the late 1920s in big urban centers, where the large proportions of women at weekly Sabbath services, apparently *arrivées* middle-class housewives with maids and without outside employment, ethnicized traditionally male-dominated Jewish religious attendance, and made it resemble more closely the feminized Anglo-Protestant pattern.[32]

Rabbi Simon also encouraged women's social participation through new forms of activities. At his suggestion, in 1931 the women reorganized the Hebrew Ladies Aid Society: some new social functions were added, and it was renamed the Ladies Auxiliary. "It sounded better," I was told, which meant "updated" or "modern" (in more decidedly Conservative congregations at that time, the properly "modern" name was Sisterhood, to suggest gender partnership in synagogue matters). Another innovation introduced by Rabbi Simon was an English-language monthly pamphlet pre-

4.3. First teachers of Tikvah Zion religious school, ca. 1920. Reprinted from the *Jewish Center of Johnstown Rodef Sholom Synagogue*, Anniversary Book, 1954.

4.4. The Ladies Auxiliary of Rodef Sholom—dinner at the Capitol Hotel, mid-1930s. Collection of Dr. Meyer and Sally Bloom Archives at Beth Sholom Temple.

pared by a group of young women, the *Rodef Sholom Bulletin*, which contained community news previously circulated only by word of mouth.[33]

Much of what was happening at Rodef Sholom during Rabbi Simon's tenure owed to his strong personality and leadership; the effects of his stay in Johnstown were yet another instance of the "causal power" of individual will and action in a small community without the bureaucratic structures that transformed socioreligious institutions in large Jewish settlements in the big cities. "We just followed him," I often heard from his congregants of that period, although the most active participants in his new programs came from the secondary Jewish settlement, and from among the second generation. (To this day, for many old-timers Rabbi Simon has remained a legend; somewhat like Maggie, perhaps, but held in a different kind of awe.) He left Johnstown in 1936 for a new pulpit in Chicago, when Rodef Sholom's financial difficulties, eased but not resolved by the affluent Glosser family's liquidation of the mortgage on the synagogue building, forced the board to substantially lower his salary. During the following fifteen years, until the synagogue finally resettled in Westmont, it remained in a state of flux, *nit ahin nit aher*, neither here nor there. After Rabbi Simon, two other Conservative rabbis led Rodef Sholom; although changes introduced in the religious services were maintained, the new spirit forcefully promoted during his tenure waned. In 1940 and 1949, the last two Orthodox rabbis in Rodef Sholom's history were elected to lead the congregation. Even though by that time the majority of its members participated in the services as modified by Rabbi Simon, "really we became Conservative only after the Synagogue-Center was established in Westmont [1952]." Even American-born residents of the secondary Jewish settlements shared this self-evaluation.[34]

At the other end of Jewish Johnstown's religious-institutional spectrum, Beth Zion Temple represented a tempered version of Reform: "Consreform" perhaps, parallel to Rodef Sholom's "Consorthodoxy." From its foundation as an informal religious congregation by a small group of German Jews in the late nineteenth century, it had followed a decidedly moderate path, most likely influenced by the more traditionalist preferences of the *poylishe* (from German-occupied Poland) among its long-term leaders, an orientation that fitted well into the generally conservative sociocultural climate of the local larger society. Main Sabbath services were held late on Friday evening, but there was no Sunday service, which in the classical Reform temple became, while not predominant, a common enough practice. Hebrew, greatly reduced or eliminated in classical Reform practices, was used to a considerable extent in services and taught as a mandatory subject in Sunday school, and traditional bar mitzvahs, which in most Reform Temples were replaced by confirmations, were maintained. When Abe Cohen, one of the early settlers in Johnstown and a founder of Beth Zion, died in 1924, at the family's request the burial service was conducted by a Conservative rabbi.[35]

In the 1920s, a dozen or so families of East European origin joined Beth Zion: some postwar immigrants and American-born couples who came to Johnstown from larger cities. In the following decade, a somewhat larger number of local families from Rodef Sholom, mostly American-born, moved to the Temple, but they usually retained their prior formal membership. The newcomers found "Consorthodox" Rodef Sholom too old-fashioned for their more decidedly Conservative practices. Among them

4.5. Social gathering, late 1930s: a get-together of the extended Beerman family. Collection of Mrs. Blanche Beerman.

were a number of professionals: over one-third of the small number of Jewish professionals in prewar Johnstown were people who settled there during the 1920s and 1930s, and they joined the Temple. Those who moved to the Temple from among Johnstown's old-time residents did so for various reasons, social and "ideological"; in the latter cases commitment to Americanism, as it was then perceived, was more important than theological preferences. Some "married into it," "joined because a friend did," or transferred as a result of personal disagreements with the Iron Street synagogue's leaders. Others, especially of the second generation, left Rodef Sholom after the departure of Rabbi Simon and his "progressive spirit"; a greater number switched to the Temple in the early 1940s, when an Orthodox rabbi once more assumed the pulpit at the Iron Street synagogue. The influx of East European families of immediate Orthodox backgrounds sustained, and likely even enhanced, the conservative elements at Beth Zion, especially since these new members' arrival coincided with the leadership of more traditionally minded (or less radically Reform) rabbis.

By mutual agreement of the officiating rabbis and the congregants, the emphasis on Hebrew was maintained in the Temple in both services and religious instruction through the 1930s. At that time there were about half a dozen six- to thirteen-year-old children in the congregation, and all went to the Sunday school, though for a few years, when Beth Zion did not have its own teacher, they attended Rodef Sholom's. Bar mitzvahs were held, and traditional *yarmlkes* (head coverings), eliminated in most Reform temples, were optional (although practically never worn) in the sanctuary. The Temple's kitchen, although not kosher according to the halakhic laws, observed biblical *kashrut,* that is, did not serve forbidden foods such as pork and shellfish.[36]

Religious and Social Life (Private)

The secularization processes transforming public religious institutions and worship in the immigrant settlements also affected private religious observance by relaxing and pluralizing the code of accepted behavior, and, generally, shrinking the scope, frequency, and strictness of ritual practices. To the outside, dominant Christian society, the members of the Jewish religious minority came to appear less "obviously" different, while on the inside, their ceremonies were being ethnicized through a fusing of old-country traditional and American middle-class elements. Inasmuch as religious practices were indeed increasingly privatized or "domesticated," as some studies have argued, the home and thus the women were becoming the main carriers of Jewish religious traditions; at the same time, it was largely the women who ethnicized this transformation of domestic religion.

As in the public sphere, however, in Johnstown all these effects, while similar in direction, differed significantly from those reported in the big cities. In the latter, a substantial diminution of Jewish religious observance occurred early, during the first-phase initial years of immigrants' stay in America, under the impact of transplantation into a new expanding urban environment with a considerably secularized mass culture. The effects of American metropolitan life were most likely stronger yet on those immigrants—a good number, as suggested in chapter 1—who came to these big cities from the already urbanized-industrialized centers in Eastern Europe and from Jewish communities in which strict religious observance had already been undermined. The diminution of Jewish religious practices intensified during the interwar period, especially among the American-born generation. Exaggerating in order to highlight the large degree of individualization—or dissipation of social control—in matters of religious practice, one observer thus characterized the situation in New York City: "Every Jew carrie[d] his own *Shulkhan Arukh* [code of Jewish conduct]," and some even embellished it, as we shall see momentarily, with American-style Christian ornaments.[37]

Asked to compare their everyday lives in Johnstown with what they remembered from the shtetls, the immigrants, men and women, emphatically described the former as "oh, MUCH less *frum* [religiously observant]!" that is, very much less regulated—in scope and rigor—by the Orthodox precepts governing daily conduct. Adjusting to the new environment, Johnstowners reshaped and diversified their *Milieufrömmigkeit,* or socially accepted ways of ritual practice. Although more pliable than in Eastern Europe, this range of group-sanctioned and practiced behavior was stricter, however, than in the big cities. When, as a teenager, Harry R. moved with his family from Johnstown to a Jewish neighborhood in Brooklyn, New York, in the 1930s, he found that before long, the whole household "became less religious [observant]."[38]

It is not possible (and, I believe, unnecessary for our purposes) to discuss here the many ritual practices required of an even moderately observant Jew of Orthodox background. I will focus on the East European group, and on three selected fundamentals: the observance of the Sabbath, *kashrut* (dietary laws), and private (unorganized) *tsdoke*.[39]

The first and foremost change my informants mentioned as evidence of a "much less *frum*" life in America was the Sabbath observance, which in the East European shtetls was a strictly practiced community affair. In America it became not only fundamentally altered, but also largely reduced to a private, family observance. With few exceptions—Johnstown did not differ in this regard from other American cities—Jews worked on the Sabbath.

The Sabbath work prohibition held strong in shtetl mores in good part because of the traditionally sanctioned cooperation of the rural Christian population, who were accustomed to the cessation of trade on Saturdays. Although the immigrants in Johnstown reestablished economic exchange with their former East European neighbors, the transplantation of the old-country Sabbath arrangement was impossible. Here, Saturday was the busiest trade day of the week, the day the mill workers and coal miners were paid their wages and went shopping with their whole families. The immigrants came to America with the determined purpose of making a better living for their families. Confronted with a new situation in which this basic goal was to be pursued, by consensus they altered the norm prohibiting Sabbath work: "It was permitted, to make a living, this was a rule among Johnstown's Jews." "In Zager [a shtetl] they'd kill you for violating Sabbath," recalled Hyman M. "Here in Portage I did work on Shabes, although I did not feel too good about it at the beginning, but I had to, to make a living, and Saturday was a business day." Nathan E. explained his father's, and other Jews', open shops on the Sabbath: "[They] came to this country without anything to make a better living, and worked very hard to give it to their families . . . it was a necessity." Benjamin I. recalled the reasons articulated by his father, an otherwise highly observant man, for working on Saturdays in his store in Boswell: "[I knew] he regretted it, but he worked on Shabes, because otherwise he would have made for us only a meager living. . . . He told us, 'One has to act in the form of *derekh erets* [way of the land, or in keeping with locally accepted social standards of behavior],' and he came to America to make a good life for the family."[40]

So conducting business on the Sabbath became from the beginning the accepted norm among Johnstown's Jews: the husbands "worked," and the wives "helped," while the young generation likewise contributed by selling and clerking. Commonly among member families of the two East European congregations, however, a family-centered and truncated form of Sabbath abstinence from work was observed. While they performed outside labor, operating the store, at home there was no work, or it was deliberately limited. Women's abstention from cooking was a prevalent observance, even in Westmont homes. In comparison, a survey conducted in 1938 in Staten Island, New York, revealed that in only 30 percent of Jewish households was there no cooking on the Sabbath; and in the early 1940s another study, focusing on families of children enrolled in religious education in one Conservative synagogue in a solidly middle-class New York City neighborhood, reported Sabbath cooking abstention in less than half the homes. In Johnstown, there was also a total or partial abstention from sewing, repairing, gardening, piano playing, and writing; these restrictions, expectedly, were most inclusive, strictly observed, and prevalent among Ahavath Achim's members; they were only minimally observed among the Temple's families of East European origin. Rodef Sholom families fell in the middle, and, generally, residence appeared a stronger influence than generational positioning: the farther the home was from the primary Jewish settlement downtown, the more permissive was the style of observance of this ethnicized Sabbath. But even in prestigious Anglo-Protestant Westmont, a considerable number of immigrant households with grown-up, coresident children kept the truncated Sabbath in a stringent manner. And although by the 1930s both generations in Westmont drove down to the synagogue, respect for the tradition prohibiting riding required symbolic compliance: cars were left out of sight some blocks from the building; in several homes, a flexible rule was the avoidance of "needless riding." The above-mentioned New York City survey reported about an equal proportion, 28 percent, of parents and children complying with this prohibition; a contemporaneous study of Sabbath observance in a "medium-size metropolitan center" in the Midwest found "an almost complete disappearance of the taboo of riding in vehicles on the Sabbath," without even a weakened, make-believe remnant.[41]

More fully shared by Johnstowners with their big-city fellow ethnics was the Friday night lighting of candles, a ritual performed by women, and the traditional family meal. Both New York studies quoted above found about 70 percent of households observing this ritual; and in the Grand Concourse section of the Bronx, the residence of newly *arrivés* middle-class Jewish families, the Friday night meal tended to be the only vestige of Sabbath observance.[42] In Johnstown, the lighting of candles and the Sabbath meal took place in most East European homes regardless of synagogue membership, residence, and generation, but when the husband or father was occupied in the store after the start of the Sabbath, he was often absent or arrived home late. Even if occasional, this socially sanctioned withdrawal of the male head of the household from the Sabbath home scene placed the observance of this ritual, traditionally female-managed in the preparatory phase, more fully under women's guardianship. This was a substantial change from the situation that had prevailed in the shtetl, where the man presided over the family gathering, reciting the *kidesh*, the blessing over wine, to welcome the holy day; leading the *zmires*, devotional songs after meals on the Sabbath; and performing the *havdole*, ceremony at its close.[43]

Two opposite theses coexist in historical studies of the transformations in religious life of American Jews: that the center of the "preservation of Jewishness" was moving away from the home and into the synagogue, and, conversely, that it was shifting in the opposite direction. This contradiction seems to result from multiple confusions in these propositions: from different understandings of the concept of "Jewishness"—ethnic (here in the sense of *folk* or a people with a common history), religious, or both; application to different branches of American Judaism—Reform or Conservative; and the vaguely specified timing of the transition in question.[44] In prewar Johnstown, among East Europeans, neither the synagogue nor the home, as I examined their operation, appeared to have absorbed or superseded the functions of the other. Nor did the recollections of my informants from that period bring back a sense of a shift in either direction. When I asked which place served as the center of religious life, after reflection, their common answer was "Both." But in surrounding townlets it was clearly the home, quite simply "because there was no shul."

As in public religion, however, we may consider the process of secularization of Jewish religious observance in the private sphere as a progressive uncoupling of its once undistinguishable religious and ethnic components, the former receding as the latter expanded, and we may assess women's role in this development.

The private counterpart to Conservative Judaism's program for transforming East European Orthodoxy in the public sphere emphasized the Jewish home as a "miniature temple" made "up to . . . modern standards." This appeal was addressed primarily to women in large part by women, the same group that had become active in the public forum in synagogue life— the Sisterhoods affiliated with the Women's League of Conservative Judaism. Such spokeswomen reiterated the importance, in fact, the primacy, of women's obligation to "the ennoblement and beautifying of the home through the Jewish life that there prevails." As indicated by numerous literary and popular memoirs, autobiographies, and oral life histories from the interwar period—most of them, again, from New York and the few largest Jewish settlements—the women indeed acted to uphold Jewishness in the home, but in popular practice not "all that is [spiritually] notable in Judaism [was] bred and fostered."[45]

Jewish domestic life in these big urban centers, as managed by women assisted by advice from proliferating middle-class magazines such as *The Jewish Woman and Her Home* or *The Jewish Home Beautiful* (see below), was acquiring more of a folk-ethnic and less of a religious character. Increasingly, especially in the second generation, the essence of the Sabbath experience was becoming the smell and taste of special foods on the table. *Fressfrömmigkeit*, gastronomic or "kitchen" Judaism—as commentators have described this reduced, secularized observance in Jewish families increasingly comfortable in their big-city middle-class homes—could be viewed as a parallel to the secularizing "pool-with-a-school-and-a-shul" development in the public religious sphere.[46]

In Johnstown, to the extent that Sabbath observance at home was also becoming focused on the celebration of food, women—the executors of this ritual—played a generally similar, instrumental role in its ethnicization qua secularization. But the decor was much more modest. I found merely two intermittent subscribers to the Jewish ladies' housekeeping magazines so popular in the 1920s–1930s among New York *arrivistes*, and the ritual objects—old-country brass candlesticks, kiddush cups, and copper pots for making the Shabes dishes—were used in active service, whereas in many an uptown New York household they were displayed, if present at all, as decorative memorabilia from a time past. Perhaps a major difference, and a sign of Johnstowners' greater traditionalism, was that even in successful Westmont the ritual meal appeared to have retained a shrunken but still clearly detectable religious dimension. By "detectable" and "religious" I mean the ready references my informants made (I did not notice gender difference) to the normative base of this residuum of the integrally observed Sabbath. In Johnstown, recollections of culinary pleasures, while no less vivid than the New Yorkers', were accompanied by an extra "we are *Jews* [so] we *should* do it" attitude toward the Friday night ritual. By evoking membership in the Jewish peoplehood as the source of obligation, they implicitly reaffirmed the core scheme-value concept of traditional Judaism: indivisibility of people and religion.

The more secularized the outer social environment of Jewish homes, the more reduced was their religious observance to "kitchen Judaism," and, at the same time, the greater was the share of American elements in Jewish eating habits. *Kashrut* or Jewish dietary laws were cast off first in public places. In large settlements of East European Jews in the big cities, particularly in diversified and cosmopolitan New York, nonkosher bars and restaurants were reportedly frequented from the beginning of the century by a number of immigrants eager to taste the new world; amid the social flux accompanying the great migration, popular opinion *nolens volens* consented to this breach of tradition. As an increasing proportion of Jews in the urban centers assumed ethnicized middle-class lifestyles during the interwar period, *oysesn*, eating out, became an accustomed recreational pursuit, and Jews increasingly patronized all-American (non-Jewish) eateries. More popular in the interwar period, however, became the new "kosher-style" restaurants and delicatessens, which responded to the need of an emerging majority (particularly among the second generation) for an "American-looking" lifestyle with built-in components of folk Jewish tradition. These institutions, another product of the secularization-ethnicization of religious observance, served foodstuffs that were not ritually kosher according to religious law, but met the criteria of ethnic Jewishness: they carried a Jewish name; the food—a mix of Jewish and American ingredients—had a traditional-looking Jewish label; the owner and clientele were Jewish, and there was a familiar Jewish aura in the place. In its genre, the kosher-style restaurant, like other Jewish adaptations of the period, was a solution to a dilemma that weighed on many minds: it allowed people to step out of tradition while still remaining within it.[47]

Like other changes in social and religious life, the practice of eating out appeared among Johnstowners of East European origin much later, on a much smaller scale, and was more closely monitored by local opinion. In a small town whose commercial and recreational hub centered on a few blocks, an unusual action could easily attract the attention of a fellow ethnic passing by or a Jewish shopkeeper looking out from his store; the news then circulated by word of mouth. By the 1930s eating in nonkosher restaurants, "but not the forbidden foods," was practiced occasionally by some—as they referred to themselves—"more modern liberal" Jews from Rodef Sholom, most of them American-born and from the newer residential locations; *oysesn* was not practiced among Ahavath Achim people. The "modern liberals" tended to hold dual membership in Rodef Sholom and Beth Zion, and many were postwar arrivals from larger cities. While the traditionalists expressed disapproval of this heterodox practice, it did not elicit the social anathema it would have triggered in the shtetl. I heard about only two instances of outright condemnation of nonkosher eating in public view. Both concerned persons in positions of leadership at Rodef Sholom who "should have known better" than to enact a public desecration that provided a negative example to others; public, in this case, referred to the Jewish audience rather than to the Gentile one, who would not have understood the significance of the action.[48]

Johnstowners apparently did not feel a strong enough need to establish a kosher-style delicatessen of the type increasingly favored by their big-city counterparts; instead, the two Jewish food markets in town, which also sold lunch sandwiches and beverages, advertised themselves in synagogue bulletins as "strictly kosher." Also kosher—not kosher-style—was a Jewish-owned hotel-restaurant where big wedding receptions were held, as were the prestigious UJA banquets at which participants made public financial pledges. The lack of a pressing social need for kosher-style eating places in prewar Johnstown delineated more narrowly the local boundaries of Jewishness; as one of my informants pointed out, reflecting on this matter, "So if you'd want to step out [of the strict rules of *kashrut*], there was no Jewish place to do so, you had to go to a Gentile [restaurant]."[49]

As shown by interwar surveys of Jewish religious practices, compared with eating behavior in public, the observance of *kashrut* in the home generally retained more of its traditional rigor. As would be expected, how-

ever, in middle-class homes in metropolitan centers, Jewish kitchens and
the cooks who presided in them secularized/ethnicized more quickly, and
absorbed more of the dominant society's middle-class standards of food
preparation and serving than did their counterparts in less "veltlekhe"
small towns like Johnstown.

Three studies conducted in the late 1930s and early 1940s in New York
City examined religious observance in middle-class Jewish families of East
European origin who identified themselves as Conservative. All three independently reported that about 70 percent ate only kosher meat at home,
and less than two-thirds observed the injunction requiring separate dishes
for meat and dairy products. Another study (1938) in a town within the
New York metropolitan area found that "kosher meat is still bought and
the dietary laws are still observed" in the majority of "nominally Orthodox" Jewish homes (no percentage figure was given), although individual
members of the same families, particularly of the American-born generation, "when not at home, seldom hesitate to eat nonkosher food, and even
forbidden meats."[50] While a growing proportion of Conservative and
"nominally Orthodox" Jews abandoned the dietary laws even in their
homes—about one-third of the families in the studies in two New York
City boroughs quoted above—those who continued to observe *kashrut*
practiced it in what they termed a "modern American style."

From the beginning of the century, Yiddish-language publications like
the New York-based *Froyen Velt* (Women's world) and home sections in
popular newspapers gave East European immigrant women lessons in
"modern housekeeping," including keeping a kosher kitchen. In New
York's Lower East Side and in other large immigrant settlements in metropolitan centers, German Jewish social workers—women already familiar
with American middle-class lifestyles—carried on a civilizing mission, as
they perceived their project, aimed at modernizing immigrant homes (an
undertaking parallel to their male counterparts' efforts in transforming the
Orthodox synagogue). Among other domestic programs for adolescent
girls, female garment workers, and young housewives from the tenements,
the instructors in settlement houses offered regular and well-attended
courses on clean and healthy cooking, aesthetic table setting, and proper
manners as practiced in genteel society.

In the interwar period, when a large number of East European Jews
moved into the white-collar strata and comfortable living quarters in more
prestigious neighborhoods, the women, "freed" into middle-class idleness,
devoted much of their time to upkeep of the family's elevated status
through activities in the kitchen and dining room. For guidance in these
domestic pursuits, greatly facilitated by technical innovations in housekeeping, Jewish housewives relied on "the science of kosher cooking" provided by an array of cookbooks; the best-sellers, like the *Jewish Cook Book*
or *Fannie Fox's Cookbook*, went through several editions, each printed in
tens of thousands of copies. Women also turned to popular food columns

in the women's journals—the Yiddish *Froyen Zhurnal* and *The Jewish Home Beautiful*, both fashioned after mainstream American magazines like *Good Housekeeping* or *Ladies Home Journal*. These culinary counsels instructed women on integrating modern American and Jewish cuisines by combining the use of commercial food products (shortening, biscuits, etc.) and the New Nutrition theories advocating "attractive-looking, healthy and well-balanced diets" with the "flavor of mother's cooking" and *kashrut*.[51] The latter, however, while taken for granted in most East European homes, had all but lost its religious symbolism, as the family cooks concentrated on the wholly mundane task of perfecting the right blend of old-country folk and American modern dishes to be served on the fashionably set dining room table.

In contrast to the large urban Jewish settlements, in prewar Johnstown almost no East European homes had abandoned *kashrut*, although a certain range of accepted deviation from the traditional norms of the shtetl was accepted: the women called it "cutting the edges" or "a more streamlined way."[52] The strictest and most traditional observance involved separate dishes for meat and dairy products (and additional sets for Passover), which were replaced or rekoshered in a prescribed ritual if a mistake occurred; food purchased at local kosher markets; and chicken for the Sabbath meal brought to the shul every week to be slaughtered by the *shoykhet*. This level of observance prevailed among the immigrant and second-generation member families of Ahavath Achim, and, even though it required a much greater effort, among families in the outlying towns. It was also practiced in a large number of Rodef Sholom's homes, though more in the primary than in the secondary Jewish settlements. Interestingly, not a few women in the latter, partisans of the Conservative reforms in the synagogue, conducted strictly kosher households. As they explained, they did this "out of deeply instilled habits and respect for tradition." Evidently, it was easier to transgress Orthodoxy by assuming new roles and identities in the public religious sphere from which traditional Jewish law had excluded women than to eradicate old habits pertaining to their familiar domain—the deeply internalized "domestic religion" absorbed from earliest childhood.[53]

A slightly relaxed but still fairly strict way of observing *kashrut* (apparently without scrupulous rekoshering of mistakenly polluted kitchen utensils), although uncommon among the East European member-families of the Reform Temple, was followed by some young American-born couples "for the parents" if the latter lived in the same household or visited their children and would not otherwise have eaten in their homes. And there was also a more "modern liberal" or "streamlined" way of keeping a kosher household: although the dishes were separate ("Everyone had them," "It was normal"), there was "no constant vigilance which plate might have been used for what," but "of course meat was koshered," and "the whole works [very involved ritual preparations] for Passover." These practices prevailed in secondary Jewish settlements and in the homes of Rodef Sholom's members; a number of Beth Zion's new affiliates, American-born women from local old-timer families of East European origin, also continued keeping their homes in this way.[54]

The modern housekeeping appliances and easy and practical commercial foods that proliferated in America during the interwar period also eased kitchen work in Johnstown. Like their big-city counterparts, local Jewish women were ethnicizing or "updating" their cooking and eating habits. Like innovations in public celebrations, however, these modifications were much smaller in form and content, and for similar reasons: first, conservative, hardworking Johnstown was no leader in fancy modern cookery, and, second, the economic condition—the insecure prosperity—of the majority of Jewish households did not permit the lavishness noted among their upwardly mobile counterparts in the big cities. Because of the greater, and steadier, economic affluence of German Jews, and because of the absence of religious dietary restrictions, it is true that their kitchens were ethnicized with a larger American component, but still far from the conspicuous consumption of their metropolitan fellow ethnics. Johnstown had none of the preparatory courses in "modern housekeeping" offered by German Jewish ladies; indeed, if a small group of the German-Jewish women had shown interest in such an undertaking, the student body would have been minuscule, so busy were the immigrant households, wives and daughters included, in collectively making a living. The women's simultaneous involvement in family businesses and household financial management put them in a field of contradictory forces, as it were, that in comparison with the situation of big-city middle-class Jewish housewives allowed on balance for less time to invest in "updating" their home life, less autonomy in decision making, and lesser spending power.

The shared primary emphasis in the Johnstown Jewish community on a "decent lifestyle" as the main goal and measure of accomplishment enhanced the authority of the women-as-managers of its domestic form and content, and motivated them toward "updating" both. At the same time, however, their firsthand knowledge of the daily running of a business made them keenly aware of its actual and potential problems. This personal involvement and practical know-how in matters of small entrepreneurship kept in check, within the clear limits of the possible, the Johnstown women's ambitions to keep their home life up to date, and, in fact, often dictated economizing on household expenditures.

Nevertheless, in the interwar period, as Jewish families were moving to nicer living quarters and better neighborhoods, their food became more diversified, lighter and greener; the latter "update" was facilitated by the possibility of purchasing fruit and vegetables very cheaply from farmers in the surrounding countryside who came with their produce to Johnstown on market days from June through October. The ethnicized diets were still kosher and retained folk Jewish dishes, but once the protein- and calorie-laden old-country dishes ceased to be the exclusive menu, they acquired a more middle-class American look and content. However, my women-informants had no recollection of "the science of kosher cooking" or the "New Nutrition theories"—so much on the public and private domestic agendas of socially mobile and culturally aspiring New Yorkers—as a matter of special personal interest, or as a subject of conversation with other housekeepers. "Things were more simple here [in Johnstown]": this recurrent motto also appeared in the context of innovations in domestic dietary habits, with no significant difference apparent between East European and German homes.

The culinary innovations introduced by Johnstown women were not only modest in scope, but also adjustable—easily reduced or entirely eliminated should the economic conditions require. This ready flexibility was particularly useful during the bad years of the Great Depression, when the ethnic(-ized) character of local Jewish kitchens became distinctly much stronger in old-country tastes and flavors. Even if the reasons for this culinary traditionalism were primarily financial, its consumers did not dislike it. The socially arrived American-born Westmonters did not recall—as did their peers from the big cities, according to common accounts—making faces "at traditional Jewish potpourri-like thick soup, and requesting that boiled cabbage, onions, and parsnips be replaced with the new-style fresh lettuce, celery, and asparagus tips." Another, and related, difference between second-generation Johnstowners and their big-city peers—in this case, young women—appears to have been the absence of conflict between the daughters and their mothers concerning "updating" family kitchens and home life in general.[55] I noted in chapter 3 occasional confrontations between fathers and sons regarding the modernization of ways of conducting business. The absence of equivalent misunderstandings between mothers and daughters in their gender-specific area of ethnicization (if I did not overlook or misinterpret something) was probably due to a combination of two factors: unlike immigrant fathers discussed in this context in the previous chapter, immigrant mothers were themselves interested in such updating, and these innovations were indeed quite modest (but young men's initiatives were not on a grand scale, either).

As mentioned earlier, neither *Froyen Zhurnal*, for the immigrant women, nor *The Jewish Home Beautiful*, addressed primarily to the American-born generation, had more than a couple of local subscribers, and I found hardly any users of Jewish-American cookbooks (or any others, for that matter). According to my informants, the immigrant women cooked mainly "from their heads." New ideas were communicated at social occasions in Johnstown, as well as during private visits or Sisterhood and Hadassah meetings in the larger cities. Sometimes new recipes were also taken from the Yiddish press. The American-born women told me they learned primarily from their mothers, and—like the latter—locally from each other, or from kin and acquaintances in Philadelphia, New York, or

4.6. Mr. Samuel
Fainberg in front of
his kosher market, and
Mrs. Helen Spiegel
leaving, early 1940s.
Collection of the
Spiegel family.

other cities where they had connections. To my questions about high
school cooking classes—one direct avenue for learning American ways and
possibly adapting them to kosher gastronomy at home—the repeated reaction was that, at Johnstown High in any case, these classes were rather
uninspiring and the menus unappetizing; the main culprit seems to have
been the ubiquitous white sauce.

Not unexpectedly, these recollections reveal two important similarities
with the public life discussed earlier in this chapter: the persistence of personal and informal means of bringing in and implementing new ways of
action, and its imitative character, or reliance on secondhand resources in
innovating. As in the public sphere, too, these characteristics reinforced
elements of continuity and slowed change in Jewish homes.

The last practice of domestic religion to be considered here is *tsdoke*—
the religiously grounded obligation to perform deeds of loving-kindness;
specifically, caring for and giving to others in need. Several studies exist on

prewar Jewish philanthropy—*tsdoke*'s public and organized form—and
there are many accounts of the generosity of outstanding individual contributors to Jewish and public causes. However, aside from scattered references in memoirs and oral history collections, I was unable to find any systematic comparative information on the observance of *tsdoke* in ordinary
American Jewish homes during the interwar period.

Of all my informants' recollections of domestic rituals, *tsdoke* seemed to
have the most explicit—or perhaps most explicitly expressed—religious reference: "religious" in the sense used earlier regarding Friday-night Sabbath
meals, as an obligation inherent in being part of *Klal Yisroel*, the Jewish
people. At the same time, this call to acts of kindness has been, among
Jewish precepts, the easiest to transfer outside group boundaries to encompass all Americans, and all humanity. This kind of extension was program-
matic in nineteenth-century German Reform Judaism; and, as attested by
both deeds and proclamations of East European Jews during the interwar
period, de-folksified *tsdoke* as universal altruism, although not the dominant trend, was professed by many, particularly among the second generation.[56] In Johnstown, however, a confluence of outer- and inner-group
circumstances sustained a predominantly particularistic, inward-oriented
practice of caring and giving.

The two preceding chapters demonstrated the prominent role of the
practice of mutual responsibility through assistance to fellow Jews in the
development and continuation of the Jewish economic niche in Johnstown. Commenting on concrete instances of such help given or received,
my informants pointed to pragmatic considerations as well as to the religiously sanctioned social norm of interpersonal relations. Assisting others
when a particular need arose was strongly emphasized by mothers and fathers, regardless of synagogue affiliation, residence, or generational status,
as a *mitsve*, a good deed or act of righteousness, and as a response to the
social expectation-obligation to keep "a good Jewish environment."

As we have seen, organized Jewish philanthropy in Johnstown in large
part retained a *gemeinschaftlich* character during the interwar period and so
blended well with domestic *tsdoke*. In addition to donations paid directly to
synagogue-related philanthropies and pledged to local collectors for outside Jewish causes, and contributions made at various social events sponsored by these organizations, the most private form of *tsdoke*, traditionally
practiced in Eastern Europe, continued in most Jewish homes throughout
the 1930s, regardless of generation and place of residence. This was the
pushkes, little boxes for charity attached to the wall or placed in the kitchen
cupboard. As noted earlier, this collection was supervised by wives and
mothers, and, within the domestic sphere, was in fact quite "organized."
In immigrant homes there were commonly several *pushkes*, each for a different purpose, and every week before Shabes small change was put into
them by the wife and children—a few pennies, a nickel perhaps; here for
Jewish hospitals, orphanages, or educational institutions in America, there

for yeshiva students, for a hospital in Palestine, for needy Jews in Eastern Europe, or for those persecuted in Germany. In second-generation homes, the number of *pushkes* was usually reduced to one or two.[57]

"All were expected to give some . . . but who was big was expected to give big"; "You gave what you could, if more comes to you, more you should give away"—so commented my informants while recollecting the ways in which public and private *tsdoke* was practiced in prewar Johnstown. Incomplete records of contributions to the German Relief Fund and later to the United Jewish Appeal during the 1930s, the only such records preserved, illustrate how it worked. Despite the Depression, the majority of Jewish families in town—over two-thirds, as name lists indicate—made donations: a total of $2,500 was collected during 1934, $2,300 in the following year, and, as the economy improved, $8,300 in 1938, and $21,000 in 1939. The "big" ones indeed gave the most: over 70 percent of the total—the greatest portion of which was collected at public fund-raisers—came from the dozen-odd most affluent families, or 5 percent of all contributors. The rest were little donations, some one-time, some from the accumulated contents of family *pushkes*, depending on the family's economic circumstances.[58]

The circumstances of particular households also dictated the amounts and regularity of financial assistance sent back to the shtetls, primarily to kin, but, means permitting, also for such communal needs as renovating an old synagogue, a new Torah scroll, or Passover wine and matzos for the local poor. This form of *tsdoke* was practiced by the immigrants rather than the second generation: assistance to families left in Eastern Europe—mostly by mail, as very few Johnstowners traveled overseas between the two wars—was sent by both men and women, while charitable donations for communal needs were given, or "authored," exclusively by men, and only the more affluent ones. The Gee Bee clan, for example, successful owners of the Johnstown department store that employed so many local Jewish youth, had one of their relatives act as manager of old-country charities: "He was the bookkeeper for between fifty and sixty families in Antopolie until Hitler destroyed them. Regularly he would send a list of names and amounts of money to be given to them by the *shames* (sexton) in Antopolie."[59]

Hakhnoses Orkhim, assisting itinerants, functioned in Johnstown in two overlapping forms: the organized form, previously discussed, and—another old-country tradition that survived through the 1930s—aid delivered privately by individual families. Such passing visitors were brought home, usually by the father or husband, from the kosher market near the railroad station, or from a store downtown, and—this role was the woman's—fed, and sometimes offered a bed for the night. This practice was more frequent (and more convenient for both guests and hosts) in the downtown sections of town, but itinerants in Westmont homes were not unusual. Isadore G.'s father "often brought fellows home after the Sabbath service, un-Americanized types, they did not speak much English, and sometimes they spent a night"; in Ruth B.'s family, "mother had open home, especially during holidays, cooked plenty and put the food out, and people were brought in to eat," and when she married and set up her own household nearby, the practice was continued. Both public and private *Hakhnoses Orkhim* ceased by the 1940s, as Jewish itinerants all but stopped coming, either because the postwar economic boom helped them gain an independent livelihood, or because the needy were by then sufficiently taken care of by professional Jewish agencies.[60]

"Plain, Orthodox Jews," as the immigrants described their families in the European shtetls, professed their religion by "living Jewish," not by theologizing. In Johnstown too, whether practiced in more old-country traditional or more ethnic-American ways, it remained experience-near, or part of the habitus: done, or felt, rather than reflected on and analyzed. There was not much discussion in Jewish homes about the reasons and meaning of the practices observed. While their life-philosophies remained in touch with the Great Tradition (see chapter 6), most immigrants, and their children as well, were not learned enough to engage in Talmudic in-terpretation. "We learned by doing, not by talking about it"; "As part of being Jewish, there were things done to fulfill the obligation"; "It was nat-urally instilled in my system"; "The parents did not articulate much about it, did not dissect, we were raised Jewish, it was what we were supposed to do"—this was the typical way children were socialized into religious prac-tices at home.[61]

A self-explanatory *du bist a yid* (You are Jewish, so you do [or you don't]) was repeated in Yiddish or English, regarding religion-related prac-tices. "You go to the religious school, Jews do this"; "You eat in a certain way [kosher, whether in a more or a less strict fashion], it's part of Jewish religion"; "There are things not done on the Sabbath [whether refrained from completely or only limited]"; "Give, or help, it's a Jewish way, a *mitsve* [whether charity to the *pushkes* or through a youth organization in a fund-raising drive, or some other form of assistance]."[62]

In the large cities during the interwar years—mostly New York, and a few other metropolises—contemporary observers noted widespread con-tention in matters of religious observance between American-born children and their East European parents.[63] Not in Johnstown: regardless of syna-gogue membership and residential location, neither the immigrants nor the second generation recalled much conflict at home between parents and children about "things done" involved in being Jewish. The children ex-pressed "some unhappiness": boys from more strictly observant homes la-mented that "instead of playing ball after school [we] had to go to the [daily] *kheyder*"; boys and girls were required to go to Sunday school rather than "for a walk or whatever"; and religious services were "so long, they *davened* and *davened* for hours." But most of them remembered that "un-happiness," though recurrent, to have been momentary, and, though without particular enthusiasm, they accepted their *du bist a yid* condition and its requirements.[64]

In the large cities, the "revolt of the second generation" regarding religious observance was facilitated by that group's much greater personal autonomy. Increased space for personal choice was created by several factors: employment outside the ethnic niche, more advanced secularization of the external environment, and the combination of greater diversification and much laxer social control within local Jewish society. In Johnstown, because of its size, conservatism, and relative isolation, conditions were of a much more settled, "of course" nature, to borrow the phrase of Robert and Helen Lynd, in their classic 1930s study, *Middletown*.[65] Inside the Jewish community, the integration of the two generations within an enclosed ethnic society, along with the lack of secular alternatives to being Jewish without alienating oneself from the group, diluted religious conflicts between parents and children. An eloquent index of the continued traditionalism of Johnstown Jews, shared by the two generations, was that the practice of installing a Christmas tree "for the children" was socially impossible in Johnstown, though reports from the late 1930s and early 1940s indicate that Christmas trees had become increasingly common in Jewish homes in the Upper West Side of Manhattan. The New Yorkers, apparently—at any rate, those who purchased the tree—stripped it of its religious, Christian symbolism, secularizing it to signify participation in a national, American festivity. For the Johnstowners, the tree retained its inherent Gentile religious symbolism and could not be adopted as an ethnic custom. My American-born informants emphatically denied even contemplating such an idea ("Not even an Easter egg!").[66]

This brings us to the last part of this section: social and other recreational activities at home and in primary group circles. General developments that shaped organized social life in Jewish settlements in America during the interwar years also influenced its private side. This period saw a rapid expansion and diversification of mass culture and popular entertainment in the society at large; simultaneously, in the Jewish group, lifestyles were ethnicized as they absorbed common urban American middle-class forms. As a result of these parallel trends, increasingly more, and new, leisure-time activities were pursued both in the homes and outside within the ethnic community as well as "out in the world." Like other changes, these transformations appeared much earlier, and occurred more thoroughly, in the big cosmopolitan cities than in towns like Johnstown, and so the primary group's social and cultural life in these two settings differed in pace and character.

Contemporary accounts, memoirs, and oral life histories of East European Jews who at the turn of the century made their homes in New York and other big cities tell how overwhelmed the immigrants were by "city lights" and the variety of new ways to spend free time the metropolis offered. The most serious-minded could (and in fact did in considerable numbers) attend educational and cultural events regularly held in American public libraries or other institutions. There were musical concerts and, for the less sophisticated, Broadway musicals, which also toured other cities. Theater was enormously popular, with offerings in Yiddish and soon also in English of acclaimed Jewish plays as well as adapted world classics; all larger Jewish urban settlements in the United States supported at least one permanent theater, and between seasons they were visited by the New York troupes. Dance halls—over thirty on the Lower East Side alone in the first decade of the century—coexisted with soda shops and nickelodeons on almost every corner. Other pastimes included boat rides, beach trips in the summer, long weekend promenades along the better streets of town, and window-shopping. In 1928, the invention of talkies made moviegoing the prime form of popular entertainment nationwide, but in the metropolises other recreational opportunities proliferated: music and theater projects, public concerts, plays, cultural festivals, art exhibits, public parks, as well as golf courses, tennis courts, and riding stables—making these previously socially exclusive sports far more accessible to the middle class.[67]

As they advanced in the American social structure, big-city Jews, particularly the second generation, made these diverse activities part of their recreational habits. A 1935 study of the social-cultural pursuits of New York youth of different economic and national backgrounds found young Jews "outstanding in the extent to which each sex engages in a wide range of recreations," including reading and visits to concert halls, theaters, and museums; and, conversely, least likely to "have the limited type of recreation" represented by the combination of moviegoing, visiting family and friends, playing cards, and "doing nothing special." The authors ascribed the interest of young Jews in more ambitious leisure activities to their relatively higher economic status and educational level, and, second, to group traditions such as "the intellectual aspirations of the Jewish people."[68]

Assuming that intellectual aspirations have indeed been an element of the Jewish people's cultural heritage, Johnstown's environment, unlike New York's, failed to stimulate these schemas-predispositions among Jews who would then apply them as resources for socioeconomic upward mobility. Compared with their big-city fellow ethnics, Jewish people in Johnstown—both the immigrant and American-born generation, and virtually regardless of occupational status (i.e., including professionals)—spent their unorganized free time on those activities the New York study called culturally limited recreation, and most of these activities remained centered on one's own and friends' extended families.

A 1937 enumeration of the town's main attractions listed the natural scenery of the surrounding hills, the municipal stadium and swimming pool, "Pennsylvania's finest department store outside of Philadelphia and Pittsburgh," the Luna Park and a picnic ground at the city's outskirts, the recreational auditorium on Main Street that served as a dance hall and arena for basketball games, boxing matches, and roller-skating, eleven theaters showing movies, Broadway and vaudeville plays by visiting troupes, and the road shows of popular magicians. Higher culture was represented by a public library with 37,500 volumes (the 1952 report counted about the same number), several choral societies performing in churches, and, still in the organizing stage, the Johnstown Municipal Symphony Orchestra, which replaced a short-lived opera company and gave irregularly scheduled concerts in the junior high school's auditorium; the orchestra acquired its own building and became a permanent feature of the town's cultural life after World War II.[69]

While Johnstown Jews did appreciate music, there were no devotees for whom, as for some of their New York counterparts, "going to the opera and to concerts was 'almost as important as food' "; nor were they frequent guests in the library. Leisure reading at home meant, in most households, Jewish and local Johnstown papers, and, time permitting, popular novels: the second generation preferred American authors, while the immigrants liked Sholom Aleichem and a few other renowned Yiddish novelists. Fewer than a dozen homes, in my estimation, had somewhat larger private libraries; about the same number subscribed on and off during the interwar period to the Jewish Publication Society, a publisher and book club with higher cultural-educational aspirations. Although it relates to postwar years, an evaluation of Johnstown Jews' intellectual interests and reading habits by a Hungarian-born Jewish owner of a fine local bookstore is also apt for the earlier period: "Johnstown is considered a very poor book market [reaches about 50 percent of the national figure in per capita expenditure on books] . . . the Jewish community [most of the Jewish families are retail merchants or nonscience professionals, lawyers, and doctors] is not in any way better or worse than other groups here . . . expresses little intellectual curiosity and spends very little on books of more than superficial meaning. . . . Novels, when asked for, must be light, humorous, or entertaining, not too highbrow or intellectual. . . . Books for pre-school and elementary school children are hardly ever purchased. . . . Junior and senior high school students do buy paperback books but rarely beyond assigned requirements."[70]

The most popular social outings "on the town" were to movies and vaudeville shows, attended, as could be expected, more keenly by the younger than the older generation. The latter usually went as husband-and-wife couples ("not often, though, because there was little free time"), the former in groups of friends or with dates, who were also taken to dances (dating non-Jewish partners will be discussed in the next chapter). In addition, young men played sports, but there were not many independent outside leisure activities for women; the case was different in New York, where already by the turn of the century immigrant girls had developed their own leisure culture, separate from the home.[71] In Johnstown, even simple activities—promenades downtown and window-shopping at the "finest department store outside Philadelphia and Pittsburgh" and a couple of other elegant ones nearby—were limited by the small size of the town, and apart from Luna Park, there were no public amusements like New York's open pageants, boat trips, and beaches for young women to attend alone.

Aside from the movie theaters, shows, dances, and sports—events young people attended by themselves—the most popular pastimes were visiting homes, playing cards, and car rides and picnics on Sundays, which involved larger groupings of family and friends that combined the two generations. Leisure social activities thus constituted yet another territory, in addition to work-group-organized life and home religious observance, that was to a large extent shared by older and younger people.

Open houses, an accustomed feature of social life in the shtetl, remained common among most families in Johnstown, both immigrant and second-generation alike, and regardless of synagogue affiliation and residence. "On Sundays [and whenever there was some free time], there were always some people, relatives or neighbors, coming to the house, just to sit, eat something, and talk." Since in America as in Eastern Europe such visits traditionally involved food, the women served at these impromptu socials, whether the conversation engaged them or the men alone. In similar gatherings of children, the girls served the boys as an "of course" matter absorbed from their parents. "We waited on boys"—second-generation women recollected their childhood—"we learned it from mothers, this deference to men, that they get [things] first."[72]

Longer prearranged visits involved playing cards, perhaps the favorite form of informal socializing across generational, economic, and congregational groups, as well as, time permitting, a common pastime of husbands and wives at home alone. An expression of the ethnicization of this leisure activity, already practiced in the European shtetls, was that it now included women, even gender-mixed groups, and that it was often accompanied by popular ethnic (Jewish-American) tunes from gramophone records, or American music from the radio. Unlike young New Yorkers, however, "keyed to the pace of city life," second-generation Johnstowners did not recollect getting "crazy about ragtime music" and, by and large culturally unrebellious, found Jewish melodies pleasant to the ear.[73]

Together with the previously mentioned "modern housekeeping" and "scientific kosher cookery," under the aegis of middle-class women a new, ethnicized form of more elaborate socializing emerged in the metropolitan centers: receptions by invitation intended to display the house as "a showcase of increased affluence," the culinary skills of the hostess, and the social graces and artistic (usually musical) talents of family members.[74] After a delay, as with other innovations, such private receptions, with invited guests, and a sit-down meal or a buffet, followed by piano- or violin-playing, or singing, first appeared in immigrant homes in the secondary settlements. These receptions were also managed by women, who had a clear-cut agenda: "To upgrade the family, to be involved [socially] with the

Jewish community"—my informant mentioned these two purposes in con-
junction—"you should have culture and a house to show." Johnstown
women were as status-conscious as their big-city counterparts, but the dis-
plays were different.[75]

"Culture" required social graces. In Johnstown homes, training in good
manners was carried out in the Yiddish idiom, combining shtetl notions of
appropriate—*sheyne*, or nice and gentle—behavior with American middle-
class rules of proper conduct. "Mother did not like boorishness, she had it
from the old country"; "[she] wanted for us culture in the house, bad manners was *dos past nit*, this isn't becoming, and *azoy nit sheyn*, that isn't
nice." "From the *Forverts*, there was the etiquette column in the *Forverts*,
and [Mother] had a special book about etiquette, in Jewish"—there had
been many similar guides on Americanization put out by the Hebrew Publishing Company; when she established her own household, my second-
generation informant purchased the English version. But, while sensitive to
making a good impression, middle-class Jewish hostesses in Johnstown did
not consciously try to remake themselves into "American ladies" like their
contemporaries in New York who, according to contemporary representations, "[went] to beauty parlors, dieted, polished their English, and even
tried to change their voices and inflections [to sound more refined]."[76]

Showing off the house was another function of private social receptions.
As discussed at length in the previous chapter, and reiterated here in connection with managing the kitchen, Jewish housewives in town, even those
in Westmont (a few of the most affluent excepted), were cautious with
spending money, even when business was good. This permanent financial
consideration, shared by the majority of women-managers of home-and-
family appearance, and the general unpretentiousness of Johnstown's surroundings, made the setting of these novel social occasions look less sump-
tuous, glittery than in the "arrived" Jewish neighborhoods of Brooklyn or
the Bronx in New York. In the latter, Jewish "American ladies" received
their guests in "parlors" decorated, if finances permitted, according to "the
prevailing American notions of home decor" depicted in *House Beautiful*
or *American Home*. In the interwar period, the style was grandiose: tufted
upholstery and gilded leather finishing, heavy cut-glass bowls, cumbrous
draperies.[77] To compose the picture for Johnstown, I asked for descriptions, and I inspected old photographs and a cross-sample of house inven-
tories provided in wills filed in Cambria County Courthouse in the 1920s
and 1930s. Even in the generally better-off German-Jewish homes more
permeated with middle-class American elements, the interiors, were, like
the cookery, more modest and functional. In prevalent practice, furnishings for the house, including the living room (not generally a "parlor")
shown off to guests, were bought on the local market, or, better yet,
bought via mail order from Sears and Roebuck—for many a socially aspiring Johnstown Jewish woman the epitome of modern elegance.[78]

Increased concern with elegant and fashionable dress was also, like an investment in home decor, a reflection of the expanding consumer culture and role of entertainment in people's everyday life. In the big cities, a combination of elements fostered a preoccupation among middle-class Jews with fashionable appearance *à l'Américaine.* Large, cosmopolitan cities, and especially New York, have generally been fashion-conscious, and access to the current *mode* was easy for large segments of the population. Inside the Jewish group, additional factors enhanced this interest. As has been pointed out in a recent study of material consumption by New York Jews "as an essential part of Americanization," the immigrants' employment in the garment industry endowed them, especially the young people, with knowledge and expertise on fashionable dress even in the early phase of their stay in America. Jews' collective movement into the white-collar strata during the interwar period, particularly as salespeople and clerks in large department stores, sustained this "professional interest" in the next, American-born generation. A "pretense not to count each penny" observed among New York Jewish *arriviste pleasurniks* in the 1920s and 1930s, when enacted in clothing stores, made this concern with fashionable dress even more spectacular.[79]

In Johnstown, all these conducive factors were lacking: the town was no more a leader in fashion than it was in fancy cookery, and the local Jews, busy in their small shops, or, the young ones, employed at the Gee Bee department store, which carried inexpensive merchandise for a working-class clientele, had neither the opportunity nor the means to keep up with current metropolitan fashion. Of course, American-looking dress was, as we have seen in the previous chapter, part of a "decent lifestyle" that Jewish households strove for, and proper attire was of considerable concern, especially for the residents in secondary areas of settlement, and for the young second generation, particularly women. But the main source of new fashion ideas, and of purchases, was local: the *Tribune*'s "Page for Women," which displayed photographs and discussed current modes; advertisements in the paper; and Johnstown's department stores, with Penn Traffic at the top of the local elegance ranking list, and Glosser Brothers' for the thrifty.

In the large cities, social receptions in middle-class Jewish homes became institutionalized as secular affairs with secular functions: to celebrate and reaffirm the family's social status in the ethnic group. In Johnstown, these ethnicized private socials were often imbued with traditional religious symbolism. Young Hadassah women and their male guests, for example, gathered privately every second Saturday in different Westmont homes to "talk about Palestine and all kinds of Jewish things, sing Hebrew songs, and tell jokes . . . we had a great time together"; they called the occasion *Oneg Shabbat*, joy of Sabbath, the traditional name for the social get-together on that day. Even when a party was given to celebrate an adopted secular American festivity—the anniversary of children's birthdays or the parents' wedding, the out-of-town relatives' arriving or leaving, and the like—the program often contained some kind of religious component. In February 1934, for instance, the *Rodef Sholom Bulletin* reported on a dinner reception at the home of Mr. and Mrs. David G., one of the most affluent families in town: "Musical selections were rendered by Rev. I. Horowitz and Irving Cohen [cantors]; the twin daughters of Mr. & Mrs. G. recited a piece in Yiddish which was favorably accepted. Rabbi Simon and Mr. Avrom W. [Hebrew school teacher] were speakers. Many out of town guests from Boswell, Cumberland, and Greensburg [in the surrounding counties] attended." In yet another reflection of the blurred boundaries between the public and private spheres in the lives of Johnstown Jews, social receptions at home were also often given for concrete, organized-religion-related purposes: in September 1934 the *Bulletin* reported that Mrs. Joseph S. "celebrated the 25th anniversary of her arrival in the United States by giving [with ten women assistants] a stag dinner and party at her home. . . . The event (beautified by piano performance by the S. family members) was a tremendous success, both socially and financially. Over seventy men were served during the evening," and, in exchange for the catering, the Ladies Auxiliary appropriated the proceeds of the affair for the needs of the Rodef Sholom Congregation.[80]

Travel on vacation to rest or visit other places, another form of entertainment of American middle-class urbanites, was also listed high among recreational activities preferred by the young New Yorkers in the 1935 study quoted above. Among Jews, trips took place on weekends, summer vacations, and Passover holidays; many a Jewish housewife was eager "to avoid the 'usual annoyances' associated with preparing for Passover by relocating elsewhere for the holiday." The destination was commonly in the Catskills or the Adirondacks, and the popularity of travel turned these places into "Jewish resorts." Various summer camps sponsored by Jewish organizations took many young people out of the city to scenic surroundings to enjoy tennis and golf, or expand their education in some specific cultural activity such as dramatics, painting, or photography.[81]

In Johnstown, short-distance recreational trips, much less diverse in purpose and involving intergenerational groupings of kin and friends, were the fourth most popular mode of informal socializing after moviegoing, playing cards, and visiting homes. "Going for a walk up on the hills, the whole family, and relatives or neighbors would join": this did not differ from East European tradition, except that it was done on Sundays rather than on the Sabbath. An evolution of this activity, a sign of economic betterment and the adoption of local customs, became "Sunday drives in a car, often several of them, for a picnic, perhaps ten miles away or to visit [relatives or friends] in Greensburg or Altoona," in similar generationally mixed groups composed of kin and close friends. A number of families shared little summer cottages in the countryside around Johnstown—a diminished version of the summer camps in the Catskills for Jewish youth from Brooklyn and the Bronx. A vacation was a rare treat, cause for excitement and an announcement in the *Rodef Sholom Bulletin*. It took the form of a weekend—or, at most, week-long—discount trip to Atlantic City with accommodation in an inexpensive Jewish hotel, or to New York itself, "to bring us out to the world," as Bill B.'s mother described such escapades.[82]

Like organized communal affairs, most of these primary-group social activities involved people from within congregational boundaries, although kin connections and residential proximity naturally generated some mixing. In the old Jewish settlements downtown, primary socializing connected Rodef Sholom's and Ahavath Achim's members, who also shared a similar lifestyle; and, likewise, in areas of secondary residence social relations also linked Rodef Sholom's and Beth Zion's East European homes. Within the Temple, however, throughout the 1930s, East European and Germans, though cooperating in the ethnic entrepreneurial niche and in organized activities, largely stayed within their own primary social circles, and mutual home visiting, cardplaying, or outings bonded only a few families. Evincing the enduring distance between these two groups, even the American-born Temple members of East European origin who did maintain these informal social contacts, while recollecting them, spontaneously referred to their fellow congregants of German background by the habitual old Yiddish term *daytshn*, still scornfully used by the larger East European group in the area, and by these few social mixers as a neutral, but still distancing term.[83]

"LOOKING FOR EDUCATIONAL OPPPORTUNITIES WAS NOT REALLY ON PEOPLE'S MINDS": ATTITUDES TO AND PRACTICE OF EXTENDED SCHOOLING

The use of extended formal education as an increasingly prevalent means toward socioeconomic advancement by growing numbers of middle-class Americans in general, and big-city Jews specifically, was treated in the previous chapter as a contrast for the distinct occupational profile and the economic bases of Johnstown Jews' livelihoods. But the increasingly common perception, and use, of advanced formal education as the main status lifter in the social stratification of the dominant (American) society can also be considered from a different perspective: as an indicator of sociocultural ethnicization—that is, the incorporation into group cultural values, and social norms and expectations, of the relevant attitudinal and behavioral patterns of the host society. In the case of Jews, ethnicization considered in terms of the appreciation for, and practice of, learning has also had a group-specific aspect, with two dimensions.

One of them is that the term "secular religion," used by historians of American education to denote the spread of college attendance among urban middle-class youth during the interwar decades,[84] represents particularly well the actual experience of Jews partaking of advanced learning in American educational institutions. Religiously sanctioned reverence for learning, and the latter's association with matters religious, have been the fundamental elements of collective Jewish tradition, both Great and Small; (religious) study sanctified the lives of its devotees and at the same time bestowed upon them the highest social status in the community. Under the impact of structural transformations of the economies and societies of Eastern Europe at the turn of the century, in the more urbanized centers the growing numbers of Jews began to pursue secular education, but its secularization on a mass scale occurred in the Jewish settlements in America. While secularized, however, the *takhlis* of learning retained in the perceptions of American Jews a normative subtext, namely, an aspect of obligatoriness inherent in group membership. In a conducive environment, this attitude could easily fuse with a new secular religion of extended schooling for status elevation that spread among the American urban middle-class.[85]

The other group-specific dimension of the educational aspect of American Jews' ethnicization was that since in several cities they actually overtook all other groups, including Anglo-Protestants, in the practice of the educational-achievement-as-secular-religion, ethnicization acquired a peculiar meaning—as the appropriation of, or pace setting for, the dominant pattern.

Like other aspects of the sociocultural transformation discussed earlier, evolving in the constraining circumstances, the educational practice of the Johnstowners developed only halfway, in that not college, but secondary education, became the social norm. Not only in reduced practice, but also in a general climate surrounding education, did the Johnstowners differ from their big-city ethnic peers. In the big-city Jewish communities, secular learning became a cultural trend, a theme-proposition fervently talked about and imbued, as one commentator put it, with a "tone of great excitement,"[86] common enough to have a ripple effect. In Johnstown, neither the public fora and primary-group circles making up the Jewish community (regardless of congregational group) nor mainstream institutions responsible for educational programs and activities promoted this theme as an object of desires, everyday conversations, and shared concern.

In the preceding chapter the educational attainment of the young generation was shown (table 3.2), indicating that the continuation of secondary schooling beyond the compulsory age of sixteen became a pursuit of the majority over the interwar years. By the mid-1920s, it involved both males and females in about equal proportions and regardless of congregational membership and residence—a significant innovation compared with the male-oriented Jewish educational tradition in East Europe, although established in Johnstown later than in larger American cities, where high school attendance of immigrant children gender-equalized more than a decade earlier.[87] Asked about secondary education, my informants from all

group subsegments responded with ready answers similar to that given by
Elmer M., born to an Orthodox family that kept a small store: "High
school, it was taken for granted among Jewish people, for boys and girls
the same, not to go through was not socially popular, it was looked at with
askance, there had to be some excuse, like father died or was sick and
mother couldn't cope, and someone had to take over. But they would try
to finish [high school] later if only possible."[88]

We have seen how through the interwar period, family economy and
intragroup employment networks overwhelmingly channeled second-generation Johnstowners into occupations within the ethnic entrepreneurial
niche, and that possession of a high school diploma did not alter this pattern, regardless of gender. Most of the jobs in the niche, excepting perhaps
higher-level managerial positions in larger business establishments, could
have been performed well enough with a minimum of high school classes,
without completion of the full curriculum; a few years of practical training
at "Gee Bee Tech" was quite effective preparation for further employment.
Much less formalized and specialized than in big cities, the functioning of
group public life did not require educational credentials. Still, proportionately, Jewish high school enrollments slightly surpassed those of youth of
American-born parentage (all West European–origin groups combined)
from white-collar family backgrounds as early as the 1920s. Even though
the great majority of Jewish high school students were not going to college, for status reasons—"It was better"; "We were kind of snobbish"—
they preferred to take the academic course.[89] It could be argued, then, that
the Jewish cultural tradition of socially rewarded respect for learning, secularized and extended to include females by the absorption of middle-class
American influences, had continued to exert an ethnicized impact in keeping children in secondary schooling in greater numbers than their native-
born American peers, and in channeling them into its more prestigious academic track.

While it was increasingly regarded as the standard for adolescents, high
school was not viewed by prevailing Jewish opinion in prewar Johnstown as
a step toward further education or professional careers. As shown in the
preceding chapter, the rate of college enrollment among the second generation rose only slightly between the 1920s and 1930s, and at the outbreak
of World War II it was merely about half (16–17 percent) of the proportion
of Jewish youth in New York who were pursuing advanced education. The
figure for young Jews of German background from the Beth Zion Reform
Temple exceeded by about 10 percent the estimated proportion among
Europeans from Rodef Sholom and Ahavath Achim combined, but since
the entire group was very small, in actual numbers it meant less than half a
dozen. I raised the question of how Johnstowners compared with New
York Jews in their attitudes toward college and formal occupational training; a reply given by Isadore S., a native Johnstowner who grew up in the
interwar period, well summarizes the prevalent local orientations: "You

should understand that in a town like this, most people were not so conscious then of cultural opportunities, advanced educational opportunities, careers for themselves and that sort of thing. They didn't think they were denied very much here, provided they made a living, and living decently, other things were much less important."[90] And in fact, none of the socially natural instigators of advanced education and professional training for young people especially promoted this course of action either from the outside or from within the Jewish group.

The Johnstown high schools, to judge from the contents of school bulletins and commencement speeches recorded in the graduation yearbooks, and from my interviews with former students and their teachers, did little to promote further education. As one of the teachers put it, "We did not discourage extraordinary talent, but there was no special emphasis on professional careers; diligence, perseverance, and work ethics were stressed." The local newspaper and other channels of public communication did not programmatically advocate college either.[91]

Nor was it promoted within the Jewish group. The theme of advanced educational training—either as a group cultural schema or a value-concept, or as a resource for socioeconomic success—was absent by and large in the community bulletins of the Rodef Sholom Center and the Beth Zion Temple. Both gazettes published the names of college students, but without fanfare—actually, more elaborate attention was given to high school graduations—and whereas announcements about religious school enrollments and confirmations clearly indicated the desirability and importance of these achievements, notices of college attendance conspicuously lacked such indicators. Occasional references in the bulletins' short editorials to "the great country America" were to its political freedom and democratic institutions, and if "the American way of life" was mentioned, the referent was lifestyles and customs, not professional career opportunities. Information about Jews in other American cities dealt with organizational events, not with their educational or professional achievements. Nor was this theme a subject in the lecture series sponsored by the two congregations, even the outward-oriented Beth Zion Forum. In the latter, however, I did notice topics related to American economic opportunities and business life.[92]

Social gatherings in public places and in private circles also served as important setters of norms and practices. In interviews with Johnstowners representing all three congregations, and both primary and secondary areas of Jewish settlement in town, I asked what they remembered as the usual topics of conversation at social occasions: "Looking for educational opportunities was not really on people's minds." Among the adults, regardless of synagogue affiliation and residence, what was on people's minds, as my informants recalled, apparently quite readily, was mostly Jewish communal and family happenings, local business conditions, economic pursuits, the acquisitions and losses of Jewish entrepreneurs in the area, or current developments in the Jewish world diaspora. But discussion about the advantages of professional training and ways of putting children through college as resources for socioeconomic success—a common theme in the *shmoozing* (*shmuesn*, to talk, or chat) of Jewish acquaintances in New York between the wars—seldom took place.[93]

The second generation who were adolescents before the war were most likely to discuss—also without much residential or congregational difference—"the usual things like who [said what] to whom and where, or just sitting and telling jokes," and also the goings-on in the Jewish community, "like plays or dances or picnics," the ways to spend the money saved from part-time work, movies, trips out of town, "girls about clothes and boys about sports," piano lessons, home and household purchases in their families. School was obviously a topic of conversation. Grades were discussed, but interests and ideas did not figure prominently in conversation (as was pointed out earlier, Johnstowners manifested limited reading interests). "We were expected to get good grades"; "Jews are supposed to be smart, so doing badly at school was looked down upon." Group self-image apparently motivated toward, and symbolically controlled, achievement, as Eva Etzioni-Halevy and Zvi Halevy argued,[94] but again on the diminished scale of a parochial small town with a stagnant occupational structure, as compared with the frenzy for excellence of Jewish college students in big, culturally vibrant cities with an expanding white-collar sector: "We didn't talk much about plans or ambitions, just doing well." In fact, as the Johnstown High School records show, most of them were good students, but not more, and there was no striking presence of Jewish names among participants in the academically oriented extracurricular activities or on the honor rolls of graduates. Between 1920 and 1935, Jewish students—two-thirds of them women—appeared in only five annual honor-roll listings; these top scholarly achievers constituted no more than 6 percent of all Jews who graduated from Johnstown High in that period; differently represented, their proportion in the entire roster of honorees did not exceed the share of Jewish students among all high school graduates.[95] In this regard, Johnstown high school students differed significantly from their New York counterparts. In a contemporary study of academic performance and extracurricular activities in different New York high schools, Jewish students were reported to have been "hyperactive" in science, academic, and literary clubs, and decidedly overrepresented among the top GPAs and on the honor rolls.[96]

At home, by and large, there was not much discussion about schooling and its purposes either. As reported in the Johnstown High School guidance files (1926–1937), Jewish parents' attitude toward their children's education was generally described as "favorable"; it certainly compared very well with that of Slavic working-class parents, who usually wanted their children out of school and at work as soon as the law permitted. But in most cases, this positive orientation did not engender active encouragement, as in the fairly typical admonitions of New Yorker Mary Jastrow's immigrant parents: "Study hard and the opportunities will open to be any-thing you wish—a teacher, maybe even a doctor." Rather, "[Johnstown] parents asked when there was some problem at school, then we had to ex-plain and try better, but otherwise we didn't talk much about it, as long as we were doing well." As for extending education beyond high school, sim-ilar comments recurred in the recollections of my second-generation infor-mants, across congregational and residential subgroups and without no-ticeable gender difference: "There was no particular encouragement from the parents"; "no push or motivation in this or other direction"; "at that age [high school], we didn't have any specific ambitions, my siblings and myself"; "A [college] 'theme' at home? No, there was no theme like that really."[97]

At times, of course, the parents' and children's wishes diverged, but the interviews suggest that these were occasional instances rather than com-mon occurrences. There were cases, as in Bea and William R.'s home, for example, in which the parents "wanted the [three] children to go on to college, or at least the oldest son, but none of us wanted to," or Dolly K., whose mother "pictured her as a teacher, but I wasn't interested." More frequently the situation was reversed: the children contemplating more schooling, and the parents arguing that their income was needed for the family's economic welfare. Harold N., "instead of to college as I thought I'd go, I went to work, because father needed my help"; similarly, Mollie K. and her two brothers "thought about going to college, but the family's needs were first"; Vivian C. "would have tried" (she was interested in nursing), but her father's salary as a buyer in a local wholesale establish-ment just sufficed for living expenses and mortgage payments on the house, and, she was told, "it was not enough for college." The young peo-ple's disappointment in such instances hurt, but—as they told me, in any case—not very deeply and not for long: in this area, too, social circum-stances muted intergenerational conflict. "Most others weren't going ei-ther" (in New York, with young people all around rushing to college, the demonstration effect worked in the opposite direction), and besides, like Vivian C.'s or Harold N.'s, these college plans were usually "not firm" and the commitment "not very forceful": "this [college] drive wasn't quite strong."[98]

Talking with my second-generation informants about this lack of educa-tional "drive," I asked about the Johnstown branch of the University of Pittsburgh, opened in 1927. It was not tuition-free, like the New York City colleges, but at least boarding expenses could be saved, and courses could be taken part-time, in the evenings or in the summer months, rather than full-time during the day. Yet the proportion of Jews enrolled there during the 1930s, which in big-city higher educational institutions far exceeded the share of the Jewish population in the total number of inhabitants, just about matched their percentage of Johnstown's population.

Commenting on the lack of a greater rush by local Jews to nearby UPJ, Isadore S., from a typical storekeeping family, again reflected the orientations then dominant in his generation, regardless of synagogue affiliation and residence: "Few of us went to college. . . . [It was the Depression], and economic reasons greatly contributed to it. When I finished high school, I went to work for my father, this was the thing to do then, go to work in some kind of business. But had we really wanted to, most of us could have found the means to go [to college]. That is evident in the fact of those who did go whose economic circumstances were not better than ours. So it could be done, we realize it now." That more promising occupational opportunities and a more stimulating sociocultural environment could have indeed encouraged many more students was evidenced in the situation in the big cities with large university centers. A New York study conducted in the late 1930s found "a tendency among [young] Jewish lawyers to obtain their training with a minimum of expense and in the shortest possible time . . . to prevent burdening the family with educational expenses by working during the day and studying at night": over 40 percent of the sample obtained their degrees through part-time evening courses.[99]

Isadore S. thought that "among those who did go to college, it was because it seemed to run in their families." I compiled the names of Jews from the area enrolled in college programs during the interwar years, first checking the rosters of the closest, the University of Pittsburgh (both main and local campuses) and Carnegie Institute, which attracted most of the students from the area, then the announcements in congregational bulletins, and the information recorded in group and individual interviews to include people who attended college elsewhere. It turned out that the bulk of college-goers indeed came from the same families. More interestingly, there was no apparent pattern in the location of these families within the group, as they dispersed across congregational and residential subgroups and household-prosperity levels. In large Jewish settlements in big urban centers, college-goers concentrated and spread from among the socioeconomically mobile. In Johnstown, too, I expected to find them clustered among the more affluent, and among those whose ethnicized lifestyles reflected a greater impact of middle-class American patterns—that is, what Johnstowners called the more "progressive" or "modern" residents of secondary Jewish settlements in town: a small but visible group that could exert a "demonstration effect" on the others. But this was apparently not the case. In Westmont, for example, which was most representative of these characteristics, the proportion of families from which young people went to college was no different from that in the areas with a greater concentration of traditional, Orthodox households.[100]

In most of the families in Johnstown and vicinity that sent children to college, attempts were made to send as many as means permitted. If choices had to be made—and with the exception of a half dozen solidly affluent families that could afford to support all who were willing, they had to be—young men had uncontested priority. Unlike secondary schooling of the immigrants' children, which after World War I achieved gender parity, at the college level the difference persisted through the 1930s. Women made up somewhat over 35 percent of my list of college attenders—a slightly higher proportion than that among all Jewish students in America at that time; only in New York did the sex ratio of Jewish students reportedly approach parity before World War II.[101]

To pay for college expenses families usually combined contributions from the parents and from the wages of the young people themselves, earmarked for this purpose. Seldom was it possible to obtain full support from the income brought in by the family enterprise. For example, rental revenues from houses owned by and supporting Fanny T., a widow, and her seven children sufficed to cover the college costs of the first two sons attending college between 1918 and 1925, and they, together with their oldest brother, a businessman, subsequently helped to support two younger siblings, a brother and a sister. David and Sarah S.'s long-established and relatively steadily prosperous clothing store in one of Johnstown's "foreign colonies" provided support for six children, five boys and a girl, while they attended schools in Pittsburgh between 1923 and 1937. Income from the business of Max and Miriam W., in the same section of town, also helped with expenses of three of their six children, two sons and a daughter, attending college between 1921 and 1932, but "it was tough and sacrifices had to be made." In Nanty-Glo, five of Aaron and Lilly E.'s seven children were enrolled in college at some point between 1928 and 1940, three sons and two daughters, drawing on a range of resources to cover their expenses: they were subsidized partly from home, "although it wasn't easy," partly from summer work at Gee Bee and—the young men—from weekend jobs during the academic year in Pittsburgh, "five dollars a week in a Jewish store." Samuel M., the sexton at the Iron Street synagogue, supported his family now from a small store, now from peddling or from the two combined; three out of four of the children enrolled in college between 1928 and 1938, with money coming mostly from the young people's summer work savings. Solomon M., a peddler in Hornerstown, "borrowed on life insurance" and then "on the house" to help out with college expenses of two of his sons, and later the youngest daughter, as they consecutively attended the University of Pittsburgh.[102]

Of all those on my list who enrolled in institutions of higher education during the interwar period, nearly half (47 percent) graduated—a proportion somewhat lower than in a sample of Russian (mostly Jewish) alumni of the prestigious Central High School in Philadelphia, but considerably higher than the less than one-third average at the University of Pittsburgh (mid-1920s to mid-1930s), and suggesting seriousness of purpose.[103] This figure includes women completing a two-year teachers' program, and men continuing on beyond college in medical, dental, and law schools—the most common choices of the persisters, a preference dictated by realism. "If you wanted to stay [in the area]"—and most college-goers did, for family reasons, and because they liked Johnstown and their life there—"what else could you do [here]? Not much other opportunities, and for Jewish people at that."

Among those who dropped out, some did so because they found out they were "not suited for college," but in the majority of cases it was because their families' economic situation not only did not permit financial assistance to students (according to contemporary estimates, standard university tuition in the 1930s absorbed 10–12 percent of a middle-class family income of $2,400) but required their full-time help. Sometimes it was the loss or incapacitation of other contributing member(s), and more often, especially during the bad years of the Depression, a faltering or bankrupt business; whenever possible, I checked these instances independently in the local sources, and I found confirmation. Such interruptions of advanced education certainly frustrated the dropouts themselves and the whole household, but, as I heard in virtually all cases, caused "no prolonged resentment since it was understood why," and "family welfare counted above all, the parents worked so hard for it, having started from scratch." I did not attempt to find out whether these reports were of sentiments actually felt at the time, or of reactions dictated by then prevalent norms; but in either instance, family welfare was at the center. When conditions improved, another family member was likely to try college.[104]

Interestingly, those few, almost exclusively young men, college-goers who went to faraway universities graduated at a considerably higher rate (over 60 percent) than their colleagues attending nearby University of Pittsburgh main and Johnstown campuses, and Carnegie Institute. Traveling a long distance to obtain advanced education could have reflected a stronger commitment to the purpose, but it also removed those young people, physically and "interactionally," from the easy grasp of local social networks and pressures of current family (business) economic needs.

"In our family, we just believed in getting all the education possible": this was the usual answer college-goers gave when I asked what moved them to the effort of pursuing extended educational training with an uncertain conclusion, not actually against, but alongside the dominant local orientations. As they remembered, in their homes, rather than an object of a latent "generic" respect without personal engagement beyond the socially sanctioned norm, learning was a customary topic of conversation. It was often discussed both as a value in itself ("what you put in your head will stay there and make your head bigger") and a practical resource, or a *takhlis* (concrete "investment for life," "to get on in the world"), although fathers apparently tended to stress more the material, and mothers more the status, aspect of this purpose.[105]

I tried to find out what this small number of families dispersed across the group could have had in common beyond personal characteristics, and what conducive blend they made up in their most immediate social environments that provided incentive and support—moral and, means permitting, financial. There seem to have been two such blends, actually. One, represented mostly among the youth of German background, from families much longer settled in this country and better-off economically than the East Europeans, contained a considerable dose of the American middle-class orientation toward advanced education. The other configuration, characteristic of the families of college-goers of East European origins, was more complex, and more unusual (in any case, not analyzed in Jewish-American historiography). In this ethnic blend, it was not a new American pattern but, rather, the enduring impact of old-country heritage that apparently played a central conducive role. What, specifically, motivated this quest for more education than was socially expected, a pursuit that brought lesser rewards in the local Jewish community than economic wealth combined with active community participation? Reflecting on this question, my informants suggested that it was immigrants' personal experience and family collective memories from Eastern Europe; and quite different ones at that.

This small group of college-goers contained, on the one hand, practically all the families, of varied economic standing, whose immigrant members received some secular education in Eastern Europe—a highly unusual and apparently transforming experience for the shtetl people, cherished in memories shared with their American-born children. On the other hand, I found among college-goers in this group the relatives of immigrant men—peddlers and established merchants—more learned in traditional Jewish scholarship, who, in private and with limited time, continued to pursue some kind of Jewish-religious (Talmudic) study and passed it on to the American-born generation, if only in conversations. It may have been, then, the experience, limited as it was, of extra-ordinary learning of either kind, recalled and transmitted in Johnstown homes, that made for the translation of a "traditional Jewish respect for education" into pursuits extending beyond the locally sanctioned practice.

Outside these families—and this observation closes the discussion of the micro-environment's influence on young Johnstowners' educational practice and ambitions—personal friendships among parents as well as students themselves, usually from no more than two or three homes, also played a role as a minuscule social support resource for college-goers. These small informal circles functioned as upholders, as it were, of the mindsets of the participants, but they were evidently too weak vis-à-vis other untoward circumstances to expand into the local Jewish community at large.[106]

To conclude, this chapter has reconstructed what I believe to have been characteristic features of Johnstown Jews' communal institutions, and public and private sociocultural activities, during the interwar period. We have seen how, evolving in specific external and intragroup circumstances, in comparison with big-city Jewish settlements the ethnicization of the

Johnstown Jews' sociocultural life contained a more substantial, and more visible, component of old-country traditional patterns, or, differently put, a proportionately larger share of continuity than of change.

Thus far this study has focused on the inside of the Jewish group: its economic networks and family strategies for a decent standard of living, and public and private sociocultural activities. The next chapter deals with the Johnstown Jews' relations with the top and bottom segments, as it were, of the local non-Jewish society: the politically and culturally dominant, mostly Anglo-Protestant, Americans, and the working-class Slavs and Hungarians, their former neighbors in Eastern Europe who became their customers in Johnstown.

In the Middle on the Periphery:
Involvement in the Local Society

PERHAPS not invisibility but all-around inconspicuousness best characterized the situation of Jews vis-à-vis the larger Johnstown society throughout
the entire period under investigation. I once asked an elderly representative
of the prewar Johnstown social elite, a former member of Bethlehem Steel
Company's management, to tell me how local ethnic groups stacked up on
the town's hierarchy of importance in those days: expectedly, he ranked
Anglo-Protestants and other West Europeans at the top (his own ancestors
came from Switzerland in the early nineteenth century), then Germans,
Irish, Slavs near the bottom, and lower yet the "colored." He did not mention Jews, but when reminded that about 1,200 of them lived in Johnstown, "Oh yes, of course," he instantly remembered, "there were Jews
here, too, quiet people . . ."[1] Quiescence, I imagine, was the last thing one
would associate with New York Jews, a great many of whom, especially
among the second generation, had developed a passion for participation in
the American political process and generally in public life.[2] But in Johnstown, in the almost identically phrased recollections of its Jewish as well as
native-born American residents, "Jews kept a low profile"; "they were not
heard much." Even at the bottom of the town's social hierarchy, Slavic mill
workers and coal miners perceived Jews similarly. One Polish octogenarian
from Minersville, a Slavic-populated neighborhood not far from the Rodef
Sholom Synagogue, employed a familiar old-country expression: "Zhidki
tutaj dobre byli, spokojne" (Jews—more accurately, "Jew-boys"—were
good here, quiet).

A brief summary of general findings from the existing studies and some
specific illustrations will help to locate the situation of Johnstown Jews in
a comparative context. Unlike economic and intragroup sociocultural adaptation, the participation of American Jews in the organized and informal
activities of the larger society has been studied in small towns as well as
large cities.[3] An inspection of twenty-odd historical investigations of American Jews' relations with the larger society in different-size localities between the 1920s and the 1940s suggests two overall conclusions. One is
that the impact of city size and the number of Jewish residents on the latter's participation in mainstream local society apparently varied depending
on the type of outside involvement. The participation of American Jews in
the civic-political affairs of their hometowns, and their involvement in
larger community services and other voluntary organizations of an inclu-

sive nature, tended to peak at opposite numerical ends, as it were: they were most significant in big urban centers with large ethnic communities and in small towns with a small number of Jews. At the same time, however, Jews' participation in voluntary organizations stressing exclusiveness of membership, such as social clubs and fraternal lodges, along with personal social relations with representatives of the dominant American society, reportedly diminished as general and Jewish populations grew.

The other conclusion further complicates this situation: together with the sheer magnitudes of general and Jewish populations, it appears that an array of economic, political, and cultural characteristics of the surrounding society and the ethnic group itself facilitated or constrained the participation of Jews in different activities of local mainstream society. The major conditions favorable to all types of involvement distinguished above (though in particular cases not necessarily present all at once) seemed to have been as follows. The fit of the Jewish group's "collective human capital," particularly occupational skills, into the profile and dynamics of the local economy (economies featuring solid commercial and/or light-industry sectors were especially favorable); pluralistic civic-political opinion and practice of the dominant group(s) in the local society concerning outsiders/newcomers in general, and Jews in particular (specifically, a low intensity of publicly displayed anti-Semitism in the civic-political life of the larger community); presence of Jews among city (town) pioneer settlers; and a low or moderate degree of sociocultural/religious self-absorption (separatism) of the Jewish group itself. In addition, facilitating, specifically, the involvement of Jews in civic-political affairs and formal organizations in their localities was the presence of outstanding Jewish group leaders and activists; while a low level of the dominant group(s)' cultural separatism and social distance vis-à-vis the outsiders/newcomers (and specifically Jews), at least in behavioral expressions, opened the door to the former's private clubs and fraternal lodges. As for informal social relations with members of the dominant groups, favorable to this type of mainstream involvement were the following additional circumstances: nonexistent or weak ethnic residential segregation; absent or weak local Jewish social-institutional networks; and, finally, residence in the South, where skin color or race was the major social partitioner, overriding ethnic divisions.[4]

To establish a comparative framework for the discussion of the Johnstown case, I have selected, and summarily characterize below, four situations—two in large-size, and two in small-size environments—that in a generally positive but nonidentical fashion influenced the involvement of Jewish residents in the local mainstream society during the interwar period: New York; Cleveland; Charleston, South Carolina; and Terre Haute, Indiana. The last two towns were chosen because of the numerical similarity of their general and Jewish populations to Johnstown's parameters.[5] In all four places Jews were reported as actively involved in mainstream civic-political process and nonsectarian organized community life; as it happened, in each city all conditions listed above as favorable to these forms of outside participation were present. However, the character of these contacts differed, as did the scope of involvement in closer social relations. Although seemingly resulting from a different set of circumstances in each setting, Jews' public relations were apparently more integrative (rather than maintaining/enhancing ethnic group boundaries) and closer social relations were more common in Cleveland and Charleston than in New York and Terre Haute.

In *Cleveland* (general population in 1930 of approximately a million, and nearly 100,000 Jews), a combination of three factors seems to have contributed most significantly to the generally integrative character of local Jews' public relations. First, there was the traditionally (since the Social Reform era) inclusive and integrative Republican spirit and practice in public life, aiming at minimizing ethnic divisiveness. Second, the long-standing involvement of Jews of German Reform background in dialogue and cooperation with members of the Anglo-Protestant group in diverse matters of public interest facilitated subsequent entry into mainstream institutions of East Europeans, who at the same time recognized the German Jews' strong organizational influence and representative legitimacy within Cleveland's Jewish community at large. And third, a tolerant civic climate and "public familiarity" between Jews and members of the dominant group had reportedly contributed to a diminution of status anxiety felt by the latter in view of a rapid upward mobility of Jews, whose 10 percent share of Cleveland's population was a third of that of its New York counterpart. As a result of all these favorable conditions, Cleveland's Jews had been accepted in many—though not "the very best," as my Cleveland Jewish informants pointed out—fraternal lodges and private clubs of the dominant, Anglo-Protestant group. These selective restrictions, as well the infrequency of lasting, close personal relations between Jews and members of the Anglo-Protestant group, indicate the persistence of "private" sociocultural distance toward the ethnoreligious outsiders on the part of the dominant group; on the part of the Jewish group, infrequency of lasting, close personal relations was an outcome of ethnic residential concentration, combined with—both a cause and an effect—their involvement in the ethnic community, and, related to it, their sense of distinct ethnoreligious identity.[6]

In *Charleston, South Carolina* (general and Jewish populations in the 1930s 65,000–70,000 and about 2,000, respectively), the nature of Jews' involvement in public life was also decidedly integrative. In this case, the major conducive circumstances seem to have been the following. The fact that the Jewish group was Caucasian facilitated contacts with local dominant society, which regarded skin color as the major social divider (Charleston's population during the interwar period was about equally divided racially). Next, Jews were a recognized presence, not only among early settlers, but, more important symbolically, among the revered patriot-heroes of the American Revolution and, later, the devoted soldiers of the Confederacy; this illustrious pedigree exerted a long *durée* extra influence in facilitating entry into the status of good American citizens for more recent Jewish arrivals. Finally, Charleston's Jews were residentially dispersed: even the East Europeans who arrived in town at the turn of the century never formed a Jewish quarter. These three factors, combined with the long-established tradition of dialogue and cooperation between representatives of the Jewish and dominant groups in public matters, and, reflecting the above circumstances, the virtual absence of the perception by the latter of local Jews as status-threatening, de-emphasized rather than highlighted ethnic group boundaries in public life. All the above elements jointly contributed in turn to a considerable involvement of Charleston Jews in private clubs and fraternal lodges frequented by members of the dominant group, as well as to informal social relations. Despite the multiple conditions facilitating social integration, however, there were certain clubs where Jews were not admitted, and while the latter's involvement in informal social relations with members of the dominant society was not uncommon overall (it was apparently more frequent than in Cleveland), it was not all-pervasive, indicating the presence here too of a measure of underlying socio-cultural distance on the part of some members of the dominant groups, invisible (and inoperative) in public. On the part of the Charleston Jews, the main factor preventing more complete social integration into the local dominant society was the Jews' active participation in their own ethnic community that, despite the absence of a Jewish neighborhood, offered a variety of activities and sustained a shared group identity.[7]

In comparison, in *New York* (general and Jewish populations in 1930 of about 6.5 million and 1.8 million, respectively), a combination of four circumstances seems to have been primarily responsible for public relations that enhanced ethnic group boundaries, rather than integrating the groups involved. The Jewish group was very large and highly residentially concentrated; as a result, in entire sections of the city Jews simply *were* "American public life," ethnically and organizationally dominating local public institutions such as schools, PTAs, local chapters of the Teachers' Association, and the like. The civic-political process, and the city's public life in general, had been pluralistic since the colonial era, but in a distinctly ethnic-conscious and competitive way. By the interwar period a majority of Jewish group leaders and public representatives were East Europeans, at once still more the outsiders vis-à-vis the dominant native-born American groups and ethnically more "inward" than were German Jews, such as those at the helm in Cleveland, for example. Finally, there was the increased, and publicly expressed, anti-Semitism of the Anglo-Protestant upper strata in reaction to the perceived status threat from upwardly mobile Jews, especially of East European origin—"the great flood of foreign blood sweeping in," as a contemporary Anglo-Protestant lawyer lamented in an apocalyptic memorandum to the New York Bar Association. These circumstances, together with the enhancing effects of ethnic group boundaries in public life, contributed to the persistence of a significant "private" social distance felt toward Jews by members of the dominant society. Complemented, on the part of the Jewish group, by a high degree of residential segregation and the absorption of its members in the institutionally complete ethnic community, this entire constellation of factors effectively prevented the participation of New York Jews in social clubs and close informal relations with upper-strata native-born American city residents.[8]

Lastly, in *Terre Haute, Indiana* (general and Jewish populations in the 1930s 65,000–70,000 and about 1,000, respectively), the situation was probably the most mixed among the four cases considered here. It represented a generally integrative kind of public relations—at any rate regarding the participation of Jews—although in a more diluted version than in either Charleston or Cleveland. While the town's civic-political process was inclusive, it was mainly in practice, without the "ideological drive" this orientation had in Cleveland; ethnic group leaders, while old-timers and recognized figures in the town's public life, had neither the meritorious civic lineage of their Charleston counterparts nor the outstanding, charismatic qualities of public representatives of the Cleveland Jews. At the same time, however, in the area of private social contacts, maintenance—not enhancement, as in New York—of ethnic group boundaries was decidedly the prevailing pattern. Lukewarm public integration had most likely contributed to this rule of "the five o'clock shadow," the routine separation of Terre Hauteans along ethnoreligious lines after work hours; and so did residential concentration of Jews as well as their involvement in the ethnoreligious community. But more important was the Ku Klux Klan. According to a couple of old-time Jewish residents of small towns in Indiana whom I approached with questions, Jews in the area perceived local Klansmen as a sort of domesticated predators: "They patronized Jewish stores," I was told, and "they said 'hallo' on the street." According to non-Jewish sources, the KKK's actual hostility in Indiana was, indeed, directed mainly against local blacks and Catholics. But while individual Klansmen in Terre Haute could have been unaggressive or even friendly, Jews and all "others"—all those who were not white Protestants—were nevertheless their ideological enemies. The silent acquiescence of Terre Haute's dominant, Anglo-Protestant, group in the symbolic manifestations of the Klan's convictions, such as cross burning and downtown parades, reflected feelings of deeper-level cultural distance vis-à-vis Jewish otherness. The fact, and the meaning, of the Klan's unchallenged presence in town upheld the tacit understanding between local Jews and the dominant group that at sunset social integration ends, and life resumes within ethnoreligious boundaries.[9]

One can hypothesize that in all four cases Jews' involvement in the affairs of the local mainstream society had had ethnicizing effects, but these occurred through different channels and in different areas of social life. In the case of Charleston, first of all, then Cleveland, and, to a lesser degree, Terre Haute, ethnicization occurred both through participation in American civic-political process and formal-organizational activities, and, in varying extents, through direct contacts and personal familiarity with the American people and their ways of life, and had, presumably, affected all these areas at once. In New York, the ethnicizing effects of participation in mainstream society occurred primarily in the specific areas of Jewish involvement: ethnic politics and formal-organizational activities.

With these complex pictures as a comparative reference, we now turn to Johnstown. The involvement of Jews in mainstream local society was much more limited, regardless of the type of participation, than that found in any of the investigated localities, big or small—too limited, apparently, to have had significant effects either by de-emphasizing or strengthening group boundaries between the Jews and members of the dominant, Anglo-Protestant society. In this case, it was not mainstream involvement but, conversely, the near-absence thereof that upheld ethnic group boundaries. This minimal participation of Jews in Johnstown's public life added to the effects of their economic and religious/cultural distinctiveness in upholding the Jewish group's "outsider" status; it also contributed to the slow pace of the ethnicization of their sociocultural life.

In what follows I first briefly review the circumstances, in the Johnstown environment as well as within the Jewish group itself, that constrained outside involvement. Next, I look somewhat more closely at three areas of Jews' limited participation in, or deliberate withdrawal from, the local institutions and people outside their own group, as shaped by the above circumstances, and, when noticeable, by generational position, gender, and synagogue membership: in civic-political life; in community affairs and the activities of organizations both inclusive (work-related, patriotic, cultural) and exclusive (social clubs); and, finally, in informal social relations. The focus is on the interwar period, because by that time Jews themselves and their ethnic community were already well established in Johnstown, and also because most historical studies of other localities concerning this subject in prewar America, including those selected here for comparison, concentrate on this era. Since Slavs and Hungarians remained the major customers of Jewish businesses, and since these groups had also been neighbors and trading partners in Eastern Europe, it makes sense to consider here other, extraeconomic aspects of their mutual relations in Johnstown, this time looking down from the middle location of Jews on the local socioeconomic ladder.[10]

A constellation of factors influenced the particular patterns of economic adaptation of Jewish families in the area and slackened the processes of sociocultural transformation within the Jewish group. A similar constellation kept Johnstown's Jews both in the midst and actually on the periphery of local society. First, there was the persisting structural marginality, or even double-marginality, of the Jewish group in the local economy. A specialist on the lower middle class has generalized that "small-scale shopkeepers . . . occupy a much more prominent, influential, and dependable position in local society and politics in small and provincial towns than they do in large cities and urban centers."[11] This may have been the case in cities with a commercial or light-industrial economic base or at least a strong commercial segment. But it certainly did not hold true in a town like prewar Johnstown, heavily dominated by steel and coal industries, and, in terms of class, by the managerial establishment of these heavy industries. Rather than being forces of economic development, trade and commerce in Johnstown performed more of a service function in feeding and clothing the population employed in the mills and coal mines. Occupation in predominantly small business in a company-run steel town was the primary source of local Jews' economic marginality and thus relative powerlessness, a situation they shared with similarly employed non-Jews. Further marginalization resulted from the enduring confinement of most Jewish businesses, as well as a handful of professionals, to the ethnic niche, namely, to the intragroup occupational network, and to servicing the largely Slavic and Hungarian working class at the lower echelons of Johnstown's economic structure. The representative of the town's upper socioeconomic layer quoted earlier could indeed have easily overlooked this small group tucked away somewhere above the crowd of "foreign" labor but a good social distance below the dominant strata.

Such an omission would not have been possible in Terre Haute, a town with a diversified economy, including, besides coal mining, prosperous light industry and strong commerce. There Jews had been well-established merchants or light manufacturers, and occupied such high-powered positions as the presidency of the local Chamber of Commerce or the directorship of a local bank.[12] For a different combination of reasons, overlooking the Jewish socioeconomic presence would also have been obviously impossible in New York (or, for that matter, in Philadelphia, Chicago, or Boston), where despite the existence of a vast ethnic occupational niche that absorbed many Jewish workers, a growing number of increasingly better-educated Jews exerted pressure on the mainstream job market in office, sales, and professional occupations.[13] In Johnstown, Jews—even a few more affluent German Jewish merchants serving the native-born American clientele—were, really, neither partners nor competitors in the local socio-economic structure, nor were German Jews recognized among the city's pioneers or as contributors to its rapid growth in the late nineteenth century.[14] As a result, the regular market or, more generally, instrumental relations, described in several studies as the base connection of Jews with representatives of the dominant, American society,[15] remained weak throughout the period investigated here.

Second, as we have seen, Johnstown's political climate and civic life were anything but liberal. Like most of Pennsylvania before and during the 1930s, the town was a Republican stronghold. It maintained this orientation in a conservative, company-town style, and with the support of a subservient press—a far cry from the progressive and reform-minded tradition of Cleveland's Republicans. When in 1935 a small group of Johnstown-born Slavs, all in middle-class occupations, sought election to higher county offices, pamphlets appeared throughout the city that read "Repel the Foreign Invasion!"[16] Closely related to the absence of a pluralist orientation and exclusionary practices in the public arena was a third pronounced characteristic of Johnstown, namely, the stratification of social life, institutional and informal, along ethnic lines. This split was neatly reflected in the treatment of social news by the local press, which, as late as the outbreak of World War II, printed announcements concerning the activities of the dominant groups and their members, that is, Anglo-Protestants and west Europeans, under the genteel headings "Evening Chat about Town" or "Social Chronicle," separate from reports about happenings among Southern and Eastern Europeans (including Jews). For eighty-seven-year-old Frances C., by birth and marriage a member of the local Anglo-Protestant upper class, "sticking with one's own [people]" was the natural, unquestioned way of doing things in the city during her youth, as "everybody took care of themselves then." So solid were these perceived divisions separating the old and new ethnic stocks that even the local version of the Americanization campaign of the 1920s, which was fiercely conducted in several big cities with large immigrant settlements, was carried out halfheartedly, as if the promoters themselves were not entirely convinced it could bear real fruit.[17]

Exclusiveness and the ascriptive treatment of ethnic membership on the part of Johnstown's dominant groups was not directed specifically at Jews; actually, it aimed primarily at other, more visible immigrant groups. Various Slavic peoples and Hungarians were the largest numerically and socioeconomically "lowliest" among the ethnic groups that had settled in town at the turn of the century. Used colloquially by Bethlehem Steel managers and townspeople in general, and occasionally in municipal documents and the local press even in the 1930s, the label "foreigners" denoted the generalized *them* and referred first and foremost to this population of nearly 17,000, including the American-born children of the immigrants.[18]

Even so, there persisted in Johnstown a detectable undercurrent of anti-Semitism among both the upper socioeconomic strata and those at the bottom of the local stratification system, who themselves faced severe ethnic prejudice. Anti-Jewish feeling escalated in several large American cities that witnessed intensified nativism and, perhaps more important, accelerated upward movement of large numbers of second-generation Jews into socioeconomic positions previously occupied almost exclusively by members of old-stock ethnic groups, who perceived this collective "invasion" as a status threat. Compared with these big-city sentiments, Johnstown's was a subdued, nonvitriolic anti-Semitism.[19] In content, it remained primarily of a more traditional kind, like many other features of the town's social organization and cultural life before World War II.

When a negative image of the "Jew-alien" appeared in public representations sponsored by the agencies of local mainstream society—in school readings and special programs, at citywide popular pageants, on the religion page and in seasonal editorials in the *Johnstown Tribune*—it was usu-

ally couched in Christian symbolism, rather than in the secular images of
economic predator, overbearing social *arriviste*, or Bolshevik (stereotypes
that ranked highest in national opinion surveys conducted in the 1930s).[20]
And so, for example, in the local newspaper's weekly section "What the
Sunday School Is Studying," the Johnstowners read, during Pentecost,
how "under Peter's tremendous proof and accusation the Jews began to
realize what they have done in crucifying Jesus." Traditionally, the Easter
season provided a special opportunity for the expression of more or less
veiled anti-Jewish religious resentment. Announced in the *Tribune*, the annual Holy Week programs in local Protestant churches customarily included, and sometimes reprinted at length, sermons on the theme of "The
Trial of Our Lord at the Hands of the Jewish Crowd."[21] In the social world
below, as it were, in the working-class Slavic communities, the Shylock
motif surfaced in public representations of Jews, in part preserved in old-
country collective memories and in part re-created in Johnstown as the
two groups reestablished their merchant-client relationship, but, as in the
dominant, Anglo-Protestant stratum, the negative imagery was rendered
primarily in religious terms. Echoing Protestant voices from the *Johnstown Tribune*, the foreign-language *Cerkovnaja Nauka*, the bulletin of
St. Mary's Uniate Catholic Slovak-Rusyn parish, thus narrated in present
tense the events of Christ's passion: "Invidious Jews have accused Jesus . . .
Him who did only but good, they call Him a thief!"[22] "Christ-killer"
(rather than "pushy kike") was the ethnic slur Jewish children typically
heard from their Protestant, Catholic, Uniate, or Russian Orthodox peers
alike, whether used in anger or just to tease.

But perhaps more than occasional open expressions of anti-Jewish prejudice, it was another aspect of the milieu that sustained a symbolic distance
between Jews and the Christian majority. The fourth and related factor
rendering the environment unfavorable to a greater involvement of Johnstown's Jews in the activities of the local dominant society was the self-
evident Christian aura of town's public life; in this regard, at least, the Slavs
were insiders, professors of the hegemonic ideology, and thus part of the
dominant society. The high proportion (about nine-tenths) of church
members among the city's residents, maintained during the interwar period, was mentioned in the previous chapter; religious, and specifically
Christian, references, also permeated most local public affairs. Daily confirmation of Jewish separateness came from public schools with their morning prayer-song "Jesus loves me, this I know, 'cause the Bible tells me so";
there were also Nativity plays and carols during the Christmas season, and
the customary end-of-the-year sermon concluding with a benediction by a
minister called in for the occasion, usually from the First Presbyterian
church downtown. Local newspapers and political campaigns were pep-
pered with references to "Christian morals," "Christ-loving citizens," and
the like.[23] Announcements about religious, organizational, and personal
events in the Jewish community appeared in the local press—with the pas-

sage of time regularly and without such lapses as "Yom Pippoor," "Rosh Ashoona," or "koschner meat."[24] Representatives of the Johnstown native-born American elite might praise the Jewish group's program on the contribution of Jews to American civilization, presented at a citywide "Americanization Pageant" organized by the Citizens' Council on Flag Day in 1935. They might congratulate a Jewish-American person on joining some community service function, or even record appreciation of an interfaith meeting; a couple such encounters during the 1930s were initiated by the Jewish side, at Beth Zion Forum or with Rabbi Simon as speaker in Protestant churches. But the terms "Hebrews" or "the Hebrew race" used at such occasions to refer to their Jewish fellow citizens reconfirmed, even in these well-meant, integrative gestures, the deep-rooted Christian sense of Jews' inherent otherness. An anniversary booklet, *Story of Johnstown Pennsylvania Illustrated*, published locally in the mid-1920s, contained photographs of city churches, Protestant and Catholic, but neither the Rodef Sholom Synagogue nor the Beth Zion Temple.[25]

This apartness was also felt by Jews themselves, immigrants as well as American-born. One of my informants, Johnstown-born Frieda S., who grew up in the 1930s, echoed the recollections of others of her generation: she "seemed to be somehow on the outside," not quite in.[26] Intertwined with this perception of outsider status, and at the same time a reaction to the multiple marginality of their existence in Johnstown, was a shared sense of group civic insecurity.

The most tangible expression of this feeling—and the fifth element in the array of interrelated circumstances constraining their participation in mainstream activities—was the preference of local Jews to remain, precisely, inconspicuous and low-profile so as not to attract attention to themselves. Different manifestations of this sense of group insecurity and how people recalled coping with it will be discussed at greater length in chapter 6, dealing with the Johnstown Jews' group self-perceptions and general life-philosophy. In this context, it suffices to point out that, generated by the Jewish group's multiple marginality in the local society, an attitude of collective self-effacement sustained Jews' nonparticipation, which, reciprocally, contributed to their continuing marginality, and, in turn, to the persistence of sharp ethnic group boundaries.

The absorbing social networks of the Jewish community—the sixth enduring condition contributing to its limited participation in the local mainstream society—upheld the inwardness of the group's members, thus adding another, inside element to the exogeneous influences. The normative *du bist nit a goy* nature of membership in the Jewish community, and the persistence of more traditional, ethno-cum-religious, meaning and practice of group identity, reinforced the distance. This group inwardness was an important resource in the achievement of local Jews' primary life-goals; but in the circumstances obtaining in the area, involvement in the ethnic entrepreneurial niche and the enjoyment of ethnic communal life were at the same time an obstacle in overcoming the predicament of sociocultural marginality. While Johnstown's Jews were concerned with their group's reputation in local society—in fact, it was "very important to look good in the eyes of the Gentiles"—it was understood that they were to maintain this good impression within the situation as it existed, namely, as Jews and from within the Jewish group's middle-but-peripheral position in the city, rather than by melting or by pushing to the fore to request a "fair share."[27]

The last, seventh, factor, also endogenous and of a voluntary or agentic nature, that worked against a more significant Jewish involvement in Johnstown's public life and in social activities with members of the dominant groups was the lack of a stable qualified leadership in the Jewish community. As one informant put it, the group did not have "any people who made a real impact [outside]" and could thus open some avenues for a greater mainstream participation of other Jews—or, we may add, apply their experience in American institutions to a deliberate ethnicization of the local Jewish community.[28] During Rabbi Simon's tenure, Jewish public visibility and outside participation did increase somewhat, but he did not stay in town very long; moreover, the economic hardships of the Depression kept people turned inward, and "minding their own business," at least in Johnstown. The Reform Temple had the Beth Zion Forum that enjoyed outside recognition, but no particular participation in local public affairs, perhaps because the most oustanding individual there was a woman (Maggie Nathan), and Johnstown at that time did not welcome female leadership in public matters.

PARTICIPATION IN CIVIC-POLITICAL AFFAIRS

The participation of Jews of the Johnstown area in city and county governments was even less than inconspicuous; it was practically nonexistent. During the half-century between the establishment of the Jewish community in the 1880s and the outbreak of World War II, there had been, at the beginning of this century, one Jewish town councilman who combined this function with serving as park commissioner, and in the 1930s the first, and only, Jewish lawyer held an appointive office in the county government as solicitor to the Cambria County controller. The highest elective office ever held by a Jew in the area during the prewar period was that of burgess in nearby Barnesboro, a coal-mining town of about four thousand. There was also, in the 1930s, a Jewish Republican party activist in political campaigns, employed on and off in city hall. His fellow ethnics referred to him, with a touch of irony, as a *makher* ("he walked around telling people to go register Republican"), while a representative of the town's political establishment at the time recalled this person, not without sympathy, as "a funny little guy" (although somehow I felt he was about to say "little Jew").[29]

Here are the characteristics of the political system in the Johnstown area that contributed to the absence of Jews in city and county offices, in addition to the general inhibiting factors noted earlier. As already mentioned, Republican rule in the area was entrenched and conservative. During the entire prewar period there was in the city only one Democratic mayor, and his election was "an aberration," according to one of my informants, who had been a member of the political establishment at the time; "he switched from Republican to Democrat during the Depression, and won on Roosevelt."[30] In practice, Republican dominance meant a decisive influence on the political processes by the local economic potentate and major employer, Bethlehem Steel Company. Staunchly antiunion—as noted earlier, the company gave in only under federal order, in 1941— through its lower-level managment in the mills and coal mines the company exerted open pressure on the workers, especially of foreign stock, to support the political establishment, that is, register with the Republican party and vote for its local candidates (reportedly there were even marked ballots in circulation).[31]

Another relevant feature of local politics, well paired with its conservatism, was the cliquishness of the participants: through the 1930s both city and county governments were pretty much controlled by an old-boy network with a strongly Masonic tinge (in contrast to some other places, the Johnstown area's Masons, or at least those from the social-political elite, were *fraters* but no egalitarians).[32] Related to this characteristic was the ethnic divisiveness of Johnstown's society, combined with the exclusiveness of its upper strata. As multiethnic, if on a much smaller scale, as New York, because of an entirely different configuration of circumstances Johnstown did not have competitive ethnic politics; but unlike Cleveland, where the purposeful downplaying of ethnicity aimed at the political integration of different groups, including recent immigrants, in Johnstown the question of ethnic representation hardly even appeared on the political agenda, preempted by the hegemony of the established cliquey elite.

The old-boy political network was also an all-boy one. As the available studies indicate, in the big cities, during the decade following the ratification of the Nineteenth Amendment in 1920, a considerable number of women (including Jewish-Americans) entered county and municipal governments, although usually in such conventional "female spheres" as public health and education; this movement was facilitated by the rapid advancement of women's education and white-collar occupational training as well as by the expansion of women's voluntary associations, including organizations with specifically political purposes. Secondary-source comparisons suggest that the situation in Cleveland was unusually favorable toward women's involvement in political processes, including those outside the traditional sphere.[33] I did not find sufficient ready information in this regard (that is, information available outside of local primary materials) about smaller towns to permit even a cautious generalization. According to one study conducted in 1930/31, all but one of the few women mayors in the United States had been elected in towns of less than 10,000 inhabitants, usually in the Midwest and Plains states. In the opinion of one of these female officials, women's election as mayors "was due to the fact that in small towns men best fitted for public office often refuse to serve on the plea that they would 'hurt their businesses.' We had no business to hurt."[34] But in neither of the two towns chosen here for comparative references, Terre Haute and Charleston, had women been involved in any local civic-political functions before the 1940s; in the latter, however—South Carolina did not ratify the Nineteenth Amendment, and the state's monopolist Democratic party excluded women—there existed throughout the interwar period an active suffrage movement among whose leaders were three outstanding Jewish women, the Pollitzer sisters.[35]

There were no women in Johnstown politics, and no suffragettes either. As already noted on several occasions, Johnstown was a "male town": in its economy and occupational structure as well as in the public implications, so to speak, of its sociocultural conservatism. A female city treasurer's clerk and registrar of deeds (the same woman for several terms) exhausted female representation in local government. A local chapter of the National League of Women Voters did not appear in town until 1961. The Republican party (but not the Democratic) had its women's auxiliary; founded in 1936, it closely collaborated with the Daughters of the American Revolution and in the political process performed mostly service functions. One of them, re-called my Jewish informants who lived in prestigious Westmont, was canvassing the homes of new residents advising them to "make sure that you register Republican"; to be nonpartisan was to be suspect in the eyes of local Republicans.

And Jews, in fact, did register Republican, with no significant difference according to generational position, residential location, or gender.[36] In the second half of the 1930s, when a majority of American Jews sided with the Democratic party,[37] over four-fifths of Jewish Johnstowners were registered Republicans. This proportion was considerably larger than the percentage—about two-thirds—of all registered Republicans in the city as a whole; only Westmont, the stronghold of the town's political establishment, ranked equally high on the side of the Republican party. Over half of the few Jewish registered Democrats were members of the largest, Conservative-Orthodox Rodef Sholom Synagogue, and the remaining divided about equally between the Orthodox Ahavath Achim and the Reform Beth Zion Temple. Since the latter two congregations were much smaller than Rodef Sholom's, outward "Democratic dissidence" within their ranks appears to have been somewhat greater if only in terms of proportionate presence; most of the Reform Temple's few registered Democrats, however, were relative newcomers to Johnstown, usually from New York, and of East European origin.[38]

According to the conventional interpretation, there has been a link, presumably causal, between Jews' marginal status in the dominant society and their political liberalism or even radical-revolutionary ideologies—orientations programmatically questioning differential treatment of citizens and groups and calling for universalist criteria of civic participation. The Johnstown case illustrates, rather, an interpretation emphasizing the contingent nature of Jews' political options as dependent primarily on their local situation as interpreted by group members in terms of their current experience and collective memory, and secondarily on the events and general political climate in the larger society and on the international scene. Specifically, as proposed by Peter Medding, "Jews will first seek to secure their [local] micro-political interests, and only then their macro-political interests. The major concern will be to achieve a maximum degree of stability and security, *irrespective of the nature of the regime*" (author's italics).[39] In prewar Johnstown, the dominant political and social forces maintaining order, security, and stability had been right-wing Republican, and, well aware of the marginality of their position in the local society, Jews supported the existing establishment by their votes, and, as we shall see shortly, by tacit if uncomfortable acquiescence in the ways this order and stability were maintained.

Although they overwhelmingly registered Republican, a good number of my interviewees emphasized, however, that in national elections they actually voted Democratic: "We were registered Republican, but supported Roosevelt"; in this declared support for FDR, and, especially, for his New Deal social policies on the domestic front and for his stand against nazism in Germany, the Johnstown Jews did not differ from their fellow ethnics across the United States. Since there were in Johnstown no precincts with a Jewish majority, there was no way to verify these claims. I could only compare the first precinct in Westmont, the area where practically all Jewish families lived in this neighborhood, known in town as the "supper side," with the more elitist "dinner side," the second and third Westmont precincts, inhabited by the managers of steel and coal companies, local bankers, and other Anglo-Protestant professionals. The first precinct voted Republican in three consecutive elections during the 1930s, but in consistently smaller proportions than did its richer and more powerful counterpart. The supper side of Westmont also contained a number of skilled steelworkers' families who were badly hurt by the Depression and would have been likely to opt for Roosevelt, but if voting Democratic for president was indeed common in the Jewish community, their votes, too, contributed to this result.[40]

In answer to the question of why Jews stayed in the local Republican camp, everyone I asked pointed to pragmatic reasons, although these did not concern a desire for political power in the form of municipal government appointments, as in the big cities with competitive ethnic politics. Ruth G., speaking for her own and other Jewish families, put it most suc-

cinctly: "In a town like this, [registering] Republican was more expedient";
Elmer M. elaborated: "to be a registered Democrat in Johnstown—and in
a small town people knew such things—where the mighty, the WASPS,
were all Republican, it lowered your class position, and not to be part of it
[the Republican majority] could also hurt your situation."[41] When asked to
specify the rewards accrued from such registered loyalty to the political establishment, my informants mentioned practical advantages. Siding with
the powerful, especially since not doing so was so readily perceptible, facilitated business-related matters such as a bank loan, mercantile license, or
adjustment of tax levied on a store building—or, in the case of the more
affluent merchants, when the county had some orders to place for clothing,
shoes, dry goods, or the like. The insecurity of Jewish businesses closely
tied to the production of the mills and coal mines, whose owners pretty
much controlled the course of local politics, naturally increased this sense
of dependence. Then, as noted by Elmer M., there was the matter of status,
especially for the *nouveaux-arrivés* in Westmont, where the prestigious address and party affiliation were two sides of the same coin. But besides individual advantages, real or potential, there was also, as Johnstown Jews perceived it, a collective purpose. Namely, by signing up Republican as did the
mighty, and keeping quiet, Jews could maintain, precisely, group inconspicuousness—a situation that New York Jews, competing for a "fair share"
in the political life of the city, would have considered, conversely, a dis-
advantage, and would have vocally contested.

This political quiescence, though, was not without a certain tension resulting from the Jewish group's ambiguous position in Johnstown's socioeconomic structure, and specifically from what the sociologists of class relations call the "contradictory class interests" of small shopkeepers.[42] As
noted above, Jews found their interests linked to those of the ruling class,
even though they were not part of it; but at the same time, as demonstrated
in the earlier chapters, the customers of Jewish businesses, and thus direct
contributors to their "insecure prosperity," were the industrial workers, or
the subordinate class.

Several of my informants commented on this inconsistency themselves,
particularly when asked about the failed strikes at Bethlehem Steel for the
independent union, in 1919 and 1937, in which the mill workers participated en masse. It was naturally in the interest of the store owners that
work should resume as quickly as possible; but, on the one hand, they did
not want to alienate their customers by openly supporting the company,
and, on the other hand, they dreaded antagonizing Bethlehem Steel management and the city government that supported it. The latter sentiment
prevailed, at least in public expression, in the largest Jewish congregation:
Rodef Sholom's rabbi joined the so-called Citizens Committee organized
during the 1937 strike at the initiative of the Westmont Presbyterian
Church's council, which ostensibly was to serve as an arbiter but actually
promoted the company's interests. But among the congregation's rank-

and-file members, the common attitude was, rather, similar to that expressed by Harry R., who kept "neutral and silent, hoping that a settlement would be reached quickly [. . .] if you had any preferences, you certainly did not show it." Like Irving L., Jewish storekeepers generally realized that "keeping quiet, it meant supporting the company . . . and [they] said among themselves how ridiculous this was, but they kept quiet." Beth Zion's rabbi, however, refused to join the antistrike Citizens Committee, apparently influenced by the radical pro–social justice orientation of the contemporary American Reform rabbinate, but this public refusal reportedly angered his congregation.[43]

Recollecting the strikes and their response to them, my informants unselfconsciously referred to the striking workers, largely Slavs and Hungarians, as "foreigners." Employing the term used by the dominant groups (Anglo-Protestants and West Europeans), they reconfirmed in this label their own in-between structural location, as well as a felt economic and social distance from the lower class. The label was doubly paradoxical, of course, considering that daily contacts in Johnstown between members of their own group and these workers were built on a long-standing old-country acquaintance, and, more ironic yet, many of the labelers were themselves immigrants. Most Jewish storekeepers commiserated with the situation of these "foreigners slaving in the mills and coal mines," "so exploited by these companies," and continued selling to the strikers' families on credit until work resumed.[44] Actually, while they recollected these feelings of commiseration and yet interpreted the complacent stand of Jewish shopkeepers during the steel strikes as the only rational option for people in their position, a number of my informants sounded somewhat defensive, as if they also remembered having felt somehow guilty of betraying a group ethical norm, namely, the traditional Jewish religious precept of acting for social justice.

"Democratic party was the place for the Jew"—Samuel K. expressed this uneasiness perhaps most clearly—"and here [in Johnstown] there was a competition between business interests and the built-in Jewish idealism."[45] This sense of a collective normative impropriety, as it were, had probably been reinforced, or induced perhaps, by the reading of *Forverts*, which consistently maintained a pro-labor orientation, and through family and social contacts in New York, where since the turn of the century liberal-democratic causes, and particularly unionism, had had a large Jewish following; in the 1937 and 1941 mayoral elections, the American Labor Party, founded by Jewish social-democrats unwilling to support the Irish-dominated Democratic party, received over 40 percent of the Jewish vote citywide. My informants remembered the awkwardness of occasional encounters between quiescent Johnstown Jews and Jewish labor organizers and lawyers from New York who visited town during and after the 1937 strike, helping to set up the informal structure of what was to become the recognized steelworkers' union in 1941. Among the different arguments offered by such visitors to persuade local Jews to take a more active stand, that emphasizing the collective "ethnic" call to social justice was most embarrassing to the listeners, although apparently not sufficient to prompt a change in behavior.

Ethnic persuasion of a more peculiar sort was used, and worked—that is, contributed to concrete action rather than mere cognitive discomfort—in different, changed circumstances a decade later. While the steelworkers' union was already firmly established in the mills, and the political power of Bethlehem Steel had considerably weakened, a small local garment factory that had been relocated to Johnstown from Philadelphia in the late 1930s by a Jewish manufacturer remained stubbornly nonunion despite repeated workers' strikes. According to a memoir by David Gingold, an International Ladies' Garment Workers' Union (ILGWU) organizer from New York who assisted these workers in their demands, the owner finally backed down in 1947 after his local Jewish lawyer set up a meeting with Gingold at a specially arranged party in a Westmont Jewish home, where the two of them engaged in a Talmudic debate. Gingold's yeshiva-trained scholarship apparently so impressed the dress manufacturer that the latter agreed to open negotations the next morning. Other ILGWU representatives and former workers who had been engaged in the Johnstown settlement confirmed this story; they added that a helpful, or perhaps central, factor in changing the manufacturer's mind was the argument, supported by members of the local Jewish community, that a Jewish-owned nonunion factory in the unionized town "reflected badly on the Jewish community by making it stand out." A desire to stay collectively inconspicuous prevailed again, except that in the transformed circumstances it now called for a pro-labor action, thus easing the discomfort of ethnic consciousness created by the previous situation.[46]

PARTICIPATION IN COMMUNITY AFFAIRS AND VOLUNTARY ORGANIZATIONS

As reported in historical studies in bigger and smaller cities, the participation of American Jews in community services and other voluntary organizations of the inclusive kind was more extensive than their involvement in local governments, and actually the most significant of all forms of outside participation.[47]

For Johnstown Jews too, involvement in general community services and inclusive-type voluntary associations was the most extensive of all forms of their participation in the local society; but, hindered by multiple factors listed earlier, it was still much more limited than that found in the four places chosen for comparison, and, for that matter, than has been reported in all other studies of different localities that I have inspected as well. And, restricted as it was, Jews' involvement in mainstream communal affairs did not alter in any sense the existing sharp group boundaries be-tween them and members of the dominant society. On the part of the lat-ter, the minimal Jewish presence in these organizations was considered to be largely inconsequential tokenism; "We would also like a member of the Hebrew race" was, as my informants remembered, a common, actually well-meaning, explanation of an occasional offer extended to a local Jew to join a board of some public charitable institution or a community function. On their part, members of the Jewish group treated these activities as pres-tigious but basically extraneous to the purview of their daily lives, which largely remained within the orbit of the ethnic community. Institutional beneficiaries named in registered wills of deceased Johnstown Jews tellingly reflected this prevalent inward orientation: in all but two or three cases, such bequests, if they were made, went to Jewish causes.[48]

For a century after the establishment of a permanent Jewish community in Johnstown, Jews held the following functions in general community ser-vices (most of them, however, were held by the same few people, all Amer-ican-born, of both German and East European origin): member (twice) of the board of the Community Chest (and Jewish organizations contributed to its campaigns), secretary of the local Tuberculosis Society, member of the Child Welfare Committee, and of the Family Welfare Society of the Council of Social Agencies. In addition, three Jews served on the boards of the Memorial Hospital and the Mercy Hospital, one on the welfare cam-paigns committee of the Citizens' Council of Greater Johnstown, and one, during the mid-Depression years, on the Johnstown Advisory Council of the Bureau of Employment of the Commonwealth of Pennsylvania's De-partment of Labor and Industry; there was also, for one term, a Jewish member of the Johnstown Civic League (the same man as in the above two functions).[49]

Nearly all the remaining few voluntary organizations with Jewish mem-bers were of an instrumental character. Before World War II, apart from church choirs and ethnic-based cultural associations that served their own public, the town had few broader-based organized activities of the expres-sive kind. For adolescents, there were high school extracurricular activities such as drama, music, or literary clubs. For adults, there was the the Amer-ican Legion, which at the local level performed symbolic-expressive memo-rial functions; some of the town's Jewish World War I veterans belonged to the American Legion, but there were no Jewish women in its auxiliary. Among the occupational associations, most relevant, was, of course, the Johnstown Chamber of Commerce. During 1921–1922 it was presided over by a member of Beth Zion Reform Temple, the son-in-law of the owner of one of the town's established better department stores, but at no time prior to World War II did more than 10 percent of the total number of Jewish merchants, predominantly of the second generation, belong to this institution; although they tended to come from the upper layers of the economic stratification of their own ethnic group, over two-thirds of the

Jewish members figured in the lowest contributor-category in the Chamber of Commerce's files. (About one-third of the total number of the Chamber's Jewish member-merchants also advertised their businesses in the local press). A small number of Johnstown's Jewish doctors, lawyers, and teachers belonged—"automatically," as one of them called this membership based on certified qualifications—to the local (county) chapters of their respective professional associations.[50]

Voluntary organizations were traditionally the main sphere of women's involvement in public affairs of their communities; in fact, it has been argued that women's voluntary work in community affairs should be treated as the equivalent of political participation, in any case before the ratification of the Nineteenth Amendment. Studies in American Jewish history suggest, in addition, that involvement in mainstream voluntary organizations was the primary avenue of Jewish women's contacts with representatives of the dominant, Anglo-Protestant group; this was indeed the case in the four localities chosen here for comparative references.[51]

In Johnstown, under the impact of circumstances described previously, even welfare and philanthropic services, which elsewhere became considerably feminized even in vertical structures, remained not only controlled by men, but also, in more elevated positions, staffed by male workers. The limited involvement of Jewish women in these activities reflected this general tendency, further reinforced from within the ethnic community. On the one hand, the latter's persistent traditionalism was particularly enduring—in this case, gender-exclusive—in matters of outside representation, wherein male dominance, even in the spheres defined by middle-class American society as "feminine," remained more solid than in other cities. On the other hand, outside participation was also restrained by the preoccupation in business of the majority of Jewish women. By contrast, neither of the above circumstances appeared to have existed to so hindering an extent in Terre Haute; in particular, by the interwar period, the great majority of Jewish merchants' wives stayed home as housewives rather than working as business companions, which enabled them to invest more time in outside activities, both within and without the Jewish community.[52]

Apart from the women teachers who belonged to the Teachers' Association, and, in the late 1930s, the few women who became actively engaged in the PTA, involvement in general community services about exhausted Jewish women's participation in organized activities. Overall, in terms of a number of civic functions fulfilled by Johnstown's Jews during the entire fifty-year period covered in this study, over two-thirds, including the conventionally female-sphere membership in child and family welfare councils, were held by men. The few Jewish women involved in Johnstown community services were all members of the Reform Beth Zion Temple, again confirming the pattern discussed in the preceding chapter, namely, of congregational differences in the scope of women's public participation. But just as the chairmanship of the outward-turned Beth Zion Forum was naturally held by Mr., and not Mrs., Nelson E., so it was he, not she, who assumed an even more public role as a member of the Johnstown Civic League, even though his wife Hulda, Maggie's resolute daughter, was more energetic and civic-minded than her quiet husband Nelson.

Next to consider is the participation of Jews in organizations that stressed, variously specified, exclusiveness of membership, such as fraternal lodges and social clubs. As we have seen, in Cleveland and Charleston Jews had been extensively involved in the public affairs of local mainstream society, and relations between them and representatives of the dominant group(s) engendered in this participation had been of an integrative character, de-emphasizing rather than strengthening ethnic boundaries. Yet even in these cities, where Jewish members were accepted in most organizations of this kind, there still remained a few where, as my local informant put it, "a certain type of WASP mentality" kept the doors closed to ethnoreligious outsiders. Studies of the relations of Jews with members of the dominant American society during the interwar period conducted in other localities—predominantly big cities—practically without exception found the former excluded from many, or even most, private social clubs and fraternal lodges frequented by members of the dominant groups. The very few places where investigators found Jews to have "mingled freely" as members of whichever clubs existed, "the Rotary, the Masons, and the Elks," were very small towns of no more than 10,000 inhabitants, with predominantly commercial economies, a very small number of residentially dispersed, and unorganized, Jewish residents occupied as merchants or professionals—and, presumably (no explicit information has been given), an integrative local public life.[53]

Not surprisingly, in Johnstown there was only strictly limited participation of Jews in exclusive social organizations, of which only two were consequential for status, connections, and power. One was the Masons, whose importance as a status marker had to do, it appears, with two characteristics of the local dominant society: it did not have a native "aristocracy" as did New England towns, for example (in several of those towns there was no Masonic lodge, or this organization was not so important), and there was no single Protestant denomination that conferred the highest social prestige. In the 1860s, before a permanent Jewish community was established in Johnstown, a few German Jews had joined the local Masonic lodge, but all of them resigned shortly (I was unable to find out why); and, early in this century, there were, apparently, two more Jewish Masons, an affluent unmarried merchant and his nephew who, to the extent that it was possible in Johnstown, had stayed aloof from the activities of the Jewish community.[54]

At the other institutional juncture of the town's status-and-power network, the prestigious Sunnehanna country club, organized in Westmont in the 1920s by Bethlehem Steel Company's management for its own and friends' leisure use, "there was an understanding that there were no Jews."

Still, during the Depression, when the club struggled with financial difficulties—my informants specified them as "piled-up laundry bills"—a few
affluent Jews were admitted, but "just those, and unmarried men only, so
that membership would not be extended to the wives and children [. . .]
more Jews did not get admitted until the 1960s." Another, less elitist club
in the area, North Fork, reportedly for similar economic reasons, decided
in the mid-1930s to admit Jewish members by quota, at a 1:10 ratio, and
a few did join. In the Jewish community, fellow ethnics' joining of these
clubs was generally met with derision, especially since the calculated reasons for their selective admission were known. Leon M., for example, a
Sunnehanna member, did not recall any unpleasant (i.e., anti-Semitic) incidents at the club; "the only abuse he ever took from anyone because of his
membership at Sunnehanna came from Jews who teased him or razzed him
a good bit."[55] While in other locations—such as New York, Cleveland, and
Terre Haute from our comparative group—status-conscious Jews, not admitted to the elite Anglo-Protestant clubs, founded their own, parallel organizations in more prestigious neighborhoods into which they moved,
Jewish residents of Westmont did not have sufficient means for this kind of
imitation and had to satisfy themselves with the Jewish Social Center serving the entire community.

In sum, Johnstown Jews' participation in organized activities of the local
mainstream society before World War II had apparently been much more
limited than in other localities, big or small; combined with other factors
noted earlier, this minimal involvement contributed to the persistence of
sharply delineated ethnic boundaries between the Jewish group and members of the dominant, Anglo-Protestant society. We may recall in this context the previous chapter's suggestion that the participation of big-city
Jews in mainstream organized activities facilitated ethnicization of their
communities by making the middle-class American sociocultural patterns
readily available; the integrative character of this involvement quickened
this process, but, as the example of New York demonstrated, was not the
necessary condition thereof. In comparison, a relative isolation of Johnstown's Jews from organized activities of the local dominant society contributed to an ethnicization of the Jewish community's institutional life
that occurred primarily "secondhand," through imitation of new developments that occurred in Jewish settlements in the big cities, rather than
through direct participation in or replication of dominant middle-class
American ways.

Yet another direction of Johnstown's Jews' involvement in external
communal affairs should be mentioned: the occasional participation of
Jews from Hungary in the organized activities of the local Hungarian Gentile community. While some informal social contacts existed at the mar-
gin of business relations between the East European Jews and Slavs in
the Johnstown area, it was only the national and cultural celebrations of
the Hungarian group that Jewish guests sometimes visited, indicating

somewhat greater "identificational closeness" between these two groups. Uniquely, too, in comparison with ethnic groups of Slavic origin, the Hungarian Gentile community counted as "theirs" the town's Jewish Hungarian businessmen and professionals, although this identification was not reciprocated.[56]

PARTICIPATION IN SOCIAL CLIQUES AND CLOSE PERSONAL RELATIONS

The last form of social participation of Johnstown's Jews outside their ethnic community to be considered here are primary social relations—understood as informal cliques, personal friendships including dating and intermarriage, and other contacts involving matters of private life: at the upper echelons of the local stratification system, with members of the dominant, Anglo-Protestant group; at its lower levels, with working-class Slavs and Hungarians, the Jews' former neighbors in Eastern Europe.

Historical and early postwar sociological studies unanimously report close personal contacts between Jews, even those of the second or third American-born generations, and members of the dominant strata as generally the least common type of the former's involvement in mainstream American society, and particularly infrequent in the contexts of numerically large, residentially concentrated, and institutionally well-organized Jewish populations in the big cities.[57] Relatively most frequent among comparative cases considered here, personal relations of Jews with members of the dominant group in Charleston and little towns seem to have been generated by their own contexts in the neighborhood, during a shopping expedition, or at the town's picnic, rather than primarily by the occasions formal association membership provided. As a matter of fact, contacts involved in formal-organizational membership—particularly in the metropolitan centers with complex institutional networks, but also, for example, in much smaller and less densely organized Terre Haute with its "five o'clock shadow" routine—have been described as largely task-oriented and superficially social, and therefore a poor transmitter for forging closer personal relations.

In Johnstown, some circumstances existed that could have generated more enduring personal relations between Jews and members of the dominant strata. The day-to-day chances of encountering non-Jews were, of course, incomparably greater than, for instance, in Cleveland, and much greater still than in New York, where *Forverts* estimated in the mid-1920s that the substantial majority "of all the Jews practically have no social contact with the Gentiles."[58] The small number and proportion of Jews in Johnstown's general population, the location of many of the Jewish businesses in the downtown area, the employment of a mixed workforce by a few larger Jewish-owned department stores, Jews' residence among

Gentiles, and their sharing with them such public facilities as schools, parks and picnic areas, movie theaters and dance halls—all these circumstances made contacts with non-Jews inevitable, and they were generally amiable. Their potentially facilitating impact, however, was neutralized by the combined effect of several restricting factors listed earlier (and absent in Charleston and little towns), so that only exceptionally—I found but a handful of cases and none without qualifications—had these daily encounters with middle-or upper-class Americans deepened into more personal enduring involvements.

Since daily occupational and organizational contacts between Jews and members of the dominant socioeconomic stratum were limited, there was also little occasion for informal socializing and forging personal friendships. Some work-related opportunities did exist, as in the Jewish-owned, larger department stores downtown that employed a mixed workforce and provided employee cafeterias, and annual picnics and dinner parties; a couple of Jewish-Gentile personal friendships among the few I located were formed between people employed at the managerial level in these establishments. Jewish and Gentile professionals also socialized at lunches if they shared the same offices, at occasional dinner parties given by the American Bar or Medical Associations, or other functions such as charity balls at local hospitals; and at similar occasions Jewish and Christian members of the local Chamber of Commerce also met. This friendly-distant socializing, however, did not transfer to homes, although the people involved on both sides resided in Westmont, often as near neighbors.

Being neighbors did not generate its own channel of social mixing, either, in any case not among the adults. On the whole, residential location did not much affect the frequency or endurance of primary social relations between Jews and their Christian neighbors; stated differently, moving to Westmont—Johnstown's equivalent of a big-city suburb—inhabited by members of the local American elite, did not lead to greater integration of Jewish residents into the elite's social circles. When the first Jewish families began settling in Westmont in the late 1910s, they were met with resistance: "Houses were for sale but you couldn't buy them." Occasionally there was open animosity: for instance, signs saying "get out of here" were placed on the front lawns of homes newly purchased by Jewish families. By the mid-1920s, however, the outward signs, at least, of opposition to the presence of Jews had disappeared, and the gradually expanding number of Jewish residents of Westmont were being met with polite *désintéressement* on the part of Christian inhabitants. The children played together on the streets and in the backyards, and there was also some home visiting, although more observant Jewish parents permitted visits of Gentile children in their own homes, but not vice versa, apparently to prevent Jewish youngsters from eating forbidden foods and perhaps becoming enchanted with Christian symbolic objects like the Christmas tree. A socioreligious distance was also maintained on the other side; a Gentile friend of thirteen-year-old Michael W., for example, was forbidden to attend the latter's bar mitzvah at Beth Zion Temple, although more likely from a sense that such a visit was improper than out of fear that the boy would become attracted to Judaism. The social mixing of children, however, did not, as one informant put it, "transfer into similar relations of parents," or adults in general.[59]

In prewar Westmont, there was apparently none of the impromptu day-time socializing reported in some studies—the domain of women, involving informal drop-ins for a cup of coffee or small talk about the neighborhood, children's school, or shopping bargains. Nor was there more formal, evening visiting, involving both husband and wife or even the whole family, such as a dinner party or a bridge game. One reason was that for the majority of Jewish resident families, maintaining the recently acquired and insecure American middle-class economic status, even on the supper side of this neighborhood, kept everyone busy, leaving little time for daytime neighborly chats over coffee, and little money to spend on dinner parties with formal guests. Another was that, as already noted earlier in this chapter, this kind of socializing was "not done" and this tacit understanding not questioned, either by a few Anglo-Protestant women I interviewed for this project, or by Jewish informant-hostesses of Westmont homes, regardless of generation and synagogue membership. One exception, Mrs. Sally W., a Beth Zion member of East European origin and resident of Westmont, remembered having once tried to strike up a closer daytime social relationship with a Gentile neighbor by offering her a volume of Sholom Aleichem's stories, but "nothing happened [. . .] she most likely never even read it, and after that I didn't try again."[60]

Expectedly, young second-generation Jewish Johnstowners had on the whole more social contacts with native-born Americans than did older cohorts, particularly the foreign-born. School was of course the main meeting ground. The average proportion of Jewish students per grade at Johnstown High School during the interwar period was about 6–7:350–400 or 1.5–2 percent (in comparison, in some New York Jewish neighborhoods at the same time, Jews constituted up to 70 percent of the student population, and 25–30 percent of schoolteachers were Jewish); and so, as one of my informants put it, "being so few Jews, automatically we had non-Jewish friends." Outside school, including extracurricular activities, my respondents also spent some leisure time with their Gentile friends, playing sports, going to the movies or vaudeville theaters, or attending public dances. The common estimate—young men mixing somewhat more often because of sports activities—of the division of entertainment time spent in exclusively Jewish versus non-Jewish or mixed company was about 70–75 percent and 25–30 percent, respectively.[61]

But the proportion of time spent with Gentile friends was not the most important issue; after all, some brief encounters can have much weightier consequence for mutual relations than regular lengthy meetings. What was more significant for most of my informants was the not quite integrative quality of these interactions. Jews and Gentiles played and did things together "as if we were the same," recalled Raphael R., and then came another school morning with its ritual Bible reading and the Lord's Prayer, and weekly Sabbath and Christian Sunday, then Jewish High Holy Days and the Christmas season: "there were moments when you thought you were like others, and then it stopped, you were different." As my second-generation informants remembered, this feeling of otherness, recurrent when they mixed socially with native-born American children and adolescents, was not primarily a matter of symbolic membership in a generalized Jewish group, as reported in studies of Jewish identity in little towns with a minimal number of Jews; rather, the otherness was anchored in concrete traditions and a lifestyle specific to their ethnoreligious group membership. "Yes, we [himself and siblings] had Gentile friends, went out together and visited them at home. . . . but our homes were different . . . theirs was not our world"—Maurice S. stated this perception in a more extreme fashion than others, but it well illustrates the point.[62]

A sense of belonging to overlapping yet somehow nonidentical worlds underlay also, and on both sides, Jewish-Gentile dating in prewar Johnstown. There was, on the whole, little of it; although its very occurrence, without general approval but also without group ostracism, was already a major departure from the strict separation in these matters that existed in the East European shtetls.[63] Jewish parental attitudes and young people's behavior regarding exogamous dating ranged considerably, according to their recollections. The categorical responses "out of the question" and "parents would have been horrified" characterized the immigrant homes of Israel and Rachel B., and Aaron and Sarah E., whose children—nine in the former and three in the latter family—obediently followed the parental wishes. In other cases, a similar parental attitude was coupled with the children's dating in defiance, like Frieda C., "just a little bit on the side." Finally, there was the more permissive if a bit apprehensive "all right, but not seriously," as in the home of Israel and Ida N. with five children. Not surprisingly, the more strictly prohibitive parental attitude and their children's willing acquiescence were reported by people from more traditionally Orthodox homes, which were less common in Westmont. But, as those who did date non-Jewish partners recollected, "it was understood that marriage was out of question"; "we dated [but] would never think of marrying." Even when the relationship developed into a serious love—I found but two such instances, although there might have been a few more—it was broken up, because the people involved apparently could not bring themselves to profoundly hurt their families and violate the norms of their ethnoreligious communities.[64]

In fact, these youthful out-of-group friendships, as well as dating relationships, tended to dissolve as the young people matured, became engaged, and established their own families. "It happened naturally, I never gave it much thought," Frances C., from a Westmont Anglo-Protestant family, reflected on this imperceptible process of sorting into ethnically homogeneous primary social circles. A few intermarriages between Jews and Gentiles did occur prior to World War II: my informants were able to count them on their fingers; they made up about 1.6 percent of all married people in both generations combined, and somewhat less than double that figure among the immigrants' American-born children. Unlike adolescent dating, however, intermarrying was unanimously regarded in the Jewish community (I did not inquire on the Christian side) as a "social disgrace" and "looked at with contempt," so that "such couples tended to stay away," and in fact the majority of them left town. For comparison, in the 1930s, the proportion of religiously outmarried Jews in the United States ranged from 4 to 10 percent, with the upper range more common on the West Coast but also obtaining in such places as Charleston, South Carolina, where, unlike Johnstown, "the majority [of intermarried] continue[d] to be regarded as members of the Jewish community."[65]

At the other end of the social spectrum, informal personal contacts between Jews and Slavic and Hungarian laborers and their families were limited, too, but the nature of these relations was quite different from contacts with members of the town's social elite. The Jews' overall marginal economic and political situation vis-à-vis Anglo-Americans in Johnstown had made them weaker partners in social interactions as well, whether as potential or actual petitioners (e.g., for social club membership), token "Hebrew" participants in a charity ball at a local hospital, or distantly tolerated neighbors in the prestigious sections of town. Working-class Slavs and Hungarians, however, as unskilled industrial laborers, were even more powerless than small shopkeepers; they were directly dependent, on the one hand, on the company managers/ruling elite, and, on the other, on the goodwill of Jewish storeowners whom they ordinarily owed money for goods purchased on credit. In relations with these Gentile East Europeans, Jews were on the whole the stronger partners (the implications of this shift in "the power balance" between the two groups for the Johnstown Jews' sense of [in]security will be discussed in the next chapter).

In practically all forms of informal social contacts between adult East European Jews and Gentiles in prewar Johnstown, the former appeared as givers, or providers, sometimes of material emergency assistance, such as small food baskets given to Slavic children coming to the doors during the particularly bad times of the Depression, but most commonly of different kinds of advice in matters concerning the latter's private lives. This role continued, on a diminished scale, the old-country tradition of Jewish ombudsmanship for the peasantry. A new function was added to it, however: mediation between East European Gentiles and the dominant society whereby Jews—from the Anglo-Protestant viewpoint "Hebrew" outsiders, but, in comparison with "Hunky" laborers, more familiar with the American system—served as Americanization agents.

Some counseling functions were performed predominantly by men. Even in the interwar period, Jewish immigrants—like the fathers of Sam K., Shirley M., Bessie S., or Miriam K.—served Gentile East Europeans as bona fide interpreters in court and other public institutions that required communication in English; though with a heavy accent, the former were more proficient in this language, and, as important, apparently less intimidated by American institutions. Jews whose domiciles or businesses remained in the "foreign colonies" occasionally also helped elderly illiterate immigrant Slavs write letters to their families in Eastern Europe, or had been asked to read letters received, learning in this way of happenings in their private lives. Israel B., owner of a well-patronized grocery in Woodvale, and of the only private automobile in the neighborhood, customarily chauffeured young Slavic couples to their nearby church for the wedding ceremony. Abe K., while peddling at the beginning of the century between coal-mining towns surrounding Johnstown, functioned for "Slavish coal miners [as] a [traveling] banker and an accountant. . . . He kept and helped calculate their savings for them." When he later settled in Beaverdale and opened a general store there, the miners still came to him from time to time for advice in more difficult financial decisions, such as taking out a loan or purchasing a house. And Harry M.'s father, also a store owner, who could converse in five Slavic languages, played the role of traditional factotum for the East Europeans "who came to him with everything, for advice, and even to help find a wife." These advisory functions were typically rendered by the immigrants, usually in an old-country-style, informal manner, on various occasions. But a modernized form of advice giving also emerged in counselor-client settings, where American-born Jewish professionals dispensed their wisdom—especially lawyers and doctors, whom their East European Christian customers often perceived, in a remnant of old-country peasant representations, as equipped with some extranatural powers.

These relations, while quite personal to the extent that Jewish advisers had insight into their advisees' private lives, did not, however, extend to home visiting. The only exception I found was, again, of a well-established Hungarian Jewish merchant in Cambria City, who was occasionally visited by—but did not visit himself—a leader of the local Hungarian Christian community "for conversation." It was also only the Jews from Hungary, it is worth noting, who reportedly felt "such a joy" at the opportunity of speaking Hungarian, also with Christians.[66]

Besides these most common kinds of primary social relations between East European Jews and Gentiles, whereby the former "participated" through advisory assistance in the latter's personal lives, there was one other form—the only type that also entailed a reciprocal insight on the part of the Gentiles. Unlike the above-mentioned contacts, this form typically involved women: informal social interactions arising from the young Slavic women's employment as servants in Jewish homes, another practice transplanted from Eastern Europe. Although this work-derived relationship gave Slavic employees access to Jewish homes and their daily happenings, differences in lifestyles, distancing mutual perceptions, and the superior/ subordinate relation between the parties effectively precluded partnerlike friendships. Like their husbands in the stores, wives in the homes (often in the back of the shop) would offer practical advice, on modern American household appliances, on hanging curtains or upholstering furniture according to current fashion, to Slavic daughters. The multiple group mediations in the process of immigrants' adaptation to the American ways of life—here, big-city Jews as intermediaries for small-town Jews, and the latter for Slavs—are only touched upon in this study, but they deserve more attention from students of ethnicity.

To conclude, a specific configuration of circumstances in the Johnstown environment and within the Jewish group constrained to a minimum all forms of Jewish participation in the activities of the local dominant society. This limited participation of Johnstown's Jews in mainstream affairs was an additional contributing factor, besides the economic and sociocultural ones discussed in earlier chapters, to the slowing down of sociocultural ethnicization inside the Jewish group, and to the persistence of sharp ethnic boundaries between the Jewish and dominant groups; and, by the same token, to the Jews' multiple marginality in the local society. Lower down on the social ladder, social relations of Jews with working-class Slavs and Hungarians, customers of Jewish businesses, were also limited, but they retained some characteristics of the traditional old-country relationship, and, in contrast to those with members of the local dominant society, the Jewish participants enjoyed the upper hand.

We shall now consider the ways Jews perceived themselves and their situation in Johnstown, and, more broadly, in America, and how they compared and evaluated it, concretely in terms of their daily experience, and in a longer, or broader, philosophical perspective, as they tried to orient their actions.

Through Several Lenses:
Making Sense of Their Lives

SHARED mental schemas for making sense of the world and oneself and coping with practical life situations have been treated in previous chapters as part of the resources used by Johnstown Jews in the pursuit of their family and communal purposes in the specific context of the town's economic opportunity structure and sociopolitical order. We now focus on these schemas in themselves as they were recollected by their bearer-practitioners. In particular, we shall look at the ways the Johnstowners—and specifically the East Europeans who have been the primary subjects of this study—appreciated, mentally and emotionally, two prominent characteristics of their experience: civic vulnerability that derived from the Jewish group's political dependence and social marginality in the local dominant society, and the instability of the material fortunes of Jewish households, or, more generally, their socioeconomic success.

Two important caveats should be noted concerning the nature of the evidence presented here and its implications for my interpretations (the matter is discussed in greater detail in appendix I, "[Self-]Reflections of a Fieldworker"). First, regarding the Johnstown evidence and the reasons why data/texts in this chapter should be considered with special awareness of their constructed and "collaborative" character. I tried to match ideas (perceptions, values, and attitudes) of my informants as closely as possible with concrete practices as recorded in contemporary sources. Nevertheless, the interpretations I heard, which are the basis of this analysis, have been reconstructed from remembered thoughts and feelings about specific and, from these, generalized life situations in the past. Perhaps more important, many of these attitudes and perceptions—especially those regarding the vicissitudes of mundane fortunes and God's involvement in human affairs—had been largely unarticulated or experience-near, and were expressed for the first time in response to my questioning during interviews. "We did not talk much about these things, it was just there, this feeling [or idea]"—such comments often accompanied Johnstowners' attempts to put into words the unspoken experience I asked them to recollect.[1] Finally, my personal situation and concerns—especially my growing involvement with Judaism—screened what I asked and heard as a researcher.

Second, the material used in this chapter for comparisons with the Johnstown "data" has also been rather unconventional. Scholarly studies contain little information about American Jews' perceptions and feelings that is directly compatible with matters of concern here. In order to maintain a comparative perspective, I decided to combine what exists, also from the early post–World War II period, with available information either indirectly related to Jewish worldviews or taken from differently conceptualized studies, which could be accommodated into my interpretive framework.

Reliance on such incomplete or indirect, or else obviously collaborative, information makes the analysis presented here admittedly the most speculative of all, and renders the discernment of what in the discussed outlooks was Jewish, and what specifically Jewish-Johnstownish, particularly difficult. However, there is a dearth of information in Jewish American studies about their subjects' schemas of interpreting and acting upon the world, information indispensable to understanding of the immigrant/ethnic experience. Therefore, the overall gains in our knowledge derived from using this evidence, and making comparisons—informed speculations, though an apparent oxymoron, seems an appropriate term—surpass, I believe, the limitations noted above.

The underlying mental schema for making sense of the world and acting upon it was the apprehension of human affairs as inherently polysemic and contradictory, and therefore underdeterminate and circumstantial— flexible and "fluxible," as one of my informant-mentors in Johnstown neologized. To repeat the caveat noted in the discussion in chapter 1 of East European Jews' shared worldviews, what was important here was not, or not mainly, that these outlooks contained heterogeneous and mutually opposite elements, since all cultural systems of course contain them, but the degree of recognition and acceptance of these incongruities in the representation of life situations.[2] Rather than readily "fleeing from ambiguity," as Donald Levine called the habitual inclination of the modern mind shaped by the ideas of the Western Enlightenment, or ignoring "biformities" in human existence, as Michael Kammen characterized, specifically, the American intellectual propensity to consider "inconsistency as a bad thing," Jewish *habitus* accommodated—even welcomed—polyvalence and the accompanying tensions built into individual and collective human existence as natural.[3]

The "Jewish mind is often self-contradictory," editorialized the *Daily Jewish Courier* in 1921, providing illustrations of apparently incongruous but "realistic" attitudes and perspectives in different spheres of life; and in Johnstown in 1936 the congregation listened without surprise to their rabbi preach approvingly on the topic "When Contradiction Makes Sense."[4] This general orientation, allowing for, even inviting, a dialectical worldview—a recognition of contradiction as one of life's operative principles—also informed the perceptions and sense Johnstown's Jews made of their civic vulnerability and of insecure economic achievement. Although they were obviously closely related, in fact formed one continuous world-view, for greater clarity the schemas Johnstown's Jews applied to apprehend and act in these situations are discussed in two separate sections—each of which, too, uses a different kind of comparative material.

"MUCH MUCH MORE SECURE INSECURITY"

The Johnstown Jewish group's civic vulnerability was appreciated, in my informants' recollections, at once through several prisms, as it were, or from different vantage points, some of which sharpened while others assuaged the shared sense of insecurity. The overall result was an intricate, multifaceted evaluation: of a "much much more secure insecurity" as Louis G. perceived the situation in Johnstown in comparison with Eastern Europe, yet nevertheless requiring, in the assessment of the local Jews, that the group remain "obviously un-obvious," as Arthur H., another of my mentor-informants, referred to the public image the Jewish community wished to project on the outside.[5]

Various accounts of the Jews' adaptation to mainstream American society in big and smaller cities, before and after World War II, suggest intergenerational persistence of a more or less intense sense of civic insecurity; this apparently held true even in places where the relations of Jews with the local dominant society had an integrative character. According to Alan Dershowitz's provocative *Chutzpah*, while largely suppressed, this insecurity haunts even solidly successful and otherwise thoroughly Americanized Jews of today.[6]

A closer look at these reports reveals three distinguishable kinds of civic insecurity experienced by American Jews during confrontations with the dominant society. One may be termed a sense of collective insecurity, that is, the perception by individual Jews of an actual or potential threat to their entire group—a general attitude captured in the "But is it good for the Jews?" reaction toward even apparently unrelated occurrences, whether local, national, or worldwide; it was often (though not necessarily) combined with a "*Shah!* Be quiet! Don't call attention to us" approach. The second type could be called individual-for-the collective insecurity, meaning the implications of individual Jews' perceptions of themselves and others as "ambassadors to the *goyim*"—that is, of their own and other Jews' behavior in public and private mainstream environments as image makers for the entire Jewish group. Finally, there is individual insecurity, stripped of the collective reference, or, more accurately, generated by an ambivalence, more or less acute, regarding membership in the Jewish group or even its outright rejection. This is the insecurity felt by those who wanted to participate in, and be accepted by, the dominant society as individuals (American citizens, lawyers or doctors, suburban residents, etc.)

and not as Jews (Jewish-Americans, Jewish lawyers, Jewish residents of a suburb). This syndrome has also been called "the vanishing Jew" phenomenon, or, in its extreme form, Jewish self-hatred, in Kurt Lewin's classical formulation, a strongly negative self-stereotype derived from the acceptance of the dominant group's status ranking that assigned low status to one's ethnoreligious group of origin. As Raphael Patai perceptively pointed out, however, this latter reaction could only have developed "if the members of the low-status minority group recognized and accepted as a fact that they were indeed a low-status group in relation to the majority," in other words, if they internalized the standards of the dominant society. Inasmuch as this reaction involved emancipation—even if only wished for—of one's personal identity from entanglement with the Jewish ethnoreligious community, it could also be thought of as a secularized, and in this specific sense, modern, insecurity.[7]

While these three kinds of insecurity could coexist and, as the reports imply, frequently did, it appears that particular circumstances tended to enhance one type or constrain another, thus making for mixtures that presumably felt different. I did not find sufficient information in the existing studies to identify different configurations of conditions contributing to particular outcomes and to set up comparative reference cases as was done in the previous chapter; and personal phone calls from an unknown historian at the University of Pennsylvania, a good enough method to find out whether there were any Jews in politics in, say, Terre Haute, Indiana, or which Anglo-Protestant social clubs did not accept Jewish members in Cleveland, would not bring satisfactory answers to inquiries about the kinds of civic insecurity experienced half a century earlier. Some propositions and a few illustrations can nevertheless be offered.

Namely, insecurity with a collective referent of either kind seems to have been lessened by the following conditions (the more of them combined, the more significant diminution, unless, of course, some drastic events outside the local or even national environment heightened it): numerically and proportionally large and residentially concentrated Jewish populations; embracing ethnic networks with resources for intragroup replication of mainstream institutional structures (such as schools, hospitals, or social organizations); a restrained level of spoken/acted-out anti-Semitism in the larger society as directed against the entire Jewish group; and a relative political empowerment of the local Jewish group. New York can serve as the prime example of such a configuration and its by and large reassuring effects—even in the era of heightened anti-Semitism between the two world wars—on the self-consciousness of local Jews, that is, on the majority who remained immersed in their large and tight-knit ethnic communities, and who could continue their lives without coming into much contact with members of the dominant society and worrying daily how well they "represented their people."

At the same time, however, the big cities with a quickly expanding opportunity structure and outwardly cosmopolitan climate provided a temptation, and a chance, for a number of American-born Jews to venture out of their ethnic communities and try making it in the mainstream. As they confronted the dominant world, they found themselves alienated as they discovered underneath cosmopolitan allure the tacit rules of conformity and social ostracism vis-à-vis the "others." Those Jews, as amply documented in autobiographies and novels, on stage, and in films, often developed severe symptoms of individual insecurity that would occasionally take on the form of self-hatred. Most of such evidence in the interwar period in fact came from New York's literary and journalistic circles, and from the Hollywood movie world, rather than from smaller cities and towns.[8]

The latter generally had more limited opportunity structures and a slower pace of life, and therefore less pressure to succeed at all costs; in this context, the reported middle-class status of the majority of Jews, along with their solid representation in local civic affairs, could be treated as indicators of ambitions by and large satisfied without this group's wishing, and trying, to negate their ethnic background. In addition, in smaller places where people knew about each other, if not through personal acquaintance, then at least by sight or hearsay, it would have been much more difficult for a Jew (or any other ethnic person), even for a convert with his/her name changed, to pass for something else, say, an Anglo-Protestant. Last but not least, economic and/or social ethnic networks that originally brought people to particular towns more often than not had endured and played crucial parts in their well-being, whereas in the big cities with large Jewish populations, such networks could be much more easily replaced.

Reports suggest that a different mixture tended to prevail in smaller cities and towns, and in suburbs (the latter have been investigated in the post–World War II era): in this case, a primary component was of the ambassadors-to-the-Gentiles type, with the resulting responsibility anxiety, and accompanied by the other kind of collective-focused insecurity. These environments shared the following features—likely contributors to the reported outcome: relatively constrained space and limited numbers and proportions of general and Jewish populations; limited or nonexistent residential segregation between Jewish and dominant groups; little developed or virtually nonexistent group ethnic networks; and the presence of routine, usually formal-institutional, social contacts between Jews and members of the dominant groups. Where the number of fellow ethnic residents was very small, the group they felt anxious about representing was apparently a generalized symbolic category, "the Jews"; where the local Jewish population was more sizable, this anxious responsibility became more local and concrete. Both types of collective-focused insecurity were often reflected in a fear that the next Jewish arrival in town might be an "agitator," a "pink," or an otherwise suspicious character who would damage the image of local

Jews in the eyes of the dominant group, spoil good relations, and possibly even endanger their position in town or suburb.[9]

Recollections of my Johnstown informants regarding their sense of civic insecurity were more vivid about the interwar period than about the initial years of their stay in the area at the beginning of the century, and so the following discussion focuses on the former. Generally, as recalled by members of the local Jewish community almost without regard to generational status, gender, residential location, or synagogue membership, these experiences resembled a pattern reported from small-town/suburban environments in that a collective-focused insecurity, a blend of the two kinds specified earlier, was the predominant type. Individual insecurity expressed by the ethnic self-denial of social climbers on the mainstream achievement ladder, as reported from metropolitan centers, was practically nonexistent. In particular, self-hatred seems to have been practically absent, mainly because most Jews in the area had been strongly and meaningfully involved in their ethnoreligious community—even, as in the case of some second-generation youngsters, when this attachment was not without a certain ambivalence; the low dynamic of the local opportunity structure did not offer much in the way of promising careers that could be achieved in exchange for renouncing one's Jewishness (and top positions in the steel and coal industries were undesired by Jews anyway); and the ethnic-divisive social organization of Johnstown was basically accepted by its resident groups. Johnstown-style "vanishing Jews" manifested some vestiges of old-country anxious demeanor, characteristic of self-effacing minority members moving about in a largely ascriptive social system, and evinced a collective desire that the Jewish group remain inconspicuous.

As they recollected the civic vulnerability of the Jewish group in prewar Johnstown—where it came from and how it "worked" on people's minds—my informants usually considered its various aspects that, as Seymour S. phrased it, "pulled in different ways" and maintained (this, in my interpretation) their insecurity in a tenuous balance of sorts.[10] Reflecting the compound marginality of the Johnstown Jews, their collective-type insecurity blend differed, it seems, in the proportioning of its components from the variety most commonly reported in other small towns. The shares were reversed: the first, collective kind of civic insecurity, as defined earlier, made up the primary element, accompanied by the ambassadors-to-the-Gentiles kind. If the Johnstowners' anxiety was indeed greater than that of their fellow ethnics in other small towns studied, it was likely also more justified, that is, reflective of the actually greater vulnerability of their economic and political condition as compared to the situations of other small-town Jewish communities.

However, the local circumstances that sustained this civic insecurity at the same time assuaged it through strong communal ties within the Jewish group. From the outside, this insecurity was alleviated by the persistent ethnic fragmentation of the town's social order that in effect shielded members of groups occupying more vulnerable positions from this very vulnerability precisely because the dominant society regarded them as socially nonthreatening.

While my informants recognized these local contingencies, this was not what they first and spontaneously referred to in recollecting how they perceived and appreciated the civic situation of the Jewish group in pre-war Johnstown. Rather, among people of East European backgrounds—the overwhelming majority of Johnstown's Jewish community—the prime qualifier was a comparison with their experience in Eastern Europe, either personally remembered or transmitted by family and group members.

In pre–World War II Johnstown, the Jews experienced a combination of economic and political marginality, and religious otherness paired with a high degree of ethnic enclosure, in a social system largely based on the ascriptive criteria of status and power. As noted earlier, this somewhat resembled features of the situation Jews had known in the East European shtetls. The instant reply of the Ukrainian-born Louis G. to my question about such possible parallels was echoed by others: "It could have seemed [similar], but it was quite different, [here] it was a *much*, much more secure insecurity!" I addressed this question mostly to the immigrant generation, but the American-born also recollected comments and comparisons made by their parents that became parts of their own worldviews.

They all stressed a sense of a qualitative difference, "in the air you breathed," a feeling of "a space having opened up, maybe not wide opened, but opened up." Johnstown, they were aware, had its limitations, and Jews' marginality in the local society unavoidably made them feel potentially vulnerable. But, first and generally, as Louis G. elaborated, the legal system in America and the official American ideology provided positive guidelines for the treatment of minorities that could be, it was believed, relied on as a firm base. For those reasons, the *Rodef Sholom Bulletin*, a congregational newsletter, referred to America as "this glorious country," even while deploring, in the 1930s, the rise of anti-Semitism in several cities. In this heartfelt appreciation of the American political system and its legal guarantees Johnstown's Jews did not differ from their fellow ethnics elsewhere in the United States.

Second and relatedly, in comparison with the experience of Jews in Eastern Europe, the unpredictability of developments actually or potentially threatening the Jewish group's civic status had greatly decreased, making the situation more controllable: in local circumstances in Johnstown, it was possible for Jews, they felt, to pursue their family purposes and communal affairs while maintaining caution and good judgment in matters concerning their ethnic community's public image. "In the shtetl of course you could not have counted on this"—American-born Ben I. repeated a comparative evaluation made by his father, typical also of the opinions of others—"[Jews] did nothing antagonistic, and there comes an *ukaz* [edict] and all Jews must pay so much extra in taxes, or say *muzhiks* [peasants] got drunk after a market day and went around breaking windows [in Jewish homes].”[11]

And third, they realized that despite their socioeconomic marginality, as petty capitalists “Hebrew” storekeepers were more akin to the dominant genre, and on much more open and hospitable territory in Johnstown (and in America generally), than Jews had ever been in that role in Eastern Europe.

A felt shift in the balance of power in relations with traditional customers of Jewish businesses—former *muzhiks* and now industrial laborers in Johnstown’s mills and coal mines—was part of this enhanced-by-comparison experience of civic security. While a sense of superiority mixed with pity generally continued to inform Jewish attitudes toward their working-class Slavic customers, another important component of this old-country relationship—an ever-present fearful and mistrustful anxiety lying beneath an accommodating demeanor on the part of the Jews—had greatly diminished in the immigrant generation, and in their American-born children it practically disappeared. In the prewar period, the smaller the locality, the more this apprehension informed Jewish immigrants’ contacts with their East European working-class customers. “In small [coal] towns here in the rural area,” Robert K.’s father had a store in one of the coal towns in Indiana County, “Gentiles brought with them their anti-Semitism [from the old country] and passed it on to their children. . . . Father never trusted them, he also brought with him this fear.” As a child, Helen M. used to accompany her father, a Johnstown-based peddler, on his commercial trips to the surrounding coal towns: “[Known among local Jews as a quiet, pensive type, and a self-taught Talmudic scholar] he was a different person when he was with his customers, told jokes and tried to make them like him. He was always careful [to accommodate] because he was Jewish, he had to make them trust him.”[12] But in Johnstown, which was bigger and had a larger, more compact and organized Jewish population, this undercurrent of fear beneath the accommodating posture in dealings with Gentile East Europeans was much less pronounced. All the same, according to the observations of their children, immigrant parents tended to bear in silence demeaning expletives like “Zhid” and “Christ killer,” now and then uttered by customers in their stores, while the second generation—young men, especially, would be more inclined to retaliate verbally.

Still, the context of the whole situation was different, and both sides were aware of it. Even in places like Johnstown and vicinity, with its divisive sociocultural order and ethnic niches for “foreigners,” Jews were, as Louis G. pointed out, protected by law as American citizens, and, as important, Jews-as-petty-capitalists were, to repeat, more closely related to the dominant economic order than were the “Hunky” common laborers in the mills and coal mines. Important primarily in their economic function as customers of Jewish businesses, beyond this East European “foreigners” were, from the Jews’ perspective, “left behind”: metaphorically, as part of the past, and actually, in the context of the dominant local society, as an insignificant and basically unthreatening group at the bottom of its socio-economic structure. Transferred from the old country and enduring under the local circumstances, their anti-Jewish feelings, for the most part latent and occasionally expressed in verbal abuse, did not interfere with individual business dealings and were taken for granted by my informants: acknowledged, and then dismissed. "You didn't expect anything else"; "Well, the usual stuff"; "They did not know any better"; "[They] repeated what the priest told them or [regarding the American-born generation] what they heard from their [immigrant] parents at home."[13]

A comparative reference to the situation in Eastern Europe, kept alive in the collective memory, thus gave Johnstown's Jews a sense of somewhat increased civic empowerment even though their actual position in local politics and society remained distinctly weak. A similar empowerment-by-comparison was also, of course, experienced by East European Jews elsewhere in America, and in all likelihood more intensely so in places where their ethnic group's situation in the dominant society was less marginal than was the Johnstowners'.

Although "much much more secure," collective-focused civic insecurity nevertheless remained a shared sentiment among Johnstown's Jews throughout the interwar period. Their preference for remaining inconspicuous or "obviously unobvious" has been noted in the previous chapter as one of the factors constraining local Jews' participation in mainstream activities, which, reciprocally, contributed to the Jewish group's continued marginality in Johnstown. This shared desire not to attract public attention expressed the felt insecurity regarding Jews' status vis-à-vis the dominant society. How different the Johnstowners' experience must have been in comparison with the "carefree" attitude of a great many of their New York contemporaries is poignantly illustrated by the recollections of Judith W., then resident of one of New York's densely Jewish neighborhoods. She recalled the surprise—annoyance, really—of her own family at the concern, recurrently voiced by family members of her Johnstown fiancé, about possible Gentile reactions to this or that action taken by the Jews. "Who cares about the goyim?!" was the spontaneous reply of her New York relatives to such anxious remarks of the Johnstowners.[14]

I identified only two instances among those remembered as positively evaluated for "put[ting] the Jewish community in a good light" in the eyes of the local dominant society that did not conform to the *Shah!* principle, that is, incidents that did not generate anxiety about—to use my informants' own terminology—making their group "stand out." Even then, however, this visibility was seen at least in part as an occasion for reasserting the image of the Jewish group as obviously unobvious—in this case, no different from the dominant society. One such instance was a series of public lectures concerning various facets of American culture, society, and politics sponsored by Beth Zion Reform Temple, the so-called Beth Zion Forum; although members of the two other East European congregations did not attend it, or attended only sporadically, several of them perceived it as an event that presented the whole local Jewish community in a good light. The other case was a person: Rabbi Ralph Simon, the first American-born rabbi of the largest synagogue, the Orthodox Rodef Sholom, a short-term but charismatic leader who introduced into the congregation some Conservative, or "Americanized," practices.

Rabbi Simon's congregants' evaluations of his "ambassadorship" for their group vis-à-vis Johnstown's social elite actually emphasized both positive visibility and inconspicuousness. He gained visibility through his participation—as a representative of "the Hebrew race"—in the few public activities Jews took part in, and in initiatives like an occasional letter writing to the *Johnstown Tribune* on general Jewish matters. Reportedly, it was also chalked up to Rabbi Simon's credit—and the renown refracted through him to the entire Jewish group—that his wife was an artist (a painter) and that the local newspaper mentioned this fact once or twice. At the same time though, the rabbi's positive representation of the community derived as well, according to my informants, from his inconspicuousness, or his similarity to members of the American middle class. An appreciation of this resemblance reflected, of course, the ethnicization of Jewish ways and customs, especially in the second generation, but there was also an element of insecurity expressed by the desire for unobviousness. And so, while recollecting what impressed her so about Rabbi Simon, besides his service within the congregation, Eleanor H. mentioned what others repeated as well: "And he also presented such a good image [on the outside], so American-looking, and he spoke so well."[15]

Aside from these two instances, each of which was ambiguous anyway, the Johnstown Jews' preferred approach in dealing with their shared sense of civic insecurity was simply avoiding public attention. For example, minutes of Rodef Sholom Synagogue meetings in the 1920s repeatedly recorded the congregation's desire to build a "*naye* [new], up to day *shul*," which, in addition to having internal improvements, would be moved from its original location next to the railroad station to a more prestigious address downtown, and would assume a more decorous exterior. Asked to elaborate on this passage, that is, to try to recollect what it was they sought to achieve by this external overhaul, my elderly informant-members of Rodef Sholom pointed to a wish for their prayer house to appear respectable, "like other modern-looking American" buildings in the area.[16]

A more poignant expression of this desire for inconspicuousness was, as discussed in the previous chapter, the Jewish community's uneasy silence during both strikes for an independent union in the local mills in 1919 and 1937, a silence that in fact supported Bethlehem Steel Company and the town's political establishment. Then, after the union was finally established and the company's hold over the city weakened, there emerged a shared wish that the local Jewish small garment manufacturer settle with his own workers and accept the union lest his failure to do so, to repeat the quotation, "reflect[ed] badly on the [Jewish] community by making it stand out." Interestingly, another argument, reportedly as effective, used on the initially reluctant factory owner by his fellow ethnics was that "holding fixed ideas [unresponsive to shifting circumstances] was completely foreign to the flexibility [of Jewish thinking]."[17]

Another, equally telling, illustration of the common sense of collective anxiety dates back to the 1930s, when United Jewish Appeal fund-raising was initiated in Johnstown: the consensus that sums collected annually for the UJA in the local Jewish community should be kept confidential, that is, not publicized in the *Tribune* or on the radio. As Meyer B., a local UJA representative, explained, the purpose of this confidentiality was "so that they [Gentiles] couldn't say Jews cared only for themselves . . . we gave here to everything, Red Cross, Community Chest, hospitals—by the way, it was better not to give too much [showing off], just as much as Gentiles gave—[but] there was a potential danger [of a critique]."[18]

While my informants' recollections indicate that civic insecurity of the collective-focused kind was a shared experience of most Johnstown Jews, some differences in these accounts were nevertheless noticeable depending on gender, generation, and local residence. Anxieties associated with the image of the Jewish community in matters concerning public affairs were spontaneously remembered almost exclusively by men—and not surprisingly so, considering all that has been said so far in this study about the absence from Johnstown public life of women in general, and Jewish women specifically. There seems, however, to have been no significant gender difference in another common expression of insecurity, namely, the precept "Be twice as nice," intended as a guidepost in encounters with members of the dominant group. I heard this attitude, coupled usually with "and try harder," mentioned by virtually all men and women with whom I discussed the subject of civic insecurity. Characteristically, the precept "Be twice as nice" was paired with "Do better," implying a perception that the effort was worth it, given that the American sociocultural system which the dominant strata represented was fundamentally approved by Jews—a perspective absent in the attitude toward East European peasant-workers, in relation to whom the Jews, even when fearful, have traditionally felt unequivocally superior.

"You're a little bit different, so you have to be a little bit nicer than everybody else and do a little bit better"—in slightly different formulations, I heard this attitude from several people as they reminisced about the ways people coped with the insecurity involved in being Jewish among Americans. "You are a Jew, so you have to be double nice to people, and try harder." It may be that a somewhat higher incidence of such reported memories among the American-born, and among residents of more prestigious neighborhoods, was indicative of a then ascending pattern; if so, then whereas the old-country fearful anxiety was on the wane, a "double-nice" attitude expressive of status intimidation experienced vis-à-vis the local social elite was an increasingly prevalent insecurity syndrome among Johnstown's Jews during the interwar period.[19]

However, even when they sought collective inconspicuousness in public matters or acceptance by personal self-effacement in social interactions with members of the dominant group, the Johnstowners remained self-consciously Jewish. One behavioral measure of this commitment was that very few had Anglicized their names over the fifty years from the late nineteenth century through the interwar period. Those who did so acted mostly for family-related rather than career reasons; and all but one remained in town and active in the Jewish community. As already noted, though, a low incidence of name changing was not surprising in a small town where the effective hiding of one's ethnic origins was much more difficult than in a big city. A more telling illustration, and symptomatic of the prevailing attitudes among local Jews regarding their ethnoreligious identity and its accompanying anxiety, was a discomfort vividly remembered by American-born Freda L. from Jeanette, a little town not far from Johnstown. Every Thursday after school her mother sent her on a train to a ritual slaughterer with a chicken for the Sabbath meal. As the bird hidden in a basket under the seat loudly "cluck[ed] and flap[ped] and squawk[ed]," the fervent desire of the embarrassed girl was by no means not to be Jewish—this circumstance of her life was obvious and inescapable—but, simply, for "that smart aleck chicken" to keep quiet in the basket; a quiet chicken would not make Freda, and her Jewishness, stand out and look funny, vulnerable in their strangeness.[20]

As my informants realized, this inescapability of membership in a Jewish group marked by its distinctiveness of ritual and daily conduct simultaneously created anxiety and assuaged it, because this very inevitability was taken for granted both inside and outside the Jewish community. On the whole, different factors that exacerbated or pacified feelings of insecurity, "pulling in different ways," balanced out so that their civic situation in prewar Johnstown appeared satisfactory. As Louis G. pointed out and people I talked to generally agreed, it was possible for the town's Jews, while collectively maintaining prudence and a low profile, and relying on each other in their socioeconomic niche, to seek, and, with good fortune, accomplish their life-goals. The pursuit of those life-purposes, however, specifically in the economic domain, involved its own uncertainties, which brings us to the second main focus of this chapter: the ways in which Johnstown's Jews perceived and appreciated their "insecure prosperity," and life success in general.

THE WHEEL OF FORTUNE

As I learned what people achieved or failed to accomplish in acting toward their primary practical purpose or *takhlis*—a good life for the family—I also wanted to know how they mentally approached and interpreted the circumstances related to these efforts, and how they perceived their own impact on these conditions as well as, more generally, human agency as cause.

Comparative information in this regard has been taken from studies that, on the basis of social mobility data—again, mainly from metropolitan centers, especially New York—have argued for the existence of a close affinity (in sociologese: functional equivalence) between component dispositions of the "Jewish achievement drive" and value-orientations comprising "the American (Protestant) success ethic" as elaborated in Florence Kluckhohn's now classic essay on "the dominant profile of cultural orientations."[21] The basic components of this profile can be specified as follows: the twin beliefs that rational mastery over nature and one's own life is possible and brings good results; the corresponding conviction that the appropriate conduct in life is to continuously engage in well-planned, future-oriented actions directed toward the achievement of defined purposes, and, relatedly, that the accomplishment of such undertakings should be the principle of judgment (evaluation) and measure of a person's success; individualism, or a primary emphasis on personal responsibility and character (rather than the environment) as the principal factor in making for the individual's achievement (or failure); and, finally, an underlying (or overriding) optimism, a "can do" attitude that sets no limits on human capabilities when aptly used.

Indeed, the traditional Jewish "cultural tool kit" did contain these elements. But, as I have already pointed out on several occasions, Jewish popular wisdom was informed by more variegated dominant value-orientations. Along with such drive as Ruth Wisse in a personal conversation once likened to the "nervous readiness of the race horses" waiting at the gate to run the steeplechase, it also included schemas-resources, well-tested in historical trials, for coping with incompletion, loss, powerlessness, lack of control, and the vicissitudes of fate, both minor and catastrophic.

The conditions the immigrants found in America, especially in the expanding metropolitan centers, very likely set in high relief and reinforced those aspects of the Jewish cultural heritage that lead to and sustain modern worldly success, such as pragmatic rationalism, individual responsibility and activism, and a future-oriented, optimistic approach to life. Specifically, students of the post-Puritan "American success spirit" emphasize the contributing role in its growth of the expansion of urban-industrial capitalism and the white-collar sector of the economy, and rapid societal differentiation combined with increasing institutionalization (bureaucratization) of social life.[22] In Jewish groups situated in such environments, the main internal factors that appear to have contributed to the mobilization of these schemas as functional equivalents of the modern American success ethos have been a rapid occupational advancement through the channel of formal education into the middle and higher strata of the dominant American social structure; the resulting separation of home and work; a corollary of this separation, namely, a significant emancipation of, especially, the second generation from family control; and a progressive ethnicization of Jewish sociocultural life, institutional and private.

Mobilized by the external and intragroup circumstances specified above, these modern-success schemas functioned, in turn, as resources in guiding actions of large numbers of big-city Jews toward mainstream middle-class socioeconomic achievement, as well as more effective organization of their ethnic communities, during the interwar period. Interestingly, similar winning-American-style life-orientations have also been strongly emphasized in a recent historical analysis of Jewish "metaphors of self" based on the oral life stories of elderly New York men and women, former garment workers and lifelong labor activists; fused with a socialist ideology, however, these attitudes made up a mix that differed from the middle-class combination.[23]

It should be kept in mind, however, that even a strong accentuation of these particular schemas-resources in the pursuits of large numbers of metropolitan Jews did not necessarily mean that other value-orientations contained in the Jewish "cultural tool kit" had not been relied on as well— by modern-American-style achievers, and also by Jewish socialists. On the contrary, I assume that the other, counterbalancing mental "tools" operated too, in the practice of successful New Yorkers, Philadelphians, or Chicagoans, although in a more subdued manner. But in view of the data showing the impressive accomplishments of metropolitan Jews in collective upward mobility, these other contents of the "kit" did not attract the attention of the investigators, and so we do not generally know what patterns these different schemas could have formed, and how they worked together. Barbara Myerhoff's anthropological study of elderly Jews at the Aliyah Senior Citizens' Center in California, *Number Our Days*, is a wonderful exception; also very unusual, and quite different in approach and in the kind of people it investigates, is a sociological study of American modern Orthodox Jews by Samuel Heilman and Steven Cohen, *Cosmopolitans and Parochials*.[24]

In Johnstown, the local circumstances sustained practical life-philosophies that encompassed the appreciation of the winning and losing sides of life, by melding schemas of rational pragmatism and the religiously grounded sense of the limitations of human understanding and control of the world, hopeful optimism and an activist approach to life together with a perception of the precariousness of good fortune, individual-and-collective responsibility tied in one. In what follows, I attempt to show how these schemas "worked," singly and together, while pointing at the same time to the intermingling—particularly noticeable in the approaches of the second generation—of East European Jewish and American elements. While immigrant versus American-born status seemed the major differentiator, I will also comment on congregational membership and gender where I thought they made a difference.

As they searched their memories for answers to "such deep philosophical questions you are asking," some of my collocutors explicitly distinguished (although leaving the boundaries imprecise), and some simply shifted between what Mildred G. called "pictures": smaller, bigger, bigger-bigger, the really big; different pictures provided different views.[25] More commonly used in the social sciences, notions such as different scales or perspectives—macro-, mezzo-, and micro-levels; or longer, shorter, and very long *durées*—convey a similar idea of multiplicity and interpenetration. I use the metaphor of the "natives" and, as I have understood it, their super-scheme of things as the main framework for presenting the Johnstowners' recollected perceptions and appreciations of different aspects of life as they appeared from different viewpoints; comparative references to the elements of dominant American/big-city Jewish ethos as specified earlier are built into this frame as we move from scale to scale.

Focusing on the ways toward achievement of Johnstowners' primary life-goal, a good life for the family, we look first at the view through a medium lens. Our conversations in this regard concerned my informants' perceptions and appreciations of the possibilities of rational mastery of their economic pursuits, and control of the outcomes thereof and therefore the welfare of their households, through the means of calculation and planning. I usually raised these issues in connection with concrete actions such as establishing, shifting, or losing business, purchasing a home or residential relocation, or improving the family standard of living. The kind of work performed by local Jews, viz., small trading, the type of enterprise in the capitalist market with great built-in risk and uncertainty; location in a town dominated by one manufacturing giant in a branch of industry with chronic arrhythmia of production, and employing over two-thirds of the local labor force; and, resulting from the above two characteristics, recurrent fluctuations in Jewish businesses—this whole situation could not but sustain in the people affected a sense that the goal of unqualified, perfect rationality would be self-defeating. The illustrations most commonly offered by my informants of why such long-term mastery over the environment—to be achieved through systematic means-to-ends management—could not have been possible were drawn from family commercial enterprises. Women were more likely to mention these rather than household matters under their management, probably because, first, so many of them were involved in the stores, and, second, because living standards at home depended directly on this main source of income (the effects of gender on my informants' perceptions of rational mastery and its limitations are discussed in somewhat greater detail below).

Johnstown shopkeepers, like Henry K., who worked in his father's store, were well aware of the limitations of planning and control in their lives—constraints that were inherent in the characteristics of jobs they had. "When you're in business, so much is a gamble," he told me while recalling his father's ups and downs in business; "even in our trade [workingmen's shoes], it did not change like fashion, you know, every season, but still you just couldn't know all that may happen." Some adverse happenings were indeed impossible to foresee or control: an earlier chapter quoted bankruptcy testimonies of people whose businesses and whole families' material welfare declined because of longer-than-usual strikes in the coal mines or mass layoffs of mill workers—the clientele of Jewish stores. More commonly, reflecting the uneven rhythm of local industrial production, trade fluctuated less sharply, but enough to make the hard-earned prosperity of Jewish homes insecure.

Moses L., a prototypical Johnstown Jewish merchant, described his enterprise as "sometimes rich, and sometimes poor, it depends," indicating that its course could not be fully masterminded either by his own efforts or by the workforce of his entire household. Bill B., son of a local wholesaler, responded to an inquiry about principles of rational economic management: "Well, planning and all that, it was possible, it was done, but to a certain extent only, for some length of time. And remember that our business [dry goods] had more versatility like moving merchandise around the area, had more maneuver than retail." And a more general perception of the situation by another local, differently formulated but similar in its underlying assumption: "There's never the 'only reason' for anything that happens, you know, there is always a lot of different things involved; some of them you're not aware of because they are invisible, others because yourself are blind."[26]

Not surprisingly, perceptions of my informants regarding the limitations of rational mastery in business pursuits were similar to the opinions of professional economists, experts on small entrepreneurship, who have strongly emphasized its unavoidably situational logic that guarantees the returns on a rational-instrumental approach only within relatively short periods of time.[27] Mixed with class-derived experiential perceptions of the structural constraints imposed on Jewish entrepreneurs' capability fully to control their economic situation had been the representations encoded in shared group memory of the shorter (Eastern Europe) and longer (the Great Tradition) *durée.*

A recurrence in the Johnstown Jews' life situations of two factors from the East European experience—occupation in small trade and flexibility of the markets on which they depended for their livelihood—sustained a sense, prevalent in the shtetls, of evident constraints on control of one's life course; however, a shift to a bigger-bigger picture with a longer time perspective made for an important qualification in outlooks on this matter. This longer view behind a bigger picture, as it were, was a deeply felt sense—discussed in the previous section dealing with Johnstown's Jews' sense of civic insecurity—that for all its apparent similarities, life in America, and Johnstown concretely, was an enormous improvement over the East European situation. The qualifying impact of this larger perspective was naturally stronger in the immigrant generation for whom life in the shtetl was once experience-near, but the second generation, who heard the old-country stories from their parents, internalized them too—enough to bring them up, unsolicited, in our conversations.

In Eastern Europe, there was relentless poverty all around with slim chance of any improvement; moreover, the Jews lived and worked "with the cards stacked against them," in the words of Johnstown-born Isadore G. who learned from his elders, as despised collective double-outcasts: religious aliens and petty capitalists amid a Christian and agricultural population. In America, while they were again small traders in the lower echelons of the entrepreneurial structure, they now belonged to the dominant economic group and operated in the expanding capitalist system. Despite the existing barriers based on ethnoreligious origin, this system was incomparably more open and amenable to rationally organized personal efforts toward a goal, especially when assisted by unimpeded group social networks.

As in the case of civic insecurity, or, more accurately, in one encompassing experience whose aspects contextualized each other, this America-versus-old-country comparison increased a sense of control they could exert over the course of their lives. Perceptions remembered personally or received from parents, quoted in previous chapters in connection with concrete economic pursuits of my informants or their family members, may be recalled here to illustrate the point. "[After] the vicissitudes of Jewish life in the Pale"—American-born Ben I. thus interpreted the attitude of his immigrant father and uncles—"when they were able to break loose from that, here they saw opportunities everywhere, and they grabbed them." And Isadore S., reviving youthful memories of how his immigrant relatives compared the situation in western Pennsylvania with that in their native Galicia: "Whatever options they had here, they went after them, if one did not work out, then something else . . . the circumstances [in America] permitted them to do it, because the marketplace was so structured that it did not deny them that opportunity."[28]

What disappears from active use in group members' repertoire of symbolic references is as good an indicator of their states of mind as that which persists. I checked sporadically which of the old Yiddish sayings widely used in the shtetls—in chapter 1 they were invoked as expressions of popular life-philosophies—were still in circulation in Johnstown in the interwar period, and in what contexts. The results of this quick survey indirectly confirm a symbolic empowerment of the collective and individual Jewish self, derived from the old-country reference framework. For example, still known and used as shorthand for a representation of the situation in the old country, sayings such as *Dem yidns simkhe iz mit a bisl shrek* (A Jew's joy is not without fright), expressing the chronic fear of people so very dependent on external and generally inimical forces, was not applied to the situation in Johnstown, despite Jews' marginality and the accompanying anxieties. Also out of currency were *Yidishe ashires iz vi shney in merts* (Jewish wealth is like snow in March: here today, tomorrow gone) and a generalized *yidishe mazl*, all-around Jewish (mis)fortune. Disclaimers popular in the shtetls and interjected in everyday speech, such as *kayn ayn-hore* (no evil eye), uttered to exorcise pervasive "bad luck," seem to have greatly narrowed in usage—primarily to matters of family health, as if hostile forces were no longer perceived as ubiquitous, leaving the other spheres of everyday life much more controllable and amenable to purposeful action.

Which brings us to a smaller picture of everyday practices, and Johnstown's Jews' appreciations of responsibility for one's own life and achievements, expressed through a flow of goal-oriented actions. While they perceived the course of life as never fully subject to rational mastery in a broader perspective because of its dynamic, fluid quality and the inherent plurality of frequently opposite possibilities, my informants saw an opportunity for, and actually an obligation to, purposeful and rational— "intelligent," in the preferred local usage—action in life's everyday becoming. The Johnstowners' perceptions in this matter, recollected as we talked about their pursuits of specific goals, have been quoted in previous chapters dealing with the economic strategies at work and in the homes of Jewish families. Let us recall some of them to illustrate, this time, the value-concept of active and purposeful life. As Abraham K. saw it, when faced with a problem a Jew always tried to find an *eytse*, "a way through," as he understood it, by scrutinizing the situation for possible opportunities it contained, and then acting in the direction deemed rational in terms of the desired goal, but always remaining open to reassessment should circumstances change. Johnstown-born Harry R. saw it in a similar way: "There are options [for action] . . . you came to a fork"—he was talking about a certain point in his occupational pursuits—"and looked around, this is what I wanted, and these were the ways to go, then you made a decision, you went there [instead of selecting another option], perhaps you had to correct where you were going, or come back." And Seymour R., commenting on his father's business initiatives during the 1930s: "From furniture business, when it didn't work out, he thought he might go into fabrics, it looked like a reasonable thing to do then, workers were laid off, so the women sew clothes at home, and also there was a Jewish [dry goods] wholesaler in town . . . [so] it made sense."[29] An activist, "intelligent" approach to life was also, of course, a strong element in the dominant profile of the cultural orientation of big-city Jews; as already pointed out, however, in that environment it was part of a different "mental configuration" and guided its carrier-practitioners onto different paths of action.

With this "look around and decide" approach applied to much more promising conditions for purposeful action toward the valued life-goals, the traditional utterance "God willing," still commonly used in Jewish homes when plans were made and tried out, expressed first and foremost— even though not entirely—a call to self-reliance; it also invoked a collective self, the family and the local ethnic community, as I will discuss below. Reflecting this shift in emphasis and the underlying increased sense of control over one's life, there disappeared (except as a piece of old-country folklore) the poignantly ironic shtetl dictum *Got vet helfn, vi helft nor Got biz*

Got vet helfn (God will provide but if only God would provide until He provides), expressing the miraculist approach of people who, like Sholom Aleichem's Tevye—the shtetl everyman always busy chasing after his daily bread—existed mainly "on air and faith." *Im yirtse HaShem*—Robert K.'s interpretation of his father's "theory and practice" in this regard was shared by others with whom I talked about these things—meant "God helps those who help themselves, [that is] who don't sit back waiting [for opportunity's knock] but make their way in life through good judgment, determination, and hard work."

In popular shtetl wisdom in Eastern Europe (and, for that matter, in Jewish tradition in general), God's omnipresent providence by no means freed humans from making decisions concerning their lives. As the Yiddish saying went, *Got heyst oykh kayn nar nit zayn* (God never told anyone to be stupid): people were to use their own reason and choose how to act. A limited secularization of the Johnstown Jews' life philosophies that had occurred in comparison with old-country orientations seems to have consisted in their placing the emphasis first and foremost on (collective) self-reliance in the "smaller picture" of everyday life, or, put differently, in leaving people alone to their personal and group devices, "grabbing chances" presented to them by the much more opportune American circumstances.

It seems, however, that this self-direction, reflecting a sense of God's noninvolvement in the events of everyday life, was stronger among the self-perceived "more modern liberal" Consorthodox residents of secondary Jewish settlements in town; at least I heard more assertive tones in their remarks. It was from or about the immigrants who were then more traditionally religious that I heard comments like Benjamin I.'s, as he answered my question about how his father reacted to a specific bad turn in the family's economic situation in the 1930s. "A Jew would ask '*Lieber Got* help me,' meaning 'please don't make things evil for me' . . . [coming] from Orthodox background, he [father] maintained a reverent hope that Lord would not do him ill . . . but never, never [would he say] 'please make me rich' and then I sit back and rest." And Samuel L. had this to say concerning his general attitude when I asked him about a concrete, difficult decision that had to be made: "God may help you along once you decided which path [of the many available] to go on, but your fate is not *bashert* [predetermined, or decided for you from above], it's up to you to make a wise choice."[30]

"God helps those who help themselves," understood as a relegation of responsibility for successful action to self-directed rational individuals, has of course also been a basic principle of the (Protestant) American ethic. It was a standard part of the public education of children, who were taught the "American way" in citizenship classes and so-called character courses; at the Johnstown High School, this theme appeared under the rubrics

"Pan-Americanism" and "Personal Development." In their activist orientations, the Jewish and American life-philosophies closely intertwined, and, like Harold N., my second-generation collocutors were unable to tell which was which: "'God will help you if you help yourself,' I heard it so often, at home and at school, I could not take it apart even if I tried." However, in reminiscing about how this attitude was inculcated in them at home and at school, the second generation used the classical idiom of the American spirit of achievement, which was not usually the phrasing of their immigrant parents.[31] "Keeping up one's drive," "pulling oneself by the bootstraps," "getting one's own breaks"—for the Johnstowners it meant, in practical application, not professional careers for the individual but the family's economic well-being. While both men and women subscribed to this activist orientation, drawn at once from the two traditions and expressed in the American idiom, the concrete illustrations offered by the women seemed assertive but less autonomous, as I will discuss below.

There has been, however, a more profound difference in the meaning of activism in the Jewish and (Protestant) American "dominant profiles of cultural orientations," and in this regard the worldviews of second-generation Johnstowners appeared distinctly closer to the Jewish cultural tradition. While the dominant American ethos has placed the major emphasis on successful accomplishment of the task undertaken, Jewish "spirit" has focused on the process itself, on the unwavering efforts toward achieving the goal. As pronounced an oft-quoted admonition in *Pirke Avot* (The Ethics of the Fathers): "The day is short, and the work is great. . . . It is not incumbent upon thee to complete the work, but neither art thou free to desist from it."[32] A thesis about the correspondence between the American and Jewish schemas of success emphasizes the strong goal-orientation of the latter but says nothing about the different foci of the two. It is reasonable to believe that a concern with the accomplishment of the task increased among Jews who, especially in large urban centers, entered the mainstream occupational world, and who actively participated in the dominant American cultural life. Those joiners, naturally, were mostly American-born, and to the extent that the above relationship held true, perceptions of members of Johnstown's and the big-city second generation regarding the practical meaning of an activist approach to life had been different.

In reply to my questions about how they coped cognitively and emotionally with adversities as we reviewed the ups and downs of businesses, difficulties in maintaining the desired standard of living at home, or unrealized plans to relocate the old synagogue to a more prestigious location, three kinds of reactions were commonly mentioned. One, related mainly though not only by the immigrant generation, again invoked the old-country reference framework: No matter how bad it was, compared with the situation in Europe America appeared a savior. The second was a coping tool more ingrained in the foreign-born, but absorbed also by their children, namely, a sense of humor, "this Jewish one, East European"; "it had irony, and some sarcasm, but it helped."[33]

The third common approach drew on the practical ethos of *Pirke Avot*; Rabbi Tarphon's wisdom was reprinted in Johnstown's *Rodef Sholom Bulletin* and was familiar to almost everyone I talked to. This kind of orientation was particularly useful vis-à-vis the unsteady fortunes of the Johnstown Jews, to sustain them in adversity and mobilize to continuous efforts. "[Ups and downs] were so common, it was expected [such was the market situation], so we looked for other opportunities, go back and try again, keep trying was the attitude"—these perceptions-schemas were quoted earlier when we considered resources used by the Johnstowners in pursuit of their life-goals—"Get up right away and try something else, you have to be doing something"; "When [plans] didn't work out, *pasirt-pasirt*, what happened, happened, [parents] did not dwell on failure, picked up and went on trying, to go on, keep on going"; "Yes, we had bad turns of events, but never took it lying down, right away tried something else."[34] (A comparative addendum outside of the framework of this discussion may be of interest. Namely, it seems that this alert counteractiveness in the face of adversity, perceived as a challenge to be met halfway, gave the Jewish attitude an extra driving edge lacking among the Slavs whose adaptation in the same town I studied prior to this project. Their lives as peasants in Europe and later as unskilled industrial laborers in Johnstown were full of insecurity and hardships; in the Slavic cultures, however, these attributes of existence seem to have been experienced more as a datum, a condition to which one succumbs "floating along," as it were, until circumstances changed. As *Chranitel*, the local Rusyn-language newspaper, philosophized, depicting human agency as an object rather than a challenger to external forces: "Life is like *morskoje plavanije*, swimming at sea [. . .] now the waves take us upward, then throw us downward again.")[35]

Talking about their own approach to life's ups and downs, the second generation, again, tended to express their attitudes in the idiom of the American success ethos—"Tie, knot, and hold on"; "Winners never quit, quitters never win,"—but like that of their immigrant parents, their emphasis was on the continuing efforts rather than on the accomplishment itself. It seems, however, that in this drive to persevere and remain active expressed in the language of "the American spirit," there was also a sense of a unique moral obligation, at once individual and collective. To what, exactly, these American-born people were not able to tell, except by repeating, men and women alike and regardless of congregational membership, "We were brought up Jewish . . ." "as Jews we were supposed to live in a certain way"—suggesting an inarticulate sense of some commanding meaning larger than that inhering in the particular goals currently being pursued.[36]

Before we move again to a "bigger picture" of the world as it appeared in the recollections of my Johnstown informants, more focused attention should be paid to gender differences in the appreciation of the constitutive elements of the dominant American "spirit of achievement." As can readily be seen, these schemas have involved traditionally male social roles and represented a masculine ideal: rational mastery over the world, a sense of responsibility for and control of one's own affairs, and an activist, goal-oriented approach to life. I have not found in the literature any discussion about the effects of gender in the specific context of the dominant American "profile of cultural orientation"; but some information on Jewish women's life-orientations can be found in autobiographies and recorded life histories, again almost exclusively from New York.[37]

A reconstruction from these sources of the self-concepts of young, unmarried Jewish women in New York in the first half of this century depicts them, generally, as quite "confident . . . that they could manipulate the environment for their ends and needs." As the editors and interpreters of these recollections point out, the main sources of this increased sense of individual control had been young women's employment outside of the home and earning their own income (even when most of it was returned to the family), along with their organization of their own leisure time, independent of family supervision, that familiarized them with "city lights" and the variety of new entertainments the metropolis offered. In the above-mentioned study of New York garment workers, the increased sense of autonomy and a sense of personal control women experienced most likely derived also from their participation in the union struggles and political activism as a source of autonomous, or individualized, self-control.[38] To these self-empowering circumstances, I would also add the intragroup factor, namely, quick ethnicization of sociocultural life in most New York Jewish communities, specifically their secularization and institutional differentiation, the effects of which on women's social position, together with the accompanying tensions, have already been discussed.

In the available women's biographies, recorded oral histories, and historical-ethnographic studies, I sought but did not find information about the reflections in women's representations of self-in-the-world of these "ministructural" intragroup tensions. One can assume, I think, that the dynamic of transformations in the big-city Jewish society during the interwar period "pulled in different ways"—to redeploy one Johnstowner's phrase—middle-class women's views on this matter. On the one hand, their entry into the middle class and the resulting withdrawal from outside employment, along with the ethnicization of values and norms concerning social status and the housewife's role, should have diminished whatever sense of personal autonomy and self-direction they had developed in their youthful unmarried phase of life, and accentuated instead a properly "feminine" sense of dependency. On the other hand, however, as they entered the middle class, women assumed responsibility for the maintenance and improvement of family social status through the female authority domains of modern-style household management and keeping the appearance of the home up-to-date; and they increasingly underook more and different functions in the organizational life of the Jewish community and on the outside. These factors tended to reinforce a sense of personal responsibility, control, and appreciation of instrumental rationality.

In Johnstown, the field of "pulling" forces was different. While Jewish women's authority was enhanced by their active involvement in family businesses, it was at the same time constrained, as we have seen earlier, by the town's heavy-industrial economy and sluggish occupational dynamic that limited their independent employment, the authoritarian political order and cultural traditionalism, and, within the Jewish group, the relatively undifferentiated institutional structure of communal life, and traditional gender roles upheld by the religious system. The same factors also shaped women's perceptions regarding rational control, a sense of personal autonomy, and an activist approach to life. Women's everyday involvement in business activities as sellers, cashiers, and buying advisers, and their personal experience with the ups and downs of these family enterprises, strengthened their practical concern with the possibilities and limitations of rational calculation and planning. While recollecting their views in these matters within the "smaller picture" of everyday life, my women-informants, as noted earlier, usually put the notion of "mastery" first and foremost in the context of management of family businesses, and their appreciations in this regard did not seem substantially different from those of the men. At the same time, both immigrant and second-generation women were subordinate in all the spheres they inhabited: in business, where they were "helpers" rather than partners; in the management of the household, where they were fully responsible only in lower-level decisions; and in the ethnic community. Women's ultimately dependent position thus did not permit significant enhancement of their sense of personal control.

In addition, the religious Consorthodoxy of the Johnstown Jewish community upheld a representation, and a normative prescription, of women's position as subordinate to men's. As my interviews indicate, this self-perception was actually shared by women of both generations, although the American-born group was, it seems, more aware of their limited autonomy. It is quite possible, however, as my informants admitted themselves, that this self-consciousness has been a more recent development, a result of increasing public awareness of gender inequality since the 1960s, as well as of the sharpened awareness of these women's own, third-generation, daughters.

While in recollections my informants shared, women's pursuits had been acquiescently seen as ultimately subordinate to the authority of men, their perceptions of the supervisory involvement of Divine Providence in their own, and generally human, everyday occupations and the results thereof did not seem very much different from schemas held by men, placing the basic responsibility on people and their actions. Among those with whom

I talked about their thoughts and feelings before World War II, or whose attitudes were described to me by their children, and who admitted to the belief in God's help in their everyday lives, most understood this assistance mainly as a call to, and perhaps a "spiritual support" in, self-directed actions; very few saw it as an assurance of providential rescue, *Got vet tsushikn,* and almost all of these were women of the immigrant generation, from the more traditional Orthodox homes either at Rodef Sholom or Ahavath Achim. Rather than embracing such a philosophy (which the men called *vaybishes verter,* women's talk, or opinions, apparently meaning "unreasoned"), Johnstown women much more commonly took the approach of Sarah I., as recollected by her nephew, who always "trusted in God's help . . . but also knew very well that were her family only to depend on the Lord, its lot would be lessened."

Despite some resemblances, however, Johnstown women's sense of control and responsibility was evidently, on the whole, less than that of men, regardless of congregational membership, residential location, and generational position. It also seems to have differed in kind, or, more accurately, had differently distributed emphases on a collective and individual component. While family welfare was, as we have seen, the main concern of the Johnstowners, male and female, and its improvement their primary life-goal, more frequent references to "us" (family) than "I" in women's recollections of their perceptions of rational control of life situations, planning for the future, and taking chances in business suggest that a family-collective sense of control, responsibility, and rational (purposeful) action was the dominant element in this set of schemas.[39]

We shall now change the lens once more, this time to a much wider, panoramic view that the Johnstowners also applied to make sense of their lives, in this case with even less gender-based difference: of the general course of the human world and, within it, of the Jewish group and personal experience. In this enlarged scale, too, the Jewish "dominant profile of cultural orientations" resembled in some aspects the dominant American model, but there were important distinctions. As outlined earlier, modern middle-class American life-philosophy has intrinsically assumed a course of human affairs that is lineal and progressive—that is, based on the premise of the successful accumulation of achievements—and its major time-focus has been on the present-turned-toward-future. Humans in such a world have been conceived of first and foremost as separate individuals, whose lives at once reflect and contribute (or should contribute) to the progressive, accumulative, forward-oriented trend of their social world. In comparison, the Jewish dominant profile of cultural orientations, to stay with Kluckhohn's concept, has contained not only these schemas but also representations that counterbalanced each of the former.

And so, alongside a lineal progressive image of the world's course (of which the traditional religious foundation has been belief in the coming of the Messiah), there was also in the Jewish dominant profile of cultural ori-

entations a cyclical one, alternating between high and low tides, and swirl-
ing people in its motions. Both these representations have been used in
traditional scholarly (Talmudic) as well as popular Jewish interpretations:
either reconciled by making the lineal dimension a higher-order, more encompassing schema, or allowed to exist side by side.

In terms of time-focus, to continue the comparison, traditional Jewish
world-philosophy, as has so often been emphasized in Jewish-American
and comparative ethnic studies, certainly has contained a strong component of present-toward-future orientation, operative particularly in the
smaller picture. But in both lineal and cyclical images of the course of
the human world, there inheres also a solid bond with the past, especially
the group (Jewish) past, a link meaningful enough to redraw the entire
picture.

There are many aspects to the significance of history in Jewish, and specifically Jewish-American, sociocultural life, and some of them have been
referred to earlier in this study; here I would like to point out one relating
particularly to the foregoing discussion. There have been in the traditional
Jewish dominant profile of cultural orientations proto-elements that in a
conducive social-structural context could, and in fact did, agglutinate into
a strong drive toward individual achievement. However, the past-in-
present orientation—that is, a binding sense of common history—has fostered a sense of ethnoreligious solidarity or a communal spirit, emphasized
much less (or even lost, in the opinion of commentators) in post-Puritan,
modern American outlooks.[40]

As attested by autobiographies, recorded oral histories, the Jewish-
American press, and literature, all these schemas—lineal-progressive and
cyclical representation of the course of human affairs, past-present-future
orientation, and individual-collectivist approach to life—were also shared
by the upwardly mobile residents of large urban centers, members of
considerably ethnicized Jewish communities. But, as already suggested,
because of these very characteristics of their social environment, the proportioning of these elements, and therefore the overall quality of life-
philosophies of those big-city Jews, was likely to have been different—
closer to the dominant profile of cultural orientations of mainstream middle-class Americans than was the case in Johnstown.

The configuration of the external and intragroup circumstances of Jews'
lives in Johnstown, recapitulated several times through this book, validated
specific aspects of their cultural outlooks, making them meaningful as tools
to interpret their own situations in America and as guideposts for action.
The shifting economic fortunes of Johnstown's Jews upheld in their perceptions a cyclical image of the course of human affairs, and, as a recourse,
also a collectivist approach to life's challenges that was strongly sustained
by several factors simultaneously: the town's sociopolitical organization,
the persistence of the ethnic economic niche, and the pronounced com-

munalism in group institutional and informal functioning that embraced members of both immigrant and American-born generations.[41]

Like the idea of responsibility to continue work even when it does not bring completion, identified as "the Jewish way" by several people I talked to, a representation of the *galgal hozer b'olam*, the revolving wheel of the world, was familiar to and shared in one way or another by most of my informants, men and women alike, who recollected the ways in which they mentally coped with ups and downs in their families' economic welfare (although they did not trace the idea specifically to the second-century C.E. Jewish sage Rabbi Ishmael ben Elisha). Isadore G., born to one of the most affluent families in town, thus elaborated this common view, which he himself learned, he said, from his immigrant father: "Money is a transient thing, it comes to you and leaves you, leaves and comes." In such a perspective, the world's wheel of changing fortune affects all and everyone: "Today I am up and you are down, tomorrow the reverse"; thus, helping out those currently in need appears not only a righteous thing to do, a *mitsve*, and a fulfillment of social expectations, but also a reasonable action, a sort of insurance. In fact, my informants usually expressed the two views at once and in linkage, like Blanche B., who explained the practical philosophy in her home when she was an adolescent before World War II: "You have and then you don't, so you should give and then it will come to you [again] . . . you should put back [into the community, for the less successful] as much as you can." Similarly, Arthur T. spoke about his approach to material accomplishments in life and how he insured against the changes of fortune by keeping up active involvement in the group: "What you take out [for yourself], you ought to put back [into others; concretely, the needs of the Jewish community]."[42]

In the published reminiscences of New York and other big-city Jews, a normative precept, "It is a *mitsve*, the righteous thing to," is typically mentioned as the reason for assisting others in need, but one can assume that to the extent that a belief in—and experience of—a cyclical movement of fortune were common in these locations, they most likely contributed as well to this shared sense of obligation. The study of New York's garment-worker labor activists quoted earlier has found them, too, collectively minded and caring for the needy. In their case, however, this orientation expressed commitments to what the author-interpreter calls "abstract categories" of class, the oppressed, the powerless, and the like, formulated in political terms, and taking precedence—as "measured" by frequency of references in life history narratives—over family and communal involvements.[43] In comparison, in Johnstown this orientation was distinctly local, concrete, and ethnic, and, while the garment workers' collectivism seems to have involved primarily a sense of responsibility for others, in Johnstown it entailed the idea of close reciprocity: responsibility for and reliance on others.

And, lastly, the big-biggest schema of the whole universe at all times, encompassing bigger and medium perspectives, as well as the "small pictures" of Johnstowners' everyday lives. As we talked about actions and attitudes related to pursuing their goals in prewar Johnstown, I explicitly asked my respondents whether they *then* felt there was a God or supreme force in the universe, and, if so, what kind of presence they thought it was. I solicited these answers because other things they commonly did (such as religious observance, the use of traditional utterances acknowledging the existence of the supernatural)—even if interpreted as calls to self-reliance, or, as will be discussed shortly, expressions of optimism or hopefulness rather than a simple rational-mastery can-do attitude—suggested an additional layer of meaning in their lives.

"God helps those who help themselves" has been, as already noted, not only the Jewish but also the accustomed American idea. Interpreters of the dominant profile of American cultural orientations (Florence Kluckhohn included) have focused, characteristically for the secular spirit of contemporary mainstream sociology, exclusively on the second, *help themselves*, part of this schema. They have left its predecessor, *God helps*, unelaborated, or, more precisely, have left its elaboration to the specialists of a (marginal) subfield of the sociology of religion. As a result, an important question has not been really or fully addressed in the literature on this subject: that of the presence or absence of the value-concept of Divine Order/God as the most encompassing schema informing the modern "American spirit of success"—or, in sociologese, of the degree of that spirit's secularization. And it has been left unaddressed despite the fact that past and contemporary reports have consistently shown the solid majority of Americans declaring that they "believe in God."[44]

I did not find, either, any hints in sociohistorical studies that posit equivalence between the dominant American and big-city middle-class Jewish life-philosophies about how secularized the latter might have been in the interwar period, that is—for the purposes of this discussion—how far stripped of belief in the supernatural as an operational force in the world on a macro-scale. In this case, too, while rare for the reasons pointed out below, investigations of this matter have been relegated to the specialized, though less marginal than in mainstream social sciences, field of religious studies.[45] One could, then, only speculate that these worldviews did secularize to the degree that their most prominent features indeed came to correspond to the secularized American ethos of achievement. (The study of self-images of New York garment workers quoted above implies such secularization, but the issue is not discussed.)

Except for theologians professionally trained to pronounce on matters of the divine, even educated people are usually quite inarticulate on the subject. In addition, as I have already pointed out, Judaism has always centered on behavior rather than beliefs, assuming God as experience rather than a concept, which makes discourse on the "meaning of God" even more difficult. However, most people whom I confronted with these questions responded upon reflection with some, if vaguely formulated, belief-statements, suggesting that those feelings-ideas, though "never dissected specifically," as one of my collocutors on this subject put it, were indeed relevant in their recollected experiences.

Almost all replies to my question of whether they then—before the war—believed there was some supreme force or meaning in the universe were in the affirmative, and for the majority this was God;[46] the remaining respondents did not know or were not sure, but I found only one self-declared atheist (his beliefs, by the way, did not prevent him from observing socially expected Jewish rituals). There was, however—or so it seemed to me—a difference in the level of involvement or intensity of recollected feelings in this matter between the immigrants and the American-born, and possibly between genders in the former group, although it may well be that women's expressive style rather than their religious fervor was more intense than men's. The immigrants, and especially women, were more prone to emphatic "oh, yes!" or "but of course!" answers. The second generation, in reminiscing about their adolescence and early adulthood in prewar Johnstown, tended to acknowledge God's existence as something taken for granted, a given scheme of things, as if, to use Clifford Geertz's apt metaphor, they were more "held by" (not unwillingly) than "holding" this belief.[47] In their parental homes these things were not talked about, "they were lived," as I heard so many times, while in their non-Jewish surroundings, and particularly at school, God—the Christian God to be sure, but still the deity for the dominant group—had been presumed as a certitude, invoked daily in the morning prayer, and referred to as self-evident in American history books and in civics classes (as in "God helps those . . ." heard so often by Jewish children in American schools).

While they said they believed in the existence of God or a supreme force/meaning in the universe, Johnstown Jews, as already noted, did not interpret this presence as directly engaged in people's daily affairs. American-born Mildred G.'s comment in this matter was one of the most elaborate I heard, but well representative of what others had to say: "Once [in her youth] we went to the woods, and there were huge trees there, they must have been there from time immemorial. I thought: they just see the tips of my shoes . . . this is how God must be. . . . Our [daily] lives are so detailed, God cannot be bothered with little details like this." However, though God was not directly involved in people's concrete plans and initiatives, my collocutors were sure that they had then been confident ("without analyzing, as you are doing") that He was the beneficent presence in the universe, a "good force of life in the general plan," as Harry R. put it—though many were not certain after the Holocaust.[48] This instinctive—*habitual* in Bourdieuse—confidence in a fundamental, life-promoting goodness within the universe could be construed as grounding the basically optimistic—to refer again to Florence Kluckhohn's cultural value-set—orientation of my collocutors' world-philosophies.

Like activism and self-reliance, optimism has been one of the main features of the "American spirit," and from the beginning of their stay in this country Jews were confronted with this prevalent approach in the institutions of the dominant society; perhaps more so than members of other contemporary immigrant groups, because the Yiddish press and cultural institutions stressed the theme of "Americanism as the confidence and optimism in life" far more strongly than, say, their Slavic counterparts.[49] American social workers and politicians, press, radio, films, and obviously school all promoted confident optimism as best-suited for "the best country in the world," another leitmotiv of public culture.

The generally optimistic approach to life was, then, another shared feature of Jewish and American dominant profiles of cultural orientations, and the greatly improved life-opportunities that big-city and small-town Jews alike encountered in the United States provided the "plausibility structure," in Peter Berger's coinage for the social-structural context of belief systems,[50] that validated this attitude drawn from both cultures. As in the case of activism and self-reliance, my second-generation respondents were at a loss to distinguish which could have been the Jewish elements, that is, acquired from immigrant parents and often in the Yiddish idiom, and which the American, that is, absorbed at school; I eventually gave up this futile inquiry and settled for just recording the overlap. "It was part of my being [this way of thinking]," Seymour S. said, for example; "it was Jewish because I was Jewish, but I was also American." In Bertha W.'s words, "It was instilled in me from my Jewish upbringing, but at school also we learned it."[51]

But as with other similarities between the Jewish and classical American "spirits," there also seems to have been a difference; in any case, so it appeared to me as I listened to my Johnstown respondents. Namely, when asked about optimism, they tended to interchange it with hopefulness, as if there was some implied limitation of the modern (secularized) American-style can-do mastery attitude, but a "trusted" limitation. Perhaps if we were to elide Paul Ricoeur's distinction between optimism and hopefulness, hopeful optimism would be the appropriate concept: a higher-order schema—the super-program—that subordinated, or made meaningful in a broader perspective, the unavoidable shorter- and longer-*durée* failures and misfortunes.[52] "Were they [the parents] optimistic? . . . oh, yes, very hopeful persons, typical for Jewish people"; "We [in the second generation] always hoped everything would be all right"; "[Optimistic?] . . . there is always tomorrow, certainly optimistic, never gave up hope"—these were rather typical answers to my questions in the matter.[53] "There must be some reason why we are here [on earth], so keep busy, you should be busy making contributions, in your [private] life, and in the community"; "This was the attitude [in Isadore G.'s home], you are only given a short while to live, a little blink of time; you cannot [do] everything, but keep working at it, keep working for the good, make something of this gift."[54]

To summarize, I have argued above that, first, the Jewish "dominant profile of cultural orientations" has been more complex and polyvalent than posited by a thesis about its functional equivalence to modern "American spirit" or the dominant life-philosophy as specified by Florence Kluckhohn and others; and, second, that while the environment of rapidly expanding large urban centers and quickly ethnicizing Jewish communities could have prompted the accentuation, or prioritization even, in cultural orientations of upwardly mobile Jews of schemas resembling those constitutive of the dominant American ethos, the circumstances prevailing in Johnstown enhanced, rather, other orientations. Assuming that value-orientations of the majority of the big-city mainstream middle-class American Jews have indeed closely resembled the dominant American "spirit of achievement," a pictorial way of comparing their worldviews and the Johnstowners' would be to set next to each other two drawings made up of similar components but colored with dissimilar intensities, so that the overall images are different.

Let me, in conclusion, briefly recapitulate the main directions of the practical effects of the schemas as reconstructed in this chapter, that is, their impact on their bearers' accommodation to the local environment. I would like to note three such consequences that seemed to me of particular importance.

The first has been the combined impact of perceptions and sense made of civic vulnerability and the precariousness of economic success on the Johnstown Jews' patterns of sociability. Both kinds of insecurity acted as reinforcements of the inwardness of the local Jewish community, an inwardness that was already strongly sustained by sociocultural and political conditions in the larger Johnstown society as well as by the internal organization of the Jewish group itself. Considering how the Jewish group's members felt about their situation in Johnstown, it made perfect sense for them to stay among, rely on, and invest in other Jews and the ethnic community: in addition to fulfilling important expressive needs, this commitment shielded them against excessive anxiety involved in occupying a marginal position amid the dominant "others," while at the same time protecting against the hard knocks expected as the wheel of fortune turned. But inasmuch as these felt insecurities contributed to the social enclosure of their ethnic group, they added to the persistence of its marginality, slowing the integrative processes, and thus perpetuating the whole pattern.

Second, the practical impact of mental schemas for apprehending life situations on the development of these situations themselves was—if my interpretation of the "unspoken connections" in these life-orientations approximates the way they actually functioned—an energizing effect on people's daily activities in the pursuit of their valued life-goals because of the underlying hopeful trust in the beneficence of a highest-order force, or God. This "realism with something extra," as the American-born Harry B. termed this approach professed in his family, called for continuous efforts, regardless of disappointments, for moving on by transcending the present and, it was hoped, expanding on it; this outlook was demonstrated in chapter 3 dealing with the economic pursuits of the Johnstown Jews in their ethnic niche.[55] In turn, energized by such an attitude, repeated efforts increased a chance of success—the hoped-for "good (and better) life for the family."

Third, and last—this point is the most speculative of all, but I feel entitled to it after this long interpretive exertion—are the adaptive effects of the general heuristic approach, namely, the evidence-sensitive, relativizing, and circumstantial way of conceiving of human affairs and the surrounding world. Ernest Gellner has called this kind of approach a "variable cognitive capital," as opposed to a "fixed" type that is characterized by "frozen notions . . . and entrenched mental habits." Gellner assigns the variable approach to modern thinking, the fixed to traditional.[56] Placed in the above categories, the traditional Jewish mentality seems to have contained elements of variability as part of the fixed cognitive capital. Under which circumstances and in which ways this tool in the Jewish "cultural tool kit" has served to facilitate Jews' adaptation to the modern world, in America and elsewhere, is a topic for a separate investigation.[57] Here, let me merely propose, locally and concretely, that the multilayered images of their life situations, perceived by the Johnstown Jews as "flexible and fluxible"—if not at a given moment, then potentially so—facilitated their adaptation to the surrounding environment by calling for alert attentiveness for a promising turn of events. As this study has shown, Jews adapted quite well—"intelligently," in the actors' own lingo—to prewar circumstances by fitting their life-goals into this framework and making the best of what conditions offered. After the Second World War, this approach also helped them quickly to adjust, by redirecting their pursuits, to the changed economic and sociopolitical circumstances in Johnstown. These developments are not part of this project, but I will outline them briefly in an epilogue.

Postwar Era: A Decline of the Community

IN PLACE of a conclusion, I will sketch out here what the Johnstowners wanted included in this book: the postwar developments in the local Jewish community. The second half of its century-long history, from the end of World War II until the present, illustrates as well as the first fifty years investigated in this study the interactive relationship between processes in the surrounding social environment and those inside the Jewish group. By the same token, it demonstrates once more the underlying theme of this project, the historicity or diversity of patterns of adaptation to American society by ethnic group members.

The postwar history of Johnstown and its Jewish community can be roughly divided into three sequences: a period of growth and diversification from 1945 through the late 1950s; a decline from the 1960s through the 1980s; and a limited but visible revival in the last few years. I will briefly outline these developments in chronological order, pointing out their main constitutive elements and consequences.[1]

As in other steel-producing centers across the country, the United States' entry into World War II in 1941 boosted Johnstown's sluggish economy, and so did the national prosperity of the postwar years. Increased residential mobility of Americans during the decade following the war, greatly facilitated by the proliferation of private cars, brought a considerable number of new people to Johnstown, many of whom were professionals from large cities. As a result of the area's economic growth and the arrival of well-educated new residents, Johnstown's white-collar sector expanded, and the occupational structure became more diversified. The expansion of the white-collar sector of the local economy created more occupational opportunities for women: their participation in the labor force increased from 18 percent in 1940 to 26 percent in 1955, although part of this growth was due to the establishment in the area of new garment-manufacturing companies. The occupational upgrading, the rise in the standard of living of many old-time Johnstown families, and the addition of better-educated new arrivals accelerated, in turn, the residential restructuring of Greater Johnstown. Its suburban areas grew rapidly; for example, the population in Westmont, the neighborhood of the "truly arrived," as my informants called it, had expanded by more than one-third between 1940 and 1955.

At the same time, the unionization of the local steel industry in 1941 broke the hold on Johnstown's political order of its longtime tacit master, Bethlehem Steel Company, and the takeover of city politics by the Democratic party opened offices and other previously inaccessible jobs to members of "new" (South and East European) ethnic groups.

The local Jewish community also grew as new families, mostly of East European origin and primarily from the big cities, arrived in Johnstown. By the mid-1950s, the Jewish group—counting adults, adolescents, and the many baby-boom children—reached the unprecedented size of 2,000-odd persons. In 1951, both Rodef Sholom Synagogue and Beth Zion Temple, each with considerably expanded membership (the latter's share had nearly tripled to about 30 percent of the total), moved to new buildings in Westmont. In the following year the Jewish Center and the Rodef Sholom Synagogue officially merged to form the synagogue-center, and the Ladies Auxiliary, renamed the Sisterhood, appointed its first representatives to the board of directors. By that time the congregation had by popular consensus become "really Conservative," and it was to remain so for the next twenty-four years. The synagogue-center, it may be noted, continued to be referred to as the "synagogue" rather than the "center."

In the prewar period only a small minority of young Jewish Johnstowners continued their education beyond the secondary level, but college attendance soon became the practice of the steadily increasing majority and the social expectation among group members, especially in the younger age cohorts. A constellation of factors contributed to this change: the previously mentioned growth of the white-collar sector combined with the loosening up of Johnstown's rigid sociopolitical organization, and the breaking of the city's isolation; the influx into the area, and into the Jewish community in particular, of educated newcomers from the big cities who brought new ideas and practices and furnished the immediate role models; the availability of college fellowships and other educational assistance under the GI Bill (the local B'nai B'rith lodge also funded a college scholarship annually for an outstanding high school senior); and, finally, local Jews' realization that the small businesses that had provided their families with a livelihood for several decades were bound to lose in a confrontation with the bigger and more versatile chain stores, and that the young should prepare themselves for other occupations.

Another change was facilitated by the loosening of the old sociopolitical organization with its rigid status hierarchy and nearly impermeable religioethnic group boundaries, although this one occurred on a smaller scale than young Jews' educational advancement and without its group transformative effects. Johnstown's Jewish community increased and expanded its involvement in the civic-political affairs and cultural activities of the local larger society, and, reciprocally—this was a novelty—mainstream organization members occasionally visited in or used the spacious synagogue-center. As before, however, closer social relations between Johnstown's Jews and Gentiles remained very limited, even though a certain number of newcomer Jewish professionals were admitted to the local country club.

The postwar growth of the Johnstown area turned out to be short-lived. As the production in mills and coal mines slumped in the early 1960s and then steadily dwindled, reflecting a nationwide trend, the local economy, still primarily dependent on the outdated smokestack industries, plunged into decline. Unlike much bigger Pittsburgh, that city's miniature sibling, as Johnstown was sometimes called, left to its own resources, was not dynamic enough to attract sufficiently large capital and innovative minds to restructure its economy.

Between 1960 and 1980, the population of Johnstown and the surrounding urbanized areas decreased by more than 7 percent; the decline accelerated in the second half of this period. During the same interval, total employment fell by 10 percent, and jobs in the manufacturing industries by about half; the latter decline affected primarily the male labor force, more than one-quarter of whom, from among those who had stayed in the area, were unemployed by the mid-1970s. The white-collar sector grew somewhat, mostly during the first part of the 1960–1980 period, but the numerical increase was limited: during the entire twenty years, the number of persons in professional occupations grew by about 400, and of those in (combined) administrative, service, and clerical employment by more than 1,500. A considerable proportion of new lower white-collar jobs were held by women, whose numbers in the labor market increased—the proportion of gainfully employed females sixteen years old and older reached 38 percent by 1980—but, again, the bulk of this growth occurred in the first decade of the twenty-year period.

Affected by processes in the larger society, in the 1960s Johnstown's Jewish community, too, began to decline. Its size progressively diminished as more people moved out and were not replaced by newcomers; for example, during one decade membership in all the local Zionist organizations combined decreased by nearly 30 percent. The losses were largest among young college graduates—the same children and grandchildren of old-time Johnstown immigrants who had rushed to colleges during the first postwar decade. As they saw little opportunity for themselves in their ever more economically depressed hometown, the majority of this group settled elsewhere, primarily in large cities. At the other end of the age structure, a growing number of retirees were leaving for Florida, where they formed the "Johnstown Club."

In 1975 the Johnstown Jewish Community Council was replaced by the United Jewish Federation—a rather belated and somewhat ironic transformation, considering the dwindling size and shrinking institutional networks of the local Jewish community. In the following year, Conservative Rodef Sholom Synagogue and Reform Beth Zion Temple merged as Beth Sholom Congregation (depopulated below the number required for public worship, Orthodox Ahavath Achim or the "little shul," as it was called by the Johnstowners, closed down a few years later). The first attempts at unification had been made in the late 1940s, when both groups were getting ready to relocate their congregational buildings to Westmont, but too many compromises would have been necessary, and, since both congregations were growing, the idea was simply abandoned. More than a quarter-century later, in view of the rapid diminution of the overall number of Jews in Johnstown, the unreasonable burden of continuing to maintain two oversize buildings almost next door to each other became apparent. In spite of strong negative emotions on both sides—feelings that were still alive when I appeared in Johnstown four years later—the merger was implemented as a pragmatic solution. It was agreed that a Reform rabbi would lead the joint congregation, but the cantor would be, as I was told by a former Rodef Sholom member, "of a more Conservative persuasion"; Friday night services were to follow the Reform ritual, but "Saturdays stayed Conservative"; High Holiday services were also to be divided, "Reform on the first day, and Conservative on the second"; and—a considerable victory for Rodef Sholom women—the new temple's kitchen was to remain kosher.

During the 1980s, "my decade" in Johnstown, the decline of the area's population and economy deepened further. The former decreased by 14 percent, and, for the first time in the postwar era, Westmont also lost some of its population; the economy, measured by the number of gainfully employed persons, declined by 13 percent. In manufacturing, this decrease was a staggering 40-odd percent in the ten years between 1980 and 1990, and—again unprecedented since World War II—there was no growth, but actually a slight decline, in the size of the administrative/service/clerical sector and, in consequence, in the number of gainfully employed women. Completing this snapshot picture of the general situation was a high 22 percent share in the total population of persons sixty-five years old and older in 1990. That group had increased by 6 percent in one decade. The corresponding national figures were 11 percent in 1980 and 13 percent in 1990; much larger and faster-growing proportions of the elderly in the Johnstown area resulted primarily from the continuing departure of considerable numbers of the younger cohort.

Further depletion of the Jewish community's vital forces during the 1980s reflected the downward trends in the surrounding society. When I began research on the history of Johnstown's Jews at the beginning of that decade, nearly all of the working adults were in professions (mostly health, legal, and managerial), a large majority resided in prestigious Westmont, and most families were comfortably situated economically. But among these successful people a mood of "gloom and doom" prevailed regarding the future of the local Jewish community. In fact, this shared sense of the impending end, as they themselves admitted, made Beth Sholom leaders all the more eager to assist me in my historical project, "to catch it before it disappears"; the historical archives and a small (permanent) exhibit in the Temple were organized in the same spirit.

Indeed, group statistics did not look promising. In 1990, a survey sponsored by Beth Sholom Temple found no more than 415 Jewish men, women, and children in the Johnstown area, or a mere one-fifth of the 1950s population. In the religious school there were 40-odd children, also a decrease to about one-fifth of the enrollments during the first postwar decade. And, perhaps most ominous for the continuing existence of the local Jewish community, the median age in the Jewish group was estimated at sixty-five. The closing down in 1991 of the Glosser Brothers' department store—the "people's store" that for several decades had served working-class families in the entire area and provided full- and part-time jobs for hundreds of Johnstowners, Jewish and Gentile—symbolized the passing of an era for many a local resident.

The future of Johnstown and of its Jewish group had appeared so bleak that positive developments inaugurated in 1991/92 were at first greeted with wariness rather than enthusiasm; indeed, during my last visit to Johnstown in the summer of 1993, I still heard expressions of disbelief that this upturn would "change things very much." As I have mentioned, Johnstown did not have sufficient resources to overhaul the economy by either building new ventures on its own or attracting them from the outside, and so it was through external political assistance—specifically, the efforts of John Murtha, the Pennsylvania congressman who grew up in Johnstown—that a number of enterprises were brought to the area. Within a couple of years, high-tech Concurrent Technologies Corporation (CTC), some defense-related industries, and, most recently, an arm of the U.S. Justice Department, the National Drug Intelligence Center (NDIC), have located in the Johnstown area. With these establishments came new people, most of whom are highly educated, urban (and urbane), younger-middle-aged professionals. Since these new establishments are growing (CTC and NDIC each intend eventually to employ 250–300 people), and since there has also been some related expansion in local educational and health service institutions, more professional newcomers are expected in the near future.

In this wave of new arrivals during 1992 and 1993, twenty-two Jewish households have settled in the Johnstown area. Of this number, fourteen households (nine families and five singles), have become members of Beth Sholom Temple, and the rest remain unaffiliated. This represented a net membership gain, as only seven "membership units" were discontinued during the same two-year period: five of those were single senior citizens who died, and two were old-time local families who moved to other cities and resumed synagogue membership there. Jewish newcomers share the demographic and socioeconomic characteristics of others who have recently come to Johnstown: they belong to third- or fourth-generation American Jewish families (mostly of East European origin); the adults are in their early to mid-forties; they are—both men and women—professionals, and usually have one or at most two children (the women generally withdraw from employment for only a few years when their children are very small); and the majority had resided in metropolitan centers or in the urban sprawl areas between them. The majority, too, apparently grew up in Reform or Conservative Jewish homes in which religious practice was largely limited to High Holidays temple/synagogue attendance and Passover family seders.

More Jews fitting this profile are likely to come to the Johnstown area as the recently established companies hire more people. Unless a serious economic downturn drives out these new ventures or their employees, the gloom-and-doom predictions from a few years ago about "the end of Johnstown's Jewish history" now seem rather improbable. What seems certain, however, is that it will be—actually, it is already—a quite different history from that told in this book.

Differing from the entire Jewish group in the past and from the dwindling number of elderly old-timers in the present, younger adults, including those who have lived in Johnstown for a long time as well as the recent arrivals, no longer make the temple their center of social life. In the past, external and intragroup circumstances would have made it very difficult, because of the prevailing cultural norms and social expectations, for newcomer Jews to remain unaffiliated with the Jewish community. Except for the pioneers in the late nineteenth century, nearly all Jews arriving in the Johnstown area followed kin-ethnic networks, and, having settled down, they naturally turned to their fellow ethnics to procure and maintain employment, participate in social life, and share cultural practices. The divisive, ethnic-ascriptive organization of the local society sustained and reinforced this group inwardness.

Today, young Jewish adults in Johnstown work for mainstream American companies, and it is these companies, not fellow Jews, that recruit newcomers to the city and provide the primary environment for everyday socializing. Successful Jewish professionals, like their counterparts from other ethnic groups, regularly participate in social functions of their occupational associations and other civic-political organizations, and are welcome as members of local country clubs, including the most chichi, Sunnehanna—which used to limit Jewish membership to few selected bachelors so as not to have to admit the offspring. There is, then, no compelling economic or social reason for Johnstown's younger Jews today to join the congregation; as noted earlier, a high 30 percent of the newcomers actually stay out. Those who do belong rarely show up at any of a dozen or so social events organized each month at Beth Sholom: unless it is "something really big or especially for the children," about 75 percent of the participants, I was told, are usually the old-timers, whereas "younger people prefer the country club," where they usually go with their professional friends. A representative of recent arrivals whom I questioned about this preference gave an answer that may reflect a common way of thinking in this entire group: "We do it [take part in mainstream social activities, especially with fellow professionals] out of necessity, as we cannot afford not to participate . . .

and there is only so much free time outside work and home life." It apparently simply did not occur to this young person that there might be reasons for different, or differently proportioned, priorities.

I asked a few of these younger Beth Sholom members what they saw as the meaning of being Jewish, and what being Jewish entailed. "Being Jewish means you want your children to have a Jewish education" and "it means maintaining Jewish rituals and religious holidays": these were the most common answers, but neither a personal need nor a normative call for the social (ethnic) embedding of these practices was mentioned. In a different context, I learned that campaigns for Zionist causes usually did well in Johnstown, suggesting that being Jewish in some way also entailed a commitment to the symbolic community, without, however, organizational involvement: over 80 percent of the membership of Hadassah, the most active of the local Zionist associations, consists of the elderly old-timers. One could, then, conclude that for the old-time Johnstown Jews their Jewishness has involved an inseparable socioreligious experience and obligation, but for their younger coreligionists today it is mainly a religious identity flown from its social nest or individualized.

The number of children in Beth Sholom's Sunday school has increased by more than 20 percent since the 1990 survey, and this has been considered a sign of the group's revitalization. Nevertheless—and this is perhaps the most telling indicator of change in the profile of Johnstown's Jewish group—only a little over 25 percent of these children have parents both of whom were born Jewish. Of those remaining, 20 percent are the offspring of marriages in which the wife (in all cases) converted to Judaism, and in the rest of the cases the non-Jewish parent agreed to have his or her children educated as Jews. In view of these figures, it may well be that the desire of the majority of Johnstown's young parents for their children to attend Jewish Sunday school expresses an anxiety to preserve the last symbolic vestiges of Jewishness threatened by dissolution more than a concern with solidifying and building on a core religious identity.

The young parents themselves do not attend services frequently, except on the High Holidays. Rather than increasing because of the recent influx of new people, attendance at Friday night temple services has dropped over the past ten years by half—to about 20–25 persons. It may be noted here that because of "this intermarrying business," as one of my informants put it, although it maintains a Conservative cantor and divides services half-and-half between Conservative and Reform, Beth Sholom had to disaffiliate with the Organization of Conservative Synagogues, in which it had retained membership after the merger in 1976 along with its association with Reform temples. Conservative services are attended almost exclusively by elderly old-timers.

Regarding temple life, a comment is in order concerning the position of women in Beth Sholom's public-religious forum. In the shared opinion of the women and men I questioned on this issue, this position, in the words of one of the former, "has been gradually evolving toward [gender] parity, but there is still a tilt toward male dominance, especially in matters religious." While they are disapprovingly aware of the persistence of gender inequality in this area, the women generally do not contest the situation, although apparently for different reasons in the older and younger generations. Older women have not been trained to participate fully in the services, and so they tend not to feel competent enough to do so, and younger ones seem largely uninterested in taking an active role. The traditional prayer address, "God of our Fathers," continues to omit "Mothers," included today in Reform and many Conservative congregations; but the local women have not requested this change. The temple's ritual committee is also the only one without female members. At the same time, however, the sparse attendance (a total of twelve persons, or about 4 percent of the adult Beth Sholom population in 1993) at two Beth Sholom religious programs—Hebrew classes for adults and weekly lunch-and-learn meetings—is overwhelmingly female; but younger women, again, remain a minority (about 30 percent). Congregational social functions, traditionally in women's hands, are not of great interest to younger members, either, who "of necessity" invest their time primarily in outside activities.

Home religious practices are minimal. Traditionally the most sanctified observance, and, considering the busy schedules of present-day professionals, not really a demanding one, women's lighting of Sabbath candles on Friday night followed by a festive family meal, is practiced only "occasionally" in most younger Jewish households. As I heard once or twice from the mothers of school-age children, "when kids come from religious school and talk about Sabbath, I think I should do it regularly, but then . . ."— but then tiredness or preoccupation with other things takes priority. In the context of everything that has been said so far about the religious life of Johnstown's Jews today, it is, of course, not a surprise that kosher kitchens are kept in no more than eight or nine, exclusively old-timers', households.

One of my key informants and interpreters of the current situation in Johnstown's Jewish group, Jon Darling, a sociologist at the University of Pittsburgh at Johnstown, made a prediction that seems to me more convincing than visions of the quickly approaching end popular among the old-timers. Should the existing trends continue, or even become reinforced by the arrival in the Johnstown area of more young professional Jews of the third and fourth generation, there will be, Jon believes, "Jews in the community, but no community of Jews."

As already noted, younger Jews are actively involved in the professional, civic-political, and social affairs of Johnstown's mainstream society. They participate in these activities first and foremost as highly skilled experts, citizens, or successful middle-class residents, even though, unless they purposely hide it, their Jewish background is recognized. Among the "carriers" of this background, according to my younger informants, there remains some insecurity related to it, in reaction to the perceived "subtle undercurrent of anti-Semitism" occasionally, and, as they view it, probably inadvertently, expressed in jokes or derogatory clichés such as "Jew him down"; however, it seems predominantly an individual rather than collective type of insecurity.

Although there will be Jews in the larger community, there may indeed cease to be a community of Jews. The dissolution in the younger group of the once strong intragroup ties sustained by multiple—economic, social, cultural/religious—reinforcements, and the resulting "decentering" of the temple, have already been noted. Disintegration of the social basis of Jewish ethnoreligious identity is also reflected in the life-orientations of the younger generation. Old-timers liked Johnstown, and, as we have seen in this book, their most valued life-goals and their reasons for remaining in town were the combination of a decent lifestyle for the family and a good environment for raising children and making friends. Younger-generation Jews of today, specifically more recent arrivals, also enjoy their life in Johnstown, and similar items appear on their priority list of valued goals. But their meaning is quite different.

Regarding a decent standard of living, the difference is self-evident, considering, first, much more developed household and consumer technologies, and, second, the much higher socioeconomic status of contemporary Jewish families; present-day newcomers also reveal their lifestyle desiderata in their preference for clean air and healthier living conditions in a smaller and geographically more remote location. Of greater consequence for this discussion is the difference regarding what constitutes a good social environment to live in. When my elderly informants recollected their goals and satisfactions from the past, it was obvious that the good social environment they had in mind was a Jewish environment. For young Jews of today, concern with and appreciation of "nice people," a "sense of being welcome," or "openness" (as opposed to big-city social anonymity) refer primarily to the environment of the larger society. In this context, their concern with good surroundings for raising children also has a different meaning from a similarly phrased concern of their Jewish predecessors in Johnstown. For the older people, the conditions in the larger society were naturally important, but it was taken for granted that a "good environment" implied as well an opportunity to raise their children in the Jewish community to become "Jewish Jews." For younger Jews today, the Jewish side of this concern seems largely limited to providing their offspring the customary number of years in Sunday school.

To conclude, it appears that unless conditions in the Johnstown area change again, a shift from the socially embedded to more individualized Jewish identity is going to accelerate and its consequences will take a more distinctive shape (I hesitate to use here the term "ethnoreligious identity" without a firmer basis in present-day ethnographic data, because clearly it means something different from what it did sixty or seventy years ago). Having spent twelve long years documenting the whys, hows, and wherefores of the Johnstown Jewish group's pronounced differences from its counterparts in other American cities as well as, more generally, the American urban middle class during the half-century preceding World War II, I find it intellectually fascinating and also in a way humbling as a historian-sociologist to see how quickly and easily these ostensibly entrenched particularities have disappeared, giving way to a configuration much more closely resembling the situation described by social scientists as characteristic of present-day American Jewish society at large.

(Self-)Reflections of a Fieldworker

To SPARE nonacademic readers lengthy theoretical divagations that might spoil their interest in the story of Johnstown's Jews, only the basic concepts used in this book were introduced in the preface, where I noted that the general sociological perspectives framing them, and, more fundamental still, the underlying philosophical assumptions about the nature of the social world we live in, would be further discussed in the appendix. Below, then, I first sketch out the intellectual traditions that have shaped my theoretical orientation and practice as a historical sociologist, and have also, more or less directly, informed this study; I then summarize the basic ontological and epistemological presuppositions of my approach, and *eo ipso* of the Johnstown project. Next, delivering on these epistemological premises, I present in one encompassing narrative the kinds of sources used, together with their sociocultural contexts of origin and possible consequences thereof for the contents of those sources; and, at the same time, the context and consequences of the interventions in this process of my own identities and interests.

The earliest lasting influence on my professional development, while I was a student at Warsaw University, was Florian Znaniecki's philosophy and social theory of culture (the latter akin to that of American symbolic interactionism). I was particularly drawn to his view of the social world as "permeated with culture" and always "pulsating with change," and of social actors as inherently creative, reproducing but also originating social situations. I was also much taken with Znaniecki's insistence that the sociologist's fundamental task is to grasp and explain these processes, but to do it with the "humanistic coefficient," that is, by reconstructing chains of actions-meanings as they are understood and represented by their carriers, concrete social actors. Another important influence on my intellectual formation from the same time and place was, Durkheimian in spirit, the cultural history of Stefan Czarnowski (1879–1937; practically unknown in the United States), particularly his careful attention to the mezzo- to microsocial embeddedness of cultural phenomena; a profound sense, exquisitely applied in research, of the temporal dimension of the social world, and, as important, his appreciation of the inseparability of historical research and theoretical reflection, and a consistent practice thereof.[1]

Both Znaniecki and Czarnowski combined ontological "humanism," i.e., a belief that the human world as predicated on symbolic communication constitutes a reality sui generis, distinct from natural phenomena, with a qualified methodological positivism, i.e., a conviction that distinct as it is, social life can and should be studied by rigorous scientific methods and explained by empirically testable theories. A similar general orientation (with "humanism" of the Durkheimian variety) has been represented by the third scholar whose work was significant in my intellectual development at that time, Robert Merton. My classmates and I first became acquainted, and impressed, with Merton's work through the readings (circulated on thin mimeographed sheets) assigned by the late Stefan Nowak in his course on Methodology of the Social Sciences. Merton's elegantly argued advocacy of disciplined, value-free research, continuous dialogue between theory and data, and empirically grounded middle-range sociological theories particularly appealed to us as an alternative to the universalist and manifestly ideologized marxist model. A few years later, still in Warsaw, I translated into Polish Merton's magnum opus, *Social Theory and Social Structure* (rev. ed. 1968). This exercise left me thoroughly exhausted and not entirely certain that I was able to convey accurately to Polish readers the meanings of unfamiliar Americana used by the author as the empirical material for theory building. I was nevertheless enormously impressed by Merton's uncanny craftsmanship at cutting amorphous social phenomena into sociological diamonds by means of a rigorously applied scientific procedure.

I have remained solidly within the humanistic tradition of sociology I learned in Warsaw, rethought and modified as time went by. But I have abandoned my youthful faith in "value-free" sociology inspired by my early mentors. As my historical ethnographic projects increasingly revealed the structure of the world as murky, multilayered mother-of-pearl rather than clear-cut diamond, my commitment to the kind of scientific study of the social world my teachers professed has largely waned as well, replaced by an option for a theoretically informed, disciplined historical interpretation-cum-analysis.

After I came to the United States in late 1979, besides the cultural anthropology of ("middle phase") Clifford Geertz that easily blended with my then essentially normative conception of society, the following influences have been of greatest consequence for my developing theoretical orientation and research: gender studies, or, more precisely, gender-sensitive sociological and historical works (having come from a society where the experience of gender discrimination was still considered as a "personal problem" of individual women, I have learned in this country to see it as a "public issue"); the cultural marxism of E. P. Thompson and Raymond Williams; the structuration theory of Anthony Giddens; and, more recently, and not without a certain intellectual resistance, the work of Pierre Bourdieu, especially in its current, apparently "mellowing" phase, and particularly in the catholic exegesis of his devoted disciple and collaborator, Loïc Wacquant.[2] Somewhat ironically, considering where I came from (but how we hated official marxism!), it is the works of Williams, Thompson, Giddens, and other neo- and reconstructed Western marxists that have turned me—a committed culturalist with an idealist bent upon arrival—into a resolute structuralist-culturalist, with a keen eye on social structures.[3] My American colleagues in social history and historical sociology have made a journey in the opposite direction: from (social-)structuralism to culture. So we are meeting halfway.

Underlying the intellectual orientation sketched above, my fundamental, or metatheoretical, beliefs about the nature of the social world and human cognition thereof can be summarized in three propositions: two ontological and one epistemological. The first assumes the social world and human experience in it to really exist *both* within and outside of our minds and bodies; differently put, "text," or representations of this social world, are the inherent aspect of human experience, but not exhaustive of it. The second views the sociocultural world and human action, joined in mutual reconstitution, as forming certain historical, i.e., time- and place-specific, patterns or regularities—ambiguous and flexible, but nevertheless discernible, at least fragmentarily. And the third assumes the ways of functioning of these "outside" and "inside" historical worlds, and their interrelations, to be knowable to human minds, although our knowledge of them is inherently incomplete and provisional, never fully reliable, and always invested with perceptions peculiar to our social situations and cultural outlooks, likewise historically contingent.

John and Jean Comaroff recently described their own position, containing similar elements, but with a greater emphasis on the "inside" (narrative) worlds than, as in the case of my own orientation, on the "inside"/"outside" reciprocity, as "*neo*modern anthropology" (authors' italics).[4] Mine, I guess, could be called "neo*modern* historical sociology"—the prefix, reflecting my resensitized epistemological (self-)consciousness, has been a relatively recent outcome of a gradual intellectual "Americanization" over the last decade, adding to my sharpened awareness of the (general) social-structural and (more specific) gender determinants of individual and collective lives. Below is a summary of the major suppositions of such a neomodern epistemological approach.

The central one acknowledges the deliberate as well as unrecognized constructive activity of the narrators engaged in producing the story: the authors of historical sources (pictorial, written, or oral) used by the researchers, as well as the researchers themselves. These different narrators are involved in multiple "epistemological structuration" (to match Giddens's "ontological" one—if anyone can stomach yet another neologism in our wordy post- and neomodern discourse). Past representations of the social world shaped the sources' and actor-informants' past narratives of that world, and, in the case of the surviving actor-narrators, also their present representations of that past; actor-informants' representations of the present situations influence, in turn, their narratives of the past; and present and, indirectly, past representations of the world informing the outlooks of the researcher interpenetrate the past stories he/she wishes to recover from historical sources/informants. As a result of these multiple entanglements, the story presented by the historian—that is, his/her depiction of past situations and the interpretation of their meaning and implications—is inescapably fragmented, imperfect, and subjective (as opposed to objective in the social-scientist paradigm).

The narratives offered by historical sources regarding the experience of Johnstown's Jews and created by them, in either written or oral form, have been treated in this project in two ways. First, and most important, they approximate the past experience of the actors, practical (actions) as well as symbolic (representations). This approach is based on two general beliefs: (1) that the past experience was narrativized by the actors who had lived it; and (2) that the acknowledgment of the narratives' constructed character does not by itself invalidate each and all of them as accounts of what *was* the actors' lived past, in meanings and practice, but, rather, the degree of approximation (or misrepresentation) should be evaluated on a case-by-case basis. In the second, complementary approach, representations provided by these sources, namely, contemporary records of group life and narrative accounts of their individual and collective experience provided by actor-informants, have also been treated as constituent of this experience—not as its textual creations, however (and, therefore, I offer no literary textual analysis of these narratives), but, rather, as theme-framing and practice-guiding "cultural programs."[5]

As for my own "narratives" that I implanted into the Johnstown story—as an immigrant (at first recently arrived, then increasingly familiar with American ways), a continuously learning professional historian-sociologist, a becoming Jew, and a woman and becoming feminist, to mention the four most significant developing social situations/identities—I tried, more determinedly as my epistemological self-consciousness grew with the passage of time, to become conscious of these implantations and their impact on my research. As neomodern research practice requires, in what follows I account, in chronological order, for my (im)positions as a multifaceted fieldworker, and for the probable effects thereof.[6] It would have been better for the "validation" of the stories presented in this book, that is, for the assessment of their blind spots and overstatements, if this accounting were built right in to the chapters. I tried this fusion, but incorporating yet another intricate text into the dense narrative of the Johnstowners' everyday lives would have made the outcome indigestible.

Before moving on, I should explain the following (and I will not repeat it in the course of this account). While I plied and flexed both the structuration and ethnicization models in concrete applications to specific research problems I was investigating, and in response to learning about new ideas and findings, in their basic premises they had remained the main interpretative frameworks throughout the duration of my project—like two concentric circles: the double structure as the outer one, the ethnicization as the inner.

I started my research at the beginning of 1980 by intense reading on the history and sociology of American immigration and ethnicity, and at the same time gathering information—from U.S. censuses, Johnstown's city directories, records available at city hall, and the local newspaper, the *Johnstown Tribune*—on the town's population, especially ethnic composition and residential patterns, economy, and political order between 1890 and 1940. Meanwhile I also collected data about general socioeconomic characteristics of the town's East European Jewish and Christian residents (I originally planned to study them together). For both groups, I inspected, first, the manuscript schedules of the 1900 local census (1910 was opened to the public in 1982), and city directories at five-year intervals between 1890 and 1940, tracing households by the Jewish and Slavic or Hungarian-sounding names of their residents; I believe my ear as a native East European, and professional training in archival work on East European history, reduced recognition errors to a passable minimum.

In comparison with Jews, the Slavic and Hungarian populations appeared to have been more considerably underestimated in these sources (I checked census and city directory information against local synagogal/parochial and other ethnic organizational records for each of these groups), most likely owing primarily to the presence in the latter's households of large numbers of boarders, and the unfamiliarity of those collecting the information with their native languages. Jewish households were smaller (most of them did not have any, or had only a few, boarders) and therefore easier to account for, and most of them were headed by small entrepreneurs, either stationary or traveling—a higher and thus more accurately labeled status than that of the unskilled industrial laborers (the lowest ranking among the former, traveling vendors or peddlers, had the highest rate of omissions in this category, but it was nevertheless lower than the latter).[7] Also important was a fact I later learned from the local newspaper: the information about Jews was collected by their fellow ethnics. In addition, as my informants suggested, Jews traditionally "stuck together," apparently counting themselves more carefully than did peasant-immigrants for a combination of pragmatic, religious, and security purposes—and there were not so many to count, after all.

While gathering this initial information about the position and characteristics of the Jewish group in Johnstown, I also made a preliminary inspection of Jewish synagogue and other organizational records held in the library of Johnstown's Beth Sholom Congregation, and, in cooperation with two synagogue officers, arranged for the instruction in oral history basics of a small group of Jewish community members so that they could record life stories "told from the beginning" by the old-timers, immigrants and their elderly American-born children, men and women. I intended to treat these two kinds of narratives both as "data" about people's activities and concrete past events, and as "texts" or self-presentations that could direct me in further research. At that time, though, soon after my arrival from Warsaw, I did not think about my purposes in these terms; rather—as in the case of the first round of my Slavic interviews—I followed Czarnowski's approach in his study of the legend of St. Patrick in Ireland.[8]

From the most extensive, five-hundred-page-long document, the 1904–1925 minutes of the Rodef Sholom Synagogue recorded in Yiddish, I learned upon the first perusal a number of things—for example, data on the synagogue officer corps and finances, the enrollments in *kheyder* (religious school), the number of tickets (seats) sold for the High Holy Days services, and the chronology of women's entry into the public life of the congregation. At the same time, the minutes-as-text revealed the persistence of collective identity of the traditional type: the congregational group had been referred to by the traditional name of the *khevre* and its members as brothers (frequent references to brothers' personal matters, recorded together with official proceedings, suggested the encompassing nature of congregational social life); dates of meetings were recorded in both secular and biblical time; and the Yiddish-language reports of the proceedings were decorated with biblical insertions in Hebrew (faulty, for that matter, in both citations and spelling, suggesting that even the supposedly better educated in Jewish lore—the recording secretaries—had not been real scholars).

I thought the idea to have local Jews collect life histories of their fellow ethnics made sense for several reasons. First, I was a multiple outsider: as a "greener" or recent immigrant unfamiliar with American ways; a person who, although self-consciously of Jewish background, was not a religious or even a cultural Jew (and for the more traditional, my paternal-only Jewish lineage disqualified even this "background"); and an academic and therefore having my own interests in doing the study, not necessarily matching the interests of its subjects-to-be. Second, it seemed a good idea to involve in this project on Johnstown Jewish history Johnstown's Jews themselves, both to invite greater cooperation in my own research and to stimulate an interest in, and assist in the realization of, a local history project. And the third reason was that, as noted above, I was interested in those life stories as a source of data, of course, but also as texts, or self-narratives as told to members of one's own community, and therefore revealing the range and contents of discourses about the past.

I will omit here the factual contents of these life stories, since they were much too detailed for a summary presentation (a good portion of them can be found in this book). At that point I was looking for what was Jewish-Johnstownish—commonalities underlying generational, gender, and other possible differences. What I found in the way of main texts or narrative themes concerning the period covered by my study, were the following: shtetl origins (immigrants), and a minority group member's sense of threat from the dominant society, but primarily economic reasons for leaving for the United States; arrival in the Johnstown area through kin networks; involvement in small business in which both men and women were occupied; residential relocation over time to better neighborhoods; and membership

in and active participation in the local Jewish community. Equally important was what did not appear, or appeared only occasionally, in these life
stories: Jewish scholarship or advanced secular education (the latter became the common theme in post–World War II narratives); the outside
local society (again, involvement in mainstream activities became a theme
in postwar life-sequences); and—less in words than in the narrative tone—
a sense of quick change during the time between settling in Johnstown and
the Second World War, either in the surrounding society, or in the Jewish
group itself and the individual lives. The exception, regarding the Jewish
community, was the short tenure at the Rodef Sholom Orthodox Congregation in the early- to mid-1930s of American-born Conservative Rabbi
Ralph Simon, whose name was connected with change.

The next step, still in the initial phase of research, consisted of several
parallel undertakings. Having learned from Jewish Johnstowners' life histories the names of their East European hometowns, I set out to find more
specific information about the demographic and socioeconomic profiles
and public culture of these shtetls, in a broader context of the turn-of-the-
century Jewish society in that region. For this purpose (moving from the
general to the particular), I read, or reread, several major works on East
European Jewish socioeconomic and political history in the late nineteenth
and early twentieth centuries; and inspected turn-of-the-century population censuses (namely, the 1897 Russian, and 1900 and 1910 Hungarian
national censuses, and the 1898 survey of the economic situation of Jews
in Russia conducted by the Jewish Colonization Society funded by Baron
de Hirsch). Further, I checked the identified localities in the encyclopedias
(primarily *Yevreyskaya* and *Judaica*), and in the existing records of the
Bund, the Jewish Socialist Party (published), and the Zionist organizations
(largely in manuscript), held at The Central Zionist Archives in Jerusalem
where I spent some time in the winter of 1982; I also consulted the "shtetl
finders," listings of shtetls with summary information, and *yitzker-bikher*,
shtetl memorial books—by no means exhaustive and always accurate
sources, but the only ones available. In addition, trying to verify the "data"
part of my informants' stories, and possibly learn more about the old-
country origins of immigrant settlers in Johnstown, I checked information
provided in their naturalization papers, and in the ship records of passengers arriving in U.S. ports (held at the National Archives in Washington,
D.C.), which listed place of residence at birth and at the time of departure, and, for adult men, the declared occupation pursued in the country of
origin. As I realized that Jewish immigrants in Johnstown had resumed
economic exchange with their former East European neighbors, I also collected information about relations between these two groups in the old
country—from the published and unpublished memoirs and autobiographies of immigrants, from contemporary ethnographic and present-day
historical studies. At the same time, I talked to a few representatives of the
former Bethlehem Steel Company management and other elderly members

of the local Anglo-Protestant elite. They were politely distant, one even slightly condescending (probably toward my foreign accent and East European origin). I asked them about the status ranking in the prewar period of different class and ethnoreligious groups in town (Jews were not mentioned at all, and I thought this was very telling about their position); and why, as I learned from local records, there had been no representatives of South and East European groups among local government officials before World War II, and but a few token Jews in the Sunnehanna country club ("Everyone kept to themselves then" was the explanation).

I also organized meetings composed of about six to eight people each on matters involved in conducting small business and on Jewish social life in a small town, for which I prepared themes-problems gathered from already collected "data" and "texts"; the idea to meet in this way, and the assistance therein, came from two Beth Sholom members. In these meetings, I mostly listened—in my relationship with my Jewish informants I still was quite insecure, or so I felt, actually in the position of a petitioner (for information), and evidently completely ignorant in matters of entrepreneurship and of life in small-town America. I was also relatively young, and a woman, while the discussants, in business groups especially, were predominantly elderly men (the invitations were issued by my Beth Sholom friend-collaborators). In addition, it is not easy, should I have wanted to try, to outtalk a gathering of Jews, discussing their own lives at that. About the same time I organized another group meeting with only women participating, devoted to similar matters: business life, social life in a small town, and, particularly, the role of women in these activities. In this meeting my obvious ignorance in most of the practical matters discussed, resulting from the recency of my arrival in the United States and my academic profession, was probably also the dominant element in my relationship with the women I listened to, but shared gender made me feel more at ease, and I therefore asked more questions.

What I learned from these meetings in evidential data were the names and gender (male) of "big shots" in the local Jewish entrepreneurial niche, the details of the operation of in-group support networks, the concrete prerogatives of women in the stores and in the public communal forum when they entered it, the very small number and the circumstances of intermarriages in the prewar era, and so forth. As for self-narrative/stories told during these meetings, ready assignation, for instance, of a synagogal identifier to my informants' mentions, in varied contexts, of individual people as well as communal events and activities indicated the inclusive, congregational character of group life ("everything revolved around the synagogue"). Spontaneous references to normatively sanctioned obligations embedded in specific behaviors—such as "Jews *should* help each other" or "He was Jewish, so it *could be expected* . . ." in the context of business and other kinds of in-group assistance—suggested the enduring traditionalism of shared life-orientations; while qualifiers such as "*today* it is a different story" or "this is how we *then* thought," inserted by women as they discussed among themselves gender roles in prewar Johnstown's Jewish community, indicated the naturalness of the past situation as they then perceived it.

By that time I had already decided to separate the "Slavic" and "Jewish" projects, and felt I had learned enough to tentatively conclude that the experience of Johnstown's Jews had been in several important respects quite distinct from what I read in studies of big-city Jews, particularly the New Yorkers. My reading list then contained mainly the classics from the 1950s and 1960s, along with more recent works, published in the late 1970s and early 1980s, that received attention in journals specializing in American Jewish studies.[9] I thought that making my case study of Johnstown's Jews into a comparative one, that is, set against contrasting references to the experience of their big-city coreligionists who came to America from the same part of the world and at the same time, but who had made their lives in quite different environments, would be both fascinating and sociologically elegant. From that moment on, it may well be that a particular focus was sharpened by my desire to deliver this project in as interesting a fashion and as elegantly as I envisioned it: my researcher's eyes and ears, and the interpreting mind, could have tuned in more to the evidence of difference than of similarity between Johnstown's Jews and their big-city counterparts, and to the signs of continuity more than change as I compared Jewish life in Johnstown and in East European shtetls.

During the remaining several years of research I moved back and forth between archival and other written sources—primarily on Johnstown and its Jewish residents, but also on other localities—and interviews with the Johnstowners that shifted thematically as I proceeded with my archival work and at the same time guided its course. My project has been collaborative in all senses of the word. In addition to the assistance I have already mentioned, my work received support grants from two local families after I presented initial and intermediate findings at three congregational meetings. And, as I proceeded with fieldwork, the Beth Sholom community independently organized a historical archives.

During 1983, when the Slavic project, selected to be completed first, required most attention, I prepared for its Jewish sequel by concentrating on reading in three areas. One of them was American Jewish history. I read (and kept reading) everything that came along, older and currently published: more general works, secondary studies of past and present Jewish communities in various localities, as well as historical and contemporary studies focused on gender, and, specifically, on the position and activities of American Jewish (and other ethnic) women, particularly in the areas of work and decision-making authority inside and outside the home. Of most immediate consequence for my own research at that time, however, was the appearance by the mid-1980s of a series of critical appraisals of the classical works in American Jewish history noted earlier. These new works pointed, generally, to a greater diversity of Jewish outlooks and lifestyles than represented in the earlier studies—outside the metropolitan centers, but also, and more important from my perspective, inside these big cities.[10] Would this undermine, I wondered, the setup of my comparative project? Somewhat reluctantly, I admit, since I was already drowning in material from my own case study, I moved to inspect some primary—that is, contemporary—information, to check for myself, at least in limited measure.

Centering on New York in the period of the reported accelerated transformations of the Jewish group's educational and occupational profile and ethnic communal life, I sample-checked the *Forverts*, the largest-circulation Jewish daily; examined some 1930s surveys of Jews' occupational mobility, educational achievement, entertainment habits, synagogal and other ethnic organizational participation, and involvement in civic-political affairs of the dominant society and social contacts with its members; and, again, looked at memoirs and autobiographies of contemporary East European Jewish immigrant and second-generation New Yorkers, as well as popular novels of prewar Jewish-American life. My abbreviated search revealed that New York Jewish lifestyles had indeed been diverse (could I have expected otherwise?), and suggested that since this diversity was not in the purview of the theoretical model—assimilation—used, usually implicitly, by the aforementioned studies, it was overlooked, or deemphasized. At the same time, however—and here I made a special effort to see with "many eyes"— the contemporary sources I looked at clearly indicated that there were among New York Jews in that period the ascending or already dominant trends of advanced education, upward occupational mobility, intragroup social differentiation, and secularization that simply did not exist in Johnstown. I decided to leave my comparative framework as it stood, with clauses and caveats, and to consider the possibility of a future project comparing small-town parts of Jewish New York or some other big city with "real" Jewish small-towners.

Motivated by both professional and personal interests, I also read intensely during that time (and, for that matter, ever since) on Judaism, and specifically Jewish philosophy, religious and secular. I looked for—or it looked for me at that stage and situation of my life—philosophical and ethical guidance, and for a practical lifestyle with some, shall we say, extra dimension beyond everyday preoccupations. This search was in part spurred by my Johnstown project; but I am sure that it also influenced my fieldwork somehow, particularly its subsequent phases. My growing interest in Jewish religious philosophy led me, in turn, to a third intellectual undertaking (also continued to this day), namely, readings in the sociology of religion, as well as, more specifically, American religious history.

Having completed the Slavic project, I resumed fieldwork on Johnstown's Jews, focusing on their economic lives, and, specifically, the operation of family businesses and the contingent realization of their shared life-goal of a decent standard of living. On the basis of the material gathered earlier I knew about the high and enduring concentration of local Jews in small business, their occupational enclosure in the ethnic entrepreneurial niche, and the existence of a strong intragroup economic support network; and I had established that life success was commonly understood primarily in terms of economic well-being. I now wanted to find out how, concretely, all this happened.

Johnstown's business guides (inspected for the period from the 1880s through the 1930s) showed, as "data," Jewish trade specialties and their persistence and change over time. As "texts," these records conformed to the gender hierarchy then prevailing in town, presenting a basically male business community: only heads of the enterprises were listed, and women-heads were undercounted. They also reflected the (middle-)class bias of the local Chamber of Commerce, where listings were prepared, limning the entrepreneurial group as more stable and more affluent than it actually was by omitting owners of minuscule stores and traveling vendors. Most of the latter I found in local city directories that also revealed a considerable shifting of Jewish businesses, particularly smaller ones (the majority), between the lines of trade; reporting on women involved in business was more complete, but, especially regarding wives, I relied primarily on interviews. Andrew Beveridge directed me to the credit reports compiled by the Dun and Bradstreet Company, a nationwide institution with local branches, regularly collecting information on the financial standing of retail and wholesale businesses. I traveled to the Baker Library in Cambridge, Massachusetts, which holds the nineteenth-century manuscript schedules of the D & B reports, and repeatedly visited the archives of the company's headquarters in New York to check printed reports for the first half of the twentieth century. As data, these records showed that although the financial standing, or net value (free of debt), of Jewish businesses in Johnstown improved over time, the majority of them had remained at the lower levels of the rating ladder throughout the entire period covered by my study. The records also reconfirmed the finding of frequent shifting between lines of trade, with a pronounced downturn during the hardest Depression years and a slight recovery in between. As group self-narratives the D & B reports, particularly from the early period of Jewish immigrant entrepreneurs' incorporation into the American business world, revealed the distinct cultural superiority and social distance of the dominant ethnoreligious strata, reflected in the use, most likely unselfconscious, of traditional negative stereotypes of the "Hebrews" in the evaluations of the Jewish merchants' economic standing and trading record.

The idea of checking the ethnic background of the providers and recipients of financial loans recorded at the Cambria County Courthouse emerged from one of the congregational meetings at Beth Sholom on the progress of "The Johnstown Jewish History Project," as our undertaking was locally known, at which comments on my report by the audience suggested a considerable measure of in-group reliance in this area. That, in turn, led me to the readings on different ethnic entrepreneurial niches in the American urban economy today and in the past, and, specifically, Ivan Light's distinction between class and ethnic resources in small business.[11] Inspection of the courthouse records gave me an insight into the amounts of money loaned and borrowed and the time needed for repayment, the gender of the involved parties, and the ethnic background and institutional affiliation (if any) of the lenders. The narrative of these records suggested that these financial transfers were highly formalized procedures; actually, according to my informants' recollections, most of them were conducted informally, "on a handshake," and extensions of payments were often granted to debtors out of court. This discrepancy indicates that—at that time, and for that group, anyway—official records should not be used as a sole source of information.

Manuscript schedules of the 1929 Small Business Census, held at the National Archives in Washington, D.C., were recommended to me as containing unusually detailed information about the operation of individual businesses, retail and wholesale. I spent a couple of weeks in Washington, laboriously copying file after file of Jewish merchants in the city of Johnstown and the surrounding area. The census provided interesting data on the economic status of individual businesses: when the business was opened and by whom, the number and gender of people it employed (family members and others) and their salaries, net sales for the previous year, the amount of financial assets clear of debt, rent paid for the store and cost of utilities, capital used to restock, and so forth. The "texts" of these records, specifically their deliberate and inadvertent misrepresentations of the actual state of affairs, remain, frankly, unclear to me, despite my having questioned both professional specialists in the area and the Johnstowners themselves, the actors/subjects of the reported stories. The reports offered to the D & B Company, if distorted in any way by the merchant-providers, were likely to have overestimated the financial status of businesses. By contrast, the presentations made to the 1929 Small Business Census takers could have gone either way: making the enterprise look stronger (for credit implications, though one wonders why, if Jewish merchants tended to rely primarily on intragroup financial support), or weaker (immigrants, especially, as one of my informants pointed out, unreflexively avoided an appearance of affluence when dealing with government agencies). I tried my best to check this information in other sources: luckily, some people preserved old business ledgers of their family enterprises, while others seem to have retained sharp memories of the details of business finances; it appears that the survey data did not so distort the actual situation as to make meaningless my analysis of the economic situation of Jewish businesses during the time in question.

With all this material (data and texts) on the Johnstowners' family enterprises, and with summary tables on particular aspects of their functioning prepared for the entire period 1890–1940, I went back to my informants and conducted a series of interviews focused specifically on business life and related issues. Although the interviews were actually informal in form and style, their procedure was as follows: I showed my informants their own family's records and asked for comments and explanations. Did they have any recollection of these things? Did the reports I showed appear true or false? Any corrections? Why? How? I wanted to know, specifically, how many employees there were in their family businesses, and who these people were: kin? other Jews? How was this employment procured? What were the wages? Did they—and if not, why not?—seek employment outside the Jewish group? What were the annual sales of the business? What was the usual markup? Did the store extend credit and how were debts repaid? Where was the merchandise bought? Which lines of trade were more profitable? Who did what in a store, and who made which business decisions? (I was especially interested in gender and generational differences.) What were the main causes of business shifting? How did they survive the Great Depression, and how much did sales go down? (I also checked census reports and Johnstown business guides for the fluctuations during that period in the number of local business establishments and the volume of trade.) What with customers unable to pay, how did they cope financially? Who helped them to stay afloat?

In all these conversations, as during group meetings devoted to business affairs, my position as a researcher-academic vis-à-vis my informants, both men and women, was a weaker one; they had, especially at the beginning of this round of interviews, a definite "power over" me in terms of know-how and familiarity with the subject matter, of which I knew zilch. Five persons among my informants, three men and two women, taught me the basics of small retail business, and I also read a good deal in this area, mainly empirical studies regularly conducted between the 1910s and the 1930s by Harvard Business School. The issues involved included practical questions, such as what should have been the maximum overhead costs at a particular level of net annual sales; how much markup was needed for a specific amount of profit; what should have been the optimal turnover rate in which kind of business; how to buy merchandise reasonably, and the like. I eventually did learn quite a bit—enough, anyway, to ask intelligent questions and understand answers, and to be able to make general estimations of the condition of businesses. I believe, however, that during the later interviews I pretended to be somewhat more ignorant of business matters than I actually was by that time, probably—I am not certain—in an expectation of being told more by informants consciously or unconsciously enjoying their "power over" a university professor. I am not at all sure that this last was actually a reason for my informants' enjoyment of these dicussions, but they obviously relished talking about the ins and outs of business (men more so than women, however), and they seemed to have remembered the details of it pretty well (with the same gender difference).

As my informants commented on the fluctuations in D & B credit ratings and on the city directory data showing frequent business shifts, they made recurrent references to the dependence of Jewish businesses on the working-class clientele employed in the local mills and coal mines. I knew from other sources that the industrial production in the area was indeed highly irregular. I thought, then, about looking at bankruptcy records, and located and compiled this material. As data, this material revealed a significant—higher than I had expected—rate of failure of the Johnstown Jewish businesses; and, considering that settlements out of court were quite common at that time, the actual rate was even higher than the official records indicated. As texts or self-narratives—particularly interesting were records of bankruptcy hearings at which the bankrupts themselves, often husband and wife together, testified—the typical story represented thrifty and hard-working merchants whose business was wiped out by external forces, most commonly a slump in the area's industries and the laying-off of workers who then could not pay off their debts.

In the next step, I shifted the focus of research to the realization of purposes served by these family businesses, namely, the achievement of a satisfactory standard of living. I concentrated on such indicators as the acquisitions and values of homes (gathered from real estate records and tax assessments of property, and represented on contemporary photographs), residential relocations to better neighborhoods (from the above sources and city directories), and the amounts of money saved by the end of life (from wills recorded at the county courthouse). As I already expected on the basis of previously gathered information, these records showed a considerable increase in material well-being of local Jewish households, punctuated by slowdowns and downturns that matched the fluctuations in business conditions and, in a larger context, the rhythm of production in the local steel and coal industries, as well as the still broader situation of the national economy. The wills revealed estates considerably burdened by debts, which was not surprising, considering that their owners' enterprises commonly functioned "on leverage," that is, on borrowed capital. I assumed that what was recorded in these wills generally exhausted the existing capital; but might some resources have remained unreported to protect the surviving family from creditors? Frankly, intimidated at the prospect of confronting my informants with records of their families' failures, I simply did not dare to inquire too specifically about this, or about whether merchandise was ever hidden away when total bankruptcy was declared. Of just a few of my friends and key informants I did ask generally, "Did it happen sometimes that. . . ? "Yes, it did," was the expected answer, "there's always been dishonest people in the world." Not very revealing.

With these records, for individual families and the entire Jewish group, I returned to my informants, but this time with considerable anxiety. The improvement over time in their standard of living was evident, but there were also failures. The latter theme—bankruptcies, unpaid mortgages, home losses—was absent in the Johnstowners' life stories "as told," which presented, rather, an image of unobstructed accomplishment of the valued life-goals. Since economic sufficiency had been one of the primary purposes of Jewish families and a core element of their understanding of success, confrontation with the records of failure in this important area could have been unpleasant. My position seemed ambiguous: although my dependence on the continuous cooperation of my informants made it weaker (will they close up and withdraw? reject me and my project, still a long way from completion?), possessing the "incriminating" information possibly strengthened it, putting my informants on the defensive. I wanted the information out in the open; in fact, an outline of the Johnstown Jewish story of "insecure prosperity," or its economic part, specifically, contrasted with big-city developments, was already taking shape in my mind, and these business failures fitted into it nicely. My informants, presumably, wanted it to remain covered and unmentioned in the published book.

The confrontation turned out to be much smoother than I had feared, virtually unproblematic, most likely because by that time, well into the fifth year of the project, my person and research were already familiar to Johnstown's Jews, and, possibly, because I approached particular people with records of both achievements and failures of their own nuclear or extended families. Showing them corroborative statistical tables for the entire group, I assured them from the start that downturns were quite common (which they of course knew), and that most losers successfully reestablished their businesses and recaptured their homes. I also explained the purpose of my inquiry into these matters: to find out the whys and hows of business failures and their effects on family welfare, and, in particular, my informants' ways and means of coping with these downturns, both practical and mental/emotional.

It was in this context, while discussing the ups and downs of little businesses and successes and adversities in accomplishing their preferred life-goals, that I first asked for—thereafter I continued to ask—and heard the schemas of practical action and coping with adversities, and higher-level schemas of the course of human life and the nature of the world. Thus I began to hear about life as "the wheel of fortune" and the world as full of contradictory forces, "flexible and fluxible," that changed constellations like images in a kaleidoscope; about the greater importance of "trying, always trying, working at it" than necessarily accomplishing it; about a strong commitment to reason paired with awareness of its limitations; and about the ethical-practical obligations (these two notions appeared inseparable) to oneself and to the community that were embedded in all these concepts. In these schemas invoked by my informants as they were reminiscing about the fluctuations of their economic fortunes, I heard echoes of my readings in Jewish philosophy, wisdom literature (e.g., Proverbs, Ecclesiastes), and old aggadic stories (nonlegal or narrative material in the Talmud and other rabbinic teachings). All these messages fascinated me, seeming to touch directly some buried half-thoughts-half-feelings that hung loose, frame- and anchorless.

It was at that time, I think, that I formed an idea of Jewish dialectical *Weltanschauung* as a "spectrum regime" (to borrow Martin Jay's term for different modes of organizing vision)[12] and as a coping tool, and I began searching for it in my readings in Jewish history, philosophy, and literature, and in conversations with the Johnstown Jews. My attraction to a view of the world as inherently plural, contradictory, and polyvalent—often cacophonous, actually—has been, I believe, influenced by my collective and personal biography, in which in-betweenness and marginality have been consistent elements: I am an offspring of a mixed marriage, half Jewish, raised in a predominantly Catholic country, and in a Polish home with a cosmopolitan rather than the prevailing nationalistic orientation; I have a double professional identity; and, five or six years after arrival in the United States, I was still a recent immigrant in a very different society, but unattached to a community of my fellow nationals that could provide a sense of familiarity and an opportunity to share difficulties of adaptation. In addition, and important, having grown up in a one-party political system that controlled information and imposed one ideology, I found plural worldviews particularly attractive. (I was at that time unaware of possible gender effects on my intellectual preferences[13]—see below for more on the circumstances of my then rather dim view of the "genderedness" of the schemas I was investigating.) Subsequent phases of my Johnstown research, particularly concerning the worldviews and schemas local Jews applied to make sense of their personal and collective existence, were probably guided not only by professional considerations, but also by my seeking to make a whole of my own life, in which in-betweenness and marginality played such a central part.

While asking about cognitive guideposts for concrete activities, in order to see the fullest possible spectrum of these schemas, I also wanted to know what my informants' sense of the "ultimate" or most encompassing meanings of human existence could have been; at that time I was reading studies recommended by a psychologist colleague on higher- and lower-level schemas and mental programs.[14] Specifically, considering what I had already learned about the enduring traditionalism of the Johnstown Jewish community, I wanted to find out what sense (if any) they had of God's presence in the world and their own lives, and what obligations (if any) this presence entailed for them. But I had a strongly personal interest as well.

Now there comes the most difficult phase of my project to account for, because the "epistemological entanglement" of the researcher and her informants was particularly close, and the narrative is, embarrassingly, even more personal than it has been so far. I will try to go quickly over this part. In the mid-1980s, a personal tragedy happened in my life, followed a couple of years later by another. My recent immigration and, in particular, the absence of relatives and old friends augmented my emotional stress, which in turn inclined me—a textbook case, I guess—toward religion. I was by then already seriously intellectually involved in, and emotionally drawn to, Judaism (though mostly to its philosophical-ethical teachings, rather than to the specifically religious lore and practice), and so the choice was natural. I was particularly attracted to what I then most desperately needed: Judaism's undefeated hopefulness focused on life, and its community-centeredness.

I then asked Johnstowners some "deep philosophical questions," as they called my inquiries, and received answers, but this investigation of the ultimate schemas, although on balance enlightening, I believe, was problematic from all sides. On my part, I treated my informants as a double source: to obtain historical information and, at the same time, for my own education (though I read intensely, and began to attend religious services, I was still a novice to the meanings they naturally understood) and to assist me in my urgent personal search. My informants, however, were not well equipped to provide clear answers to my inquiries; as already noted, Judaism's primary emphasis is on practice rather than beliefs, and the Johnstowners were unfamiliar with advanced Jewish learning. When I asked about such schemas as the obligation upon each individual to collaborate with God in shaping the world and their own lives, or divine involvement in human everyday affairs,[15] I always made every effort to link them with concrete happenings at that time in my informants' personal lives, in the local Jewish community, or in the larger world; nonetheless, I found that I was forcing most of my informants to speak of things they had never articulated before. (There were, however, a few people with whom I had spontaneous long conversations on different aspects of "the ultimate," and whose insights have had a lasting influence on my emerging spiritual Jewish self.) As if things were not complicated enough, my questions concerned ideas-feelings, largely unarticulated or experience-near as they were, from times long past. I felt somewhat reassured about the validity of the answers—that is, their approximate correspondence with how it *was*—by the fact that several of my informants spontaneously drew a dividing line between their pre-and post-Holocaust feelings regarding unreflexive acknowledgment of and trust in God.[16] On the whole, though, I do not think I know how to separate "data" and "texts" (theirs and mine) in the results of my inquiry. I decided to use what I found, and to inform my readers (as I have just done) why and how this information was collected.

Before moving on to the next issue, I should comment on two more matters regarding this particular part and phase of my research: the "genderlessness" of my investigation at that time of these ultimate schemas, and the way I went about reconstructing the popular worldviews in the turn-of-the-century East European shtetls from which the Johnstowners came. Concerning gender differences in these ultimate schemas, I did not pay much attention to that issue then, apparently assuming these ultimate values to be universal. I did not look into these differences (even while I pursued such investigations in other areas of the Johnstowners' lives) for what I now see as three reasons. First, I was learning Judaism from zero, and the received tradition was so immense that it entirely filled my cognitive field, as I made the bits and pieces I was learning into a meaningful whole. It seemed simply impossible to absorb at the same time a fundamental Jewish feminist critique of this tradition (evidently male-centered) that I had just begun to digest. Second, the liberal-progressive environment in which the bulk of my Jewish philosophical-religious education was taking place dulled the immediate experience of gender inequality in matters of the mind and soul. These are rational—or, better, reasoned—explanations. The third circumstance was emotional. As have mentioned, a prolonged personal tragedy made me desperately search for hope and community grounded in some "vertical" dimension of human existence—that is, a dimension larger than, or transcending, the "horizontal" or here-and-now perspective. I think that these strongly felt concerns and my related need for the integral life philosophy "overrode" gender considerations, which would in this case have been fracturing. (I subsequently went back to my women informants in Johnstown to talk about God-ideas and the related issues, as I will discuss below.)

Like the Johnstown immigrants' socioeconomic origins in Eastern Europe, the old-country background of their worldviews was investigated in the reverse order, as it were—after I recorded and gathered together by themes and levels all references made by my informants to the interpretive and coping schemas that presumably guided their actions. In resuming research on turn-of-the-century East European shtetls I was motivated by professional interests, to find out which of these schemas had been transplanted from the old country, as well as by personal curiosity: in Poland, I had taught myself the economic and political history of Jews in Eastern Europe, but not the sociocultural, including religious, history. Curiously, reading in cultural theory at Warsaw University had not translated into expanding in this direction my limited knowledge of Jewish history—or was it, perhaps, the striking absence of living Jewish culture around me that made this limitation unobvious? I began reading broadly—I drowned in the literature for several months—concentrating on sources either created by immigrants themselves or whose content was likely to have been familiar to "simple Orthodox Jews," as most of my foreign-born informants described their old-country origins: immigrants' letters written shortly after their arrival in America and in large part concerning old-country matters (a unique collection exists from the years 1890–1891);[17] published and unpublished autobiographies and memoirs of immigrant men and women;

contemporary realist novels of renowned Yiddish writers, as well as commentaries on them by literary critics, folklorists, and historians of Jewish religion; contemporary ethnographic studies of some localities (a few have been preserved); Yiddish proverbs and folktales; sermons of the *magidim* (traveling preachers); and *Tz'enah Ur'enah*, the Yiddish translation of the Bible for women, with commentary, popular in Eastern Europe.

Scholars who used these sources noted that the beautifying or "turpidifying" narratives in many of them—especially the literary and memoiristic genres—colored the data on the shtetl and its people that they depicted. If I was more inclined toward some representations than others—again, it is the question of balance—it was probably, for personal reasons already explained, toward the beautifying-as-hopeful, the orientation accepting life and meeting its challenges, rather than to the image of the aimlessly floating and abstracted *batlonim*. I also read these sources with a synthesizing lens, especially keen on themes that surfaced in my Johnstown interviews, as I wanted to reconstruct a composite picture of the traditional "cultural tool kit," and also the forms and range of public and home ritual observance, the functioning of the communal institutions and social relations, that could serve as the background comparative reference for my interpretation of the pace and content of the Johnstown Jews' sociocultural ethnicization. Although I am not entirely happy with this "synthetic" approach—after all, even the economically and culturally more traditional shtetls were not identical, either with each other or inside—I believe (or want to believe) that my "reverse" method, from the Johnstown themes back to Eastern Europe, defends such a composite reconstruction. Besides, it simply would not have been feasible to obtain enough information from the individual shtetls from which my immigrants came.

In the next step of research I planned to gather information about the continuity and change, in the context of local conditions, of Johnstown Jews' communal life, and public and private religious observance. But two of my colleagues, American Jewish historians, who read early drafts of my economic chapters expressed in their comments a disappointment at the absence of a discussion, and statistical tables, on "the educational and occupational mobility that has been one of the central issues in American Jewish studies," and so I decided to fill in this gap first. I gathered the enrollment and graduation data (recorded separately for boys and girls) of Johnstown's elementary and high schools; high school honor rolls and listings of participants in academically oriented extracurricular activities; and a name-file of young Jewish men and women who enrolled in and/or graduated from the University of Pittsburgh main and Johnstown branches and the Carnegie Institute (as I learned from nationwide surveys of college students conducted in the 1930s, the great majority of them attended schools near their homes, and this was also true of the Johnstowners).

Problems of incompleteness and uncertain reliability of historical records on young Americans' schooling—those preserved in the schools as well as those published in local and national censuses—have a considerable literature produced by researchers in this area. These researchers also offer reasonable suggestions about ways to deal with these imperfections in calculating estimates—no better measures are feasible—of school enrollments and graduations at different levels of educational careers. Advised by historians of American education among my colleagues, I read some of these studies and calculated the Johnstown estimates accordingly. The records and data-estimates I gathered added interesting information but basically confirmed what I already knew, namely, that strong interests in advanced education (honor rolls and academic extracurricula) were not common, and college attendance, proportionwise, was more limited among Johnstowners than among their big-city fellow ethnics; and that regardless of the amount of formal education (in particular, enrollment in college), the majority of Jewish youth, including some of the college graduates, entered the ethnic entrepreneurial niche. As for these records as texts, two narratives caught my attention while I was researching these sources, enhancing a picture of the enduring sociocultural distance between the dominant and Jewish groups in Johnstown. One was embedded in the notations made by elementary school teachers in students' files that occasionally—but commonly enough for me to start a count on the side of my own notes—referred to their Jewish pupils as "Hebrews." The other was in the high school records: a glaring absence, throughout the interwar period, of Jewish names among top class officers, and among the lead actors in school theater performances.

As in the previously investigated problems, with all this information, individual records and tabulations, as well as big-city data, I went back to my informants. I was interested in their comments on these findings, and in particular, their explanations of their own and their family members' educational pursuits and gender differences therein, of the figures for college attendance (Johnstown's Jews in comparison with New York's), and of the table showing weak occupational effects of more advanced education. I also wanted to find out whether advanced training and professional careers had been present as themes in Jewish homes and in informal social gatherings of the Jewish community members. I checked, too, and counted, topics in the congregational bulletins as well as high school special programs, commencement speeches, and the like, and talked to a few retired high school teachers about educators' activity, or, as it turned out, the lack thereof, in encouraging students to pursue college education and professional careers.

This time—the seventh year into the project—I was no longer anxious concerning "unpleasant" data, and our conversations went very well, although several of my informants did seem somewhat on the defensive, as representatives of the local Jewish community rather than as individuals, when confronted with the impressive data of New York college attendance, as if the Johnstown statistics implied that as a group they had fallen short of some Jewish standard. However, as I listened to their interpretations, especially those emphasizing the specific time and place as contexts of their educational practice ("You must understand that in a town like this . . ." and "You should consider that at that time . . ."; or "But Johnstown was not New York"), I realized that by requesting explanations I implicitly assumed there was something to explain—*at that time*, that is, and I saw that it was my tables, and the present-day context of our conversations, that imposed this "Jewish standard" of college attendance that in those days was actually the ascending trend only among upwardly mobile American Jews.

The project was interrupted for practically all of 1987 owing to my preoccupation with personal problems. When it was possible to resume it, I focused on Johnstown's Jews' communal institutions and activities, and on their religious observance. The sources included the previously mentioned Rodef Sholom congregational minutes (from the beginning of this century through the mid-twenties) and monthly bulletin (1931–1936), and Talmud Torah (religious school) records; some interwar records of two other, much smaller, congregations, (Reform) Beth Zion and (Orthodox) Ahavath Achim; information about the Johnstown Jewish community printed occasionally in the local newspaper, the *Johnstown Tribune*, and in the Pittsburgh Jewish press, and, more regularly (together with coverage of other localities with Jewish populations), *American Jewish Year Books*; contemporary photographs; and a history of Johnstown's Jewish community compiled by one of its postwar (Reform) rabbis.[18] And, of course, the interviews, in which I asked for comments on the information about communal institutions and public activities I collected in historical records, and inquired also about the home practices.

As data, the written records provided further information about congregational membership, leadership, religious school attendance, finances and social activities, and the participation of women in each of the three synagogues. Regarding the largest, the Rodef Sholom Congregation, these additional records documented what I noted earlier as a difference of tone in life stories as told by the Johnstown men and women, namely, the quickening of change in public religious practice and social organization at Rodef Sholom under the leadership of Rabbi Ralph Simon during the first half of the 1930s, and the subsequent loss of dynamism in these transformations after he left town. But despite evidence of updating the old ways in terms of decisions made and implemented at both Rodef Sholom and Beth Zion (the resolutely Orthodox Ahavath Achim had been the least concerned with the novelties), these records, as data and as self-narratives, enhanced rather than weakened the image of Johnstown's Jewish group as significantly more traditional: more inclusive, and less institutionally differentiated, than those depicted in studies of its big-city counterparts during the interwar period, particularly in New York. The readers should be reminded, however, about the caveat noted earlier concerning the persistence of traditional communal life and forms of worship among big-city Jews, as well as qualifications concerning my own professional vested interests likely to have influenced my researcher's vision.

Proceeding in the usual way, after I collected information from these sources, I prepared summary findings and presented them to my informants (separately to members of each of the three then-existing synagogues), asking for comments and explanations about specific aspects of the communal/religious life of the group at that time and the content and pace of its transformation. I also talked to the surviving former rabbis of Johnstown's three congregations. Besides the professional concerns that could have influenced my perception, it was my gender interests that strongly, though certainly not exclusively, motivated my investigation. At that time, in the late 1980s, I felt that the base of my Jewish identity was already in place (I was formally converted—membership in a Conservative synagogue required conversion because of my non-Jewish mother—and a regular participant in religious services and a Talmud study group). As I read extensively on the topic of women's—especially American Jewish women's—involvement in communal and, specifically, religious-institutional life, I was drawn, as a historical sociologist, a woman, and a Jew at the same time, to those issues.

Considering that in traditional Judaism the woman's temple was her home, gender, and, specifically, change and continuity over time in gender role expectations and activities, and the sociocultural context thereof, was of evident importance in the conversations about family and personal religious practices that I conducted with individual Johnstowners, in group meetings with members of households as they were then constituted, and with prewar local rabbis; since the Jewish community was numerically small, its rabbis by and large knew, and apparently remembered, the general scope of ritual observance among their congregationist-families. I was especially interested in comparisons of those remembered practices, accompanied by explanatory comments, with forms and extent of religious observance in Eastern Europe as remembered by immigrant men and women; in comparisons between immigrant and American-born generations, and among the three synagogues and the varied residential locations. In these interviews, both on the communal institutions and public worship and on religious observance at home, my status as a recent immigrant and an aspiring Jew had become, I felt, of considerably lesser significance as a "disempowering" element in my relations with people I talked to than they had been in the earlier phases of my research: I was by that time familiarized enough with American, and past and present American Jewish ways, to pass for an insider with a foreign accent. As before, however, I was aware that my informants' Jewishness came "from the roots," while mine, as it were, grew from the head, and though no one ever hinted at it in my presence, I still felt a bit vulnerable on this point.

During these conversations on religious practices I asked again about God's presence in the world and in directing human affairs, and also about the schemas of a good Jew and the religiously grounded reciprocal obligations of the Jewish community and its members. As before, I used concrete past events as references but this time kept in mind potential gender differences reflecting different social situations of men and women in private and public realms. It seemed to me that in comparison with comments offered by the men, the women's implied a generally lesser sense of individual control and responsibility in personal matters; but then all my readings, as well as my Johnstown evidence on the ultimate subordination of women to the authority of men in economic and social matters suggested it should be just so, and so my ear could have been pretuned to identifying some differences. Asked to comment on a new-and-improved version of my discussion of schemas, Barbara Laslett, my personal arbiter on matters of gender analysis in historical sociology, found it "strangely genderless" still. I then expanded and elaborated it somewhat more, including a comparative discussion of some autobiographical and oral history materials from New York, but the final product is, I am aware, unsatisfactory. I have since read several interesting works on American Jewish (and Christian) women's spirituality,[19] and I realize that important questions that would have considerably enriched my interpretation were left out of the interviews. I especially regret not having tried to investigate the link between the maleness of God's image and the derivative male-oriented ideas in Judaism, on the one hand, and, on the other, the religiously grounded schemas of the ways of the world and human action held by Johnstown's women.

After I drafted the chapter on communal life and religious practices, I was about to turn to research on the last aspect of Johnstown's Jews' experience to be included in my study, namely, their relations with the larger local society. But at that point new readings on the "Americanization" of home lives and consumer habits of New York Jews between the turn of the century and the Second World War, along with the discovery that an exhibition on a similar topic was about to open at the YIVO Institute for Jewish Research in New York,[20] made me decide to return again to issues I had thought I was done with. This time, it was the treatment of home life. Neither my investigation of home economics nor my research on family religious practices paid attention, I now realized, to the material culture and consumer habits of the Johnstowners—two aspects of lifestyles, including religiously regulated practices, that primarily involved what could be conceptualized, and "measured" in terms of ethnicization, and that primarily involved women, who could then be considered as agents of ethnicization. In short, a new and interesting field of investigation. Back, then, to my female informants: I made one short visit to Johnstown, and, following it, over a dozen phone calls; unfortunately, a number of women of the immigrant generation already died by that time or their health had deteriorated too much to permit questioning, and so I talked mainly to American-born persons. Following my (verbal) presentation of items treated in the New York exhibition (and later a published study), which at the same time provided a framework for comparison, I asked for old pictures and comments on the "updating" of material objects and consumer goods, those of general use and, in particular, those pertaining to Jewish-American ethno-religious folklore. At the same time, I inquired about similar innovations in public or congregational life, for example, at parties and other social occasions; the source of these novelties; the authorization of small, middle, and ultimate decisions regarding the acquisition of particular items (expectedly, the ultimate ones usually belonged to men); and the financial constraints on the scope of ethnicization of consumer lifestyles due to the local economic conditions and Johnstown's small-townish tastes.

For the concluding part of my project, dealing with Jews' participation in civic-political and informal social affairs of the larger Johnstown society, and, specifically, its dominant (Anglo- and other West European–Protestant) groups, I already had considerable information gathered during the previous phases of research: on the town's general political climate and social organization; the content and tone of local press references to new (South and East European) ethnic groups; admission policies at local country clubs; membership in the Johnstown Chamber of Commerce and other voluntary organizations; and the knowledge gleaned from interviews with elderly members of the Anglo-Protestant elite. I also compiled into one file several references made by my Jewish informants in earlier interviews to the generally limited involvement of Jewish group in Johnstown's larger society and concrete instances of such participation, as well as their recollected views on these matters and more general schemas for making sense of the situation and directing relevant behavior. The image revealed by these sources—and a representation already preformed in my mind as I turned to the subject of Jews' relations with Johnstown's dominant society—was that of the restricted Jewish involvement in outside activities upheld by Johnstown's circumstances and characteristics of the Jewish group, and of the enduring sense of collective insecurity in the latter, resulting from this situation. I had also preclassified this limited outside participation as a factor that further contributed to slowing down the pace of ethnicization and sustaining traditional sociocultural patterns in the Jewish group, on the one hand, and, on the other hand, the self-consciously ambivalent perceptions accompanying the latter's marginality as an expression of "Jewish dialectics."

Choosing, and making sense of, the comparative material for my Johnstown case turned out to have been the greatest difficulty in this final phase of my research, and a cause of considerable aggravation for me; on the point of celebrating the tenth anniversary of this project, I was by that time tired and eager to conclude it as soon as possible. I began reading seriously on the issues in question only then; unlike other aspects of Jews' American experience, their relations with the dominant society have been studied in small towns as well as big cities. I was overwhelmed by the diversity of the reported patterns, especially regarding civic-political matters, and did not seem able to find the interpretative key to this abundance. An additional difficulty in resolving this puzzle and, by the same token, finding guidance for my investigation in Johnstown was caused by my lack of expertise in the functioning of the American political system and "making politics." This incompetence, resulted, in turn, from my preoccupation with establishing myself professionally in a new and different academic environment, and with the exigencies of my personal life; besides, during the greater part of the 1980s, my political attention was still habitually more strongly drawn to and consciously focused on the Soviet bloc than on U.S. politics.

Instead of speedily concluding the study, I engaged, then, and without much enthusiasm, I must say, in a quick-but-intense reading course on the history of American, and, specifically, ethnic urban politics, and other forms of mainstream institutional activities between the 1880s and 1940. As my education progressed, making things more intelligible but also producing new questions, I selected for comparison four cities in each of which, as my readings suggested, the political constellation "differently differed" from the Johnstown case, and wrote to or phoned about ten people, professional or amateur historians of these places identified by a method of chain references, to ask specific questions pertinent to my study. I also briefly revisited Johnstown two more times between 1990 and 1991, where I checked voter registration records at the county courthouse and actual voting returns (in the local press); looked in the *Johnstown Tribune* and in high school programs for Christian themes (which, as I already knew from the earlier interviews, used to alienate my informants); found, and interviewed, a nonprofessional but very well informed historian of Johnstown's politics; talked to a few more representatives of the Anglo-Protestant elite, especially residents of the most prestigious section in town, about neighborly and other social relations with local Jews; and discussed with an elderly representative of the ILGWU local the course and conclusion of a strike in a Jewish-owned small garment factory in the late 1930s.

During these visits I also, of course, called again on my informants—my key informant-friends, precisely, about nine persons altogether, men and women—asking for comments and explanations concerning the material I gathered. They by and large confirmed the information I collected, and we talked more about causes and consequences of Jews' restricted participation in the affairs of the larger society in prewar Johnstown; possible gender and generational differences in different forms of outside involvement; the Jewish group's desire for inconspicuousness, schemas used to cope with a sense of civic insecurity, and, again, possible indicators of their ethnicization (as before, I tried to link questions about these meanings and coping feelings-thoughts with concrete actions or events). A second draft of the chapter, produced after my last visit in Johnstown, was promptly "deconstructed" by Charles Tilly, who found its comparative material still rather confusing (I agreed) and suggested, as did my other readers, especially Jonathan Sarna and Ronald Bayor, some useful modifications. I rewrote the blasted thing and resolutely decided, by the summer of 1992, to conclude my research. I spent the following year making alterations and cleaning up the manuscript, mainly in front of the computer. During that final phase of the project I also acquired information on the present-day Jewish community, collected by my Johnstown friends, needed for the book's epilogue.

When the manuscript was finally completed, I took it, as promised, for inspection to the board members of Beth Sholom Congregation. They approved of it as "generally true"—that is, approximating to a passable extent the whats and hows in the local Jewish community before the Second World War, although one of the elderly board members who personally knew most of the actors in my story felt that some of the people I talked to in the project tended to present "the nice side" of their family members: not that this side did not exist, but there were also less pleasant aspects. As I was driving home to Philadelphia, this observation of my Johnstown friend made me realize that my professional interests (the choice of the ethnicization theory as the major analytical framework, and the decision to keep a comparative approach throughout the book that meant dependence on the existing historical studies), along with my personal situation and concerns, had made me leave unexamined as well another less "nice" but important aspect of Johnstown's Jews' history. Namely, intragroup conflicts, particularly between congregational factions; between big fish and small merchants; between friends; and inside the homes between husbands and wives, and parents and children (the latter I had touched upon). "Too bad, too late," I thought to myself (admittedly with relief—by that time the very idea of resuming research on the Johnstown project made my mind shrink). But this omission, if it has not been obvious to the readers as they plowed through the book, should be brought out in this place.

Throughout the book, social relations within the Jewish community have been discussed in terms of "authority" understood as power viewed as legitimate by those subject to it, and specifically, conditions and consequences of the differential access to and execution of authority by gender, generational status, and economic position-cum-community leadership. In the sociocultural context of the lives of Johnstown's Jews during the time covered by my study, the priority of representatives of certain social categories—such as husbands and fathers, male heads of family enterprises, the most economically successful businessmen–community leaders—to define situations and make decisions involving others (wives and children, rank-and-file group members) was apparently accepted as "natural," or, in Weberian terms, as based on traditional authority, with an admixture of pragmatic consent, by those with more limited autonomy. Rather than as traditional authority, this "naturalness" could have been interpreted in terms of symbolic violence—Bourdieu's coinage for the domination that is misrecognized by the victim, or "exercised upon a social agent by his or her complicity."[21] I used the former concept because most of the existing historical studies of gender and generational relations among big-city Jews discuss them in terms of "spheres of authority." (Another reason may be that—thankfully for the sake of my comparative purposes—I began learning Bourdieuse more than two-thirds of the way into my project. At that point it was too late for me to even consider overhauling it, which would have required, of course, much more than a mere change of concepts.) Still, occasional frictions and conflicts in various areas of Johnstown Jews' lives could have been more systematically identified, and a discussion thereof effectively accommodated in the authority framework I chose for the interpretation of in-group social relations. The reason for their near-absence in this story, has been, I believe, a semiconscious desire on my part, resulting from my feelings of various kinds of insecurity as a researcher in the Jewish Johnstown community, to steer clear of the issues of intra-group conflicts that the "power over" approach would unavoidably bring up for analysis.

To conclude. The objective of this study has been an approximate reconstruction, within the interpretative framework of ethnicization theory and its area-specifications, of the experience of Jews in a small American town during the fifty years between turn-of-the-century mass migration from Europe and the outbreak of World War II, as compared with that of their big-city fellow ethnics. The research method for the case study was historical-ethnographic, involving repeated rounds of checking and counter-checking against each other of various kinds of information gathered from diverse written and pictorial sources and from the recollections of the involved actors, and, for comparative analysis, the selective collection of mainly secondary data from the most studied metropolitan centers, particularly New York. Has anything valid and reliable been left of this historical account, woven of hundreds of tiny facts and micro-data, after this confessional exegesis, disclosing the researcher's views read into these materials and uncovering many other epistemic impositions? I strongly believe there has, and a considerable amount—otherwise I would not be able to involve myself in this exacting research and would not dare to publish this book. I do consider historians' depictions of past situations and interpretations of their contexts, meanings, and consequences to be inescapably imperfect, fragmented and particular (or subjective), due to multiple entanglements of cognitive vantage points and perspectives of actors and spectators involved in making these stories. But I certainly do not suffer from the "epistemological hypochondria"[22] that has afflicted some sociological and historical quarters, that is, the defensive apprehension that in view of radical criticism from the postmodernist camp (camps, rather, as they are diverse), the objectives and analytical methods of these disciplines have become entirely invalidated, and their results cognitively worthless. Rather, I believe, it is by combining these objectives and methods with the systematic exploration of the reciprocal effects of different narratives involved in creating particular pieces of the story and its final composition that we may be able to produce more valid and reliable approximations of the ways things are/ were in the social world. Though imperfect and incomplete, such approximations, accounted for from all sides, will be the best possible.

Before closing, I would like to address the question of the Johnstown case's representativity. Concern with this issue belongs, of course, to the scientistic paradigm of gathering knowledge about society. From a postmodernist perspective, the matter is either utterly irrelevant (a radical approach), or else the answer to questions about typicality is resolutely negative (a moderate stand). My position as a self-proclaimed epistemological neo*modernist* assumes, let us recall, that the social world and human experience form certain patterns that are always underdeterminate (i.e., plural in composition and ridden with ambiguities and contradictions) and historical (i.e. time- and place-specific), but nonetheless knowable in approximate and incomplete ways. Thus it recognizes the question of representativity as legitimate but provides open-ended and contingent answers.

As mentioned in the preface, the dearth of knowledge concerning the adaptation of no less than one-quarter of turn-of-the-century Jewish immigrants and their offspring, who had resided in small towns during the half-century preceding the Second World War, was one of my main reasons for undertaking this project. This scarcity means, of course, that we simply do not know enough about different social contexts of the pace and composition of the ethnicization of lifestyles and group institutions in small-town Jewish communities at that period to estimate Johnstown's representativity. I can, therefore, propose only some reasonable guesses.

First, I would expect to find the pace and composition of the ethnicization of other small-town Jews during the period investigated in this study generally similar to the Johnstown case—that is, relatively slow and occasionally recursive, with a larger component of traditional or old-country elements than new or middle-class American ones, and with innovations introduced primarily "secondhand," through the national Jewish press and social contacts in metropolitan Jewish communities—under the following external and intragroup circumstances.

Regarding *the surrounding environment*, I would expect a similar pattern of ethnicization in towns approximating what Rogers Hollingsworth and Ellen Hollingsworth have called the "autocratic" or "oligarchic," not the "polyarchic," type.[23] The Hollingsworths' autocratic ideal-type city possessed an undifferentiated economic base and a low level of horizontal socioeconomic differentiation; a pyramid-shaped social structure (pronounced inequality in the distribution of status and wealth, with a small homogeneous elite and a large lower class); a rigid stratification system with sharp ethnic cleavages, and a corresponding ascriptive (or near-ascriptive) normative system; an autocratic and centralized political system with

overlapping political and economic elites; a relatively high level of local autonomy; and a traditionalist political culture, marked by low participation,
"bossism," and a perception of the political process as based on ascriptive-
particularist rather than rationalist-legal criteria. The oligarchic type of city
had a somewhat more complex socioeconomic structure, slightly less rigid
social divisions, and somewhat less autonomy. Prewar Johnstown, in my
evaluation (it is not on the Hollingsworths' list), was an essentially autocratic type, with certain characteristics of the oligarchic pattern. It would
have been comparable to such places as (from the Hollingsworths' list)
Irontown, Pennsylvania; Marinette, Wisconsin; Shenandoah, Pennsylvania;
Spartanburg, South Carolina; or Wilkinsburg, Pennsylvania.

Regarding, in turn, *the internal characteristics of the Jewish group*, an
ethnicization process similar to the kind found in Johnstown could be expected in situations with the following characteristics: the Jewish group's
marginal position in the town's economy, particularly when enhanced by
their enclosure in the ethnic economic niche; absence of publicly recognized Jews among the city's first settlers or other pioneer-benefactors (this
is actually both an external and intragroup condition); residential stability;
presence of developed intragroup organizational and informal social networks (a condition requiring, of course, a sufficient number of Jewish residents in town), particularly in combination with social cultural/religious
separatism of the ethnic group (actually a one-in-two condition acting simultaneously as a cause and an effect regarding the pace and composition
of ethnicization)—group separatism seems, in turn, enhanced by the traditional old-country backgrounds of the immigrants; and, the last factor on
my (certainly incomplete) list, absence of outstanding and charismatic
group leaders interested in speeding up the ethnicization process and capable of implementing it. (The same combination of internal factors could
serve as the initial tester-anticipator for small-town settings of what William Yancey, Eugene Ericksen, and Richard Juliani called "emergent ethnicity,"[24] except that—and this too suggests plurality of patterns—their
list, apparently derived from analyses of ethnic groups in big urban centers,
contains different contributing factors from those enumerated above, such
as, for example, a large ethnic population and residential concentration.)

The simplest proposition would be that the probability of finding a
Johnstown-like pattern of ethnicization should be the highest in localities
where all or almost all of the external and intragroup conditions listed
above were present (or absent, as specified) at the same time, and diminish-
ing with a decrease in the number of these factors. But then relative
weights or causal effects of particular contributing conditions most likely
differed, so that a weakening of a more influential condition could have had
a greater transformative effect than did a similar manipulation of a less significant factor. And these weights or causal effects of the contributing
conditions probably differed as well depending on how many factors were
present at once and with what intensity.

I would be inclined to assume that the economic/occupational position of the Jewish group in the local larger society (reflecting the external and intragroup circumstances) was in most situations a particularly, though by no means exclusively, mighty factor, both in its direct effects on the course of ethnicization and indirectly, through influencing other contributing factors. In comparison, group leadership, for example, seems more contingent and volatile, and the effects of its absence were probably more readily enhanced or weakened depending on the strength and configuration of other conditions. A combination in a town X of the absence of leadership with, say, a somewhat more open and dynamic economic structure (the "oligarchic" type), and a somewhat less socially inward Jewish community than was the case in Johnstown, could have had different effects on the pace and content of ethnicization in that town, even though all or most of the external and intragroup contributing factors could have been marked as present. There is also a question of the replaceability of these conditions, or, more accurately, of a possibility of counterbalancing. To stay with absence of leadership: if, in a town Z sharing with Johnstown the external and intragroup characteristics listed above, this absence combined with a low rate of residential stability and greater proximity to a metropolis, its effects could have been counterbalanced by the influx of new ways and ideas brought in by the newcomers and by traveling residents, resulting in the overall acceleration, in this case, of the ethnicization process.

And, to make the picture more complex still, these combined effects, as well as impacts of particular conditions listed above on the pace and content of ethnicization, could have differed as a result of different temporal arrangements of configurations of these conditions differing in weights and intensities. For example, it is reasonable to expect that, *ceteribus paribus*, the concurrence over several decades in a town Y of two trends (on the outside, the growing dynamism of the economy, and, in the Jewish group, the weakening of the communal institutional bonds) would have had effects on the pace and composition of ethnicization different from those in Johnstown during the same period of increasingly sluggish economic growth, on the one hand, and, on the other, the solidifying of intragroup ethnic networks.

Clearly, the matter is highly complex, involving many more diverse interacting factors than simply the size of the general and Jewish populations. The question of the Johnstown case's representativity, and, more broadly, of the historical specification of social contexts within and outside differently located Jewish groups conducive to particular kinds of ethnicization patterns, cannot be answered in an even partially satisfactory manner without—a perennial appeal—much more research. Continuing individual research in particular localities, including understudied small towns and "small-town" parts of the big cities—projects especially well suited to young scholars working with limited financial means on their doctoral dissertations or first books—will certainly provide more useful information at the micro-level. It seems to me, however, that to the extent that arriving at some middle-range historical generalizations regarding this diversity of ethnicization patterns, and their contexts and consequences, among American Jews is at all possible, and desirable, it requires a comparative-historical team project, and, better yet, project*s*, focused simultaneously on a few wisely selected locations.

Members of the Jewish Community in Johnstown and Vicinity Who Participated in This Study (Alphabetical List)

Frieda Bass; Blanche and Abe Beerman; Dr. Curtis and Mary June Beerman; Fanny Berman; Gwen, Lottie, and Bill Berney; Atty. Samuel and Sally Block; Dr. Meyer Bloom; Rabbi Mordecai Brill (former member); Dr. Jerome and Frieda Cohen; Bellah Coppersmith; Atty. Louis Coppersmith; Mary and Bernie Covitch; Vivian and Millard Cummins; Dr. Jon Darling; Esther Dorfman; Nathan and Lester Edelstein; Edith, Phillip, and Herman Eisenberg; Samuel and Jane Epstein; Dr. Louis and Faye Finkelstein; Judith Finkelstein; Rhoda Friedman; Herbert Freeman; Isabelle and Wallace Friedman; Louis Fruhlinger; Mildred and Gilbert Ginsburg; Ruth, Isadore, Rita, Daniel, David, Alvin, and Bill Glosser; Babe Goldberg; David Goldfeder; Martin Goldhaber; Florence and Louis Green; Jenny and Isadore Greenberg; Pauline and Arthur Hagadus; Sarah Harris; Alberta Herring; Eleanor Herskowitz; Naomi Holtzman; Louis Horowitz (former member); Atty. Harry and Cecelia Isaacson; Benjamin Isaacson; Esther Jacovitz; Atty. Samuel Kaminsky; Rose and Henry Kaplan; Joseph Kapolitz; Harriet Katz; Eva Katzenstein; Mollie Klater; Abe Kleinstub; Alfred Kline; Dolly Koff; Rabbi Nathan Kollin (former member); Miriam Kranich; Robert Krantzler; Samuel Kwait; Rabbi Morris Landes (former member); Rose Leshner; Lillian Leuin; Meyer Levin; Dr. Yale Lewine; Cecelia and Irving London; Atty. Gustav Margolis; Hilda Markovitz; Dr. Elmer and Betty Match; Lucille Mendelson; Shirley Miller; Betty Misler; Golda, Helene (former member), Harry, and Ben Morrow; Joyce and Harry Moskat; Atty. Morton Myers; Morris Nathan; Harold Neafach; Belle Nederlander; Lillian Oker; Sidney and Molly Osip; Helen Paul; Rabbi Hayim Perelmuter (former member); Harry Rabinowitz; Seymour and Betty Rabinowitz; Bea Rabinowitz; Samuel Rapoport; Ida Reese; Pearl and Raphael Rose; David, and Charlotte Rudel; Nathan Ruder; Jack Sacks; Lena and Dr. Freda Sattel; Sally and Jack Schmerin; Martin and Manny Schwartz; Bessie and Max Schwartz; Sarah Schwartz; Sam and Louis Segal; Atty. Maurice Shadden; Mildred Sherer; Olga Sherman; Ida Shonberg; Eleanor Silverman; Dr. William and Betty Silverstein; Atty. Seymour Silverstone; Rabbi Ralph Simon (former member); Freda Sinberg; Rabbi Rav and Mrs. Harriet Soloff (former members); Isadore and Rose Suchman; Dr. Israel and Rita Teitelbaum; Ida and Morris Torledsky; Ruth Turgelsky; Sally Walzer (former member); Helma Weisberg (on tape); Betty Weissberg; Rabbi Leonard Winograd (former member); Irene Wollitzer; and Bertha Wulfe.

NOTES

PREFACE

1. The concept of structuration is, of course, Anthony Giddens's—see, especially, his *New Rules of Sociological Method: A Positive Critique of Interpretative Sociologies* (London: Hutchinson, 1976), and *The Constitution of Society* (Cambridge: Polity Press, 1984). Giddens's theory/framework of structuration has since acquired a considerable literature—for a critical assessment thereof, see, e.g., C.G.A. Bryant and D. Jary, eds., *Giddens' Theory of Structuration* (London: Routledge, 1991); J. Clark et al., eds., *Anthony Giddens: Consensus and Controversy* (London: The Falmer Press, 1990); D. Held and J. B. Thompson, eds., *Social Theory of Modern Societies: Anthony Giddens and His Critics* (Cambridge: Cambridge University Press, 1989). The idea of social actors as defined by their attributes of material and symbolic purposiveness and responsiveness is akin to the conception of "minimal actors" (i.e., minimally defined for theoretical purposes) as proposed by Edward Lawler et al., in "Structural Social Psychology and the Micro-macro Problem," *Sociological Theory* 11 (1994): 268–90. See also Piotr Sztompka, *Society in Action: The Theory of Social Becoming* (Chicago: University of Chicago Press, 1991).

2. The issue of whether the "generative weights" of each of the two sides of the action-structure reciprocity in Giddens's model are equivalent, and, if they are not, which is assigned a greater significance, has been subject to different, in fact, opposite, interpretations by the commentators on his opus—on this matter, see, e.g., John Thompson, "The Theory of Structuration," in Held and Thompson, *Social Theory of Modern Societies*, 56–76; Zygmunt Bauman, "Hermeneutics and Modern Social Theory," in ibid., 34–55; Ian Craib, *Anthony Giddens* (London: Routledge, 1992): 181–83.

3. For synthesizing reviews of these models, see Ewa Morawska, "The Sociology and Historiography of Immigration," in *Immigration Reconsidered: History, Sociology, and Politics*, ed. Virginia Yans-McLaughlin (New York: Oxford University Press, 1990): 189–90, 212–16; Peter Kivisto, "Beyond Assimilation and Pluralism: Towards Situationally Sensitive Theoretical Models of Ethnicity" (paper presented at the 1992 Annual Meeting of the American Sociological Association, Pittsburgh); Werner Sollors, *Beyond Ethnicity: Consent and Descent in American Culture* (New York: Oxford University Press, 1986), introduction.

4. The term "ethnicization" was first used, I believe, by Victor Greene, in *For God and Country: The Rise of Polish and Lithuanian Consciousness in America* (Madison: State Historical Society of Wisconsin, 1975); the concept was subsequently elaborated by Jonathan Sarna in "From Immigrants to Ethnics: Toward a New Theory of Ethnicization," *Ethnicity* 5 (December 1978): 73–78. Two variants of the ethnicization model actually exist in the literature: one, the mobilizationist model, wherein ethnic-group boundaries and collective ethnic identity arise or strengthen, usually in response to the perceived mistreatment of the ethnic group's members by the institutions of the dominant society, or else in reaction to some international event involving the group's ancestral homeland; and the other, a more common, accommodative type, used in this study. Both variants of the ethnicization model, by the way, accommodate the "invented ethnicity" approach:

group members use schemas and resources to build ethnic communal institutions and establish social networks and a sense of shared membership, but they do it in a historically specific social context.

5. Among the most persuasive critiques of these assumptions in the classical modernization theory that have significantly contributed to its demise in the late 1970s have been Reinhard Bendix's "Tradition and Modernity Reconsidered," *Comparative Studies in Society and History* 9 (1967): 292–346; Joseph Gusfield's "Tradition and Modernity: Misplaced Polarities in the Study of Social Change," *American Journal of Sociology* 72 (January 1967): 357–63; Leon Mayhew's "Ascription in Modern Societies," *Sociological Inquiry* 38 (Spring 1968): 105–21; and Dean Tipps's "Modernization Theory and the Comparative Study of Societies: A Critical Perspective," *Comparative Studies in Society and History* 15 (January 1973): 199–226.

6. William H. Sewell, "A Theory of Structure: Duality, Agency, and Transformation," *American Journal of Sociology* 98 (July 1992): 1–29.

7. Ann Swidler, "Culture in Action: Symbols and Strategies," *American Sociological Review* 51 (April 1986): 273–86.

8. E. P. Thompson, *The Poverty of Theory and Other Essays* (New York: Monthly Review Press, 1978), 1–2.

9. Theda Skocpol, "Emerging Agendas and Recurrent Strategies," in *Vision and Method in Historical Sociology*, ed. Theda Skocpol (New York: Cambridge University Press, 1984), 368–74.

CHAPTER 1
IN THE SHTETLS AND OUT

1. The first part, entitled "Ways of Life," uses information about old-country backgrounds of the founders of the Johnstown Jewish community gathered from and about the concrete people and their concrete hometowns; the second one, "Popular Worldviews," is a reconstruction derived from the collective symbols and references in a repertoire of the turn-of-the-century popular Jewish culture in Eastern Europe.

2. On the dependent character of Eastern Europe's economic development in the period 1870–1914, see Ivan Berend and Gÿorgi Ranki, *Economic Development of East Central Europe in the Nineteenth and Twentieth Centuries* (New York: Columbia University Press, 1974); idem, *The European Periphery and Industrialization, 1780–1914* (New York: Columbia University Press, 1982); William Blackwell, ed., *Russian Economic Development from Peter the Great to Stalin* (Princeton: Princeton University Press, 1974).

3. General information obtained and average statistical figures for the region calculated from: Berend and Ranki, *Economic Development of East Central Europe*, 15–22, 128–38; idem, *The European Periphery*, 25, 144, 157–59; Clive Trebilcock, *The Industrialization of the Continental Powers* (New York: Longman, 1981), 233–35, 300–301, 351, 358–59; Blackwell, *Russian Economic Development*, 11–35; Thomas Fedor, *Patterns of Urban Growth in the Russian Empire during the Nineteenth Century* (Chicago: University of Chicago, Department of Geography, 1975), 95–97, 128–38, 145–50, 174–75, 183–214; Joseph Bradley, *Muzhik and Muscovite: Urbanization in the Late Imperial Russia* (Berkeley and Los Angeles: University of California Press, 1985); Ivan Berend and Gÿorgy Ranki, *Underdevel-*

opment and Economic Growth: Studies in Hungarian Social and Economic History (Budapest: Hungarian Academy of Science, 1979), 81–84, 142–43; *Polish Encyclopedia* (Geneva: Atar, 1922), 2:398, 426, 913–15, 933, 3:242–43, 267, 343, 390–99, 420–26, 562, 588.

4. Of 7 million Jews in Eastern Europe, about 5 million resided in Russia (together with Congress Poland), while the remaining were about equally divided between the Galician and the Hungarian part of the Austrian Monarchy—approximately 850,000 in each—and over 250,000 Jews lived in Romania. See Arthur Ruppin, *The Jews of To-Day* (London: G. Bell and Sons, 1913), 38–41. On anti-Jewish policies and popular disturbances in turn-of-the-century Eastern Europe, see, for Russia (including Congress Poland), Simon Dubnow, *History of the Jews in Russia and Poland* (Philadelphia: The Jewish Publication Society, 1916), 2:340–64, 3:28–38, 80–101, 116–19; Salo Baron, *The Russian Jew under Tsars and Soviets* (New York: Macmillan, 1964), 13–62, 124–31, 136–51; *Encyclopedia Judaica*, 2:84–85, 123–24, 3:86, 123–24, 6:711–16, 13:694–98, 732–38, 14:435–51. For Galicia, see Yitzhak Schiper, *Zydzi w Polsce Odrodzonej* (Warsaw: Nak. Wydawn. "Zydzi w Polsce Odrodzonej," 1932–1933), 2:239, 380–412, 423–87; *Encyclopedia Judaica*, 3:84–85, 123–24, 893–96; 8:1079–95; 16:1325–31. For Hungary, see Randolph Braham, ed., *Hungarian Jewish Studies* (New York: World Federation of Hungarian Jews, 1966–1973), 1:61–72, 90–114, 2:35–85, and "Hungarian Jewry," *Journal of Central European Affairs* 20 (April 1960): 1–23.

5. The data on the urbanization, industrialization, and pauperization of Jewish populations in particular regions of Eastern Europe presented in this and the following two paragraphs have been compiled from: Isaac Rubinow, *Economic Condition of the Jews in Russia* (1907; reprint, New York: Arno, 1975), 493–95, 503–66; Jewish Colonization Association, *Sbornik materialov ob ekonomicheskom polozhenii evreev v Rossii* (St. Petersburg: Jewish Colonization Association, 1904), 1:xxxvii–xxxix 189–94, 205–7, 220–48, 285–86, 395, 2:2, 8–9, 113–19, 16–68, 182–92, 209–20; *Yevreyskaya Entsiklopedya*, 13:650–59, 600, 668–70; Baron, *The Russian Jew under Tsars and Soviets* 145–46; Simon Kuznets, "Immigration of Russian Jews to the United States: Background and Structure," *Perspectives in American History* 9 (1975): 70–73; Arcadius Kahan, "The Impact of Industrialization in Tsarist Russia on the Socioeconomic Conditions of the Jewish Population," in Arcadius Kahan, *Essays in Jewish Social and Economic History* (Chicago: University of Chicago Press, 1982), 1–69; *Historia Polski* (Warsaw: Państwowe Wydawnictwo Naukowe, 1963), vol. 3 (1850/1864–1918), pt. 2, 61–63, 87–89, 189; Schiper, *Zydzi w Polsce Odrodzonej*, 1:192–93, 377–80, 401–406, and idem, *Dzieje Handlu Zydowskiego na Ziemiach Polskich* (Warsaw: Nakład Centrali Związku Kupców, 1937), 441–53, 478–96, 505–52, 558–61; Raphael Mahler, "The Economic Background of Jewish Emigration from Galicia to the United States," *Yivo Annual of Jewish Social Science* 7 (1952): 256–63; Berend and Ranki, *Underdevelopment and Economic Growth*, 80–89, 106–7; Braham, *Hungarian Jewish Studies*, 2:73–76; *Magyar Statisztikai Kozlemenyek: 1910 Evi Nepszamlalasa* 56 (1915): 324–29, 436–513, 581–89; *Magyar Varosok Statisztikai Evkonyve* 1 (1912): 64–77.

6. On different depictions of the shtetl in contemporary Yiddish literature, see, e.g., introduction to Irving Howe and Eliezer Greenberg, *A Treasury of Yiddish Stories* (New York: Schocken Books, 1973); Ruth Wisse, ed., *A Shtetl and Other Yiddish Novellas* (New York: Behrman House, 1973), 1–22; Chone Shmeruk, "Yiddish Literature," *Encyclopedia Judaica*, 16:798–833.

7. The beautifying representation of the shtetl, motivated by the desire to preserve what was best in the past, irrevocably vanished in the Holocaust, informed the widely acclaimed anthropological work of Mark Zborowski and Elisabeth Herzog, *Life Is with People: The Culture of the Shtetl* (New York: Schocken Books, 1952), which soon after its publication became the standard reference in sociological and historical studies of the Jewish group in America. In scholarly debate on the evolution of modern Judaism, the portrayal of the East European shtetl as the mainstay of intransigent traditionalism against a disintegrative American/modern experience has been repeatedly challenged since the 1950s. It has been argued that the immigrants' ready and widespread abandonment of fundamental religious practices, observed by contemporaries in the large Jewish settlements in America, and especially in New York, in fact originated in emancipatory forces that had already undermined the "faithfulness of the Jewish masses" in their East European homelands, and could not be attributed solely to their confrontation with the modern way of life and opportunities found in the United States. For this argument, see Herbert Parzen, "When Secularism Came to the Russian Jewry," *Commentary* 13 (April 1952): 355–62; idem, "East European Immigrants and Jewish Secularism in America, 1882–1915," *Judaism* 3 (Spring 1954): 154–64; Charles Liebman, "Orthodoxy in American Jewish Life," *American Jewish Year Book* 66 (1965): 27–30; David Singer, "David Levinsky's Fall: A Note on the Liebman Thesis," *American Quarterly* 19 (Winter 1967): 696–706. Similar in emphasis, but more consequential in that they have altered the representation of the shtetl in mainstream ethnic studies, are two subsequent classics in American-Jewish historiography: Moses Rischin's *The Promised City: New York's Jews, 1870–1914* (Cambridge: Harvard University Press, 1962), a social history of Jewish immigrants in New York before World War I, and Irving Howe's more popular treatment, *World of Our Fathers* (New York: Simon and Schuster, 1976).

8. See, e.g., Joshua Rothenberg, "Demythologizing the Shtetl," *Midstream* 27 (March 1971): 25–33; Calvin Goldscheider and Alan Zuckerman, *The Transformation of the Jews* (Chicago: University of Chicago Press, 1984), pt. 3, "The Transformation of European Jewish Communities."

9. The following sources were consulted: *Yevreyskaya Entsiclopedya, The Jewish Encyclopedia* (New York and London: Funk and Wagnalls, 1901–1906); *Encyclopedia Judaica; Shtetl Finder,* ed. Chester Cohen (Los Angeles: Periday Co., 1980); *yizker-bikher* (collection at the Hebrew University, Jerusalem); *Magyar Statisztikai Kozlemenyek: 1910; Menoslov Obci na Slovensku* (Bratislava: Nakladom Vlasnim, 1910); *Vlastivedny Slovnik Obci na Slovensku* (Bratislava: VEDA, 1977–1978).

10. For sources of these data, see n. 5 in this chapter.

11. On the economic activities of shtetl women in particular, see Zborowski and Herzog, *Life Is with People,* chap. 5, "People of the Week"; Charlotte Baum, Paula Hyman, and Sonya Michel, *The Jewish Woman in America* (New York: The Dial Press, 1976), chap. 3, "Fight for Survival: Jewish Women in Eastern Europe." Sydelle Kramer and Jenny Masur, eds., *Jewish Grandmothers* (Boston: Beacon Press, 1976); Charlotte Baum, "What Made Yetta Work? The Economic Role of Eastern European Jewish Women in the Family," in *The Jewish Woman: New Perspectives,* ed. Liz Koltun (New York: Schocken Books, 1976), 32–40, and, in the same volume, Paula Hyman, "The Other Half: Women in the Jewish Tradition," 67–76; Sydney Stahl Weinberg, *The World of Our Mothers: The Lives of Immigrant Jewish Women* (Chapel Hill: University of North Carolina Press, 1988), chap. 1;

Susan Glenn, *Daughters of the Shtetl: Life and Labor in the Immigrant Generation* (Ithaca, NY: Cornell University Press, 1990), chap. 1, "The Girl Wasn't Much." The proportion (21 percent) of employed Jewish women in the Russian Pale as reported in the 1897 Russian census quoted from Kahan, "The Impact of Industrialization in Tsarist Russia on the Socioeconomic Condition of the Jewish Population," 6, 49–51, 64n.10. (Kahan brings this estimate up to about 28 percent, but this figure is probably still much too low.)

12. Interviews with Bella C., 8/4/1980; David R., 5/3/1986; Samuel M., 8/21/1980; Esther J., 8/10/1981; Joseph K., 8/6/1986. Max Wagner's story is recorded in his memoir, part of the collection held at the YIVO Institute for Jewish Research in New York, no. 289, 4–5.

13. Interview with Esther J., 8/21/1984.

14. Interview with Martin S., 8/14–20/1980. Figures for Limanowa from Franciszek Bujak, *Limanowa: Miasteczko Powiatu Rzeszowskiego* (Cracow: Gebethner, 1902), 158, also 83–90, 104–7; for Sniatyń, from Joachim Schoenfeld, *Shtetl Memoirs* (Hoboken, NJ: Ktav, 1985), 22–23. The 1898 survey data on paupers in the shtetls, in *Sbornik materyalov ob polozhenii evreev v Rossii*, 2:221–35, 245, 282. Urban dwellers, especially in some larger cities such as Odessa or Ekaterinoslav, seem to have been even more affected by pauperism than those in shtetls (the latter were closer to sources of food). Overall, the Jewish Colonization Association estimated that the proportion of Russian Jewish families in need of outside assistance was as high as 30 percent or over (ibid.). In Galicia, poorer than the Russian Pale, the Agudas Akhim Society's 1890 report to the Polish Parliamentary Club in the Austrian Parliament estimated such needy families as constituting over 50 percent of the total (Jacob Bross, "The Beginning of the Jewish Labor Movement in Galicia," *Yivo Annual of Jewish Social Science* 5 [1950]: 58).

15. Morris Rubin, Autobiography, 1847–1931 (at the Balch Institute for Ethnic Studies, MS no. 141), 65; interview with Bella C., in Johnstown, 8/12/1986.

16. Stanisław Szczepanowski, *Nędza Galicji w Cyfrach i Program Energicznego Rozwoju Gospodarstwa Krajowego* (Lvov: Gubrynowicz and Schmidt, 1888), 57.

17. On the location of the Jewish minority in the "status gap" within the social structure of traditional societies and its consequences for intergroup social relations, see Irwin Rinder, "Strangers in the Land: Social Relations in the Status Gap," *Social Problems* 6 (Winter 1958–1959): 253–60, and a critical elaboration of this model by Sheldon Stryker, "Social Structure and Prejudice," ibid. 6 (Spring 1959): 340–54. Generally on Jews as "middleman minority," see Walter Zenner, "Middleman Minority Theories and the Jews: Historical Survey and Assessment," *Working Papers in Yiddish and East European Jewish Studies*, no. 31 (1978).

18. For sources of these data, see n. 5 in this chapter.

19. On economic complementarity between peasants and Jews in the East European countryside at the turn of the century, see William I. Thomas and Florian Znaniecki, *The Polish Peasant in Europe and America* (Boston: G. Badger, 1918–1920), 1:138–39; also Jack Kugelmass, "Native Aliens: The Jews of Poland as a Middleman Minority" (Ph.D. diss., The New School for Social Research, 1980).

20. *Pinkes Khmelnik* (Tel Aviv, 1960), 360 (quoted from Kugelmass, "Native Aliens," 24).

21. Similar and further information on the forms of Jews' contacts with peasants in turn-of-the-century Eastern Europe can be found in Kugelmass, "Native Aliens," 24, 68, 104–8, 115, 121, 225, 238–46; Alexander Hertz, *Żydzi w Kulturze*

Polskiej (Paris: Institut Litteraire Kultura, 1961), 98–105, 250–65; Alina Cała, "Wizerunek Zyda w Polskiej Kulturze Ludowej" (Ph.D. diss., Department of Ethnography, Warsaw University, 1985); Hirsch Abramovitch, "Rural Jewish Occupations in Lithuania," *Yivo Annual of Jewish Social Science* 1–2 (1947–1948): 206; Israel Bartal, "On Top of a Volcano: Jewish-Ukrainian Coexistence as Depicted in Modern East European Jewish Literature" (paper delivered at a conference on Jewish-Ukrainian Relations, MacMaster University, Hamilton, Canada, October 1982); Herman Dicker, *Piety and Perseverance: Jews from the Carpathian Mountains* (New York: Sepher-Hermon Press, 1981), 478 and passim. On Slavic girl-servants and *Shabes goyim*, see *yizker-bikher*, e.g., the English-language collection by Jack Kugelmass and Jonathan Boyarin, *From a Ruined Garden: The Memorial Books of Polish Jewry* (New York: Schocken Books, 1983), and published as well as unpublished immigrant memoirs (large collections of the latter can be found at the YIVO Institute in New York, the Balch Institute for Ethnic Studies in Philadelphia, and the American Jewish Historical Society in Waltham, Massachussets.

22. Kugelmass, "Native Aliens"; Livia Rothkirchen, "Deep-Rooted Yet Alien: Some Aspects of the History of the Jews in Subcarpathian Ruthenia," *Carpatho-Rusyn Research Center Monograph*, 1986, 147–91.

23. Cf. *Über den Stand der Ungarischen und Galizischen Ruthenen-Bewegung*, Osterreichisches Staatsarchiv, Wien. Informations-buro, Annexe 27, 150–63 (as quoted in Rothkirchen, "Deep-Rooted Yet Alien," 163); Thomas and Znaniecki, *Polish Peasant*, 1:139; Kugelmass, "Native Aliens," 32–33, 38.

24. Robert Rothstein, "Jews in Slavic Eyes: The Paremiological Evidence," *Proceedings of the Ninth World Congress of Jewish Studies* (Jerusalem, 1986), Division D, II: 185–86; *Nowa Księga Przysłów i Wyrażeń Przysłowiowych Polskich w Oparciu o Dzieło Samuela Adalberga*, ed. Julian Krzyżanowski (Warsaw: Państwowe Wydawnictwo Naukowe, 1969–1978), 3:981–99; Cała, "Wizerunek Zyda," 104–9, 112–25. Neither Christian Jewish imagery nor folk beliefs in the magical powers of the Jews were obviously unique to Eastern Europe, but almost universal throughout Christendom (cf. Joshua Trachtenberg's excellent study on this topic, *The Devil and the Jews* [Cleveland: World Publishing Co., 1943]).

25. Cała, "Wizerunek Zyda," 45–51; Olga Goldberg-Mulkiewicz, "The Stereotype of the Jew in Polish Folklore," in *Studies in Aggadah and Jewish Folklore*, ed. Issachar Ben-Ami et al. (Jerusalem: Hebrew University, 1983), 85–90; Schoenfeld, *Shtetl Memoirs*, 12–13; also published and unpublished memoirs of Jewish immigrants in America.

26. For discussion of this equation of *goy*-and-peasant, and of the connotations of the term in the shtetl culture, see Zborowski and Herzog, *Life Is with People*, 151–57; Marshall Sklare, "The Values of Eastern European Jewry and of American Society," *Jewish Frontier* 28 (July 1961): 7–11; Kugelmass, "Native Aliens," 109–10 and passim; Hertz, *Zydzi w Kulturze Polskiej*, 92–99. This image of the peasant was, however, not universally pejorative: in fact, more approving of their characteristics (such as laboriousness, physical "productivity," and endurance) were the Hebrew and Yiddish belles lettres of the late nineteenth century, particularly works authored by writers influenced by *Haskalah* ideas (see Israel Bartal, "Non-Jews and Gentile Society in East European Hebrew and Yiddish Literature, 1856–1914" [Ph.D. diss., The Hebrew University, 1980] [in Hebrew], and idem, "On Top of a Volcano").

27. On the partial absorption by East European Jews of sociocultural percep-

tions of the dominant (gentry) classes in the societies in which they resided, see Hertz, *Żydzi w Kulturze Polskiej*, 96 and passim; Bartal, "Non-Jews and Gentile Society"; Victor Karady and Istvan Kemeny, "Les juifs dans la structure des classes en Hongrie: Essai sur les antecedents historiques des crises d'antisemitisme du XXe siècle," *Actes de la Recherche en Sciences Sociales* 22 (June 1978): 43–55. We may add here that peasant representations of Jews reflected, too, values of the dominant (gentry) cultural system and attitudes of the ruling class.

28. It was not, however, that there was no appreciation whatsoever among Jews of peasant wisdom—a number of Hasidic *tsadikim*, for instance, were known to acknowledge and value it.

29. Benjamin Gordon, *Between Two Worlds* (New York: Bookman Associates, 1952), 21; interview with Joseph K., 8/6/1986.

30. Interviews with Ivan V., 6/20/1986, and with Joseph K., 8/6/1986. As noted earlier, turn-of-the-century Hungary was the friendliest, or the least inimical, toward its Jewish minority; among the future Johnstowners less than 10 percent— including, incidentally, two leaseholders mentioned earlier who remembered, and not unsympathetically, "our gentry"—originated there. Still, as reported by early-twentieth-century ethnographers, there circulated at that time throughout the Hungarian countryside rumors that every fall the Jews snatch away a Christian boy or girl and suffocate the victim with their *teffilin* (*Handwörterbuch des deutschen Aberglaubens* [Berlin, 1927–1942], 1:1439—as quoted in Chaim Chajes, "Baal-Szem Tov u Chrześcijan," *Miesięcznik Żydowski* [Warsaw], 4 [May 1934]: 442).

31. Of all provinces of Eastern Europe, these new trends were most intense and had the greatest influence in the Russian Pale, where Jews were the most numerous and residentially concentrated, and where Jewish intellectual life traditionally centered—see Dubnow, *History of the Jews*, 2:340–64, 3:20–38, 80–101; David Vital, *Zionism: The Formative Years* (Oxford: Clarendon Press, 1982); Ezra Mendelsohn, *Class Struggle in the Pale: The Formative Years of the Jewish Workers Movement* (New York: Cambridge University Press, 1970); Henry Tobias, *The Jewish Bund in Russia: From Origins to 1905* (Stanford: Stanford University Press, 1972); Jonathan Frankel, *Prophecy and Politics: Socialism, Nationalism, and the Russian Jews, 1862–1917* (New York: Cambridge University Press, 1981); cf. also Moshe Mishkinsky, "Regional Factors in the Formation of the Jewish Labor Movement in Czarist Russia," *Yivo Annual of Jewish Social Science* 16 (1969): 27–52. A much paler replica of these ideological movements, from bourgeois and revolutionary integrationism to Jewish socialism and Zionisms, developed in Galicia; see Raphael Mahler, "The Social and Political Aspects of the Haskalah in Galicia," *Yivo Annual of Jewish Social Science* 1 (1946): 65–85; Bross, "The Beginning of the Jewish Labor Movement in Galicia," 55–84; Shabtai Unger, "The Jewish Workers' Movement in Galicia on the Eve of World War I: The Failure to Unify," in *Gal-Ed: On The History of the Jews in Poland* (Tel Aviv) 10 (1987): 12–13 (in Hebrew); N. M. Gelber, *Dzieje Ruchu Syjonistycznego w Galicji, 1875–1918* (Jerusalem: Hebrew University, 1958) (in Hebrew). The Jews of Hungary, especially residents of the largest cities in central parts of the country (by 1910, they constituted nearly 60 percent of the entire Jewish population), had by the turn of the century been considerably magyarized culturally, and the influence of Zionism was generally very limited; it was somewhat greater among the least assimilated town dwellers in more remote northeastern provinces. As for the labor movement, Hungarian Jews joined mainstream Hungarian parties. See Michael Silber, "The Historical Experience of

German Jewry and Its Impact on the Haskalah and Reform in Hungary," in *Toward Modernity: The European Jewish Model*, ed. Jacob Katz (New Brunswick, NJ: Transaction Books, 1987), 107–59; Isaiah Friedman, "The Austro-Hungarian Government and Zionism, 1897–1918," *Jewish Social Studies* 27 (July 1965): 147–67, and (October 1965): 236–49; George Barany, "Magyar Jew or Jewish Magyar?" *Canadian-American Slavic Studies* 8 (Spring 1974): 1–45; personal correspondence with Professor Victor Karady, Centre de Sociologie Européene, Ecole des Hautes Etudes en Sciences Sociales, Paris.

32. Information about these movements in the shtetls in which future Johnstowners originated was gathered, for the period between the late 1890s and the early 1900s, from *yizker-bikher*, *Yevreiskaya Encyclopedya*, The Central Zionist Archives in Jerusalem, the Bund archives in New York (presently at YIVO), the list of localities provided in *Di geshikhte fun Bund*, 2 vols. (New York: Unser Tsayt, 1960–1962), and from Johnstown interviews.

33. According to the 1898 survey of the Jewish Colonization Association, 25–30 percent of all Jewish children of elementary-school age in Russia and Congress Poland did not receive any education. Among those who did, fewer than 5 percent attended public grade schools (the *ukaze*, regulations requiring Jewish students to do written work on the Sabbath, virtually excluded children from Orthodox families). In the Austro-Hungarian Monarchy, elementary public schooling was officially mandatory, but in the rural areas and in the strictly Orthodox Jewish communities, parents often did not comply; in Galicia by 1900, about two-thirds of the Jewish children in the 7–14 age group attended public schools; in Hungary in 1910, inability to read and write non-Hebrew characters among Jewish children of elementary-school age was reported as 10 percent in Budapest, but as high as 70 percent in a rural Maramos county. (This information was compiled from sources listed in n. 5 in this chapter; see also Goldscheider and Zuckerman, *The Transformation of the Jews*, 106–7.)

34. Main sources for this comparative generalization are immigrant memoirs and autobiographies; in fact, in their major features the lifestyles as recollected by my informants resembled the depiction of Zborowski and Herzog in *Life Is with People*, which, as already noted, has been more recently replaced by a representation of the shtetl with its traditions shattered. It may be that Zborowski and Herzog's account was more accurate for certain types of shtetls—e.g., the types in which the prospective Johnstowners originated.

A thesis that Jews in rural shtetls were more bound by tradition than their urbanized fellow ethnics does not imply, however, that the latter were freed from it. Rather, the latter's lifestyles and worldviews had come to contain, and fuse, more different elements. On the continuing connection with Jewish traditions of the Bund and still more radical marxist devotees, see e.g., Mendelsohn, *Class Struggle in the Pale*, and Gerald Sorin, *The Prophetic Minority: American Jewish Immigrant Radicals, 1880–1920* (Bloomington: Indiana University Press, 1985), chap. 1, "Roots of Radicalism: Life, Work, and Politics in the Old Country."

35. Peter Berger, *The Sacred Canopy: Elements of a Sociological Theory of Religion* (New York: Doubleday, 1969).

36. On the organic relationship of religion and ethnicity in traditional Judaism, see, e.g., Charles Liebman, "Religion, Class, and Culture in American Jewish History," *Jewish Journal of Sociology* 9 (December 1967): 227–32. On the collusion of religion and ethnicity among non-Jewish East Europeans at the turn of the century, particularly in rural areas, see Timothy Smith, "Religion and Ethnicity in America,"

American Historical Review 83 (December 1978): 1165–68 and passim; the quotation regarding conflation of religious and Polish identities among the peasantry is from Joshua Fishman and Vladimir Nahirny, *Language Loyalty* (The Hague: Mouton, 1966), 328.

37. *Pinkes Antopolie: Yizkor Book* (Tel Aviv, 1972), 19.

38. This recollection is from a memoir of Rose Pesotta, *Days of Our Lives* (Boston: Excelsior Publishers, 1958), 204.

39. Johnstown interviews; also immigrants' memoirs and autobiographies, published, and from the manuscript collection in the archives of the YIVO Institute in New York (the Zhitkovitz quotation from memoir of Jacob Doroshkin, no. 305, 21).

40. The same survey of life conditions among Russian Jewry reported that the average family contributed as charitable donations between $0.15 and $0.50 of their weekly earnings, which ranged from $1.50 to $5.00. *Sbornik materyalov*, 2:207, 221–35, 245.

41. *Tz'enah Ur'enah*, translated as "Come out and see" (*Shir HaShirim*, 3:11), was published by an itinerant preacher from Yanov near Lublin in Poland, Yaakov ben Yizchak Ashkenazi (1550–1624/28). The quotation is from *Tz'enah Ur'enah*, trans. from the Yiddish by Miriam Stark Zakon (Jerusalem: Hillel Press, 1984), 2:632. See also Joseph Schultz, "The Tze'enah U-Re'enah: Torah for the Folk," *Judaism* 36 (Winter 1987): 84–96.

42. Kahan, *Essays in Jewish Social and Economic History*, 124. On the meaning and place of *tsdoke* in Judaism, see Jacob Neusner, "Righteousness, Not Charity: Judaism's View of Philanthropy," *Liberal Education* 74 (September–October 1988): 16–18. In turn-of-the-century Eastern Europe, see Natalie Joffe, "The Dynamics of Benefice among East European Jews," *Social Forces* 27 (March 1949): 238–47.

43. Quotation from an interview with Mildred G., 6/1/1986. It is not possible, I believe, to make a percentage estimate of the proportion of turn-of-the-century East European women who did this kind of reading. Zborowski and Herzog in *Life Is with People* (125) claimed that a tattered volume of *Tz'enah Ur'enah*, "the most popular Yiddish book, [was] found in every shtetl household." My interviews indicate that it was much more popular among the generation of immigrants' mothers (and grandmothers) than among the immigrants themselves; it might have been that the immigrants were simply too young to be interested in such readings, or, more likely, that preference for traditional readings was waning, while the interest in secular Yiddish literature was on the increase. *Tkhines*, or supplicatory prayers, also apparently popular among pious East European Jewish women during the time under consideration here, were not mentioned by my interviewees. On the content and use of *tkhines*, see Chava Weissler, "The Traditional Piety of Ashkenazic Women," in *Jewish Spirituality: From the Sixteenth Century Revival to the Present*, ed. Arthur Green (New York: Crossroad, 1988), 2:245–75.

44. Information about Lemberg in Abraham Kahan, *Bleter fun mayn leben* (New York: Forverts, 1913), 5:144–46, after Arthur Goren, "Preaching American Jewish History: A Review Essay," *American Jewish History* 79 (Summer 1990): 546; Steve Zipperstein, *The Jews of Odessa: A Cultural History, 1794–1881* (Stanford, CA: Stanford University Press, 1985), 131.

45. Interview with Hyman M., 8/11/1980.

46. Concepts of the scope, i.e., the range of social contexts in which religion has relevance, and the force or "psychological grip" it has on people's lives, are Clifford

Geertz's, from his *Islam Observed: Religious Development in Morocco and Indonesia* (New Haven: Yale University Press, 1968), 11–15.

47. *Tz'enah Ur'enah*, 1:255. Quotation from a new *tkhine* is from Chava Weissler, "American Transformations of the Tkhines" (paper presented at a conference on American Jewish Women's History, University of Maryland, November 3–5, 1993), 10 (see pp. 1–12 of this paper for an interesting discussion of new themes in women's *tkhines* of *maskilic* origin). On *bitokhn* as the fundamental life-orientation of shtetl residents, see also Zborowski and Herzog, *Life Is with People*, 257–65.

48. Quotations from Louis I. Newman, *Maggidim and Hasidim: Their Wisdom* (New York: Bloch Publishing Co., 1962), 52, 19, and *T'zenah Ur'enah*, 1:26. On the idea, and applications thereof, of *takhlis* in East European Jewish society, see Moses Kliegsberg, "Jewish Immigrants in Business: A Sociological Study," in *The Jewish Experience in America*, ed. Abraham Karp (Waltham, MA: American Jewish Historical Society, 1969), 5:254–60.

49. Such an interpretation of the basic schemas in the Jewish "spectrum regime" has been proposed in studies of different genres, from cultural anthropology, exegeses of the "logic" of Talmudic study, to psychology: see, for example, Raphael Patai, *The Jewish Mind* (New York: Charles Scribner, 1952), or Max Kadushin, *The Rabbinic Mind* (New York: Jewish Theological Seminary of America, 1952). It should be pointed out that there also exist different—in fact, opposite—interpretations of the ideal-typical Jewish cognitive *habitus*, emphasizing, rather, its dichotomizing tendency: see, for example, literary essays of Cynthia Ozick, or a recent study of Suzanne Klingenstein, *Jews in the American Academy, 1900–1940: The Dynamics of Intellectual Assimilation* (New Haven: Yale University Press, 1991); see also the reviews of the latter by Alan Mintz, "Manners, Morals, and the Academy," *New Republic* 79 (March 9, 1992): 41–44; and by Stephen Whitfield, "Polite Ivy League Pioneers," *New Leader* 65 (December 30, 1991): 10–11.

It appears possible to reconcile these two interpretations by distinguishing between matters relating to ideas and beliefs (in rabbinic Judaism: pertaining to the aggadic, or nonlegal portion of rabbinic literature), and to the rituals and religiously prescribed practices (pertaining to the halakhic or legal and regulatory portion of the above): while the former—generally, the schemas—permit, or even invite, ambiguity and contradiction, the latter require unequivocal stands. To clarify: as a masterly study by Jacob Katz, *The "Shabbes Goy": A Study in Halakhic Flexibility* (Philadelphia: The Jewish Publication Society, 1989), has demonstrated, using as an example the rabbinic rulings over several centuries regarding the employment of a non-Jew to perform works forbidden on the Sabbath, also in matters of *halakhah* the rabbinic interpretations allowed for flexibility. The point is that while particular rabbis in particular circumstances may offer different interpretations of the law, their pronouncements regarding matters of concrete conduct derived from the accepted position must be clear and unequivocal. But see also "(Self-)Reflections of a Fieldworker" in appendix I for a discussion of the circumstances of my interpretative preferences in this matter.

50. "Forty-nine faces" of the Torah—in Gen. R. 25.1; "Interpret me!" is ascribed to Rashi, a renowned eleventh-century scholar of the Bible and Talmud (*Pesiqta Rabbati* 34a).

51. For a collection of popular Yiddish maxims and proverbs, see *Yiddish Proverbs*, ed. Hanan Ayalti (New York: Schocken Books, 1963). As is well known in studies of folk maxims and proverbs, this "wisdom of many" is itself dialectical in

the sense that one proverb can almost always be found to cite against any other; the argument here, let me repeat, is that "Jewish wisdom" at the scholarly as well as folk level, consistently places a strong emphasis on the polyvalent and contradictory nature of human affairs. The Ladier rabbi quotation is from Newman, *Maggidim and Hasidim*, 18.

52. *Tz'enah Ur'enah*, 3:1089; this commentary is on a verse in Koheleth (Eccles. 3:1), "To each, a time."

53. *Tz'enah Ur'enah*, 3:689, expounding on the Psalmist's "Your righteousness is like the mighty mountains; Your judgements are like the great depths"(Ps. 36:7).

54. Especially Proverbs, Job, and Koheleth—see, e.g., Robert Gordis, *Koheleth: The Man and His World. A Study of Ecclesiastes* (New York: Schocken Books, 1955); idem, *The Book of Job* (New York: Jewish Theological Seminary of America, 1978). The seven-volume *Legends of the Jews*, compiled by Louis Ginzberg (Philadelphia: The Jewish Publication Society, 1913), is a rich source of these and other schemas; see vol. 7, index. Also Gerhard Von Rad, *Wisdom in Israel* (London: SCM Press, 1972); and R.B.Y. Scott, *The Way of Wisdom in the Old Testament* (New York: Macmillan, 1971).

55. See *Yiddish Proverbs*; also *Blessings, Curses, Hopes and Fears: Psycho-Ostensive Expressions in Yiddish*, ed. James Matisoff (Philadelphia: Institute for the Study of Human Issues, 1979), 8–13, 26–28, 47–51.

56. *Tz'enah Ur'enah*, 3:918.

57. See, e.g., David Berger, ed., *The Legacy of Jewish Migration: 1881 and Its Impact* (New York: Columbia University Press, 1983); Howe, *World of Our Fathers*, introduction.

58. Imre Ferenczi and Walter Willcox, eds., *International Migrations* (New York: National Bureau of Economic Research, 1929–1931), 1:91, 167, 175, 183, 385–92, 461–69, 483–84, 2:415–16, 471–82, 524–30; Kuznets, "Immigration of Russian Jews," 39, 44, 87–88; Samuel Joseph, *Jewish Immigration to the United States from 1881 to 1910* (New York: Columbia University, 1914), 93, 110; Mahler, "The Economic Background of Jewish Emigration from Galicia," 266–67; Julianna Puśkas, *From Hungary to the United States, 1880–1914* (Budapest: Akademia Kiado, 1983), 18–19, 28–29.

59. Data on Jewish versus non-Jewish emigration to America from Joseph, *Jewish Immigration to the United States*, 101–2; see also Arthur Goren, "The Jews," in *Harvard Encyclopedia of American Ethnic Groups*, ed. Stephen Thernstrom and Ann Orloff (Cambridge: Harvard University Press, Belknap Press, 1980), 571–81; Mahler, "The Economic Background of Jewish Emigration from Galicia," 255–67; *Magyar Statisztikai Evkonyv* (Budapest: Kozponti Statisztikai Hivatal, 1909), table 5, 57–59. Generally on mass population movements across and outside of Eastern Europe in that period, see Walter Nugent, *Crossings: The Great Transatlantic Migrations, 1870–1914* (Bloomington: Indiana University Press, 1992), chap. 9.

60. Data compiled from Hersch Liebman, "International Migration of the Jews," in Ferenczi and Willcox, *International Migrations*, 2:472–82; Kuznets, "Immigration of Russian Jews," 41–43, 50–51, 87–88; Kahan, *Essays in Jewish Social and Economic History*, 31–32; Rubinow, *Economic Conditions of the Jews in Russia*, chap. 4, 503–4n.3; *Evreiskaia Entsiklopedia*, 16 (1913): 264–65; Andrzej Pilch, ed., *Emigracja z Ziem Polskich w Czasach Nowożytnich i Najnowszych* (Warsaw: Państwowe Wydawnictwo Naukowe, 1984), 259–65; Mahler, "The Economic Background of Jewish Emigration from Galicia," 255, 266–67; *Magyar Varosok Statisztikai Evkonyve*, table 5, 57–60.

61. Data according to Liebman, "International Migration of the Jews," 483–87; Kuznets, "Immigration of Russian Jews," 94–96. A compilation of 1890–1891 immigrant letters in *Writing Home: Immigrants in Brazil and the United States, 1890–1891*, ed. Witold Kula, Nina Assorodobraj-Kula, Marcin Kula, trans. Josephine Wtulich (New York: Columbia University Press, 1986). Jonathan Sarna has estimated on the basis of U.S. government figures that in the period 1881–1900 Jewish immigrants were returning to Europe at a considerable rate of 20-odd percent; after that—as the result, on the one hand, of the deteriorating climate for Jews in Russia, and, on the other, the solidifying social embeddedness of immigrants in America—the return rate dropped to about 6–7 percent (Jonathan Sarna, "The Myth of No Return: Jewish Return Migration to Eastern Europe, 1881–1914," *American Jewish History* 71 [March 1981]: 256–69). Much higher, the return rates in the same period of non-Jewish immigrants from East Europe varied from 35 to 50 percent (depending on the nationality and region of emigration) and did not show a comparable drop anywhere near that of the Jewish case, even in times of economic depression in the United States; the latter was reflected, rather, in considerable drops in emigration from Eastern Europe, as people learned through letters about the bad work situation (see Ewa Morawska, "Return Migrations: Theoretical and Research Agenda," in *A Century of European Migrations, 1830 to 1930: Comparative Perspectives*, ed. Rudolph Vecoli [Urbana: University of Illinois Press, 1991], 277–92).

62. Irving Howe has been the main advocate of the idea of the symbolization of Jews' American emigration as a replay of Exodus (see, e.g., Irving Howe, introduction to *The Legacy of Jewish Migration*); the Mary Antin quotation is from her autobiographical *The Promised Land* (1916; reprint, New York: Arno Press, 1980), 141.

63. *Reports of the Immigration Commission*, 61st Congress, 3d Session, Sen. Doc. 748, *Emigration Conditions in Europe* (Washington, DC: Government Printing Office: 1911), 377; Kuznets, "Immigration of Russian Jews," 106–7.

64. Figures quoted from Kuznets, "Immigration of Russian Jews," 113. I have not found any comparable data for emigrants from Austro-Hungary.

65. Quotations from letters no. 123, 140, and 231, in *Writing Home*, 240, 262, 376.

66. *Antopolie: Yizkor Book*, 44.

67. Lawrence Glosser, "After the Horse Died: An Historical and Sociological Study of the Glosser Family of Johnstown, Pennsylvania" (M.A. thesis, Hebrew Union College, 1972), 22, 30; see also *Antopolie: Yizkor Book*, 44.

68. Interview with Wolf G., 7/26/1987.

69. Percentage figures for the general population of emigrants from Joseph, *Jewish Immigration to the United States*, 140–45; Ruppin, *The Jews of To-Day*, 89.

CHAPTER 2
FITTING OLD-COUNTRY RESOURCES INTO A NEW PLACE:
THE FORMATION OF A (MULTI-)ETHNIC ECONOMIC NICHE

1. For a review of literature on various modes of immigrants' incorporation into the American economy, in the past and at the present, see Ewa Morawska, "The Sociology and Historiography of Immigration," in *Immigration Reconsidered: History, Sociology, and Politics*, ed. Virginia Yans-McLaughlin (New York: Oxford Uni-

versity Press, 1990), 196–212. Specifically on ethnic enclaves (called also ethnic or coethnic economies, and ethnic economic niches), among the best known (though often differently conceptualized) discussions are Edna Bonacich and John Modell, *The Economic Basis of Ethnic Solidarity* (Berkeley and Los Angeles: University of California Press, 1980); Ivan Light, *Ethnic Enterprise in America: Business and Welfare among Chinese, Japanese, and Blacks* (Berkeley and Los Angeles: University of California Press, 1972); *The Ethnic Economy*, special issue of *Sociological Perspectives* 30 (October 1987); Alejandro Portes and Robert Manning, "The Immigrant Enclave: Theory and Empirical Examples," in *Competitive Ethnic Relations*, ed. Suzan Olzak and Joanne Nagel (Orlando, FL: Academic Press, 1986), 47–68 (the modes of immigrants' access to primary sector have not been much researched thus far).

2. Statistical figures on the employment of Jews in New York and in industrial, and specifically garment, manufacturing, can be found in Charles Bernheimer, *The Russian Jew in the United States* (Philadelphia: The John Winston Co., 1905), 104, 108–9, 112, 120, 122–23; U.S. Bureau of the Census, *Twelfth Census of the United States: 1900*, Population, pt. 2 (Washington, DC: Government Printing Office, 1901), 578–85; U.S. Immigration Commission, *Reports of the Immigration Commission*, 61st Congress, 2d Session, Sen. Doc. 338: Immigrants in Cities, vol. 1 (Washington, DC: Government Printing Office, 1911), 216–17, 309, 397; Jacob Lestschinsky, "Economic and Social Development of American Jewry," *The Jewish People: Past and Present* (New York: Jewish Encyclopedic Handbook, 1955), 4:82, 87, 90–93. The above sources (on pages included in citations) also provide statistical figures, generally similar in terms of a high-level concentration, 60 to 65 percent, of Jews in the manufacturing and/or garment industry, for Philadelphia, Boston, and Chicago. On the expansion of the garment industry at the turn of the century, see Joel Seidman, *The Needle Trades* (New York: Farrar & Rhinehort, 1942); Jesse Pope, *The Clothing Industry in New York* (Columbia: University of Missouri Press, 1905), chap. 1. Specifically on the employment of Jews in the New York garment industry, see Irving Howe, *World of Our Fathers* (New York: Simon & Schuster, 1976), chap. 4; Susan Glenn, *Daughters of the Shtetl: Life and Labor in the Immigrant Generation* (Ithaca, NY: Cornell University Press, 1990), chaps. 2 and 3. On Jews' reliance on ethnic networks in procuring employment and improving occupational position, see Suzanne Model, "Mode of Job Entry and the Ethnic Composition of Firms: Early Twentieth-Century Migrants to New York City," *Sociological Forum* 3 (Winter 1988): 110–27; and idem, "Italian and Jewish Intergenerational Mobility: New York, 1910," *Social Science History* 12 (Spring 1988): 31–48.

3. Data on big-city Jews employed in manufacturing from Lestschinsky, "Economic and Social Development of American Jewry," 82, 87; on the preponderance of trade and trade-related occupations among Jews inhabiting smaller cities, see, e.g., Joel Perlmann, "Beyond New York: The Occupations of Russian Jewish Immigrants in Providence, R.I., and in Other Small Jewish Communities, 1900–1915," *American Jewish History* 72 (March 1983): 369–94; Charles Reznikoff and Uriah Engelman, *The Jews of Charleston* (Philadelphia: The Jewish Publication Society, 1950); Joshua Trachtenberg, *Consider the Years: The Story of the Jewish Community of Easton, Pennsylvania, 1752–1942* (Easton, PA: Temple Brith Sholom, 1944); William Toll, *The Making of an Ethnic Middle Class: Portland Jewry over Four Generations* (Albany: SUNY Press, 1982). A similar commercial concentration

and reliance on coethnics in business has been reported in the nineteenth-century South where Jews, few in numbers and geographically mobile, did not organize stable ethnoreligious communities: see Elliott Ashkenazi, *The Business of Jews in Louisiana, 1840–1875* (Tuscaloosa: University of Alabama Press, 1988). The only contemporary study of the Jewish entrepreneurial niche, and that in a large city, that I have come upon, is Morton Weinfeld's "The Ethnic Sub-Economy: Explication and Analysis of a Case Study of the Jews of Montreal," *Contemporary Jewry* 6 (Winter 1983): 6–25.

4. On ethnic entrepreneurship, see, e.g., Robin Ward and Richard Jenkins, *Ethnic Communities in Business* (London: Cambridge University Press, 1984); Bonacich and Modell, *The Economic Basis of Ethnic Solidarity*; Light, *Ethnic Enterprise in America*; Howard Aldrich and Roger Waldinger, "Ethnicity and Entrepreneurship," *Annual Review of Sociology* 16 (1990): 111–35; Roger Waldinger et al., *Ethnic Entrepreneurs: Immigrant Business in Industrial Societies* (Newbury, CA: Sage, 1990); Calvin Goldscheider and Frances Kobrin, "Ethnic Community and the Process of Employment," *Ethnicity* 7 (September 1980): 256–78. There exists also a substantial literature, in part overlapping with the above, on so-called middleman minorities; for a review, see Walter Zenner, *Middleman Minority Theories* (Albany: SUNY Press, 1991).

5. Quotations from Ivan Light, "Immigrant Entrepreneurs in America: Koreans in Los Angeles," in *Clamor at the Gates*, ed. Nathan Glazer (San Francisco: ICS Press, 1985), 173.

6. John J. McLaurin, *The Story of Johnstown* (Harrisburg, PA: Published by the author, 1891), 40–46; *Souvenir History of Johnstown, Pennsylvania, 1800–1939* (Johnstown, PA: Johnstown Chamber of Commerce, 1939); Henry W. Storey, *History of Cambria County, Pennsylvania* (New York: Louis Publishing Co., 1907), 3 vols.; and *Statistical Review of Greater Johnstown, Pennsylvania* (Johnstown: Johnstown Chamber of Commerce, 1952), 7–8; John W. Boucher, "The Cambria Iron Company," in Pennsylvania Bureau of Industrial Statistics, *Annual Report, 1887*, E1–2; William Hogan, *Economic History of the Iron and Steel Industry in the United States* (Lexington, MA: Heath, 1973), vol. 3, pt. 4, 933–37; *Johnstown Works: United States Steel Corporation* (June 1976), vol. 4, no. 2, pt. 1; *Reports of the Immigration Commission*, Immigrants in Industries, pt. 2: Iron and Steel Manufacturing, vol. 1, 61st Congress, 2d Session, Sen. Doc. 633 (Washington, DC: Government Printing Office, 1911), "Community A," 329.

7. The figures compiled from: U.S. Bureau of the Census, *Eleventh Census of the United States: 1890*, Compendium of the Eleventh Census of the United States, pt. 1, Population (Washington, DC: Government Printing Office, 1897), 138:36–37, 426–27, 606–8, 691–97, 654; U.S. Bureau of the Census, *Twelfth Census of the United States: 1900*, Population, vol. 1 (Washington, DC: Government Printing Office, 1901), 334–35; U.S. Bureau of the Census, *Thirteenth Census of the United States: 1910*, Population (Washington, DC: Government Printing Office, 1914), 1:242, 531, 571; 3:563, 567–69, 574–80, 893–95, 900, 935–42.

8. *Twelfth Census of the United States: 1900*, Special Reports: Occupations, 448–50. The occupational data for the four counties are not available before 1930, so the figures presented are actually for that year (U.S. Bureau of the Census, *Fifteenth Census of the United States: 1930*, Population, vol. 3, pt. 2 [Washington, DC: Government Printing Office, 1933], 709–13).

9. Herbert Gutman, "Two Lockouts in Pennsylvania, 1873–1874," *Pennsyl-*

vania Magazine 63 (July 1959): 307–27; Bruce Williams and Michael Yates, *Upward Struggle: A Bicentennial Tribute to Labor in Cambria and Somerset Counties* (Harrisburg, PA: AFL-CIO, 1976), 4–5, 10, 20; Nathan Shappee, "A History of Johnstown and the Great Flood of 1889: A Study of Disaster and Rehabilitation" (Ph.D. diss., University of Pittsburgh, 1940), 75–76, 101, 528–59; David Brody, *Steelworkers in America: The Non-Union Era* (Cambridge: Harvard University Press, 1960), 233–36; Donald Sofchalk, "Steelworkers of America, United (U.S.W.A.)," in *Labor Unions*, ed. Gary Fink (Westport, CT: Greenwood Press, 1977), 357–59.

10. The information gathered—from the naturalization records at Cambria County Courthouse, Ebensburg, Pennsylvania; manuscript schedules of the 1900 and 1910 censuses; passenger lists of the ships arriving in the ports of New York and Boston, National Archives, Washington, DC; in Philadelphia, Federal Records Center, and "Philadelphia Ship Manifest Records" in the archives of the Balch Institute for Ethnic Studies in Philadelphia; the 1915 city directory, and the 1900 and 1910 census SOUNDEX, which lists previous place of residence, Johnstown Jewish merchants as listed in Dun and Bradstreet credit reports, 1890–1910, and interviews with members of the Jewish community in Johnstown—permitted tracing of 108 people, men who by the outbreak of World War I formed the majority of the local East European adult male Jewish population.

11. Interviews with Martin G., 8/10/1984; Betty W. and Helen P., 7/7/1984; Lawrence Glosser, "After the Horse Died: An Historical and Sociological Study of the Glosser Family of Johnstown, Pennsylvania" (M.A. thesis, Hebrew Union College, 1977), 50–54; Industrial Removal Office records (American Jewish Historical Society, Waltham, Massachussetts).

12. Interviews with Louis F., 1/13/1980; Moses S., 8/13/980; Robert K., 8/16/1984; Sarah H., 6/29/1980; Harry M., 8/11/1980; Morris T., 8/9/1984. Difficult conditions of everyday life on the Lower East Side at the beginning of the century have been described in several studies and a number of immigrant memoirs; see, e.g., Jacob Riis, *How the Other Half Lives: Studies among Tenements of New York* (New York: Scribner's Sons, 1903); Moses Rischin, *The Promised City: New York's Jews, 1870–1914* (Cambridge: Harvard University Press, 1962), 76–94; Howe, *World of Our Fathers*, pt. 2., "The East Side." Although the situation in the immigrant section of Philadelphia, where the second-largest number of the prospective Johnstowners originally resided, was not as bad as that in New York, it had basically similar features disliked by the immigrants; see e.g., Carroll Wright, *The Slums of Baltimore, Chicago, New York, and Philadelphia*, Special Report of the Commissioner of Labor, 53d Congress, 2d Session., Ex. Doc. no. 257 (Washington, DC: Government Printing Office, 1894); also *Reports of the Immigration Commission*, Immigrants in Cities, pt. 4, vol. 1, "Philadelphia" (Washington, DC: Government Printing Office, 1911), 42, 345–421. In a study of Jews in small towns in upstate New York conducted in the mid-1950s, the immigrants were also reported to have left New York at the beginning of the century to get away from the unpleasantness of the big city (unfortunately, no information has been provided as to their old-country backgrounds); see Peter Rose, *Strangers in Their Midst: Small-Town Jews and Their Neighbors* (Merrick, NY: Richwood Publishing Co., 1977), chap. 3.

13. Interviews with Frieda Z., 8/25/1980; Philip E., 8/11/1982; Moses S., 8/13/1980; Robert K., 6/14/1986; Harry M., 8/11/1980.

14. Interviews with Cecelia I., 9/23/1980; Robert K., 6/14/1986; Harry M., 8/11/1980; Jack S., 8/15/1984.

15. The manuscript schedules of the (1900 and 1910) censuses, while not free from enumeration bias against the new arrivals who often gained their livelihood from peddling around the area, have been generally a more accurate source than city directories. I supplemented the information gathered from this source with name listings found in Rodef Sholom synagogal minutes, tax assessment records, and local interviews. A higher figure, about fifty German families, has been reported in Leonard Winograd's *"The Horse Died at Windber": A History of Johnstown Jewry* (Bristol, IN: Wyndham Hall, 1988), 154–55 (after the *Johnstown Tribune*, October 4, 1910, p. 6); my calculation from the manuscript schedules of the 1910 census indicates a smaller number.

16. The information I gathered from personal interviews with the Johnstowners in 1984–1985 indicates that the average number of children per East European immigrant family was 6.4. This figure, however, represents the total number of children, reported long after immigrant women had passed childbearing age; in 1910, half of the women reporting for the census were younger than thirty-five.

17. Were we to apply the conventional division into white-collar (nonmanual) and blue-collar (manual) occupations, no less than 95 percent of the Johnstown Jews at the beginning of the century—as compared with 23 percent of the city's general population—could be classified as part of the white-collar stratum. I decided against such a gross tabulation, not only so as to avoid losing interesting information, but, more important, because of the hybrid character of several occupations actually performed by the immigrants (not unlike their experience in East European shtetls).

One such category was artisanry, performed by 23 percent of the immigrants: over half of them were tailors, and the rest shoemakers, goldsmiths and jewelers, coopers, tinners, and blacksmiths, most of whom worked in their own small shops where they produced (entirely or in part) and sold their merchandise, thus working as laborer-businessmen. (In larger American cities, an estimated 20 to 30 percent of Jews classified under the "manufacturing pursuits" category were shop-owning artisans; see Nathan Goldberg, "Occupational Patterns of American Jews," *Jewish Review* 3 [April 1945]: 1–23, Lestschinsky, "Economic and Social Development of American Jewry," 90–93.) Another ambiguous category were peddlers who constituted 27 percent of the gainfully employed Johnstown immigrants in 1910. They have usually been assigned to the category of (lower) white-collar occupations (e.g., Stephen Thernstrom, *The Other Bostonians* [Cambridge: Harvard University Press, 1973]; Thomas Kessner, *The Golden Door: Italian and Jewish Immigrant Mobility in New York City, 1880–1915* [New York: Oxford University Press, 1977]; Judith Smith, *Family Connections: A History of Italian and Jewish Immigrant Lives in Providence, Rhode Island, 1900–1940* [Albany: SUNY Press, 1985]), but peddling, too, represented a mixture of manual (labor) and buying-and-selling (business) activities. Johnstown city directories at the beginning of the century listed some of the men thus occupied as "laborers," while manuscript schedules of the census and tax assessments specified possession of "a horse"—a clear indication that a person was in the peddling business. Peddlers, in studies dealing with this occupational category, have usually been treated as salesmen, and therefore as employees. I assigned them to the self-employed group (keeping them separate from others involved in trade and services), since—at least in the Johnstown area—most of them worked "on own account," managing credit, merchandise, and sales. Another reason for the assignment of peddlers to this category—admittedly an unorthodox consideration for standard occupational classifications, but valid in my opinion—was that, as the interviews clearly indicated, they perceived themselves as independent businessmen (or proto-businessmen perhaps), on their way toward establishing proprietary enterprises.

18. Calculation based on information concerning ninety immigrant men, gathered from the manuscript schedules of the 1910 censuses (Cambria and three surrounding counties), tax assessment records, and local interviews.

19. I have dealt more extensively with this replica of the old-country relationship in an article, "A Replica of the 'Old-Country' Relationship in the Ethnic Niche: East European Jews and Gentiles in Small-Town Western Pennsylvania, 1880s–1930s," *American Jewish History* 77 (September 1987): 87–105. A number of studies contain passing references indicating that to a greater or lesser degree the trading relations between Jewish and Gentile East European immigrants had also been reestablished in large cities such as Chicago, Detroit, Buffalo, Philadelphia, Pittsburgh, and Boston, as well as in Canada. In Johnstown, because of specific circumstances as described in this chapter, this transplant appears to have been particularly extensive and durable. See Lestschinsky, "Economic and Social Development of American Jewry," 76–77; Robert A. Woods and Albert J. Kennedy, eds., *Handbook of Settlements* (New York: Charities Publication Committee, 1911); Louis Wirth, *The Ghetto* (Chicago: University of Chicago Press, 1928), 229–32; Jerome Davis, *The Russian Immigrant* (New York: Macmillan, 1922), 55–56; Caroline Golab, *Immigrant Destinations* (Philadelphia: Temple University Press, 1977); Myrna Silverman, "Jewish Family and Kinship in Pittsburgh: An Exploration into the Significance of Kinship, Ethnicity, and Social Class Mobility" (Ph.D. diss., University of Pittsburgh, 1976), 47–49; Jonathan D. Sarna, "Jewish Immigrants to North America: The Canadian Experience (1870–1900)," *Jewish Journal of Sociology* 18 (June 1976): 36–37.

20. Business panels, 7/15–16/1981; small town panel, 7/30/1981; interviews with Helma W., 4/5/1980; Harry R., 8/15/1981.

21. Interviews with Olga S., 8/14/1984; Abe K., 11/30/1980 (a similar recollection, "chicken for merchandise," from Alfred K. from Bolivar in the same county, 8/16/1984); Seymour R., 8/11/1984; Isadore S., 8/16/1984.

22. Business panel, 7/15/1981; interview with Anthony C., 6/27/1984.

23. Manuscript schedules of the 1910 census, Johnstown—enumeration of members of Jewish immigrant households. Keeping servants has been used in social-historical studies as an indicator of wealth; it was not so in the foreign quarters of Johnstown at the beginning of the century, especially in such familiar intergroup relations as those described here. A weekly expenditure of $1.50 for a Slavic servant was affordable for somewhat more established Jewish immigrant families.

24. Estimated on the basis of the last occupations prior to emigration of the prospective Johnstowners ($N = 51$) as recorded by the passenger lists of ships arriving in U.S. ports, and local interviews.

25. Interview with Benjamin I., 4/6/1986 (also quotation about his father, Samuel I.); Bob K., 6/4/1986 (see also Winograd, *A History of Johnstown's Jews*, 252); Isadore S., 8/16/84; business panels, 7/15–16/1981.

26. Mark Granovetter, "Economic Action and Social Structure: The Problem of Embeddedness," *American Journal of Sociology* 91 (November 1985): 481–510.

27. Record Book of the Hebrew Cemetery Association of Johnstown, Pennsylvania, 1888–1909, n.p.; Rodef Sholom Synagogue minute book, 12/25/1904; Winograd, *A History of Johnstown's Jews*, 148–55; employment of American-born East Europeans in German-Jewish stores from 1915 Johnstown city directory. On strained relations between the German and East European Jewish communities in the early years of their encounter in America, see Esther Panitz, "In Defense of the Jewish Immigrant," *American Jewish Historical Quarterly* 53 (December 1963): 99–130; Selma Berroll, "In Their Image: German Jews and the Americanization of the *Ost Juden* in New York," *New York History* 63 (October 1982): 578–92; for a reappraisal of these relations, see Zosa Szajkowski, "The Yahudi and the Immigrant: A Reappraisal," *American Jewish Historical Quarterly* 63 (September 1973): 13–44; Gerald Sorin, "Mutual Contempt, Mutual Benefit: The Strained Encounter between German and East European Jews in America, 1880–1920," *American Jewish History* 81 (Autumn 1993): 34–59.

28. On the functioning of these organizations in assisting the economic needs of the immigrants, see, e.g., Michael Weisser, *A Brotherhood of Memory: Jewish Landsmanshaftn in the New World* (New York: Basic Books, 1985); Shelly Tennenbaum, "Immigrants and Capital: Jewish Loan Societies in the United States," *American Jewish History* 76 (March 1986): 67–78; Nathan Kaganoff, "The Jewish Landsmanshaftn in New York before World War I," *American Jewish History* 76 (March 1986): 56–67; Terry Fisher, "Lending as Philanthropy: The Philadelphia Jewish Experience, 1847–1954" (Ph.D. diss., Bryn Mawr College, 1987). See also William Mitchell, *Mishpokhe: A Study of New York City Jewish Family Clubs* (The Hague: Mouton, 1978).

29. A possible connection of *Tikvah Zion* in Johnstown with the Mizrachi is suggested by frequent visits at Rodef Sholom—especially during the period when the synagogue was being constructed and the *Tikvah Zion* society founded—of Rabbi Aaron Ashinsky, a leader of the Orthodox community in Pittsburgh and actively involved in the religious Zionist movement. One of my informants, however, whose family was very involved in Zionist activities in Johnstown from the beginning, thought that commitment to Zionism was originally transplanted there from Palestine, where one of her relative-pioneers had lived for some time and then regularly revisited from Johnstown (interview with Bella C., 8/4/1980).

30. Rodef Sholom minute book, 1904–1914, 1–327: applications of new members, donations and contributions, reports of the committee on the status of new arrivals to town.

31. On peddling as a common initial occupation of Jewish immigrants in small towns, nineteenth century Germans and turn-of-the-century East Europeans alike, see, e.g., Rudolph Glanz, "Notes on Early Jewish Peddling," *Jewish Social Studies* 7 (April 1945): 119–36; Marc Lee Raphael, *Jews and Judaism in a Midwestern Community: Columbus, Ohio, 1840–1975* (Columbus: Ohio Historical Society, 1979), chap. 9; Stephen Mostov, "A 'Jerusalem' on the Ohio: The Social and Economic History of Cincinnati's Jewish Community, 1840–1875" (Ph.D. diss., Brandeis University, 1981), chap. 4; Perlmann, "Beyond New York," 369–94; Smith, *Family Connections*, chap. 2; Eleanor Horwitz, "Old Bottles, Rags, Junk!" *Rhode Island Jewish Historical Notes* 7 (November 1976): 189–257.

32. Business panel, 7/15–16/1981; interviews with Maurice S., 8/16/1981; Samuel M., 8/21/1980; Isadore G., 8/7/1980; Isadore S., 8/16/1984; Robert K., 8/2/1982; Ben I., 7/30/1981.

33. Business panel, 7/16/1981; interviews with Sarah H., 6/29/1980; with Joseph P.—quoted from Winograd, *A History of Johnstown's Jews*, 307; Alfred K., 8/16/1984; Henry K., 8/16/1984; bankruptcy testimony of Samuel B., 1921, Federal Archives and Records Center, Philadelphia, bankruptcy files of the western district of Pennsylvania.

34. Transcript of bankruptcy hearing, testimony of Abraham F., 1909, Federal Archives and Records Center, Philadelphia; interviews with Bernie C., 7/10/1980; Robert K., 8/14/1984; Bill B., 8/12/1984; Isadore G., 8/17/1984; business panel, 7/15/1981.

35. Quotations from manuscript credit ledgers of the Dun and Bradstreet Company's notations on Jewish entrepreneurs in Cambria County, 1862–1891, vols. 33–34, Baker Library, Harvard University. On the nineteenth-century American business establishment's attitudes toward (German) Jewish entrepreneurs as reflected in D & B reports, see David Gerber, "Cutting Out Shylock: Elite Anti-Semitism and the Quest for Moral Order in the Mid-Nineteenth Century American Market Place," *Journal of American History* 69 (December 1982): 615–37, and idem, "Ethnics, Enterprise, and Middle-Class Formation: Using the Dun and Bradstreet Collection for Research in Ethnic History," *Immigration History Newsletter* 12 (May 1980): 1–7. See also Peter Decker, "Jewish Merchants in San Francisco: Social Mobility on the Urban Frontier," in *The Jews of the West: The Metropolitan Years*, ed. Moses Rischin (Waltham, MA: American Jewish Historical Society, 1979), 12–23; Stephen Mostov, "Dun and Bradstreet Reports as a Source of Jewish Economic History: Cincinnati, 1840–1875," *American Jewish History* 72 (March 1983): 333–53. It may be of interest to note that Mostov found a similar (to Johnstown's) low rate of coverage by D & B reports of German Jewish businesses in Cincinnati in the 1850s–1860s—the initial years of that group's settlement there (p. 337).

36. Interviews with Abe B., 6/2/1982, 8/2/1982. On kinwork or sustaining kinship bonds for instrumental and expressive purposes as a "female sphere" in immigrant communities, see Donna Gabaccia, *From the Other Side: Women, Gender, and Immigrant Life in the U.S. 1820–1990* (Bloomington: Indiana University Press, 1994), chap. 5, "All Her Kin," and bibliography.

37. Information on loans obtained from Judgement Dockets: Ejectment and Miscellaneous, Cambria County Courthouse, Ebensburg, Prothonotary's Office.

38. Mostov, "A 'Jerusalem' on the Ohio"; Decker, "Jewish Merchants in San Francisco"; Ashkenazi, *The Business of Jews in Louisiana*.

39. As in other immigrant communities, there was in Johnstown a considerable correlation between economic status and leadership in the Jewish community. Of the total of twenty-seven officers who served on the board of Rodef Sholom from 1904 through World War I, the proportion of homeowners (as of 1915) was a high 59 percent as compared with 27 percent in the entire Jewish population in the city (see the discussion below); the average value of the officers' homes was $5,112 as compared with $3,459 for the rank-and-file synagogue members (from Rodef Sholom Synagogue minute book, 1904–1925, 1915 tax assessments, Johnstown, Cambria County Courthouse, Ebensburg, Pennsylvania). On the relationship between economic status and institutional leadership in other Jewish communities, see, e.g., Steven Hertzberg, *Strangers within the Gate City: The Jews of Atlanta, 1845–1915* (Philadelphia: The Jewish Publication Society, 1978), chaps. 5 and 6; William Toll, "Mobility, Fraternalism and Jewish Cultural Change: Portland, Ore-

gon, 1910–1930," in Rischin, *Jews of the West*, 75–107; Smith, *Family Connections*, chap. 4. A similar correlation obtained also among Slavic and Hungarian East Europeans in Johnstown; see Ewa Morawska, *For Bread with Butter: Lifeworlds of the East Central Europeans in Johnstown, Pennsylvania, 1890–1940* (New York: Cambridge University Press, 1985), chap. 5.

40. Interviews with Louis F., 8/13/1980; William B., 8/15/1984; Isadore S., 6/8/1986; Ruth T., 8/14/1984.

41. Calculated from lists of creditors of these establishments as listed in the bankruptcy records (U.S. Bankruptcy Court, District Court for the Western District of Pennsylvania, Federal Archives and Records Center, Philadelphia). There was in Pittsburgh at the beginning of this century a Jewish-owned bank that, among other services, offered mercantile loans (Jacob Feldman, *The Jewish Experience in Western Pennsylvania: A History, 1755–1945* [Pittsburgh: The Historical Society of Western Pennsylvania, 1986], 173–74). Very likely some of the Johnstowners obtained funds from this bank, but I was unable to identify any such cases.

42. Information gathered from bankruptcy records, 1909–1915 (Federal Archives and Records Center, Philadelphia). To survive in business, some bankrupts turned to maneuvers of dubious legality, practiced, as noted with chagrin in contemporary D & B reports and confirmed in historical studies, by small-scale entrepreneurs of native-born American as well as ethnic backgrounds (cf. Clyde Griffen and Sally Griffen, "Small Business and Occupational Mobility in Mid-Nineteenth-Century Poughkeepsie," in *Small Business in American Life*, ed. Stuart Bruchey [New York: Columbia University Press, 1980], 114–15; Charles Warren, *Bankruptcy in the United States History* [Cambridge: Harvard University Press, 1935], chap. 3). These included transferring the existing assets of a bankrupt operation to another person, usually a family member (wife or adult son) to forestall their seizure by the creditors, or hiding the stock at someone else's place until after the sheriff's sale.

43. Interviews with Isadore S., 8/16/1982; Isadore G., 8/7/1980.

44. Extensive reliance on kin and informal social networks demonstrated in studies of small nonethnic shopkeepers has been reported, e.g., in Sally Griffen and Clyde Griffen, "Family and Business in a Small City: Poughkeepsie, New York, 1850–1880," in *Family and Kin in Urban Communities, 1700–1930*, ed. Tamara Hareven (New York: New Viewpoints, 1977), 144–63, or Michael Katz, "The Entrepreneurial Class in a Canadian City," *Journal of Social History* 8 (Winter 1974): 1–29; see also Howard Aldrich and Catherine Zimmer, "Entrepreneurship through Social Networks," in *The Art and Science of Entrepreneurship*, ed. Donald Sexton and Raymond Smilor (Cambridge, MA: Ballinger, 1986), 3–24.

45. Interviews with Isadore S., 8/16/1982; Bill B., 8/15/1982.

46. Interview with Millard C., 6/3/1984.

47. Interviews with Harry R., 8/2/1982; Abe B., 8/2/1984 (a similar recollection appears in the interview with Abe K., as quoted in Winograd, *A History of Johnstown's Jews*, 252).

48. Interview with Abe B., 6/2/1982; Nathan E., 6/2/1984.

49. For the first interpretation, see, e.g., John Modell, "Changing Risks, Changing Adaptations: American Families in the Nineteenth and Twentieth Centuries," in *Kin and Communities: Families in America*, ed. Allan Lichtman and Joan Chalinor (Washington, DC: Smithsonian Press, 1979), 119–44, or John Bodnar, *The Transplanted: A History of Immigrants in Urban America* (Bloomington:

Indiana University Press, 1985), esp. chaps. 2 and 6; for the "achievement" emphasis, see, e.g., my earlier study of Slavic and Hungarian working-class families in
Johnstown: Morawska, *For Bread with Butter*, esp. chap. 4.

50. Alfred Schutz, *Collected Papers*, vol. 1, *The Problem of Social Reality* (The
Hague: M. Nijhoff, 1962), 69–71.

51. Information about New York Jews' family economy and the employment
figures can be found in Glenn, *Daughters of the Shtetl*, 67–69, 72–80; see also Maxine Schwartz Seller, "Beyond the Stereotype: A New Look at the Immigrant
Woman, 1880–1924," *Journal of Ethnic Studies* 3 (Spring 1975): 59–71; Thomas
Kessner and Betty Boyd Caroli, "New Immigrant Women at Work: Italians and
Jews in New York City, 1880–1905," *Journal of Ethnic Studies* 5 (Winter 1978):
9–32. Autobiographical narratives of New York Jewish women on the themes of
work, wages, contributions to family budgets, during the same period, can be
found in Sydney Stahl Weinberg, *The World of Our Mothers: The Lives of Jewish
Immigrant Women* (Chapel Hill: University of North Carolina Press, 1988); Sydelle Kramer and Jenny Masur, eds., *Jewish Grandmothers* (Boston: Beacon Press,
1978); Maxine Schwartz Seller, *Immigrant Women* (Philadelphia: Temple University Press, 1981). On homework as a family economic strategy, see Eileen Boris and
Cynthia R. Daniels, eds., *Homework: Historical and Contemporary Perspectives on
Paid Labor at Home* (Urbana: University of Illinois Press, 1989). Among Jews it
was largely the Orthodox who continued homework as a "religious strategy" in
order to be able to work on the Sabbath.

52. Cf. Irene D. Neu, "The Jewish Businesswoman in America," *American Jewish Historical Quarterly* 66 (September 1976): 135–55; Charlotte Baum, Paula
Hyman, and Sonya Michel, *The Jewish Woman in America* (New York: The Dial
Press, 1976); Charlotte Baum, "What Made Yetta Work? The Economic Role of
East European Jewish Women in the Family," in *The Jewish Woman: New Perspectives*, ed. Liz Koltun (New York: Schocken Books, 1973), 32–40; Glenn, *Daughters of the Shtetl*, chaps. 1–3; also immigrant women's autobiographical narratives—
see n. 51 above.

53. Interview with Esther J., 8/10/1982.

54. The figure for Gentile East European children in Johnstown quoted from
Morawska, *For Bread with Butter*, 132. The proportion, about one-fourth, of Jewish children in Johnstown who did not complete elementary education did not differ from the general population of 6–14-year-olds in the city school in 1910; similar
proportions of dropouts among Russian Jewish children were reported for 1908 by
the U.S. Immigration Commission in Boston, New York, and Chicago (*Reports of
the Immigration Commission*, 61st Congress, 3d Session, Sen. Doc. 749: The Children of Immigrants in Schools, table 4 for each city). In combining school with
work, young Johnstown Jews did not differ from the national pattern for their ethnic group estimated from the 1910 manuscript census data. Information about
Jewish children combining school with work appears in Jerry Jacobs and Margaret
Greene, "Race, Ethnicity, Social Class, and Schooling," in *After Ellis Island: Newcomers and Natives in the 1910 Census*, ed. Susan Cotts Watkins (New York: Russell
Sage, 1994), 209–56. Jacobs and Greene found 13 percent of the Jewish boys and
7 percent of the girls in the age group 14–18 reported as working and attending
school at the same time.

55. The proportion of Russian Jewish schoolchildren reported by the Immigration Commission as retarded, i.e., two or more years older than the normal age for

his/her grade starting at the age of six, has been quoted from David Tyack, *The One Best System: A History of American Urban Education* (Cambridge: Harvard University Press, 1974), 242–43. The Providence data are from Smith, *Family Connections*, 59.

56. Business panel, 7/15/1981; women's panel, 7/22/1981; individual interviews. The practice of giving the parents—the mother was the direct recipient—either the entire or a significant part of the wage or salary was also common among working children of non-Jewish immigrants, in Johnstown and elsewhere; as documented in written and oral histories and autobiographical narratives, it was common among contemporary young Jews in large cities as well.

57. Weinberg in *The World of Our Mothers* (chap. 7), and Glenn in *Daughters of the Shtetl* (chap. 2) draw very convincing pictures of this newly gained assertiveness of the young women.

58. Jews in Johnstown: calculations on the basis of information provided in the manuscript schedules of the 1900 and 1910 censuses, traced in the 1915 city directory. The figure for Slavs: Morawska, *For Bread with Butter*, 399. The data on Boston Jews in Thernstrom, *The Other Bostonians*, 164–65; on Jews in New York, from Kessner, *The Golden Door*, 143, 152–53. In Providence, Rhode Island, however, the persistence rate among Russian Jewish immigrants during the same time was apparently similar to that of the Johnstown Jews, 61 percent (see Alice Goldstein, "Mobility of Natives and Jews in Providence, Rhode Island, 1900–1920," *Rhode Island Jewish History Notes* 8 [November 1971]: 84).

59. Data on Jewish merchants from Johnstown city directories and business guides, 1890/1900–1918/1919; bankruptcy records, Johnstown (Federal Archives and Records Center, Philadelphia). Figures on business withdrawals among non-Jewish merchants calculated from 1900 and 1910 Johnstown business guides (I calculated the average for apparel, shoes, general merchandise, jewelry, grocery, and tailor shops—the lines of trade in which Jewish merchants were concentrated). Figures on non-Jewish East European businesses from Morawska, *For Bread with Butter*, 151–54, 405. On the chronic precariousness of small businesses in North American cities in the nineteenth and early twentieth centuries, and on the common occurrence of shifting between manual (factory) labor and small entrepreneurial ventures, see Griffen and Griffen, "Small Business and Occupational Mobility," 123–211; Michael Katz, *The People of Hamilton, Canada West: Family and Class in a Mid-Nineteenth-Century City* (Cambridge: Harvard University Press, 1975); Melanie Archer, "Self-Employment and Occupational Structure in an Industrializing City: Detroit, 1880," *Social Forces* 69 (March 1991): 785–810.

60. Interviews with Bella C., 8/4/1980; Meyer B., 8/7/1984. This kind of evaluative comparison can be found in many an immigrant memoir, not only Jewish. Slavic immigrants, for instance, used similar criteria of kitchen and sanitary facilities, and the amount and quality of food, in assessing their improved living standards in America. See, e.g., a collection of letters written by Polish and Jewish immigrants from America to their families and friends in Eastern Europe, edited by Witold Kula, Nina Assorodobraj-Kula, and Marcin Kula, *Writing Home: Immigrants in Brazil and the United States, 1890–1891*, trans. Josephine Wtulich (New York: Columbia University Press, 1986).

61. Interview with Isadore S. 7/23/1981.

62. Data for Jews come from tax assessments of property and mortgage books,

Johnstown, 1915, at Cambria County Courthouse, Ebensburg, Pennsylvania. The figure for the city of Johnstown, and this and following data on Gentile East Europeans in Johnstown, are from Morawska, *For Bread with Butter*, 89, 147–49.

63. All this information comes from the minutes of the Rodef Sholom Congregation's monthly minutes, 1904–1916/17.

CHAPTER 3
INSECURE PROSPERITY

1. Data on the doubling of the American white-collar sector between 1910 and 1930 are from President's Research Committee on Social Trends, *Recent Social Trends in the United States* (New York: McGraw-Hill, 1933), 281–82; similar data for the five largest U.S. cities in the same period in Thomas Lyson, "Industrial Shifts, Occupational Recomposition, and the Changing Sexual Division of Labor in the Five Largest U.S. Cities: 1910–1930," *Sociological Forum* 6 (March 1991): 160. An interpretation of the middle class's increased educational aspirations during the interwar period as a new American religion—a common metaphor at that time—was offered in 1936 by the law educator Roscoe Pound: "In its hold upon popular faith and popular imagination, organized higher learning has the place in American society today which organized religion had in the society of the Middle Ages"—as cited in David Levine, *The American College and the Culture of Aspiration, 1915–1940* (Ithaca, NY: Cornell University Press, 1986), 87; quotation about education as the most promising route to social advancement also from Levine, ibid., 87. See also Burton Bledstein, *The Culture of Professionalism: The Middle-Class and the Development of Higher Education* (New York: Norton, 1976); and Christopher Jenks and David Riesman, *The Academic Revolution* (Chicago: University of Chicago Press, 1968).

2. For the interpretation of the interwar decades as the "watershed" in restructuring American Jewish society, see, e.g., C. Bezalel Sherman, *The Jews within American Society* (Detroit: Wayne State University Press, 1965), chaps. 5, 9; Deborah Dash Moore, *At Home in America: Second Generation New York Jews* (New York: Columbia University Press, 1981); Nathan Goldberg, "Occupational Patterns of American Jews," *Jewish Review* 3 (January 1946): 262–90; Nathan Glazer, "The American Jew and the Attainment of Middle-Class Rank: Some Trends and Explanations," in *The Jews: Social Patterns of an American Group*, ed. Marshall Sklare (New York: The Free Press, 1958). Occupational figures compiled from Jacob Lestschinsky, "Economic and Social Development of American Jewry," in *The Jewish Past and Present* (New York: Jewish Encyclopedic Handbook, 1955), 4:82–91; Nathan Goldberg, "Occupational Patterns of American Jews," *Jewish Review* 3 (April 1945): 3–24, and 4 (January 1946): 262–90, and idem, "Economic Trends among American Jews," *Jewish Affairs*, October 1, 1946, 3–19. Jewish college attendance in New York estimated from data in Ira Rosenwaike, *Population History of New York City* (Syracuse, NY: Syracuse University Press, 1972), 123–29, table B3; *American Jewish Year Book* 39 (1937/38): 72; Lee Levinger, *The Jewish Student in America* (Cincinnati, OH: B'nai B'rith, 1937), 91–94, tables 25–26; and personal communications from Selma Berroll and Deborah Dash Moore. Quotations are from Henry Feingold, "Investing in Themselves: The Harvard Case and the Origins of the Third American-Jewish Commercial Elite," *American Jewish History* 77 (June 1988): 530, 537. On the dominant society's response to this

"passion for learning" in the form of discrimination in college and university admissions, see Marcia Synnot, "Anti-Semitism and American Universities: Did Quotas Follow the Jews?" in *Anti-Semitism in American History*, ed. David Gerber (Urbana: University of Illinois Press, 1986), 241–42; Levine, *The American College*, chap. 7, "Discrimination in College Admissions."

3. Feingold, "Investing in Themselves," 543.

4. Calculated from U.S. Bureau of the Census, *Twelfth Census of the United States: 1900*, Abstract of the Twelfth Census of the United States (Washington, DC: Government Printing Office, 1901), 101; ibid., Population, pt. 1, 334–35; U.S. Bureau of the Census, *Thirteenth Census of the United States: 1910*, Population, vol. 3 (Washington, DC: Government Printing Office, 1914), 567–69; ibid., *Abstract of the Thirteenth Census of the United States with Supplement for Pennsylvania*, 579–80; U.S. Bureau of the Census, *Fourteenth Census of the United States: 1920*, vol. 1, Population, Number and Distribution of Inhabitants (Washington, DC: Government Printing Office, 1923), 285–91; ibid., vol. 3, Population, Characteristics by States, 893–94; U.S. Bureau of the Census, *Fifteenth Census of the United States: 1930*, Population, vol. 3, Report by States, pt. 2 (Washington, DC: Government Printing Office, 1933), 670, 722–23; U.S. Bureau of the Census, *Sixteenth Census of the United States: 1940*, Population, vol. 1, Number of Inhabitants (Washington, DC: Government Printing Office, 1943), 915; ibid., vol. 2, Characteristics of the Population, 66, 197–98.

5. Data compiled from *Fourteenth Census of the United States: 1920*, vol. 4, Population. Occupations, 276–80; *Fifteenth Census of the United States: 1930*, vol. 4, Population, Occupations by States, 1395–97; *Sixteenth Census of the United States: 1940*, Population, vol. 2, Characteristics of the Population, pt. 6, 189, 287.

6. Information compiled from *Fourteenth Census of the United States: 1920*, Occupations, 276–81; ibid., *Abstract of the Fourteenth Census of the United States: 1920*, 261; *Fifteenth Census of the United States: 1930*, Population, vol. 4, Occupations by States, 1395–97; Commonwealth of Pennsylvania, Department of Labor and Industry, *Employment Fluctuations in Pennsylvania, 1921–27*, Special Bulletin, no. 24 (Harrisburg, PA: Pennsylvania Bureau of Industrial Statistics, 1928), 185; William Hogan, *Economic History of the Iron and Steel Industry in the United States* (Lexington, MA: Heath, 1973), vol. 2, pt. 3, 899–900; *Johnstown Tribune*, September 20, 1922, 18; October 26, 1922, 3; April 7, 1926, 27; July 1, 1926, 11; July 24, 1926, 1; May–July 1927; Commonwealth of Pennsylvania, Department of Labor and Industry, "Review of Industrial Statistics" (monthly prepared by the Department's Bureau of Statistics), a sample from the period 1924–1934; Commonwealth of Pennsylvania, Department of Labor and Industry, *How Many Are Jobless in Pennsylvania: An Estimate of the Number of Unemployed and an Analysis of Industrial Employment and Wage Payments in Pennsylvania*, Special Bulletin, no. 33 (Harrisburg, PA: Pennsylvania Bureau of Industrial Statistics, 1931), 7, 13; Pennsylvania State Emergency Relief Board, Social Surveys Section, "Unemployment in Cambria County," *Bulletin 50-A*, April 1934, MS, National Archives, Industrial-Social Branch, RG-207, 1, 9–10; *Seventh Industrial Directory of the Commonwealth of Pennsylvania* (1931), 158–59; U.S. Department of Labor, Division of Research and Statistics, "HOLC Survey File: Johnstown, Pennsylvania," 1937, MS, National Archives, Industrial-Social Branch, RG-207, 4.

7. Data compiled from *Twelfth Census of the United States: 1900*, Special Reports: Occupations, 448–50; *Fourteenth Census of the United States: 1920*, Popula-

tion, vol. 4, Occupations, 276–82; *Sixteenth Census of the United States: 1940*, Population, vol. 2, Characteristics of the Population, pt. 6, 57–64, 215–22, 261–63; *Comparative Statistics for the United States, 1870 to 1940*, 185, and *The Labor Force*, vol. 3, pt. 4, 460–61, pt. 5, 94–97; H. Dewey Anderson and P. Davidson, *Occupational Trends in the United States* (Stanford: Stanford University Press, 1940), 16–17.

8. Bruce Williams and Michael Yates, *Upward Struggle: A Bicentennial Tribute to Labor in Cambria and Somerset Counties* (Harrisburg, PA: AFL-CIO, 1976); David Brody, *Steel Workers in America: The Non-Union Era* (Cambridge: Harvard University Press, 1960), 233–36; Donald Sofchalk, "Steel Workers of America, United (U.S.W.A.)," in *Labor Unions*, ed. Gary Fink, 2d ed. (Westport, CT: Greenwood Press, 1971), 357–59.

9. A small community of African Americans in Johnstown, which had numbered a few hundred people before World War I, was joined by over 1,000 more, most of them imported by the Cambria Company during the steel strike of 1919. During the 1920s and 1930s, the number of African Americans in Johnstown fluctuated between 1,600 and 1,700, or 2.5 percent of the city's population. In 1919 the company also brought in a small group of Mexican workers from Chicago. Data compiled from *Fourteenth Census of the United States: 1920*, Population, 2:954–57, and 3:866–76; ibid., State Compendium for Pennsylvania, 74–75; *Fifteenth Census of the United States: 1930*, Population, vol. 3, pt. 2, Report by States, 798; ibid., Population, Special Report on Foreign-Born Families by Country of Birth of Head, 151; *Sixteenth Census of the United States: 1940*, Population, vol. 2: Characteristics of the Population, pt. 6, 68, 253–56.

10. Intermarriage estimate based on the inspection of interwar marriage records in Johnstown's Christian parishes (see Ewa Morawska, *For Bread with Butter: Life-worlds of the East Central Europeans in Johnstown, Pennsylvania, 1890–1940* [New York: Cambridge University Press, 1985], chap. 5, "Johnstown and the Immigrant Communities between the Wars"); on the intermarriage of Jews, see chap. 5 in this volume.

11. Data on the number of Jews, their residential persistence, and family relatedness have been estimated from the enumeration of households in tax assessment records, 1925, 1940 (Cambria County Courthouse, Ebensburg, Pennsylvania); Johnstown city directories, 1920, 1925, 1930, 1935, 1940/41; Johnstown Street Guide, 1940; *Rodef Sholom Bulletin*, September–October 1935; ledgers of the Israel Isaiah Beneficial Society, 2 vols., 1918–1939/40; Rodef Sholom Talmud Torah minutes, 6/8/1928; Beth Zion Temple membership lists, 1940–1943; and local interviews. *American Jewish Year Books* consistently underestimated, by about one-fifth, the number of Jews in Johnstown during the 1920s and 1930s; see "Jewish Population of the United States," *American Jewish Year Book* 30 (1928/29): 192–93; 32 (1930/31): 223; Harry Linfeld, "Statistics of the Jews," *American Jewish Year Book* 33 (1931/32): 279.

12. A similar concentration in secondary areas of settlement occurred also during the interwar period among other immigrant groups in Johnstown: Slavs, Hungarians, and Italians (see Morawska, *For Bread with Butter*, chap. 3). While Johnstown conditions could have been particularly conducive to such enduring residential clustering, as numerous studies indicate, in other, larger and very big (New York) cities, ethnic groups, Jewish ones included, also tended to relocate in this pattern.

13. Percentages calculated from tax assessments and Johnstown city directories, 1937–1940.

14. Merchants' offspring's ($N = 64$) occupational careers were traced through Johnstown city directories and business guides from 1910 through 1937 every five years, and, whenever possible, checked in the interviews.

15. See, e.g., Louis Allen, "Factors Affecting the Profitability of Small Firms," in *The Vital Majority: Small Business in the American Economy,* ed. Deane Carson, ed., (Washington, DC: Government Printing Office, 1973), 244–48, 250–51.

16. In addition, a couple of Jewish-owned clothing and jewelry wholesale establishments were in business during the interwar period, but they did not survive more than a few years.

17. On the concentration of Jewish businesses in a few lines of trade during the interwar period, see Lestschinsky, "Economic and Social Development of American Jewry," 86–87, 90, 93; Ben Seligman, "Some Aspects of Jewish Demography," in Sklare, *The Jews,* 76–79; Maurice Taylor, *The Jewish Community of Pittsburgh* (Pittsburgh: Federation of Jewish Philanthropies, 1941), 117, 122; Henry Meyer, "The Structure of the Jewish Community in the City of Detroit" (Ph.D. diss., University of Michigan, 1939), 194–95, 313; Samuel Koenig, "The Socioeconomic Structure of an American Jewish Community," in *Jews in a Gentile World,* ed. Isacque Graeber (New York: Macmillan, 1942), 200–242. Data on the proportion of Jewish doctors, lawyers, and dentists in these entire professional groups in New York and Cleveland are from Arthur Goren, "The Jews," *Harvard Encyclopedia of American Ethnic Groups* (Cambridge: Harvard University Press, Belknap Press, 1980), 589; Lestschinsky, "Economic and Social Development of American Jewry," 94.

18. On the basis of information in Johnstown city directories and business guides, 1933, 1937, and 1940; Morawska, *For Bread with Butter,* 97.

19. Business panel, 7/16/1981; interviews with Helma W., 4/5/1980; Naomi S., 8/20/1984; Abe B., 5/24/1981; Nathan E., 8/17/1984; Martin G., 8/10/1984; Olga S., 8/14/1984; Ben I., 7/30/1981; Henry K., 8/15/1984; Yale L., 8/7/1984; Isadore G., 4/5/1980, 8/7/1980.

20. *Chranitel* (Johnstown), "Svoj ko Svojem," November 1, 1920, 5–7.

21. Percentages calculated from data provided in the manuscript schedules of the business census conducted in 1929 by the U.S. Department of Commerce, Bureau of the Census, and located at the National Archives, Suitland Branch: Pennsylvania: box 1381 (retail trade), file 23/71–74, and box 661 (wholesale trade), file 16817. Similar figures were reported for "Jewish" lines of business in the 1933 census of retail trade in Johnstown (U.S. Bureau of the Census, *Census of American Business: 1933,* Retail Distribution, vol. 5 [Washington, DC: Government Printing Office, 1935], 39).

22. Interviews with Meyer B., 8/24/1980; Samuel K., 7/29/1981; Morton M., 8/22/1980; Seymour S., 8/9/1984; Maurice S., 8/16/1981; Louis F., 7/23/1981.

23. Interviews with Gene E., 8/9/1984; Alberta H., 8/6/1981; Isadore G., 8/7/1980, and his letter to this author dated 4/25/1987; Glosser Brothers' department store, payroll records, 1928–1941.

24. From local synagogal and organizational sources (presently at Beth Sholom Temple, in a collection of the local Jewish Historical Archives); and Leonard Winograd, *"The Horse Died at Windber": A History of Johnstown's Jews of Penn-*

sylvania (Bristol, IN: Wyndham Hall Press, 1988), 156–57, 180–87, 200–202, 205–36.

25. Interview with Betty W. and Helen P., 5/10/1986.

26. Local interviews; Glosser Brothers' department store—payroll records, 1930–1941.

27. Payroll data for Jewish-owned department stores, from Gee Bee payroll records, 1930–1941; Lawrence Glosser, "After the Horse Died: An Historical and Sociological Study of the Glosser Family of Johnstown, Pennsylvania" (M.A. thesis, Hebrew Union College, Los Angeles, 1977), 77–9, 180–82; interviews with Mr. Martin Schwartz, 8/14–20/1980; current information in the *Johnstown Tribune*; and employment figures reported by individual businesses, manuscript schedules of the 1929 business census.

Getting jobs through ethnic networks was also, as indicated in studies, common during the interwar period in the big cities. But from New York, for example, contemporary reports appear contradictory (which does not mean, of course, that the opposing trends did not occur at the same time): while a 1935 survey of young people 16–24 years old (a sample of 9,000 contained 2,800 Jews) found 60 percent of them to have obtained their last job through friends or relatives, a study published a few years later reported that many Jewish firms preferred to (and did) hire Christian employees. See Nettie P. McGill and Ellen Matthews, *The Youth of New York City* (New York: Macmillan, 1940), 132; also Moore, *At Home in America*, 13; on pro-Christian preferences of Jewish employers, Heywood Broun and George Britt, *Christians Only: A Study in Prejudice* (New York: Da Capo Press, 1974), 296–99. A relevant point for this study is that in Johnstown it would have been unthinkable for a Jewish employer to refuse to hire a Jewish person in need of a job.

28. The Recorder of Wills, Cambria County Courthouse, Ebensburg, Pennsylvania, doc. no. 22182.

29. Israel Isaiah Beneficial Society, minute books, 1923–1929; interview with Irving L., 10/31/1980.

30. Business panels, 7/15–16/1981; social life panel, 7/21/1981; interviews with Isadore G., 8/7/1980; Abe B., 24/5/1981; Bill B., 8/15/1984; bankruptcy hearing of Isaac R., 1924 (Federal Archives and Records Center, Philadelphia).

31. Interviews with Bill B., 8/15/1984; Abe B., 5/2/1986.

32. Interviews with Bill B., 8/15/1984; Isadore S., 8/16/1984; Henry K., 8/15/1984; Morris T., 8/9/1984; Millard C., 8/13/1984; Nathan E., 8/17/1984.

33. Bankruptcy hearings of Morris R., 1920; Israel L., 1929; Samuel E., 1931 (Federal Archives and Records Center, Philadelphia); interviews with Nathan E., 8/17/1984; Lester E., 6/11/1982; Irving L., 5/12/1982; Seymour S., 8/11/1984.

34. As quoted in Virginia Yans McLaughlin, "Metaphors of Self in History: Subjectivity, Oral Narrative, and Immigration Studies," in *Immigration Reconsidered: History, Sociology, and Politics*, ed. Virginia Yans-McLaughlin (New York: Oxford University Press, 1990), 280.

35. Interviews with Rita B., 8/16/1984; Frieda C., 8/28/80.

36. Women's panel, 7/22/1981; interview with Bella C., 7/4/1986.

37. Interviews with Esther J., 8/10/1984; Martin G., 5/4/1986; Israel and Rita T., 8/16/1984; Elmer M., 6/11/1984; Raphael R., 6/2/1984; Ida T.,

4/4/1980; Naomi S., 8/20/1984; Glosser, "An Historical and Sociological Study of the Glosser Family," 54–55. Sydney Weinberg reported similar recollections of her New York female interviewees about maintaining the "language" and "posturing" of women's subordination, even when the important decisions were actually in the hands of the women (*The World of Our Mothers: The Lives of Immigrant Jewish Women* [Chapel Hill: University of North Carolina Press, 1988], passim).

38. Women's panel, 7/22/1981; local interviews.

39. Interview with Fanny B., 8/1/1986; local interviews.

40. Regrettably, I did not separate, while gathering these data from local sources, married from unmarried coresidents—information that a couple of my colleagues who read drafts of this chapter would have liked to know. The interviews suggest that such temporary cohabitation was, if not typical, not uncommon. The average age of marriage in the American-born generation was 25 for men and 22 for women in the 1920s, and in the 1930s, evidently owing to the Depression, 28 and 24, respectively; most unmarried young adults lived in their parents' homes. I estimated these figures from records, inspected at the Cambria County Courthouse in Ebensburg, Pennsylvania, of marriages concluded in Johnstown and vicinity during the 1920s and 1930s by American-born Jews.

41. Interviews with Henry K., 8/16/1984; Lester E., 8/8/1984; Isadore S., 7/23/1981; Millard C., 8/13/1984; business panels, 7/15–16/1981.

42. Andrew Heinze, *Adapting to Abundance: Jewish Immigrants, Mass Consumption, and the Search for American Identity* (New York: Columbia University Press, 1990), 3, 8. See also Susan Braunstein and Jenna Weissman Joselit, eds., *Getting Comfortable in New York: The American Jewish Home, 1880–1950* (New York: The Jewish Museum, 1990).

43. The quotation is from Otis Pease, *The Responsibilities of American Advertising* (New Haven: Yale University Press, 1958), 40–41. See also Robert Lynd, "The People as Consumers," in *Recent Social Trends, II*, ed. William Fielding Ogburn (Chicago: University of Chicago Press, 1958), chap. 17; Elaine Tyler May, *Great Expectations* (Chicago: University of Chicago Press, 1980), chap. 8.

44. Broun and Britt, *Christians Only*, 49; Heinze, *Adapting to Abundance*, 121, 130–45.

45. New York estimates, from Moore, *At Home in America*, 66; Johnstown figures are based on local data from the 1929 business census. Calculation of the average income in the best neighborhood (Westmont) excludes young second-generation recently established households, in which the (male) breadwinners were employed in lower-level sales/clerical jobs; including these would have increased the discrepancy even further.

46. Interviews with Arthur T., 4/4/1980; Isadore S., 7/23/1981, and others.

47. Local data calculated from manuscript schedules of the 1929 business census. National data are from Anderson and Davidson, *Occupational Trends in the United States*, 452. In comparison, 38 percent of a sample of (general population) retail stores in Buffalo—I was unable to find any other studies of this kind for the comparable time period—surveyed between 1918 and 1928, reported annual net sales of less than $10,000 (in Edmund D. McGarry, *Retail Trade Mortality in Buffalo* [Buffalo, NY: The University of Buffalo, Bureau of Business and Social Research, 3, 1929], 65).

48. Excluding reported stock at hand, I estimated for each case the amount of money needed to purchase merchandise at cost so as to make the same net sales as

in 1929. The information about customary markups for particular lines of merchandise carried by Jewish storekeepers in Johnstown and vicinity during the interwar period has been provided by my local informants. National statistic is from Joseph Philips, *Little Business in the American Economy* (Urbana: University of Illinois Press, 1958), 51.

49. Morawska, *For Bread with Butter*, 211–13.

50. Calculations based on the information in manuscript schedules of the 1929 business census—Johnstown; Glosser Brothers' department store—payroll records, newspaper clippings; local interviews.

51. Royal Mecker, "What Is the American Standard of Living?" *Monthly Labor Review* 9 (July 1919): 1–13; Marian D. Savage, "Family Budgets and Living Conditions," Bureau of Industrial Commission of Inquiry, Interchurch World Movement Research (New York, 1920), 4–5; Faith M. Williams, "Changes in Family Expenditures in the Post War Period," *Monthly Labor Review* 47 (November 1938): 967–79; "Family Expenditures for Housefurnishings" (editorial), ibid., 49 (June 1940): 1352–55; Winifred D. Wandersee Bolin, "The Economics of Middle-Income Family Life: Working Women during the Great Depression," *Journal of American History* 65 (June 1978): 64–66.

52. Data on the costs of living are calculated from "Changes in the Cost of Living in the United States" (editorial), *Monthly Labor Review* 31 (August 1930): 516–31; "Standard of Living of Professional Man's Family in 1816/17 and Compared with 1926/27" (editorial), ibid., 29 (December 1929): 222–28; Ada Beney, *The Cost of Living in the United States, 1914–1936* (New York: National Industrial Conference Board, 1936), 47–51, 57–59, 62–65, 74–77, 80–81; idem, *Differentials in Industrial Wages and Hours in the United States* (New York: National Industrial Conference Board, 1938), 2, 13, 37–38, 178–80, 202–3; idem, "The Cost of Living in Fifty-Nine Communities," *National Industrial Conference Board Bulletin* 11 (July 1931): 85–99; and idem, "Local Variations in the Cost of Living," *National Industrial Conference Board Bulletin* 11 (December 1935): 89–95; *The Cost of Living among Wage-Earners* (New York: National Industrial Conference Board, 1924), Research Reports nos. 22, 24; *The Cost of Living in New York City, 1926* (New York: National Industrial Conference Board, 1928), 34, 43, 48–49, 72, 75–76, 87, 100.

53. Interviews with Nathan E., 3/19/1981; Isadore G., 8/8/1984; Herman E., 8/9/1984 (I also had an opportunity to inspect a notebook from the 1930s with weekly sales and business expenditures of Herman's late father, a truck vendor); Sidney O., 8/7/1981; Jack S., 9/29/1981; Moe S., 8/5/1981 and 8/9/1984 (in this case, too, I also looked at his father's business ledger); Henry K., 8/15/1984; Harry R., 8/15/1984; Meyer B., 8/7/1984; Rabbi Ralph Simon, 9/11/1986.

54. Calculated from contemporary studies of operating expenses in retail stores in specialties in which Johnstown Jews concentrated: *Operating Expenses in Retail Jewelry Stores in 1920*, Harvard Bureau of Business Research, 27 (1921); *Operating Expenses in Retail Shoe Stores in 1920*, ibid., 28 (1921); *Operating Expenses in Retail Grocery Stores in 1924*, ibid., 52 (1925), *Operating Expenses in Retail Jewelry Stores in 1924*, ibid., 53 (1925). A similar figure, 27 percent of the average total overhead, was reported for the "going firms" in a study of retail stores in Chicago in the early 1930s: John C. Cover, "Business and Personal Failure and Readjustment in Chicago," *Journal of Business of the University of Chicago* 7 (July 1933),

pt. 2, 45; on the reduction of overhead costs as common practice in small businesses, see Philips, *Little Business in the American Economy*, 50–68.

55. Calculated from the manuscript schedules of the 1929 business census—Johnstown; personal business records of Isadore K., 1938–1942.

56. Average proportion of rentals below $300 annually, and data for individual businesses cited were calculated from the manuscript schedules of the 1929 business census (Johnstown and vicinity), checked against deeds recorded in Grantee and Grantor Books at Cambria County Courthouse, Ebensburg, Pennsylvania. For comparison, a study of small retail businesses in Poughkeepsie, New York, conducted in 1923–1926, showed 59 percent of such stores located in homes of the owners (quoted after Philips, *Little Business in the American Economy*, 64); in Buffalo, a survey of small retail businesses during the period 1918–1926 showed such arrangements in half the cases (McGarry, *Retail Trade Mortality in Buffalo*, 72).

57. Bankruptcy hearings of Morris L. (1928), Max S. (1922)—Federal Archives and Records Center, Philadelphia (Dun and Bradstreet Company's local credit assessors evaluated the net worth of each merchant's business at less than $1,000 in these respective years); interviews with Morris T., 8/9/1984; Hyman R., 8/2/1986.

58. National figures from Anderson and Davidson, *Occupational Trends in the United States*, 460. However, I have been told by New Yorkers who held paid jobs in that city during the interwar period that there, too, salaries paid to the employees of ethnic (Jewish) enterprises were lower than those received for the same kind of work in mainstream establishments (personal communications).

59. Calculated from the manuscript schedules of the 1929 business census (Johnstown), with each case traced in the 1929 Johnstown city directory for recorded employment; local interviews.

60. Information based on the report of Abe M. as recorded in the 1929 business census, and interviews with his three children, 8/10/1981; business panel, 7/16/1981.

61. Interview with Herman E., 8/9/1984.

62. Quotations from conversations with Millard C. and Isadore S.; similar recollections also from Isadore G., Ray R., Abe B., Harold N., Gilbert G.—all these interviews were conducted on 10/19–20/1984.

63. It did not make sense to ask my informants, who were trying to recollect things from times long since past, about the "gender distribution" of decision-making authority regarding item-by-item details of household management, as is done in present-day studies on this subject (see, e.g., Nelson Foote, ed., *Household Decision-Making* [New York: New York University Press, 1984]). Instead, I asked generally about categories of expenditures, replicating contemporary surveys of the American standard of living.

64. According to my estimates, the mean number of children born to the (East European) immigrant women in Johnstown in the early 1930s was 4.4 (and in smaller towns in the area 4.9). It was significantly lower than the mean for their mothers in Eastern Europe, 6.2, but still considerably higher than figures reported in contemporary studies of both large and small American cities: e.g., 3.4 in Buffalo, 3.3 in New London, Connecticut, 2.4 in Passaic, New Jersey, and 2.0 in Trenton, New Jersey—after Sophia Robison, ed., "Jewish Population Studies," *Jewish Social Studies*, Publication no. 3 (New York: Conference on Jewish Relations, 1943), 19, 29, 45, 63–65. I do not have a satisfactory explanation as to why there

seems to have been such a big difference in the number of children in immigrant families between Johnstown and even smaller towns, such as New London. Two possible contributing factors come to mind. The first pertains to class: small shop-keepers generally tend to have larger families (and close to one-fifth of New London's Jews were industrial workers). The second has to do with varying sociocul-tural contexts, in this case, the fact that all smaller cities mentioned above are located near metropolitan centers (New York), and therefore were more open to modernization, including fertility behavior, especially since, as other data reported in the same studies indicate, a considerable proportion of residents in these places were relatively new residents—presumably from big metropolitan centers such as New York—and brought with them new cultural ways. In comparison, Johnstown was relatively isolated, and its Jewish residents residentially stable and socially "inward."

65. Local interviews with American-born women.

66. Interviews with Moe S., 8/12/1984; Blanche B., 6/18/1989. I intended to include here a comparison with the decision-making authority in household management of women (wives) in upwardly mobile families in the large cities who withdrew from gainful employment and became full-time housewives. There ap-pears, however, to be no consensus in different studies of this matter. Some inter-pretations argue that with the separation of home and work and the retreat of mar-ried women into the house, the key to their power became the management of the household, and that, in fact, they gained a decisive control over it. A different claim has been that even though wives did manage household economies, they actually remained "silent partners" of their husbands, either acquiescing to them in more important decisions or at any rate upholding an image—not only in public, but also in the personal interactions of the couple—of man as the supreme man-ager and supervisor. This latter thesis (image maintenance), by the way, is not nec-essarily irreconcilable with the interpretation ascribing the decisive authority to wives.

67. As the interviews quoted by Sydney Weinberg and her own interpretation thereof suggest, conflicts about the "Americanization" of lifestyles between Jewish immigrant mothers and their American-born daughters in New York were not un-common, but they did not seem to be particularly disruptive for their relations. See Weinberg, *World of Our Mothers*, chap. 7, and idem, "Jewish Mothers and Immi-grant Daughters: Positive and Negative Role Models," *Journal of American Ethnic History* 6 (Spring 1987): 45 and passim.

68. Local interviews; women's panel, 7/22/1981.

69. Local interviews with immigrant women and their American-born children.

70. University of Pittsburgh Bulletins: School of Law, School of Medicine, 1920s–1930s (Archives of the Industrial Society, Hillman Library, University of Pittsburgh); interviews with Samuel B., 6/26/1986; Maurice S., 8/13/1980; Louis F., 5/3/1986; Meyer B., 2/24/1986.

71. The estimate of annual mortgage payments has been calculated from "Home Ownership and the Family Budget," *Monthly Labor Review* 28 (May 1929): 243–49.

72. Benjamin K.'s bankruptcy hearing record, 1933 (Federal Archives and Rec-ords Center, Philadelphia), deed book 401:260 (Cambria County Courthouse, Ebensburg, Pennsylvania); interviews with Samuel P., Ruth S., and Molly W., 8/10/1984.

73. Calculated from manuscript schedules of the 1929 business census (Johnstown) checked against local city directory of the same year for recorded employment of children of immigrant store owners.

74. Data on merchant-homeowners from the lowest sales groups are from the manuscript schedules of the 1929 business census compared with local tax assessments of Jewish persons for that year. The figure for Slavs and Hungarians from Morawska, *For Bread with Butter*, 206.

75. Prices of homes purchased by Jewish families in different Johnstown neighborhoods between 1922–1926 and 1938–1941, from deed books, Cambria County Courthouse, Ebensburg, Pennsylvania. General data for Johnstown from *Sixteenth Census of the United States: 1940*, Housing (Pennsylvania), vol. 4, 89. Information about house purchases by Chicago Jews, from Foreign Language Press Survey, *Daily Jewish Courier*, Immigration History Research Center, St. Paul, Minnesota. Lieberson and Waters have reported, however, quoting from the 1930 housing census, the figure of $7,546 as the average value of homes owned by Russian-born (presumably Jewish) immigrants in that year (Stanley Lieberson and Mary Waters, *From Many Strands: Ethnic and Racial Groups in Contemporary America* [New York: Russell Sage, 1990], 141).

76. I traced the mortgage records of those who did not complete their payments by 1940 beyond that year. Data on real estate transactions of Johnstown Jews, and mortgage loans and payments they took and made, are calculated from deed books, 1920–1940, and mortgage books, 1920–1960, Cambria County Courthouse, Ebensburg, Pennsylvania. The information about New York Jewish builders' constituting 40 percent of the total number in this city is from Moore, *At Home in America*, 43–50.

77. On the chronic precariousness of small businesses in the United States and elsewhere in the world, see, e.g., Frank Knight, *Risk, Uncertainty, and Profit* (Boston: Houghton Mifflin, 1964); Stuart Bruchey, ed., *Small Business in American Life* (New York: Columbia University Press, 1980).

78. Interview with Henry K., 8/16/1984; sales figures from the manuscript schedules of bankruptcy hearings of Samuel I., 1930; Samuel Z., 1923; Abraham S., 1924, and Moses L., 1928 (U.S. Bankruptcy Court, Western District of Pennsylvania, Pittsburgh, and Federal Archives and Records Center, Philadelphia). The majority of my informants acknowledged these fluctuations in their own or their parents' businesses before World War II.

79. Calculated from *Census of American Business: 1933*, Retail Distribution, 3:46, 91, 146–55; U.S. Bureau of the Census, *Census of American Business: 1935*, Retail Distribution, vol. 2 (Washington, DC: Government Printing Office, 1937), 140; ibid., Retail Distribution, 3:224–30; *Sixteenth Census of the United States: 1940*, Census of Business, Retail Trade: 1939, pt. 3, 424–33, 775.

80. Data calculated from U.S. Department of Commerce, Bureau of the Census, *Survey of Current Business*, no. 90, February 1929, 3, 34–35, 109; ibid., no. 91, March 1929, 18–19; ibid., no. 102, February 1930, 4–5, 34–40; *Census of American Business: 1933*, Retail Distribution, 3:46, 91, 146–55; U.S. Department of Commerce, Bureau of the Census, *Census of American Business: 1935*, Retail Distribution, 2:140; 3:224–30; *Sixteenth Census of the United States: 1940*, Census of Business, vol. 1, Retail Trade, 1939, pt. 3, 424–33, 775; cost of the damage by the flood in March 1936 from "Property Losses by Wards in Johnstown," *Johnstown Tribune*, March 17, 1936, 13.

81. Manuscript schedules of bankruptcy hearings of Hyman B., 1924; Hyman G., 1928; Joseph R., 1926—Federal Archives and Records Center, Philadelphia; the figure for average liabilities calculated from the same sources.

82. Figures for business persisters in Chicago and Poughkeepsie in the 1930s calculated from the data provided in Cover, "Business and Personal Failure," 83; Mabel Newcomer, "The Little Businessman: The Study of Business Proprietors in Poughkeepsie, New York," *Business History Review* 35 (Winter 1961): 503–5, 529.

83. Data from Philips, *Little Business in American Economy*, 53–59; McGarry, *Retail Trade Mortality*, 68, 83, 92; Cover, "Business and Personal Failure," 17–18, 22; Newcomer, "The Little Businessman," 507, 511; A. E. Boer, "Mortality Costs in Retail Trades," *Journal of Marketing* 2 (July 1937): 55–57. See also n. 59 in chapter 2 of this book for studies of instability of little businesses in nineteenth- and early-twentieth-century America.

84. Business panels, 7/15–16/1981.

85. Interviews with Isadore S. 8/16/1984; Harry M., 6/14/1984; Henry K., 8/6/1984; Sam M., 8/27/1980; the manuscript schedule of bankruptcy hearing of David B., 1924 (Federal Archives and Research Center, Philadelphia); business panels, 7/15–16/1981; interview with Seymour R., 8/11/1984.

86. Manuscript schedules of bankruptcy hearings of Samuel G., 1930; Louis C., 1930; Isadore and Joseph O., 1931; Nathan B., 1938; Federal Archives and Records Center, Philadelphia, traced in Johnstown business guides and city directories until 1940; Glosser Brothers' department store—payroll records, 1930–1940.

87. Figures compiled from Nathan Glazer, "Social Characteristics of American Jews, 1654–1954," *American Jewish Year Book* 56 (1955): 21–22; and Lloyd Gartner, "The Midpassage of American Jewry," in *The American Jewish Experience*, ed. Jonathan Sarna (New York: Holmes & Meier, 1986), 225–27. These proportions, however, must have varied considerably from city to city, depending on the occupational profile of Jewish communities there and local economic conditions. In Buffalo, for instance, the unemployment rate among Jews at the same time was only 5 percent.

88. Calculated from *Census of American Business: 1933*, Retail Distribution, vol. 3, County and City Summaries, 36–37, 104–5; *Census of American Business: 1935*, Retail of Business, by Areas, States, Counties, and Cities, 193–96; *Sixteenth Census of the United States: 1940*, Census of Business, vol. 1, Retail Trade: 1939, pt. 3, 161–69, 729–31. This "swelling" of Jewish businesses during particularly bad years of the Depression has not been, however, reported in a recent study of New York Jewish families during the Great Depression; the author emphasizes, rather, a high rate of unemployment of New York Jewish youth (Beth Wenger, "Ethnic Community in Economic Crisis: New York Jews and the Great Depression" [Ph.D. diss., Yale University, 1992], chaps. 1 and 2).

89. Between 1929 and 1936, it should be added, the average cost of living in the United States decreased by about 25 percent; food 20 by percent, rent by 32 percent, clothing by 26 percent. The average income of Jewish proprietors in Detroit is reported in Meyer, "The Structure of the Jewish Community in Detroit," 220; a decrease in the average cost of living in the United States, in Beney, *Cost of Living in the United States, 1914–1936*, 43–46.

90. Manuscript schedule of bankruptcy hearing of Abraham M., 1930 (Federal Archives and Records Center, Philadelphia); interview with Ephraim B., 8/9/ 1984. Barter exchange was also practiced during the Depression between Jewish

professionals and their Gentile East European customers, at the latter's initiative, since they had no ready money to pay for services—dental, for example (interview with Rita F., 6/3/1981).

91. Interviews with Moses S., 8/9/1982; Martin G. and Esther J., 8/10/1982; Lena S., 8/14/1984; Betty W., Helen P., and Harold N., 8/10/1984.

92. More common is a somewhat different interpretation, namely, the deprivation thesis holding that people reared during the Depression became—and stayed so in the following years—fixated on values such as money, family comforts, and security, because "they were deprived of these objects or experiences in the 1930s" (Glen Elder, Jr., *Children of the Great Depression* [Chicago: University of Chicago Press, 1974], 184–85). The "uncertainty thesis," or possibly similar effects of a chronic economic volatility, would also be worth investigating.

93. Calculated from deed and mortgage books, 1920–1940 (Cambria County Courthouse, Ebensburg, Pennsylvania); Dun and Bradstreet Company's credit ratings of Jewish merchants checked against home ownership as recorded in tax assessments of property, 1920–1940.

CHAPTER 4
SMALL TOWN, SLOW PACE:
TRANSFORMATIONS IN JEWISH SOCIOCULTURAL LIFE

1. The earliest classical studies propounding these twin theses were Louis Wirth's *The Ghetto* (Chicago: University of Chicago Press, 1928), chap. 12, "The Vanishing Ghetto"; then Nathan Glazer's *American Judaism* (Chicago: University of Chicago Press, 1957); Marshall Sklare's *Conservative Judaism: An American Religious Movement* (Glencoe, IL: The Free Press, 1958); and idem, ed., *The Jew in American Society* (New York: Behrman House Publishers, 1974). More recently, the middle-class modernization thesis has been argued by Deborah Dash Moore in *At Home in America: Second Generation New York Jews* (New York: Columbia University Press, 1981), and for American Jewry in general, e.g., by Steven Cohen, *American Modernity and Jewish Identity* (New York: Tavistock Publications, 1983), chap. 3 on, and, in a strongly structuralist interpretation, by Calvin Goldscheider and Alan Zuckerman in *The Transformation of the Jews* (Chicago: University of Chicago Press, 1986), pt. 4. The reference to Jewish adaptation in New York as "the master pattern" is Robert Warshow's in "Poet of the Jewish Middle Class," *Commentary* 7 (May 1946): 17–18. The quotation about "a new Jewish community" having come into being between the two wars is from Gibson Winter, "The Jewish Development," in *The Emergent American Society*, ed. W. Lloyd Warner (New Haven: Yale University Press, 1967), 1:467.

2. Karl Mannheim, "The Problem of Generations," in *Essays on the Sociology of Knowledge* (1928; reprint, New York: Oxford University Press, 1952), 276–332.

3. On these processes affecting the entire Jewish group, see, e.g., Oscar Janowsky, *The JWB Survey* (New York: The Dial Press, 1948); Herman Stein, "Jewish Social Work in the United States: 1920–1955," in *The Jews: Social Patterns of an American Group*, ed. Marshall Sklare (Glencoe, IL: Urbana University Press, 1958), 173–204; Daniel Elazar, *Community and Polity: The Organizational Dynamics of American Jewry* (Philadelphia: The Jewish Publication Society, 1980). Arthur Goren's *New York Jews and the Quest for Community* (New York: Columbia University Press, 1970)—a study of the failure, already at the beginning of the cen-

tury, of the attempts at establishing in New York the inclusive *kehila*, a multifunctional umbrella organization patterned on the traditional Jewish institution—could also be considered as an illustration of the differentiation-secularization thesis. On secularization-"Protestantization"/Americanization of Judaism, see, e.g., Sklare, *Conservative Judaism*; Glazer, *American Judaism*; also Jonathan Sarna, "Is Judaism Compatible with American Civil Religion?" in *Religion and the Life of the Nation*, ed. Rowland Sherrill (Urbana: University of Illinois Press, 1990), 154–74. Specifically on Protestant/American influences on the Reform Movement, see Michael Meyer, *Response to Modernity: A History of the Reform Movement in Judaism* (New York: Oxford University Press, 1988). On particular cities: Moore, *At Home in America*, esp. chap. 5; Selig Adler and Thomas Connolly, *From Ararat to Suburbia: The History of the Jewish Community in Buffalo* (Philadelphia: The Jewish Publication Society, 1960), chaps. 7, 8; Lloyd Gartner, *History of the Jews of Cleveland* (Cleveland: Western Reserve Historical Society, 1978), chaps. 8, 9, 10; Louis Swichkow and Lloyd Gartner, *The History of the Jews of Milwaukee* (Philadelphia: The Jewish Publication Society, 1963), esp. chaps. 7, 8 in pt. 2, and chap. 2 in pt. 3; Stuart Rosenberg, *The Jewish Community in Rochester, 1843–1925* (New York: Columbia University Press, 1954), pt. 4; Max Vorspan and Lloyd Gartner, *History of the Jews of Los Angeles* (San Marino, CA: The Huntington Library, 1970), chaps. 11, 12, 13. On the secularization of the dominant, Anglo-Protestant society and the acceleration of this process during the interwar period, see Martin Marty, *The Righteous Empire: The Protestant Experience in America* (New York: Dial Press, 1970).

4. On the (East European) Jewish women's participation in group institutional life and religious change, and their role in the ethnicization ("Americanization" in the studies) of the above, see, e.g., Jenna Weissman Joselit, "The Special Sphere of the Middle-Class American Jewish Woman: The Synagogue Sisterhood, 1890–1940," in *The American Synagogue: A Sanctuary Transformed*, ed. Jack Wertheimer (New York: Cambridge University Press, 1987), 206–30; Paula Hyman, "The Volunteer Organizations: Vanguard or Rear Guard?" *Lilith* 5 (1978): 12–22; Norma Fain Pratt, "Transitions in Judaism: The Jewish American Woman through the 1930s," *American Quarterly* 30 (Winter 1978): 681–702.

5. Local interviews with Jews, and with representatives of the former municipal leadership; content analysis of the *Johnstown Tribune*, 1890s–1930s, for "ethnic" mentions; Johnstown city directories, 1920s–1930s; *Statistical Review: Greater Johnstown, Pennsylvania* (Johnstown: Greater Johnstown Chamber of Commerce, 1950), 2; U.S. Bureau of the Census, *Abstract of the Fifteenth Census of the United States: 1930* (Washington, DC: Government Printing Office, 1933), 21, 32; U.S. Bureau of the Census, *Religious Bodies: 1926* (Washington, DC: Government Printing Office, 1930), 1:13–19, 441–42, 486–93, 507–12; U.S. Bureau of the Census, *Religious Bodies: 1936* (Washington, DC: Government Printing Office, 1941), 1:17–23, table 31. In both censuses, unfortunately, Jewish congregations reported the total number of Jews in the city/town, rather than members of the synagogues, so even though these two figures were not far apart, the censuses could not be used as a source for adult synagogue membership.

6. The Johnstown data from *Rodef Sholom Bulletin* and *Beth Zion Temple Tidings*, 1930s, synagogue memorial books, interviews with the rabbis and former leaders of local congregations, former synagogue secretaries, and community members. Estimates for New York from Robert Park and Herbert Miller, *Old World*

Traits Transplanted (New York: Harper, 1921; reprint, Arno Press, 1969), 209. Information on Pittsburgh from Maurice Taylor, *The Jewish Community of Pittsburgh* (Pittsburgh: Federation of Jewish Philanthropies, 1941), 69. Pittsburgh in the 1930s had approximately 15,000 Jewish households, as compared to about 300 in Johnstown. The local environment clearly influenced the proportions of synagogue affiliation: in Stamford, Connecticut, for example, a town similar in size to Johnstown, but located in "that vast suburban area called metropolitan New York" and with nearly 1,000 Jewish households supporting a well-developed network of over 30 organizations, only about 30 percent were formally affiliated (Samuel Koenig, "The Socioeconomic Structure of an American Jewish Community," in *Jews in a Gentile World*, ed. Isacque Graeber [New York: Macmillan, 1942], 201, 218, 232).

7. Interview with the former Rodef Sholom rabbi, Ralph Simon, 11/6/1986. Residents of the surrounding towns also remained at the fringes—there were usually enough families in each to conduct regular prayers in private homes, but not enough to erect a synagogue. For major holidays they either came to Johnstown or went to equidistant Altoona; a number maintained formal synagogue membership in one or the other place, but tracing these switches would have been too time-consuming, so I did not attempt to calculate the proportions. Deborah Dash Moore called the membership of New York Jews in their ethnic institutional structures "semi-voluntary" (*At Home in America*, 16); in Johnstown, then, the degree of voluntarism must have been one-quarter or less.

8. Quotation from David de Sola Pool, "Judaism and the Synagogue," in *The American Jew: A Composite Portrait*, ed. Oscar Janowsky (Freeport, NY: Books for Libraries Press, 1942), 52.

9. Minutes of the Rodef Sholom board meetings; *Rodef Sholom Bulletin*, 1930s; *Jewish Center of Johnstown Rodef Sholom Synagogue*, 73–85; minutes of the Talmud Torah board meetings, 9/19–21/1924; National Council of Jewish Women– Johnstown branch, memorial booklet, 1928; ledgers of the Israel Isaiah Beneficial Society (incomplete), 1919–1940; local interviews. On the socialist tradition of the Workmen's Circle, see Maximilian Hurwitz, *The Workmen's Circle: Its History, Ideals, Organization and Institutions* (New York: The Workmen's Circle, 1936). Already in the early twentieth century the Rodef Sholom Congregation had among its leaders committed Zionists (its Sunday school, founded in 1911, was managed by a Zionist group, *Tikvah Zion* society—see chapter 2), and since the interwar period Zionism had become a common interest of the community at large, including—especially since the 1930s, under the influence of Rabbi Abram Granison— members of the Reform Beth Zion Temple (see *Rodef Sholom Bulletin*, May–June 1935: "History of Zionism in Johnstown"; Leonard Winograd, *"The Horse Died at Windber": A History of Johnstown's Jews in Pennsylvania* [Bristol, IN: Wyndham Press, 1988], 164–68, 201–2, 233–34). In addition to Beth Zion Forum, occasional interfaith meetings took place between local Protestant clergy and Jewish rabbis (Reform, and in the 1930s also Conservative)—see chapter 5.

10. Winograd, *A History of Johnstown's Jews*, 229–30; local interviews. Interestingly, I found a record of a similar approach to professionalized social work as "simply assisting" the needy people rather than "working on cases" in one of the Jewish agencies in Buffalo, New York (Norman Miller, "The Jewish Leadership of Lakeport [Buffalo]," in *Studies in Leadership*, ed. Alvin Gouldner [New York: Harper & Row, 1950], 201); it suggests—a nice research topic for the interested—that the

old-country, *gemeinschaftliche* ways of dealing with social problems could have been preserved within the "updated" Jewish-American philanthropic institutions in big urban centers as well.

11. Minutes of the Rodef Sholom board meetings, 2/26/1922; local interviews.

12. See Henry Rosenfelt, *This Thing of Giving* (New York: Plymouth Press, 1924); Winter, "The Jewish Development," 463–83; Milton Goldin, *Why They Give: American Jews and Their Philanthropies* (New York: Macmillan, 1976), 82–83; Elazar, *Community and Polity*, 165ff.; Moore, "A Collective Enterprise," in *At Home in America*; Kenneth Roseman, "American Jewish Institutions in Their Historical Context," *Jewish Journal of Sociology* 16 (June 1974): 25–38.

13. Dr. Meyer Bloom's personal archives, presently part of Dr. Meyer and Sally Bloom Archives at the Beth Sholom Congregation in Johnstown; *Tri-State Zionist Pinkus* (Pittsburgh, 1941), 190–91; Winograd, *A History of Johnstown's Jews*, 121–23, 237–38, and passim; local interviews.

14. The Jewish "social center" developed from the late-nineteenth-century YMHA, which, in turn, was created as an adaptation of the Protestant YMCA. It was, however, a prominent religious philosopher, Rabbi Mordecai Kaplan, who gave it an ideological framework: the community-synagogue-center was to reintegrate into organic unity, but in a (modern) American way, the rupturing bond between Judaism (religion) and the Jewish people (ethnicity). See Mordecai Kaplan, *Judaism as a Civilization: Toward a Reconstruction of American Jewish Life* (1934; reprint, Philadelphia: The Jewish Publication Society, 1981); also Louis Blumenthal, "Developments in the Jewish Community Center Movement," *Jewish Social Service Quarterly* 15 (March 1938): 155–63; Abraham Duker, "Structure of the Jewish Community," in Janowsky, *The American Jew*, 147–50; Janowsky, *The JWB Survey*; Winter, "The Jewish Development," 463–83. Citations from Moore, *At Home in America*, 134–35, 139.

15. I thought of calling the interwar Rodef Sholom Congregation "Modern Orthodox" or "Conservadox," similar to those in uptown New York City, but in comparison with how the latter have been described, the Johnstowners appear to have been, on the one hand, less committedly and self-consciously Orthodox than were modern Orthodox (see below on the scope and character of the religious observance of the Rodef Sholom members), and, on the other, less modern in their religious organization and practice than big-city "Conservadox" Jews. See, e.g., Jeffrey Gurock, *When Harlem Was Jewish, 1870–1930* (New York: Columbia University Press, 1979); and two special issues of *American Jewish History*—74 (December 1984) and 77 (December 1987)—reexamining Sklare's *Conservative Judaism* and Glazer's *American Judaism*, respectively; also a comment on the persistence during the interwar era and into the present times of Jewish religious Orthodoxy in America in n. 27 in this chapter.

16. Quotations from minutes of the Rodef Sholom board meetings on 12/26/1920 and 4/6/1924.

17. National figure from Uriah Zvi Engelman, "Jewish Statistics in the U.S. Census of Religious Bodies (1850–1936)," *Jewish Social Studies* 9 (April 1947): 164–65; New York data from Moore, *At Home in America*, 135, 141; estimate of the costs of Rodef Sholom upkeep from income and expenses records in the synagogue minutes, 1920s; minutes of the Johnstown Talmud Torah, 1924–1928; and local interviews.

18. William Toll, "A Quiet Revolution: Jewish Women's Clubs and the Widening Female Sphere, 1870–1920," *American Jewish Archives* 41 (Spring–Summer 1989): 8–25; see also n. 4 in this chapter.

19. Minutes of the Rodef Sholom board meeting on 11/1/1921; also minutes of the Johnstown Talmud Torah, 1924–1928; *Jewish Center of Johnstown Rodef Sholom Synagogue*, 48–52, 64–67; and local interviews.

20. Local interviews; Winograd, *A History of Johnstown's Jews*, 231.

21. Local interviews; the Johnstown subscribers to *Forverts* and *Tageblat* (in 1928 absorbed by *Morgen Zhurnal*), and the *Forverts* records of readership, and commercial advertisements, from the archives at the YIVO Institute for Jewish Research in New York; *Jewish Criterion*, November 10, 1922; and content analysis of the *Johnstown Tribune*, 1890s–1930s. On the Yiddish press as an agent of Americanization, see Mordecai Soltes, *The Yiddish Press: An Americanizing Agency* (New York: Columbia University, 1925; reprint, Arno Press, 1969); Isidore Passow, "The Role of the Yiddish Press in the Acculturation Process," *Gratz College Annual of Jewish Studies* 5 (1976): 69–80. Also Susan Braunstein and Jenna Weissman Joselit, eds., *Getting Comfortable in New York: The American Jewish Home, 1880–1950* (New York: The Jewish Museum, 1990).

22. Information about only 25 percent of the congregants' having paid their dues from *Rodef Sholom Bulletin*, February 1934. The insufficient congregational budget was frequently supplemented from the "personal funds" of local "bigshots" (*Jewish Center of Johnstown Rodef Sholom Synagogue*, 74; small town panel [7/30/1981] and individual interviews). Over 50 percent of the UJA collections from Johnstown in the late 1930s—these records are the most systematic and can be used as an illustration of the congregation's economic dependence on a small group of supporters—were made up by donations from members of one family clan, and another 25 percent came from a dozen-odd families (Dr. Meyer Bloom's personal archives). The minicenter, eventual relocation to Westmont, and social activities, from *Jewish Center of Johnstown Rodef Sholom Synagogue*, 29–35; "News about Town," *Johnstown Tribune*, May 22, 1933; individual interviews and small town panel (7/30/1981).

23. Women's panel (7/22/1981) and individual interviews with American-born Johnstown women; quotations from conversations with Blanche B., 7/1/1989, and Lillian C., 6/5/1988; quotation about "exhibitions of vanity" in New York from Ira Eisenstein, "The Rabbi and His Congregation," *Proceedings of the Rabbinical Assembly of America*, 40th Annual Convention, Detroit, Michigan, June 25–27, 1940, Appendix D, 203—a similar observation about the difference between Johnstown and New York Jews' styles of religious celebrations was made by the former Rodef Sholom rabbi, Mordecai Brill, in a conversation with this author (7/1/1988). Besides interviews, information about the activities of the Ladies Auxiliary and the participation of women in congregational decision making from *Jewish Center of Johnstown Rodef Sholom Synagogue*, 64–67, 90, 103. For selected studies on women in American Judaism, see n. 4 in this chapter.

24. *Dedication of the New Beth Zion Temple*, Johnstown, Pennsylvania, September 14th and 15th, 1951; *Year Book and Program, 1928–1929*, Johnstown Section, National Council of Jewish Women; *Beth Zion Temple Tidings*, 1930s; Winograd, *A History of Johnstown's Jews*, 156–58, 233–34; local interviews. On the increasing influence on Reform Judaism of Kaplan's ideas about the all-inclusive synagogue–social center, see Meyer, *Response to Modernity*, 303–4.

25. On women in Reform Judaism, see, e.g., Ellen Umansky, "Women in Judaism: From the Reform Movement to Contemporary Jewish Religious Feminism," in *Women of Spirit*, ed. Rosemary Ruether and Elanor McLaughlin (New York: Simon and Schuster, 1979), 333–54; Beth Wenger, "Jewish Women of the Club: The Changing Public Role of Atlanta's Jewish Women (1870–1930)," *American Jewish History* 76 (December 1987): 311–33; Toll, "A Quiet Revolution," 8–25; Meyer, *Response to Modernity*, 306; Ann Braude, "The Jewish Woman's Encounter with American Culture," in *Women and Religion in America*, ed. Rosemary Radford Ruether and Rosemary Skinner Keller (New York: Harper & Row), 1:150–92.

26. Local interviews, and personal communications from the former Beth Zion rabbi, Hayim Perelmuter (4/6/1989, 7/4/1989); *Beth Zion Temple Tidings*, 1930s; *Dedication of the New Beth Zion Temple*; Winograd, *A History of Johnstown's Jews*, 74–75, 269–70, 322.

27. The quotation about celebrating God "in an American accent" from Lawrence Hoffman, "Jewish Liturgy and American Experience," *Religion and Intellectual Life* 5 (Fall 1987): 72; about making East European Orthodox Jews "thoroughly American" from Solomon Schechter, rabbinic scholar and president of the Jewish Theological Seminary, a bulwark of Conservative Judaism in the first decades of the twentieth century (as cited in Marc Lee Raphael, *Profiles in American Judaism* [San Francisco: Harper & Row, 1984], 91). The most concise information on the early influence of Reform Judaism on the emerging Conservative Movement is in *Encyclopedia Judaica* 5: 901–6 (on the Protestant influences on American Reform Judaism, see n. 3 in this chapter); see also *Conservative Judaism in America: A Biographical Dictionary Sourcebook*, ed. Pamela Nadell (Westport, CT: Greenwood Press, 1988). A thesis that the end of World War I marked the replacement of the Orthodox by the Conservative religious-institutional form in big-city Jewish settlements has been challenged by recent historical studies showing that in particular neighborhoods and informal social circles in large cities, Jewish religious Orthodoxy as a communal organization and lifestyle was at once more stubborn and more flexible than the conventional thesis assumed, and that it not only persisted well into the interwar period but "traveled" with upwardly mobile American Jewish families to economically more affluent and socially prestigious residential areas (for bibliographic references, see n. 15 in this chapter).

28. Interview with Isadore G., 8/16/84.

29. The style of worship at Rodef Sholom from local interviews; High Holiday sermons in English from minutes of the Rodef Sholom board meetings, 5/28/1922, 7/25/1922 (the English-speaking preacher insulted, 7/27/1913); the issue of the inclined plane on Sabbath in Lawrence Glosser, "After the Horse Died: An Historical and Sociological Study of the Glosser Family of Johnstown, Pennsylvania" (M.A. thesis, Hebrew Union College, Los Angeles, 1977), 101–2.

30. In the latter category, the proportions varied considerably: for instance, depending on the source of the estimation, about 50 percent in Pittsburgh, between 30 and 45 percent in Boston, 30–40 percent in Philadelphia, 20–30 percent in Chicago, around 30 percent in Milwaukee, and about 24 percent in the whole city of New York, but in Brownsville as much as 33 percent, and in Brooklyn reportedly only 12 percent. Estimate for Johnstown from the *Census of Religious Bodies: 1936*, 1:549; Johnstown Talmud Torah minutes, 1924–1928; *Rodef Sholom Bulletin* and *Beth Zion Temple Tidings*, 1930s; *Jewish Center of Johnstown Rodef Sholom Synagogue*, 73–85; interviews with the Johnstowners and prewar local rabbis. Estimates

of Jewish religious school enrollments nationwide from Harry Linfield, "The Communal Organizations of the Jews in the United States," *American Jewish Year Book* 31 (1929/30): 102–3, 148–49; Israel Chipkin, "Twenty-Five Years of Jewish Education in the United States," *American Jewish Year Book* 38 (1936/37): 34–43, 87; Engelman, "Jewish Statistics," 170–72. Data for Jewish agricultural colonies from Philip Goldstein, *Social Aspects of the Jewish Colonies of South Jersey* (New York: The League Printing Co., 1928), 50; calculations for the six cities quoted after Meir Ben-Horin, "From the Turn of the Century to the Late Thirties," in *A History of Jewish Education in America*, ed. Judah Pilch (New York: American Association for Jewish Education, 1969), 82–83; Noah Nardi, "A Study of Afternoon Hebrew Schools in the United States," *Jewish Social Studies* 8 (April 1946): 58–64. Data for Brooklyn in the 1920s from Michael Weisser, *A Brotherhood of Memory: Jewish Landsmanshaftn in the New World* (New York: Basic Books, 1985), 150–51.

31. Local interviews; minutes of the Johnstown Talmud Torah, 1/14/1924, 5/5/1924, 9/21/1925, 9/29/1925, 10/12/1925, 10/26/1925; Winograd, *A History of Johnstown's Jews*, 198–200. In the large cities, religious education became increasingly professionalized (since 1928, there has appeared a specialized journal, *Jewish Education*, published by the National Council for Jewish Education); see Alexander Dushkin, "The Role of the Professional Worker in Jewish Education," *Jewish Education* 5 (January–March 1933): 3–19; Alexander Dushkin and Leo Honor, "Aims and Activities of Jewish Educational Organization in America," ibid., 136–258; Chipkin, "Twenty-Five Years of Jewish Education in the United States," 78–86.

32. On the "feminization of the synagogue," see Alter Landesman, "Synagogue Attendance," *Proceedings of the Rabbinical Assembly* (1928), 50, cited in Jack Wertheimer, "The Conservative Synagogue Revisited," *American Jewish History* 74 (December 1984): 125; Jacob Golub and Noah Nardi, "A Study in Jewish Observance," *The Reconstructionist* 11 (June 1945): 14; also Sklare, *Conservative Judaism*, 86ff. According to my informants' recollections, during Rabbi Simon's tenure at Rodef Sholom, on Friday nights three to four times as many women attended as did on Saturday mornings, when the service was conducted in a traditional Orthodox way. Generally, men worshipers (Friday night and Saturday morning services combined) typically outnumbered the women 3 to 1.

33. Local interviews with women; conversations with Rabbi Ralph Simon (the quotations regarding changes in Rodef Sholom are from an interview conducted on 11/6/1986); and telephone conversations with Rabbis Morris Landes (7/4/1989) and Nathan Kollin (7/2/1989), his successors at the Rodef Sholom pulpit; *Jewish Center of Johnstown Rodef Sholom Synagogue*, 25, 64–65, 73–74, 85. In an interview with Abraham Karp on reforms introduced in Rodef Sholom in the 1930s, Rabbi Simon recollects the young people in Johnstown as eager for changes, and the older generation as more suspicious of innovation (Abraham Karp, "The Conservative Rabbi—'Dissatisfied But Not Unhappy,'" in *The American Rabbinate: A Century of Continuity and Change, 1883–1983*, ed. Jacob Rader Marcus and Abraham Peck [Hoboken, NJ: Ktav, 1985], 126). This was indeed, and naturally, a general tendency, but more important was a previously noted earlier difference between more traditionally inclined residents of the primary, downtown Jewish settlement, around the old synagogue, and those, of both generations, in prestigious, all-American Westmont. If there was a conflict during and after Rabbi Simon's tenure, it seems to have been more a clash of personalities between the contending

leaders, who used the then current issue of Conservative reforms for political reasons, than a generational ideological confrontation over the "right" way in Judaism; the congregants, aware of their small number and the practical (financial) impossibility of forming two separate institutions, accommodated their differences of orientation within the same synagogue by praying in their preferred way, and attending their preferred kind of Sabbath services (Winograd, *A History of Johnstown's Jews*, 140–41). There also exists different information regarding the time when the Hebrew Ladies Aid Society was renamed the Auxiliary. According to the Pittsburgh *Jewish Criterion* (as quoted by Winograd, ibid., 230), the latter was already in place in 1916; it seems more likely, however, that the English-language *Criterion* used that "modern" name (common at that time in Conservative and Reform congregations) to describe a traditional-type organization.

34. Local interviews; conversations and correspondence with Rabbis Simon, Kollin, and Landes; *Jewish Center of Johnstown Rodef Sholom Synagogue*, 25–28, 31; Glosser, "An Historical and Sociological Study of the Glosser Family," 103–4. It is a recurring theme in the literature on early twentieth-century American Judaism that the grass-roots transformation of East European congregations in America into Conservative ones had been the work of the laity. In Johnstown, although of course "the laity" invited Rabbi Simon to the pulpit of Rodef Sholom, it was primarily his personal charisma and dynamic leadership that effected the synagogue's remaking. On the role of individual rabbis in quickening or hindering change in "congregational" American Judaism, see Marcus and Peck, *The American Rabbinate*, chaps. on Orthodox, Conservative, and Reform synagogues; Jack Wertheimer, "The Conservative Synagogue," in Wertheimer, *The American Synagogue*, 114–17 (and a short bibliography of personal congregational histories in 143–44n.16).

35. Winograd, *A History of Johnstown's Jews*, 81, 148–50, 201, 269–70; *Johnstown Tribune*, February 24, 1924, 7. Founded in the late nineteenth century, Johnstown's Beth Zion Temple never shared the then radical Reform orientation of her big-city sisters, which focused on the religious-ethical dimension of Judaism and programmatically denounced the ethnic (as *folk*) part (cf. Meyer, *Response to Modernity*, chap. 7, "Classical Reform Judaism"; Leon Jick, "The Reform Synagogue," in Wertheimer, *The American Synagogue*, 85–96; David Polish, "The Changing and the Constant in the Reform Rabbinate," in Marcus and Peck, *The American Rabbinate*, 173–92. An expression of the persistent ethnoreligious identity of the Beth Zion Reform Congregation was, for example, its celebration in the 1930s of popular holidays commemorating the salvation of the Jewish people from the hands of their enemies, such as Purim (celebrating the rescue of the Jewish people from destruction at the hands of the Persian leader Haman in the fifth century B.C.E.) and Hannukah (celebrating the defeat of Syrian Greeks by Maccabees in 165 B.C.E.). It could also have been, however, that the observance of these "folk" religious holidays reflected an increase of East European members at the Temple, rather than an original greater traditionalism of the old-timers. Jonathan Sarna suggested another possibility, namely, that the celebration of Purim in the 1930s expressed symbolic resistance of American Jews against German nazism (Haman = Hitler) and hope for the ultimate victory of the Jewish people; while the celebration of Hannukah was a response to the all-pervasive celebration of Christmas (personal communication, 10/8/1991).

36. Local interviews, and conversations and correspondence with the former Beth Zion rabbi, Hayim Perelmuter (4/6/1989, 7/4/1989); Winograd, *A His-*

tory of Johnstown's Jews, 163–64, 203. As time showed, Beth Zion's "Consreform," which appeared backward vis-à-vis the mainline Reform Movement at the turn of the century, by the late 1930s–1940s turned out to have been the avant-garde, as Reform Judaism increasingly returned to an appreciation of the history and religious tradition of the Jewish people as an organic part of Judaism (see Meyer, *Response to Modernity,* chap. 8, "Reorientation"; Jick, "The Reform Synagogue," 96–99; Polish, "The Changing and the Constant in the Reform Rabbinate," 192–96, 207.

37. The quotation is from Abraham Duker, "Emerging Culture Patterns in American Jewish Life," *Publications of the American Jewish Historical Society* 39 (September–June 1949/50): 376n.65. On the rapid diminution of Jewish religious observance in American cities during the interwar period, see idem, "On Religious Trends in American Jewish Life," *Yivo Annual of Jewish Social Science* 4 (1940): 51–63; Golub and Nardi, "A Study in Jewish Observance"; Nathan Goldberg, "Religious and Social Attitudes of Jewish Youth in the U.S.," *Jewish Review* 1 (July 1943): 135–68; Marvin Nathan's national survey of religious practices of Jewish youth in America during the 1930s—cited in Stephen Sharot, "The Three Generations Thesis and the American Jews," *British Journal of Sociology* 24 (June 1973): 155–57. On minimal religious observance of the second-generation women in New York City—Sydney Stahl Weinberg, *The World of Our Mothers: The Lives of Immigrant Jewish Women* (Chapel Hill: University of North Carolina Press, 1988), 115–16, 122; a 1935 survey reported that three-quarters of the second-generation young Jews 15–25 years of age in New York had not attended any religious service during the preceding twelve months (after Charles Silberman, *A Certain People: American Jews and Their Lives Today* [New York: Summit Books, 1985], 172).

38. Interview with Harry R., 7/2/1986.

39. I selected the basic practices about which I could, I believed, obtain more reliable information from my Johnstown informants. On the standard sets of Jewish ritual retention (usually eleven to thirteen items) used in post–World War II studies, the majority of prewar Johnstowners would have generally scored rather high, considerably higher than either immigrant or second-generation respondents in postwar studies. For examples of standard question-sets on "ritual retention" in postwar sociological studies of Jewish religious observance, see Marshall Sklare and Joseph Greenblum, *Jewish Identity on the Suburban Frontier: A Study of Group Survival in the Open Society* (New York: Basic Books, 1967); Calvin Goldscheider and Frances Kobrin Goldscheider, *Jewish Americans: Three Generations in a Jewish Community* (Englewood Cliffs, NJ: Prentice Hall, 1968); or Ralph Segalman, "Jewish Identity Scales: A Report," *Jewish Social Studies* 29 (April 1967): 92–111. See also Samuel Heilman and Steven Cohen, *Cosmopolitans and Parochials: Modern Orthodox Jews in America* (Chicago: University of Chicago Press, 1989), chap. 2, "Ritual Practices"; and Jack Wertheimer, "Recent Trends in American Judaism," *American Jewish Year Book* 89 (1989): 85–91. Unfortunately, I was unable to obtain a good enough estimate of the proportion of Johnstown women-members of two East European synagogues who visited the *mikve*: it was still in operation in the 1930s but was apparently used more or less regularly only by a small group of older immigrants from the neighborhood near Rodef Sholom and members of Ahavath Achim. The women from secondary settlements denied, with considerable emotion, ever having used the local *mikve*. These strong feelings were evoked either by

memories of the *mikve*'s unsanitary conditions, or by a recollection—in any case as reported to me—that unlike *kashrut*, they found the traditional religious laws of female purity "old-country fanatic," or by the two factors combined.

40. Interviews with Hyman M., 8/11/1980; Ben I., 6/11/1985; and Nathan E., 4/18/1986.

41. The New York City survey data from Golub and Nardi, "A Study in Jewish Observance," 11–15; and Isadore Steinbaum, "A Study of the Jewishness of Twenty New York Families," *Yivo Annual of Jewish Social Science* 5 (1950): 247 (the same study cites a much larger religious survey conducted in 1940 among nearly four hundred Jewish families in Staten Island, New York); a midwestern city from Leonard Bloom, "The Jews of Buna," in Graeber, *Jews in a Gentile World*, 187. Information about Johnstown's Jews from local interviews. My cautious estimate of Sabbath synagogue attendance during the 1930s in two East European congregations combined is between 15 percent and 20 percent of total membership (Friday night and Saturday morning services together); a few contemporary surveys in small towns reported similar figures—as cited in Wertheimer, "The Conservative Synagogue," 120–21.

42. The Staten Island survey data cited in Steinbaum, "A Study of the Jewishness," 235; see also Abraham Fleischman, "Some Aspects of the Jewish Population of Staten Island" (unpublished MS, Graduate School for Jewish Social Work, New York, 1937); Golub and Nardi, "A Study in Jewish Observance," 11, 15; data from the Bronx after Moore, *At Home in America*, 77–78; a similar impression of the Friday night lighting of candles as a common ritual among the New Yorkers before the war appears in women's oral histories as recorded by Weinberg, *The World of Our Mothers*, 94.

43. A contemporary study of immigrants' religious practices in New York City found special Friday evening meals celebrated in 70 percent of the homes, but *kiddush* (blessing over wine) was regularly recited in 23 percent, and occasionally in 18 percent of the surveyed families (Golub and Nardi, "A Study in Jewish Observance," 12, 15).

44. A thesis that "the center of Jewishness" shifted to the home in Sklare, *Conservative Judaism*; a similar impression in the recollections of New York's women in Weinberg, *The World of Our Mothers*, 140, 285n.54. In Canada, see Stuart Schoenfeld, "Canadian Judaism," in *Canadian Jewish Mosaic*, ed. Morton Weinfeld et al. (New York: Wiley, 1981), 141–45. An opposite thesis, that "the center of Jewishness" shifted to the (Conservative) synagogue, and religious school served "a surrogate parental role," in Lucy Dawidowicz, *The Jewish Presence* (New York: Holt, Rinehart & Winston, 1977), 64–67; to the synagogue-center in Moore, *At Home in America*, chap. 5. In American Reform Judaism, according to its historians, this shift from home to the temple occurred earlier, at the turn of the nineteenth and twentieth centuries; see *People Walk on Their Heads: Moses Weinberger's Jews and Judaism in New York*, trans. from Hebrew and ed. Jonathan Sarna (New York: Holmes & Meier, 1982), 9; Walter Jacob, *The Changing World of Reform Judaism in Retrospect* (Pittsburgh: Rodef Sholom Congregation, 1985), 96, 115.

45. The quotation is from "Jewish Home-Making of the [Conservative] Women's League," *The United Synagogue Recorder* 1 (July 1, 1920): 1 (cited in Pamela Nadell, "The Beginnings of the Religious Emancipation of American Jewish Women" [paper presented at the Berkshire Conference of Women Historians,

June 10, 1990]). On women's role as upholders of Jewishness in the home: "Under modern conditions, it is the mother who becomes the guardian of the Sabbath and its interpreter"; see Deborah Melamed, *The Three Pillars: Thought, Practice, and Worship* (New York: Women's League of the United Synagogue, 1927)—a widely read guide for (Conservative) Jewish women. Also Braunstein and Joselit, *Getting Comfortable in New York*, 50–51, 72; Charlotte Baum, Paula Hyman, and Sonya Michel, *The Jewish Woman in America* (New York: The Dial Press, 1976), 13, 57, 63ff.; Paula Hyman, "The Modern Jewish Family: Image and Reality," in *The Jewish Family: Metaphor and Memory*, ed. David Kraemer (New York: Oxford University Press, 1989), esp. 189–90.

46. *Fressfrömmigkeit* was already practiced by the acculturated Jews of the Habsburg Empire in the second half of the nineteenth century (the term "gastronomic Judaism" dates even earlier: it was (first?) used by Heinrich Heine in the eighteenth century)—see Norman Friedman, "Jewish Popular Culture in Contemporary America," *Judaism* 24 (Summer 1975): 266–68; Herbert Gans, "American Jewry: Present and Future," *Commentary* 21 (May 1956): 429; Barbara Kirshenblatt-Gimblett, "Kitchen Judaism," in Braunstein and Joselit, *Getting Comfortable in New York*, 75–106; Weinberg, *The World of Our Mothers*; and Neil Cowan and Ruth Cowan, *Our Parents' Lives: The Americanization of Eastern European Jews* (New York: Basic Books, 1989) on the interlinking of food, women, and Jewishness. Generally on the function of food in the preservation of group identity and social integration, see Mary Douglas, "Standard Social Uses of Food," in *Food in the Social Order*, ed. Mary Douglas (New York: Russell Sage, 1984), 1–40.

47. Advertisements of kosher-style delicatessens were a permanent feature in the Yiddish- and English-language papers in large American cities; references to kosher-style eateries appear also in novels and memoirs describing life in Jewish communities in American urban centers during the interwar period.

48. Interviews with individual Johnstowners; also social life panel (7/30/1981) and small town panel (7/21/1981), and telephone conversations with Rabbis Ralph Simon (11/9/86, 5/1/1987) and Morris Landes (7/2/1989). Among those who ate out some never ordered meat "for safety," while others only refrained from eating shellfish, pork, and the unpurged hindquarters of beef (forbidden by Jewish law).

49. Interview with Millard C., 3/2/1989.

50. Duker, "On Religious Trends in American Jewish Life," 54; a Staten Island religious survey as reported in Steinbaum, "A Study of the Jewishness," 234; Golub and Nardi, "A Study in Jewish Observance," 12; Koenig, "Socioeconomic Structure of an American Jewish Community," 228; Bloom, "The Jews of Buna," 187–89.

51. On a variety of cookery books and recipes *spetsyel far der yidisher kikh*, prepared specially for the Jewish kitchen, and "the science of kosher cooking," see Jenna Weissman Joselit, "'A Set Table': Jewish Domestic Culture in the New World, 1880–1950," in Braunstein and Joselit, *Getting Comfortable in New York*, 55–58; and Kirshenblatt-Gimblett, "Kitchen Judaism," 75–100.

52. In very small towns, however, located a long distance from a bigger city in which a kosher butcher could be found, and where Jews were very few in number and unorganized, the observance of *kashrut* in Jewish homes was often practically nonexistent; for example, such was apparently the situation in the town of Columbus, Indiana, during the interwar period (Gladys Kaminsky, *History of the Jewish*

Community in Columbus, Indiana [Fort Wayne: The Indiana Jewish Historical Society: 1978], 29 and passim).

53. The term "domestic religion" is Basha's from Barbara Myerhoff, *Number Our Days* (New York: Dutton, 1978), 256; on the deeply ingrained, unreflective "domestic religiosity" of Jewish women, see also Baum, Hyman, and Michel, *The Jewish Woman in America*, 12, 57–62, 120.

54. I selected for illustration here the most typical of my women informants' replies to my questions.

55. This particular account of an American-born girl's dislike for the old-country dishes prepared by her mother is from Jessie Bernard, "Biculturality: A Study in Social Schizophrenia," in Graeber, *Jews in a Gentile World*, 276–77. Although comparatively more frequent and more intense than in Johnstown, a lesser conflict over lifestyles in general between immigrant mothers and American-born daughters than between their respective male counterparts has also been recorded in oral life-histories of New Yorkers: see, e.g., Sydney Stahl Weinberg, "Jewish Mothers and Immigrant Daughters: Positive and Negative Role Models," *Journal of American Ethnic History* 6 (Spring 1987): 39–55, and idem, *The World of Our Mothers*, chap. 7, "Mothers, Fathers, and Daughters," and passim; Susan Glenn, *Daughters of the Shtetl: Life and Labor in the Immigrant Generation* (Ithaca, NY: Cornell University Press, 1990), chap. 2, "Mothers and Daughters: Remaking the Jewish Family Economy in America," and chap. 4, "'All of Us Young People': The Social and Cultural Dimensions of Work."

56. Elaborating in a somewhat different direction Will Herberg's interpretation of the adherence to socialist or communist ideologies among Jews as an expression of secularized Jewish Messianism ("Socialism, Zionism, and Messianic Passion," *Midstream* 2 [Summer 1956]: 65–74), one might argue that the Jewish Left's commitment to helping the world's exploited and needy out of their troubles has been a form of the secularized-universalized *tsdoke*.

57. Local interviews with women, social life panel (7/21/1981), women's panel (7/22/1981), *Rodef Sholom Bulletin*, 1931–1936. Written memoirs and recorded oral histories of big-city Jews make frequent references to the charity *pushkes* attached to kitchen cupboards, but they do not tell how far this ritual of private *tsdoke* traveled with the economically and residentially mobile Jewish families.

58. UJA donations calculated from personal records of Dr. Meyer Bloom (presently at Dr. Meyer and Sally Bloom Archives at the Beth Sholom Congregation in Johnstown). Post–World War II data indicate that a considerably greater proportion of Jewish households in small towns than in big cities contribute to the annual UJA campaigns: 66–75 percent, and 20–25 percent, respectively (cited after Silberman, *A Certain People*, 193). Many more unaffiliated Jews live in large cities than in small towns, and this of course to a significant degree explains the low figure in the former; another likely factor is that among the institutionally affiliated, social expectations regarding communal obligations are more imposing and social control more effective in small towns than in large cities.

59. Local interviews; the Gee Bee clan's sending money to their shtetl in Europe from interview with Bella C. (November 1965), as quoted in Winograd, *A History of Johnstown's Jews*, 133.

60. Interviews with Isadore G., 6/2/1986, and Lottie B., 8/25/1980; also small town and women's panels. As in the case of charity *pushkes*, immigrant memoirs and oral histories of big-city Jews also contain mentions of this private form of

Hakhnoses Orkhim, but not much more can be said about the persistence of this practice in metropolitan centers during the interwar period without closer inquiry into the matter.

61. Interviews with Abe B., 7/18/1988; Fanny B., 7/16/1988; Nathan E., 6/2/1986; Millard C., 7/16/1988.

62. Interviews with Sadie W., 11/25/1988; Isadore G., 7/18/1988; Harriet K,. 7/15/1988; Isadore S., 8/16/1984.

63. See, e.g., Moshe Davis, "Jewish Religious Life and Institutions in America (An Historical Study)," in *The Jews: Their History, Culture, and Religion*, ed. Louis Finkelstein (New York: Harper & Brothers, 1949), 1:354–453; Sharot, "The Three Generations Thesis and the American Jews," 156; Weinberg, *The World of Our Mothers*, 117–21, 253, 258, 268–69; Cowan and Cowan, *Our Parents' Lives*, 265–77. A sharp generational conflict regarding religious and related matters has also been recorded in memoirs and novels written by the American-born offspring of immigrants: see, for example, Leah Morton's memoir *I Am a Woman and a Jew* (New York: J. H. Sears & Co, 1926), or Anzia Yezierska's novels *All I Could Never Be* (New York: Brower, Warren, & Putnam, 1932) and *Bread Givers* (New York: Braziller, 1925).

64. These quotations are typical comments made by my informants while they reminisced about the "naturalness" of their religious practices and occasional conflicts they caused. Interestingly—here is another instance of "individual effects" upon cultural change—a number of the second-generation Johnstowners spoke of the influence of Rabbi Ralph Simon at Rodef Sholom, and at Ahavath Achim that of Herman Rockoff, a young American-born Orthodox rabbi who stayed there for a short period. Under the impact of these rabbis' "wonderful sermons" and "beautiful [biblical] stories and old legends" vividly narrated, the young people reflected on their Jewishness and found it "interesting" for the first time in their lives. (Having repeatedly heard statements about the experience-near "of course" nature of their religiosity, I explicitly asked whether there was in it anything of interest to them.)

65. Robert Lynd and Helen Merrell Lynd, *Middletown in Transition* (New York: Harcourt, Brace & World, 1937), 403.

66. This last was Jennie G.'s immediate reply to my inquiry about the prospect of a Christmas tree in her parents' home (interview on 7/16/1988); my other respondents' denial was as quick, if less emphatic. On Christmas trees in Jewish homes in New York City before World War II: Duker, "On Religious Trends in American Jewish Life," 52; Kenneth Nathan White, "American Jewish Responses to Christmas" (M.A. thesis, Hebrew Union College at Cincinnati, 1982); Sarna, "Is Judaism Compatible with American Civil Religion?" 152–73. On the same issue after the Second World War, see Milton Matz, "The Meaning of the Christmas Tree to the American Jew," *Jewish Journal of Sociology* 3 (April 1961): 129–37.

67. On public recreation in New York City, see, e.g., Kathy Peiss, *Cheap Amusements: Working Women and Leisure in Turn-of-the-Century New York* (Philadelphia: Temple University Press, 1986); Glenn, *Daughters of the Shtetl*, 159–63; and Elisabeth Ewen, *Immigrant Women in the Land of Dollars* (New York: Monthly Review Press, 1985), chap. 12, "City Lights." On Yiddish- and English-language Jewish-American entertainment: Irving Howe, *World of Our Fathers* (New York: Simon and Schuster, 1976), pt. 3; Nahma Sandrow, *Vagabond Stars: A World History of Yiddish Theater* (New York: Limelight Editions, 1983), chaps. 5, 7, 8, 10;

Sarah Blacher Cohen, ed., *From Hester Street to Hollywood: The Jewish-American Stage and Screen* (Bloomington: Indiana University Press, 1983). Generally on a rapid diversification of mass entertainment and the growth of recreational consumption in America from the turn of the century through the interwar period, see Richard Wightman Fox and T. J. Jackson Lears, eds., *The Culture of Consumption: Critical Essays in American History, 1880–1980* (New York: Pantheon Books, 1983).

68. Nettie McGill, "Some Characteristics of Jewish Youth in New York City," *Jewish Social Service Quarterly* 14 (June 1937): 251–72; Nettie McGill and Ellen Matthews, *The Youth of New York* (New York: Macmillan, 1940), 258ff.

69. *Johnstown—The Friendly City* (Johnstown: Johnstown Chamber of Commerce, 1937); 1920s and 1930s Johnstown city directories; *Review of Greater Johnstown, Pennsylvania* (Johnstown: Greater Johnstown Chamber of Commerce, 1952); Jean Crichton, "Music and Lights of Main Street," in *Johnstown: A Story of a Unique Valley*, ed. Karl Berger (Johnstown: The Johnstown Flood Museum, 1982), 666–706.

70. The New York quotation from Weinberg, *The World of Our Mothers*, 99. Information about Johnstown's Jews from local interviews; annual lists of subscribers to the Jewish Publication Society, 1920–1940. The quotation about general Johnstown and Jewish reading habits from Winograd, *A History of Johnstown's Jews*, 262–63. (Arthur H. confirmed this opinion in several conversations with me as well.)

71. Local interviews. On young women's leisure activities in New York City, see Peiss, *Cheap Amusements*; Ewen, *Immigrant Women in the Land of Dollars*, and idem, "City Lights: Immigrant Women and the Rise of the Movies," *Signs* 5 (1980), suppl. issue, 45–66.

72. Women's panel, 7/22/1981.

73. Local interviews, social life panel (7/21/1981). On ragtime music fans in New York City, see Ewen, *Immigrant Women in the Land of Dollars*, 214.

74. Quotation from Joselit, "'A Set Table,'" 48–49ff.; see also Ewen, *Immigrant Women in the Land of Dollars*, 158–59; Charlotte Baum et al., "Pearls around the Neck, a Stone upon the Heart: Becoming an American Lady," in *Immigrant Women*, ed. Maxine Schwartz Seller (Philadelphia: Temple University Press, 1981), 140–45; Gwen Gibson Schwartz and Barbara Wyden, "Culture, Culture, Culture," in Gwen Gibson Schwartz and Barbara Wyden, *The Jewish Wife* (New York: Peter H. Wyden, 1969), 231–38.

75. Interview with Moe S., 6/6/1986. In her very interesting discussion on the role of women as managers of family social life, Micaela Di Leonardo seems to restrict this function to "the work of kinship," in her own phrase (Micaela Di Leonardo, "The Female World of Cards and Holidays: Women, Families, and the Work of Kinship," *Signs* 12 [Spring 1987]: 440–53). The experience in the management of informal social life of Jewish women in Johnstown—and, I believe, outside of it as well—extended beyond circles of relatives into the larger (ethnic, in this case) community: more than "the work of kinship," it was, rather, "community work."

76. Interviews with Moe and Dolly S., 8/9/1986; Joe K., 6/18/1990; Mildred G., 6/20/1990. On various etiquette guidebooks for Jewish readers, see Braunstein and Joselit, *Getting Comfortable in New York*, 38–39; and Eli Lederhendler, "Guides for the Perplexed: Sex, Manners, and Mores for the Yiddish

Readers in America," *Modern Judaism* 11 (October 1991): 138–77. The quotation about "American ladies" from Baum et al., "Pearls around the Neck, a Stone upon the Heart," 206–7.

77. A description (and pictures) of the interiors in Joselit, "'A Set Table,'" 48–49ff.

78. Local interviews and private collections of old photographs; the contents of wills on record at Cambria County Courthouse, Ebensburg, Pennsylvania.

79. "Pretense not to count every penny" from Andrew Heinze, *Adapting to Abundance: Jewish Immigrants, Mass Consumption, and the Search for American Identity* (New York: Columbia University Press, 1990), 121. On New York Jews' preoccupation with stylish dress, see ibid., chap. 5; cf. also *Becoming American Women: Clothing and the Jewish Immigrant Experience, 1880–1920*—an exhibition at the Chicago Historical Society, March 1994–January 1995, catalog (same title) by Barbara Schreier (Chicago: Chicago Historical Society, 1994).

80. *Oneg Shabbat*—interview with Bella C., 8/4/1980; announcements from *Rodef Sholom Bulletins* of February 1934, n.p., and September 1934, n.p.

81. The quotation from Joselit, "'A Set Table,'" 43; summers in the Catskills in Judd Teller, *Strangers and Natives* (New York: Delacorte Press, 1968), 87, 141ff.; Heinze, *Adapting to Abundance*, chap. 7; also memoirs and novels. Summer camps in the Catskills, Poconos, and Adirondacks were also places where young New Yorkers, dressed in "flamboyant sport shirts, flowered organdy dresses, "*costumes pour le sport*," engaged in the games of mating. An interesting discussion of this practice-as-ethnicization can be found in Phyllis Deutsch's "Theater of Mating: Jewish Summer Camps and Cultural Transformation," *American Jewish History* 75 (March 1986): 307–21. Regrettably, I did not investigate Johnstowners' ways of dating in a systematic enough manner to be able to make comparisons.

82. Local interviews (quotation from a conversation with Bill B., 8/15/1984); *Rodef Sholom Bulletin*—personal announcements, 1931–1936.

83. Interviews with Rodef Sholom members; Winograd, *A History of Johnstown's Jews*, 162, 210.

84. The term "secular religion" is from David Levine, *The American College and the Culture of Aspiration, 1915–1940* (Ithaca, NY: Cornell University Press, 1986), 87; see also Burton Bledstein, *The Culture of Professionalism: The Middle-Class and the Development of Higher Education* (New York: Norton, 1976); and n. 1 in chapter 3 of this book.

85. There exist in Jewish-American studies contrary opinions regarding the "translatability" of the traditional Jewish reverence for and practice of religious (Talmudic) scholarship onto secular education: an interpretation of the latter as a functional equivalent of the former applied to different circumstances can be found, for instance, in Nathan Glazer, "The American Jew and the Attainment of Middle-Class Rank: Some Trends and Explanations," in Sklare, *The Jews*, 138–47; for an argument that the two have been of qualitatively distinct kinds, see, e.g., Miriam Slater, "My Son the Doctor: Aspects of Mobility among American Jews," *American Sociological Review* 34 (June 1969): 359–73.

86. A "tone of great excitement" from Henry Feingold, "Investing in Themselves: The Harvard Case and the Origins of the Third American-Jewish Commercial Elite," *American Jewish History* 77 (June 1988): 543; see also Leonard Dinnerstein, "Education and the Advancement of American Jews," in *American Education and the European Immigrant, 1840–1940*, ed. Bernard Weiss (Urbana:

University of Illinois Press, 1982), 49; Glazer, *American Judaism*, 81. On the dominant society's response to this "passion for learning" in the form of discrimination in college and university admissions: Marcia Synnot, *The Half-Open Door: Discrimination and Admissions at Harvard, Yale, and Princeton, 1900–1970* (Westport, CT: Greenwood Press, 1979); Levine, *The American College*, chap. 7, "Discrimination in College Admissions."

87. In Providence, Rhode Island, for example, gender parity in Jewish enrollments had nearly been reached by 1915 (Joel Perlmann, *Ethnic Differences, Schooling and Social Structure among the Irish, Italians, Jews, and Blacks in an American City, 1915–1935* [New York: Cambridge University Press, 1989], 146–49); for similar findings nationwide based on the 1910 census, see Jerry Jacobs and Margaret Greene, "Race and Ethnicity, Social Class and Schooling," in *After Ellis Island: Newcomers and Natives in the 1910 Census*, ed. Susan Cotts Watkins (New York: Russell Sage: 1994), 209–56.

88. Quotation from interview with Elmer M., 6/11/1986.

89. Quotations from interviews with Betty W. and Helen P., 6/3/1986. Such status-motivated preference for the academic course in high school were not unique to Jewish students: see David Labaree, *The Making of an American High School: The Credentials Market and the Central High School of Philadelphia, 1838–1939* (New Haven: Yale University Press, 1986), 155–60.

90. Interview with Isadore S., 8/16/1984.

91. Graduation yearbooks: Johnstown High School, 1920–1940; Westmont High School, 1930–1940; content analysis of the *Johnstown Tribune*, 1920–1940; interview with Marian V., a retired high school teacher (6/12/1986).

92. *Rodef Sholom Bulletin*, 1931–1936; *Beth Zion Temple Tidings*, 1941–1942.

93. This is my general evaluation based on individual interviews, and small town and business panels.

94. Eva Etzioni-Halevy and Zvi Halevy, "'The Jewish Ethic' and the Spirit of Achievement," *Jewish Journal of Sociology* 19 (June 1977): 49–66.

95. Jewish names traced in the Johnstown High School records, and in *The Spectator*, graduation yearbooks of the Johnstown High School, 1920–1935.

96. Paula Fass, "'Americanizing' the High Schools: New York in the 1930s and '40s," in Paula Fass, *Outside In: Minorities and the Transformation of American Education* (New York: Oxford University Press, 1989), chap. 3, esp. 80–97, 105–11. Jewish students' average grades as generally higher than those of members of other ethnic groups have also been reported in Perlmann's study in Providence, Rhode Island, *Ethnic Differences*, 151–54; and in Labaree's investigation of school curriculum, academic performance, and future plans of students of an elite high school in Philadelphia, *The Making of an American High School*, 159–60 and passim. In public schools with intellectually stimulating extracurricular programs in smaller cities, too, Jewish students excelled academically—see, e.g., a (narrative) report by Jeanette Goldhar and Frances Nelson, *"As We Remember": Early History of the Jewish Community in Gary, Indiana*, The Indiana Jewish Historical Society, Publication no. 28 (June 1992), 45. Rather than seeing it as mainly a result of a stimulating environment, however, Fass interprets this "hyperactivity" of Jewish students as "produced by a lack of manifest status and assured social position" ("'Americanizing' the High Schools," 94).

97. Johnstown High School guidance files, 1926–1937 (not systematic), on microfilm at Meadowvale Media Center in Johnstown; Mary Jastrow quotation

from her autobiography, *Looking Back: The American Dream through Immigrant Eyes* (New York: Norton, 1986), 97; Johnstown quotations from interviews with Isadore S., 6/8/1986; Eleanor H., 6/7/1986; Abe B., 6/2/1986); Mildred G., 6/1/1986.

98. Interviews with Bea R., 6/3/1986; Dolly K., 8/5/1981; Harold N., 6/3/1986; Mollie K. 6/4/1986; Vivian C. 6/3/1986.

99. University of Pittsburgh at Johnstown enrollment records, 1928–1940, *Scrapbook UPJ*; interview with Isadore S., 6/8/1986. The New York study of Jewish law students: Melvin Fagen, "The Status of Jewish Lawyers in New York City," *Jewish Social Studies* 1 (January 1939): 73–104; a similar survey conducted in the 1930s among students in Boston also reported "a majority of students working their way through college"—cited in Levine, *The American College*, 86–87.

100. Information gathered from the University of Pittsburgh enrollment records, 1918/19–1939/40 (University of Pittsburgh, Hillman Library, Archives of the Industrial Society; Office of the Registrar), and Carnegie Institute enrollment records, 1918/19–1939/40 (Carnegie-Mellon University Library).

101. Estimates based on the applications for entry, and enrollment records— University of Pittsburgh, Office of the Registrar, 1930/31–1939/40 (I also sample-checked gender composition of the applicants two decades earlier, 1910–1920, and found nearly 70 percent of the candidates to have been men). National and New York data on Jewish college enrollments and the approximate gender parity among New York Jewish students from Lee Levinger, *The Jewish Student in America* (Cincinnati: B'nai B'rith, 1937), 41–42. However, recollections of the second-generation female New Yorkers suggest that young men did have a priority in college education (cf., e.g., Baum, Hyman, and Michel, *The Jewish Woman in America*, 123–28); it may be that these were representatives of the earlier cohorts of American-born children of immigrants.

102. Interviews with Israel T., 8/16/1984; Naomi S., 6/2/1988; Ruth W., 6/2/1986; Harriet K., 6/2/1988; Shirley M., 6/3/1986; Ben M., 8/14/1984.

103. Interviews with former college students and their families in Johnstown; Labaree, *The Making of an American High School*, 159–61; University of Pittsburgh—enrollments and graduations (Jewish-sounding names), 1918/19–1926/27, 1930/31–1936/37.

104. Interviews with former students (graduates and dropouts) in Johnstown. In large cities, Jewish students also disproportionately chose medical and legal professions (Levinger, *The Jewish Student in America*, 70, 72, 80, 86), but it made even more sense in Johnstown where there were practically no other employment opportunities for Jewish college graduates.

105. Quotations from interviews with Naomi S., 6/2/1988; Ben I., 6/6/1986; Harriet K., 6/2/1988.

106. Interviews with former college students and their families about their old-country origins, religious and secular training of family members in Europe, and social micro-networks.

CHAPTER 5
IN THE MIDDLE ON THE PERIPHERY: INVOLVEMENT IN THE LOCAL SOCIETY

1. Interview with Louis M., retired superintendent at Bethlehem Steel Company in Johnstown, 10/31/1981. Regarding a small African-American community in Johnstown, see n. 9 in chapter 3.

2. After Deborah Dash Moore, *At Home in America: Second Generation New York Jews* (New York: Columbia University Press, 1981), 201.

3. Following the prevailing usage in the historiography of American urbanism in the period of main concern in this chapter (i.e., about two and a half decades between the two world wars), in my investigation of the existing studies, I used less-than-100,000 inhabitants as a cutoff point dividing "small" from "large" cities. Regarding the size of an ethnic (Jewish) group, I followed the common usage among historians of American Jews in the same time period: I have classified the number of Jewish residents in a city as "large" when it was 10,000 and more (a "large share" in the total population has been assigned an arbitrary cutoff value of 10 percent).

Among studies conducted in the metropolitan centers and larger cities that either wholly or in part deal with the period prior to World War II, the following have devoted specific attention to one or more aspects of the participation of Jews in the dominant (American) local society: in New York—Irving Howe, "Getting into American Politics," in *World of Our Fathers* (New York: Simon and Schuster, 1976); Heywood Broun and George Britt, *Christians Only: A Study in Prejudice* (New York: Da Capo Press, 1974); Moore, *At Home in America*; Ronald Bayor, *Neighbors in Conflict: The Irish, Germans, Jews, and Italians of New York City, 1929–1941* (Urbana: University of Illinois Press, 1988); Lawrence Fuchs's study, *The Political Behavior of American Jews* (Glencoe, IL: The Free Press, 1956), contains data on Jewish political participation in New York, Boston, Chicago, and Philadelphia; Digby Balzell, "The Jewish Communities in Philadelphia and Boston: A Tale of Two Cities," in *Jewish Life in Philadelphia, 1830–1940*, ed. Murray Friedman (Philadelphia: Institute for the Study of Human Issues, 1983), 290–313; Henry Meyer, "The Structure of the Jewish Community in the City of Detroit" (Ph.D. diss., University of Michigan, 1939); Edward Herbert Mazur, *Minyans for a Prairie City: The Politics of Chicago Jewry, 1850–1940* (New York: Garland Publishing, 1990); Erich Rosenthal, "Acculturation without Assimilation? Jewish Community of Chicago, Illinois," *American Journal of Sociology* 65 (November 1960): 275–88; Judith Endleman, *The Jewish Community of Indianapolis 1849 to the Present* (Bloomington: Indiana University Press, 1984); Lloyd Gartner, *History of the Jews of Cleveland* (Cleveland: Western Reserve Historical Society, 1978); Max Vorspan and Lloyd Gartner, *History of the Jews of Los Angeles* (Philadelphia: The Jewish Publication Society, 1970); Marc Lee Raphael, *Jews and Judaism in a Midwestern Community: Columbus, Ohio, 1840–1975* (Columbus: Ohio Historical Society, 1979); Richard Zweigenhaft, "Two Cities in North Carolina: A Comparative Study of Jews in the Upper Class," *Jewish Social Studies* 41 (Summer–Fall 1971): 291–300; Judith Kramer and Seymour Leventman, "The Jews in North City: The Emergence of a Community," in *Children of the Gilden Ghetto* (New Haven: Yale University Press, 1961); Jonathan Sarna, "'A Sort of Paradise for the Hebrews': The Lofty Vision of Cincinnati Jews," in *Ethnic Diversity and Civic Identity: Patterns of Conflict and Cohesion in Cincinnati since 1820*, ed. Henry Shapiro and Jonathan Sarna (Urbana: University of Illinois Press, 1992), esp. 140–49.

The participation of Jews in the local mainstream society in smaller cities and towns has for the most part been investigated by sociologists in the early postwar era. Among the classical studies are Ben Kaplan, *The Eternal Stranger: A Study of Jewish Life in the Small Community* (New York: Bookman Associates, 1957); Peter Rose, *Strangers in Their Midst: Small-Town Jews and Their Neighbors* (Merrick, NY: Richwood Publishing Co., 1977); Charles Reznikoff and Uriah Engelman, *The*

Jews of Charleston (Philadelphia: The Jewish Publication Society, 1950); Joseph
Greenblum and Marshall Sklare, "The Attitude of the Small-Town Jew toward His
Community," in *The Jews: Social Patterns of an American Group*, ed. Marshall
Sklare (NewYork: The Free Press, 1958). Also Joshua Trachtenberg, *Consider the
Years: The Story of the Jewish Community of Easton, 1752–1942* (Easton, Pennsylva-
nia: The Centennial Committee of Temple B'rith Sholom, 1944); Jonathan Sarna,
Jews of New Haven (New Haven, CT: Jewish Historical Society of New Haven,
1978); Gerald Gold, "A Tale of Two Communities: The Growth and Decline of
Small-Town Jewish Communities in Northern Ontario and Southwestern
Louisiana," in *The Jews of North America*, ed. Moses Rischin (Detroit: Wayne State
University Press, 1987); Leonard Dinnerstein's and Mary Dale Palsson's edited
volume, *Jews in the South* (Baton Rouge: Louisiana State University Press, 1973),
containing several references to small-town Jews' relations with mainstream local
society; Eugen Schoenfeld, "Small-Town Jews: A Study in Identity and Integra-
tion" (Ph.D. diss., Southern Illinois University, 1957); Robert Shosteck, *Small-
Town Jewry Tell Their Story* (New York: B'nai B'rith Vocational Service, 1953);
John Dean, "Patterns of Socialization and Association between Jews and Non-
Jews," and the discussion following the paper with Julian Greifer, Leo Srole, and
Joshua Trachtenberg participating—*Jewish Social Studies* 17 (July 1955): 77–110.
About a dozen short local histories of Jewish communities in different small towns
in Indiana, prepared by their own members, have been published by the Indiana
Jewish Historical Society, but they are of unequal value as sources for sociological
analysis. Also noteworthy is vol. 2 of the so-called Lakeville Studies conducted in
the 1950s in a midwestern suburb under the direction of Marshall Sklare, and entirely devoted to Jewish-Gentile relations: *A Study of Jewish-Gentile Relations: The
Edge of Friendliness*, by Benjamin Ringer (New York: Basic Books, 1967).

4. Although the information is insufficient for a more accurate assessment, it
appears that transiency of Jewish residents, particularly in "small-size" environments, apparently neutralized the effects of weak (or absent) organized ethnic
group networks as well as white skin color, both otherwise conducive to Jews' participation in the local mainstream society. On the transiency of Jews in Southern
rural towns in the nineteenth century and their (resulting?) limited outside involvement, see Elliott Ashkenazi, *The Business of Jews in Louisiana, 1840–1875* (Tuscaloosa: University of Alabama Press, 1988), and Dinnerstein and Palsson, *Jews in
the South*; also Lee Shai Weissbach, "Stability and Mobility in the Small Jewish
Community: Examples from Kentucky History," *American Jewish History* 79
(Spring 1990): 355–75.

5. I was tempted to take for comparison the town of Muncie, Indiana, because
it has been repeatedly studied by Robert and Helen Lynd during the interwar period (*Middletown* and *Middletown in Transition* [New York: Harcourt Brace, 1929
and 1937]). At the time of my writing this book, however, there did not exist
enough information for this town pertinent to the subject of this chapter; on the
Muncie Jewish residents, see Whitney Gordon, "Jews and Gentiles in Middletown," *American Jewish Archives* 18 (April 1966): 41–72, and Dwight Hoover,
Magic Middletown (Bloomington: Indiana University Press, 1986), passim. Only
after having completed the manuscript of my Johnstown study did I learn about
Messrs. Martin Schwartz and Daniel Rotenberg's oral history project-in-progress
on the past and present of the Muncie Jewish community.

6. Sources of information about Cleveland's Jews can be found in n. 3 in this

chapter; information about the city comes from Philip Porter, *Confused City on a Seesaw* (Cleveland: Ohio State University Press, 1976); Thomas Campbell and Edward Miggins, eds., *The Birth of Modern Cleveland, 1865–1930* (Cleveland: Western Reserve Historical Society, 1988); Edward Miggins, ed., *A Guide to Studying Neighborhoods and Resources in Cleveland* (Cleveland: The Cleveland Public Library, 1984)—the volume also contains a chapter entitled "Cleveland's Jewish Community"; David Van Tassel and John Grabowski, eds., *Cleveland: A Tradition of Reform* (Kent, OH: Kent State University Press, 1986); personal communications from Edward Miggins, Thomas Campbell, Scott Cline, John Grabowski, and Yehuda Rubinstein (4/5–6/1991). It should be noted, because it most likely also contributed to the overall integrative character of Cleveland Jews' public relations, that their involvement in the local political process had originated, and had by and large remained throughout the interwar period, under Republican tutelage at both city and ward levels, and therefore without the competitive presence of other ethnic groups of recent origins. (One of the most widely acclaimed and charismatic leaders who opened up and multiplied communication channels between the Jewish as well as other "new" ethnic groups and the dominant society was during the 1920s a devoted Republican, Attorney Maurice Mashke, an American-born son of German-Hungarian parents.) All the combined circumstances promoting the integrating rather than divisive character of Cleveland Jews' public relations, and this very effect itself, made possible two public events symbolically expressing intergroup civic solidarity during periods of intensified anti-Semitic sentiments and actions across the country (no such events, we may add, took place in New York): in 1920, a mass rally was held against the anti-Semitic propaganda of Henry Ford's *Dearborn Independent*, and in 1938 a mass demonstration protested Nazi persecution of German Jews. A similar integrative situation regarding civic-political participation of local Jews obtained also in Cincinnati (see Sarna, "'A Sort of Paradise for the Hebrews,'" 140–49).

7. Besides Reznikoff's and Engelman's *The Jews of Charleston*, and (during the final round of checking and revisions of the book manuscript) James Hagy's *This Happy Land: The Jews of Colonial and Ante-Bellum Charleston* (Tuscaloosa: University of Alabama Press, 1993), I have relied on personal communications (4/21–22/1991) from Mr. Salomon Breibart from Temple Beth Elohim in Charleston. A majority of Charleston's Jews in the 1940s were affiliated with the Orthodox synagogue, but apparently these were different, that is, considerably less separatist or more outgoing, Orthodox Jews than elsewhere in America; a contemporary study reports, in fact, regular cooperation between the Reform and Orthodox segments of the Charleston Jewish community, in both internal group matters and outside representation, with the Reform leaders usually at the helm. It may also be of interest to some readers that apparently the very first merger of a Reform temple and an Orthodox synagogue in American Jewish history occurred in Charleston, as early as 1866 (Reznikoff and Engelman, *The Jews of Charleston*, 164–65 and passim).

8. General bibliographic sources for the information about New York can be found in n. 3 in this chapter. New York East European Jews—the overwhelming majority of the city's Jewish population—entered and participated in the American political process at the local level primarily through the Democratic party, dominated by the Irish-ruled Tammany machine that fended off attempts by "new" ethnic groups to break, or at least diminish, its control. The quotation about "the foreign [Jewish] blood sweeping in" is from Jerold Auerbach, *Unequal Justice:*

Lawyers and Social Change in Modern America (New York: Oxford University Press, 1976), 107.

9. Information about Terre Haute is from Jacob Rader Marcus, *To Count a People: American Jewish Population Data, 1585–1984* (New York: Lanham, 1990), 68; Herman Koren, *From Generation to Generation: A History of the Terre Haute Jewish Community*, The Indiana Jewish Historical Society, Publication no. 20 (Fort Wayne, IN, 1986); personal communications from old-time residents of the area, Messrs. Max Einstandig and Martin Schwartz, 4/7–8–9/1991. Terre Haute's Jews were, actually, accepted in the Masonic lodge, but not in social clubs (*From Generation to Generation*, 49). Regarding my informants' resolute denials that Indiana Jews were afraid of the Klan, I report what I heard, but I am not sure whether, and if so, how, these statements should be "deconstructed," that is, searched for possible hidden (suppressed) meanings. Neil Betten, the (non-Jewish) author of a history of Gary, Indiana, confirmed, however, this evaluation of local Klansmen as hostile mainly against Catholics and blacks, and generally more "civilized," so to say, than their Southern brethren—personal communication, 4/20/1991. See also Raymond Mohl and Neil Betten, *Steel City: Urban and Ethnic Patterns in Gary, Indiana, 1906–1950* (New York: Holmes & Meier, 1986).

10. While there exist studies of the social, and especially political, relations in different cities between Jews and Irish, Germans, and Italians, excepting a few investigations of Jewish-Ukrainian relations in Canada and the United States, there is, curiously, practically no research on such interactions between Jews and Slavic groups. On Jewish-Ukrainian relations, see Harold Troper and Morton Weinfeld, "Jewish-Ukrainian Relations in Canada since World War II," *American Jewish History* 77 (September 1987): 106–34; see also Morton Weinfeld et al., eds., *The Jews in Canada* (Don Mills, Ont.: Oxford University Press, 1993). Contacts of Jewish socialists and union activists with Slavic workers in American cities have been mentioned in passing, but not specifically investigated, by historians of American, and particularly Jewish, political and labor radicalism during the first half of this century. A history of Jewish-Hungarian social relations, and cultural and ethnic-political cooperation in the United States prior to World War I—unusually friendly in comparison with any other (Christian) immigrant group from East Europe—has been described in Robert Perlman's *Bridging Three Worlds: Hungarian-Jewish Americans, 1848–1914* (Amherst: University of Massachusetts Press, 1991).

11. Arno Mayer, "The Lower Middle Class as Historical Problem," *Journal of Modern History* 47 (September 1975): 427.

12. Koren, *From Generation to Generation*.

13. Regarding Jews competing for mainstream office and sales jobs in New York City, Broun and Britt cite a report of the Bureau of Jewish Social Research's survey of June 1929 on employment discrimination, and similar observations reported by Bruno Lasker in a 1926 study. According to Broun and Britt, a number of Jews nevertheless managed to obtain these jobs, by changing names and otherwise concealing their ethnic origin (*Christians Only*, 125, 148–49, 213, 224–31).

14. It is interesting, however, that during the 1870s and through the mid-1880s—when Jews from Germany, most of them prosperous merchants who regularly advertised in the *Johnstown Tribune*, constituted the majority of the small Jewish population in town—the local paper not infrequently carried information, presented in a positive light, about "Jewish" events around the world and different aspects of Jewish history. Most likely these items were brought to the paper by the

local Jews themselves, but they were nevertheless accepted. With the arrival of larger numbers of East Europeans, these news items, excepting notes about religious holidays, practically disappeared for several decades.

15. On market/work relations as the main area of Jewish-Gentile contacts see, especially, the Lakeville study: Ringer, *The Edge of Frendliness*, 2:188–94 and passim.

16. Information from Attorney Samuel DiFrancesco, Sr., Johnstown, 12/18/1980.

17. On the basis of content analysis of the *Johnstown Tribune*, 1890s–1930s; interview with Frances C., 6/9/1980; YMCA, Johnstown, scrapbook; "Americanization Program—Johnstown, Pennsylvania," loose documents 1915–1927, The National Archives, Washington, DC; Judicial and Fiscal Branch, NARS (E587, box 92).

18. Ewa Morawska, "Immigrant Communities between the Wars," in *For Bread with Butter: Lifeworlds of East Central Europeans in Johnstown, Pennsylvania, 1890–1940* (New York: Cambridge University Press, 1985).

19. On anti-Semitism in America during the period covered in this study, with some regional and interurban comparisons, see, e.g., Jonathan Sarna, "American Anti-Semitism," in *History and Hate: The Dimensions of Anti-Semitism*, ed. David Berger (Philadelphia: The Jewish Publication Society, 1986), 115–28; specifically on so-called social anti-Semitism, see John Higham's classic, *Send These to Me* (New York: Atheneum, 1975), and idem, "Social Discrimination against Jews in America, 1830–1930, in *The Jewish Experience in America*, ed. Abraham Karp (New York: Ktav, 1969), 5:349–82. Charles Herbert Stember et al., in *Jews in the Mind of America* (New York: Basic Books, 1966), assembled public opinion surveys from the years 1937–1963 dealing with Americans' attitudes toward Jews. According to a survey conducted in 1930 by the *Jewish Daily Bulletin* among Jewish college students, anti-Semitic occurrences were less frequent in small towns than in large cities—after Broun and Britt, *Christians Only*, 96–97 (on anti-Semitism in particular cities, see case studies listed in n. 3 in this chapter).

On anti-Semitism and Jewish quotas in American universities, see Marcia Synnot, *The Half-Open Door: Discrimination and Admissions at Harvard, Yale, and Princeton, 1900–1970* (Westport, CT: Greenwood Press, 1979); and Harold Wechsler, "Anti-Semitism in the Academy: Jewish Learning in American Universities, 1914–1939," *American Jewish Archives* 42 (Spring–Summer 1990): 9–21; David Levine, *The American College and the Culture of Aspiration, 1915–1940* (Ithaca, NY: Cornell University Press, 1986), pt. 2, "Discrimination in College Admissions."

20. As related in Stember, *Jews in the Mind of America*, 65 and passim.

21. Content analysis of the *Johnstown Tribune*, Johnstown High School's graduation programs, special publications related to important local events (anniversaries, celebrations, etc.). Quotations (in the order that they appear in the text) from *Johnstown Tribune*, January 3, 1920, 3; April 4, 1925, 8. The emphasis here on the religious character of Johnstown's public anti-Semitism does not imply, however, that it did not exist in the big cities in which Jews had been perceived as economic competitors and a status threat: see, e.g., Broun and Britt, *Christians Only*; also, Charles Glock and Rodney Stark, *Christian Beliefs and Anti-Semitism* (New York: Harper & Row, 1966). Robert Wuthnow (*The Restructuring of American Religion* [Princeton University Press, 1988], 77) cites a 1930s study in the San

Francisco area reporting that "Protestant and Catholic church members were prone to think of Jews as 'Christ-killers' who were still experiencing the wrath of God for not believing in Christ."

22. "Hory Bratja Serdca Nasa," *Cerkovnaja Nauka*, March 3, 1903.

23. Johnstown High School holiday programs, high school yearbooks—Johnstown Public Library, Johnstown High School archives (Media Center), Westmont High School, Dale High School, content analysis of the *Johnstown Tribune*; local interviews. *Story of Johnstown, Pennsylvania, Illustrated* (Johnstown: Clarence Weaver Publisher, n.d).

Robert Lynd and Helen Merrell Lynd reported in *Middletown* (1929) a local opinion survey showing nearly 90 percent of the town's high school students as having agreed with the statement that "Christianity is the one true religion" (pt. 5, "Religious Practices," 316). In all likelihood, the results of a similar quiz in Johnstown in the same period would not have been different. On Jewish reactions to religious instruction in American public schools, see Joakim Isaacs, "The Struggle for the Soul: A Jewish Response to Bible Reading and Religion in American Public Schools, 1900–1925," *American Jewish Archives* 42 (Spring–Summer 1990): 119–34.

24. Quotations from *Johnstown Tribune*, September 24, 1902, 2; September 23, 1911, 4; "koschner meat"—as cited in Leonard Winograd, *"The Horse Died at Windber": A History of Johnstown's Jews of Pennsylvania* (Bristol, IN: Wyndham Hall Press, 1988), 109.

25. Content analysis of the *Johnstown Tribune*, 1920s–1930s, *Rodef Sholom Bulletin*, 1931–1936; *Jewish Center of Johnstown–Rodef Sholom Synagogue*, Johnstown, (1954), 27; interviews with Isadore S., 7/23/1981; and Rabbi Ralph Simon, 11/9/1986; Winograd, *A History of Johnstown's Jews*, 158, 225; YMCA archives, Johnstown. It may be added that the term "race," with its implication of immutable difference, was applied to Jews rather widely and across the country; Stember et al. report on the mid-1940s national opinion survey in which over 40 percent of the respondents defined Jews as a "race" rather than as a nationality or a religious group (*Jews in the Mind of America*, 50, 59 and passim).

26. Interview with Frieda S., 6/3/1989.

27. Quotation from interview with Rita T., 4/18/1986.

28. Social life panel, Johnstown, 7/21/1981. On the Americanizing role of ethnic leadership, see Victor Greene, *American Immigrant Leaders, 1800–1910: Marginality and Identity* (Baltimore: Johns Hopkins University Press, 1987).

29. Winograd, *A History of Johnstown's Jews*, 80–83, 277 (a–b, h–k); *Jewish Criterion*, Pittsburgh, March 1916, n.p.; *The Universal Jewish Encyclopaedia* (New York: The Universal Jewish Encyclopedia, 1944), 8:430–31; interviews with Maurice S., 8/13/1980; Samuel K., 7/29/1981; Meyer B., 8/7/1984; Isadore S., 7/23/1981; Ben I. (the first quotation), 8/18–19, 26/1980; Blanche B., 6/2/1986; Andrew G., (the second quotation), 10/11/1991. There was yet another case of a Johnstown Jew eulogized by his family (also in the local paper after his death) as a Republican party activist, whose name my informants from the prewar local political establishment were unable to recognize.

30. *Johnstown Tribune*, municipal election reports, 1890s–1930s; interview with Mr. Andrew Gleason, 10/16/1991. (There were in Johnstown during the interwar period a total of 10–25 registered Socialists, and 150–250 actual Socialist

voters, depending on the year and election level.) Should anyone interested in a history of American small-town politics before World War II like to see the Johnstown data (registered voters, voting returns by city precincts, etc., for local and national elections), I would be glad to share my small archive.

31. Interviews with the late Attorney Samuel diFransesco, Sr. (12/18/1980), arrested by the mayor of Johnstown during the 1937 steel strike at Bethlehem Steel Company for trying to represent the workers; Andrew G., 10/11/1991; Robert F., 6/11/1989; also Morawska, *For Bread with Butter*, 159–60, 246–47.

32. Masonic lodges in Johnstown (about fifteen) as listed in Johnstown city directories, 1890s–1930s; on the influence of Masons in local politics, interviews with Andrew G., 10/16/1991, and Jack P., 11/16/1991. On the Masons in Pennsylvania: "Freemasonry in Pennsylvania," in *Gould's History of Freemasonry throughout the World*, rev. Dudley Wright (New York: Charles Scribner's Sons, 1936), 6:144–68. On different kinds of Masonic orders in the United States, from the egalitarian to the most exclusive: Mary Ann Clawson, *Constructing Brotherhood: Class, Gender, and Fraternalism* (Princeton: Princeton University Press, 1989).

33. On women's involvement in American politics before and after the Nineteenth Amendment, see Suzanne Lebsock, "Women and American Politics, 1880–1920," in *Women, Politics, and Change*, ed. Louise Tilly and Patricia Gurin (New York: Russell Sage, 1990), 35–62; in the same volume, Nancy Cott, "Across the Divide: Women in Politics before and after 1920," 153–76, and Kristi Andersen, "Women and Citizenship in the 1920s," 177–198. As for Cleveland, Sophonisba Breckinridge's contemporary classic, *Women in the Twentieth Century: A Study of Their Political, Social, and Economic Activities* (New York: McGraw-Hill, 1933), makes frequent references to Cleveland women's engagement at all levels of city politics; see also Thomas Campbell, "Mounting Crisis and Reform: Cleveland's Political Development," in Campbell and Miggins, *The Birth of Modern Cleveland*, 298–324; Lois Sharf, "The Women's Movement in Cleveland from 1850," in Van Tassel and Grabowski, *Cleveland: A Tradition of Reform*, 67–90; also personal communication from Lois Sharf (12/31/1991).

Surprisingly, unless I missed something, there seem to exist no historical studies devoted specifically to women's political participation in prewar New York City. My impression from bits and pieces gathered from different studies has been, however, that Cleveland was more progressive, or open, in this regard than New York (in the latter, Bella Moskovitz, a powerful assistant to Al Smith, seems to have overshadowed other women, in any case in historical accounts).

34. Quotation after Breckinridge, *Women in the Twentieth Century*, 332. A "small town" category, however, was defined as containing "up to 50,000 inhabitants," and it is probable that the reported phenomenon occurred mainly in very small towns of less than 10,000 inhabitants.

35. In the one-party system the most important—actually, the only—local elections are the primaries, and in the period considered here the way they were conducted, i.e., who was included and who was out, was decided by the ruling party. Information about Charleston interwar politics comes from my telephone interviews with Dr. Amy McCandless from the History Department at the University of Charleston (4/21/1991), and with Mr. Salomon Breibart, a native and longtime resident of the town. The Pollitzer sisters' papers are deposited at the South Carolina Historical Society in Charleston. On states that did not ratify the Nineteenth

Amendment, see Carrie Chapman Catt and Nettie Rogers Shuler, "The States That Did Not Ratify," in their *Woman Suffrage and Politics* (New York: Charles Scribner's Sons: 1926), 462–89.

36. This and the following voter registration figures for Johnstown Jews come from the Election Office at Cambria County Courthouse in Ebensburg, Pennsylvania (the only prewar years for which there exist personal voter registration records are 1936/37 and 1940, and these have been used). Women had a smaller share, 37 percent, in the total number of registered Jewish voters in the 1930s, which was slightly lower than the average figure, 43 percent, reported for that period in the United States generally. The information on women voters in the United States from Breckinridge, *Women in the Twentieth Century*, 246–47, and Andersen, "Women and Citizenship in the 1920s," 193. In comparison with the general registration figures in Pennsylvania in the 1930s, 56 percent and 44 percent, respectively (Breckinridge, 251), the proportions of registered Jewish voters, especially men, were considerably higher: 75–80 percent among men, and nearly 50 percent among women, perhaps as a result of the combined persuasive efforts of Max B. (the fellow ethnic *makher*) and the Westmont (and other) canvassers. Unfortunately, I was unable to locate any similar data for Jews in smaller towns, but Ronald Bayor, a specialist on interwar ethnic voting (*Neighbors in Conflict*) believes that in comparison with other immigrant groups, Jews generally tended to register in high proportions, and my figures did not surprise him (personal communication, 1/17/1991).

37. Since the great majority, about three-quarters, of American Jews were big-city dwellers, this statement applies primarily to that category, and, in particular, to the New Yorkers, who constituted a majority of big-city Jews. On the Democratic party preference of the majority of American Jews by the late 1930s, see Fuchs, *The Political Behavior of American Jews*, 73–75. According to the *American Jewish Year Book* 39 (1937/38): 735, 90 percent of all (ten) Jewish members of the U.S. Congress were Democrats. Historical studies in larger cities indicate, however, a considerable differentiation of Jewish voting patterns in local elections (I have not found any voter registration data for small-town Jews prior to World War II; shortly after the war, a study of Jewish communities in several small towns in southern Illinois found Jews there to have been "politically more conservative and [to have] vote[d] more often Republican than their urban counterparts": Schoenfeld, "Small-Town Jews: A Study in Identity and Integration," 97).

38. Data gathered from the Election Office, Cambria County Courthouse, Ebensburg, Pennsylvania. There were only a handful of instances—less than 5 percent of the total number of families for whom records exist—of "split registration," i.e., different for parents and children, or husband and wife. Regarding the latter, it was, interestingly, without exception the wives who registered as Democrats, the husbands as Republicans; unfortunately, all of these few people had either died or left town by the time I arrived so there was no one to ask.

39. On the relationship between Jews' marginality and political liberalism or radicalism, see work of Michels and Lipset—as discussed in Charles Liebman, *The Ambivalent American Jew* (Philadelphia: The Jewish Publication Society, 1973), 135–68; also Gerhard Lensky, *The Religious Factor* (Garden City, NY: Doubleday, 1961), 137–40, 319–21, and passim. On the "localism" of the Jewish vote, see Oscar Handlin, *The Uprooted* (New York: Little, Brown & Co., 1951), 211, and idem, *Adventure in Freedom: Three Hundred Years of Jewish Life in America* (New

York: McGraw-Hill, 1954), 128; generally on the contingent nature of Jews' political orientations, see Samuel Heilman and Steven Cohen, *Cosmopolitans and Parochials: Modern Orthodox Jews in America* (Chicago: University of Chicago Press, 1989), 163–64 and passim; on this issue, see also Stephen Cohen, *American Modernity and Jewish Identity* (New York: Tavistock, 1983), chap. 7, "Liberalism as the Politics of Group Integration." Quotation from Peter Medding, "Towards a General Theory of Jewish Political Interests and Behavior," in *Kinship and Consent: The Jewish Political Tradition and Its Contemporary Uses*, ed. Daniel Elazar (Washington, DC: University Press of America, 1983), 321. In another interpretation, Jewish voting behavior has been primarily determined by the civic insecurity of the voters; see, e.g., Stephen Isaacs, *Jews and American Politics* (New York: Doubleday, 1974), 140–43.

40. Local interviews; data for Westmont calculated from voting returns as printed in *Johnstown Tribune*, November 5, 1936, 16; November 6, 1940, 13. In the 1936 presidential election, over 40 percent of Westmont's "supper side" and 30 percent of its "dinner side" voted for Roosevelt. For the entire city, this vote was 59 percent, reflecting in large part the sentiments prevailing in densely populated working-class wards. (In comparison, 74 percent of the New York voters cast their votes for Roosevelt). A colleague who is a historian of American Jewry pointed out to me that the pattern of split voting was actually quite common among Jews in that era; I did not succeed, however, in locating any concrete information, whether quantitative or narrative, on this matter.

41. Quotations from interviews with Ruth G., 7/15/1990, and Elmer M., 9/11/1990.

42. There exists a considerable sociological literature on this subject; a good review discussion, and an extensive bibliography, can be found in Frank Bechhofer and Brian Elliott, "The Voice of Small Business and the Politics of Survival," *Sociological Review* 26 (February 1978): 57–88. See also Erik O. Wright, "Class Boundaries and Contradictory Class Locations," in *Classes, Power, and Conflict: Classical and Contemporary Debates*, ed. Anthony Giddens and David Held (Berkeley and Los Angeles: University of California Press, 1982), 112–30.

43. On the Rodef Sholom rabbi as a member of the Citizens Committee during the 1937 steel strike, see Robert Peles, "Crisis in Johnstown: The 'Little Steel' Strike of 1937" (unpublished seminar paper, University of Pittsburgh at Johnstown, 1975), 32–34, 38, 66; also Bruce Williams and Michael Yates, "Labor in Johnstown," in *Johnstown: The Story of a Unique Valley*, ed. Karl Berger (Johnstown: The Johnstown Flood Museum, 1984), 589–638. Interviews with Harry R., 8/15/1984, and Irving L., 10/31/1980; also with Maurice S., 8/13/1980; Isadore G., 8/25/1980; Morton M., 8/22/1980; Isadore G., 8/13/1980; Samuel R., 8/25/1980. On the Beth Zion rabbi's refusal to join the Citizens Committee, see Leonard Winograd, "A History of Johnstown's Jews" (Ph.D. diss., Hebrew Union College-Cincinnati, 1967), 168–69 (the information about the congregation's unhappiness about the rabbi's public stand does not appear in the published version of Winograd's study). There was also an earlier, similar incident, during the 1919 steel strike, when a rabbinical student invited from Hebrew Union College delivered a High Holiday sermon in which he openly defended the strike, and was met with icy silence (ibid., 305–6). On the American Reform rabbinate's "social justice platform," see Michael Meyer, *Response to Modernity: A History of the Reform Movement in Judaism* (New York: Oxford University Press, 1988), 309–14.

44. Quotations from interviews with Ben I., 7/30/1981; Henry K., 8/6/1986.

45. Interview with Samuel K., 7/29/1981.

46. Percentage of Jewish vote for American Labor Party in New York from Bayor, *Neighbors in Conflict*, 41. David Gingold's story as recorded by Harry Crone, *35 Northeast: A Short Story of the Northeast Department International Ladies' Garment Workers' Union, AFL-CIO, Based on the Reminiscences and Diaries of David Gingold and Official ILGWU Records* (New York: ILGWU Publications, 1970), 57–60; also interviews with Martin Morand, the ILGWU activist, 10/18/91; labor historian Alice Hoffman, 10/18/91; Ruth Whitehead, former employee at Goldstein and Levine in Johnstown, 10/11/1991; telephone conversation with Patricia Raines, Western Pennsylvania District Council, ILGWU, Johnstown, 11/17/91; and local interviews with members of the Jewish community. The first Jewish labor arbitration lawyers from Johnstown appeared in the area in the late 1940s. The United States' entry into the war, and, locally, the establishment of the independent union at Bethlehem mills in 1941 and subsequent weakening of the company's grip over the town's public life, must have created a sufficient cluster of motivations for Johnstown Jews increasingly to switch their party allegiance from the Republican to the Democratic party (on the basis of voter registration records, Election Office, Cambria County Courthouse, Ebensburg, Pennsylvania, 1940s–1950s).

47. For example, according to an investigation conducted in 1948–1951 in over two hundred urban communities of different sizes and varying proportions of Jews in their general populations, regardless of these numerical parameters, about 85–90 percent reported Jewish involvement in nonsectarian organizations, but in only between 45 and 75 percent did Jews hold elective and/or appointive political offices: Dean, "Patterns of Socialization and Association between Jews and Non-Jews," 91–93. Historical studies (see n. 3 in this chapter) do not provide comparable statistical figures, but their analyses indicate a similar general pattern (New York could have been an exception, in that, during the interwar period, political participation of Jews was very considerable, while intense "occupational" anti-Semitism kept many Jewish professionals out of work-related associations; see Broun and Britt, *Christians Only*, chap. 5, "Professional Prejudice"). There exists some evidence indicating a retrogression of Jewish participation in general organizational activities in the 1920s and 1930s, during the time of increased "urban" (or secular) anti-Semitism in the United States; in fact, this occurrence has been reported not in small towns but in the big cities. Cleveland seems to have been, again, a notable exception: there an uncommonly favorable and stable constellation of factors allowed for the maintenance over time of the undiminished substantial Jewish involvement in the city's community affairs that was apparently on a par with Anglo-Protestant contributions (Gartner, *History of the Jews of Cleveland*, 84; also 74 75, 226–41).

48. Local interviews; bequests from Registrar of Wills, Cambria County Courthouse, Ebensburg, Pennsylvania, 1920–1950.

49. *Greater Johnstown, Pennsylvania* (Greater Johnstown Chamber of Commerce, 1950), 5; *Pennsylvania Labor and Industry in the Depression*, Commonwealth of Pennsylvania, Department of Labor and Industry, Special Bulletin no. 39 (Harrisburg, 1934), 124; Winograd, *A History of Johnstown's Jews*, 80, 158, 228–

29; *Johnstown Tribune*, content analysis (news related to Jews and Jewish community, 1890s–1930s); *Rodef Sholom Bulletin*, 1932–1935; local interviews.

50. The Johnstown Chamber of Commerce, "Capital Contributors," continuous file 1936–1947; *Johnstown Tribune*, February 3, 1936, 4; business panel 7/15–16/1981; individual interviews with Meyer B., 8/21/1980; Henry K., 8/15/84; Blanche B., 1/7/1989. The Johnstown Symphony Orchestra, the town's chief cultural institution, was not fully established until the mid-1940s, although its origins (in local German bands) date back to the 1920s (Jean Crichton, "Music and Lights of Main Street," in *Johnstown: The Story of a Unique Valley*, ed. Karl Berger [Johnstown: The Johnstown Flood Museum, 1984], 666–705).

51. Tilly and Gurin, *Women, Politics, and Change*; Lebsock, "Women and American Politics." Discussions of the implications for the Jewish group's "assimilation" (the term conventionally used in pre-1970s studies) of such facilitating functions of women's membership in nonsectarian voluntary organizations can be found in several historical studies; see, especially, the Lakeville study (Ringer, *The Edge of Friendliness*, chap. 11, " The Voluntary Association and Social Contact").

52. Telephone conversation with Mr. Max Einstandig, 4/23/92.

53. Minuscule Jewish participation in private clubs and lodges: e.g., Kaplan, *Eternal Stranger*, and Rose, *Strangers in Their Midst*. The quotation about small-town Jews in Rotary and Elks clubs, and the like, from Lee Levinger, "The Disappearing Small-Town Jew," *Commentary* 14 (May 1952): 159. While the exclusionary admission policies of New York social clubs prior to World War II are often stated by American Jewish historians, one seldom finds contemporary data to this effect; some information is provided in Broun and Britt, *Christians Only*, 222, 282–84, 289–93, and passim. On the exclusion of Jews from Cleveland's Union and University clubs, see Gartner, *History of the Jews in Cleveland*, 84–85. In Los Angeles, for comparison, which had long retained the qualities of an open frontier town, and where Jews freely joined nonsectarian social clubs, since the mid-1920s a tangible increase in anti-Semitism resulted in a dwindling of this membership (Vorspan and Gartner, *History of the Jews of Los Angeles*, 144–45).

54. See n. 32 in this chapter for bibliographical references on the history of U.S. and Pennsylvania Masonry. Local interviews with Martin S., 8/20/1980; members of the local elite, Jack P., 11/24/90; Andrew G., 11/15/91. On Jewish members of the Masons in the 1860s–1870s, see Winograd, *A History of Johnstown's Jews*, 34–35 and passim.

55. Jewish members at Sunnehanna country club from the club's membership file; Winograd, *A History of Johnstown's Jews*, 7–13, 320–27, 163 (quotation about Leon M.); other quotations from interviews with Robert F., 6/11/89; Irving L., 5/12/1982; also interviews with members of the local elite, Andrew G., 10/11/91; Matthew S., 6/14/89.

56. On the American Jewish-Hungarians' triple identity, see Perlman, *Bridging Three Worlds*; see also Ewa Morawska, "A Replica of the 'Old-Country' Relationship in the Ethnic Niche: East European Jews and Gentiles in Small-Town Western Pennsylvania, 1880s–1930s," *American Jewish History* 77 (September 1987): 72–73. Interviews with Arthur H., 7/23/1981; Olga S., 8/7/84; Martin G., 8/6/84, 5/4/86; Esther J., 5/4/86; Irene W., 8/7/84; Joe K., 6/8/86. This particular carry-over from the old country, where the cultural integration of Jews and Gentiles had been more pronounced in Hungary than in the surrounding Slavic-popu-

lated areas, suggests, by the way, that participation in formally organized activities, and specifically in the symbolic-expressive kind, may be in certain situations more significant as an indicator of ethnic group identification than primary social involvement, which in the classical assimilation model has been treated as a stronger predictor of ethnic bonds' maintenance (or weakening).

57. See, e.g., Baltzell, "The Jewish Communities in Philadelphia and Boston"; Rosenthal, "Acculturation without Assimilation?"; Raphael, *Jews and Judaism in a Midwestern Community*; Meyer, "The Structure of the Jewish Community in Detroit"; Kramer and Leventman, *Children of the Gilden Ghetto*. An early postwar study of a Midwestern suburb found on the average about 85 percent of close circles of friends reported by Jewish respondents to have been ethnically homogeneous, even though—especially in the residential areas with a predominance of Gentiles—the majority of Jews did socialize informally in some manner with their neighbors, including occasional home visiting (Ringer, *The Edge of Friendliness*, 120, 223–28). In Cleveland, although there occurred Jewish-Gentile friendships formed on the basis of shared participation in public affairs and organizational activities, very little of such relations was carried into private domiciles; on residential segregation in Cleveland prior to World War II, see, especially, Edward Miggins, "The Ethnic Mosaic: The Settlement of Cleveland by the New Immigrants and Migrants," in Campbell and Miggins, *The Birth of Modern Cleveland*, 104–40. Also personal communications from Scott Cline, John Grabowski, Edward Miggins, and Yehuda Rubinstein (December 1991).

58. *Forverts* (1926)—quotation from Moore, *At Home in America*, chap. 3. "A World of Its Own," 85.

59. Business panels, 7/15–16/1981; interviews with Lilly L. and Rose L., 8/16/1984 (also Winograd, *A History of Johnstown's Jews*, 142 and n.576); Sally W., 11/25/1988 (bar mitzvah story); Isadore G., 6/3/1986 (no transfer to parents).

60. Quotation from interview with Sally W., 11/25/1988. Local interviews with Jewish and Anglo-Protestant women; social life panel, 7/21/1981. I located only one report—an early postwar study of Jewish-Gentile relations in a Midwestern middle-class suburban community—in which more systematic data have been provided regarding this kind of informal relations in the neighborhood; even while it reported close ("meaningful") friendships as for the most part ethnically homogeneous, the study found these two forms of socializing to have been a quite common occurrence among Jewish (male and female) respondents whose neighbors were predominantly (70 percent or more) Gentile—see Ringer, *The Edge of Friendliness*, 223–27.

61. Estimates calculated from the Johnstown High School school records, 1920s–1930s; New York (Grand Concourse and Flatbush, 1937) from Moore, *At Home in America*, 98; see also Broun and Britt, *Christians Only*, 72, and Bayor, *Neighbors in Conflict*, 26. Quotation from interview with Frieda C., 8/28/1980; estimation of a "division of entertainment time" from local interviews.

62. Local interviews; quotations from interviews with Raphael R., 6/2/1986, and Maurice S., 8/13/1980.

63. In bigger cities this complete separation was beginning to break somewhat at the turn of the century as young Jewish people occasionally dated Gentile partners; on this development, see Sydney Stahl Weinberg, *The World of Our Mothers: The Lives of Jewish Immigrant Women* (Chapel Hill: University of North Carolina

Press, 1988), 50–53; Weinberg also notes a considerable independence from parental opinion of second-generation young Jewish girls' dating behavior (not necessarily with Gentile boys) (ibid., 205–12).

64. Local interviews; specific examples and quotations from interviews with Abe and Blanche B., 5/2/1986; Harriett K., 6/2/1989; Frieda C., 8/28/1980; Betty W., Helen P., and Gloria M., 6/3/1986; Moe S., 8/13/1980; Maurice S., 8/6/1980; two broken relationships from interviews with Fanny B., 8/1/1986; Robert K., 6/11/1986. A similar "dating but no marriage" principle has been reported in other Jewish settlements in big and small cities, after World War II; for a review, see Louis Berman, *Jews and Intermarriage: A Study in Personality and Culture* (New York: Thomas Yoseloff, 1968).

65. Local interviews. Quotations from interviews (in the order that they appear in text) with Frances C., 6/9/1980; Abe K., 5/31/1984; Betty W., 8/10/1982; Irving L., 5/12/1982. Several people remembered an incident when parents of one such intermarried son sat *shivah*, i.e., mourned the departed family member in a traditional ritual for the dead. Intermarriage estimates for the United States and selected cities from C. Bezalel Sherman, *The Jew within American Society* (Detroit: Wayne State University Press, 1965), 183–87; Sidney Goldstein, "American Jewry: A Demographic Analysis," in *The Future of the Jewish Community in America*, ed. David Sidorsky (Philadelphia: The Jewish Publication Society, 1973), 81–88; in Charleston: Reznikoff and Engelman, *The Jews of Charleston*, 239; in Stamford (and quotation): Samuel Koenig, "The Socioeconomic Structure of an American Jewish Community," in *Jews in a Gentile World*, ed. Isacque Graeber (New York: Macmillan, 1942), 236–38.

66. Interviews with Sam K., 7/29/1986; Shirley M., 6/3/1986; Miriam K., 8/3/1984; Bessie S., 6/1/1986; Blanche B., 6/2/1986; Abe K., 10/30/1984; Harry M., 8/11/1980; Martin G. and Esther J., 5/4/1986.

CHAPTER 6
THROUGH SEVERAL LENSES: MAKING SENSE OF THEIR LIVES

1. Interview with Blanche B., 6/2/1986.
2. "Flexible and fluxible" from a conversation with Ben I., 6/4/1984.
3. On Western and American minds, see Donald Levine, *The Flight from Ambiguity: Essays in Social and Cultural Theory* (Chicago: University of Chicago Press, 1985); Michael Kammen, *People of Paradox: An Inquiry Concerning the Origins of American Civilization* (New York: Knopf, 1973), chap. 4, "Biformity: A Frame of Reference," 107. While discussing the appreciation by modern Americans of their existential situations, Robert Bellah et al. point out several "ambivalences" therein, but what they have in mind are *sociological* ambivalences (as elaborated by Robert Merton), more often than not unacknowledged by the actors. See Robert Bellah et al., *Habits of the Heart: Individualism and Commitment in American Life* (New York: Harper & Row, 1985); Robert Merton and Elinor Barber, "Sociological Ambivalence," in Robert Merton, *Sociological Ambivalence and Other Essays* (New York: The Free Press, 1976), 3–32. Ambivalence as the inherent feature of modern (Western) experience is also discussed by Andrew Weigart and David Franks in "Ambivalence: A Touchstone of the Modern Temper," in *The Sociology of Emotions*, ed. David Franks and Doyle McCarthy (Greenwich, CT: Jai Press, 1989), 205–28, but the authors' primary concern is to demonstrate *that* such ambivalence exists

and identify its social sources, rather than to analyze mental and emotional ways in which the moderns approach and handle this condition. On "dialectical" and other interpretations of Jewish outlooks in this matter, see n. 49 in chapter 1 of this book.

4. "Whatever We Do Is Not Satisfactory," *Daily Jewish Courier*, September 26, 1921 (Foreign-Language Press Survey, 1936—at the Immigration History Research Center, St. Paul, Minnesota); "Rabbi Will Preach: 'When Contradiction Makes Sense,'" *Beth Zion Temple Tidings*, Johnstown, October 1936.

5. Quotations from conversations with Louis G., 5/4/1984, and Arthur H., 8/4/1984.

6. Most studies used as a comparative base in the preceding chapter contain at least a passing note about this persistent sense of insecurity: see n. 3 in chapter 5, and also Peter Rose, *The Ghetto and Beyond: Essays on Jewish Life in America* (New York: Random House, 1969); Jessie Bernard, "Biculturality: A Study in Social Schizophrenia," in *Jews in a Gentile World*, ed. Isacque Graeber (New York: Macmillan, 1942), 264–93. A sense of vulnerability-insecurity has also been conveyed, tacitly or explicitly, in the autobiographical sources—memoirs and novels, particularly by the first American-born generation, the immigrants' children: see, e.g., Norman Podhoretz, *Making It* (New York: Harper & Row, 1980); Charles Silberman, *A Certain People: American Jews and Their Lives Today* (New York: Summit Books, 1985), esp. 29–40, 222–24; Henry Popkin, "The Vanishing Jew of Our Popular Culture," *Commentary* 42 (July 14, 1952): 46–55; Alan Dershowitz, *Chutzpah* (Boston: Little, Brown, 1991).

7. The coinage "ambassadors to the *goyim*" in studies of American Jews' relations with and attitudes toward Gentiles seems to be Peter Rose's, who in turn heard it from his informants while conducting research in little towns in upstate New York in the 1950s (*Strangers in Their Midst: Small-Town Jews and Their Neighbors* [Merrick, NY: Richwood Publishing Co., 1977], 76–79). "The vanishing Jew" comes from Popkin's essay, "The Vanishing Jew"; see also the essays in Rose, *The Ghetto and Beyond*, in the part entitled "Outsiders Within," 421–94. Jewish self-hatred has a substantial literature; for a classical statement, see Kurt Lewin, *Resolving Social Conflicts* (New York: Harper & Brothers, 1948), 193, cf. also 169–200; a cogent discussion of the problem and a review of literature can be found in Raphael Patai, *The Jewish Mind* (New York: Charles Scribner's Sons, 1977), chap. 17, "Jewish Self-Hate," 456–81 (the quoted statement can be found on p. 462).

8. See, e.g., Podhoretz, *Making It*, esp. chap. 1, "The Brutal Bargain"; Joseph Mersand, *Traditions in American Literature: A Study of Jewish Characters and Authors* (Port Washington, NY: Kennikat Press, 1939); Patricia Erens, *The Jew in American Cinema* (Bloomington: Indiana University Press, 1984); Lester Friedman, *Hollywood's Image of the Jew* (New York: Frederick Ungar Publishing Company, 1982), 66–67; Popkin, "The Vanishing Jew."

9. See, e.g., Rose, *Strangers in Their Midst*, and small-town studies of Ben Kaplan, Eugene Schoenfeld, Joseph Greenblum and Marshall Sklare, and Benjamin Ringer—all cited in n. 3 in chapter 5.

10. Quotation from interview with Seymour S., 6/4/1986.

11. Quotations from interviews with Louis G., 5/4/1984, and Ben I., 8/16/1984; America as "this glorious country" from *Rodef Sholom Bulletin*, July 1936, 27.

12. Interviews with Robert K., 6/4/1986, and Helen M., 6/8/1986.

13. Quotations from interviews with Moses S., 7/30/1980; Morris N., 9/12/1981; Nathan E., 3/19/1986. On the subject of mutual perceptions of Jewish and Gentile East Europeans in western Pennsylvania small towns during the first half of this century, see Ewa Morawska, "A Replica of the 'Old-Country' Relationship in the Ethnic Niche: East European Jews and Gentiles in Small-Town Western Pennsylvania, 1880s–1930s," *American Jewish History* 77 (September 1987): 27–86.

14. Interview with Judith W., 4/7/1992.

15. Local interviews, social life panel, 7/21/1981; small town panel, 7/30/1981, and conversations with Eleanor H., 6/7/1988; Betty W. and Helen P., 6/3/1986; Rabbi Ralph Simon, 11/9/1986.

16. To judge from the imposing synagogue buildings constructed during the same period by upwardly mobile Jews in metropolitan centers, the motives there were the opposite of a desire for inconspicuousness. But these structures usually stood in the middle of dense ethnic neighborhoods seldom visited by the Anglo-Protestant middle class, so the impressed were apparently usually the Jews themselves. Social life panel, 7/21/1981; small town panel, 7/30/1981, and individual interviews. " *Naye* up to day *shul*" from minutes of Rodef Sholom Synagogue board meetings, 12/26/1920. On the imposing synagogue buildings in New York, for example, see Deborah Dash Moore, *At Home in America: Second Generation New York Jews* (New York: Columbia University Press, 1981), chap. 5, "From Chevra to Center."

17. See "Participation in Civic-Political Affairs" in chapter 5 of this book; the argument that holding on to fixed ideas is alien to the Jewish way of thinking was reportedly used by David Gingold, an ILGWU organizer from New York, during a dinner party held in a Jewish home in the Westmont section of Johnstown, as he was persuading Mr. G., owner of a local garment factory, to permit in his establishment an independent labor union—quotation from *35 Northeast: A Short History of the Northeast Department International Ladies' Garment Workers' Union, AFL-CIO, Based on the Reminiscences and Diaries of David Gingold and Official ILGWU Records*, booklet prepared by Harry Crone (1970), 59.

18. Interview with Meyer B., 8/24/1980.

19. Notes from interviews with Phil E., 8/11/1982, and Nathan E., 6/2/1986.

20. Anglicized names from Ejectment and Miscellaneous Docket, Cambria County Courthouse, Ebensburg, Pennsylvania, Prothonotary Office (1880–1940). The story of traveling with a chicken to the *shochet* from Freda LaVictoire, *Who Sing and Spring: A Somewhat Sardonic Sound-Off* (MS, Hebrew Union College Archives, Cincinnati, n.d.). I heard reminiscences with a similar underlying meaning from my second-generation informants in the Johnstown area: the most common seems to have been a discomfort with visibility connected with coming from and going to the synagogue at "odd times" from the viewpoint of the Christian ritual calendar; but the Jewish observance was never negated.

21. On parallelism between the Protestant and Jewish ethos of achievement, with particular reference to America, see Fred Strodbeck, "Family Interaction, Values, and Achievement," in *Talent and Society*, ed. David McClelland et al. (Princeton: D. Van Nostrand Company, 1958), 135–94; Nathan Glazer, "The American Jew and the Attainment of Middle-Class Rank: Some Trends and Explanations," in *The Jews: Social Patterns of an American Group*, ed. Marshall Sklare (New York: The Free Press, 1958), 138–47; Gerhard Lensky, *The Religious Factor*

(Garden City, NY: Doubleday, 1961), 113–14ff. For comments and polemics, see, e.g., Eva Etzioni-Halevy and Zvi Halevy, "The 'Jewish Ethic' and the 'Spirit of Achievement,'" *Jewish Journal of Sociology* 19 (June 1977): 49–66; Mariam Slater, "My Son the Doctor: Aspects of Mobility among American Jews," *American Sociological Review* 34 (June 1969): 359–73. The question of comparability of the modern Protestant and Judaic ethos has its roots in the classical studies of Max Weber and Werner Sombart (Max Weber, *Ancient Judaism*, trans. and ed. Hans Gerth and Don Martindale [Glencoe, IL: The Free Press, 1952]; Werner Sombart, *The Jews and Modern Capitalism* [Glencoe, IL: The Free Press, 1951]); for Jewish and other scholars' discussion of this issue, see Paul Mendes-Flohr, "Werner Sombart's: The Jews and Modern Capitalism. An Analysis of Its Ideological Premises," *Leo Baeck Institute Yearbook* 21 (1976): 87–107; Werner Mosse, "Judaism, Jews, and Capitalism: Weber, Sombart, and Beyond,' *Leo Baeck Institute Yearbook* 24 (1979): 3–17; Freddy Raphael, "Max Weber and Ancient Judaism," *Leo Baeck Institute Yearbook* 18 (1973): 41–62. See also Mathew Schoffeleers and Daniel Meijers, "Judaism and Capitalism," in *Religion, Nationalism, and Economic Action: Critical Questions on Durkheim and Weber* (Assen: Van Gorcum, 1978). Florence Kluckhohn's essay, "Dominant and Substitute Profiles of Cultural Orientations: Their Significance for the Analysis of Social Stratification," was published in *Social Forces* 28 (May 1950): 376–93.

22. Sociological literature on these processes, under the general heading of "modernization," and under specific subjects, is much too large for even a fragmentary listing. Pertinent to the issues discussed here are, for instance, Robert Bellah's classic, *The Broken Covenant* (New York: Seabury, 1975), and a more recent, and more popular, study by this author and others, *Habits of the Heart*.

23. Virginia Yans-McLaughlin, "Metaphors of Self in History: Subjectivity, Oral Narrative, and Immigration Studies," in *Immigration Reconsidered: History, Sociology, and Politics*, ed. Virginia Yans-McLaughlin (New York: Oxford University Press, 1990), 254–90. Collected during the epoch of social history "from the bottom up," these interviews have now been reexamined in a moderately postmodernist fashion.

24. Barbara Myerhoff, *Number Our Days* (New York: Dutton, 1979); Samuel Heilman and Steven Cohen, *Cosmopolitans and Parochials: Modern Orthodox Jews in America* (Chicago: University of Chicago Press, 1989).

25. Interview with Mildred G., 6/1/1986.

26. Interviews with Henry K., 8/16/84; Bill B., 10/2/81; Irving L., 10/2/81.

27. Risk and uncertainty as inherent in small (and bigger, for that matter) entrepreneurship in the capitalist market have of course been noted in the social science literature, and there also exist interesting investigations of "the psychology of coping" with economic uncertainty; see Frank Knight, "The Meaning of Risk and Uncertainty," in *Risk, Uncertainty and Profit* (Boston: Houghton & Mifflin, 1968); George Katona, *Essays on Behavioral Economics* (Ann Arbor: Michigan Institute for Social Research, 1980), 28–35 and passim. See also Ellen Langer, "The Psychology of Chance," *Journal for the Theory of Social Behaviour* 7 (October 1977): 187–267. But I have not been able to find studies looking at consequences of these work circumstances for the meaning content of the Protestant ethos of achievement, and specifically for its basic rationalism and sense of controllability of the world of one's calling. On the basis of evidence provided in the above quoted

works, it is difficult to imagine any small shopkeepers, including the most faithfully Protestant, operating in a modern capitalist market, to have actually displayed in full the orientation posited by the Protestant ethos. It may be that the worldviews of Jews, especially those occupied in trade (but this employment has traditionally been so common in the Jewish group that the accompanying attitude set could well have spread to the larger community), and Christian small entrepreneurs have had in common precisely this element: a sense of a limited rational mastery.

28. Quotations from interviews with Isadore G., 8/18/1980; Ben I., 4/18/1986; Isadore S., 8/16/1984.

29. Quotations from interviews with Abe K. (cited in Leonard Winograd, "A History of Johnstown's Jews" (MS), 303—this fragment does not appear in the published version); Harry R., 6/4/1986; Seymour R., 8/10/1984.

30. The quotations are typical of what I heard from my respondents: interviews with Robert K., 6/4/1986; Ben I., 6/2/1986; Samuel L., 11/2/1988. An interesting attempt to capture religious *Weltanschauungen*, and specifically beliefs about God's interventions in the course of people's actions, among today's Orthodox American Jews can be found in Heilman and Cohen, "The Religious Faith and Fervency of Orthodox Jews," in *Cosmopolitans and Parochials*; see also William McCready and Andrew Greeley, *The Ultimate Values of the American Population* (Beverly Hills, CA: Sage Publications, 1976).

31. On "the American spirit" in the public school system, see David Tyack, *The One Best System: A History of American Urban Education* (Cambridge: Harvard University Press, 1974), esp. pt. 5, "Inside the System: The Character of Urban Schools, 1890–1940." In Johnstown: *The Johnstown High School Spectator* (graduation books), 1918–1940. Quotation from interview with Harold N., 6/4/1986.

32. *Pirke Avot* 2.21 (text, translation, and commentaries by R. Travers Herford (New York: Schocken Books, 1945), 62.

33. Quotations—quite typical of what I heard in connection with "coping tactics"—from interviews with Henry K., 6/1/1986, and Helen M., 6/8/1986. On Jewish humor and its practical uses, see Theodore Reik, *Jewish Wit* (New York: Gamut Press, 1962); also interesting is a contemporary essay of Abraham Klein, "Of Hebrew Humor," *Opinion* 5 (November 1935): 15–19.

34. Local interviews; quotations from my conversations with Isadore S., 6/8/1986; Naomi S., 4/18/1986; Abe B., 4/18/1986; Rita T., 6/10/1986.

35. On the Slavic worldviews, see Ewa Morawska, *For Bread with Butter: Lifeworlds of the East-Central Europeans in Johnstown, Pennsylvania, 1890–1940* (New York: Cambridge University Press, 1985), esp. chaps. 6 and 8; quotation on *morskoje plavanije* from St. Mary's Greek Catholic *Chranitel* (Johnstown), February 1921, 4. In "Metaphors of Self in History," Virginia Yans-McLaughlin makes similar observations about self-concepts of the Italians (described as "passive") as compared with those of the Jews ("active"), but she seems to deny—incorrectly— the emphasis on inner-worldly activism in the traditional (religious) Jewish culture, ascribing the difference between the two worldviews practically entirely to the socioeconomic conditions of the Italian and Jewish everyday lives in New York.

36. Local interviews. Quotations from Jack S., 6/4/1986; Ruth G., 6/3/1986; Ben I., 7/30/1980; and Isadore G., 7/2/1988.

37. Gender effects regarding particular elements of what is considered here inclusively as "the American ethos" have been analyzed by specialized scholarly fields: e.g., a sense of individual autonomy and control by psychologists; instrumental

rationalism and task-orientation by the sociologists of organizations. On Jewish women's worldviews, see, for example, *Writing Our Lives: Autobiographies of American Jews, 1890–1990*, ed. Steven Rubin (Philadelphia: The Jewish Publication Society, 1991); *Jewish Grandmothers*, ed. Sydelle Kramer and Jenny Masur (Boston: Beacon Press, 1977); Sydney Stahl Weinberg, *The World of Our Mothers: The Lives of Jewish Immigrant Women* (Chapel Hill: University of North Carolina Press, 1988); Susan Glenn, *Daughters of the Shtetl: Life and Labor in the Immigrant Generation* (Ithaca, NY: Cornell University Press, 1990); Myerhoff, *Number Our Days*; Yans-McLaughlin, "Metaphors of Self in History."

38. The quotation is from Yans-McLaughlin's "Metaphors of Self in History," 276. On young women's sense of empowerment stemming from independent employment and income, see also Kathy Peiss, *Cheap Amusements: Working Women and Leisure in Turn-of-the-Century New York* (Philadelphia: Temple University Press, 1986); and Weinberg, *The World of Our Mothers*.

39. The quotation is from a conversation with Ben I., 4/18/1986. See also Y. Rim and Z. E. Kurzweil, "A Note on Attitudes to Risk-Taking of Observant and Non-Observant Jews," *Jewish Journal of Sociology* 5 (December 1965): 238–45; and Heilman and Cohen, *Cosmopolitans and Parochials*, 109–10. For a similar interpretation of the practical religious philosophy of American Jewish women in the period under consideration here (those women, of course, who had not broken away from Judaism, i.e., God-trusting yet not passively dependent, and primarily home-oriented), see Chava Weissler's "American Transformations of the *Tkhines*" (paper delivered at a conference on American Jewish Women's History, University of Maryland, November 3–5, 1993). On the significance of God's maleness for Jewish women's spirituality, see Judith Plaskow, *Standing Again at Sinai: Judaism from a Feminist Perspective* (New York: Harper & Row, 1990).

40. Literature on the eroded sense of and obligation to community in the modern (capitalist) American ethos is too large to be cited here; classical discussion can be found in Bellah, *The Broken Covenant*.

41. This is no place to embark on a polemic with different theses found in the sociological literature regarding social conditions conducive to individualist versus collectivist orientations in the "dominant profiles of cultural orientations," but I would like to mention just two such propositions that I find rather unconvincing as overly generalized or ahistorical. One is Frank Bechhoffer and Brian Elliott's idea that "radical individualism" is inherent in the class location of small shopkeepers (see, e.g., "An Approach to a Study of Small Shopkeepers and the Class Structure," *Archives Européennes de Sociologie* 9 [1968]: 180–204); not only the Jewish case in Johnstown, but evidence of strong collectivism of small storekeepers documented in studies on so-called middleman minorities, as well as ethnic groups prone to establish "economic enclaves," undermines this proposition (see, e.g., Walter Zenner, *Minorities in the Middle: A Cross-Cultural Analysis* [Albany: SUNY Press, 1991]). The other thesis I find unconvincing is Robert Wuthnow's generalization that it has been the stability of social conditions that sustains collectivist orientations, while social instability, conversely, breeds individualism (Robert Wuthnow, *Meaning and Moral Order: Explorations in Cultural Analysis* [Berkeley and Los Angeles: University of California Press, 1987], 167–68, 201, and chap. 6, "Social Selection among Ideological Forms"). Wuthnow's proposition seems to me too general, or, differently put, insufficiently contextualized: to take the Jewish case, for example—for the greater part of this group's history it was, precisely, a continuous

threatening "social instability" of the surrounding environment that sustained a strongly collectivist in-group orientation. However, more interesting, and certainly better fitting Jewish history in the modern era, is Wuthnow's (unelaborated) suggestion that "collectivism and individualism may sometimes combine in curious ways," although, he maintains (and I disagree), that these two are "essentially opposites of each other" (ibid., 167). But it may be that we understand the terms "stability," "instability," and "essentially" in different ways. For a historical account of the opposite attitudinal consequences of unstable conditions, see, e.g., John Modell, "Changing Risks, Changing Adaptations: American Families in the Nineteenth and Twentieth Centuries," in *Kin and Communities: Families in America*, ed. A. J. Lichtman and J. R. Challinor (Washington, DC: Smithsonian Press, 1979), 119–44.

42. Quotations from interviews with Isadore G., 6/2/1986; Blanche B., 6/2/1986; Arthur T., 8/8/1980. Charles Silberman believes that even today "among American Jews still close to their East European roots . . . there is a deep-rooted, if unconscious, belief that good fortune is always precarious" (*A Certain People*, 162).

43. Yans-McLaughlin, "Metaphors of Self in History."

44. There are, of course, a great many empirical studies of the "religiosity" of the American people treated as a subject in and of itself, and—closer to the matters of concern here, but still on a different path, so to speak—a considerable literature on the link between American (Protestant) religion and the civil-political "spirit." But I have in mind here, specifically, the consideration of Divine Presence/God in relation to the post-Puritan, modern capitalist ethos of success. Andrew Greeley and William McCready's studies of the "ultimate meanings" in modern American culture are exceptions in this regard (see, for example, McCready and Greeley, *The Ultimate Values of the American Population*).

45. Samuel Heilman's ethnographic studies of the lives of contemporary Orthodox Jews in America are perhaps the most outstanding: see *Cosmopolitans and Parochials* (coauthored with Steven Cohen), and his earlier study *Synagogue Life: A Study in Symbolic Interaction* (Chicago: University of Chicago Press, 1973).

46. For Jews, the God-idea, if grasped at all, appears as the supreme life-promoting force, rather than personified in a concrete figure. Such interpretation can be found in popular-level or didactic essays on this subject published by Conservative authors during the interwar period: Samuel Dinin, "Teaching the God-Idea to Children," *Jewish Education* 6 (April–June 1934): 65–75; also Mordecai Kaplan, "The Place of the Rabbi in American Jewish Life," *Proceedings of the Rabbinical Assembly of America*, 40th Annual Convention at Detroit, Michigan, June 25–27, 1940, esp. 282–87, and discussion, 291–97. Rabbi Simon, a graduate of the (Conservative) Jewish Theological Seminary and the leader of Johnstown's Rodef Sholom Congregation between 1931 and 1936, shared, as I understand, this interpretation of the God-Idea as the creative, life-promoting force. For a good and cogent discussion of the idea of God in Judaism, see Samuel T. Lachs, *Humanism in Talmud and Midrash* (London: Associated University Press, 1993), chap. 2, "God."

47. Clifford Geertz, *Islam Observed: Religious Development in Morocco and Indonesia* (New Haven: Yale University Press, 1968), 17.

48. Interviews with Mildred G., 6/1/1988, and Harry R., 6/4/1988.

49. Cf. Ewa Morawska, "Changing Images of the Old Country in the Development of Ethnic Identity among East European Immigrants, 1880s–1930s: A

Comparison of Jewish and Slavic Representations," *Yivo Annual of Jewish Social Science* 29 (1992): 273–341.

50. Peter Berger and Thomas Luckmann, *The Social Construction of Reality* (Garden City, NY: Doubleday, 1966).

51. Local interviews; quotations from conversations with Seymour S., 6/4/1986, and Bertha W., 6/3/1986.

52. Paul Ricoeur's distinction between optimism and hopefulness can be found in his classic *The Symbolism of Evil* (New York: Harper & Row, 1967); on hopefulness as the higher-order schema, see Ezra Stotland, *The Psychology of Hope* (San Francisco: Jossey Bass, 1969); on "Jewish hope," see Yosef Hayim Yerushalmi, "Vers une histoire de l'espoir juif," *Esprit* 8–9 (August–September 1985): 24–38.

53. Quotations from interviews with Isadore S., 8/16/1986; Joe K., 6/8/1986; and Lillian and Rose C., 8/16/1986. See also Stotland, *The Psychology of Hope*; and McCready and Greeley, *The Ultimate Values of the American Population*.

54. From interviews with Isadore G., 6/2/1988, and Harry R., 6/4/1986.

55. Interview with Harold B., 4/2/1989. The psychologists emphasize the energizing effects of hopefulness on action: see, e.g., Stotland, *The Psychology of Hope*.

56. Ernest Gellner, *Relativism and the Social Sciences* (Cambridge: Cambridge University Press, 1985), 77–78, 81–82.

57. Not by the social scientists, the following studies known to me address this issue in some way: Max Kadushin, *The Rabbinic Mind* (New York: Jewish Theological Seminary of America, 1952); Susan Handelman, *The Slayers of Moses: The Emergence of Rabbinic Interpretation in Modern Literary Theory* (Albany: SUNY Press, 1982); see also (a quite different genre) Ruth Wisse, *Shlemiel as Modern Hero* (Chicago: University of Chicago Press, 1971); and Ellen Schiff, *From Stereotype to Metaphor: The Jew in Contemporary Drama* (Albany: SUNY Press, 1982), esp. chap. 8, "The Jew as Metaphor."

EPILOGUE
POSTWAR ERA: A DECLINE OF THE COMMUNITY

1. I relied on the following sources in this reconstruction: demographic and occupational data for the "Johnstown urbanized area" from the U.S. population censuses in 1950, 1960, 1970, 1980, and 1990 (*urbanized area*, the unit introduced by the 1950 U.S. census, is defined by the Census Bureau as "a central city [or cities] and the surrounding closely settled territory ['urban fringe'] that together have a minimum population of 50,000"); *A Guide to State and Local Census Geography* (U.S. Department of Commerce, Washington, DC: Government Printing Office, 1990), 4; Rodef Sholom Synagogue, Beth Zion Temple, and, after their merger in 1976, Beth Sholom Temple records, 1945–1993; Leonard Winograd's study, *"The Horse Died at Windber": A History of Johnstown's Jews of Pennsylvania* (Bristol, IN: Wyndham Hall Press, 1988); and local interviews with city officials, members of the editorial staff of the local paper, representatives of various religio-ethnic groups, and Johnstown's Jews, men and women in different generational and age groups. Since the discussion in this epilogue is but a quick overview of the main developments in the city and in the Jewish community during the last fifty years, I decided to forgo the usual bibliographic annotations.

APPENDIX I
(SELF-)REFLECTIONS OF A FIELDWORKER

1. Znaniecki's theory of culture remains largely unfamiliar to American sociologists, although it was much more central in his scholarly work over a lifetime than his collaboration with W. I. Thomas on *The Polish Peasant in Europe and America* (Boston: G. Badger, 1918–1920). For Znaniecki's major studies available in English, see *Cultural Reality* (Chicago: University of Chicago Press, 1919); *The Method of Sociology* (Chicago: University of Chicago Press, 1934); *On Humanistic Sociology*, ed. R. Bierstadt (Chicago: University of Chicago Press, 1969); *Approaches to Social Theory*, ed. S. Lindenberg et al. (New York: Russell Sage, 1987). Stefan Czarnowski's collected works are published in the five-volume *Dzieła* (Warsaw: Państwowe Wydawnictwo Naukowe, 1956). Between 1902 and 1912 Czarnowski lived in Paris, where he attended Durkheim's lectures and was a member of the intellectual circle of his disciples. Durkheim's social theory was a lasting influence on Czarnowski's thinking, but in his own work he used a more dynamic approach and strongly stressed the inherent historicity of the sociocultural world. His most renowned historical studies concerned various aspects of collective consciousness (in particular, national, ethnic, and religious) and the social contexts of their transformation. Critical evaluations of theoretical positions and research of each of these two scholars can be found in Piotr Sztompka, ed., *Masters of Polish Sociology* (Cracow: Zakład Narodowy im. Ossolińskich, 1984).

2. For time-mellowed Bourdieu, that is, allowing for a greater role of the creative agency and a more fluxible-flexible *habitus*, see, e.g., his *Les règles de l'art* (Paris: Seuil, 1992). For Loïc Wacquant's extensive, annotated introduction to Bourdieu's work, see Pierre Bourdieu and Loïc Wacquant, *An Invitation to Reflexive Sociology* (Chicago: University of Chicago Press, 1992).

3. I should perhaps explain at this point that "my" Robert K. Merton, the author of *Social Theory and Social Structure* (New York: The Free Press, 1968), was a self-declared functionalist (and was interpreted as such by Stefan Nowak, himself of a similar persuasion). Only after I came to this country in 1979 did I read structuralist interpretations of Merton's work and his own later writings with the explicit structuralist focus. See Lewis Coser, ed., *The Idea of Social Structure: Papers in Honor of Robert K. Merton* (New York: Harcourt Brace Jovanovich, 1975); Jon Clark et al., eds., *Robert K. Merton: Consensus and Controversy* (London: The Falmer Press, 1990).

4. John and Jean Comaroff, *Ethnography and the Historical Imagination* (Boulder, CO: Westview Press, 1992), xi.

5. I borrow here from an interesting, and, in my opinion, very persuasive, defense of the representational treatment of historical narratives, which can be found in Andrew Norman's article "Telling It Like It Was: Historical Narratives on Their Own Terms," *History and Theory* 2 (1991): 119–35. See also Joyce Appleby, Lynn Hunt, and Margaret Jacob, *Telling the Truth about History* (New York: W. W. Norton, 1994). In a recent study of nineteenth-century workers' autobiographies and class formation, Mary Jo Maynes has called a similar combination (i.e., the use of the narratives at once as "data" and as "text") "a contradictory epistemological position"—see her "Autobiography and Class Formation in Nineteenth-Century Europe: Methodological Considerations," *Social Science History* 16 (Fall 1992):

517–37. It seems that this combination appears contradictory only because the social scientists have made it so.

6. On a "constructionist" approach to or "politics" of ethnographic interpretation, and the "accounting for ourselves" as researchers, see Norman Denzin and Yvonna Lincoln, eds., *Handbook of Qualitative Research* (London: Sage, 1994), and, especially, Maurice Punch, "Politics and Ethics in Qualitative Research," 83–98; Egon Guba and Yvonna Lincoln, "Competing Paradigms in Qualitative Research," 105–17; Paul Atkinson and Martyn Hemmersley, "Ethnography and Participant Observation," 248–61; David Altheide and John Johnson, "Criteria for Assessing Interpretive Validity in Qualitative Research," 485–99; and Norman Denzin, "The Art and Politics of Interpretation," 500–515.

7. On the undercounting, and misrepresentations, of lower-level occupational categories in the U.S. censuses at that time, see Margo Anderson, *The American Census* (New Haven: Yale University Press, 1988).

8. Stefan Czarnowski, *Le culte des héros et ses conditions sociales: Saint Patrick, héros national de l'Irlande* (Paris: Librairie Felix Alcan, 1919).

9. I was beginning my education from scratch and did not have any guidance at that time, so this reading list was unavoidably eclectic. For those unfamiliar with but interested in the basic classics in American Jewish studies, this introductory reading list included works of Jacob Rader Marcus, John Higham, Oscar Handlin, Marshall Sklare, Moses Rischin, Nathan Glazer, Peter Rose, Irving Howe, Will Herberg, Daniel Elazar, Paula Hyman, Jonathan Sarna, Barbara Myerhoff, Deborah Dash Moore, Maxine Seller, Simon Kuznets, Arthur Goren, Samuel Heilman, Charles Liebman, Sidney and Alice Goldstein, Calvin Goldscheider and Frances Kobrin Goldscheider. (I mention here only the names of the authors I started with; the specific titles can be found either—a laborious way—in the notes to particular chapters of this book, or—much easier—in the bibliography that may be obtained directly from the author.)

10. See, for example, "Moses Rischin's *The Promised City*, Twenty Years Later," special issue of *American Jewish History* 73 (December 1983); "Marshall Sklare's *Conservative Judaism*, Thirty Years Later," special issue of *American Jewish History* 74 (December 1984); "John Higham's *Strangers in the Land*," special issue of *American Jewish History* 76 (December 1986); "Revisiting a Classic: Nathan Glazer's *American Judaism*," special issue of *American Jewish History* 77 (September 1987). On the inadequacy of Kessner's data, see, for example, Nancy Fitch, "Statistical Fantasies and Historical Facts: History in Crisis and Its Methodological Implications," *Historical Methods Newsletter* 4 (Fall 1984): 245–46.

11. For bibliographic references in this matter, see nn. 1–5 in chapter 2 of this book.

12. Martin Jay, *Downcast Eyes: The Denigration of Vision in Twentieth-Century French Thought* (Berkeley and Los Angeles: University of California Press, 1993).

13. On feminism as a "differencing" epistemology, see, e.g., Shulamit Reinharz, with Lynn Davidman, *Feminist Methods in Social Research* (New York: Oxford University Press, 1992); Virginia Olesen, "Feminisms and Models of Qualitative Research," in Denzin and Lincoln, *Handbook of Qualitative Research*, 158–74. In a different context, Judith Plaskow makes a similar suggestion while discussing gendered perceptions of God in *Standing Again at Sinai: Judaism from a Feminist Perspective* (New York: Harper & Row, 1990), chap. 4, "God: Reimagining the Unimaginable."

14. A good review of these works can be found in Ezra Stotland's *The Psychology of Hope* (San Francisco: Jossey-Bass Publishers, 1969), chap. 4, "Schemas."

15. Samuel Heilman and Steven Cohen asked somewhat similar questions in their study of religious images among members of an Orthodox Jewish synagogue in the American urban Northeast: see their *Cosmopolitans and Parochials: Modern Orthodox Jews in America* (Chicago: University of Chicago Press, 1989), chap. 3, "The Religious Faith and Fervency of Orthodox Jews."

16. In his studies of "the ultimate values" of present-day Christian Americans, Andrew Greeley uses retrospective questions and obtains apparently "valid" answers, i.e., answers approximating how it *was*. See Andrew Greeley, *Religious Change in America* (Cambridge: Harvard University Press, 1989), and idem, with William McCready, *The Ultimate Values of the American Population* (Beverly Hills, CA: Sage, 1976).

17. For the bibliographic information, see n. 65 in chapter 1.

18. Leonard Winograd, *"The Horse Died at Windber": A History of Johnstown's Jews of Pennsylvania* (Bristol, IN: Wyndham Hall Press, 1988).

19. I learned especially from studies of Judith Plaskow, *Standing Again at Sinai*; Ellen Umansky and Dianne Ashton, eds., *Four Centuries of Jewish Women's Spirituality* (Boston: Beacon Press, 1992). Studies of women's spirituality by Christian feminists have likewise been very enlightening, e.g., Mary Daly, *Beyond God the Father: Toward a Philosophy of Women's Liberation* (Boston: Beacon Press, 1973); Rosemary Ruether, *Sexism and God-Talk: Toward a Feminist Theology* (Boston: Beacon Press, 1983); Elisabeth Schussler Fiorenza, *In Memory of Her: A Feminist Theological Reconstruction of Christian Origins* (London: SCM, 1983). See also two interesting volumes: Carol Christ and Judith Plaskow, eds., *Womanspirit Rising: A Feminist Reader in Religion* (San Francisco: Harper & Row, 1979); and Judith Plaskow and Carol Christ, eds., *Weaving the Visions: New Patterns of Feminist Spirituality* (San Francisco: Harper & Row, 1989).

20. These readings included, for example, Jenna Weissman Joselit, "The Special Sphere of Middle-Class American Jewish Women: The Synagogue Sisterhood, 1890–1940," in *The American Synagogue: A Sanctuary Transformed*, ed. Jack Wertheimer (New York: Cambridge University Press, 1987), 206–30; Barbara Kirshenblatt-Gimblett, "Kitchen Judaism," then in MS, subsequently published in *Getting Comfortable in New York: The American Jewish Home, 1880–1950*, ed. Susan Braunstein and Jenna Weissman Joselit (New York: The Jewish Museum, 1990), 75–106; Sydney Stahl Weinberg, *The World of Our Mothers: The Lives of Immigrant Jewish Women* (Chapel Hill: University of North Carolina Press, 1988); Neil Cowan and Ruth Schwartz Cowan, *Our Parents Our Lives: The Americanization of Eastern European Jews* (New York: Basic Books, 1989). The exhibition, entitled *Getting Comfortable in New York: The American Jewish Home, 1880–1950*, was shown at the YIVO Institute in the fall of 1990.

21. The quotation is from Pierre Bourdieu's conversation with Loïc Wacquant, in "The Purpose of Reflexive Sociology (The Chicago Workshop)," in Bourdieu and Wacquant, *An Invitation to Reflexive Sociology*, 167; cf. also 170–74; and Pierre Bourdieu, "The Force of Law: Toward a Sociology of the Juridical Field," *Hastings Law Journal* 38 (July 1987): 814–53; and idem, "La domination masculine," *Actes de la recherche en sciences sociales* 84 (March 1990): 2–31.

22. I found this term—referred to as "the so-called epistemological hypochondria," suggesting prior currency—in Jean and John Comaroff's recent discussion of

the current postmodernist malaise in the field of anthropology: *Of Revelation and Revolution: Christianity, Colonialism, and Consciousness in South Africa* (Chicago: University of Chicago Press, 1991), xiii.

23. J. Rogers Hollingsworth and Ellen Hollingsworth, *Dimensions in Urban History: Historical and Social Science Perspectives on Middle-Size American Cities* (Madison: University of Wisconsin Press, 1979). I also used this classification in my previous study on Johnstown's Slavic and Hungarian working-class families (Ewa Morawska, *For Bread with Butter: Lifeworlds of the East Central Europeans in Johnstown, Pennsylvania, 1890–1940* [New York: Cambridge University Press, 1985], 19–20).

24. William Yancey, Eugene Ericksen, and Richard Juliani, "Emergent Ethnicity: A Review and Reformulation," *American Sociological Review* 41 (June 1976): 391–403.

26–27; employment patterns in, 3, 5, 7, 12; intensifying nationalism in, 12, 17; Jewish organizations in, 20–21; mass labor migrations, within and without, 3, 26; poverty in, 12, 26–27; urbanization-industrialization of, 3, 5, 7

Education of Johnstown Jews. *See* Second generation: educational attainment of

Ethnic economic niche, 31–33, 73–74; literature on, 31–32. *See also* Jewish entrepreneurial niche

Ethnicization, xviii–xix, 287–88; theoretical models of, 287–88; understanding of, in this study, xviii–xix. *See also* Ethnicization, big-city Jews; Ethnicization, Johnstown Jews

Ethnicization, big-city Jews, 133, 135, 139–40, 142, 147, 150, 154, 157–61, 168–74, 176, 323n.27; as diversification of lifestyles, 133, 139, 176, 323 n.27; as linked with collective upward mobility, 133, 139, 152–54, 158–59, 168–69, 176, 323n.27; resulting in the emergence of "a new (American) Jewish community" between two world wars, 133, 139, 150, 154–56, 158–59, 173; as secularization of lifestyles, 133, 139, 147, 154, 157–61, 168–74; as secularization of synagogue centers, 135, 140; women, as ethnicizers, 138–40, 142, 172–73; and women's entry into public arena, 135, 139–40, 142

Ethnicization, Johnstown Jews, xix, 86–87, 98, 114–16, 133–36, 139–45, 148–51, 155, 164, 171–76, 191, 206, 232–34, 240–42; of economic resources, 86–87, 98–99; of education, as value and practice, 175–78; effects of limited participation in larger society on, 133–34, 191, 206; of entertainment and social activities, private and public, 140–51, 170–75; of family lifestyles, 114, 116, 155–64, 170–74, 317n.67; of popular schemas-worldviews, 232–34, 240, 242; of religious observance, 155–62; as retaining considerable measure of old-country components, 133–34, 138, 140–42, 147, 150, 165–67, 171; as "second-hand," 143–44, 163–64, 206; as shaped by the external and intragroup circumstances of Johnstown Jews, 133–35, 159; and synagogues, 140–45, 149–51; women's role in, 114–16, 140–45, 149–54, 171–74

Fannie Fox's Cookbook, 160

Forverts, 144, 201, 264; Johnstown subscribers to, 144; reasons for reading, 144

Free Loan Society (*Gemilut Hasadim*), 97–98, 139

Froyen Velt, 160

Froyen Zhurnal, 161, 163

Gee Bee, Gee Bee Tech. *See* Glosser Brothers department store

Glosser Brothers department store, 92, 95–96, 104, 108–9, 114, 129, 166, 249; as competitor for small Jewish businesses in town, 95; as employer of East European Gentiles, 95; as provider of part-time employment for Jewish youth, 129; as provider of business apprenticeship for Jewish youth, 95

Good Housekeeping, 161

Great Depression, in Johnstown, 75, 113, 118, 121–31, 137, 144, 163; general employment and, 75, 123; Jewish businesses/family economies and, 118, 122–31; Jewish kitchens and, 130, 163; synagogue budgets and, 144

Hadassah, 94, 138, 145, 163, 173, 251

Hakhnoses Orkhim society, for assistance to transients, 51, 71, 140, 143, 166–67

Hebrew Ladies Aid Society, 143, 150, 326–27n.33

Homeownership among Johnstown Jews, 70, 77, 119–21, 131; average prices paid for, 119–22; in different sections of town, 131; East Europeans and, 119–21; effects of Great Depression on, 121–23, 131; in "foreign" sections of town, 131; Germans and, 119–21; proportion of homeowners, 119–21

Household economies, operation of. *See* Immigrants in Johnstown: household incomes and expenditures of; Jewish family businesses: finances of; Jewish family businesses: space-sharing of home and work; Second generation: household incomes and expenditures of

Immigrants, in East European shtetls, 3–30, 231n.14; civic-political situation of, 5, 293n.31; collective insecurity of, 12–17; contact with modern Jewish ideological movements of, 17; occupations of, 7–8, 10–12; popular schemas-worldviews of,

91–92; 221–22; social interactions between, 206–7, 347–48n.56; symbolic
194, 201–2
Religious participation/observance of Johnstown Jews, 135–39, 142–47, 168, 246–
52, 326n.32, 326–27n.33, 327n.35,
328–29n.39, 329n.41, 332n.64; in comparison with East European shtetl practices, 154–55; ethnicization of, 141–52,
156–68; factors facilitating maintenance
of, 133–38, 167–68; and generational position, 148–49, 155–68; and *kashrut*,
158–64; and *mikve*, 70, 148, 328–
29n.39; *Millieufrömmigkeit* nature of,
154–56; and religious education of children, 148–49, 153, 332n.64; and residential location, 156–58, 161–66; and observance of the Sabbath, 155–58, 326n.32,
329n.41; sense of "should do," 157, 165,
167; and synagogue affiliation, 50–51,
135–38, 156–67, 249–50; and *tsdoke*,
114–16, 164–68; women's involvement
in, 70, 114–16, 140–51, 156–63, 165–
67, 174, 198, 209, 236, 246, 251–52,
275, 326n.32, 328–29n.39. *See also*
Ahavath Achim Synagogue; Beth Sholom
Temple; Beth Zion Temple; Rodef Sholom Synagogue
Representativity of Johnstown Jewish case,
reflections on, 282–84
Research for this study, discussion of, 259–
81; on American Jewish history, general
and in particular localities, 263–64, 279;
on Johnstown Jewish women's position
and activities, 260, 262, 267, 271–72,
276–77, 280–81; on Johnstown Jews'
communal life, 259–62, 275–76, 280–81;
on Johnstown Jews' East European origins and route to Johnstown, 260–61,
272–73; on Johnstown Jews' economic
pursuits and operation of family businesses, 259–62, 264–78; on Johnstown
Jews' education, attitudes to and practice
of, 261, 273–75; on Johnstown Jews' family economies and lifestyles, 268–69,
277–78; on Johnstown Jews' group support networks, 262, 265–66; on Johnstown Jews' life-goals and accomplishments, 260, 264–65, 268; on Johnstown
Jews' occupational mobility, 273–75; on
Johnston Jews' participation in local society, 278–79; on Johnstown Jews' religious practices, 275–76; on Johnstown

Jews' schemas-worldviews, 262–63, 269–
71, 277; on Johnstown's economy, society, and politics, 259, 261–62, 274, 278;
on Johnstown synagogues, 260, 275–76
Residential locations of Johnstown Jews,
41–49, 77–80, 119–21, 131; in better
neighborhoods, 77, 80, 90, 119–21; in
downtown area, 41–47, 77–79; in "foreign colonies," 46, 49, 77–80; in "peddler's place," 41, 48–49, 77; in proximity
to East European Gentiles, 41–47, 77; in
Westmont, 77, 80, 119–121
Rodef Sholom Bulletin, 151, 174–75, 220,
234
Rodef Sholom Ladies' Auxiliary, 150–51,
174, 246, 327n.33
Rodef Sholom Synagogue, 38, 51, 52, 70–
71, 81, 94, 135, 137–39, 140–52, 156–
63, 165–67, 178, 195–96, 198, 200,
222–23, 260, 275, 305–6n.39, 323n.15,
326n.32, 326–27n.33, 328–29n.39,
332n.64; "Consorthodox" reform at,
149–52, 326n.32, 326–27n.33, 332n.64;
finances of, 70–71, 141, 144; founding
of, 51; introduction of English into services at, 148, 150; location of, 38, 51,
52; membership in, 51, 135–38; overlap
of congregational leadership and high economic status in, 53, 94, 305–6n.39; religious affiliation of, 51, 94; religious education at, 148–52; religious observance
among members of, 147–52, 155–68,
326n.32, 326–27n.33, 332n.64; role of
Rabbi Ralph Simon in ethnicization of,
149–52, 223, 326–27n.33, 327n.34,
332n.64; and second generation, 149–51,
326–27n.33, 332n.64; social-religious activities at, 143–46; women's role in, 140–
44, 148–51, 173–74, 246, 326n.32, 326–
27n.33. *See also* Ethnicization, Johnstown
Jews: and synagogues

Schwartz Brothers department store, 95, 97
Second generation, 41, 66–67, 77, 80, 82–
86, 88, 95, 103–20, 131–32, 143–46,
149–51, 152–53, 175–84, 219, 221,
223, 228–34, 241–42, 273–75, 314n.40,
326n.32, 326–327n.33, 329n.41; attitudes toward education among, 175–84;
businesses of, 41, 66–67, 80, 82–83, 85–
86, 88, 95, 103–18; civic insecurity
among, 219, 221, 223–24; and "Consorthodox" reform, 148–52, 326–27n.33;

About the Author

EWA MORAWSKA is Professor of Sociology and History and a member of the Jewish Studies Program at the University of Pennsylvania. She is the author of a study of Johnstown Slavic immigrants, *For Bread with Butter*.